SOCIALIST *senses*

For Gohar and Jules,
The craftspeople and artists — with truly emancipated sen<u>ses</u>.
All my love and thanks,

Emma

SOCIALIST
senses

FILM, FEELING, AND
THE SOVIET SUBJECT, 1917–1940

EMMA WIDDIS

INDIANA UNIVERSITY PRESS

This book is a publication of

Indiana University Press
Office of Scholarly Publishing
Herman B Wells Library 350
1320 East 10th Street
Bloomington, Indiana 47405 USA

iupress.indiana.edu

© 2017 by Emma K. Widdis

All rights reserved

No part of this book may be reproduced or utilized in any form or by any means, electronic or mechanical, including photocopying and recording, or by any information storage and retrieval system, without permission in writing from the publisher.
The Association of American University Presses' Resolution on Permissions constitutes the only exception to this prohibition.

⊛ The paper used in this publication meets the minimum requirements of the American National Standard for Information Sciences—Permanence of Paper for Printed Library Materials, ANSI Z39.48-1992.

Manufactured in the United States of America

Library of Congress Cataloging-in-Publication Data

Names: Widdis, Emma, 1970- author.
Title: Socialist senses : film, feeling, and the Soviet subject, 1917-1940 / Emma Widdis.
Description: Bloomington : Indiana University Press, 2017. | Includes bibliographical references and index.
Identifiers: LCCN 2017014166 (print) | LCCN 2017028835 (ebook) |
  ISBN 9780253027078 (eb) | ISBN 9780253026330 (cl : alk. paper) |
  ISBN 9780253026941 (pb : alk. paper)
Subjects: LCSH: Motion pictures—Soviet Union—History and criticism.
Classification: LCC PN1993.5.R9 (ebook) | LCC PN1993.5.R9 W525 2017 (print) |
  DDC 791.430947—dc23
LC record available at https://lccn.loc.gov/2017014166

1 2 3 4 5 22 21 20 19 18 17

For Jason, Barney, and Iona

CONTENTS

	Preface	*ix*
	Acknowledgments	*xi*
	Note on Translation and Transliteration	*xv*
	Introduction: Feeling Soviet	*1*
1	Avant-Garde Sensations	27
2	Material Sensations	51
3	Textile Sensations	85
4	Socialist Sensations	123
5	Primitive Sensations	165
6	Modern Sensations	203
7	Socialist Feelings	227
8	Socialist Transformations	265
9	Socialist Pleasures	297
	Conclusion: The Death of Sensation	337
	Glossary of Russian Terms	353
	Bibliography	355
	Index	395

PREFACE

My first book, *Visions of a New Land*, was a spatial history of Soviet Russia on-screen before the Second World War. This one is a sensory history. It uncovers film's role in an imagined remaking of the Soviet self through the senses, revealing a potent dream that the Bolshevik revolution in social and political structures might be accompanied by a revolution in human sensory experience. It is both a new account of Soviet cinema in the vital years from the revolutionary avant-garde to established Socialist Realism, and a new cultural history of Soviet Russia. *Socialist Senses* tells a story of early Soviet culture through touch, texture, and material, showing the importance of embodied experience in the creation of models of Soviet subjectivity during this formative period. Focusing on the twin concepts of sensation (*oshchushchenie*) and texture (*faktura*), I challenge established narratives of Soviet culture, offering an original perspective on the core preoccupations of the age.

Socialist Senses reveals the scale and reach of the materialist-sensory ambition in Soviet culture, and its impact on cinema. The book operates at macro- and microlevels. It is at once a close reading of films' surfaces and textures, an account of the evolution of Soviet cultural ideology, and a picture of how filmmakers negotiated and adapted their formal preoccupations to meet the demands of a rapidly changing world. It can be read as a series of "close-ups," exploring how the relationship between the body and the world was configured. But it is also organized to provide a chronological (and conceptual) overview of this complex period from 1917 to 1941. Each chapter explores a particular manifestation of the materialist-sensory project in Soviet culture; within these broad conceptual frameworks, each examines a number of films, some known and canonical, and others less so. Throughout the book, I show how these films emerged as part of a wider shared social and political context.

Together, the chapters of this book reveal an ambitious project for the remaking of the Soviet subject in the postrevolutionary years: the forging of an alternative psychological model in which the psyche would be formed in direct relation to a sensory, embodied encounter with the world. They also track a historical evolution. By the late 1930s, "emotion" and "consciousness" had replaced "sensation" as the index of a specifically Soviet selfhood. The utopian dream of sensory revolution was at an end. Against the background of this evolution, the book traces the continuities and ruptures in Soviet cinema's materialist project. It charts the flowering, and the failure, of the dream of socialist sensations.

ACKNOWLEDGMENTS

I AM PRIVILEGED to belong to two institutions that have supported my work on this book generously: my thanks go to Trinity College and the University of Cambridge. I am also grateful to the Arts and Humanities Research Council and the Cambridge Humanities Research Grants Scheme, for research leave and technical support.

It is impossible to do justice to the debt of gratitude that I owe to Julian Graffy. His support for my work, and willingness to read the text with characteristic intellectual generosity, vast breadth of knowledge, and a remarkably acute eye, have been extraordinary. The wonderful Susan Larsen, Joan Neuberger, Simon Franklin, Michael Kunichika, and Rosalind Blakesley have also all read sections of the text, and I have profited greatly from their careful input, spirited argument, and wry humor. I have been stimulated by conversation with, and suggestions from, so many scholars, including Petr Bagrov, Phil Cavendish, Katerina Clark, Evgenii Dobrenko, Anne Eakin Moss, Samuel Goff, Nikolai Izvolov, Lilya Kaganovsky, Sergei Kapterev, Christina Kiaer, Antonia Lant (and Klemens Gruber and the Texture Matters team), Stephen Lovell, Rachel Morley, Evgenii Margolit, Eric Naiman, Anne Nesbet, Ana Olenina, Sergei Oushakine, Elizabeth Papazian, Jan Plamper, Susan Reid, JD Rhodes, Jane Sharp, Nariman Skakov, Susanne Strätling, Mark Steinberg, and Maia Turovskaia. I am extremely grateful to the anonymous readers of the manuscript for their valuable suggestions and support. The book has also benefited from colleagues' responses when I have presented portions of it in institutions including Stanford University, Princeton University, Bristol University, University College London, and the University of Sheffield. I owe a great debt to all my colleagues in the Department of Slavonic Studies, as well as to my graduate and undergraduate students, who continually stimulate my passion for this period of Soviet cultural history. Viktor Listov remains an important interlocutor—absent or present—in all my thinking about Soviet cinema.

Other people have provided invaluable practical support. Isobel Palmer and Anna Toropova were invaluable research assistants. Max Anley and Olenka Dmytrk both helped greatly with practical matters. The director and staff at Gosfil'mofond of Russia (Nikolai Borodachev, Oleg Bochkov, Petr Bagrov, and particularly Alisa Nasrtdinova, who was extremely generous with her time) have been unfailingly helpful: unless otherwise mentioned, all frame stills are reproduced with their kind permission. I also always owe a debt of gratitude to the wonderful team at the Museum of Cinema (Moscow)—Naum Kleiman, of course, but also Kristina Iur'eva and Elena Dolgopiat. For help with the preparation of images, I thank also Chris Jones, and the staff at the Tretyakov, Novgorod, and Kyiv Museums of Art, and at the Hillwood Museum, Tate Gallery, and McDougall Auction House. The book found a perfect home with Indiana University Press, and I am profoundly grateful to Raina Polivka, Gary Dunham, Janice Frisch, David Miller, and Melissa Dalton, without whose enthusiasm and care it would not have been possible.

While I have been writing this book, friends and family have provided much needed sustenance, both literal and metaphorical. I thank them all, and in particular: Cherry Goddard, Su Goddard, Suzanne Nicholas, Jan Pester, Rachel Polonsky, Laura Robson-Brown, Anne and Jerry Toner, Sally Standley, Muriel Zagha, Dianna Widdis, and Michael Widdis.

Finally, it does not seem merely coincidental to me that this book has sheets, laundry, material, and "making" at its center. It has been produced during a period of my life that has involved quite a lot of textile, and a great deal of making. The other (human) things that I have "made" in this period are far more significant than this book. My deepest thanks go to Jason, Barney, and Iona, for providing the joy in the midst of it all.

Material emerging from research undertaken for this book appeared in the following publications: "Cinema and the Art of Being: Towards a History of Early Soviet Set Design," in *A Companion to Russian and Soviet Cinema*, edited by Birgit Beumers, 314–336. London: Palgrave Macmillan, 2016; "Making Sense without Speech: the Use of Silence in Early Soviet Sound Film," in *Sound, Speech, Music in Russian and Soviet Cinema*, edited by Lilya

Kaganovsky and Maria Salazkina, 100–116. Bloomington: Indiana University Press, 2014; "Child's Play: Pleasure and the Soviet Hero in Savchenko's A Chance Meeting (1936)," *Studies in Russian and Soviet Cinema* 6: 3 (2013), 319–333; "Socialist Feelings: Film and the Creation of Soviet Subjectivity," *Slavic Review* 71, no. 3 (Fall 2012), 590–618. It has been significantly changed in preparation of *Socialist Senses*.

NOTE ON TRANSLATION AND TRANSLITERATION

TRANSLITERATION OF RUSSIAN is according to the Library of Congress system, with diacritics, except when Russian names are of Germanic origin (e.g., Eisenstein rather than Eizenshtein). Titles in the text are given in Russian and English at first mention, and thereafter in English. Titles in the notes are in Russian only. Although most citations are in English, key Russian terms used throughout the text will be explained, given in Russian and English at first mention, and thereafter cited in Russian. They are italicized only when first used, and appear subsequently in roman. A brief glossary of key Russian terms is provided. All translations from the Russian are mine unless otherwise noted. Note most foreign terms are rendered first in italics and then in roman type on subsequent mention.

SOCIALIST *senses*

INTRODUCTION

Feeling Soviet

> In a strict sense, all senses come down to one—to touch.
> Dal', *Tolkovyi slovar' russkogo iazyka* (1909)

IN *THE THIRD Manuscript of 1844*, Karl Marx made a perplexing claim:

> The abolition of private property is ... the complete emancipation of all the human qualities and senses. It is an emancipation because these qualities and senses have become human, from the subjective as well as the objective point of view. The eye has become a human eye when its object has become a human, social object, created by man and destined for him. The senses therefore become directly theoretical in practice.[1]

What did Marx mean by the senses becoming "directly theoretical in practice"? The human senses, he proposed, are shaped in relation to the object world that surrounds them, determined by the relationship between bodies and things. This relationship is transformed by social and economic organization. Capitalism ("private property") creates a rupture between the human body and the material. *Capitalist senses* are impoverished: people are unable to feel the world. So socialist revolution must, and would, create *socialist senses*.

In the Soviet Union in the decades preceding the Second World War, such ideas had potent appeal. The revolution in social structures was to be accompanied by a revolution in sensory experience. This book will uncover film's role in that sensory revolution—in the creation of revolutionary models of subjecthood. According to Marx, after all, the sensuous world was "not a thing given direct from all eternity, remaining ever the same, but the product of industry and of the state of society."[2] Soviet man or woman would feel the world differently, reborn into a revitalized sensory apprehension of the material. In the words of Marxist ideologue Nikolai Bukharin in 1927, "The cultural revolution has a socio-biological equivalent that reaches down to the very physiological nature of the [human] organism."[3]

A study of cinema in the first two decades of Soviet power provides a lens onto this larger cultural history. Film was a privileged site for the exploration of new modes of perception, a space for working through the complex relationship between body, mind, and world that had particular ideological potency in early Soviet Russia.[4] Like the young state itself, cinema was a new medium, the definition of which took place alongside the shaping of Soviet culture—and specifically, of the contours of the Soviet subject. Filmmakers operated in close dialogue with fields such as psychological and physiological science, architecture and design, as well as broader ideological contexts.[4] With its capacity for sensory and emotional affect, cinema was a laboratory through which new models of subjectivity could be tested.

There are two ways in which film can help us to understand the imagined contours of the new Soviet subject. First, film presents visual evidence of material culture as both lived and imagined. What do people touch in Soviet cinema of the 1920s and 1930s, and how do they touch it? What are the symbolic meanings ascribed to textures, surfaces, and objects in film? What are the relationships between protagonists on-screen and the world that they inhabit? Second—and most important—how does film seek to engage its spectator? What is the nature of the sensory encounter between spectator and screen, and how do filmmakers aim to alter it? Film spectatorship offered a microcosmic model of the relationship between human subject and world. Film could both discover the world anew, and model a way of inhabiting it.

Soviet filmmakers in the years before the Second World War were very much aware of this two-stranded project. Indeed, it acquired particular urgency in the Soviet context, where the "reconstruction of everyday life" was a specific priority for the new regime. As Christina Kiaer has shown, avant-garde artists and Bolshevik ideologues shared a desire to remake the world of objects according to new ideological priorities, identifying the interface between the human body and the material world as a site of revolutionary significance.[5] In parallel, early Soviet psychological science saw

Fig. 0.1 El Lissitskii, *The New Man* (Neuer) from Figurines: The Three-Dimensional Design of the Electro-Mechanical Show "Victory over the Sun" (1920–1921, published 1923). ©Tate, London 2016.

the experience of the body as the core element in the creation of human consciousness. El Lissitskii's design for the "New Man" (to be realized on stage in the 1920 production of the Futurist opera *Victory Over the Sun*) captures the potency of this reformulated vision of the subject (figure 0.1): it pictures the human body rendered transparent—metaphorically turned inside out. This body is not subject but object—and is in constant interface with the external world.

Lissitskii's image reflects the wider Soviet ambition that revolution would create "New People," which found its most famous expression in Lev Trotskii's *Literature and Revolution* (1923): "Man will make it his purpose to master his own feelings . . . to raise himself to a new plane, to create a higher social-biological type."[6] Trotskii's suggestion that this elevation of the self would be brought about by "*social* construction and *psycho-physical* self-education" points to the matrix of mind, body, and world that inflected Soviet models of the self during this formative period. This book will examine how the relationship between external life (the body and its sensations) and inner life (consciousness and emotion) was imagined, as the contours of the New Soviet Person were elaborated in the 1920s and 1930s. It will explore the emphasis on the sensory experiences and physical surfaces of the body and its material contexts, across a series of fields, showing film theory and practice to be entangled with discussions about the creation of a new way of living in the world.

Specifically, the chapters that follow tell a story of early Soviet culture through touch, texture, and sensation. Yet theorists of both Russian and non-Russian modernity have tended to emphasize *vision* as the quintessential modern sense. In 1903, Georg Simmel, one of the most eloquent early commentators on the "modern condition," discussed the "rapid crowding of changing images" and the "unexpectedness of onrushing impressions" characteristic of life in the city as creating an "intensification of nervous stimulation."[7] This emphasis on vision has been decisive in shaping narratives of modernity and its cultural forms. Following Simmel, Walter Benjamin and others such as Wolfgang Shivelbusch and Jonathan Crary have described modernity—particularly the dynamic stimuli of modern urban experience—as launching a radical challenge to accepted models of vision, and traced a preoccupation with the category of "attention" in late-nineteenth- and early-twentieth-century art.[8] Other historians and theorists have focused on a concomitant search for regulation, discipline, and order as a fundamental feature of modern society, a response to this pervasive sense of visual destabilization. Casetti, for example, sees early cinema as engaged in a project of regulating and disciplining the eye.[9] In the Soviet context, much scholarship has emphasized such control and regulation: Irina Sandomirskaia is one of several who have insisted on the primacy of vision in Soviet culture and ideology, arguing that a "politics of vision" underlies Soviet culture. Film technology, she suggests, had a key role here.[10] Marx's call for senses that were "theoretical in practice" was realized in the ideal of the camera eye put forward by Dziga Vertov, which, she suggests, sought to replace the individual gaze with a hegemonic "collectivization of vision."[11] The single (collective) mechanical eye of the camera regulates the (multiple) unruly human body(ies), and creates a new Soviet vision of the world.

With its focus on tactile senses, this book tells an alternative story. It shows that physical sensation and embodied experience occupied a central place in the anticipated remaking of the Soviet subject. I suggest that bodies and senses—rather than being seen as subversive, transgressive threats to the Soviet project—were envisaged as part of a specifically Soviet refashioning of human life. In Marx's terms, they would be "emancipated" by communism.[12] This is not to deny that the ideal of the liberation of the body in Soviet revolutionary culture went hand in hand with projects for its mechanization and organization. The metaphorical opposition between vision and sensation, the eye and the body, mirrors the dialectical relationship, in early Soviet revolutionary culture, between consciousness (*soznatel'nost*) and spontaneity (*stikhiinost'*).[13] On the one hand, revolutionary iconoclasm celebrated what the poet Aleksandr Blok called the "savage chorus" of the masses, the spontaneity and elemental energy of liberated, rebellious bodies.[14] On the other, the organization of this innate revolutionary energy was a key imperative for the new regime.

Projects of regulation and emancipation existed in a creative tension that was particularly evident in debates around cinema. For Sergei Tret'iakov, for example, cinema was both an "intellectualizer" and an "emotionalizer."[15] It must make the viewer both think and feel. Film's emotional impact, however, was achieved through the senses. It was, Tret'iakov claimed, a *kinoaffektorium*: its bodily (sensory) impact on the spectator could act as a form of social gunpowder.[16] Although Treti'akov used the term "affekt" (drawn from the Latin) here, in this book, I will generally use "sensation" (*oshchushchenie*), because it had more immediate relevance for the theorists and practitioners that I will be discussing.[17] I will trace the resonance of a cluster of terms relating to sensation—and specifically tactile sensation (*oshchup'*).[18] The term "oshchushchenie" had particular potency in the period under consideration, when the relationship between body, mind, and matter was a subject of intense preoccupation. Defined by Vladimir Lenin himself in "Materialism and Empiric-criticism" (first published in 1909, and re-published in Moscow in 1920) as "the direct connection between consciousness and the external world," oshchushchenie was a key term in early Soviet psychology.[19] In Lenin's much-quoted phrase, it was "the transformation of the energy of external excitation into a state of consciousness."[20] With its emphasis on the sensory experience of the body as a determinant of consciousness, this definition signals the positivist-materialist grounding of early Soviet physiological and psychological science. And it provides a focus for this inquiry into Soviet senses.

Of course, this project is not an attempt to map the *real* sensory experience of individuals in Soviet Russia. I do not claim to discover what Soviet subjects actually felt. Rather, *Socialist Senses* will trace shifts in the imagined relationship between sensation (oshchushchenie), feeling (*chuvstvo*), and emotion (*emotsiia*), and between the human body and the physical world, as they were articulated and refracted in cultural texts. These shifts mirror transformations in the ideological climate—and allow us to interrogate historical periodizations. The years 1917–1941 are generally seen as incorporating four distinct stages in Soviet history. They take us first from the early revolutionary years into the diversity and complexity of the NEP (New Economic Policy, 1921–1928), when the need to kick-start the economy led to a series of political compromises. The period from 1928 to 1932, marked by the launching of the first Five-Year Plan and the Cultural Revolution, is usually described as a transitional phase in Soviet culture: it was a time of considerable debate, as the social and economic frameworks that would come to define Soviet society were tested and refined. Finally, the years from approximately 1932 until the beginning of the Great Fatherland War (1941) are shaped by Socialist Realism and Stalinism. Treating source material across this time frame, this cinematic sensory history reveals continuities and ruptures that cut across common periodizations. *Socialist Senses* traces an evolution from the immediately postrevolutionary years to established Stalinism. It uncovers a potent utopian dream for the remaking of the Soviet subject: the forging of an alternative psychological model in which the psyche would be formed in direct relation to a sensory, embodied encounter with the world. And it traces the shifting contours of that dream.

Theoretical Frameworks

This is a book about the revolutionary significance of sensation—with a focus on touch. I think about touch in three distinct but interrelated ways: as literal touching; as emotional touching/feeling; and in terms of touch-as-perception. These categories map onto the three principal theoretical frameworks that have shaped this project: sensory history; theories of Soviet subjectivity/history of emotions; and haptic film theory.

First, literal touch: what (and how) do people touch, and how does it shape them? Such questions are the focus of scholars in the fields of sensory history and anthropology of the senses.[21] Historians of the senses take as their starting point a deceptively simple statement by Lucien Febvre: "A series of fascinating studies could be done on the sensory underpinnings of thought in different periods."[22] How people sense the world (through the body) shapes the way that they think. And sensory experience is not innate, but shaped by society and environment. So historians and anthropologists must enter a domain that has traditionally seemed inaccessible to scholarly analysis.

Although the discipline of sensory history has developed rapidly in recent years, only limited work has been done in Russian and Slavic fields. Smell in particular has been a subject of some research: from Ol′ga Vainshtein's edited collection in 2003, to Vladimir Lapin's monograph on the sounds and smells of Saint Petersburg.[23] Tricia Starks and Igor′ Bogdanov have written on the history of tobacco in Russia; Alison Smith has studied Russian food culture; and Alexander Martin includes a study of the smells and sensory experiences of Moscow as part of his recent monograph.[24] Such work complicates and enriches our historical picture, but the field remains underdeveloped. For the Soviet period, such work is of particular importance: the young state was explicitly engaged with the creation of "new" Soviet bodies. Clare Shaw's excellent work on deaf culture in Soviet Russia alerts us to the political discourses surrounding and shaping sensory experience.[25] Similarly, Sandomirskaia proposes that the Soviet case can be regarded as an instance of "biopolitics."[26] Irina Sirotkina and Igor′ Chubarov have begun to investigate the avant-garde's preoccupation with sensory experience.[27] In film studies, the work of Oksana Bulgakowa (Bulgakova), Lilya Kaganovsky, and Ana Olenina considers the ways in which film sought to condition the body of the spectator, and Anna Toropova explores Stalinist cinema, genre, and affective emotional education.[28]

This list makes clear the tension inevitable to sensory history. The desire to study actual sensory experience leads to a study not of life itself, but of how sensory experience has been written about, thought about, and conceptualized. There is a gap between the "real" life of the body and the discursive frameworks that seek to shape it. In the Soviet case, such tensions have been the focus of the second historical/theoretical field with which this book is in dialogue: Soviet subjectivity and history of emotions. The "Soviet subjectivity" movement, pioneered by Igal Halfin and Jochen Hellbeck, starts from the premise that a specifically Soviet human subject was actually created by discursive frameworks: real people internalized and *lived* the doctrines of Sovietness.[29] Eric Naiman sees Hellbeck's and Halfin's work as the culmination of a scholarly tendency to read the Soviet experience as "textuality triumphant"—that is, to see Stalinism (in particular) as underpinned by a view of language as creative, collapsing the distance between reality and its representation.[30] Soviet slogans were not exhortations, but incantations. So scholars of Soviet subjectivity study not bodies, but words.

In one sense, the history of emotions (exemplified in the work of Jan Plamper, Mark D. Steinberg and Valeria Sobol) starts from a different impulse.[31] Scholars in this field seek a way of writing about something that seems to be outside language: feeling. They view emotions as agents of historical change, and see emotional expression as shaped by historical context. Historians of emotion operate at what Steinberg and Sobol call "the knotty intersections of body, self, society, culture and power."[32] Here, too, however, language matters: discursive frameworks articulate how it is possible and/or appropriate to feel. Historians of emotions in the Soviet context, moreover, share with those in the Soviet subjectivity school a tendency to view Soviet culture in terms of regulation and consciousness, emphasizing how individual human emotion was to be disciplined in the service of the collective, creating appropriate socialist feelings.

A sensory history of Soviet Russia may provide an alternative narrative to these dominant models, excavating a different kind of (sensory) feeling as part of the Soviet project. In particular, it may uncover an emphasis on emancipation, and bodily experience, alongside that of regulation and consciousness. How, though, can film contribute to a sensory history—particularly to a history of touch? What can film tell us about bodies and feelings? Here, my third category, touch-as-perception, is important.[33] To what extent does touch (the sensations of the body) provide a primary level of perception? What is its relationship with vision and consciousness? This book is an attempt not to answer those questions, but to trace how they were thought about in the Soviet context, and how they inflected the development of film form. Here, this project intersects with theoretical accounts of haptic cinema. Theorists such as Laura Marks, Vivian Sobchak, Jennifer Barker, and Giuliana Bruno have sought to account for an impact of film on the spectator that exceeds the visual: to understand cinema not as a purely specular experience, but as *embodied* and multisensory. The spectatorial eye, they suggest, can operate imaginatively as an organ of touch.[34]

The term "haptic" comes from Greek *haptikos* (ἁπτικός), and means "able to touch," referring to perception by tactile means. Perhaps the most useful prehistory of the application of the haptic to visual culture lies in the work of Viennese art-historian Alois Riegl. Riegl proposed that the history of visual art could be understood as a passage from haptical to optical modes of perception—from a decorative art of ornamental surfaces (Egyptian art, for example), toward a representational art of depth, perspective, and figuration.[35] Early abstract ornamental art provokes haptic perception: the lack of distinction between figure and ground impedes the process of recognition. Since the viewer cannot recognize objects, he/she is drawn into an alternative mode of contemplation—one that encounters the *surface* and material of the work of art, and is multisensory. When an object cannot be recognized, it is encountered instead as surface: it is felt. Thus, Riegl suggested, abstract art encourages an imaginatively tactile (haptic) response that figurative representation does not.[36]

Riegl's suggestion that the eye can operate as an organ of touch has had considerable impact on recent film theory, where "haptic" has been used to describe a mode of spectatorship that can be loosely termed "embodied." Vivian Sobchak memorably describes her experience of the opening scene of Jane Campion's *The Piano* (1993)—despite the blurring of the visual image, she writes: "My fingers knew what I was looking at." An imaginary tactile experience occurs, Sobchak suggests, because "we see and comprehend and feel films with our entire bodily being, informed by the full history and carnal knowledge of our acculturated sensorium."[37] Laura Marks has sought more precision in distinguishing what she calls "haptic looking" from nonhaptic looking in cinema.[38] Echoing Riegl, she defines haptic images as those in which the eye is led to move *over the surface* of its object rather than to plunge into illusionistic depth, not to distinguish form so much as to discern texture."[39] Haptic perception privileges not what the object *is*, but *what-it-is-made-from*, so it brings the spectator to an awareness of what we might call the "thinginess" of the thing. Jennifer Barker also emphasizes what she calls film's ability to "caress" and "palpate" objects and surfaces, insisting on how close-up shots of texture and material can create a reciprocity between spectator and film.[40] Haptic looking, she suggests, creates an intensified relationship between the viewing body and the objects on-screen.

This book explores how the relationship between speaking, seeing, and feeling (language, vision, and sensation) was articulated in Soviet culture.

It operates at the nexus of the three theoretical frameworks (sensory history, Soviet subjectivity/history of emotions, haptic film theory) discussed above. It is a sensory history in directing attention to the importance of bodily sensation in Soviet ideology and culture, and in using (largely silent) film to uncover what Soviet subjectivity was supposed to feel like. It engages with studies of Soviet subjectivity in suggesting that the imaginary Soviet subject was to be created not just through language, but through the body. This emphasis on the body allows us to challenge not only logocentric readings of Soviet culture, but also those that overemphasize vision: the hegemonic eye. It reveals that a history of Soviet emotions must be accompanied by consideration of Soviet senses—particularly in this period, when the relationship between the two was such a sustained point of focus. Finally, this book is a haptic analysis of Soviet cinema. Although the application of haptic theory to Soviet material has been limited to date, there is rich potential in thinking about early Soviet filmmakers' manipulation of film's all-body address to the spectator. A haptic analysis of early Soviet cinema will reveal how Marxist-inflected theories of the self placed the body at the center of a new model of knowledge of the world.

This is not to suggest that haptic theory should be merely applied to Soviet cinema, however. Rather, I suggest that Soviet film theorists and practitioners anticipated many of the concerns and preoccupations that have shaped contemporary haptic theory. In tracing a prehistory of a Soviet haptic, I start from the premise that the role of cinema in this period was not to present a picture of the world, but to articulate a relationship with it. This relationship was to be one of heightened sensory proximity, enabled by the conditions of socialist revolution. In the materialist climate of Soviet Russia, cinema had a twofold task. According to the Marxist-materialist worldview, Soviet man and woman would be constituted from the outside in, in concrete relationship with the world. Cinema was uniquely equipped, first, to *reveal* those material conditions that shape and determine human life, uncovering the physical world in all its plenitude. Film's second purpose, however, went further: it must seek not only to reveal, but also to *shape* a new relationship with those material conditions—through its address to the spectator. This is a particularity, I suggest, of Soviet cinema's project of sensory realism. Filmmakers exploited the textures and surfaces of material on-screen, seeking to provoke fresh, embodied awareness of the world.

How, then, does sense take form in film? Of course, the world caught on film is inescapably full of objects. And full of people touching objects. How, though, is tactility rendered on-screen, and how can it be the object of analysis? These were the very questions that preoccupied Soviet film theorists and filmmakers in this early period. In the Soviet context, they were caught up in larger questions about the relationship between the human and the material, between the machine and handcraft. The film camera mediated between body and world. Its lens permitted a technical-scientific encounter with the material that was not normally available to the naked eye. But that lens could also operate proprioceptively, as an extension of, or substitute for, the human senses (the hand). In the chapters that follow, I will trace the different ways in which filmmakers sought to articulate a proximate, hands-on relationship with material, emphasizing the textural and material qualities of objects, and their relationship with human subjects.

A Soviet Science of the Self

This book will explore how cinema reflected and refracted a wider discourse relating to the relationship between body, mind, and world.[41] It is important, therefore, to understand core shifts in the development of psychological science in the Soviet Union in this period, against which to map the evolutionary trajectory of Soviet sensation. In general, the years from the revolution until the mid-1930s were a period of considerable state investment in psychology, with a rich diversity of theoretical positions and debates, and ambitious projects for applied psychology and experiment. Psychology was at the very heart of the Soviet project, an applied science for the utopian vision of a new Soviet subject. In the words of Aron Zalkind in 1929: "In the USSR, as nowhere else, enormous attention is drawn to the study of *human personality*."[42] As psychologist Lev Vygotskii wrote: "In the new society, our [psychological] science will be at the center of life."[43] Several Bolshevik luminaries (notably Nikolai Bukharin and Lenin himself) were interested in psychology—and specifically in the idea of developing a particular Soviet psychology. The challenges faced by psychological science in the Soviet context were considerable, however. First, it must offer an explanatory model for the self within the new ideological frameworks of Marxism. Second, it must not only analyze the human psyche, but also seek to *remodel* it. At stake was nothing less than the shape of the new Soviet person.

Through the 1920s and into the early 1930s, Soviet psychological science was a space for competing ideologies and ideals, in which different models of a potential "Soviet self" were tested. The first All-Russian Psychoneurological Conference took place in January 1923, and thereafter was held annually. State-subsidized psychological research grew: according to Margarete Vöhringer, of fifty-five research institutions established by Narkompros during the 1920s, twenty-four were explicitly linked to physiology and psychology.[44] Despite a considerable diversity of positions in the early years, certain core principles were evident. In particular, there was a shared preoccupation with overcoming the dualistic view that had traditionally separated mind and body, the spiritual and the physical. This ambition was underpinned by the materialist philosophical basis of Marxism. As Vladimir Borovskii stated in 1927, Marxism revealed the "spiritual and the psychical" to be inextricably tied to the material body—and hence to the material world.[45]

The key to understanding the Marxist frameworks within which psychological science operated is the principle of monism—the conception of mind and body as a single reality, which could therefore be described and ultimately shaped by a single science.[46] This monistic mind-body was, moreover, embedded in the material world. Lenin stated categorically that "matter is the philosophic category which is given to a man in his sensations, which is copied, photographed and reflected in our sensations, although existing independently of them."[47] The world, that is, exists a priori. "To be a materialist," Lenin asserted, "is to acknowledge objective truth which is revealed to us by our sense organs."[48] In broad terms, then, the focus of psychological science through much of the 1920s was on understanding the relationship between the human subject and the (physical) world. This accorded sensation (oshchushchenie) a key role: things act upon subjects, and subjects are formed from sensations of things.[49]

Here the political imperatives of early Soviet Russia coincided with the scientific ambitions that had been guiding the development of psychological research before the revolution, in Russia and elsewhere.[50] In a broader Western context, the influence of William James was particularly important. James called for the conventionally understood "I cry because I am afraid" to be reformulated as "I am afraid *because I cry*." Physiological reactions are not caused *by* emotions, but produce them. James's 1890 work, *Principles of Psychology*, was not published in Russian translation until 1902, but it was much reviewed and discussed, and an abridged version was published earlier.[51] Meanwhile, Russia had its own materialist psychological school, led by the work of Ivan Sechenov, a convinced materialist and mechanist, whose theory of "biological psychology" (articulated in works published between 1863 and 1900) viewed bodily reflexes as underpinning all acts of conscious or unconscious life. Sechenov's work was, in Sirotkina's words, an "effort to describe the human being in terms of reflexes without any reference to the will."[52] In the political context of late nineteenth-century Russia, this was received as a liberating, scientific ideal—politically radical in its denial of the soul. For the radicals, it had the additional political benefit of presupposing collective (and equal) experience: all bodies share the same basic reflexes.[53] It was within this broad context of psychological research that the work of Vladimir Bekhterev and Ivan Pavlov emerged. Bekhterev's *Objective Psychology* (published 1907) described the use of tests to investigate the sensory reflexes of the human body and their link with cognition and emotion.

By 1917, then, psychological science in Russia was well positioned to respond to the materialist imperatives of the new regime, and the period from 1917 to the mid-1930s was one of intense experimentation.[54] It is possible to draw a rough three-phase chronology, mapping shifts in Soviet psychological science, and their relationship with the ideological priorities of the state. The first phase, up to the mid-1920s, was one of considerable diversity: a single state line on psychology had not been clarified; there was a clear need to shape a Marxist model for understanding the human psyche; and the utopian ambitions of the Soviet project to create a "new man" gave scope for experiment. The immediate and urgent project was to integrate psychological science with Marxist orthodoxy. Any psychologists with links to "idealism" (such as Semen Frank and Nikolai Losskii) quickly lost their positions. Others, such as Georgii Chelpanov, sought what Graham calls "a position of neutral empirical psychology."[55] And a third group continued the project, initiated by Sechenov, Bekhterev, and Pavlov, among others, of using the study of reflexes to seek a scientific, objective understanding of human behavior—and positioned this approach strategically under a Marxist-inflected materialist umbrella.[56] Through the 1920s, the latter group was broadly dominant. Bekhterev, who had been removed from his post as head of the Saint Petersburg Psychoneurological Institute in 1913, publicly embraced the revolution and its ideology, and was reinstated in 1918. He founded a group in Petrograd dedicated to the study of the physiological and psychological responses of the human subject to external stimuli and environment.[57]

Reflexology found a natural support base in Marxist materialism, as a scientific demonstration of the mantra that being determines consciousness, praised for its materialist grounding in tangible physical phenomena.[58] Bukharin, for instance, famously characterized the individual person (*lichnost'*) as "a sausage skin stuffed with the influences of the environment."[59] The potency of such metaphors, and their reach across diverse fields of cultural discourse, is a key to understanding the sensory project in early Soviet culture. As Halfin notes, "Science was a crucial weapon in the hands of the communist hermeneuts of the soul."[60] For if the psyche was formed by the sensory encounter between the body and the material world, then it followed that changes in the conditions that provoked or created sensations could bring about changes in psychological makeup—that is, could create a new Soviet subject. Thus, in the postrevolutionary context, reflexology was challenged to move from being a science of observation to being one of *intervention*: the conditioning of reflexes could be a means of conditioning the self.[61] Indeed, many schools of Soviet psychology during this period shared the desire to move from *understanding* to remodeling. For Kornilov, for example, the task of psychology was not only to explain the human psyche, but to master (*ovladet'*) it; for Borovskii, psychology had two tasks: to study human behavior and to direct it.[62] At its most ambitious, the project was nothing less than the creation of a new model of subjectivity. Aron Zalkind was confident enough to set out a "communist psychogram," enumerating the key qualities of this ideal subject.[63]

A broad interest in the possibility of using psychological-scientific methods (psychotechnics) to create new people was evident across diverse fields of Soviet theory and practice through the 1920s, and their intersection with the arts will be discussed in chapter 1.[64] In the latter part of the decade, however, although reflexology (and associated applied sciences) retained considerable dominance, a growing number of voices began to call for a more nuanced understanding of the role of the psyche. For all the popularity of mechanistic theories of the relationship between body and mind, certain theorists were perceived to have gone too far.[65] *Biolizirovat'* (describing an excessively mechanistic view of the psyche) became a negative term. There was a pressing need for a Marxist recognition of the influence (on the body) of an environment that was not only *material* but also *social*. Kornilov, who displaced Chelpanov as head of the Moscow Institute of Psychology in 1923, used the term "biosocial" to describe a Marxist version of psycho-physiological theory that was distinguished from the reflexology of Bekhterev and his followers. His theory of "reactology" sought to reconcile mechanistic theories of the reflex with a more socially grounded vision of the psyche, describing human behavior as stemming from reactions, which were both physiological and social in origin. In 1927, Lev Vygotskii and his close associate Aleksandr Luriia published an essay describing a "crisis" in psychology, which they identified as a failure (in overly mechanistic theories) to account for the culturally and socially situated nature of the self.[66] In 1931, speaking at the Seventh International Conference of Psychotechnics, (and no doubt trying to stem the growing tide of official disapproval), Isaak Shpielrein accused bourgeois psychotechnics of too much focus on biology at the expense of social factors; in contrast, he claimed that Soviet (Marxist) psychotechnics was alert to the relationship between individual human bodies and their social *and* material context.[67]

The second phase of Soviet psychology, then, was marked by this growing emphasis on the importance of social context. Toward the end of the 1920s, however, and into the mid-1930s, psychological debate was increasingly marked by discussion of consciousness (*soznanie*). This signaled the end of psychotechnics and the beginning of what I will call the third phase in Soviet psychological science. It provides a useful explanatory framework for cultural Socialist Realism. Loren Graham has identified what he calls a "great struggle for consciousness" in psychological science at the beginning of the 1930s.[68] Vygotskii was unambiguous: "The study of only those reactions that are visible to the naked eye is totally powerless and untenable in explaining even the simplest problems of human behaviour."[69] The challenge for psychology, then, was to find a way of understanding consciousness. As such, Vygotskii advocated that psychology should be the study not of reflexes, but of behavior—understood as a more complex matrix of influences than only the physiological. This marked a shift from a focus on sensation, and a reconceptualization of feeling as a mental as well as a physical process, shaped by social and historical developments.

In the hands of scholars such as Vygotskii and Aleksandr Luriia, this was undoubtedly a more complex and nuanced understanding of the human than the mechanistic visions that underpinned reflexology and associated applied sciences.[70] In a wider ideological context, however, the shift away from reflexology and toward an interest in "consciousness" paved the way for a simplified Marxist understanding of the relationship between the human body and the material world, and (crucially) a reduced sense of the potential for *changing* that relationship.[71] This marked the end of one phase of Soviet utopianism and corresponded with shifting ideological frameworks. If early Soviet psychology was marked by a revolutionary ideal of mutual interdependence between the human self and the material world (a reanimated sensory relationship), this gave way in the early to mid-1930s to a model of control: the human mind (consciousness) *processes* and ultimately organizes the material world. And consciousness controls and modulates sensation. This shift away from mechanistic understandings of the relationship between body and mind shifted focus from sensation (oshchushchenie) to emotion (emotsii). Rather than being passive reflections of bodily states, emotions were increasingly seen as having the potential to motivate human action. Gaivorovskii, for example, focused on the question of emotion as a way of demonstrating the failure of "purely physiological analysis" of the psyche for a vision of the Soviet subject as more than just a machine. It was vital, he suggested, to recognize the influence not just of physical reflexes, but also of the *social environment*, on the development of emotions. This led, of course, to increasing discussion of what might be specifically Soviet emotions, and for increasing distinction between "good" and "bad" feelings. Gaivorovskii was one of many who stressed the need for emotional and sensory *education*: "It is essential to teach the masses not only to think, but also to feel."[72]

Key Terms: Sensation, Feeling, Emotion

This three-stage broad-brush account of early Soviet psychological science maps a shift from a focus on bodily sensation as a key to consciousness, through a growing interest in the social *and* material world as the context in which the psyche is formed, and finally toward an emphasis on the psyche, and on the relationship between consciousness and emotion. This evolution provides a structuring axis for the shifting story of Soviet sensations in this book. It can be clearly seen in the changing popular-scientific definitions of three key terms: sensation (oshchushchenie), feeling (chuvstvo), and emotion (emotsiia) in major encyclopedias published between 1900 and 1950. The authoritative prerevolutionary Brokgauz and Efron encyclopedia, for example, contained a detailed entry for oshshushchenie, (written by the eminent physiologist I. Tarakhanov), which focused on the evolving science of reflexology and the importance of bodily sensation in relation to consciousness.[73] By contrast, it contained no entry at all for emotion (emotsiia), simply cross-listing it with the term *chuvstvovanie*, which translates more directly as "feeling," and which was itself notable in its emphasis on sensation as an empirically verifiable source for feeling.[74] In simple terms, then, oshchushchenie appeared in this prerevolutionary context as the key determinant of the psyche.

After 1917, in the first edition of the Great Soviet Encyclopedia (which began publication in 1926), the definitions of all three key terms—oshchushchenie, chuvstvo, emotsii—reflect a similar focus on the relationship between the human body and the material world as a condition for psychic response (feeling).[75] V. Teplov noted that recent scientific research had explored the relationship between chuvstvo and oshchushchenie, locating the roots of emotion in material, physical phenomena.[76] The entry for emotsii (written by psychologist Aleksei Leont'ev, a colleague of Vygotskii and Luriia), described emotion as produced by, and located in, the body and its sensations.[77]

Between this first edition of the encyclopedia and its second iteration, produced in the late 1940s and 1950s, however, a marked change took place, as Soviet ideological frameworks clarified and hardened.[78] In the second edition, the definitions of both chuvstvo and oshchushchenie were more ideologically inflected: feelings (chuvstva) were no longer only scientific and empirically verifiable; they were also value driven. The social quality of emotion was strongly underlined.[79] There was also a marked emphasis on important higher feelings (moral, aesthetic, and intellectual), which had been absent from the more scientifically inflected first edition.[80] The "content of feelings," it was proclaimed, "changes from era to era."[81] And as such, human feelings could—and should—be educated (vospitany).

Alongside this discussion of "higher" feelings, oshchushchenie was relegated in the second edition of the encyclopedia to the "merely" physiological.[82] The category of thinking (myshlenie) emerged as a key element: "The dialectical path of cognition ... goes from living perception to thought (myshlenie) and from that to practical action."[83] This introduced the category of consciousness as a force that moderates and controls sensation, enabling the elimination of "bad" feelings and the creation of good ones. This was particularly emphatic in the 1950 entry on affect. Where in the early period affect was seen as holding the possibility of the transformation of body and mind (through reflexology), now it represented a threat to social order. Fortunately, however, "Soviet man has gained self-control and restraint, a conscious and responsible relationship with all his actions and deeds. This quality, developed through communist education and through the action of the socialist collective, creates the ability to master the affective qualities of behaviour."[84] The new Soviet science proclaimed the victory of consciousness over affect.

These changing definitions, aimed at a popular audience, trace the evolution of Soviet conceptions of the relationship between body, mind, and world, from the immediately prerevolutionary period, into established

Stalinism. They reveal the shifting status of bodily sensation, and a broad shift toward conscious emotion as a determinant of the new Soviet subjectivity. In simple terms, they map a shift from body to mind as the core determinant of the Soviet vision of self. The chapters of this book trace that same evolution, from the immediately postrevolutionary years to established Stalinism. They explore, in different ways, how the relationship between sensation, consciousness, and emotion was discussed and understood in (and beyond) cinema. They demonstrate that by the late 1930s, emotion and consciousness had replaced sensation as the index of a specifically Soviet selfhood.

How, then, did the dream of socialist sensation develop alongside this changing context? This book traces a continuity of interest in material, texture, and sensation across the 1920s and 1930s, in the face of a rapidly changing ideological field. It reveals the scale and reach of the materialist ambition in Soviet culture, and its impact on cinema. Each chapter explores a particular manifestation of the materialist ambition, showing how it took form in attitudes toward, for example, domestic interiors, handcraft, mechanized production, the non-Russian periphery, and toys and games. Beneath broad conceptual headings, each chapter seeks to strike a balance between developed close readings of individual films, and a revelation of their wider, shared, social and political context. The chapters are organized along a loose chronological framework, but they also treat material that cuts across this chronology. My emphasis throughout is as much on continuity as it is on change.

Chapter 1 ("Avant-Garde Sensations") provides a conceptual and historical overview of the potency of the idea of bodily sensation in artistic theory and practice. It introduces three key terms that structure the book's analysis as a whole: *faktura* (texture, materiality), oshchushchenie (sensation), and *material* (material), and explores the multivalent application of the term "faktura" across the broad range of Soviet avant-garde artistic production. It suggests that the avant-garde preoccupation with material was part of a broader interest in the capacity of art to reformulate the relationship between the human body and the physical world—and to do so in revolutionary terms.

Chapter 2 ("Material Sensations") extends these abstract conceptions of faktura and material into concrete details, examining the debates and practicalities surrounding film production design in the Soviet 1920s and 1930s. This is not a total history of early Soviet set design; rather, it sets out the core preoccupations that shaped the evolution of design theory and practice in this formative period.[85] It focuses particularly on a number of costume dramas of the 1920s, and argues that faktura—texture, set, costume—plays a vital, largely overlooked part in the evolution of Soviet film culture in this period. In that sense, this chapter displaces the montage story from its supposed centrality in Russian film history, suggesting that historical/costume dramas can be seen as a first stage in Soviet filmmakers' working through of their complex relationship with the pleasures of material on-screen.

Chapter 3 ("Textile Sensations") turns from the costume dramas of chapter 2, to the dramas of everyday life that proliferated in Soviet cinema of the later 1920s. This chapter examines the role played by decorative textile in interior film sets during the 1920s, in both provincial and urban settings, and shows how textile (as decorative item and as a product of women's handwork) carried ideological and formal meaning. Tracing how decorative textiles were configured in Soviet filmed interiors during the 1920s, and the emphasis on material and "making," it complicates visions of the Soviet "modern" and reveals an emphasis on homemaking as central to emerging discourses on the Soviet self.

In different ways, chapters 4, 5, and 6 all explore the relationship between body and world both on-screen and in emerging models of spectatorship. Chapter 4 ("Socialist Sensations") develops the previous chapter's analysis of textile craft into an examination of the category of labor and making. Noting the symbolic importance of the human hand in industrial narratives, it tells a new story of the Soviet preoccupation with industrial production, suggesting that the relationship between the human body and the tool (modeled in handcraft) was central to the ideological value of labor in Soviet culture. Chapter 5 ("Primitive Sensations") continues this inquiry into craft in a study of attitudes toward the ethnic other and his/her (imagined) sensory experience, tracing the potent myth of a "primitive" mentality as a model for a heightened sensory relationship with the world. The chapter treats the representation of the Soviet "East" (Central Asia and the Caucasus) in cinema and the development of *local* cinema in the national republics themselves. As the last of this group, chapter 6, "Modern Sensations," turns away from the handwork and crafts that have provided the focus of previous chapters, and looks at the status of modern interiors in Soviet cinema from the 1920s into the first Five-Year Plan. It examines how the textures and surfaces of new interiors encoded an ideologically framed relationship between the body and the material world.

The final three chapters of the book analyze the transition to Socialist Realist (sound) cinema, and trace the continuities and ruptures in Soviet cinema's materialist project in the face of increasing calls for films to model new Soviet feelings. Rather than tracing the evolution of Soviet screened emotion per se, however, these chapters suggest that the years from approximately 1932 to 1937 are best understood as a *testing ground* for Socialist Realism, and for socialist sensations—at a time when the formal and ideological parameters of Socialist Realism were still unclear. They show how Socialist Realism changed the treatment of sensation and texture on-screen. Chapter 7 ("Socialist Feelings") explores how the representation of the relationship between self and world evolved to meet the changing ideological demands of the new aesthetic. It traces a shift from the exploration of sensation as the basis for a new model of subjectivity, toward the search for specifically Soviet feelings, and explores how this changed the treatment of cinematic material, and of oshchushchenie. The remaining two chapters trace two different afterlives of socialist sensation and the materialist impulse during this period of change. Chapter 8 ("Socialist Transformations") returns to the cinema of the national republics to consider how the shifting relationship between sensation-feeling and consciousness-emotion was reflected in the representation of "primitive" life and the need for its modernization and transformation. It traces the changing image of the faktura of the Soviet "East," and reveals how the multisensory encounter with difference that marked the "Eastern" (*vostochnyi*) cinema of the 1920s was increasingly uneasy in the cinema of the 1930s. Finally, chapter 9 ("Socialist Pleasures") examines the material surfaces of Stalinist cinema of the 1930s. Focusing specifically on the representation of play (toys, childhood) as a locus of sensory pleasure, it traces how the cinematic pleasure in texture, touch, and embodied experience endured in 1930s cinema, and how it was part of the negotiation of the consolidating norms of Socialist Realism.

As is clear from these synopses, this book is not a history of Soviet cinema. It does not offer a sustained account of the social and material conditions of film production. I do not discuss spectatorship in terms of shifting class and gender affiliations, even though these undoubtedly inflected the representation of sensory experience on-screen. Nor do I provide full history of the technical innovations in set design, sound technology, and cinematography that transformed Soviet cinema in this period. Rather, I use film as a lens through which to understand a wider Soviet cultural preoccupation with sensation; and in turn, I reflect that wider story of sensation back onto Soviet cinema itself, offering a fresh perspective on film's formal strategies and thematic preoccupations during this complex period. This book is a cultural history of the Soviet sensory project and the dream of sensory revolution.

What, then, are the claims of *Socialist Senses*? I have stated that I do not seek to reveal how people actually felt in Soviet Russia during the 1920s and 1930s. Nor do I argue for any innate sensory specificity for Soviet Russia (although during Margaret Mead's anthropological study of 1953, a Russian respondent noted that in Russian textbooks on the senses, the sense of touch is always placed first: "The dictionary of the Russian language . . . defines the sense of touch as follows: 'In reality, all five senses can be reduced to one—the sense of touch . . . It means to ascertain, to perceive, by body, hand, or fingers.'")[86]

I do, however, suggest that tactile experience occupied a particularly resonant place in articulations of what a new Soviet selfhood might feel like. Marxist "materialism" was not an empty term. Ideology demanded an interest in the material world (broadly understood)—what it was, and how people should live with/within it. There was a drive to appropriate the intuitive, spontaneous potential of sensory, embodied experience to the ideological frameworks of Marxism, and to discover what it might feel like to live that way.

The arguments that follow do not seek to overturn those existing understandings of Soviet culture that emphasize regulation, consciousness, logos (the word) and vision (the all-seeing eye), but rather to uncover an element of Soviet aesthetics that is all too often overlooked. If we put the sensory back into aesthetics in our reading of Soviet culture—and show its potency across a number of related fields—we will reveal the place of sensations, touch, and feelings both within the Soviet ideological framework and in a wider modernist context.[87] Walter Benjamin, for example, described revolutionary experience as a form of "innervation," or bodily transformation: "Revolutions are innervations of the collective—or more precisely, efforts at innervation on the part of a new, historically unique collective." For Benjamin, this new collective had "its organs in the new technology."[88] Film in particular was one of these new sensory "organs"—with the potential to create a new relationship between the human subject and the material world, as the basis for a fresh, embodied (innervated) model of selfhood. A similar ambition underlay Soviet culture of the 1920s, and continued into the 1930s. "Feeling" Soviet would be distinctive and definitive. In 1928, Béla

Balázs, in an attack on the sterile "machine" culture of some (German) socialist art, described Soviet proletarian literature by contrast as creating a new sensibility (*Sensibilität*).[89] This sensibility, he clarified, was marked by a proximity with the material world: it reacts directly to "the things of reality (*die Dinge der Wirklichkeit*)."[90] Here, Balázs blurred the terms "feeling" and "sensation" in ways that reflect the dominant impulse that is the subject of this book: the mobilization of the body as the transformation of self. The proletarian individual, he said, "wants to feel himself (Sich selber will es fühlen), and not to be ashamed of this feeling."[91] This book will trace the shaping of that proletarian sensibility.

NOTES

1. Marx, "Economic and Philosophical Manuscripts," 300.
2. Marx and Engels, *The German Ideology*, 35.
3. Bukharin's Speech to the First Pedological Conference in 1927, cited in Etkind, *Eros of the Impossible*, 264–65.
4. Francesco Casetti describes his work on early twentieth-century cinema as locating film within the "network of social discourses that extend within and around it," reading the visual images of film alongside the larger practices, and discursive frameworks, that surround them. Casetti argues that social discourses create "glosses" for the cinematic phenomenon, which "help, if not directly determine, its intelligence and understanding." A parallel argument shapes my own methodology: Casetti, *Eye of the Century*, 170.
5. Kiaer, *Imagine No Possessions*.
6. Trotskii, *Literatura i revoliutsiia*, 189. = The Soviet project to create a "new man" has been much studied. See, for example, Hellebust, *Flesh to Metal*.
7. Simmel, "The Metropolis and Mental Life," 175.
8. Crary, *Suspensions of Perception* (and *Techniques of the Observer*). For Walter Benjamin's discussion of the stimuli that characterize modernity, see his *Charles Baudelaire* and *The Arcades Project*. Wolfgang Schivelbusch's treatment of similar ideas can be found in *The Railway Journey*.
9. Casetti, 178. Other examples are too numerous to list here. See, for example, Jameson, *Signatures of the Visible*; Debord, *Society of the Spectacle*; Comolli, "Machines of the Visible." Of course, many accounts of modernism and visuality are influenced by Foucault's theories of surveillance: Foucault, *Discipline and Punish*. For a detailed critique of ocularcentrism, see Jay, *Downcast Eyes*. For narratives of the relationship between technologies of seeing (in particular cinema) and modernist culture, see, inter alia, Trotter, *Cinema and Modernism*, and Marcus, "Modernism and Visual Culture." See also Jacobs, *The Eye's Mind*, and Danius, *The Senses of Modernism*.
10. Sandomirskaia, "One Sixth of the World."
11. Ibid., 18.
12. Marx, "Economic and Philosophical Manuscripts," 300.

13. As Anna Krylova shows, this binary opposition has provided a structuring metaphor for much scholarship of Soviet Russia, in all fields. Krylova, "Beyond the Spontaneity-Consciousness Paradigm." In literary/cultural analysis, the most important iteration of this binary came in Clark, *The Soviet Novel*.
14. Blok, "Krushenie gumanizma," 112.
15. Tret′iakov, "Chem zhivo kino?" 25.
16. Ibid., 24.
17. As will become clear, however, much of my discussion will emphasize the noncognitive *embodied* experience of feeling that is commonly described as affect. For a useful account of the term, see Flatley, *Affective Mapping*, 20–36, and Leys, "The Turn to Affect."
18. Russian has two verbs that translate the English "to feel/sense": *osiazat′* (to feel by means of touch (sensation), is distinct from the broader *oshchushchat′*, (to sense). In the 1938 *Tolkovyi slovar′ russkogo iazyka*, ed. by B. M. Volin and D. N. Ushakov, for example, *osiazat′* is defined as "perception by means of touch" (oshchup′) (890); *oshchutit′/oshchushchat′* is described as "to grasp by means of sensation" (1039). The other term, *chuvstvovat′* can be translated as "feel/sense," but also has the emotional meaning, to feel. Its derivative, chuvstvo, carries the dual meaning of the physical senses (the five *chuvstva*) and feeling/emotion that are present in the English "feeling." These terms will be discussed in further detail below.
19. Lenin, "Materialism and Empirio-criticism." Cited in *BSE* 1-oe izdanie, 727.
20. Ibid.
21. See, for example, Classen and Howes, *Ways of Sensing*; Classen, *The Deepest Sense*; Smith, *Sensing the Past*; Paterson, *The Senses of Touch*; Garrington, *Haptic Modernism*.
22. Febvre, *The Problem of Unbelief*, 436, cited in Classen, *The Deepest Sense*, xv.
23. Vainshtein, *Aromaty i zapakhi v kul′ture*; Lapin, *Peterburg: Zapakhi i zvuki*.
24. Romaniello and Starks, eds., *Tobacco in Russian History and Culture*; Bogdanov, *Dym otechestva*; Smith, *Recipes for Russia*; Martin, "Sewage and the City," (and his book *Enlightened Metropolis*). See also Romaniello and Starks, eds., *Russian History through the Senses*.
25. Shaw, "'We Have No Need to Lock Ourselves Away.'" See also Shaw, *Deaf in the USSR*.
26. Sandomirskaia, *Blokada v slove*.
27. Chubarov, *Kollektivnaia chuvstvennost′*. Sirotkina, *Shestoe chuvstvo avangarda*.
28. Bulgakova, *Sovetskii slukhoglaz*; Kaganovsky, *How the Soviet Man was Unmade*; Olenina, "Psychomotor Aesthetics"; Toropova, "Educating the Emotions."
29. Halfin, *Terror in My Soul*; Hellbeck, *Revolution on My Mind*. These (and subsequent) monographs emerged after key articles by both scholars, and had prompted considerable debate even before their publication. See, for example, the debates in *Kritika* 6, 1 (2005).
30. Naiman, "On Soviet Subjects, 309.
31. See, for example, Plamper, "Introduction," in Jan Plamper, ed., "Emotional Turn?" See also Plamper, *The History of Emotions*. Notable other works include Plamper, Shakhadat, and Eli, eds., *Rossiiskaia imperiia chuvstv*, and Steinberg and Sobol, eds., *Interpreting Emotions*.
32. Steinberg and Sobol, "Introduction," 6.
33. There is, of course, a vast philosophical history here. In recent history, a particularly important attempt to redress the dominance of vision (and reason) in accounts

of human experience has come from French theoretical school (emerging in part from the phenomenology of Edmund Husserl and Maurice Merleau-Ponty): see in particular Serres, *Les Cinq sens*; Nancy, *Le Sens du Monde*; Deleuze, *Francis Bacon: Logique de la sensation*; Derrida, *Le Toucher*. Obviously, the philosophical history of theories of touch is longer than this, reaching back to Aristotle's "hierarchy of the senses," and assumes particular importance in the works of Denis Diderot and Etienne Bonnot de Condillac. Heller-Roazan provides a theoretically rich account of the intellectual history of touch in his *The Inner Touch*.

34. Marks, *The Skin of the Film*; Sobchak, *Carnal Thoughts*; Bruno, *Atlas of Emotion*; Barker, *The Tactile Eye*.

35. Riegl, *Late Roman Art Industry*.

36. As such, Riegl suggested that haptical art had disappeared with the rise of perspective and figuration—that is, in post-Roman art.

37. Sobchak, *Carnal Thoughts*, 63.

38. Ibid., 162.

39. Ibid.

40. Barker, *The Tactile Eye*, 36, 77.

41. The literature here is extensive, but key works in English include Joravsky, *Russian Psychology*; Graham, *Science and Philosophy*; Etkind, *Eros of the Impossible*. The work of Irina Sirotkina is of particular importance. See, for example, Sirotkina and Smith, "The Russian Federation"; Sirotkina, *Diagnosing Literary Genius*; Sirotkina, Barbara, Dupont, eds., *History of the Neurosciences in France and Russia*, and Sirotkina, "The Ubiquitous Reflex."

42. Zalkind, *Estestvoznanie i marksizm*, 3 (1929): 216, cited in Joravsky, *Russian Psychology*, 250.

43. Vygotskii, "Istoricheskii smysl psikhologicheskogo krizisa," 436.

44. Vöhringer, "Professionalisiertes Laientum," 333. Etkind calculates that in 1922, there were at least thirteen research institutes directly focused on forms of psychological research in Moscow and Petrograd alone. See Etkind, *Eros of the Impossible*, 16–17.

45. Borovskii, "Chto takoe psikhologiia?" 158.

46. Joravsky, *Russian Psychology*, 264.

47. Lenin, "Materialism and Empirio-criticism," 13, cited in Kornilov, "Psychology in the Light of Dialectic Materialism," 246.

48. Lenin, "Materialism and Empirio-criticism," 130. Lenin's analysis was in part a critique of Ernst Mach's sensationalism, which was, as Graham states, "the late nineteenth century's most formidable criticism of the philosophic belief in a material world independent of man's mind" (Graham, *Science and Philosophy*, 42). In *Analysis of Sensations* (1897), Mach asserted that the "world consists only of our sensations." This view had significant influence on some Marxist philosophers such as Aleksandr Bogdanov and Anatolii Lunacharskii. It placed emphasis on the human *organization* of the perception of matter; for Bogdanov in particular, this principle of *organization* became the basis for his theory of the relationship between the human and the material world. In simple terms, however, Mach's thesis denied the objective existence of the material world, and its capacity to *shape* human subjects. As such, it was, in Lenin's view, antithetical to the materialism that was at the heart of the Marxist project.

49. See Lenin's commentary on Diderot's "Conversations between d'Alembert and Diderot," in "Materialism and Empirio-criticism," 36.

50. Gustav Fechner coined the term "psychophysics" in his *Elemente der Psychophysik* (1860). See Hawkings, "William James, Gustav Fechner and Early Psychophysics," 68.

51. For a complete list of James's translations into Russian, see Delaney Grossman and Rischin, *William James in Russian Culture*, 224. See also page 3 in that volume for a discussion of the translation of James's work.

52. Sirotkina, "The Art and Science of Movement," 184.

53. Crary, *Suspensions of Perception*, 169.

54. Daniel Beer has noticed the importance of social psychology—and in particular of theories of crowd psychology and suggestion in the conceptualization of revolutionary action as mental contagion. See Beer, *Renovating Russia*.

55. Graham, *Science and Philosophy*, 363.

56. Ivan Sechenov's interest in the "human machine" had much in common with the theories of Jules Amar in France. Amar's *Le rendement de la machine humaine* (1908) was published in Russia in 1922 (Amar, *Chelovecheskaia mashina*).

57. Bekhterev, *Kollektivnaia refleksologiia*. Despite his eventual lionization, Pavlov had an initially more complex relationship with the Soviet regime. See Todes, *Ivan Pavlov*.

58. Joravsky, *Russian Psychology*, 224, 274. For discussion of the prominence of reflex theory in Russia in this period, see Sirotkina, "The Ubiquitous Reflex."

59. Bukharin, *Historical Materialism*, 98.

60. Halfin, *Terror in My Soul*, 97.

61. Joravsky, *Russian Psychology*, 213.

62. Kornilov, "Psychology in the Light of Dialectic Materialism," 16; Borovskii, "Chto takoe psikhologiia," 157.

63. Aron Zalkind, *Ocherki kul′tury revoliutsionnogo vremeni*, 74. Zalkind enumerated the following qualities: revolutionary monoidealism, dynamism, avant-gardism, a sense of risk, capacity for analysis, sociocentrism, and "higher sublimation" (advocating that sexual energy must be sublimated into the revolutionary project).

64. One extreme interpretation of early Soviet mechanism is Emanuil Enchmen's theory of new biology, first announced in a pamphlet published in 1920: Enchmen, *Vosemnadtsat′ tezisov*. Enchmen announced the death of the psyche, which, along with consciousness and reason, he condemned as a method of capitalist exploitation: all cognition was based in physiological reaction. The human self is thus entirely knowable. Thus as Naiman notes, Enchmen envisaged the "collectivization of [that] body's functions, pleasures and desires." See Naiman, *Sex in Public*, 77.

65. In 1924, Bukharin became an outspoken critic of "Enchmeniada," challenging Enchmen for the "the practical expulsion of the psychical and the emotional." Bukharin, "Enchmeniada"; see Naiman, *Sex in Public*, 75.

66. Vygotskii, "Istoricheskii smysl psikhologicheskogo krizisa."

67. Several new psychological periodicals were established in 1928 and 1929: *Psychology* (*Psikhologiia* [closed 1932]); *Pedology* (*Pedologiia* [closed 1932]), and *Psycho-physiology of labour and Psychotechnics* (*Psikhofiziologiia truda i psikhotekhniki* [renamed *Sovetskaia psikhotekhnika* in 1932—and closed in 1934]); see Kozulin, *Psychology in Utopia*, x. Shpielrein's attempt at rebranding psychotechnics was unsuccessful, however: in 1934, the journal *Soviet Psychotechnics* was closed down; twenty-nine research institutes were closed; Shpielrein himself was arrested in 1935, and executed in 1937. For discussion of the end of psychotechnics in Soviet Russia, see Kurek, "Razrushenie psikhotekhniki."

68. Graham, *Science and Philosophy*, 365.

69. Vygotskii, "Soznanie kak problema psikhologii povedeniia."

70. Vygotskii and Luriia were by no means part of the scientific mainstream, however; and their position in the Psychological Institute under the leadership of Kornilov became rapidly untenable.

71. Graham, *Science and Philosophy*, 366.

72. Gaivorovskii, "Chuvstva i emotsii."

73. Tarkhanov, "Oshchushchenie."

74. Lapshin, "Chuvstvovanie." Lapshin provides a lengthy history of the changing understanding of feeling (broadly understood as the senses).

75. Anon, "Oshchushchenie," *BSE*, 1-oe izdanie, 727. Teplov, "Chuvstvo," 727. The latter volume was published in 1934, but the entry was probably written during the early 1930s or even before. The first edition of the *BSE* was under the general editorship of Otto Shmidt (note that Shmidt's wife, Vera Shmidt, became the head of the Psychoanalytical Kindergarten, which was opened in Moscow in August 1921, and secretary of the Russian Psychoanalytical Society from 1927). The second edition of the Encyclopedia was begun in 1949, and edited, from 1951 by B. A. Vvedenskii.

76. Teplov, "Chuvstvo."

77. Leont'ev, "Emotsiia." Leont'ev's work focused on sensation (Sirotkina, *Shestoe chuvstvo avangarda*, 64); and he was particularly interested in the importance of touch in the differentiation of color. See, for example, Leont'ev and Luriia, "Issledovanie ob"ektivnykh simptomov affektivnykh reaktskii." The definition of "affect" itself, meanwhile, was provided by Luriia himself (and cross-referenced with "emotsii"). Affect was, Luriia claimed, "passionately occurring emotion" *manifest in the body*. Luriia, "Affekt," 150–51.

78. See Kassof, "A Book of Socialism," 55–95.

79. Anon, "Emotsii," 31–32.

80. Anon, "Chuvstvo," 459.

81. Ibid., 459.

82. Anon, "Oshchushchenie," *BSE*, 2-oe izdanie, 504.

83. Ibid., 504.

84. Anon, "Affekt," 558.

85. For more detail on set design, see Widdis, "Cinema and the Art of Being."

86. Mead and Métraux, eds., *The Study of Culture*, 175.

87. The original etymology of the term "aesthetics" (*aisthetikos*) describes something that is "perceptible by the senses." The definition of the term as relating to beauty develops in the course of the eighteenth century.

88. Benjamin, "The Work of Art in the Age of its Reproducibility: Second Version," 124. Benjamin used the term "innervation" frequently in relation to revolution and technology. See, for example, "Surrealism," 217–18.

89. Balázs, "Sachlichkeit und sozialismus," 918.

90. Ibid.

91. Ibid.

Chapter One

AVANT-GARDE SENSATIONS

> For without touch it is impossible to have any other sense.
> Aristotle, *De Anima*

In January 1921, Italian Futurist Filippo Marinetti announced a new art of "Tactilism," exhibiting a series of panels covered with different textures and materials to be perceived by the hand, and not by the eye. These "tactile boards" were part of a broader project for the "education of the sense of touch," involving tactile dresses, tactile beds, sofas, pillows, streets, and theaters.[1]

Although the Russian and Soviet avant-garde has no single example of such a vivid preoccupation with the sense of touch, an interest in the relationship between art and physical sensation runs through avant-garde and early revolutionary culture: Viktor Shklovskii's famous essay of 1917, "Art as Device," identified the goal of art as to give the "sensation" (oshchushchenie) of things; Dziga Vertov celebrated the camera's power to create a "cinematic sensation" (kinooshchushchenie) of the world.[2] This chapter will trace the preoccupation with material that underlies such statements, showing how the Russian and Soviet avant-garde imagined themselves to be engaged in a project for a reeducation of the senses, at the heart of which lay a dream of a reanimated sensory proximity between the human body and the world.

It is a well-recognized characteristic of modernist artistic production that the focus shifts from the object of representation to the *experience* of representation. The spectator—and the transformation of his/her body and mind—becomes the product of the artwork. For László Moholy-Nagy, for example, art was a means of schooling the senses to meet the complex perceptual tasks and physiological aspects of modernity.[3] In the Soviet context, this was linked to a broader, more ambitious project: the creation of the new Soviet man and woman. According to Tret′iakov's declaration of 1923, the artist must be a psycho-engineer, a psycho-constructor.[4] Tret′iakov's emphasis on the psyche, however, is misleading: the early revolutionary avant-garde envisaged the construction of the new Soviet subject as taking place first and foremost through the body. Art was a means through which the senses could be transformed. And one crucial element of this transformation was the remaking of the relationship between the human and material worlds. There was, however, an unresolved tension between two apparently opposing aims: the search for an unmediated, embodied *encounter* between the human body and the material, and the need to *transform*, control, or process that material.

This chapter will explore this project, and its tensions, in three areas of Soviet avant-garde culture. First, I will discuss pre- and postrevolutionary theories of art as an encounter with material and texture (faktura), and show how, in the postrevolutionary context, art was seen as a means of direct intervention in the interface between the human body and the world. Second, I will trace how these preoccupations were part of a wider dialogue between artistic production and psychological science, which was particularly potent in relation to arts such as dance and theater. Finally, I will examine the particular role that cinema was seen to occupy in the sensory project. In sum, the chapter will reveal the wide discursive range of the avant-garde preoccupation with *material*, positioning it as part of a broader interest in the capacity of art to create a relationship between the human body and the physical world—in revolutionary terms.

Material Sensations

The history of the Russian avant-garde's interest in material and volume is well-established.[5] It is perhaps most vividly evident in the work of Vladimir Tatlin, whose prerevolutionary counter-reliefs, composed of different material textures and surfaces protruding above a base canvas, sought to allow material to shape form.[6] Tatlin referred to his work as a "culture of materials." In a 1920 statement accompanying his famous "Monument to the Third International" (the Tatlin Tower), he wrote decisively: "Distrusting the eye, we place it under the control of touch."[7]

Maria Gough has described Tatlin's prerevolutionary work as guided by the "volition of the material"; it was also marked by what Margit Rowell calls a desire to "return to primary experience."[8] In this sense, Tatlin had common ground with many members of diverse avant-garde groupings. In particular, Viktor Shklovskii's notion of "estrangement" (*ostranenie*), first coined in a lecture of 1913, described the "making strange" of objects, through the formal devices of art, in order to prompt renewed perception.[9] Its purpose was to restore to human experience the full sensory immediacy of the world, which had implicitly been lost in modern life: "The goal of art is to give the sensation (oshchushchenie) of the world—as seeing (*videnie*), and not as recognition."[10] Shklovskii was explicit in giving this sensation material, and even tactile, qualities: art exists, he proclaimed, in order "to make the stone stony."

Shklovskii's use of the term "oshchushchenie" will be considered further below. For now, it should be noted that it, and Tatlin's call toward tactility, were linked to a key term in avant-garde aesthetic theory: faktura. This word, which has no easy translation into English, had considerable resonance in artistic discussions in all fields during this period.[11] At its simplest, faktura describes texture or materiality, but it also refers to the working of that material in an artistic context. Hansen-Löve provides a rich genealogy of the use of faktura in Russian avant-garde theory, pointing to the importance of texts such as David Burliuk's "Cubism" (1912) and Vladimir Markov's, "Principles of Creation in the Plastic Arts" (1914), as well as Nikolai Tarabukin's "Towards a Theory of Painting" (1916).[12] For Markov, faktura was the "noise of the material," and art must reflect the "love for material" that was at the root of human existence.[13] In an essay notably entitled "On Faktura and Counter-reliefs," Shklovskii himself wrote that the key task of both writers and visual artists consists primarily in creating an "object that ... can be felt (*oshchutimuiu*) in every place—a textural (*fakturnuiu*) object."[14]

Shklovskii's blurring of visual and verbal faktura here points to the wider applicability of the term in the pre- and postrevolutionary context, and links it to the project of ostranenie: rediscovering the sensory plenitude of experience, through the body.[15] This was a common emphasis. For Formalist theorists of language (and for Futurist poets), for example, the release of the word from its denotative meaning was seen as enabling a discovery of its material qualities: the faktura of language itself. Formalist theories of poetry explored the relationship between corporeal experience (the physical sensation of the mouth in forming particular sounds) and psychological response (the emotions created *by* these movements). In Shklovskii's own words, "Perhaps it is the articulatory aspect—something akin to the dance of the organs of speech—that is responsible for most of the pleasure given to us by poetry."[16]

In sum, before 1917, for all the nuanced differences between diverse practitioners and theorists, faktura described material as apprehended through the senses, with particular emphasis on corporeal sensation. After the revolution, however, the concept of faktura acquired ideological resonance. It became a potent "index of material presence," a marker of the essential proximitiy between art and lived experience that was a condition of the revolutionary avant-garde.[17] Constructivist theorist Aleksei Gan distinguished the postrevolutionary avant-garde view of faktura from what he called a traditional artistic understanding. Where the term might traditionally describe simply "the handling of a surface," for the avant-garde it meant "the selection and processing (*obrabotka*) of the raw material."[18] Two important concepts are blurred here. Certainly, faktura remained linked to a broader emphasis on the sensory rediscovery of the material world (the *raw material*).[19] As Gough points out, however, the "principle of materiological determination" was supplemented by the idea of the processing of the material.[20] This shift reflects the key tension that underlay the materialist impulse in Soviet culture: between the desire for enhanced proximity with the world as it was, and the desire to transform that world.[21] The three core principles put forward by Gan in his manifesto of Constructivism make this tension visible. Gan proposed that Constructivist art should depend on an understanding of the texture and material (faktura) of an object, and its volumetric presence in space (*tektonika*).[22] His final principle, however, was that of *konstruktsiia* (construction)—described by Buchloh as the "organization of the kinetic life of objects." This organization is an act of processing (obrabotka)—transforming the raw material into a socialist object. As such, faktura incorporated both a primitive rediscovery of the material, and its transformation.

Nikolai Chuzhak, key member of the Left Front of Art (LEF) movement, made a programmatic differentiation between two models of art that underlines this dual emphasis. Art was both a means of knowing the world, and means of constructing it.[23] And socialist art must aim to *construct*. Yet the project of construction and reconstruction was still premised on a sensory proximity with the material. For Chuzhak, the "dialectical 'sensing' (chuvstvovanie) of the world through the material" was the first stage in art's project of transforming human life.²⁴ The world is felt (and known) through the material; it is then organized and *processed* through art; finally, it is *refelt* as a new and specifically Soviet sensate experience.

Constructivism, then, as it evolved in the early to mid-1920s, was at its base a vision of art as a reshaping of material reality—a model of direct human interaction with the material. This was particularly evident in the project of *zhiznestroenie* (life-building), articulated by Chuzhak and other members of LEF. Convinced by the materialist vision of the human subject as shaped in an interface with the object world, LEF members were committed to altering that interface. From 1924 to 1925, Tatlin's studio in the Leningrad branch of the Institute of Artistic Culture (INKhUK) was named the Section for Material Culture, and underpinned by "research into material as the shaping principle of culture production and experience."²⁵ In Moscow, VKhUTEMAS, which focused on providing "highly qualified artist-practitioners for modern industry," training artists, architects, metalworkers, ceramicists, textile designers etc., drew in artists such as Aleksandr Rodchenko, Varvara Stepanova, and Liubov' Popova as teachers and designers.²⁶

A glance at the VKhUTEMAS core curriculum in the mid-1920s reveals how avant-garde theorists and practitioners during the first postrevolutionary decade were interested in the possibilities of multisensory experience in both the creation and the reception of art. It also shows the complex relationship between the twin imperatives of encountering and processing the material. In the foundational "Space" course, for example (organized by Nikolai Ladovskii, Vladimir Krinskii, and Nikolai Dokuchaev, with Konstantin Mel'nikov as an instructor), students used clay to visualize space, shaping and molding their architectural ideas by hand, from malleable (claggy) organic material (figure 1.1). This method was informed by Ladovskii's interest in the relationship between tactile experience and cognition. Clay, he argued, would prompt an automatic connection between mind, body, and matter, which would enable cognitive leaps, and ultimately provoke the creation of new forms.²⁷

This emphasis on a reanimated contact between the (creating) body and the material world in the Soviet 1920s was increasingly linked to a broader focus on the relationship between human and object worlds, and a desire to shape that relationship. As Marx had recognized, the bourgeois relationship with things was principally one of consumption, and this produced a

Fig. 1.1 Hands-on Modernism. Students at VKhUTEMAS in the Space laboratory, during a lesson on the evaluation of mass and weight (1925). Private collection.

condition of alienation. According to LEF theorist Boris Arvatov, this separation of consumption from production had produced not only unresponsive *bodies*, but also unresponsive *things*. In his words: "The construction of proletarian culture . . . requires the elimination of that rupture between things and people that characterized bourgeois society."[28] Arvatov argued that the "thing" in bourgeois society was finished, fixed, and inert, for it was in no active contact with the human subject.[29] In the imagined socialist utopia, by contrast, there would be "a giant system of collaboration between humanity and the spontaneous forces of nature." In Kiaer's words: "Only under socialism will the object be animated by the living force of nature; socialism must foster the forms of technology that unite nature with production and with everyday life."[30] As Kiaer has suggested, Arvatov and the

Constructivists conceived of the new industrial objects of socialism as "co-worker(s), fulfilling or amplifying the sensory capacities of the human organism."[31] Thus Marx's theory of fully sensuous human activity was to be realized by Constructivism: industrial design and production transformed the object world into one designed by man—and thus in sensory harmony with him.

Bodily Sensations

Arvatov's understanding of the Soviet individual as psycho-piological directly echoes Trotskii's call for the psychophysical education of the new Soviet man, and in turn the longer history of Russian and Soviet psychology.[32] Indeed, this phrase recurred frequently during the early Soviet period and signified two things: the dominance of the monistic vision of mind and body, and the proximity between cultural production and psychological/physiological science. It was common for artistic training to include a grounding in psychology. Alongside Tatlin's Section for Material Culture, the Leningrad INKhUK contained a psycho-physiological department, led by Mikhail Matiushin.[33] Largely through the initiative of Vasilii Kandinskii, the Moscow INKhUK and the Academy for Artistic Sciences (GAKhN) also had psycho-physiological departments, carrying out research into the scientific, sensory basis of artistic perception. GAKhN's department in particular became a cradle for research into the role of sensation and emotion, stimulus and affect, in both the creation and the reception of art, and there was considerable cross-fertilization and dialogue between the more clearly avant-garde INKhUK and GAKhN, with many scholars, artists, and scientists moving regularly between the two.[34]

Although it was diverse and informed by many different psychological theories (such as psychoanalysis, gestalt, etc.[35]), much of the research in GAKhN reflected the broad influence of reflexology on the development of theories of artistic perception and production during the first decade after 1917. As Zalkind stated in 1925: "The materialist endeavors of the proletariat, the only revolutionary class today, go along well with reflexology—this objective, experimental, monistic, and materialist doctrine.... Reflexology... will provide us with invaluable means for educating and reeducating man according to the goals of the proletarian revolution."[36]

This principle underlay the spread of applied psychology in Soviet society more widely, in the form of psychotechnics (*psikhotekhnika*). In broad terms, psychotechnics describes projects for the transformation of the psyche via the manipulation of the body. In Soviet Russia, it found its most famous realization in Aleksei Gastev's experiments in his Central Institute of Labor (TsIT), founded in 1921 with the aim of investigating, and ultimately creating, the optimal conditions for efficient, rationalized labor processes.[37] Work in Gastev's institute was influenced by Western theories of labor (Frederick Taylor's time-efficiency charts, the Fordist production line), as well as by the motion-studies work initiated by Etienne-Jules Marey.[38] Its chief neuropsychologist during the 1920s was Nikolai Bernstein, whose work focused on the analysis of human movement using recording apparatus, and whose theory of "biomechanics" had profound influence across the wide field of Soviet culture.[39]

In the Institute of Labor, biomechanics was a scientifically organized series of exercises, seeking to maximize the efficiency of what Gastev called "that magnificent machine that is so close to us—the human organism."[40] Biomechanics sought to change the relationship between the human body and its tasks, establishing what Gastev called a new physical *ustanovka*—a set of "biological and social qualities."[41] This term, "ustanovka," recurs in works of the period, with different inflections. Olenina translates it in Gastev's usage as a bodily tune-up, describing a combination of physical positioning and mental attitude.[42] According to Zalkind, the new socialist world order would change the very ustanovka not just of the outer body, but of its internal organs: Soviet man or woman would have more perfectly realized sensory organs—the ability to see farther, to smell and taste better.[43]

Such ideas had considerable resonance across diverse fields of Soviet art and culture.[44] Perhaps most obviously, reflexology and psychotechnics influenced the conceptualization of physical movement and emotional expression in acting and dance, not only in theater director Vsevolod Meierkhol'd's famous training system of biomechanics. There was an active relationship between Gastev's Institute of Labor and the Dance Studio of Rhythmo-plastics run by Nikolai Pozniakov; Bernstein was active in the Institutes of Musicology and Choreography; and the Institute of Labor and the GAKhN Laboratory of Choreology (which focused on the relationship between mental state and plastic pose[45]) ran a collaborative exhibition in 1926.[46] The principle of mechanization and efficiency was not the only framework that structured dreams of broadening the perceptual capacities of the human body, however. The Organic schools that centered around Matiushin's laboratory in the Leningrad Academy of Artistic Sciences (such as the Geptakhor Dance Studio, active between 1924 and 1927) were focused on achieving freedom of bodily movement and expression that would expand human perceptual capacities and enable a closer relationship with nature.[47] Ultimately, all these movements had in common the project of teaching human bodies how to *feel* more intensively. The training of the body enables its liberation, and in turn, it permits a new, proximate relationship with (and apprehension of) the material world. Intrinsic to biomechanics and its realization in performance art, however, was a dialectical relationship between freedom and control.

Film Sensations

Film practitioners were very much aware of movements in psychological science—and indeed were often in direct dialogue with it. Vsevolod Pudovkin's *Mechanics of the Brain* (*Mekhanika golovnogo mozga*, 1926) was an investigation into Ivan Pavlov's experiments in conditioned reflexes.[48] It was not alone. Olenina notes that, shortly after the production of *Mechanics of the Brain*, Mezhrabpom-Rus' advertised a forthcoming film *Modern Neuroses* (*Sovremennye nevrozy*), based on a script by Zalkind, with Bekhterev as chief scientific consultant.[49] Between 1928 and 1929, two intriguing documentaries directly reflected recent research into psychological science: *For Your Health* (*Za vashe zdorov'e*, dir. Aleksandr Dubrovskii, 1929); and *Nervous Illness* (*Bol'nye nervy*, dir. Noi Galkin, 1929).

The interest was mutual. For psychologists, film had two potential benefits. First, as Bekhterev wrote in a 1915 article, film was a scientific resource, enabling new knowledge of human experience.[50] In an essay published in *Kinofot* in 1922, Nikolai Tikhonov suggested that cinema enabled humanity to "reach a deeper level of knowledge."[51] The camera's observational power could improve study of the mechanics of human movement and sensation, and their relationship to the psyche.[52] Second, film could act on the spectator: a study of the spectatorial response to different filmic phenomena could help scientific investigations of perception. Ultimately, it might even enable the *transformation* of perception itself. An article in a 1919 collection argued that cinema had "practical significance for consciousness."[53]

There was considerable direct cross-fertilization between film and psychology during the early Soviet period. It is well known that Dziga Vertov studied at Bekhterev's Psychoneurological Institute in Saint Petersburg between 1914 and 1916.[54] Abram Room was a fellow student at the institute (alongside author and journalist Larisa Reisner and filmmaker Grigorii Boltianskii) and later described how, when teaching at the State Film Academy (GTK) during the 1920s, he sought to use Bekhterev's theories of collective reflexology in training actors.[55] Olenina has studied in depth how reflexology and psychotechnics had a wider influence on developing theories of theatrical and cinematic performance—in the work of Lev Kuleshov in particular.[56]

Sergei Eisenstein also had well-documented connections with psychologists. In the early 1920s, he was close to Zalkind, and made considerable notes on Bekhterev's reflexology: his early writings—in particular the theory of "expressive movement," and the principle of the "montage of attractions"—were directly influenced by the idea of the reflex.[57] Later, Eisenstein worked closely with Vygotskii, Luriia, and linguist Nikolai Marr (see chapter 5).[58] Possibly through this contact, Aleksei Leont'ev, a close associate of Luriia and Vygotskii, taught at the State Film Academy between 1928 and 1930, when his position in the Psychological Institute became untenable under the leadership of Kornilov.[59]

Of course, pre- and postrevolutionary Russian film practitioners were by no means unique in their interest in film's affiliation with psychological research. In the United States, Hugo Münsterberg, a pioneer of experimental psychology who insisted on the relation between body and mind, was one of the first to conceptualize the relationship between film and the creation of specific emotional and sensory responses in the spectator.[60] For Münsterberg, film had a dual ability. It could *show* emotion on-screen (characters experiencing anger, pain, or joy, for example); but it could also *provoke* emotion. And crucially, it would do so through the *sensory* impact of formal devices. In Münsterberg's words: "Of course, impressions which come to our eye can at first awaken only sensations, and a sensation is not an emotion. But it is well known that in the view of modern physiological psychology our consciousness of the emotion itself is shaped and marked by the sensations which arise from our bodily organs."[61]

Münsterberg saw film as a form of psychotechnical education, which had the potential to remodel human consciousness: "The massive outer world has lost its weight, it has been freed from space, time and causality, and it has been clothed in the forms of our own consciousness. The mind has triumphed over matter and the pictures roll on with the ease of musical tones."[62]

Cinematic Material(s)

Münsterberg's vision was one of control—envisaging a human mastery over nature. As such, it prompts us to consider the specificity of the Soviet ideological context, and how it shaped notions of film's potential. In the Marxist materialist climate of early Soviet Russia, cinema's indexical link with reality gave it particular potency—felt not only by film theorists, but more widely. Commissar of Enlightenment Anatolii Lunacharskii emphasized film's capacity to reveal the details of the physical world: "No theater can show you some tiny flower, trembling in the wind, covered with dew."[63] Cinema was an art born of technology, yet it seemed *material* (and materialist). In Lunacharskii's words, it "flies with steel, electrified wings, but maintains an entirely human face."[64] It was this human link with lived experience that provided cinema's most important ideological validation in Soviet Russia during the 1920s. It seemed a unique lens through which to understand—to *feel*—the material conditions of everyday life as they shaped the human subject. In the words of Gan, "The technical system of contemporary society demands from us other ways of moving, of explaining ourselves and orientating ourselves above all in its material-object (*material'no-veshchestvennoi*) dimension."[65] Cinema was an explanatory aid for this new "material-object" life, an epistemological tool for the new age.

Soviet theorists were by no means alone here. Much early film theory was preoccupied with the phenomenological impact of cinema, and marked by a conviction that cinema might be able to articulate a new relationship between human and object worlds. As noted by Trotter, many filmmakers (and writers) shared "a conviction . . . that the instrumentality of the new recording media had made it possible for the first time to represent (as well as to record) *existence as such*."[66] In the words of Antonin Artaud, writing in 1927: "The human skin of things, the epidermis of reality: this is the primary raw material of cinema. Cinema exalts matter and reveals it to us in its profound spirituality."[67]

Film was not just an explanatory aid, however; it had the potential to change the relationship between the human body and the world. The roots of materialist-phenomenological early film theories lay in Marxism: in contrast to the sterile commodity fetishism of capitalism, socialism must have a reanimated relationship with the material world. Georg Lukács, for example, criticized the abstract "thinginess" (*Dinghaftigkeit*) that was a condition of capitalist society, and called for the release of the object world from commodification into a new, proximate relationship with the human subject.[68] Many Marxist theorists saw film as playing a key role here. As is well known, Walter Benjamin feared that technological-industrial advance would rupture the sensucus relationship between body and material that was, he believed, intrinsic to handcraft. Apparently paradoxically, however, Benjamin argued that technologies such as cinema had the potential to restore that relationship, to remake it in terms appropriate to the modern age: "Evidently a different nature opens itself to the camera than opens to the naked eye—if only because an unconsciously penetrated space is substituted for a space consciously explored by man."[69]

Film's optical unconscious enabled what Benjamin called a "tactical tactility," which could recreate the embodied link between the human and the material, implicitly lost under capitalism. In essays written in the late 1920s, Benjamin's contemporary Siegfried Kracauer lamented (German) filmmakers' failure to exploit cinema's capacity to remake the human sensorium, and to fully engage the details of the material everyday.[70] Much later, in 1960, Kracauer diagnosed the problem of modern man as an insufficiently tactile relationship with the world.[71] What was needed, he suggested, was "to touch reality not only with the finger tips but to seize it and shake hands with it."[72] In the face of this condition, film had particular potential: "It effectively assists us in discovering the material world with its psychophysical correspondences. We literally redeem this world from its dormant state, its state of virtual nonexistence, by endeavouring to experience it through the camera."[73] Film's redemptive capacity lay in part in its capacity to stimulate what, in his unpublished notes, Kracauer called "the material layers of the human being: his nerves, his senses, his entire physiological substance."[74] Cinema proceeds from the senses to the mind, and not the other way around.[75] As such, it has the capacity to forge a reanimated relationship with the world.

A similar redemptive impulse underpinned the Soviet cinematic project in the 1920s. Indeed, it had particular ideological urgency. Although ostranenie was framed as a theory of literature, and Shklovskii himself never linked it directly to cinema, it had clear relevance for other arts—and perhaps even for cinema in particular.[76] Indeed, Annie van den Oever sees estrangement as an early iteration of what became a core element of film theory by the mid to late 1920s: the idea that, in the conditions of modernity, film was well equipped to teach the human subject how to see again.[77] The question, however, was twofold. *What* should be seen? And *how* would cinema do that teaching? And how could filmic "seeing" offer a new model of experience?

Soviet film practitioners were in constant dialogue with Western theory and practice during the 1920s and into the 1930s, and the shaping of an ideologically appropriate vision of cinema's phenomenological capacity took place in relation to this dialogue. Many of the most influential Western film theories in Russia during the 1920s were those that emphasized film's ability to reveal the lost or hidden truth of the material world, particularly those theories of French impressionist filmmaker and theorist Louis Delluc, and Hungarian theorist Béla Balázs. In 1924, publishers in both Moscow and Leningrad advertised the publication of a Russian translation of Delluc's short book, *Photogénie* (first published in French in 1920).[78] Balázs's work *The Visible Man* was published in Russian in early 1925.[79] Both works provoked a storm of debates in the Soviet film press, which reveal a search for a specifically Soviet theory of film's phenomenological power.

Delluc proclaimed that cinema could bypass rational perception, enabling a "pure" act of seeing: "*Photogénie*, you see, is the law of cinema. In order to recognize it you have to have eyes that are *real eyes*."[80] Film was a means of creating a "lived" experience for the spectator, in which the world was "alive." To this end, Delluc provided a list of objects that were innately photogenic—natural phenomena such as the sea and clouds, and new industrial phenomena such as the locomotive, steamboat, airplane, and railway—and celebrated the power of cinema to reveal their full material presence.[81] This emphasis on cinema's capacity to provoke a heightened apprehension of the textures and surfaces of the world had considerable resonance for Soviet cinema's own materialist project. Responses to Delluc made visible, however, the tension in Soviet culture between those twin imperatives: to encounter the material, or to *process* it. Delluc's emphasis was described as "impressionistic" and lacking in ideological focus—a pantheistic celebration of the natural world.[82] Vsevolod Pudovkin, for one, took issue with his "lyricism," and declared *Photogénie* "alien (*chuzhdaia*) and almost useless to us."[83] He did, however, acknowledge the photogenic quality of the filmed material as the most important question in cinema, the importance of choice of material, and specifically the necessity of faktura.[84] He also shared the conviction that film could enable a deeper understanding of material reality: "The film apparatus as if unceasingly, intently, penetrates to the depths of life; it tries to get to places that an average observer could never reach, as they superficially grasp, with their passing glance, the world that surrounds them."[85]

Despite these shared emphases, Pudovkin's theory differed from Delluc's in two key ways. First, he defined the task of film explicitly as one of the *organization* of matter: the filmmaker must "exclude chaos and contingency."[86] Second, he stated emphatically that it was the rhythm of editing, not the innate power of material, that created the power of a film.[87] Editing (montage) was a cinematic form of processing the material. Pudovkin's emphasis on organization was echoed in Eisenstein's important essay, "A Materialist Approach to Film Form" (published alongside Pudovkin's essay in 1925). Eisenstein went characteristically further, however: the task of revolutionary form in cinema was "the creation of a new view of, and approach (*podkhod*) to, things."[88] Film form (montage) had the capacity not just to reveal reality, but to recarve it.

Béla Balázs, who lived in Moscow during the 1930s, had a closer and more complex relationship with the Soviet film community than Delluc. In *The Visible Man*, Balázs seemed to share a core Soviet belief that film could play a role in creating the new embodied human being that would emerge out of the ashes of capitalist alienation.[89] "Man will become visible again," he declared. "It is film that will have the ability to raise up and make visible once more human beings who are now buried under mountains of words and concepts."[90] In contrast to Delluc, moreover, Balázs's work had clear political inflection as what Erica Carter has called "utopian modernism." For him, cinema was an instrument of what Carter terms "phenomenological epistemology"—a new means of knowing the world through the senses.[91] It uncovered "the hidden mainsprings of a life we had thought we already knew so well."[92] As such, film spectatorship was an act of apperception: it could provoke an intensified sensory awareness of empirical phenomena, and have a profound impact on psychic development.[93]

Here too, the tension between discovery of the material and its recarving provided the poles of debate in the Soviet press. Balázs's theory depended on a sense of the material world as *living material*. For him, the task of film was to reveal the "living physiognomy that all things possess."[94] His, then, was an unproblematic celebration of the material *as it is*. In the Soviet context, the challenge was to process it, for it was by processing the material that spectators themselves could be transformed. Responding directly to Balázs's work, Eisenstein asserted that only montage could achieve that dual purpose.[95] He took issue with Balázs's emphasis on the value of the individual shot; the power of cinema lay entirely in the *combination of shots*. Montage permitted what Eisenstein had earlier called the "organization of the spectator through organized material."[96] It shaped (and controlled) the sensory-emotional response of the spectator.[97]

It is clear, then, that the relationship between body, mind, and world was a major preoccupation in early film theory, and raised difficult questions in the Soviet context. Here we return to Viktor Shklovskii—a key protagonist in my sensory story. Shklovskii's evolving theories of cinema through the 1920s reflect the complexity of Soviet attitudes toward cinema's capacity to provoke a sensory encounter with the raw material of the world. As the theory of ostranenie demonstrates, Shklovskii was interested in bodies and senses, yet his own writings on cinema during the 1920s lack the sensory emphasis of ostranenie, and speak to his evolution within the ideological frameworks of LEF: it is notable that Shklovskii does not use the term "ostranenie" in relation to cinema at all.

The root of Shklovskii's problematic relationship with film lay in his understanding of film's indexical relationship with the world. For Shklovskii, film's difficulty lay in the fact that, as a photographic medium, it was *unable* to alter the material essence of its objects: "Film is concerned ... with an unchanged object."[98] The challenge for the filmmaker was to discover methods that enabled the photographic image to be "made strange." This was necessary in order that the object be *felt*, in Shklovskii's terms, and it was achievable through montage.[99] Disagreeing with Delluc, Shklovskii and his fellow Formalists argued that *any object* could be photogenic, provided the correct means of filming and editing were used. The material properties of the object remain vital, but the filmmaker's task is to organize them. As Boris Kazanskii noted, "the dramatic character of a film is simply the result of the special organization of its textures (faktura)."[100]

The picture is not as simple as it may appear, however. It is notable that Kazanskii emphasized faktura: the film enables an encounter with the filmed object in sensory plenitude. Despite the gradual evolution through the 1920s toward a model of cinema as processing the material, a phenomenological-epistemological impetus was visible in Formalist film theory and practice throughout the decade. Shklovskii himself was unquestionably interested in the affective power of cinema: in a pamphlet of 1927, he described the task of the director as working with the "building blocks" of "cinematic sensation (*kinematograficheskoe oshchushchenie*)."[101] He sought to identify what he called the "source of film's artistic *oshchutimost'*, its capacity to make itself *felt* through the senses."[102] In related terms, Eikhenbaum echoed Balázs and Delluc's emphasis on the power of cinema as bypassing rational, language-based cognition, describing film as enabling its spectator to "see things afresh and sense them as unfamiliar things."[103] This new form of perception was, moreover, explicity nontextual: "The film viewer seeks relief from the word; he wishes only to see and divine."[104]

This phenomenological impulse was inflected by—indeed it could be justified by—Marxist materialism. And the materialist underpinning complicated Shklovskii's attitude toward the filmed object. From 1926 on, Shklovskii began to refer consistently to film "material"—a term that also had considerable resonance in the evolution of Formalist theory.[105] This term, "material," will recur frequently in our discussions in this book, for it was at the center of Soviet inquiries film's capacity to engage the spectator in a renewed sensory relationship with the world. During the 1920s, "material" had many meanings for the Formalists. It was consistently used to refer to both the external material (reality, historical fact, etc.) that provides the stimulus for the work of art, and to the already-processed-by-the-artist material (i.e., words, images) that is organized into the work of art. For our purposes, the former category is of particular interest. Hansen-Löve notes that, in his early writings, Shklovskii envisages a sensualist (phenomenological) encounter with the material, enabled by defamiliarization.[106] Such an emphasis was equally evident in Boris Eikhenbaum's 1916 statement: "The material is not passive—it has its own laws, its own life, its own truth, which the artist must discover in order to learn how to master."[107] Eikhenbaum's use of the term "master" (ovladet'), however, points to the tension that was, as we have seen, to become a central issue in the theory and practice of Soviet art during the 1920s: between the desire to encounter the material and the desire to control/process/transform it.

The evolution of Shklovskii's film theory and his attitude to cinematic material shows increasing emphasis on transformation (processing) of material through artistic form.[108] In an essay of 1925, Shklovskii criticized Vertov for not respecting the core rule of cinema: the selection of the material, likening the kinoki to people with thick fingers who cannot apprehend detail.[109] This was the first articulation of what was to become Shklovskii's key idea: that cinema must show not only the object but also *a relationship* with the object. At a LEF meeting in 1927, he affirmed that the task of editing was to overcome the indiscriminate relationship of the camera to the material, and to articulate a socialist relationship with the world.[110]

Shklovskii's project, in these and other writings about cinema, was an attempt to combine a celebration of film's capacity to provoke an embodied, sensory encounter with the world with an appropriately Marxist emphasis on the human *transformation* of the material. In this respect, he echoed the wider context of film criticism. Delluc's pantheistic celebration of the material world was generally discredited in Russia by 1927, criticized for passivity.[111] In the context of these shifting parameters, the power of cinema was not simply to reveal the world, but to remake it.

Nevertheless, the influence of *Photogénie* can still be felt across much discussion of film through the last years of the 1920s. A 1927 article by N. O. Kaufman reveals the complexity surrounding the relationship between cinema and "things." Kaufman claimed that cinema is the only art in which material objects acquire life. While careful to reject the overaestheticized "fetishism of things" that characterized the work of some Western avant-garde filmmakers (Kaufman was certainly alluding here to Delluc), he suggested that film could "take a dead thing . . . and make a poem from it . . . reveal its independent essence, its internal beauty." Cinema had, moreover, the power to extend this transformative power beyond the limits of the screen, to alter our perception of the material world.[112] In 1929, V. Kolomarov declared that "film is the only art that is capable of conveying the living faktura of the real world in all its clarity and plastic expressivity."[113] Kolomarov quoted Balázs's claim that no other art reveals "things" as fully as cinema.[114] In similar terms, in an article on set design published in Russian in 1928, Léon Moussinac quoted Balázs's description of the camera as a microscope, which could redeem the physical world: "It . . . brings to life a whole rank of phenomena that are unavailable to our eye."[115] While rejecting the poetic aspirations of the impressionists, therefore, Soviet critics and practitioners called for cinema to reveal the faktura of the physical world, to better acquaint them with the objects that surrounded them—and ultimately, to aid in the project of reformulating the relationship between man and material world.

A Soviet Haptic?

In this chapter, we have shown how faktura—commonly understood in the narrow terms of avant-garde artistic practice—was part of a wider discursive framework relating to the senses, and caught up in the ambitious project of remaking the relationship between the human body and the object world. This project is particularly visible in early Soviet film theory. Early Soviet Marxist-inflected phenomenological materialism has much in common with contemporary haptic film theory. Like Soviet film theorists and practitioners, much recent haptic theory has a political agenda. Marks, for example, suggests that the haptic gaze that Riegl had seen as *erased* in the development of Western art, has in fact been sublimated: it has taken refuge in nonmainstream, independent art production. It is affiliated with marginality, emblematic of an oppositional stance—a refusal of the ideological framings of mainstream Hollywood. Such a point of view has framed much work on haptic cinema. Haptic is seen as potentially redemptive. In Marks' words, "By engaging with an object in a haptic way, I come to the surface of myself."[116] For Barker, touch is "a profound manner of being" in the world."[117]

Both Marks and Barker emphasize the reciprocity of the relationship between film and spectator—they see film as having the potential to open up a space of sensory exchange between the viewing body and the screen. This emphasis on reciprocity is a further key to understanding the relevance of haptic theories to the Soviet case. Haptical and phenomenological approaches to film insist on a constant sensory-emotional interaction between film and spectator that echoes Soviet film theorists' understanding of filmic power. The Soviet case, however, contests the assumption—prevalent in haptic theory (and in contemporary affect theory) that sensation, touch, and affect always work against the dominant ideology. The Soviet project sought to appropriate the spontaneous, dynamic, intuitive force of bodily sensation to Marxist ideological frameworks.

Soviet filmmakers were interested in film's capacity to enact what Bruno calls a "movement of rematerialization"[118]—to transform the surfaces and volumes of the world into light projected on-screen, and thereby return to them a *material* presence that had been lost under capitalism. Yet this was not straightforward. Two tensions structured the development of Soviet culture through the 1920s and into the 1930s: between the emancipation of the senses and the control of the senses; and between the desire to encounter the material, and the need to transform it. To enable an unmediated, embodied encounter with the physical world *as it is*; and to allow the screen to *mediate* and reconstruct the relationship between self and world. In this context, film had potential in its capacity to capture the "real" on-screen; but also in its *processing* of that material. It is this twin purpose that distinguishes the Soviet haptic.

In the chapters that follow, I will analyze how sensation took shape on the Soviet film screen in films produced between the early 1920s and the late 1930s. How did Soviet haptic images mutate or endure as silent cinema was replaced by sound? How did emerging forms of Socialist Realist narrative cinema challenge cinema's textural, material project? I will view these films in terms that benefit both from contemporary haptics, and from the particularity of its Soviet precursor. I will focus on how films pictured materials, and their interaction with bodies, on-screen. I will pay attention to shots in which the surfaces and textures of objects are filmed in ways that provoke the spectator to move beyond recognition and into an apprehension of material presence. This apprehension of material presence was the key to the project of Soviet sensory realism. It sought, I suggest, to create socialist sensations. The textures of objects and material could be used to articulate the relationship between surface and depth on-screen, creating a newly mobile, sensually alert spectator, whose embodied *navigation* of the screen approximated to a new model of being in the world. Cinema's "virtual materiality" had potent appeal in the Soviet context.[119]

NOTES

1. Marinetti, "Le tactilisme." See Antonello, "'Out of Touch.'"
2. Shklovskii, "Iskusstvo kak priem," 13; Vertov, "Kinoki. Perevorot," 141.
3. Elsaesser and Hagener, *Film Theory*, 120.
4. Tret'iakov, "Otkuda i kuda?" 202.
5. See, for example, Gough, *The Artist as Producer*.
6. Gough, *The Artist as Producer*, 11.
7. Tatlin, Shapiro, Meerson, and Vinogradov, "Nasha predstoiashchaia rabota," 11.
8. Rowell, "Vladimir Tatlin," 96. See also Milner, *Vladimir Tatlin*.
9. Shklovskii, "Iskusstvo kak priem," 13.
10. Ibid.
11. T'ai Smith has discussed the importance of the category of "facture" in relation to Bauhaus aesthetics: Smith, *Bauhaus Weaving Theory*, 90–93.
12. Hansen-Löve, *Russkii formalizm*, 85–88. See also see Bois, "Malevitch," and Rowell, "Vladimir Tatlin: Form/Faktura." It is important to note that the wider interest in the capacity of art to extend sensory perception beyond the limits of the everyday (and in particular the possibility of synaesthesia) was important to the prerevolutionary avant-garde more broadly and had particular potency for the Symbolists in particular.
13. Markov, *Printsipy tvorchestva*, 2, 6.
14. Shklovskii, "O fakture i kontr-rel'efakh," 103.
15. Tihanov notes Shklovskii's emphasis on the inate material presence of the object world, and calls this a "norm of authenticity." Tihanov, "The Politics of Estrangement," 672.
16. Shklovkii, "O poezii i zaumnom iazyke," 24, cited in Olenina, "Psychomotor Aesthetics," 15. Olenina (40–44) offers a sustained analysis of how Shklovskii's conception of the relationship between emotion and sensation was influenced by late-nineteenth- and early-twentieth-century psychological theory, particularly by the work of Wilhelm Wundt.
17. Gough, *The Artist as Producer*, 11–12.
18. Gan, *Konstruktivizm*, 62–64. See Cooke, *Russian Avant-garde*, 105.
19. Note that the term used here could be *syr'e* (raw materials or resources) as well as the more general "material". See Widdis, *Visions of a New Land*, 64–70.
20. Gough identifies, however, a paradox in constructivist artists' turn toward technology, particularly after the Revolution: "The more technologically advanced the process of the object's production, the less corporeal, tangible and object like that object, in fact,

becomes" (Gough, *The Artist as Producer*, 146). For a more elaborated account of the complexities of the term "faktura" in avant-garde theory and practice see Gough, "Faktura: The Making of the Russian Avant-garde."

21. Gough, *The Artist as Producer*, 58.
22. Gan, *Konstruktivism*, 61, 62, 64.
23. Nikolai Chuzhak, "Pod znakom zhiznestroeniia," 36.
24. Ibid., 35. Art, Chuzhak suggested, was primarily emotional in impact (36); the challenge for artists, however, was to organize that emotional potential in the project of *zhiznestroenie*.
25. INKhUK (Institut Khudozhestvennoi kul´tury). In 1925, INKhUK became GINKhUK (Gosudarstvennyi Institut Khudozhestvennoi kul´tury), cited in Kiaer, *Imagine No Possessions*, 67.
26. VKhUTEMAS (Vysshie Khudozhestvenno-tekhnicheskie Masterskie; Higher Artistic and Technical Studios). This became VKhUTEIN (Vysshii Khudozhestvenno-tekhnicheskii Institut; Higher Artistic-Technical Institute) in 1926.
27. Bokov, "VKhUTEMAS training." See Ladovsky, "Psikhotekhnicheskaia laboratoriia arkhitektury," 352.
28. Arvatov, "Everyday Life and the Culture of the Thing," 121.
29. Ibid., 124.
30. Kiaer, "Boris Arvatov's Socialist Objects," 116.
31. Kiaer, *Imagine No Possessions*, 37.
32. Trotskii, *Literatura i revoliutsiia*, 189.
33. Sirotkina, *Shestoe chuvstvo avangarda*, 63.
34. GAKhN (Gosudarstvennaia Akademiia Khudozhestvennoi nauki); GAKhN was formed as the Russian Academy of Artistic Sciences (RAKhN) in 1921, and renamed in 1925. GAKhN involved members of the avant-garde (such as Arvatov and Tarabukin, as well as Kandinskii) together with more figurative artists such as Pavel Kuznetsov. See Kandinskii, "Plan for the Physico-Psychological Department of the Russian Academy of Artistic Sciences." In addition, GAKhN had a Philosophical Department (headed by Gustav Shpet), and a Sociological Department (headed by Vladimir Friche). See Misler, "A Citadel of Idealism." An extended study of the work of GAKhN is offered in Hansen-Löve, Obermayr, Witte, eds., *Form und Wirkung*.
35. Under Chelpanov's leadership, from 1925 there was increasing focus on emergent Gestalt psychology and its relevance to an understanding of artistic perception.
36. Aron Zalkind, "Refleksologiia i nasha sovremennost´," v-vii.
37. TsIT (Tsentral´nyi institut truda). See Johansson, *Aleksej Gastev*. For a general history of the influence of Taylorism in Russia before and after the October Revolution, see Kravchenko, *Istoriia menedzhmenta*.
38. See Braun, *Picturing Time*.
39. Bernshtein, *Obshchaia biomekhanika*. See also Bernshtein, *O lovkosti i ee razvitii*. For excellent discussion of Bernstein's work, see the many articles of Irina Sirotkina, including "Nikolai Bernstein."
40. Gastev, *Kak nado rabotat´*, 41.
41. Gastev, *Trudovye ustanovki*. See also *Kak nado rabotat´*, 63–67.
42. Olenina, "Psychomotor Aesthetics," 193.
43. Zalkind, "Die Psychologie des Menschen der Zukunft," 671.
44. See Vaingurt, "Poetry of Labor."

45. Zhdan, "Art History and Psychology at RAKhN," 70.

46. Misler, "A Citadel of Idealism," 93. Ippolit Sokolov's theory of "labor gymnastics" also called for a synergy between production theory and artistic performance. Sokolov, *Sistema trudovoi gimnastiki*; Sokolov, "Industrial'naia zhestikuliatsiia."

47. See Povelikhina, "Introducing the Catalogue," and the articles in that special issue of *Experiment*. See also Wünsche, "The Evolution of Human Eyesight," and *Kunst & Leben*; and Til'berg, *Tsvetnaia vselennaia*. On Geptakhor, see Zacharias, "Movement within Nature."

48. See Vöhringer, *Avantgarde und Psychotechnik*, 107–68; and also Sargeant, *Vsevolod Pudovkin*, 29–45.

49. Anon., "My v sezone 1926–27." See Olenina, "Psychomotor Aesthetics," 311.

50. Bekhterev, "Kinematograf i nauka."

51. Tikhonov, "Fotografii," 4. In the same 1919 volume as Chebotarevskii, Tikhonov published an essay also focused on the scientific potential of cinema (and its technical capacities). Tikhonov, "Kinematograf v nauke i tekhnike."

52. Wurm, "Gastevs Medien." In the same volume, Holl notes the influence of Bekhterev on Dziga Vertov: Holl, "Die Bildung des Menschen im Kino-Experiment."

53. Chebotarevskii. "Kinematograf, kak metod," 56.

54. Pozner, "Vertov before Vertov." John Mackay offers an important analysis of Vertov's *The Eleventh Year* in terms of the energeticist philosophies to which the director was exposed while in Bekhterev's institute. Mackay, "Film Energy."

55. See Room's series of essays in *Kino*, each with the title "Akter-polpred idei."

56. Olenina, "Psychomotor Aesthetics," 193–200.

57. For an excellent account of these relationships, see Bulgakowa, "From Expressive Movement to the 'Basic Problem.'"

58. Eizenshtein, *Metod*, Tom 1, 136.

59. Leont'ev, "Biograficheskii ocherk." Leont'ev's involvement in the film community is evident in an article published in *Kino* in 1931, in which he discusses the need for a closer relationship between film practice and science/education: Leont'ev, "Nauka dlia kino." Further research into his input into the development of film theory in VGIK (particularly in relation to his interest in sensory experience and color) would be of great interest.

60. Münsterberg, *The Photoplay*.

61. Ibid., 129.

62. Ibid., 220.

63. Lunacharskii, "O kino," 46.

64. Ibid., 40.

65. Gan, "Kinematograf i kinematografiia," 1.

66. Trotter, *Cinema and Modernism*, 3–4.

67. Artaud, "Cinema and Reality," 411.

68. Lukács, *History and Class Consciousness*, 83–110. For an insightful discussion, see Hansen, *Cinema and Experience*, 20–21.

69. Benjamin, "The Work of Art in the Age of Mechanical Reproduction," 236–37.

70. Siegfried Kracauer, "Film 1928." Other essays written during this period (published in *The Mass Ornament*) reveal Kracauer's dissatisfaction with the fracturing of human experience that (bad) film is bringing about, but also mark his interest in the potential of film (and photography) to reconstruct the relationship between human and material.

71. Kracauer, *Theory of Film*, 294.
72. Ibid., 297.
73. Ibid., 300.
74. Cited in Hansen, "Introduction," in Kracauer, *Theory of Film*, xxi. See also her "With Skin and Hair," 437–69.
75. Kracauer, *Theory of Film*, 309.
76. See Borislavov, "'O zakonakh kino' V. Shklovskogo."
77. van den Oever, "Ostranenie," 33.
78. Delluc, *Fotogeniia kino*. Note that there is less evidence of the Russian reception of Jean Epstein but, as we will discuss below (see especially chapter 7), it is likely that Soviet filmmakers were very much aware of his work. Epstein was explicitly concerned to emphasize cinema's capacity to reinvigorate the human apprehension of the material world. See, for example, "Le sens 1 Bis," 27–44. For discussion of Epstein's theory of film as corporeal, see Wall-Romana, *Jean Epstein*.
79. Two translations of Balázs's *Der Sichtbare Mensch* were published in Russian in 1925, in Moscow and Leningrad. See "Vidimyi chelovek" v kontse stoletiia." For further discussion of Balázs in relation to other theorists see Turvey, "Balázs: Realist or Modernist?"
80. Delluc, *Ecrits cinématographiques I*, 66.
81. Ibid., 56.
82. The introduction to the 1924 Russian version of the book acknowledged the problematic "ideological neutrality" of Delluc, while praising his emphasis on the particularity of film's relationship with reality: "Only cinema is capable of conveying the colossal rhythmical impact of the industrial era, the age of electrification and radio, the era of mass agitation." Iu. Potekhin, "Predislovie," 8.
83. Pudovkin, "Fotogeniia," 90.
84. Ibid., 90.
85. Pudovkin, *Kinorezhisser i kinomaterial*, 100.
86. Pudovkin, "Fotogeniia," 92.
87. Ibid., 92–93. In an essay also published in *Kinozhurnal ARK*, Leo Mur rejected all notion that certain materials were more innately photogenic. While acknowledging that the best material for cinema is that which is real, he maintained that anything that is not false could be photogenic if it was well photographed and well lit. Thus Mur's article was a call for improvements in technical efficiency, rather than abstract theory. See Mur, "Fotogeniia," 3.
88. Eisenstein, "K voprosu o materialisticheskom podkhode," 111.
89. Balázs, "Visible Man," 10.
90. Ibid., 11.
91. Carter, "Introduction," xxv.
92. Balázs, "The Close-Up," 260.
93. Carter points out how Balázs's theory of film is influenced by William James's interpretation of Kant's term "apperception," to describe a mental process that "brings sensory awareness of empirical phenomena into association with inner mental processes" (Carter, "Introduction," xxiv).
94. Balázs, "Visible Man," 46.
95. Eisenstein, "O pozitsii Bela Balasha," and "Bela zabyvaet nozhnitsy."
96. Eisenstein, "K voprosu o materialisticheskom podkhode," 115.

97. This emphasis on organization was common in Eisenstein's early writings, and was inflected by theories of psychotechnics: in an essay jointly authored with Sergei Tret'iakov, for example, he noted that "unorganized movement does not evoke a direct emotional reaction." Eisenstein and Tret'iakov, "Vyrazitel'noe dvizhenie," 188.
98. Shklovskii, "O zakonakh kino," 246.
99. Ibid., 252.
100. Ibid., 96.
101. Shklovskii, "Ikh nastoiashchee," 334.
102. Ibid.
103. Eikhenbaum, "Problemy kinostilistiki," 15.
104. Ibid., 13. Eikhenbaum's terms here directly echo those of Balázs. His broader position, however, was more complex, and influenced by Vygotskii's conception of "inner speech"—a form of cognition that is *between* image and language. For Eikhenbaum, film spectatorship was a form of thinking through images but it was not, crucially, limited by images.
105. See Pozner, "Shklovskii/Eisenshtein-dvadtsatye gody." For discussion of the complexity of Formalist theories of material (in literary works) see Anley, "The Wisdom of Brainless Knights."
106. Hansen-Löve distinguishes two stages (Material I and Material II) in the Formalist understanding of external material, and maps them onto a parallel Sensation I and Sensation II. It is in the first stage of Material and Sensation that he locates a "sensualist" emphasis. Hansen-Löve, *Russkii formalizm*, especially 180–189, 206–213. The relationship between early Formalist thinking and phenomenology (both Western phenomenology and its Russian forms) would benefit from further research. See, for example, Hansen-Löve, Obermayr, and Witte, eds, *Form und Wirkung*.
107. Eikhenbaum, *Skvoz' literaturu*, 9.
108. Where in Formalist literary theory, the term "material" mutated in complex ways through the 1920s, and always signified *both* the (real, material) world represented in a text and the material of language itself, in the filmic context, it seems to have referred consistently to the *filmed material*—the photographed object. For Shklovskii, for example, a filmic trick (or device) is "a piece of material experienced aesthetically." Viktor Shklovskii, "Kuda shagaet Dziga Vertov?" 78.
109. Shklovskii, "Semantika kino," 30–32.
110. Shklovskii, in Osip Brik et al, "Lef i kino: stenogramma soveshchaniia," 57.
111. Mur, "Aktivnaia i passivnaia fotogeniia."
112. Kaufman, "Veshch' na ekrane," 5.
113. Kolomarov, "Veshch' v kino," 29. See Deriabin, ed., *Letopis' rossiiskogo kino 1863–1929*, 653.
114. Ibid., 29.
115. Moussinac, "Dekoratsiia i kostium v kino," 6.
116. Marks, *The Skin of the Film*, 184.
117. Barker, *The Tactile Eye*, 2.
118. Bruno, *Surface*, 135.
119. Ibid., 143.

Chapter Two

MATERIAL SENSATIONS

> Hanging carpets remain the true walls, the visible boundaries of space.
> Gottfried Semper, 1861

THIS CHAPTER STEPS back from the theoretical and ideological frameworks that shaped the Soviet preoccupation with faktura, and explores the practical challenges that defined its realization on-screen. How do film images become "haptic"? What combination of set, lighting, camerawork, and other production elements, works to create embodied spectatorship? Here, attention to the actual material—objects, textiles, walls—of film is important. Yet the production designer is the forgotten figure in film scholarship, and early Soviet cinematic set design has received particularly scant attention. In this early period, however, in Russia and elsewhere, the hegemony of the director was not yet established; the very structure and organization of the filmmaking process was in formation. In the pages of the Soviet cinema press in the mid to late 1920s, we can trace a battle over the role of the production designer (*khudozhnik*) in film. This was not merely a question of practical organization. It touched on the very nature of filmic representation itself: the creation of filmic space and spectatorial experience. As the technical capabilities of the still-young medium were tested and explored, debates about set design reflected the emergent aesthetics of Soviet cinema.

Attention to the actual material of set and costume is rare in film scholarship.[1] And it is still rarer to think about it in relation to spectatorial experience. The limited existing work on production design has tended to focus on the relationship between set and narrative. Charles and Mirella Affron, for example, offer a taxonomy of film design, ranging from "Sets as Denotation" (largely invisible, nonsignifying background), through to "Sets as Artifice" (highly visual and responsible for a large part of the film's overall impact).[2] These categories are useful, reflecting a key tension in the evolution of film set design, which was particularly acute in the period under consideration here: is the set an independently expressive part of the film in itself, or a servant of the plot? This question underpinned debates on the role of the production designer in the Soviet cinema press during the 1920s. The Affrons' categories are limited, however, by the assumption that a good set is one that serves the narrative. Charles Tashiro, by contrast, suggests that objects on-screen can have meanings of their own that *exceed* the limits of narrative.[3] He proposes that we engage with the affective power of the material mise-en-scène, envisaging cinematic spectatorship as embodied *participation* in the space of the film, such that "things" on-screen provoke sensations.[4] Such a view of spectatorship was, as we have seen, shared by Soviet theorists and filmmakers.

In this chapter, I will explore how the theory and practice of production design evolved in Soviet film during the second half of the 1920s. Discovering the practical exigencies that shaped the construction and decoration of cinematic space, and how film-practitioners grappled with them, we can trace evolving understandings of filmic representation. This is not a complete history of Soviet set design, but rather explores the evolution of the practice as shaped by two key questions.[5] First, early film theorists and practitioners were preoccupied by the paradoxical relationship between the flatness of the cinematic screen and the illusion of life in three dimensions that it was so uniquely equipped to portray. How were the material properties of mise-en-scène used to create patterns, planar intersections, and volumes on-screen? How did cinema practitioners exploit objects, textile, and texture to maximize the sensory impact of their film on its spectators? Second, how did production design reflect the ideological complexity of objects themselves during this period? Abram Room's declaration in 1925 that "theater is an art of 'seeming,' but cinema is 'being,'" threw down a gauntlet for production designers.[6] If film was reality itself, then the way that it presented material objects was not just a question of film aesthetics, but was central to the construction of the new Soviet world.

The Prerevolutionary Legacy

Although the revolution of 1917 brought new ideological imperatives to Soviet cinema, it did not bring an entirely new cast of characters—or new equipment. The first production designers working in Soviet cinema during the 1920s had almost all been in the profession before 1917. Even those young directors (such as Eisenstein, Vertov, and Pudovkin) who came to film after 1917 were often working alongside veterans in technical areas such as set construction. In this context, a broad understanding of the conditions and achievements of prerevolutionary production design is important.

For the very first Russian films, individually constructed sets were rare: standard painted flat backdrops were used on many different films; furniture, props, and costumes were taken from studio stores, or simply hired. Décor was often prepared merely days—even hours—before filming.[7] As the new film art developed in Russia between 1908 and 1913, the elaboration of the so-called fundus system enabled more complex designs. The fundus consisted of a series of standard partitions and screens (flats), together with columns, doorways, staircases, and so forth, which allowed designers to construct sets with multiple layers and create the illusion of depth, offering several different positions for the camera.[8] In this way, set design evolved from two-dimensional surface toward three-dimensionality.

This development reflected a growing understanding of the specificity of cinematic space. It was linked to improvements in other technical aspects of the film process—in particular, camera mobility and lighting technique. When not on location, very early cinema had been largely filmed in so-called glass houses, with glass roofs allowing daylight to illuminate the set from above. Although Hollywood introduced studio lighting around 1907, Europe, including Russia, continued to use glass roofs for some time.[9] By the midteens, however, techniques for artificial studio lighting were developing rapidly in Russia. This placed new demands on set architecture, objects, and costumes: the better lit the space, the more "real" things needed to appear. In addition, developing interest in the creation of depth of field on-screen meant greater attention to the material properties of the set. In Russia, this is particularly evident in the films of Evgenii Bauer, whose complex architectural interiors are usually seen as a pinnacle of prerevolutionary Russian set design. Bauer's "psychological" cinema depended for its impact on the architecture of domestic interiors, often positioning the spectator as voyeur,

Fig. 2.1 Depth and Surface. Still from *Child of the Big City* (*Ditia bol´shogo goroda*, dir. Evgenii Bauer, production design by Evgenii Bauer, 1914).

penetrating private space (figure 2.1).[10] The set played a key role in organizing filmic space: Bauer replaced many solid elements with drapery, curtains, and tulle, and made extensive use of columns and foregrounded details (architectural shapes or single objects, known as the *dikovinka* ["curiosity"]) to create perspective.[11] The three-dimensional "relief" of real objects in the foreground structures the spectator's reception of the shot, giving the illusion of depth.[12] Finally, production design (and lighting) also played a key part in the patterning of the screen as *surface*, maximizing the expressive potential of the untinted orthochromatic film stock, which offered a range of tones from deep black to extreme white. Alongside architectural detail, the designs and textures of patterned textile were used to create contrast and variation.

Early set design, then, was both an architectural and a pictorial process, which sought to exploit volume and texture.[13] Here, the background and training of production designers is important. The majority of designers working in Russian and Soviet cinema before the revolution had artistic training. Many (such as Vladimir Egorov and Aleksei Utkin), had been educated in the Moscow Stroganov Institute for Technical Drawing.

A significant proportion (e.g., Egorov, Dmitrii Kolupaev, Czesław Sabiński) had gone on to apply that training to work in theater, in particular with the Moscow Art Theater, where they worked directly with Konstantin Stanislavskii. There they were exposed to the naturalist school of set design (with its emphasis on authentic materials and verisimilitude), exemplified by Stanislavskii's collaborations with Valentin Simov, who himself worked as a set designer in pre- and postrevolutionary cinema. The influence of the Moscow Art Theater was not solely that of naturalism, however. Egorov, for one, worked with Vsevolod Meierkhol'd in the experimental studio set up by Stanislavskii in 1905, which was an early cradle for modernist (and symbolist) theater in Russia. More broadly, the ornamental *moderne* aesthetic, with its interest in *dekorativnost'* and patterning (exemplified in the set designs for Sergei Diaghilev's Ballets Russes but also evident in, for example, the designs for Meierkhol'd's 1917 production of Mikhail Lermontov's *Maskarad*) was another core influence in early Russian film set design. The sets and costumes of the Ballets Russes productions between 1909 and 1928 had far-reaching impact on theatrical design across Europe, and, after 1917, the so-called Russian spirit in décor found its way into film, when émigré Russian designers in Paris formed L'albatros, a production company initially under the leadership of Ermol'ev (and later Lazare Meerson).[14] Leon Barsacq suggests that the Albatros filmmakers were influenced by the Ballet Russes' unique combination of the naturalism of the Moscow Art Theater and the decorative impulse of the symbolist World of Art group (a broad artistic grouping to which several artist-designers, including Vladimir Balliuzek, were linked).[15] In similar terms, John Bowlt has described the Ballets Russes as viewing stage set as decoration—that is, as two-dimensional backdrop.[16]

Bowlt distinguishes this tradition from the innovations of Russian avant-garde (Constructivist) theater design in terms of a distinction between surface and space.[17] The Ballets Russes, with their luxuriant excess of decorative pattern, were an art of surface. So too, he suggests, were the naturalist stage designs of Simov for Stanislavskii. By contrast, Constructivism was an art of volumes: the organization of forms in their interaction with space. This latter was the third key influence on evolving film set production in Russian. Budding production designers who received their training in Meierkhol'd's studio, for example, would have been exposed to a growing interest in the manipulation of spatial volume in the construction of stage sets. Many of them also had architectural/technical training: the Stroganov Institute, for instance, educated them alongside architects and technical designers.[18]

These influences are particularly evident, for example, in Egorov's designs for Meierkhol´d's lost 1915 film adaptation of Oscar Wilde's *The Picture of Dorian Grey* (*Portret Doriana Greia*), which exploited volume, depth, and contrast—exhibiting a blend of influences that merged Russian avant-garde forms with exaggerated use of shade and light characteristic of the films of the Danish film school during the 1910s.[19]

Soviet Beginnings

It is clear, then, that prerevolutionary production designers operated within a matrix of different influences, which shaped the working through of key questions: in particular, the importance of "real" materials, and the relationship between surface, depth, and volume on-screen. And of course, this did not change in 1917. By the mid-1920s, there were effectively three generations of production designer working in Soviet cinema: the first khudozhniki (such as Simov himself) remained linked to traditions exemplified by the naturalism of the Moscow Art Theater. A second younger group included Sergei Kozlovskii, Egorov, and Balliuzek (most of whom had also begun their careers in theater and had worked in prerevolutionary cinema). A third generation of designers, many of whom came to prominence in the 1920s, consisted of men who had worked almost exclusively in film, not theater: Kuleshov, Utkin, Vasilii Rakhal´s, and Evgenii Enei. The evolution of practice and theory across these generations tracks growing understandings of the unique capabilities of film.

In their study of the development of set design in France, Britain, and Germany, Bergfelder, Harris, and Street focus on the period from the 1920s to the late 1930s, as "the moment in film history in which set design was given more prominence and attention than perhaps during any other period."[20] In Hollywood, the establishment of the studio system brought ever more lavish production design;[21] in Germany, the influence of expressionism brought a revolution in the role of film design, most famously realized in Wiene's *The Cabinet of Dr. Caligari* (1920); in Paris, émigré Russian designers linked to L'albatros group were pioneering "a modern, performative conception of décor," with a new emphasis on multidimensional space.[22] Despite the influence of Russian émigrés on film design in the period under discussion, Bergfelder et al. do not discuss Soviet cinema itself. This omission is consistent in histories of production design: Barsacq, one of the only writers on production design even to address the question of Soviet cinema, roundly discounts its studio/interior shots, praising it instead for the "perfection of its exterior shots."²³ A closer look at interior sets of this period, however, and at the debates surrounding design in the film press, reveals a rich vein of experimentation, in particular regarding the shifting role of faktura on-screen.

The so-called poverty of early Soviet set design is commonly attributed to the underfunded state of film production during the 1920s. Certainly, although ideological exigencies did shape film form in the early Soviet years, the importance of practical and technical issues should not be underestimated. Film studios were underequipped, and there was little or no money available for complex set design. By the middle of the 1920s, however, the situation had improved, and the second half of the decade—a time of immense productivity in terms of the number and quality of films released—was also a period of technical consolidation and professionalization.²⁴ This had an impact on the practices of set design. Kozlovskii was named head of production design at Mezhrabpom; Vasilii Rakhal's filled the same role in the state-run Goskinofabrika (later Sovkino). A new fundus system was elaborated, and better equipment gradually made available. Improvements in technical provision were accompanied by a focus on professional training: in 1924, an "architectural-decorative" department opened as part of the new State Film Academy (GTK).²⁵ Its instructors included Kozlovskii, together with the artist-architect Konstantin Mel'nikov; the first cohort of students graduated in 1927, and a new generation emerged into professional practice.²⁶

Not all set designers coming new to cinema during the late 1920s and into the 1930s went through this training, however. Indeed, it was not yet clear exactly what kind of professional or specialist training a production designer needed.²⁷ Many active khudozhniki graduated from VKhUTEMAS/VKhUTEIN.²⁸ Others went to GTK only *after* initial broader arts training.²⁹ And of course, the field of influence was wider still: director and set designer Vladimir Kaplunovskii, for example, emerged from an art institute in Kiev, and Evgenii Enei, who began working in cinema in 1923, had been trained in architecture. Such fluidity of professional formation reflected an uncertainty about the role and purpose of the production designer, which found expression in an energetic debate in the pages of the Soviet film press in the mid-1920s. Part of broader discussions around the professionalization of the film production process, this was also a process of definition, marking the boundaries between different members of the filmmaking collective. For the designers themselves, the key task was to carve out a clear role and appropriate recognition. Dmitrii Kolupaev, for example, argued that the khudozhnik must have overall responsibility for all "artistic-decorative elements" of the film: set, costume, props, and overall "style."[30] Aleksandr Rodchenko, who was at that time working as a production designer for Sovkino, called for the designer to have control of a film's entire "material environment."[31] In February 1928, khudozhniki published a resolution, seeking to define their role as a valuable member of the filmmaking collective, and insisting that their names must feature on a film's promotional material.[32] The battle was not easily won, however: there was an enduring tendency to consider the designer a lesser partner alongside director and cameraman. Almost a decade later, Natan Al´tman still felt the need to state that the artist "must be a fully-fledged creative partner in the process."[33]

In any case, focus on such practical issues did not resolve the core question at the heart of these debates. What was the appropriate aesthetic for Soviet cinema? Here, production design came in for considerable criticism. It was clear that the new Soviet films should look different—both from what had gone before (prerevolutionary film), and from what was made elsewhere ("bourgeois" or capitalist cinema). Particular criticism was leveled at the dominance of costume drama in cinema before 1917. Production designers were under attack: in addition to complaints of poor quality work, they were frequently accused of "excess" and "pomposity."[34] It was difficult to know what Soviet films should look like, however. With the decorative excesses of prerevolutionary Russian cinema deemed unacceptable, so too should Soviet set designers avoid the traps of Western modernist films. Expressionist currents in German cinema provoked particular discussion. A pseudonymous opinion piece in *Soviet Screen* dismissed the "self-indulgence" and "absurdity" of the striking design of *The Cabinet of Dr. Caligari*; and the sets by Russian émigré Andrei Andreev for Wiene's *Raskolnikow* of 1923 were criticized for their painterly style—for treating the screen only as a pictorial surface.[35] There were increasing suggestions in the press that a good set was one that was fully integrated with the film's narrative. According to Pudovkin, for example, the task of a true film artist was to "create a calm décor, which does not attract the eye."[36] Similarly, Kuleshov suggested that film décor must be subtle and unobtrusive.[37]

In fact, at their most extreme, Soviet ideological frameworks seemed to put the very idea of production design under threat. That same pseudonymous reviewer, for example, praised the outdoor shooting and "reality" of Eisenstein's *Strike*, and declared, provocatively, that the Soviet realist agenda meant that perhaps it was time for the khudozhnik to disappear entirely from cinema.[38] Rakhal's' designs for Eisenstein's next film, *Battleship Potemkin* (1926), were praised for their lack of artifice, for their "real energy." Soviet cinema would distinguish itself by an entirely new attitude to the material world—a rejection of the staged quality of prerevolutionary cinema, and an embracing of the new, the real and authentic. In contrast to the expressionist sets of *Caligari*, and to the vast studio sets emerging in Hollywood, Soviet filmmakers would favor the energy of outdoor shooting, the life of the streets.

Faced with rapidly changing ideological imperatives, Soviet production designers sought to align aesthetic and political demands. They blamed poor-quality equipment for their failings, suggesting that the resources available did not enable them to create realistic sets.[39] In 1925, Kolupaev bemoaned the insufficient funds accorded to set and costume design in the Soviet production process. Using the example of folk (*narodnyi*) and peasant films, he described how "in the studio, village style dominates, with its uniform huts, barns, and basic details of peasant life," and called for greater accuracy and ethnographic detail: "We need to improve our stocks with sketches and photographs of the village. We must organize an artistic/photographic commission and send them out into the countryside."[40] Such a call for authenticity was not just a way of improving quality, however. It was also a key strategy by which production designers attempted to carve themselves a role within contemporary ideological frameworks. Here, material and faktura also had key roles to play. Sergei Kozlovskii emphasized that the production designer had a vital role in shaping the impact of material on-screen, sourcing the objects that created faktura, and later recalled the mid-1920s as a period when "I experimented in seeking out new textures."[41] Faktura was also consistently linked in the film press to terms that emphasized three-dimensionality in descriptions of film sets (specifically "relief"/"in relief" [*rel'efno*] and "volume" [*ob"em*]).[42] This was vital to the incorporation of set design within new ideological frameworks. In a careful sleight of hand, Kozlovskii claimed that the khudozhnik was not a "decorator," but a "builder" (*konstruktor*)—at once an engineer and an architect. After all, if the decorative had no role in the new ideological value system, construction certainly did. This shift defined production design as an art of volumes and not surfaces, of three dimensions rather than two. As such, it provides a revealing framework through which to consider experiments in cinematic space during this period.

In practice, however, the blend of influences (naturalism, ornamentalism, and Constructivist experiment with volume) that had characterized prerevolutionary set design continued to be significant after 1917. Although the impact of Constructivist-influenced training (in VKhUTEIN and GTK) was evident in the development of Soviet production design through the 1920s, so filmmakers demonstrated an ongoing interest in the cinema screen as decorative surface. The play between the flat and the volumetric was a fundamental feature of silent cinema.[43] The flat screen, and the black-and-white film stock, posed particular challenges in the presentation of the object world in all its textural and three-dimensional reality. But that very surface was equally a source of filmic power. During the 1920s, Soviet production designers worked to maximize the impact of filmic faktura on spectatorial experience. Their conscious exploitation of the tension between two and three dimensions (surface and depth, decoration and volume) is particularly visible in the curious genre that is early Soviet costume drama.

Historical Material

In debates about production design, costume dramas were a frequent target of criticism. They were a problematic throwback to prerevolutionary cinema. The tradition of historical cinema/costume drama had begun in Russia long before 1917, in particular with the Golden Series of films (produced by the Thiemann and Reinhardt Studio), for which the young Moscow Art Theater–trained set designer Vladimir Egorov was employed.[44] Several key figures who were involved in this prerevolutionary tradition continued to work after 1917, and private production companies continued to make and release historical dramas. Egorov himself was the designer for Konstantin Eggert's *The Bear's Wedding* (*Medvezh´ia svad´ba*, 1926), and for Iurii Tarich's *Wings of a Serf* (*Kryl´ia kholopa*, 1926). Director Ivanovskii worked with Utkin for his *Stepan Khalturin* (1925). Other notable films of this type include Ivanovskii's *Palace and Fortress* (*Dvorets i krepost´*, 1923), and *The Decembrists* (*Dekabristy*, 1927), as well as Gardin's *The Poet and the Tsar* (*Poet i tsar´*, 1927), and Eggert's *The Ice House* (*Ledianoi dom*, 1928).

The reception of historical films was complex. For although the category of costume drama (as established in the prerevolutionary context) was increasingly negatively coded during the 1920s, the historical film could attempt to claim a role within the new ideological climate, provided that it told historical stories with revolutionary credentials.[45] And the scale and scope of historical filmmaking was important evidence of Soviet cinema's status on a world stage. Ivanovskii's *Palace and Fortress*, for example, was positively described by one reviewer as "the first and only Russian film that has the right (to be called) monumental."[46] This review praised the film for equaling German historical blockbusters, such as *Lady Hamilton* (Oswald, 1921), in its "immaculate precision" and detail, and for even surpassing them in outdoor shots and in ideological purpose.[47] Other critics, however, criticized *Palace and Fortress* for peddling its historical material as exotic visual pleasure, rather than seeking an authentic or meaningful representation of revolutionary history.[48] There was a clear need for a new type of ideologically sound costume drama.

In effect, historical films became a focus for debates about the status of decorative/authentic material in film in the mid-1920s, which were inflected by a growing interest in the expressive power of the set. The year 1926 saw the release of two important historical films—radically different in their approach to the challenge of how to represent the past: Tarich's *Wings of a Serf* and the FEKS collective's *The Overcoat* (*Shinel*). Both can be seen as an attempt to answer the difficult question of what a Soviet historical film might look (and feel) like. Critic Mikhail Bleiman expressly praised *Wings of a Serf* for its quest for what he called "authentic historicity," claiming that the film avoided the flaws of other historical dramas where history served merely as decorative backdrop.[49] The achievement was partly social and ideological: in its representation of the life of the serf Nikita, the film pictured the nonphotogenic past of a poor man alongside the grandeur of Ivan the Terrible's court. But the film was also, according to Bleiman, a formal success, within the new ideological frameworks, in presenting authentic material on-screen. Bleiman's arguments here echoed common strategies that were used to distinguish "new" Soviet historical film from the decorative prerevolutionary tradition, and to forge a place for historical drama within the new repertoire. Typical in this regard was Babenchikov's survey essay of 1927, which suggested that Soviet historical films must be as focused on "everyday reality" as films focused on contemporary life. After all, he pointed out, "people are the same; only their material circumstances are different."[50] As a result, he announced: "We need ethnography, mass heroics. And, of course, we need everyday life, at all levels, including the historical."

Bleiman was not unanimously positive in his review of *Wings of a Serf*, however, and overall, the film was badly received—seen as continuing the obsolete genre of historical melodrama. The ideal form of Soviet historical film had not yet been found. Yet the past—its architecture, interiors, objects, and costumes—retained particular allure in the quest for expressive visual material on-screen. This was the ideological minefield that the FEKS collective set out to navigate with their three historical films, produced between 1926 and 1929: *The Overcoat*, *SVD* (*Soiuz velikogo dela*, 1927) and *New Babylon* (*Novyi Vavilon*, 1929). Their aim was to create a new kind of historical film: one that would be both politically appropriate *and* formally innovative. These films were certainly a polemic with other "pompous" costume dramas; but they were also a challenge to the simplistic naturalistic impulse, seeking instead a new way of representing the affective power of the past, and its material pleasures, for a contemporary audience.

In one sense, *The Overcoat* is neither a historical film nor a costume drama; loosely adapted from Nikolai Gogol''s novel of the same name, it is a psychological study of the protagonist Akakii Akakievich Bashmachkin. Yet this is a film in which historical material matters. As Grigorii Kozintsev himself recalled, "We delved into the materials."[51] In contrast to the visual extravagance of many historical films of the mid to late 1920s, nineteenth-century Saint Petersburg appears on-screen through the eyes of the protagonist, as what scriptwriter Iurii Tynianov called the "corpse of the Nikolaievan capital."[52] It lacks grand facades and emerges instead as a series of distorted forms, looming shadows, and fragmented facades. This uncanny effect was achieved by a combination of lighting, cinematography, and set design. Designer Evgenii Enei replaced realism with stylization: distortions of scale invert the proportions of human figures and landscape, showing Bashmachkin dwarfed by the imperial city.[53] And Bashmachkin's tiny domestic space, with its oversized teapot, speaks eloquently of his longing for comfort, his self-protection from the onslaught of the city.

Enei's work was consistently singled out for praise in reviews of the film: Sokolov, for example, mentioned particularly its "polished surfaces," and linked it to Andreev's designs for *Raskolnikow*.[54] Enei occupied a privileged place in the FEKS collective, working closely with cinematographer Andrei Moskvin to achieve the group's signature style. Kozintsev was explicit in describing FEKS's interest in film's *faktura*, and described his work on this film as teaching him how to make filmed material "plastic" and "poetic."[55] In *The Overcoat*, material matters: as Bleiman noted, "things (monuments, a walking stick, the coat) are magnificently shown."[56]

This is not merely formal experiment, however. Bashmachkin's sensory-emotional relationships with things—most obviously his coat, but also the few oversized objects in his small home—are a surrogate for relationships with people, which he lacks. They are articulated on-screen through intense exploitation of faktura. The eponymous overcoat is literally sewn together out of the rich textures and fabrics that Bashmachkin selects with sensual rapture: thick padding, soft lining, and rich fur, which dominate the surface of the screen. When Bashmachkin visits the tailor's workshop for the first time, the frame distorts the scale of the tailor's model and the clothes and hat hanging upon it (figure 2.2a). And his reverential touching of the suits foreshadows his intensely sensual relationship with his own coat later in the film. Later, he sensually caresses the fur that will be used for his new collar (figure 2.2b) as it is draped around his shoulder. Careful lighting emphasizes the frayed and ragged edges of his disintegrating old coat, in contrast to the dense materiality of the new.

On-screen, as in Gogol''s tale, the relationship between human subject and material object is inverted: the coat is more substantial—more *material*—than Bashmachkin himself. It embodies a dream of the future, enabling a fuller physical existence amid the shifting, ephemeral spaces of the modernist city of Saint Petersburg. In one scene, as Bashmachkin leaves a party and looks to wrap himself within the coat's comforting embrace. His hand reaches, unseeing, for his hat and coat, and finds only an empty space: it gropes, grasping at air. They are gone. Panic. Without the coat, Bashmachkin appears once more insubstantial, naked, and unprotected. When the coat is retrieved, the spectator feels the reassurance of its padded weight settling upon its owner's shoulders. It affords Bashmachkin, briefly, material presence in the city.

In *The Overcoat*, then, the faktura of the material constructs the plot and its meaning. This "psychological" study is not carried out through realism or subject-identification, but rather through an intense, exaggerated encounter with the material, which enables for the spectator an affective encounter with Bashmachkin's physio-psychological experience. The film seeks to exploit the visual and sensory pleasures of its historical material, but without allowing them to be mere decoration. In the changing ideological climate, this was a landmark statement of what could be achieved, in formal terms, within the so-called costume genre.

Pattern and Surface

The Overcoat exploited texture and volume in order to explore the affective potential of material on-screen. Other films explored the power of ornament and pattern. Notable in this respect was Abram Room's *The Traitor*

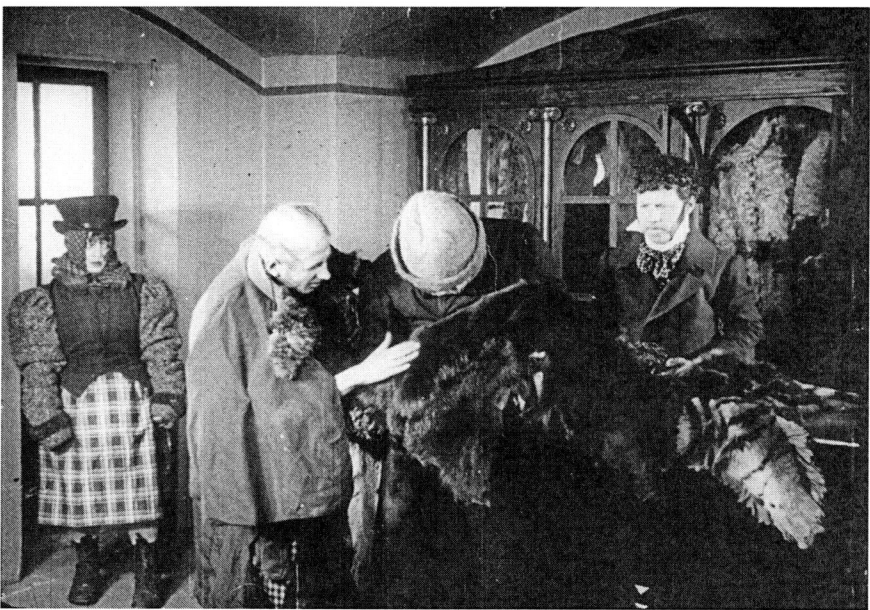

Fig. 2.2 Textile Pleasures: At the Tailor's Workshop. Still from *The Overcoat* (*Shinel'*, dir. G. Kozintsev and Leonid Trauberg, production design by E. Enei, 1926).

(*Predatel'*), produced in the same year as *The Overcoat*, and featuring one of FEKS's earliest collaborators, Sergei Iutkevich, as designer. Iutkevich's artistic training and work in avant-garde theater had given him an interest in new connections between background (set) and action.[57] Before becoming an independent director, he worked as production designer for Room in *The Traitor*, and in Room's better-known film of 1927, *Bed and Sofa* (*Tret'ia Meshchanskaia*, 1927). In both films, Iutkevich experimented with the power of the set and the relationship between surface and depth on-screen.[58]

The Traitor was Room's second film and has been described as an "eccentric melodrama."[59] With a narrative that transformed an ideologically appropriate revolutionary tale of a saboteur into an adventure yarn, it was one of the popular genre of *detektivy* (detective/adventure films) that proliferated in Soviet film production in the mid-1920s. The first half of the film was set in prerevolutionary Russia, the second in the Soviet period. Despite this ostensibly contemporary section, however, *The Traitor* is in essence a costume drama, in which the textures and patterns of historical setting play an important part. It was not a critical success, and recent scholarship, based on the limited extant material, has largely concurred.[60] Iutkevich's designs, however, attracted significant attention and even praise. The pseudonymous reviewer "Prim," for example, commented that Iutkevich broke away from "simple naturalism," and took set design to a new level, making the set into "a participant in the action."[61] Other critics were less generous. Khersonskii wrote a scathing review of *The Traitor*.[62] He categorized the film as an "aesthetic rebellion," a "pure experiment in formalism," and even described some of the sets as "cardboard."[63] In his later writing, Iutkevich himself suggested that the set in *The Traitor* was unsuccessful because it was not organically tied to the narrative of the film. It was, he said, a technical exercise: "Since it was my 'debut,' I decided to show off everything I could do, to produce what they call a 'calling card.'" The film involved thirty specially constructed pavilions, an enormous number by contemporary standards.[64]

To dismiss *The Traitor*'s set as simply an exercise in artistic self-promotion, however, is to do it an injustice. In his later writings, Iutkevich discussed the three key tasks of the set designer: first, the organization of space; second, control of the relationship of volumes and structures within the set; and third, responsibility for cinematic *faktura*, for "capturing and conveying different materials."[65] The set of *The Traitor* can be described as an attempt to use *faktura* as a means of structuring cinematic space. In an article of 1925, with a revealingly material metaphor, Iutkevich called decoration the "dressing" of a film.⁶⁶ And indeed, the set of *The Traitor* is constructed around a stylized excess of contrasting decorative textures and patterns. It is, in Iutkevich's words, an exercise in "the volumes and textures of surfaces, silken, shiny, lacquered."⁶⁷

This play of textures is particularly evident in the brothel that provides the principal location in the film's prerevolutionary section—an overdecorated blend of baroque and art deco. Pattern is overwhelming. The courtesan Wanda's boudoir, for example, has a raised platform at the rear of the set, covered with oriental carpet and functioning as bed/divan (figure 2.3). This is distanced from the spectator by multiple levels of decoration and textile: an apparently diaphanous folded curtain in the foreground creates an almost theatrical "stage." It is framed by a decorative wallpaper frieze of stylized ships and waves. Later, the folded curtain turns out to be a screen that descends suggestively in the shape and design of a fan, illuminated from behind, creating a strong geometric pattern, which sits alongside the striking design of the wallpaper that surrounds it (figure 2.4). A further beaded curtain to the left simultaneously screens and reveals the bed as site of carnal pleasure.

At a primary level, of course, this excess signals the retrograde and decadent morals of the protagonists, and Iutkevich's conscious exploitation of baroque style tapped into an established ideological meaning-system: "A parody of the over-padded style of a Russian Watteau."⁶⁸ In this respect, the art-deco style of *The Traitor* echoes that of many Western films of the period, with similar intent. In 1928, Robert Mallet-Stevens observed with regret that modern (and specifically art deco) sets were habitually used to signal debauched or at best demimondain environments.⁶⁹ *The Traitor* features a playful "bath," which turns out to be a divan, in a direct echo of what Donald Albrecht describes as a fascination with luxurious bathrooms in modern film design during the late 1920s and 1930s, specifically "to heighten a scenario's exotic titillation."⁷⁰

In Soviet Russia, art-deco style had additional ideological inflection. Its influence on Soviet studio sets is clear in other films, particularly in the work of Vladimir Egorov.⁷¹ Aleksei Utkin's sketches for Bassalygo's *Mr. Lloyd's Journey* (*Reis mistera Lloida*, 1927) feature high-shine surfaces and geometric patterning. In its self-conscious excess, however, *The Traitor* went further than these, and as such it bears comparison with Marcel L'Herbier's *The Inhuman* (*L'Inhumaine*) of 1924.⁷² *The Inhuman* was a self-conscious homage to modern design, for which the director recruited a remarkable roll

Fig. 2.3 Wanda's Boudoir. Still from *The Traitor* (*Predatel'*, dir. A. Room; production design by S. Iutkevich, 1926).

Fig. 2.4 The Boudoir: The Screen as Surface. Still from *The Traitor* (*Predatel'*, dir. A. Room; production design by S. Iutkevich, 1926).

call of the foremost representatives of the new style: Fernand Léger, Robert Mallet-Stevens, and René Lalique for props, and Cavalcanti for the film's interiors. The interior shots of singer Claire Lescot's home are marked by the ornamental excess that characterized deco: geometric flooring, lozenge patterning, and heavily patterned, sculpted fabric.[73]

This comparison invites us to go beyond the ideological signification and to think about the impact of the design of *The Traitor* in formal terms. Like *The Inhuman*, *The Traitor* is a mirror of the many diverse artistic movements that played a part in the development of Soviet set design. In addition to the flirtation with art deco, its flattened and distorted perspective echoes Iutkevich's earliest theater designs, which were characteristic of the cubo-futurist art of the period.[74] Maia Turovskaia suggests that the influence of German expressionism can also be seen in the film. And the plenitude of contrasting patterns echoes the work of Henri Matisse, very well known in Russia at the time, as well as the decorative excesses of the Ballets Russes productions.[75] This combination of influences prompts consideration of the film's provocative play with spectatorial experience. How do these hybrid styles operate in formal terms on-screen?

Above all, *The Traitor* plays consciously with two- and three-dimensional space. In Wanda's boudoir, the foregrounded patterns seem first to *flatten* the screen, drawing attention to its surface. This is a characteristic of the film's style. In a later scene, two men sit playing chess against a background textile with a design of vines heavy with grapes, mountains, and even a large stork. The pattern competes aggressively for attention with the protagonists and the action. Its refusal to operate as backdrop upsets perspective, constructs the screen as a two-dimensional plane, and distorts the illusion of depth. Despite the frontal impact of this patterning of the screen, however, Iutkevich's set design also plays consistently with depth of field. Back in Wanda's boudoir, the intense patterns in the foreground coexist with decorated carpets and wall hangings in the depth of field (a guitar suspended above the bed, scattered cushions, etc.). Diaphanous fabrics such as net and tulle create transparent partitions and vary the levels of action within the frame, drawing the spectator's eye toward the intimate depths of the shot. These transparent screens draw our attention to the nature of the screen as two-dimensional surface; at the same time, however, they engage us in an act of seeing *through* that surface and invite perception of depth and three-dimensionality. As such, they set up a play between surface and depth. Antonia Lant has analyzed the use of transparent curtains in de Cordova and Samuelson's *She* of 1925. She suggests that the layering of textile is used to make two- and three-dimensional spaces (the surface of the curtain and that which lies beyond) coexist: "The curtain itself, with its figures, slight folds and undulations, slight thickness, not quite one with the skin of the screen, portends this spatial rending."[76] Such play between surface and depth is characteristic of Iutkevich's work in *The Traitor*. While the stylized excess of pattern is painterly in feel, treating the screen as a flat, pictorial surface, the film does not allow the spectator's eye to rest at a distance from this surface, drawing it instead, through those transparent screens, into three-dimensionality.

So Iutkevich and Room playfully seduce the spectator into a process of constant readjustment. Appearances are deceptive: a bath turns out to be a divan; a curtain turns into a fan-shaped screen. Expected hierarchies of significance are thrown into question: action does not dominate over set; characters appear no more "alive" than the things that surround them. As one contemporary reviewer exclaimed: "Everything is acting/playing (*igraet*)."⁷⁷ This "play" cannot be interpreted; it yields no obvious meaning. It is in its very meaninglessness, however—in the consistent blurring of figure and ground—that Iutkevich's most significant experiment in cinematic faktura lies. For this play compels the spectator to move between what, following Riegl, we might call the "haptical" and the "optical" modes of seeing. As Lant notes, Riegl's original formulation of the haptic as a term of art criticism referred to the "pure surface" of Egyptian art. In Egyptian art, he suggested, space relations were transformed into relations on a plane: there was no depth. As a result, the spectator remains fixed in a position *external* to the work of art. For Riegl, therefore, haptic perception is objective: an encounter with the surface material of the object. By contrast, optical modes of spectatorship are subjective: perspective and depth encourage a mobile spectator engaged in an act of imaginative identification with the image.⁷⁸

Notably, however, for Riegl *neither* mode of spectatorship takes place through his or her identification with a represented human figure. It operates instead at the level of design—as a relationship with the material.⁷⁹ These terms provide an interesting approach to *The Traitor*—and, indeed, for thinking more broadly about Soviet filmmakers' exploitation of the construction of models of spectatorship during the 1920s. They invite us to consider how filmmakers sought to manipulate spectatorial response not only via editing, but also through the material of the film. In *The Traitor*, the clashing patterns and textures in the set are part of the film's conscious play between surface and depth. Their frontal nature repels the spectator's instinctive attempts to penetrate the space, forcing us to rest in a position that Riegl would describe as "objective." We are acutely aware of faktura—of the densely textural, heavily decorative *stuff* of which the set is made. We move between objective and subjective, optical and haptical experiences of the screen. As such, the film can be viewed as part of the inquiry into film's relationship with material that was a vital part of Soviet film practice in this period.

Depth and Volume

These two films of 1926, *The Traitor* and *The Overcoat*, have revealed a strand of avant-garde filmmaking in which faktura is as stylistically important as editing: a vital element of the film's address to the spectator. Room and Iutkevich used textile and pattern to experiment with the construction of cinematic space. This appears directly opposed to standard narratives of the Soviet avant-garde. As Kozintsev recalled, "The 1920s taught us to hate fakes, papier-mâché. Directors and cameramen learned to capture the authenticity of material, the character of its surface."[80] Yet, as we shall see, many films of this period display an ambivalent relationship with what might be called the surplus pleasure of the material. As Kozintsev himself acknowledged, "I grew up infatuated with faktura—beloved word of young artists."[81] These films thus navigate a careful path between an (ideologically inappropriate) *pleasure in* the material and an (ideologically sanctioned) *encounter with* the material. They explore how cinematic faktura can be used to create new modes of (embodied) spectatorship—and the place of such embodied spectatorship in the new Soviet cinema. In the mid-1920s, costume drama provided a space for the working out of these complex questions.

FEKS's next film, SVD, came out in 1927—closely following Ivanovskii's *The Decembrists* and shortly before Gardin's *The Poet and the Tsar*. This timing is not coincidental: these were two of the most lavishly funded, heavily discussed, and critically doomed historical epics of the period, and their production and reception directly shaped FEKS's approach to the historical film genre. *The Poet and the Tsar* is a classic example of the costume drama genre. Starring Evgenii Cherviakov (later to become an important director; see chapter 7) as Pushkin, it offered a politically appropriate narrative of Pushkin as poet of the people, repelled by the artifice of the Russian nobility. But its plot focused above all on the crowd-pleasing narrative of Pushkin's doomed love, and his tragic death. Production designer Anatolii Arapov (who was also responsible for the design of *The Decembrists*) seems to have relished the opportunity to recreate the baroque extravagances of imperial Russia on-screen. His designs for both films emphasize decorative excess and surface patterning—no doubt reflecting Arapov's earlier affiliation with the symbolist *Blue Rose* and *World of Art* groups before the revolution. Particular emphasis is given to the pleasure gardens of Peterhof: its extravagant fountains create visually striking patterns on-screen, their glistening arcs complementing the curves and flourishes of the baroque architecture, and echoing the shapes created by the feathers adorning women's costumes. In *The Decembrists*—a film with an even larger budget than *The Poet and the Tsar*—the interiors of noble families are similarly marked by an excess of pattern, and visual emphasis on the faktura of moldings, cornices, mirror frames, and the like, alongside heavily patterned wall coverings.

Both *The Poet and the Tsar* and *The Decembrists* were critical failures. Their sins were partly thematic and ideological. Bleiman, for one, noted that *The Decembrists* showed good work with costumes and makeup, but that it failed to convey the vital revolutionary message attached to the story of the Decembrists. In the end, he lamented, "This entire film consists of sets and uniforms."[82] He was even more uncompromising in his condemnation of *The Poet and the Tsar*—criticizing it for turning the tragic story of Pushkin (as liberal critic of an oppressive regime) into a petty "family-historical" drama.[83] Neznamov, however, directed his criticism at the production design itself, criticizing Gardin (and Arapov) for an overemphasis on the visual pleasures of imperial Russia, and for treating the Peterhof palace as nothing more than a "special effect." The costumes were so luxurious, he noted, that they might as well "be sent straight to Hollywood," but the social-historical context that was essential to a Soviet historical film was completely absent.[84] Shneider was equally damning, describing the set and the costumes in *The Poet and the Tsar* as "artificial" (*maskaradnye*): Gardin copied the portraits, engravings, and other historical materials "too slavishly," rather than trying to capture the spirit of the age.[85]

The terms of these criticisms are revealing. Neznamov used familiar language in calling for a more "everyday" presentation of Pushkin's Russia—for a focus on the real life of ordinary people. For both Shneider and Bleiman, however, even the tried and tested "authenticity" argument held no weight. Shneider described the costume genre per se as a "dead form." In 1928, Bleiman wrote a scathing indictment of what he called the "genre" film, which he described as "history in costumes": "Whatever the material of the film, it is not contemporary, not everyday, and not historical-revolutionary. It is stylized and aesthetically sanitized."[86] This polemic gathered weight toward the end of the decade. If authentic historical material was not the answer, however, the question of what might be an appropriate mode for a specifically Soviet historical film remained unresolved. FEKS, first in *SVD* and later in *New Babylon*, tried to answer that question.

According to Bleiman, Arapov's focus on decoration and surface flattened the lived reality of the past. It prevented an encounter with the three-dimensional faktura of material on-screen, and transformed it into mere visual spectacle. In *SVD*, the FEKS collective attempted a different approach to the material pleasures of the past. Like that of *The Overcoat*, the screenplay for this film was written by Tynianov (here together with Iulian Oksman). The film treated the same historical period as *The Decembrists*—in this case the uprising of the Chernigov regiment that was a key event in the Southern Decembrist revolt. But Tynianov was explicit in framing *SVD* as a polemic with *The Decembrists*: "We wanted to illuminate the sharp, leftist Decembrist movement as a counterbalance to the uniforms, the tastelessness and the showiness of *The Decembrists*."[87] He noted that the appeal of the narrative for FEKS lay not in its historical basis, but in its potential for "cinematographic pathos." And indeed, the film operates through the narrative codes of romantic melodrama. But this pathos lies equally in the affective power of the production design. Several reviewers recognized *SVD* as a new stage in Soviet historical cinema. Bleiman praised FEKS's approach to historical material, suggesting that they used it as a "trampoline" from which a new image of the epoch could be created.[88] Sokolov praised the directors' ambition of presenting a stylized vision of history.[89] Béla Balázs was even more explicit. In a riposte to those critics who claimed that Soviet cinema could and should not treat historical material, Balázs suggested that revolutionary filmmakers had a duty to do so "in order to firmly connect the past with real life problems."[90] Rather than being afraid of the aesthetic pleasures of the material, revolutionary filmmakers should feel free to enjoy it— to appropriate the devices of "beauty" and "mood–effects." Indeed, Balázs lambasted those who criticized them for it: "Does that mean that beauty is a bourgeois privilege? Does that mean that proletarian-revolutionary poetry cannot be beautiful?"[91] *SVD*, he suggested, succeeded as an "optical ballad." It might not externally resemble any particular reality, but it was "sincerely authentic in its internal orchestration of feelings (chuvstva), which—like music—can only be deeply felt."

We will return to Balázs's description of the "orchestration of feelings" below. How, though, was this "stylized" history presented through *SVD*'s production design? Much of the impact of this film comes from Moskvin's exceptional cinematography and lighting, which throw into relief Enei's carefully chosen costumes and sets. The film's key set of a bar, for instance, is striking for its frontal, flat arrangement, and its almost empty space: a single table (figure 2.5). Shot in static midrange, the set is framed theatrically, and against the almost empty set, the stark patterns of the character's costume (his thin, curling sideburns, his patterned braces against a white shirt) are striking. Such contrasts mark the visual style of *SVD*: the white of the crossed ribbons on the soldiers' uniforms, for example, and of the internal ruff on the heroine's dark cloak, stand out vividly against the shadows of often-bare sets. Where in both *The Poet and the Tsar* and *The Decembrists*, visual impact is created by ornate pattern on-screen (decorative wallpapers, mouldings, draped fabrics), in this film it comes from the positioning of rare patterns against an otherwise empty surface. The drama of a card

Fig. 2.5 Surface Patterns. Still from *SVD (Soiuz velikogo dela)* (*SVD*, dir. G. Kozintsev and L. Trauberg, production design by E. Enei, 1927).

game is marked by the visual play of smoke rings.[92] The smoke renders the screen opaque, drawing attention to it as surface. The light of candles vacillates through that surface, illuminating only the contrasting black and white of the cards themselves, and the gleaming *faktura* of perspiring faces seen in close-up.

This shadow play was to become the signature style of Andrei Moskvin, and had already been developed in *The Overcoat*, where, as Kozintsev recalls, the team had worked to light "only the outlines" of objects and people.[93] It depended equally, however, on set. In *SVD*, Enei's design is a complex blend of different styles. In places, as contemporary critics observed, the influence of expressionism is clear in distorted and exaggerated shapes (an oversized chair, a twisting staircase), which enable Moskvin's rich play with light and dark, drawing out the expressive possibilities of texture on-screen. Elsewhere, the film exhibits clear impressionist influence. The consistent use of smoke and fog recalls the devices of filmmakers such as Kirsanoff and Epstein, and the central ice-skating scene is marked by distinctive impressionistic elements.[94] Shifting perspective, the camera looks first across at the scene, and then down upon the mirrored surface of the iced lake, which glistens and blurs as the skaters whirl around it. The screen is transformed into the surface of the lake, marked by the patterns of skates. Ultimately, however, the film cannot be reduced to either expressionism or impressionism; as Sokolov noted, its principle aesthetic style is that of romantic melodrama. And its eclectic formal "devices" serve to emphasize that style: in this scene, as the lovers kiss, rapid montage transforms the swirling skates into a visualization of the protagonists' swirling emotions.[95]

Critics agreed that *SVD* represented a particular step forward in the genre of historical cinema, and its success was frequently described in terms that emphasized the formal impact of materials and their affective power. For Balázs in particular, the achievement of *SVD* lay in its ability to convey not the facts of history, but its *feeling*: the "warm pathos, which can nowhere appear more clearly than in the great feeling of revolutionary inspiration."[96] The orchestration of this feeling in the spectator was achieved via the sensations provoked by historical material (shapes and surfaces) on-screen. Such emphasis was a consistent element of Balázs's emerging theories of film, but took shape here in surprising relation to historical films. And it seemed to offer a way forward for the troubled genre of costume drama.

FEKS's exploitation of cinematographic potential of material was particularly evident in the 1929 film, *New Babylon*. Alongside the play of light and shadow that dominated *SVD*, however, *New Babylon* also used pattern and textile. Set in a Parisian department store, and directly inspired by Emile Zola's *Au Bonheur des Dames* (and his other works), *New Babylon* tells a story of the Paris Commune.[97] As in *The Overcoat*, the human relationship with material objects (commodities) is a thematic focus, and explored as part of the film's expressive style. In Kozintsev's words, in *New Babylon*, "things acted alongside people. They entered the film as motifs, metaphors, and participated in events, had their own development."[98] This material emphasis is most obvious in the film's early scenes of the department store, which picture rapturous consumers amid an overwhelming profusion of textiles—lace, chiffon, silk, velvet. This may be early Soviet cinema's most striking instance of cinematic faktura. Contrasting textures and (moving) materials transform the screen into an undulating surface: lace parasols swirl; fabric cascades. This scene is at once a two-dimensional plane and a three-dimensional coming-to-life of the commodity.

New Babylon makes its thematic—and ideological—argument through material. It draws a clear contrast between two types of sensory experience of the world: between the surface (and superficial) textures and patterns of bourgeois Paris, and the life of shopworker Louise Poirier and her comrades; between the glitter of the department store, and the intense physical experience of implicitly "real" life. The montage switches from the phantasmagoria of textiles, to the gruelling labor of sewing machinists, shoemakers, and laundrywomen; between the commodity, and the (hidden) work that goes into creating it (figure 2.6a).[99] In these scenes of workers' life, however, faktura still has a key part to play. All of these workers labor with their hands—a fact that is particularly visually striking in the recurring images of laundrywomen, their hands covered in soap, moving their garments amid the water as the steam rises around them. One woman stands out for her gaunt face, skin gleaming with sweat, and her labored, difficult breathing (figure 2.6b). For the characters, the decorative surfaces of bourgeois experience signal a lack of authentic sensory engagement with the world, which is in contrast with the intense physicality of working life.

The contrasting sensory modes represented by the bourgeoisie and the workers are echoed in cinematographic style. Kozintsev recalled his trip to Paris in preparation for the film, where they shot material on location. There the FEKS group met Léon Moussinac, as well as the young Jean Renoir and Kirsanoff. Kozintsev wrote notably of the "sensations" (oshchushcheniia) of Paris and of his ambition in transforming those sensations into film: "Sensations are capable of being given flesh, of thickening to a point where they take on a particular form."[100] This emphasis on sensation is consistent in Kozintsev's discussion of *New Babylon*, and linked to the creation of spectatorial affect: he writes of his desire to make the celluloid start to "feel (*chuvstvovat'*)."[101] This process was not straightforward, however. Kozintsev recalls a long and difficult struggle with the tendency of the material to appear merely historical, and to lack affective materiality: "In the frames you couldn't feel the power of the energy of the plastic material. Rather, it all looked decorative, stylized."[102] It was only when Moskvin—in a final attempt—shot the wide scenes of bourgeois Paris through a lens normally used for portraits that Kozintsev saw what he had been hoping for: a "translucent, fantastical, feverish world."

In contrast with this phantasmagoric world of consumption, the world of the commune operates with a different visual and sensory code: it is, as Kozintsev notes, "close up."[103] In *New Babylon*, then, different relationships with the material articulate social identities, and faktura plays a key role in conveying this to the spectator as *felt* knowledge—through the body. This is characteristic of FEKS's approach to the historical film. They sought to exploit the impact of physical material on-screen to convey a sensory (felt)

Fig. 2.6 Contrasting Worlds. Stills from *New Babylon* (*Novyi vavilon*, dir. G. Kozintsev and L. Trauberg, production design by E. Enei, 1927).

Fig. 2.7 Redeeming Lace. Still from *New Babylon* (*Novyi vavilon*, dir. G. Kozintsev and L. Trauberg, production design by E. Enei, 1927).

experience of a historical time. For FEKS, however, this film was also a transitional text, a swan song for a particular kind of infatuation with faktura, made vividly clear in the shifting image of the department store mannequin. Initially a blandly smiling symbol of the bourgeois enslavement to the commodity, she/it becomes increasingly dishevelled and grotesque, before its eventual desecration and burning in the commune. It is perhaps this emblematic moment that Kozintsev described as the film's "breakdown of material (*raspad materii*)."[104] In this sense, *New Babylon* can be read as a renunciation of the (cinematographic) pleasures of textiles—exemplified in Louise's desperate waving of rags over the revolutionary barricade, accompanied by a frenzied echo of "For Sale." Where in Kirsanoff's *Ménilmontant*, lace is an inviting, seductive veil, simultaneously screening and revealing the body, in *New Babylon* it is scrunched up and wound messily around an otherwise naked mannequin, in a grotesque parody of lace's sensual invitation. Later, it is wrapped around a wounded revolutionary's foot (figure 2.7). Thus transformed, lace takes on an assertive (rebarbative) materiality that refuses its customary sensory pleasure, while drawing the spectator nevertheless into an almost tactile encounter with the physical textile.

To some extent, then, *New Babylon* can be seen as an inquiry into how cinema might articulate a different kind of relationship with the material—and in particular with material pleasure. It rejects the spectacular allure of the patterned textiles and laces of the department store, and embraces the hands-on close-up of manual labor. As such, it reflects back on the story that this chapter has uncovered. Through these historical dramas, we have seen how production design could function as part of a film's poetic style—and in particular, how the textures and materials of set could be exploited to create particular models of spectatorship, and to play with the relationship between surface and depth. Noël Burch has described the development of cinema during its first two decades as a journey toward Renaissance perspective, as "a recapitulation of the decades of work which went into the constitution of monocular perspective in painting."[105] For Burch, this journey was one of progress—from flat, planar models with a fixed camera, evenness of lighting, and painted backdrops toward the illusion of depth that was cinema's "three dimensional vocation."[106] In these early Soviet costume films, however, we discover a much more complex—and conscious—interplay between surface and depth. And one that in the Soviet case was increasingly ideologically coded. Many of my protagonists in this chapter were part of a small avant-garde group. They shared an interest in formal experiment, and in their production design they sought both haptical and optical modes of spectatorship, and explored the relationship between the two as an index of possible modes of revolutionary sensation. This preoccupation was not unique to the avant-garde, however. As I have shown, these films must be seen alongside more mainstream costume drama, as part of a wider interest in the role and function of faktura on-screen. For all their apparent historical and costume focus, the diverse films treated in this chapter share the key aim articulated by Kozintsev: to make the screen (and the spectator) *feel*.

NOTES

1. A notable recent exception is Fischer, ed., *Art Direction*. This book focuses almost exclusively on Hollywood, however.

2. Affron and Affron, *Sets in Motion*, 37–40. An excellent overview of different critical approaches to set design can be found in Bergfelder, Harris, and Street, *Film Architecture*, 11–25. Other works that treat set design include Berthomé, *Le décor au cinema*; Barsacq, *Caligari's Cabinet*; Neumann, ed., *Film Architecture*.

3. Tashiro, *Pretty Pictures*, 6.

4. Ibid., 18–38.

5. For a fuller (but still introductory) account of production design in this period, see Widdis, "Cinema and the Art of Being."

6. Room, "Kino i teatr," 56 cited in Iampol′skii, "Rossiia," 14.

7. Cavendish, "The Hand that Turns the Handle," 206.

8. Mikhin suggests that this system was introduced in 1911 for Chardynin's *Kreuzer Sonata* (*Kreitserova sonata*, 1911): Mikhin, "Rozhdenie fundusa," 148–54. Sobolev, however, suggests that Czesław Sabiński was working in parallel on a similar system: Sobolev, *Liudi i fil′my dorevoliutsionnogo kino*, 61–63.

9. Bergfelder, Harris, and Street, *Film Architecture*, 41.

10. Tsivian, "Two 'Stylists' of the Teens"; DeBlasio, "Choreographing Space, Time and *Dikovinki*."

11. Khanzhonkova, "Iz vospominanii o dorevoliutsionnom kino," 126.

12. When he was employed as a young set designer for Bauer, Lev Kuleshov's role was to find this defining detail (known as the *dikovinka*, or "curiosity") for every shot: "The foreground has to be based around some object or other, sometimes particular, sometimes ordinary, but characteristic of the style of the frame. Objects have a rather great significance in the construction of filmic material" (Kuleshov, "Znamia kinematografii," 83). Furthermore, Kuleshov stresses the director's emphasis on creating depth of field. If a set was to consist of two rooms, then they must be at different levels, and connected by a staircase. Columns, architectural friezes, drapery, and the like, were used to provide further "relief" and contrasting volumes (ibid., 79). Kuleshov published earlier articles dealing explicitly with the role of the khudozhnik in cinema, most notably the paired essays "O zadachakh khudozhnika," and "Zadachi kinokhudozhnika." It is notable that these are Kuleshov's first theoretical articles (indeed they could be called the first examples of Russian film theory), and that they are focused on the role of the khudozhnik.

13. Lisakovskaia, "Nezamechennyi avangard," 27; Gromov, *Vladimir Egorov*, 13.

14. Albéra, *Albatros: Des russes à Paris*.

15. Barsacq, *Caligari's Cabinet*, 38.

16. Bowlt, "Constructivism and Russian Stage Design," 62.

17. Ibid., 63.

18. Egorov, for instance, studied architecture at the Stroganov Institute under Fedor Shekhtel′ and Ivan Zholtovskii. Shekhtel′ is best known as a pioneer of *style moderne* architecture in prerevolutionary Russia. Zholtovskii began his career in 1908 (having worked with the more senior Shekhtel′ in the Stroganov Institute from 1898); he came to particular prominence, however, in postrevolutionary Russia, and in particular in the 1930s, when his neoclassical style was celebrated as an appropriate direction for Socialist Realist architecture.

19. See Voevodin, "V. Egorov," 27.

20. Bergfelder, Harris, and Street, *Film Architecture*, 25.

21. See Fischer, ed., *Art Direction*, and Ramirez, *Architecture for the Screen*.

22. Bergfelder, Harris, and Street, *Film Architecture*, 58.

23. Barsacq, *Caligari's Cabinet*, 47. Berthomé also suggests poverty as the principle reason for the weakness of Soviet studio work, and the preference for location shooting. Berthomé, *Le décor au cinéma*, 82.

24. In 1927, the Mezhrabpom-Rus′ studio moved to new, bigger premises: new pavilions were constructed, and Sergei Kozlovskii elaborated a special "fundus" system

of moveable flats. See Miasnikov, *Ocherki istorii*, 66; Kozlovskii describes his system in "Tekhnika kinoatel'e," and in his book of 1930. An article in 1925 boasts of Mezhrabpom-Rus''s advanced lighting techniques ("Genri," "Kartonnyi domik," 56), and indicates that Goskino was still using the glass house system of illumination.

25. GTK (Gosudarstvennyi tekhnikum kinematografii) was founded in 1922. In 1930 the Tekhnikum (academy) became an Institute (GIK), and from 1938, (V)GIK had a designated art faculty (established and run by Fedor Bogorodskii until 1959), which incorporated set design, animation, and, later, costume design.

26. See Widdis, "Cinema and the Art of Being."

27. Kozlovskii and Kolin, *Khudozhnik-arkhitektor v kino*, 37.

28. Miasnikov, *Ocherki istorii*, 92; Kozlovskii, *Khudozhnik-arkhitektor v kino*, 40.

29. Ibid., 38. Kozlovskii notes that a special department for film art direction was opened in the Academy of Arts in 1929 (121).

30. Kolupaev, "Khudozhnik v kino-proizvodstve," 18.

31. Rodchenko, "Khudozhnik i 'material'naia sreda,'" 15–16.

32. Anon., "Rezoliutsiia sektsii khudozhnikov arkhitektorov," 12–13.

33. Al'tman, "Khudozhnik v kino," 22. For more information on how the practical work of production design was organized in this period, see Widdis, "Cinema and the Art of Being."

34. Agden, "Kino-khudozhnik," 16–18.

35. The French Impressionist filmmakers grouped around Delluc and Epstein (and including another émigré, Dmitrii Kirsanoff) were also well known, largely due to Il'ia Erenburg and Vladimir Pozner (Cavendish, *Soviet Mainstream Cinematography*, 43). For an indication of Soviet filmmakers' familiarity with French films, see Erenburg, "Novoe frantsuzskoe kino," 24.

36. Pudovkin, "O khudozhnike v kino," 117.

37. Kuleshov, "Iskusstvo kino (moi opyt)," 185.

38. Irinin. "Arkhitektura i dekoratsii," 32.

39. Ibid.

40. Kolupaev, "O dekoratsiiakh," 34. There is evidence that such expeditions did take place. Kozlovskii recalls, for example, a visit to the Donbass to see coal mines: RGALI f. 2394, op. 1, ed. khr 85, cited in Miasnikov, *Ocherki istorii*, 27.

41. Miasnikov, *Ocherki istorii*, 45.

42. See Kuleshov, "Iskusstvo kino (moi opyt)," 188.

43. Lant, "Haptical Cinema."

44. Gromov, *Vladimir Egorov*, 13.

45. The Russian term is generally "historical film," but discussion revolves frequently around "costume" in discussion of the "wrong" kind of film in ways that allow us to think of this opposition between "costume drama" and "historical film."

46. B-Shtein, "Dvorets i krepost," 2.

47. Ibid.

48. See, for example, the review in *Izvestiia* (November 12, 1923).

49. Bleiman, "Kry'lia kholopa," 3.

50. Babenchikov, "Kino—geroi—byt," 13.

51. Kozintsev, "Glubokii ekran," 112.

52. Tynianov, "Libretto kino-fil'ma 'Shinel,'" 78, cited in Kozintsev, "Glubokii ekran," 107.

53. Kozintsev, "Glubokii ekran," 114.
54. Sokolov, "Shinel'," 28.
55. Kozintsev, "Glubokii ekran," 112.
56. Bleiman, "Shinel'," 62.
57. See Moldavskii, *S Maiakovskim v teatre i kino* for full biographical details.
58. Room himself played an active part in the construction of his films' sets—indeed, Dmitrii Kolupaev criticized him directly for treating the *khudozhnik* as a mere laborer. Kolupaev, "Khudozhnik v kino-proizvodstve," 18.
59. Bagrov, "Sovetskii dendi," 74.
60. Grashchenkova, *Abram Room*, 34.
61. Prim, "O predatele," 2. Another reviewer, Kh. Khersonskii, was largely negative, but did comment on the "artistic" success of the design. Khersonskii, "Predatel'," 5.
62. Khersonskii, "Bor'ba faktov," 24–25.
63. Such Formalist criticism has been applied to much of Iutkevich's work—Jay Leyda, for example, describes "a pleasure in plastic effects that sometimes diluted the dramatic aims of his films." Leyda, *Kino*, 256.
64. Iutkevich, *Chelovek na ekrane*, 135.
65. Ibid., 136.
66. Iutkevich, "Plat'e kartiny," 7.
67. Iutkevich, "Dekorativnoe oformlenie fil'ma," 8.
68. Ibid., 8.
69. Mallet-Stevens, *Le décor moderne*, cited in Albrecht, *Designing Dreams*, 52.
70. Albrecht, *Designing Dreams*, 120.
71. See for instance the designs for Meierkhol'd's 1916 *Portret Doriana Greia*, Protazanov's *Ego prizyv* (1925), and Fedorov's *Mertvyi dom* (1932, not released at the time). The Moscow Museum of Cinema holds a number of Egorov's design sketches, together with those of Aleksei Utkin. See f. 153, op. 07–24.
72. Anon., "Frantsuzskie nemye fil'my," 356, 477. Although the only one of L'Herbier's films to be released in Russia was *Le Torrent* (The Flood, 1923), Soviet filmmakers were familiar with French productions of the period. L'Herbier is mentioned, alongside Abel Gance and Jean Epstein, in a discussion of good French cinema published in ARK in 1925: Pozner, "Frantsuzskii kinematograf v 1924 godu," 27–29.
73. Felicia Miller Frank describes the decorative 'moderne' interiors of the film as evidence of the heroine's coldness. Frank, "'L'Inhumaine."
74. Turovskaia and Chanutin, *Sergei Jutkewitsch*, 42.
75. Iutkevich was later acquainted with Matisse—and greatly prized the sketch caricature that Matisse did of him. See Bagrov, "Sovetskii dendi," 73.
76. Lant, "Haptical Cinema," 53.
77. Prim, "O predatele," 2.
78. Riegl's somewhat reductive account of the evolution of Western art charts a move from the haptic to the optical, from the objective to the subjective, and thus away from the confrontation with materiality that Egyptian art had offered. Alois Riegl, *Late Roman Art Industry*.
79. Lant, "Haptical Cinema," 62.
80. Kozintsev, "Glubokii ekran," 190–1.
81. Ibid., 191.
82. Bleiman, "Dekabristy," 78.

83. Bleiman, "Poet i tsar'," 82.
84. Neznamov, "Poet i tsar'," 3.
85. Shneider, "SVD," 20.
86. Bleiman, "'Mezhrabpom-Rus''- zhanr," 1.
87. Tynianov, "O feksakh," 10.
88. Bleiman, "Kuda rastut 'feksy'?," 112.
89. Sokolov, "SVD."
90. Bálázs, "Russkaia fil'ma i ee kritika," 3.
91. Ibid.
92. Kozinstev recalled that it was the young Fridrikh Ermler who, hidden from the camera, smoked and blew these stupendous rings throughout the scene. See "Glubokii ekran," 119–20.
93. Kozintsev, "Glubokii ekran," 113.
94. Shneider noted this influence. Shneider, "SVD," 20. For excellent analysis of this scene, see Cavendish, *The Men with the Movie Camera*, 218–24.
95. Sokolov, "SVD," 21.
96. Bálázs, "Russkaia fil'ma i ee kritika," 3.
97. Zola is an author distinguished by his "naturalism"—his attempt to capture the fleshy materiality of lived reality. He also had a marked interest in the capacity of language to create word-pictures: there is a clear reciprocity between Zola's literary style and the painterly experiments of his artistic contemporaries in Paris, most particularly impressionist painters such as Manet and Renoir, with whom he worked closely. In a sense, *New Babylon* shares Zola's twin ambitions.
98. Kozintsev, "Glubokii ekran," 151.
99. Nesbet, "Émile Zola, Kozintsev and Trauberg," 105–6.
100. Kozintsev, "Glubokii ekran," 142.
101. Ibid., 143.
102. Ibid., 144.
103. Ibid., 152.
104. Ibid., 152.
105. Burch, *Life to Those Shadows*, 2, cited in Lant, "Haptical Cinema," 69.
106. Ibid.

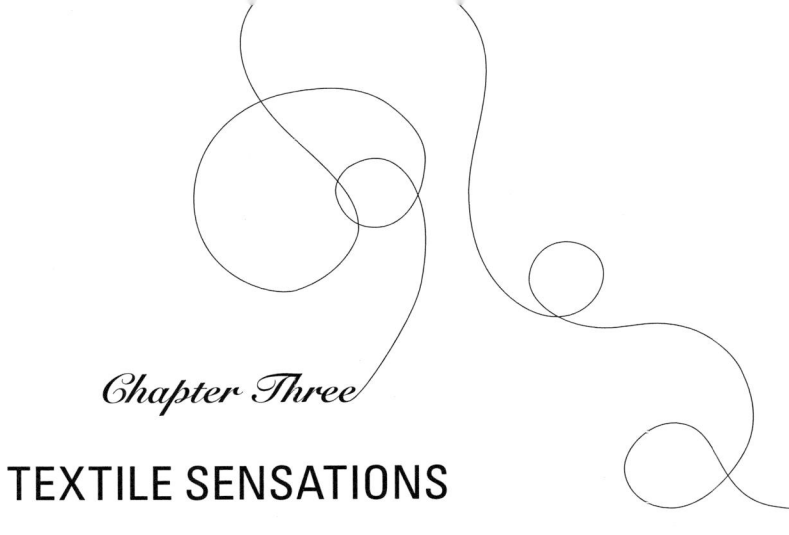

Chapter Three

TEXTILE SENSATIONS

> Tissue, textile, and fabric provide excellent models of knowledge, excellent quasi-abstract objects, primal varieties: the world is a mass of laundry.
>
> Michel Serres, 1985

CHAPTER 2 HAS explored the place of decorative textile in film production design, and its role in the creation of cinematic faktura. This chapter will trace the fate of such textile in the shaping of Soviet domestic style on-screen. In Soviet Russia, of course, the place of textile was not straightforward. Decorative cloth could retain a legitimate place in "historical" interiors on-screen, but pattern and ornament were not ideologically neutral in Soviet Russia. By the mid-1920s, it was becoming increasingly clear that cinema's chief mission was to picture Soviet reality: to show real people living in new ways in the new world. The task of filmmakers was to picture the domestic interiors of the present. How should they configure new models of the relationship between characters and the world of objects that surrounds them? And in vital parallel, how could these relationships be mirrored in a film's address to the spectator? What was the "material" of the new cinema?

In the second half of the 1920s, and particularly with the beginning of the first Five-Year Plan in 1928, these questions became increasingly acute. In 1928, prompted by the first All-Union Party Conference on Film in Moscow, calls went out for a new stylistic and thematic framework for the maturing Soviet film industry.[1] Vigorous debates before, during, and after the conference left no doubt that cinema had its part to play in the first Five-Year Plan.

There were two key elements to these discussions. First, subject matter: the newly centralized film studio Sovkino announced a production plan in July 1928, with clear thematic guidelines for filmmakers and scriptwriters, and a call for films to reflect Soviet *byt* (everyday life), and to model the path for its improvement.[2] Second, as a reaction to what Adrian Piotrovskii designated the "intellectualism" of the Soviet avant-garde, and in particular to the "mass" heroes of Sergei Eisenstein's revolutionary cinema, filmmakers were called upon to create developed, three-dimensional characters, who would make ideological messages "real."[3] In the words of Gazdenko in 1927, "We have outgrown propaganda."[4]

Notwithstanding the obvious ironies of Gazdenko's claim, such statements reflect the imperatives that shaped Soviet film production. Films must show "real" Soviet people, living a real Soviet life. But how? What should the socialist interior look like? This was a complex question in Soviet Russia of the 1920s. And it was particularly acute in cinema. Early Soviet cinema, after all, was celebrated for its outdoor shots, for capturing the "life of the masses." Leo Mur had gone so far as to proclaim the "the life of the interior" to be "a forbidden arena for the film camera."[5] The problem faced by filmmakers, however, as Mur himself acknowledged, was that "the greater part of a person's life takes place not under the sky but under a ceiling." If cinema was to picture Soviet everyday life, and to offer ideological lessons for its improvement, then it needed to find a way to picture interior spaces.

Here, filmmaking intersects with a wider history of Soviet interior design. The mainstream of design theory during the 1920s aimed—according to rhetoric at least—at the elimination of ornament, the creation of clean-lined clothing, furniture, and housing to suit the new age of production. The drive toward functionalism and efficiency seemed to work against comfort, against the softness of pillows and eiderdowns, against extraneous decoration, and toward a lived environment of maximum simplicity. Of course, Soviet Russia was not alone here. Le Corbusier's influential pamphlet *The Decorative Art of Today* (1925) viewed ornament as superfluous, and as a false mask or disguise. Following Adolf Loos's aphoristic essay "Ornament as Crime," Le Corbusier suggested that ornament satisfied the base sensory desires of the human; the evolution of civilization could be seen as a move from the sensual to the intellectual, from the sensuality of decoration to the abstraction of form.[6] In the modern world, the mind had conquered the senses, and so modern architecture and design should eschew decoration; their form must be defined by function alone.

At first glance, Soviet revolutionary ideology seemed to adopt this position: the decorated home was the petty-bourgeois home, satirized in Maiakovskii's well-known propaganda poem "On [Domestic] Trash" (1920), when a portrait of Marx begins to howl, lamenting the possibility "that the revolution [would] be destroyed by canaries."[7] In propaganda, excessive pattern, heavy furniture, and ornamental clutter became key signifiers of "former" people. In practice, however, the picture was more complex. First, of course, domestic interiors had not been (could not be) transformed wholesale in 1917. During the 1920s, traces of prerevolutionary domestic architecture and decoration were still very much in evidence. Second, and more interestingly, attitudes toward ornament were not as straightforward as histories of Soviet design may lead us to believe. They were tied to the elaboration of a new aesthetic—and this process was nuanced and complex. For Russian modernists, as for their European counterparts, the elimination of the extraneous ornamentation intrinsic to bourgeois decoration was a vital first step in the creation of the new, modern style. This did not necessarily mean, however, that there was no place for the decorative. It was just a question of finding the right type.

In this respect, Le Corbusier's and Loos's emphasis on sensory pleasure as a threat to the modern project is important. But it is also misleading. In fact, modernism had an ambivalent relationship with the sensory impact of ornament and textile. In Soviet culture, this is particularly visible in the evolution of domestic space in cinema. Domestic interiors in films set in the contemporary Soviet Union in the mid to late 1920s reveal a complex picture. In schematic terms, they can be divided into three basic categories: the traditional rural provincial interior; the (retrograde) bourgeois urban interior; and the new socialist interior. This chapter will treat only the first two of these interiors: the rural and the bourgeois urban. Later, chapter 6 will explore the tentative outlines of new socialist interiors with a focus on "modern sensations." In both chapters, however, my focus is on hybrid spaces *in transition*, and specifically, on how films picture characters' lives as shaped by material context, where textiles and objects play a particularly important role. Things matter. The elaboration of domestic space on-screen was a project that worked in parallel with the real project of creating a new socialist interior, constructing new relationships between the spectator and the material objects of everyday life.

Material as Background

Although the center of gravity of Bolshevik ideology lay in the urban proletariat, 83 percent of the Soviet population in 1926 lived in villages.[8] Traditional peasant life was very much alive, and attitudes to the village were complex. On the one hand, narratives of modernization were clear in viewing peasant life as backward and retrograde, and to be eliminated in the passage to socialism. From another perspective, however, peasant Russia could be seen as the locus of a specifically Russian form of precapitalist life—one that made the particular Soviet form of socialism not just possible, but inevitable. In the course of the 1920s, shifting images of rural Russia on-screen reveal this ambivalence—and its gradual resolution.

The representation of provincial domestic interiors is of particular interest in this respect. In Soviet cinema of the mid-1920s, rural interiors were commonly signaled by traditional embroidered and floral textile. The shifting meanings of this signifier can be traced across two indicative films: Iakov Protazanov's 1925 comedy, *The Tailor from Torzhok* (*Zakroishchik iz Torzhka*), and Ol′ga Preobrazhenskaia and Ivan Pravov's *Women of Riazan Province* (*Baby riazanskie*, 1927). Both films were self-reflexively engaged with the history of representations of rural life in Russia, reflecting and refracting key visual tropes, and raising questions about their relevance for the present. This was a rich and potent field of meaning. Through the nineteenth century, the changing representation of traditional (peasant) Russia had been intricately connected to the articulation of a specifically Russian national identity. In very different ways, Protazanov and Preobrazhenskaia used both theme and form to navigate the visual pleasures of rural Russia, seeking to articulate a new Soviet provincial aesthetic—and perhaps to pave the way for a new Soviet identity.

The Tailor from Torzhok is set in provincial Russia during the 1920s, in a small town not far from Petrograd. It is designated a "lyrical comedy" and is a gentle satire on the collision between old and new ways of life. Directed by Protazanov, with Egorov as production designer, the film's image of provincial space drew much from those men's shared experience in prerevolutionary filmmaking. They had, after all, worked together on the prestigious Golden Series of Russian films, and in the Ermol′ev studio. In *The Tailor from Torzhok*, they present domestic interiors that are a blend of traditional folk and provincial merchant culture, located within familiar visual frameworks. Melan′ia Ivanovna (figure 3.1), proprietor of a tailor's workshop, is

Fig. 3.1 Melan´ia Ivanovna: The Merchant Woman. Still from *The Tailor from Torzhok* (*Zakroishchik iz Torzhka*, dir. Ia. Protazanov; production design by V. Egorov, 1925).

an archetypal provincial merchant woman, apparently drawn directly from Boris Kustodiev's many portraits of the same name produced between 1910 and 1925 (figure 3.2).[9] She is dressed in richly patterned textile, her hair covered with a headscarf, her ears decorated by earrings. Such images acted as ideological shorthand in representations of provincial life in this period. Though her business is threatened by the new Soviet cooperative store that has opened in the village, Melan´ia Ivanovna's merchant life goes on as always, alongside the new world of pioneers and communist workers, and also alongside the simpler world of the traditional Russian village. The world of 1920s Russia is shown as a space of transition, a hybrid composite of different lives and different values.

What is the role of textile in *The Tailor from Torzhok*? Set in a tailor's workshop, the film features a plethora of fabric. Melan´ia Ivanovna's home (described by one of her friends as "a horn of plenty") is bedecked with textile, and its patterns have both thematic and formal significance. In one

Fig. 3.2 Boris Kustodiev, *The Merchant Woman* (1923), oil on canvas, 97.5cm × 77cm. Private collection. Courtesy of MacDougall Arts Ltd.

scene, for example, when Melan′ia Ivanovna is dreaming of romance with her mistreated young employee, Petel′kin, her fantasies are played out in tactile images, in which textiles play an important role. She discovers her old bridal gown in her dowry chest, and reverently hangs it on a tailor's model

Fig. 3.3 Melan′ia Ivanovna: Self and Textile. Still from *The Tailor from Torzhok* (*Zakroishchik iz Torzhka*, dir. Ia. Protazanov; production design by V. Egorov, 1925).

(figure 3.3). Cloth is a repository of sensory and emotional memory. As she touches these fabrics, Melan′ia Ivanovna rediscovers the feelings linked to them. The film needs no title cards to explain this. Sensation creates emotion; the object is an externalization of the self, evoking past experience.

This sequence is also of interest from a formal perspective, however. It exemplifies the density of textile that continually surrounds Melan′ia Ivanovna, and how its different designs articulate cinematic deep space. The tailor's model occupies (and constructs) the foreground, and the spectator's eye is led from there, through a curtain, to a dressing table, and then to Melan′ia Ivanovna herself, clothed in a patterned dress that renders her part of the film's textural surface. In the depth of the frame lies a bed piled with cushions; behind it there are at least five further textures and patterns. As in *The Traitor* (see chapter 2), this set initiates a play between surface and depth. The overloading of textiles and textures turns the screen into a surface, upon which the human subject competes for attention. Such visual equivalence between human protagonist and set speaks thematically to

Melan′ia Ivanovna's double-entrapment—in the object world and (through those objects) in the past. And although she may relish this world of layered textile, for young Petel′kin (played by comic actor Igor′ Il′inski) it is emphatically a form of captivity. Later, in an act of desperate rebellion, he pushes Melan′ia Ivanovna's interfering friends into her dowry chest, enclosing them within that mass of oppressive, memory-bearing material, in a visual realization of the film's principal metaphor.

The key impact of (patterned) textile in this film is to emphasize the failure of the provincial merchant class to embrace the future, and production design works to ensure that the spectatorial experience mirrors this suffocation. The film does offer a glimpse of an alternative model of sensory experience, however. Petel'kin forms an alliance with the equally naïve, and equally oppressed, young Katia, and his attraction to her is shown in images that operate through a different sensory code. Katia and the other women of the village are washing their clothes in the river. Her bare feet are in the water; her toes grip the stone on which she stands (figure 3.4a); her hands swirl the textile beneath the water's surface. The tangible physicality of these images of Katia is consistent throughout the film. The relationship between her and Petel′kin is marked out by minute physical details that are sharply different from the broad brushstrokes that signal other characters. They sit on a tree trunk, their bodies lightly touching (figure 3.4b); they wind ribbon nervously around their fingers as they flirt. Such affecting physicality prevents these two otherwise comic characters from descending into caricature, and provides, for the spectator, a space of respite from the decorative assault of provincial textile.

In *The Tailor from Torzhok*, then, two types of sensory experience are set against one another. Petel′kin's escape from the amorous clutches of Melan′ia Ivanovna, into the innocent arms of young Katia is an escape from the suffocation of comfort. The minute and signifying physical sensations of Katia and Petel′kin contrast with the inhibiting morass of sensory indulgence that surrounds Melan′ia Ivanovna. The new world against the old world. This is not a straightforward binary, however: sensory pleasure is not eliminated in the "new" world, but mediated; attention is drawn to the tactile experiences of the human body. It matters that Petel′kin and Katia touch; and it matters that they touch the world—that Katia washes her linen, and that Petel′kin cuts and sews. In the figure of Katia in particular, the film posits an implicitly unspoiled, rural peasant body as the site of authentic sensory (and implicitly emotional and moral) experience. It posits that body

Fig. 3.4 Redemptive Touch. Still from *The Tailor from Torzhok* (*Zakroishchik iz Torzhka*, dir. Ia. Protazanov; production design by V. Egorov, 1925).

(with bare feet, always dressed in a curious mix of peasant headscarf and komsomolesque white blouse) as the positive future image of Soviet society. However, the romantic plot makes it subtly clear that the space of a Soviet future is not yet formed. Petel´kin and Katia have no alternative "home." There is no modern socialist alternative to the old world. Rather they move into a future that as yet has no form.

The Tailor from Torzhok is a comedy. It does not seek to make complex points about the new Soviet self. Yet its use of textile focuses our attention on key elements in the evolving representation of the Russian village. This picture of rural Russia embeds peasant tradition (the wedding feast, traditional textile, etc.) within a merchant milieu, rather than focusing on labor, craft, or hardship. The domestic interior, with its textiles, provides a merely decorative backdrop for its characters. They do not live in connection with it; and for the spectator it is little more than an ornamental frame. The challenge for Soviet filmmakers, however, was to transform decorative background into lived material.

Touching Cloth

In this respect, it is significant that Petel´kin and Katia's relationship has its starting point in the vivid scene where she washes her linen in the river. Images of laundry recur in the visual culture of the period as a marker of the lived experience or ordinary people. Ivan Shagin's 1929 photograph, *The Laundry Women (Prachki)*, for example, captures the industry of women washing linen in a (probably urban) river (figure 3.5).[10] In Kozintsev and Trauberg's *New Babylon*, the working women of Paris are shown amid soapsuds and sheets. Laundry, it seems, marked a hands-on connection with the world that was the beginning of politicization—and possible salvation. On this basis it is not by chance that Ol´ga Preobrazhenskaia's *Women of Riazan Province* opens with a scene of laundry. With a village in the background, women stand on boulders in a river, treading their cloth with their feet and swirling it in the water, before stretching out the plain white textile in vivid ribbons across the riverbanks to dry. The impact here is both aesthetic and thematic: this film is set in a traditional textile-making community, and this opening scene links linen and labor in a combination that turns out to be central to the film's narrative.

Women of Riazan Province was produced in 1927, two years after *The Tailor from Torzhok*. Although Preobrazhenskaia had worked for Protazanov as an actress before the revolution, in this film she set out to do

Fig. 3.5 Ivan Shagin, *Washerwomen (Prachki)*, photograph, 1929. Private collection.

something very distinct from the older director.[11] Where Protazanov's film was a comedy, *Women of Riazan Province* is a dark melodrama.[12] Its central story is that of young bride Anna, who is raped by her father-in-law while her husband Ivan is at war, bears an illegitimate baby by him, and eventually commits suicide from shame when Ivan returns. Although undoubtedly a critique of traditional patriarchal rural society—and in particular of the widespread tradition of *snokhachestvo* (sexual abuse of daughter-in-law by the male head of a peasant household[13])—the film is remarkable for its relative lack of political message. Despite its plot spanning 1914 to 1918, *Women of Riazan Province* lacks overt Bolshevik ideology, or indeed any evidence of revolutionary history. Instead, its principal impact lies in its vivid picture of the life of a wealthy peasant family during the First World War.

This film was widely seen as marking a new stage in the filmic representation of the Russian village, and much discussed as an ethnographic picture of rural life. It was one of two films that appeared in 1927 that pointedly advertised anthropologist Ol'ga Vishnevskaia as coauthor of their screenplay and "ethnographic consultant."[14] *Women of Riazan Province* was shot on location in the village of Sapozhok, "fifty kilometres from the nearest railway line."[15] Dmitrii Kolupaev was set designer, and here had a chance to put into practice his desire for authentic sets, aided by ethnographic research (see chapter 2), and by direct input from Vishnevskaia. Although lamenting its lack of a clear political message, reviews in the press praised the film's ethnographic truth-to-life.[16]

This emphasis on ethnographic verisimilitude may be misleading, however. This is a film saturated with textile, and its presence has symbolic and formal impact that goes beyond truth-to-life. *Women of Riazan Province* is set in textile-producing communities, and the lives of its female protagonists are intertwined with textile: they are dressed in heavy traditional costume; they spin, weave, wash, and fold linen. In this traditional community, cloth is capital: a woman's worth is measured in textile. The mean-spirited Luker´ia retorts to Viktor, looking at Anna's meager linen hung out on the washing line: "Your wife does not take up much space when she hangs out her trousseau." When the evil father-in-law Vasilii returns, drunk, from the market, he brings gifts of shawls and scarves for his womenfolk. As he moves to rape Anna, he seems to enclose her within the large dark-colored shawl that is her (unwanted) gift.

The darker symbolism attached to textile shadows the film's images of rural life. At the end of the film, markedly, Anna's suicide takes place during the village's annual Assumption feast while the other villagers dance and play in what appears to be a decorative idyll. Their various patterned dresses and shirts create an overwhelming concatenation of fabric. But the parallel montage here serves to transform these textiles into cruelly indifferent witnesses, signifiers of a rural idyll, a joy and peace, that has no place in Preobrazhenskaia's brutal picture of village life. Defamiliarized, they are more than mere background or decoration: they shape and constrain lives. In this patriarchal system, women are both literally and symbolically oppressed by the suffocating weight of textile. Anna is shown rigidly contained by the ceremonial headdress (*kokoshnik*) of the bride. Even the bodies of children are constrained by fabric. Authentic life is bound up, limited by the weight of tradition.

This thematic focus on the binding weight of tradition is directly mirrored in the film's formal devices. Textile patterns are overwhelming in their visual impact on-screen. In one particularly striking scene, the film revels in portraying the rituals of the traditional folk wedding.[17] Anna and Ivan kiss beneath an arch made from woven and embroidered wedding

Fig. 3.6 Costume on Display. Still from *Women of Riazan Province* (*Baby riazanskie*, dir. O. Preobrazhenskaia (and I. Pravov); production design by D. Kolupaev).

cloths (*rushnyki*). Women dance, their patterned skirts swirling, as they twirl cloths above their heads. Ivan and Anna's families hold aloft an icon and a symbolic loaf of bread enclosed within more woven textile. At the formal wedding feast, the camera pans from right to left along a table of seated women, all clothed alike in embroidered or patterned blouses, with sarafan and patterned headscarf. As if this display were not enough, the background walls and windows are hung with an array of different textiles; and through the window peep the faces of female onlookers in patterned headscarves. Anna and her new husband are on show (figure 3.6): although the women remain facing the camera, arms folded, their bodies immobile as in a tableau, their eyes move insistently and curiously toward the newly-weds (Figure 3.7). The next shot, panning left to right, shows the assembled men at the table similarly looking surreptitiously at the married couple. A group of uninvited villagers peers through an open door; others through windows (figure 3.7). Thus Anna and Ivan are displayed for public consumption. And the spectator is fixed as observer in relation to the screen's patterned surface.

TEXTILE SENSATIONS

Fig. 3.7 Pattern and Surface. Stills from *Women of Riazan Province* (*Baby riazanskie*, dir. O. Preobrazhenskaia (and I. Pravov); production design by D. Kolupaev).

Preobrazhenskaia emphasizes here the traditional rural society's preoccupation with display. But the scene, and its visual excesses, might also be a self-reflexive comment on the film's own display of village ethnography and, by association, on a century-long Russian tradition of representing peasant life in visual art, literature, and cinema. The film's position here is complex. In its theme, *Women of Riazan Province* echoes the nineteenth-century "Critical Realist" tradition of representations of rural life, which sought to avoid false romanticizing of peasant Russia, and to indict its social (and in this case moral) backwardness. In visual art, this was evident in the canvases of the Peredvizhnik group, who offered not picturesque landscapes, but images of the real, labor-marked earth of rural Russia. Yet the visual code of this film is close not to the muted shades that marked the canvases of the Peredvizhniks, but rather to the rich patterns and colors of paintings such as Mikhail Shibanov's *The Marriage Contract* (1777, figure 3.8), which pictures a fully dressed and rigidly posed potential bride, displayed for selection by suitors (surely an influence for the equivalent scene here). It also echoes, in particular, the colorful paintings of Ukrainian rural life by Konstantin Makovskii (such as *A Boyar's Wedding Feast*, 1883, figure 3.9), and his brother Vladimir Makovskii (e.g., *The Bride's Party* of 1883, which features a row of seated women at a feast, directly mirroring the shot described above [figure 3.10]).[18]

On camera instead of canvas, the rich colors of such painted representations of peasant costume are replaced, on black-and-white film stock, by excessive pattern.[19] This is particularly vivid in the wedding feast and fête scenes, but is part of the film's visual impact throughout, and reveals the filmmakers' have a formal interest in the cinematographic representation of patterned and unpatterned material. Textile articulates and decorates the surface of the screen, and shapes spectatorial experience. In the wedding feast scene, the textile initiates a play between two- and three-dimensional space. Excessive pattern turns the screen into a surface, flattening and smoothing the faktura of filmed objects, transforming them into abstract shapes. The women in the shot (figure 3.7) appear as a tableau, but their stillness appears enforced: Their (often fleshy) bodies are as if captured within the framing surfaces of textile. As a result, pectatorial experience is caught uncomfortably between processing the flattened, two-dimensional patterns of the tableau and sensing the embodied fleshiness of the women's bodies.

Fig. 3.8 Mikhail Shibanov, *Celebrating the Marriage* Contract (Prazdnestvo svadebnogo dogovora), 1777, oil on canvas, 199cm × 244 cm. Courtesy of State Tretyakov Gallery, Moscow.

Fig. 3.9 Konstantin Makovskii, *A Boyar's Wedding Feast* (*Boiarskii svadebnyi pir v xvii veke*), 1883, oil on canvas, 391cm × 236cm. Courtesy of Hillwood Estate, Museum & Gardens; Image by Google.

Fig. 3.10 Vladimir Makovskii, *The Bride's Party* (*Devichnik*), oil on canvas, 189cm × 125cm. Courtesy of the Kyiv National Museum of Russian Art.

In *Women of Riazan Province*, then, the excessive dressing of both women and homes is revealed as a layer that contains (and restrains) the authentic body. Preobrazhenskaia and Pravov manipulated the visual pleasures of traditional life in order to articulate a revolutionary (and feminist) message. The film navigates the specific appeal of the decorative on-screen. It is explicitly interested in textile not just as background, but as shaping human experience. And it makes this interest clear not just through its theme, but also in its formal address to the spectator.

Processing the Material

Women of Riazan Province was not only a critique of traditional life, however. It also sought to suggest a new possible (revolutionary) relationship between people and world. And here textile was directly thematic. The female protagonists in *Women of Riazan Province* do not only inhabit a world of textile, they also *produce* and process that textile. They spin and weave thread. Several scenes in the film show the older women of the village at spinning wheels, gossiping while they work (figure 3.11). These wheels appear as a symbol of a traditional system, part of a retrograde world.[20] Here,

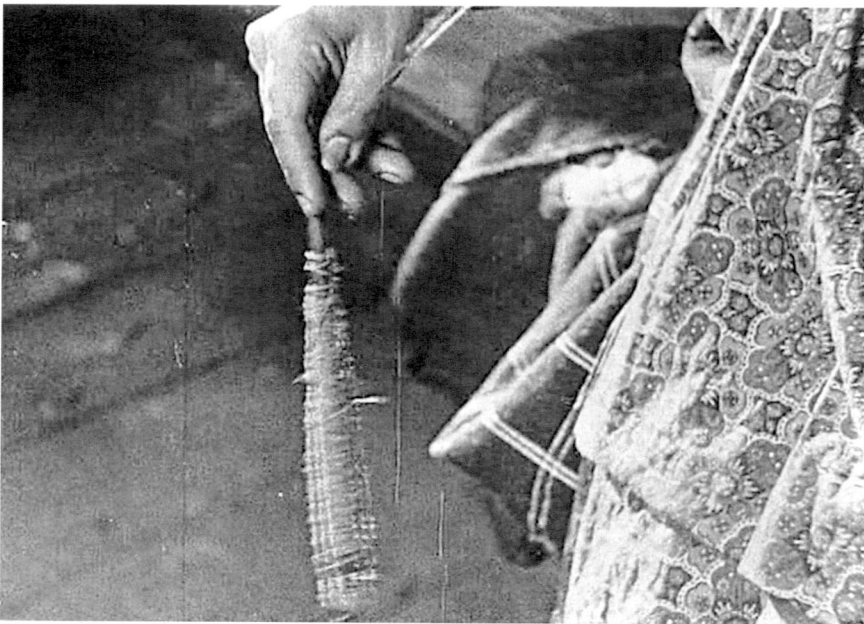

Fig. 3.11 The Binding Threads of Textile. Stills from *Women of Riazan Province* (*Baby riazanskie*, dir. O. Preobrazhenskaia (and I. Pravov); production design by D. Kolupaev).

Preobrazhenskaia plays with folkloric echoes: the spindle is a recurring trope in Russian folklore; the goddess Mokosh´, protector of women, traditionally watches over spinning and weaving; even Baba Iaga, the archetypal witch, is sometimes pictured spinning thread.[21] In this film, however, the thread that the women spin represents the thread of gossip that holds Anna captive in the patriarchal system, ashamed to be the mother of an illegitimate child. It is another symbol of the enclosing weight of textile that structures the film's theme and style.

This is the primary level at which Preobrazhenskaia's picture of textile craft operates. Yet the film is more complex than this interpretation suggests, and in some ways anticipates the more subtle views of "female" crafts that have emerged in recent (feminist) scholarship, where crafts such as sewing and embroidery are seen as constitutive of female identity and seen as forms of tacit opposition (to patriarchal structures). Rozsika Parker's work on embroidery (tellingly entitled *The Subversive Stitch*), for example, makes a case for embroidery as a site of the creation of female identity and resistance.[22] Nadia Seremetakis sees embroidery as a form of female communication: "Women circulate knowledge through multiple designs and spaces, which they cover, protect and ornament. It is this transfer of the self into substance that disseminates a history of the person in dispersal." For Seremetakis, this is not a feature of female oppression, but one of potential liberation: "Embroidering engages a self-reflexive femininity: she will endow artefacts with her content and yet allow them to speak for themselves."[23]

Women of Riazan Province offers an ambiguous perspective on the relationship between traditional peasant textile, craft, and subjectivity. Not all textile craft is negative. As the plot progresses, and Anna is transformed from symbolic bride and folkloric archetype into laboring member (and eventually oppressed victim) of a patriarchal system, her physical appearance changes. Her feet are bare as she shovels dirty straw outside the home. She sleeps with a calf in a barn. These are images of hardship, but they are ideologically coded. Anna's body becomes the body of a worker, not of a virgin bride. Later, while the older women of the village gossip at their spinning wheels, Anna works at a larger wooden handloom (figure 3.12). This places her apart and also emphasizes her physical strength: by weaving rather than spinning, operating the loom rather than the wheel, Anna moves symbolically out of one traditional sphere of women's work. Her weaving can be described as protoindustrial; it is positioned between handcraft and manufacture. The shots of her at the loom emphasize the embodied act of making: her feet on

Fig. 3.12 Handcraft and Emancipation. Stills from *Women of Riazan Province* (*Baby riazanskie*, dir. O. Preobrazhenskaia (and I. Pravov); production design by D. Kolupaev).

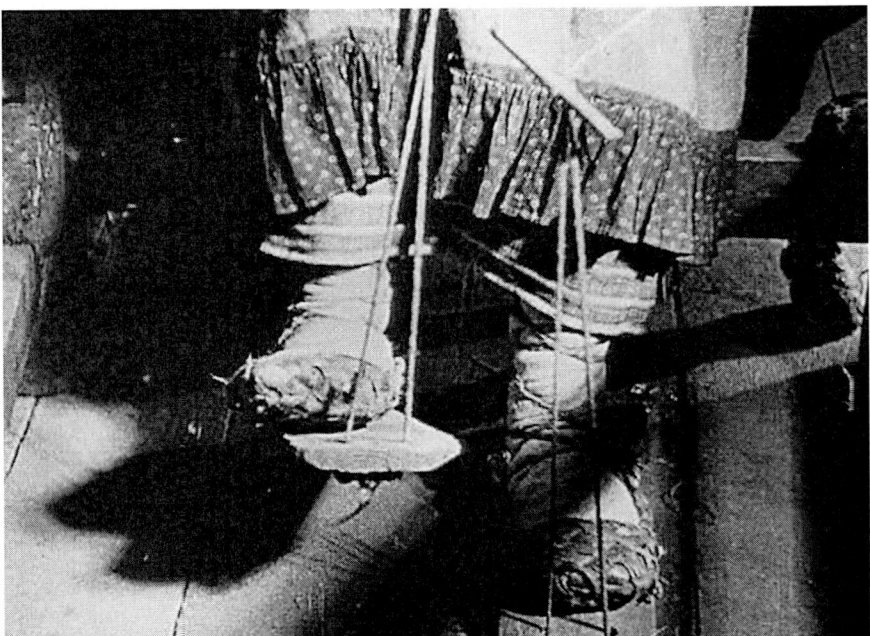

Fig. 3.12 (Continued).

treadles, her hand moving the heddle and shuttle of the machinery, passing the thread. As she works, she smiles—there is implied pleasure in her absorption, removed from the cruel gazes and gossip of the other women.[24]

On the one hand, Anna's imprisonment by the loom shows peasant textile craft as intrinsically retrograde. Yet weaving is pictured here as different from spinning and sewing. Here, the specificity of weaving is important. Marx and Engels had identified the development of the textile industry—the replacement of handlooms by mechanized looms—as an inevitable step toward the politicization of the working class. Industrial weaving, they suggested, ruptured the relationship between the worker's body and the act of making that was intrinsic to the handloom. So the textile factory worker's body was an archetypal symbol of the estranged labor of the alienated proletariat.[25] From this perspective, then, Anna's *hand*loom is a site of authentic handcraft. We can posit perhaps that Preobrazhenskaia's picture of Anna's weaving was a double symbol: of her oppression, and of her potential salvation. The brief sequences of the loom offer a vision of embodied labor that may mark a way out of the binding threads of peasant textile craft. As Anna handles and shapes the textiles that hold her captive, so textile is transformed from background into *material*. It is processed by the human hand. And with that comes the potential for change.

As we shall see in chapter 4, such metaphors of making had particular potency in the Soviet context. They offered a peculiarly Soviet salvation. Although for Anna herself the path offered by labor is barred by tragedy, the narrative of her sister-in-law Vasilisa offers a "positive" vision of a (socialist) future. Expelled by her father from her traditional home because of her love of a "mere" blacksmith, Nikolai, Vasilisa moves symbolically outside the provincial patriarchy, and sets up in a modern state of cohabitation with the man she loves. As a blacksmith, her Nikolai is a protoindustrial figure, and he and Vasilisa are shown operating smelting machinery. Empowered by her move into the world of production, toward the close of the film Vasilisa sets up an orphanage in a grand disused house, the white porticos and large windows of which mark a radical shift from the dark wooden homes of the villagers. Here, too, however, just as in *The Tailor from Torzhok*, the future is an undefined space: the film can only hint at Vasilisa's future village school and its white open spaces. The future remained unformed; the challenge for filmmakers was to form it.

Folk Craft

Preobrazhenskaia's direct engagement with peasant textile production was part of a wider interest in folk (*narodnyi*) craft during the 1920s. Despite their rejection of bourgeois ornament and decoration, Soviet modernists in this early period were greatly interested in peasant crafts such as embroidery, weaving, and lace-making. In fact, in the search for a "modern," ideologically sanctioned form of ornament, folk cultures provided a valuable resource for avant-garde designers the world over. True ornament, according to Bauhaus director Walter Gropius, was the product of the collective consciousness over a period of time. Folk ornament, therefore, could be permissible in modern design: "Forward to Tradition. The Ornament is dead," Gropius pronounced in 1938. "Long live the Ornament!"[26] For those searching for a new aesthetic for Russian textile and clothing design, folk craft was a particularly important resource. Roginskaia, writing in 1926, suggested that two key influences could and must be combined in new Soviet textile design: first, decorative elements and techniques drawn from the peasant background (embroidery, appliqué, lace, etc.); second, decorative elements drawn from Constructivism. Geometric motifs could be appliquéd onto fabric, for example.[27]

A similar emphasis on folk heritage is evident in the avant-garde artist-led fashion journal *Atel´e* (the first and only issue of which was produced in 1923). Evgeniia Pribyl´skaia, who worked for some time in a peasant embroidery collective, sought to justify a continuing role for embroidery in Russian clothing design, despite the fact that "our life must not be overburdened with purely aesthetic objects." According to Pribyl´skaia, folk textiles were distinguished by their handmade quality: "In folk costumes, made by the peasants themselves out of flax, hemp, wool and leather, the external working/processing (obrabotka) of the material is essential."[28] As these rough fabrics are difficult to sew, she points out, folk techniques have recourse to externally visible stitching, which forms part of the structure of the finished item. It was in these terms (as an act of processing) that Pribyl´skaia framed her rehabilitation of embroidery: "Here embroidery does not play a role of pointless decorative element; it constructs the object alongside the base material."[29]

Of course, there is a longer Russian history here. There had been a significant revival of elite interest in *kustar´* (craft) industries, in defiance of large-scale industrialization, in the latter decades of the nineteenth century—particularly evident in the well-known enterprises of Talashkino and Abramtsevo, which fostered traditional crafts (lace-making, embroidery, weaving) as well as the Solomenko embroidery workshops, set up by Mariia Fedorovna Iakunchikova in 1891.[30] In 1900, the Russian exhibit at the Universal Exhibition in Paris showcased a Russian village kustar´ corner, with Solomenko embroideries, wall hangings, and carved furniture. The kustar´ industries enjoyed great success in the decades preceding the First World War. This, however, speaks of the commercialization of folk design for a bourgeois audience. Of more particular interest for our purposes is the relationship between avant-garde art and folk craft that developed in the 1910s in particular. In Verbovka in Ukraine, a workshop was set up by Natal´ia Mikhailovna Davydova, where peasant women would embroider textiles according to designs by avant-garde artists.[31] From 1915, Aleksandra Ekster was its artistic director, and Liubov´ Popova produced many and varied designs for its skilled seamstresses. In the village of Skoptsy, also in Ukraine, another workshop was established, where Pribyl´skaia led rug design between 1910 and 1916.[32] Such productive enterprises were in direct interaction with the "mainstream" Soviet avant-garde, before and after the revolution. Work from the Verbovka workshops featured in two exhibitions in Moscow: in 1915 at the First Exhibition of Modern Decorative Art, where suprematist canvases by Malevich were also exhibited for the first time; and in December 1917, at the Second Russian Decorative Arts Exhibition. That exhibition showed over sixty works based on sketches by Ol´ga Rozanova, alongside a suprematist pillow design by Malevich executed in appliqué. the State Exhibition of Applied Arts in 1919 also showed embroidery from the Verbovka workshops, to designs by Rozanova and others.

In fact, after 1917, folk-style ornament acquired particular ideological justification, and an interest in peasant tradition was frequently evident in Soviet clothing and textile design—both avant-garde and mainstream. The artist-driven publication *Art in Everyday Life* of 1925, for instance, featured a kaftan made from two traditionally embroidered towels from the Vladimir province, alongside a Young Pioneer suit made from what is described as "peasant canvas."[33] This and other patterns in *Art and Everyday Life* sought to appropriate an implied peasant ethics of simplicity and economy in revolutionary terms. In similar terms, the prerevolutionary couturier Nadezhda Lamanova, who embraced the revolution with apparent enthusiasm, transferred her prerevolutionary designs, often inspired by folk costume, into ideologically justified shapes for the new era: "Folk costumes are ... work clothes, devised for hard physical work.... Combining the lively picturesqueness of folk costume with modern techniques of mass production, we achieve a type of clothing that responds to the needs dictated by our contemporary life."[34] Such ideological legitimation of peasant craft in the leftist avant-garde filtered down into the mainstream press. In magazines such as *Women's Journal* and *The Art of Dressing* (issued as a supplement to *Krasnaia panorama* in 1928 and 1929), aimed at the emerging Soviet consumer, we see similar traces of what was increasingly dubbed "Russian style."[35]

In Soviet Russia, then, the hands-on crafts and styles of traditional peasant culture had a triple justification for the avant-garde. First, their social roots in peasant Russia gave them ideological value as the labor of the working classes. Second, and more intriguingly, the very nature of their making—their hands-on "processing"—was suited to the Soviet avant-garde focus on material. The sewing "patterns" in *Art in Everyday Life* deconstruct clothing, revealing the how-it-is-made. Finally, the handcrafts of peasant culture could be seen in relation to the broader value that was placed on the act of making. *Art in Everyday Life* was dedicated to the homemade (clothing, children's toys, and objects for domestic and public space); its patterns sought, in effect, to turn everyone into a potential "maker." This three-part rationale positioned embroidery, and appliqué, at the heart of the Soviet project.

Handcraft: Sewing the Home

A parallel emphasis on "making" filtered down into the models of urban domestic space. From 1926 until the early 1930s, each issue of the popular magazine *Women's Journal* contained a one-page section with the heading "Handcraft" (*rukodelie*), and instructions on how to make objects for the home. In 1930, the heading was changed to the more portentous "Craft and Applied Arts," but the content remained essentially unchanged. Similarly, in the more obviously worker-targeted journal *Working Woman*, a regular page entitled "What's New and Practical?" introduced a host of useful tips for the homemaker. Appliqué, "open-work stitching," and other forms of basic embroidery formed part of the ballast of skills that—with the help of her magazines and their pages of rukodelie—the ordinary Soviet woman would master.[36]

Such acts of making were of particular importance in relation to urban domestic spaces, and became part of a discourse of homemaking in this formative period. In June of 1926, the title of an editorial article in *Women's Journal* posed the difficult question: "How to create domestic comfort/coziness (*uiut*)?"[37] "An absolute absence of comfort distinguishes the great majority of our workers' apartments," it acknowledged. How, the author asked, in the crowded conditions that were the reality of Soviet housing in the mid-1920s, could domestic comfort exist? The careful balance of this article points to the complexities of sensory pleasure in the early Soviet years. On the one hand, it stated unambiguously that some "rationalization" of the domestic environment was needed, that "there must be no superfluous objects in the Soviet worker's home," and that unwieldy "old-style" furnishings had no place in new socialist spaces. Despite this, however, it claimed without prevarication that comfort and coziness were essential.

How should we understand the continuing presence of the homemade within the emerging Soviet command economy? How can appliqué, of all things, be considered Soviet? What need for wall hangings in the new world? Surely the encouragement of rukodelie, of individual practices aimed at the creation of nonstandard objects, at the embellishment of the self, or of one's personal space, worked against the collective imperative of Soviet socialism? Why did such exhortations in the female press not disappear after 1917? There are several interrelated answers here. On the one hand, we can see this emphasis on rukodelie as simply pragmatic. The individual acts of homemaking implied by do-it-yourself craft patterns were of particular urgency in the real conditions of Soviet Russia during the NEP years. They were a straightforward response to shortage: a way of acquiring things that the Soviet market could not provide (or, during the difficult years of the New Economic Policy, of obtaining articles that ordinary workers could not afford). Appliqué, for instance, served a basic and practical function, creating patterned textile, when most available fabric was unprinted (linen canvas, tarpaulin, low-grade woolens, or calico).[38]

Second, these handmade craft projects can be seen as a response to the situation of urban overcrowding in Soviet cities of the 1920s. As another article acknowledged, "In our living conditions, with our living space, the bedroom often serves also as an office, a dining room, and a living room."[39] Strategies by which these spaces could be differentiated were needed. Appliqué, for instance, could be used to make a door curtain or screen; a large floral design, cut out of "colored linen or satin," was to be sewn onto the simple linen, by appliqué: "Once you can reproduce the designs below, it is easy to make a beautiful and cheap door curtain out of unbleached linen."[40] The hanging of such textile within domestic space was not merely a sign of the endurance of bourgeois bad taste. The textural, tactile environment creates the conditions for human experience and interaction. In Wigley's words, "It is not that the fabrics are arranged in a way that provides physical shelter. Rather, their texture, their sensuous play, their textuality . . . opens up a space of exchange."[41]

Finally, and most importantly, rukodelie and making could find ideological justification within emerging Soviet discourse relating to texture, touch, and material. Here we can think specifically about appliqué. Appliqué is practical and hands-on. It is an act of bottom-up homemaking that has its roots in the manual processing of the material that was so praised in folk craft. Second, appliqué is multilayered and intrinsically textural: sewing fabric shapes on top of one another to create ornamental designs upon a plain base, the seamstress creates a fabric that is three-dimensional. It rewards not just the eye but also the hand. For all its absurd petty-bourgeois connotations, therefore, appliqué could find its place in Soviet culture: that Verbovka cushion, appliquéd to Malevich's suprematist design, turns out to be an important symbol of the developing revolutionary aesthetic.[42]

Cinematic Homemaking

It is clear that the magazines discussed above were aimed at an urban population; in the case of *Women's Journal* and *The Art of Dressing*, moreover, the actual readership seems to have largely comprised a moderately affluent social group (even though the rhetoric of both journals suggested a readership of working women). The fact that a similar discourse of rukodelie was present in directly worker-targeted journals such as *The Delegate* and *The Worker*, however, indicates a more widespread aspiration toward the "dressing" of the home, and a less straightforward ideological divide between the functional and the decorative than we might expect. A similar ambivalence was evident in cinematic interiors during the mid to late 1920s. Indeed, it could be exploited to mark the emergence of a new way of being in the world—one that we can think of as proto-Soviet, and which had its roots in the project of sensory remaking that is the subject of this book.

One of the key directors of the so-called everyday genre that emerged in Soviet cinema during the second half of the 1920s is Boris Barnet, who worked extensively with Kozlovskii (then the principal production designer at Mezhrabpom), as production designer for his key films of this period: *Girl with a Hatbox* (*Devushka s korobkoi*, 1927) and *House on Trubnaia* (*Dom na Trubnoi*, 1928). Through these films, we can see how different domestic environments interacted and acquired ideological meaning. In *Girl with a Hatbox*, for example, the differing interiors of provincial and urban bourgeois life are set against one another. First, there is the traditionally furnished village home of the milliner Natasha (the eponymous girl with a hatbox) and her grandfather, with its wooden furniture and floral textile. Second, the modern bourgeois urban home of shop mistress Madame Irene and her husband, to which Natasha delivers hats, and where she is the nominal inhabitant of a room that is in fact used by Irene and her husband themselves, in defiance of Soviet housing allocation laws (which restricted space allocated per family). This space is marked by an excess of heavy furniture, drapes, carpets, and ornament. In contrast to these two visually and sensually rich worlds, the film pictures a third space: Natasha's single room in Madame Irene's home (rapidly emptied by Madame Irene when the housing officers inspect), which she offers to homeless Il´ia, a young worker-peasant that she meets on the train, freshly arrived from the country. This room functions in the film as an unformed proto-Soviet space, in which Il´ia sets out to make a home.

One of the most striking interior sequences in this film comes the morning after Il´ia has spent his first night in the room that Natasha has claimed for him. It is almost entirely bare. The arrival of morning is signaled first by the awakening of Il´ia, and then by the telling contrast of a shot of a plump eiderdown and two pairs of slippers on an oriental carpet. Bare feet emerge and fill the slippers (figure 3.13): Madame Irene and her husband awaken. This collision of textures and patterns (the corner of a lace sheet peeps out from beneath the eiderdown) draws the spectator's attention to the physical opulence of Irene's world, in contrast to the spartan simplicity of that of Il´ia. The plush excesses of Madame Irene's domestic space are familiar signs of bourgeois aspiration: heavy furniture, wall hangings, oriental carpets, and a divan piled high with cushions act as visual shorthand, ideologically encoded for the Soviet viewer (Barnet's next film, *The House on Trubnaia*, showed bourgeois hairdresser Golikov's wife in a similar environment). In contrast, Il´ia's room is inhospitable: an anomalous crystal chandelier, remnant of the room's previous form, serves to emphasize its current lack of decoration.

The opposition between plush bourgeois space and simple worker's is not straightforward, however—particularly in terms of spectatorial experience.

Fig. 3.13 Bourgeois Surfaces. Still from *Girl with a Hatbox* (*Devushka s korobkoi*, dir. B. Barnet, production design by S. Kozlovskii, 1927).

Rather, the excesses of Irene's space throw the few objects of material texture in Il´ia's almost empty room into relief. A single patterned blind covers the window; a few clothes and a towel (with folk-style embroidery) hang in a corner. Il´ia sleeps with a risibly small sheet, and the pathos of his attempts to cover himself gives the spectator a tangible sense of the body's quest for comfort. Il´ia's project is one of homemaking, and the spectator is implicated in it. Likewise, the implicitly sheltered, indulged bodies of Irene and her husband emphasize Il´ia's robust physicality. After an enthusiastic set of exercises, he sets off, bare chested, to find a washbasin. Outside, he navigates a labyrinth of sheets that have been hung out to dry, forming a network of textile walls (figure 3.14). Il´ia's progression through the sheets, before he finds a tap, is comic, and reveals what we might call the underside of domestic life; but it also draws the spectator into a sensory apprehension of the experience of his body, of the sensations of his flesh, as he brushes against the fabric of the sheets. This is enhanced when he places his head beneath cold running water, rubbing his neck with an improvised loofah.

Il´ia's bare room reveals the new socialist interior as an unformed space in *Girl with a Hatbox*—as it is in most of the "everyday" comedies of the

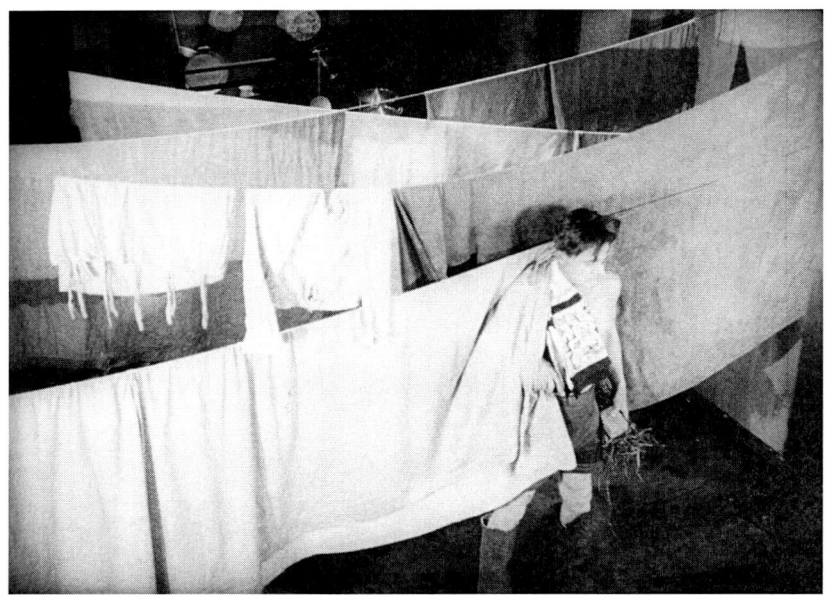

Fig. 3.14 Textile Walls. Still from *Girl with a Hatbox* (*Devushka s korobkoi*, dir. B. Barnet, production design by S. Kozlovskii, 1927).

1920s. It also shows how the choice of textures and objects in a film set play a key role in meaning and in spectatorial experience.[43] The sensory and the sensual are by no means the domain of the bourgeoisie alone. Rather, the film interpolates the spectator into an intensified sensory awareness of the life of the body. A similar complexity is evident in Fridrikh Ermler's 1926 film, *Kat´ka's Reinette Apples* (*Kat´ka—bumazhnyi ranet*). Initially, a simplified opposition between petty-bourgeois and workers' domestic space appears to operate. The textile-bedecked, densely patterned interior in which the corrupt Sen´ka and his aspirational coquette Vera operate signifies *meshchanstvo*, its inhabitants enmeshed in the trappings of the old world, prey to the allure of material possessions. In contrast, the bare room in which Kat´ka and her baby make their home, and into which the simple Vad´ka is gradually assimilated, appears initially unadorned. Where Vera's mother's bed is symbolically stacked high with four feather pillows, Kat´ka's is covered in a single eiderdown, with one pillow. Within this simplified ideological opposition, however, Ermler introduces important subtlety. The overarching narrative of the film is one of homemaking: Kat´ka and Vad´ka gradually appropriate a corner of the urban world as their own, find their place in the new world, just as Sen´ka and Vera are increasingly excluded. This appropriation is expressed through minute but important transformations in their domestic space. Vad´ka, initially alone and apparently unable to cope in society, finds shelter in Kat´ka's world: in a strikingly tactile image, he nestles within her eiderdown, his head resting on her pillow, as she darns his worn clothes. Later in the film, Vad´ka's growing ease, and the increasing comfort and intimacy of his and Kat´ka's domestic arrangement, is mirrored in a softer domestic environment, in which texture and textile play a subtle but important role: a small dressing table covered by a lace cloth, a sewing basket, a covered window. Alongside the swaddling of the baby, and the mending of Vad´ka's clothing, these objects serve to dress Kat´ka's simple home, and to shelter their nuclear family.

Thus, although *Kat´ka's Reinette Apples* is structured along clear ideological lines, where simple workers flourish, and profiteers and petty-bourgeoisie fall, and although Kat´ka and Vad´ka are finally affiliated to the Soviet world via their employment in a factory, nevertheless a more ambiguous discourse on homemaking carries much of the film's emotional weight. The domestic space acts as a stark contrast to the frenetic urban space of NEP-era Leningrad; its softened contours invite the spectator into a sensory understanding of the protagonists' need for comfort and protection.

Feeling Film?

Girl with a Hatbox and *Kat´ka's Reinette Apples* are just two examples of a broader genre of everyday films from the 1920s in which the new domestic interior was an unrealized space. In a sense, the characters' search for a home echoes cinema's own search for an appropriate socialist interior. The protagonists' enhanced proximity with a few objects of comfort mirrors the film's impact on the spectator. Throughout this chapter, I have suggested that, in their search for a new model of Soviet socialist experience, filmmakers presented a tentative alternative to the inhibiting morass of objects that represents so-called bourgeois life. This alternative is signaled by enhanced proximity with the material—through acts of touching or making. The films offer their characters a sensory relationship with the faktura of the world, which marks a new way of being in the world. How was this mirrored in films' formal address to the spectator? Certainly, an interest in using filmed objects and textures to provoke different kinds of spectatorial experience can be traced in many films of this period. In *Girl with a Hatbox*, for example, we have noted the textural impact of the combination of oriental carpet, brocade slippers, eiderdown, and human feet. Closer attention to that shot reveals something else: two discarded cigarette butts on the carpet. These filmed objects serve a formal purpose. More than just a symbol of the protagonist's evil habits, the cigarette butts interrupt the spectatorial process. In Shklovskii's terms, they defamiliarize, interrupting "recognition," drawing the spectator instead into a sensory encounter with the multiple textures that make up the shot: the weave of carpet, the lace of the eiderdown, and human skin. There are many such moments in the film. In Natasha's village home, the camera looks through a window covered by a network of snowflakes; in another scene, Madame Irene's shop window is obscured by soapy smears as it is cleaned, and it is only as the soap is wiped away that we acquire again the illusory sense of the screen as window, of the visual omnipotence of the camera lens.

Strategies such as this are common in cinema of this period, their self-reflexivity seeking to make the spectator aware of the act of looking, and of the specificity of cinema. But they also draw our attention to the presence, on-screen, of surfaces and textures. In Laura Marks's terms, they force our eye "not to distinguish form so much as to discern texture."[44] They encourage so-called haptic looking. In these terms, we may return to *Girl with a Hatbox*, and to Il´ia and his "textile walls" of sheets (figure 3.14). In this sequence, the sheets create a pattern across the surface of the screen that, with its intersecting geometric shapes, is almost a parody of cubist art. But this pattern is not flat: it is textural, volumetric, and *material*; ll´ia's movement through his textile labyrinth creates depth of field. As his body moves through the sheets, we feel their faktura, their material presence. For this moment, sensation predominates over narrative, or meaning. This is another act of touching—and it is shared between the character and the spectator. The surfaces of film provoke a form of spectatorship that approximates to the hands-on experience of touch. They can offer a sensory equivalent of the cold water splashing on Il´ia's bare skin. They can, that is, represent the bare reality of living in the world.

Sewing the Future

My argument in this chapter has been that, contrary to views that see them as intrinsically anti-Soviet and as working against the revolutionary project, decorative textiles could be used to articulate on-screen a new protorevolutionary model of living in the world. Aleksei Popov's 1930 comedy, *A Major Nuisance* (*Krupnaia nepriatnost´*), is of interest in this respect. Produced in 1930, in the middle of the first Five-Year Plan, it pictures a subtly different kind of provincial space from those discussed above. This is a traditional provincial space *with new people in it*. It explicitly contrasts younger and older generations, and does so by suggesting that they represent different relationships with the world—and with the new world in particular. For my purposes it is of interest that these relationships are articulated through different attitudes to textile, decoration, and making.

A Major Nuisance was produced by the newly formed Soiuzkino (Moscow) studio, which replaced Sovkino in 1930. Dmitrii Kolupaev (by now apparently specializing in "rural" films) was production designer; literary satirist Mikhail Zoshchenko had oversight of the film's intertitles. *A Major Nuisance* is explicit in contrasting the "ancient" time of the provincial town symbolically named Otshib (which translates as "at a distance," "outskirts") with the forward-moving real time of contemporary Soviet life. The film's narrative focuses on two events that propel the town into the present. First, the connection of the village to a bus line, and thereby to mechanized transport, prompting a larger battle between traditional and modern belief systems. Second, the simultaneous arrival of two important figures: the regional bishop and a Bolshevik ideologue and speech-giver. Two different "churches" (as a title announces ironically) are shown preparing their respective receptions. In the film's conclusion, the "old" (religious) church is ridiculed, and the new communist temple (the workers' club) is the clear victor in the battle for the hearts and minds of the future.

In the sequences introducing Otshib, familiar tropes evoke provincial timelessness: women washing clothes in the river; wooden fretwork on houses; churches and their bells; striking montages of lined faces, wrapped in headscarves. The pace of the film from its first frames, however, offers a different temporality. It is set from the beginning by the arrival of the bus and, implicitly, by the crowds of young people who appear to celebrate its arrival. Even the church bells seem to ring with a faster beat. The bus, then, becomes a shared project for the village's younger generation. To the question "American car or Russian cart?" a group of school children reply with unbridled enthusiasm, "The car!" Young men and women help to build a road suitable for it. And the mystique (and indeed fear) of the machine itself is dispelled when the bus driver shows the young heroine Evlagiia how easily its engine can be understood—and hence how easily fixed. In this way, the engine is implicitly appropriated: it is no more mysterious—and no more alien—than the now outdated machinery that makes up the traditional horse and cart.

In contrast with this appropriative vision of technology, those who are against the bus, and for the traditional horse-drawn cart, are pictured according to familiar visual codes. Indeed, the decorative faktura of the old world provides a large element of the film's visual impact. This is particularly evident as the two different groups prepare for their important guests, when the confrontation between different belief systems is staged at the level of visual style, as a battle between decoration and plainness. In the local merchant's store, the two groups seek out the materials they need to decorate their different "churches." On the left are the young komsomol members, in their black-and-white jerseys, selecting the plain textiles they need to decorate their club. On the right are the richly embroidered textiles of traditional church celebrations; the village elders try on various religious cloths and adornments as if they were fashion items.

In ideological terms, it is inevitable that in this battle of adornment, the light of the modern will prevail over the dark of the old world. What is important in this film, however, is how a new Soviet "modern," represented in the young komsomol members, appropriates the values of making that are intrinsic to needlework and handcraft—but in new terms. Though the rich patterned cloths of the traditional church contrast with the plain white cloth chosen by the young workers to bedeck their modern temple, it matters that the young men and women sew their banners and flags. Theirs is a hands-on construction of a new world. The younger generation does not reject the crafts of the village, but they adapt them to the new age. This is a new pastoral: folk culture remade in revolutionary terms, a new pastoral, which offers the young generation the tactile experience of making that is a precondition for Soviet salvation.

This has been a chapter about cloth, in its different forms, and its role in Soviet everyday life. It has uncovered the discreet presence of fabric in hidden corners of the Soviet interior, and revealed that, alongside the official drive for pared-down and functional interiors, an urge to decorate the home with layers of texture and textile remains. This counternarrative of Soviet interiors, I suggest, is more than just an argument for the realm of (individual) everyday life as constantly threatening the success of the Soviet collective project.[45] Instead, I have revealed the presence of textile in Soviet cinema of the 1920s as part of a wider discourse on homemaking. It was not opposed to the ideological project, but worked alongside it. Wall hangings, door curtains, sofa covers—all these appliquéd objects served to dress the bare walls of mass housing, to clothe the new Soviet spaces, to enrich the sensual texture of the lived environment.

But it is more than that: textiles speak of an act of *making* that had particular value in Soviet culture. In picturing textile, films revealed what Maxine Bristow has called "a dense accumulation of subtly modulated surfaces that silently speak of the process of their making."[46] They embedded those textiles within an emergent discourse about craft that was central to the Soviet ideological system. Rukodelie was a form of participation in the wider Soviet project of making revolution, linked to the validation of labor that was at the heart of Soviet ideology. In contrast to the indolent consumer of bourgeois luxury, the Soviet homemaker is resourceful and self-reliant, able to use his or her hands. The labor carried out in factories and workshops across the nation during the day is mirrored in the home during one's free time. As such, according to this interpretation, Soviet society was not only built, at a macro level, it was also made (even homemade) at a micro one. The ideologically sanctioned encouragement of rukodelie, of the processing of material, by hand, in the home, could be justified as part of the broader ideological project.

NOTES

1. The conference took place March 15–21, 1928, and minutes were published a year later: Ol'khovyi, ed., *Puti kino*. See Miller, *Soviet Cinema*; Taylor, *The Politics of the Soviet Cinema*, 106–13; Youngblood, *Soviet Cinema in the Silent Era*, 155–61; Kenez, "The Cultural Revolution in Cinema," 418–19.

2. Early in 1929, Pavel Bliakhin (official of Sovkino) noted that of 135 films made between 1927 and 1928, only 58.5 percent were on "contemporary Soviet material," and called for more on workers' life in particular. Bliakhin, "K itogam kino-sezona," 10. See also Krinitskii, "Nuzhen reshitel'nyi sdvig."

3. N. K., "Byt 'ideologicheskii,'" 5.

4. Gazdenko, "Sovetskii byt na sovetskom ekrane," 9.

5. Mur, "S''emki na nature i v atel'e," 3.

6. Le Corbusier, *L'art décoratif*. Loos, "Ornament und Verbrechen" (1908, 1913).

7. Maiakovskii, "O driani," 145. For excellent discussion of the resonance of these debates, see Boym, *Common Places*. See also Graffy, *Bed and Sofa*, 25–29.

8. Becker, Mendelsohn, and Benderskaya, *Russian Urbanization*, 6.

9. In one scene, where Melania Ivanovna is seated by a samovar, attempting to seduce Petel'kin, she appears to be consciously staged to echo Kustodiev's image of a merchant woman drinking tea. See, for example, *The Merchant Woman at the Tea Table* (*Kupchikha za chaem*, 1918); *Merchant Woman Drinking Tea* (*Kupchikha, piushchaia chai*, 1923).

10. There is a further striking sequence of women washing laundry in *The Prostitute* (*Prostituka*, dir. Oleg Freilikh, 1927).

11. There is little existing scholarship on Preobrazhenskaia and Pravov. For background details, and an account of their relationship, see Bagrov and Nussinova, "Preobrazhenskaya e Pravov."

12. The studio released an accompanying brochure: *Baby riazanskie* (Moscow: Teakinopechat, 1927).

13. In 1912, another film had treated the same theme: *Snokach* (dir. Unknown but attributed to Aleksandr Ivanov-Gai and/or Petr Chardynin). For discussion, see Morley, "The Incestuous Father in Law," 331–2.

14. The other, *Whirlpool* (*Vodovorot*), directed by Pavel Petrov-Bytov, has not been preserved, but told the story of a battle between a kulak miller and a Bolshevik peasant-worker in early Soviet Russia. See *Sovetskie khudozhestvennye fil'my*, Tom 1, 184. For excellent discussion of this film see Grashchenkova, *Kinoantropologiia XX/20*, 378–383.

15. Anon., "Smotrim na etoi nedele," 4.

16. Ibid., and Neznamov, "*Baby riazanskie*," 3.

17. See Kelly, "The Ritual Fabrics," 151–176; Hilton, *Russian Folk Art*, 93.

18. This painting formed part of a cycle of paintings produced by Vladimir Makovskii that was exhibited in Moscow in 1902. See Nesterova, "The Brothers Konstantin and Vladimir Makovskii."

19. Panchromatic film stock was largely used for Soviet film from 1928 onward (the choice between orthochromatic and panchromatic largely depending on whether incandescent or arc lighting was used for filming in the studio), but Soviet film units continued to have access to foreign panchromatic film on a sporadic basis from 1928 onward. From 1932, Soviet-made film stock became available, initially orthochromatic, but then, with increasing frequency, panchromatic. I am grateful to Philip Cavendish for sharing this information. For further discussion, see Cavendish, *The Men with a Movie Camera*.

20. For discussion of the symbolism of spinning in Slavic folk culture, see Ivleva, "Functions of Textile," and Mencej, "Connecting Threads."

21. As in the famous tale Rumpelstiltskin, the production of thread, cloth, or garments is often a test enabling a women's initiation into society. See Ivleva, "Functions of Textile," 289.

22. Parker, *The Subversive Stitch*. It is worth noting that Parker's view of textile as a form through which the female can externalize the self is actually central to the role of traditional textile (and wedding textile in particular) in Russian culture. See Kelly, "The Ritual Fabrics," 152–76.

23. Seremetakis, "The Memory of the Senses," 15.

24. I reference here Michael Fried's conception of absorption: *Absorption and Theatricality*.

25. See Ward, *Russia's Cotton Workers*.

26. Gropius, "Towards a Living Architecture," cited in Wigley, *White Walls*, 110.

27. Roginskaia, "Problemy kostiuma," 63–67.

28. Pribylskaia, "Vyshivka v nastoiashchem proizvodstve," 7–8.

29. See Douglas, "Bespredmetnost' i dekorativnost'." T'ai Smith's excellent account of the development of Bauhaus theories of weaving tells a compelling story of how the relation between material, texture and design was envisaged in that context: Smith, *Bauhaus Weaving Theory*.

30. Salmond, "The Solomenko Embroidery Workshops."

31. Gurianova, *Exploring Color*, 128–30; Adaskina, "Constructivist Fabrics and Dress Design." Davydova was also very interested in lace (see chapter 4).

32. Myzelev, "Handcrafting Revolution."

33. Mukhina and Lamanova, "Kaftan iz 2-kh vladimirskikh polotents," 19.

34. Lamanova, "Russkaia moda," 32.
35. Semashko, "Gigiena kostiuma," 5.
36. Anon., "Rukodelie," 24.
37. Anon., "Kak sozdaetsia domashnii uiut?," 13.
38. Strizhenova, *Iz istorii*, 15.
39. Anon., "Ugolok khoziaiki," 13.
40. Anon., "Portera iz kholsta," 16.
41. Wigley, *White Walls*, 11.
42. Gurianova notes the relationship between collage and appliqué in the work of Ol'ga Rozanova. See Gurianova, *Exploring Color*, 97, 173.
43. Archival production papers for this film give us a sense of the contribution of the set designer, and give an indication of the role played by the process of censorship. The documents tracing the approval process of the film include a note from the censor Denisov, which criticizes the original plan to show Il'ia in a completely empty room, insisting that the room "must, all the same, have a table and chairs, a cupboard, a commode and a bed" (Sek. 1. f. 2, op. 1, ed. khr. 2, 92). For Denisov, it seems, the emergent socialist interior could not be entirely unformed—and implicitly unformable. In the film's final realization, I suggest, the sheer vitality of Il'ia's act of makeshift homemaking goes some way to answering Denisov's concerns.
44. Marks, *Touch*, 8.
45. Boym, *Common Places*; see also Lebina, *Povsednevnaia zhizn'*. Note that Susan Reid's work further complicates straightforward binaries in analysis of domestic interiors in the post-war period. Reid, "Makeshift Modernity"; Reid, "Everyday Aesthetics."
46. Bristow, "Continuity of Touch," 49.

Chapter Four

SOCIALIST SENSATIONS

> Perhaps the key to the ontology of making is to be found in a length of twine.
>
> Tim Ingold

MANY OF THE films discussed in chapter 3 had "makers" as their protagonists: tailors, hat-makers, blacksmiths, and weavers. Through such figures, these films visualize Soviet Russia's transition from traditional to industrial production. That transition is the subject of this chapter. I will trace the evolution of models of making on-screen—from handcraft to industry—and their relation to the core question of the transformation of the human sensorium. The focus will be on the relationship between the human and object world: how was the world of objects to be transformed by changes in methods of production? And in turn, how might it transform the human subject? Why did craftsmen and women play such an important role in film during the late 1920s?

Underlying this inquiry is a question about the symbolic value of the human hand—and handwork—in Soviet culture, and its place in the story of Socialist sensation. These traditional makers work with their hands; they produce handwork (rukodelie). Hands, indeed, played an important role in the iconography of the Soviet avant-garde.[1] Aleksandr Rodchenko and Varvara Stepanova's 1933 poster *Results of the First Five Year Plan*, features a hand unrolling a scrolled map; El Lissitskii's series of self-portraits as "Konstruktor" (1924) feature the artist's hand holding a compass; Eleazar Langman's 1934 photograph *The Student* shows its subject's hand in close-up, again holding a compass. In these images, the hand is a symbol of the reconstructed Soviet self, the artist turned worker, or the newly educated youth, building a new world. The specificity of these and other Soviet hands is the subject of this chapter. Looking at the prevalence of hands in French Surrealist texts and images, Kirsten Powell identifies what she calls a "kind of anti-modernist gesture": "Even when hands are juxtaposed with machines or repeated elements that recall the factory assembly line, there is something that wilfully counters the idea of mechanical reproduction in the ubiquitous presence of the hand, that timeless sign for declaring human presence, human marking, and art-making."[2]

In the Soviet case, by contrast, I suggest that the human hand functioned as a symbol of a reanimated sensory encounter with the world, and was certainly not opposed to the ideal of industrialization. Here, then, the metaphor of haptic imagery that has run through previous chapters takes a literal turn. I will trace the symbolic importance of the hand—and more broadly, of tactile sensation—in relation to models of production, and its role in the construction of specifically Soviet models of subjectivity, in which the human and material world would exist in a relationship of productive reciprocity. Films of this period reveal an attempt to humanize the industrial, envisaging a possible sensory rapprochement between man and tool.

Encountering the Material

Dziga Vertov's interest in the relationship between human hands and objects is evident throughout his work. *Man with a Movie Camera* (1929) shows the hands of women in a textile factory, of cigarette makers, and of switchboard operators, and the labor of miners and masons. But a manuscript for a film that Vertov imagined, but never made, makes this preoccupation even more evident. In 1927, he produced a study (*etiud*) for a film called *Hands*, which was to consist only of shots of hands.[3] The study lists 127 shots: hands twirling moustaches, a hand opening a cigarette case, a hand lacing up a dress, hands cranking up a car and a propeller. Fingers wrung in grief. Hands washing laundry, and praying. The hands of a cobbler. The hands of a tailor. And, of course, the hands of a cameraman.

Although *Hands* never came to fruition, Vertov's interest in the human hand—and specifically in the relationship between the human hand and the object world—is evident even in his earliest work. The first *Film Week* (*Kino-nedelia*, 1919) ends with an odd sequence entitled "Hand-made Toys"

(*Kustarnye igrushki*). The camera shoots from behind a market stall selling wooden toys. In the foreground a hand holds a series of toys and manipulates them, revealing their mechanics. Although Iurii Tsivian's most recent research suggests that this issue of *Film Week* may precede Dziga Vertov's supervision of the series, this scene is indicative of an interest in film's capacity to enable a closer encounter with the construction and faktura of material objects.[4] The handmade toy has an ideological weight as a counter to the industrially manufactured commodities of capitalism: it speaks of a closer relationship between the human and the object. Yet the camera's interest in the object goes further. As it is touched, the toy's three-dimensional presence constructs the surface of the screen. The plastic possibilities of the handmade, hand-operated toy as a thing in itself are exploited alongside its ideological significance.

Whether or not this particular *Film Week* was his work, Vertov's overarching interest in the relationship between people and things is evident through his work of the 1920s. His 1924 feature-length *Film Eye* (*Kino-glaz*) features two sequences that are of particular importance for our purposes. Both use the potential of cinema to run backward in order to show where basic commodities—bread and meat—come from: the beef is turned back into a bull; the loaf of bread returns to dough, to flour, and to grain. In one sense, these are straightforward visualizations of Marx's disclosure of the origins of the consumer commodity, showing the processes that have transformed a bull from living animal to object for consumption. The film investigates commodities as organic matter and reveals them as products of interaction between (wo)man and nature. The object is revealed as a "human object," in Marx's terms.[5]

In both cases, however, material texture—of meat and of dough—is a key focus of the sequence. The camera lingers closely as a slaughterman handles the bull's slippery, bloody innards: "We return to the bull his intestines." The mottled surface of the intestine fills the screen. Where a close-up of the intestine alone, however, would have reduced its material to pure abstraction and pattern, the presence of the human hand insists upon the meat as material object (figure 4.1). The emphasis on contact between hand and object draws the spectator into a visceral understanding of its texture: we encounter the material through an imaginative substitution of our eye for the hand on-screen. Similarly, a crusty loaf of bread is transformed back into damp, claggy dough, stirred and kneaded by several hands. This spectatorial encounter with organic matter has a double ideological significance.

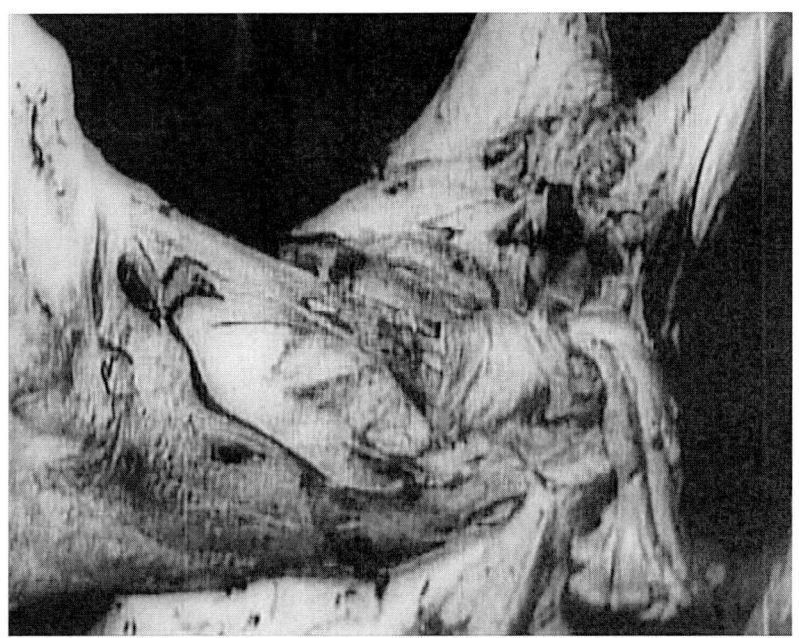

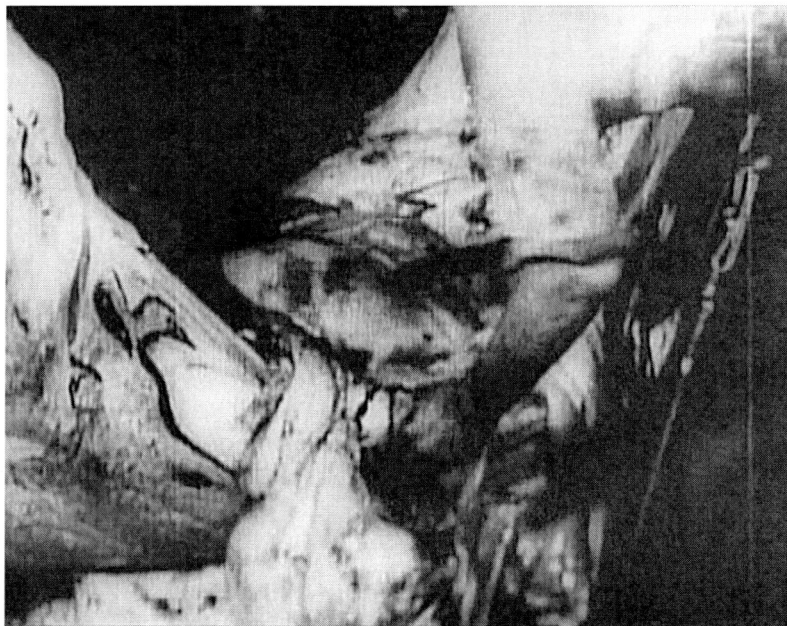

Fig. 4.1 Touching the Material: Hands-on. Stills from *Film Eye* (*Kino-glaz*, dir. D. Vertov, 1924).

First, as an explanation of the origins of the commodity, it seeks to make the (implicitly proletarian) spectator complicit in the act of production—to give them a direct sense of ownership, a new proximity with the material of everyday life. Second, that complicity operates through the body, through an emphasis on the embodied experience of making that underlies the socialist product—the interaction between the human hand and the world. In this way, using Marx's terms, Vertov uses film to make his spectator's senses "directly theoretical in practice."

We might compare Vertov's use of bulls and slaughter in *Film Eye* with that of Eisenstein in a film of the following year: *Strike*.[6] In the famous closing sequence of *Strike*, Eisenstein intercut footage of slaughtered bulls in an abattoir, blood pumping out of their necks, with scenes of the suppression of the workers' revolt. In this striking early example of the director's "montage of attractions," the combination of shots works to create a shocking "path to consciousness" for the proletarian spectator: the bourgeois factory owner treats the workers like meat.[7] Both directors, then, have an ideological point to make. And both are concerned with the visceral impact of the camera's rendering of real blood and flesh. There are vital differences, however. Vertov wants the spectator to encounter the slaughter, and the carcass of the bull, *for its own sake*. For Eisenstein, the bull is a means of exerting emotional influence on the spectator. For Vertov, the film eye is an agent for the discovery of the material presence of the world; for Eisenstein, the physical matter of the bull's carcass creates a visceral shock on the spectatorial eye, but that shock is not an end in itself. Vertov stops at sensation, where Eisenstein proceeds to "consciousness." It was for this that Eisenstein criticized Vertov's use of the slaughterhouse in *Film Eye*: "The abattoir that is merely recorded in *Film Eye*," he claimed, "[is] gorily effective in *Strike*."[8]

This emphasis on cinematographic material for its own sake was central to Vertov's work in the 1920s, and it had direct ideological justification—not only in Marxism itself, but also in specifically Soviet Marxism. Devin Fore reads Vertov's work as a vision of how "politics emerges out of matter," and not out of language.[9] As such, he reads Vertov's films as a counter to arguments that have seen industrialization as dehumanizing. Fore argues that in Vertov's work of this period, verbal communication (between people) is replaced with intuitive empathy (between people and the world). This affinity works outside language, and through the body. In the reverse-time sequences of *Film Eye*, the spectator is led to feel an embodied affinity with the commodities of meat and bread: a specifically communist relationship with the products of consumption. And the film's emphasis on material and matter is fundamental to the creation of spectatorial affect.

Material

I have had frequent occasion in this book so far to refer to "material"—of cinema, and of the world. Indeed, it may appear that my use of this term is frustratingly vague at times. I hope that this vagueness is attributable not to me, but to my subjects themselves: the term was used in multiple ways in Soviet Russia during the 1920s. It was, as productionist art theorist Toporkov observed in 1929, a "fashionable" word—an easy legitimation of diverse ideas in appropriately Marxist terms.[10] What it meant, however, was variable, and often unclear.

In chapter 1, we explored how Shklovskii's use of the term "material" in relation to cinema changed in the second half of the 1920s. Shklovskii held two apparently contradictory views. On the one hand, he was uncompromising in his belief that cinema was hindered by its photographic quality, its inability to alter the essence of the material. At the same time, however, from 1927 on, the camera's proximity with "real" material was also the basis of an evolving view of the potency of cinema in relation to an affective-materialist agenda. In a short book of 1927, he wrote: "Contemporary art lives through the material, and not through its construction (that is, its form) . . . In its orientation toward texture-material (*faktura-material*), toward photography, Constructivism itself is, at its best, 'materialism.'"[11] Apparently rejecting Formalist emphasis on form, then, Shklovskii turned emphatically towards the a refashioned materialism.

Also in 1927, Shklovskii published an article entitled "Wool, Glass and Lace," where he discussed three films: Sergei Iutkevich's *Lace* (*Kruzheva*, 1927, set in a lace factory); Abram Room's *Potholes* (*Ukhaby*, 1927, set in a glass factory), and Boris Svetozavrov's *Golden Fleece* (*Zolotoe runo*, 1928, about wool production).[12] He praised these films for two things: for attempting to capture real "workers' everyday life," and for a "clearly expressed orientation toward the material (*ustanovka na material*)."[13] The first category is straightforward: like other critics, Shklovskii argued that Soviet everyday life had yet to make its appearance in film; the urgent task was to capture real life, to show *rabochii byt* (workers' everyday life) as "photogenic" (using Delluc's term—see chapter 1). Shklovskii's second criterion for praise—the films' "ustanovka na material"—bears further consideration. It was the duty of film, Shklovskii suggested later in the essay, to "convey our relationship to the object." In another article of 1927, he made the statement that Soviet cinema was entering a new phase, a "second stage," in which it would become "a factory of the relationship (*otnoshenie*) with things."[14] And that relationship, he suggested, must be intensely material. The task of the film was to provoke a renewed relationship with the object world.

These statements mark a complex moment in Shklovskii's developing film theories. They signal a shift in attitudes to material on-screen. Specifically, they attempt to link "material" with an evolving interest in the cinematic representation of the individual. The term "ustanovka" is important in this respect. We have discussed the recurrence of this term (drawn from behavioral psychology) in diverse fields during this period. Here it marks a focus on the *relationship*—between characters on-screen and the material world and, more fundamentally, between the spectator and the material on-screen. Ustanovka is a "tuning" of the human subject that takes place through the senses; and film spectatorship was a space in which such tuning was possible.

Shklovskii's statements engaged in a key debate that began in Soviet cinema in 1927, and that continued to have potency (and ideological resonance) through the 1930s. How to represent the new Soviet subject on-screen? With the first Party Conference on Film in 1928, and its call for a "new stage" in Soviet cinema, the question of how to render the particular psychology of Sovietness on-screen became ever more urgent. Replacing the mass heroes of revolutionary cinema, the mature Soviet cinema would feature real individuals. How, though, should filmmakers negotiate the relationship between the individual and the collective, and picture the inner life of the new Soviet subject? What was the shape of Soviet feelings, and how could they be expressed on-screen? The new film heroes must be individuals (not a mass), but also distinctly Soviet: critic I. Davydov criticized filmmakers for showing people "with individual, but not social characteristics," and suggested that social identity (*sotsial'nost'*) must become the structuring principle of film characterization.[15] Films should show characters motivated by a love "for ideas," and "for the great project of construction."

Shklovskii's focus on "material" and "relationships with things" can be seen in relation to these increasingly urgent ideological imperatives. They were an attempt to articulate a new model of human feeling—one based on a sensory proximity between human and world, and in which material mattered. Here, Shklovskii was part of the shared project that is the subject of this book. The new Soviet individual must be pictured in everyday life. This, after all, was the founding principle of Marxist materialism. Indeed, according to materialist philosophy, Soviet man or woman was not just in everyday life; he/she was *created* by the conditions of everyday life. As an article in *Soviet Screen* suggested, "A person's relationship with objects leaves an impression on the everyday conditions of his life; for he is organically linked with objects by production, craft, or trade."[16] In the words of another critic in 1928, "The human individual is not a homunculus, locked up in a transparent cube."[17] Body and mind are shaped in sensory interface with the world.

In this context, cinema had a double mission. The camera was uniquely equipped, first, to bring awareness of those material conditions that shape and determine human life, uncovering the physical world in all its plenitude. In the words of one critic, "It makes us sense (*vvodit v oshchushchenie*) everyday life first and foremost through the representation of surroundings, of objects."[18] Film's second purpose, however, was more complex: it should not only reveal, but also transform, the human relationship with those material conditions—it could articulate alternative models of selfhood. This second project could work on two levels. Most obviously, film could picture, on-screen, new relationships between human and material. But it could also, more crucially, use the affective potential of its address to the spectator to carry out its own sensory revolution.

The remaining sections of this chapter will explore this two-stranded project through the prism of production, focusing on how cinema pictured the relationship between artisanal and industrial production. First, I will explore how theories of production in Soviet Russia treated industrial and traditional modes of making, uncovering an important focus on handcraft as a model for a new Soviet relationship between human and material world. I will then examine a range of Soviet production movies, showing how films pictured the three-way relationship, in any act of making, between the human subject, the tool/machine, and the made product. Soviet filmmakers were, I suggest, concerned to ask—and perhaps to answer—the following questions: What might a specifically Soviet model of labor look like? What was the relationship between human and material that was at stake in the act of production? Finally, how might film itself be understood as a new model of making?

THE TOOLMAKER

In early Soviet Russia, evolving attitudes to the relationship between the human and object worlds were rooted in reflections on industrialization, modernity and labor, and their transformation by Soviet socialism. In a letter written in Berlin as part of *Zoo* (but not included in the first published version of 1923), Shklovskii wrote of the relationship between man and material objects. A man, he wrote, "is changed by his trade": "A tool not only extends the arm of a man, but also makes him an extension of itself."[19] He went on: "What changes a man most of all is the machine."[20] This change was not negative, however—Shklovskii was clear in this text about his fascination with, even love of, machines ("I love automobiles!"), and the potential for a productive connection between man and object. Here, Shklovskii's thinking overlapped with a broader current in LEF and Constructivism. In chapter 1, I noted that the relationship between the human and the object world was a key point of focus for the Soviet revolutionary avant-garde. This relationship was envisaged as one of reciprocity: an emotional affinity between the human and object worlds that was created through the body.

As we have seen, the interest in the relationship between human bodies and the inanimate world in Soviet Russia was part of a wider project for the scientific study of the body and movement. It was particularly evident in relation to psychotechnical science and its associated fields, where concepts of labor and work had particular importance. Bernstein's biomechanics, for example, began with the analysis of the movements of a blacksmith at a forge, observing that the hammer landed in the same spot on the anvil with each stroke, but that each movement made was different. From this Bernstein noted the instinctive capacity of the laboring body to "tune" (or adapt; again the term ustanovka is important) its movements to the emergent task.[21] Bernstein's notion of "technical intelligence" underlay the growing concept of "technicity" in Soviet production aesthetics: the act of making engenders a special kind of movement, which is the key to the refashioned self.[22] The Soviet interest in the possibilities of enhanced bodily efficiency through psychotechnics is well documented. But discussions about the particular relationship between the laborer and his tools were also part of a wider interest in the act of making—as a model for a sensate relationship between man and the object world.

In an essay of 1919, Lenin set out to describe the qualities that would distinguish proletarian labor from that of capitalist workers, and he did so by emphasizing the workers' investment of "care" (*zabota*), not only for his/her own machinery and product, but for all the products of a given society.[23] This term, "zabota," notably evokes a relationship between worker and product (and worker and machine) that, in its emphasis on proximity and affect, echoes that usually described as between the handworker and his devices and product. As Devon Fore notes, "Lenin defines communism not as an abstract political program, but as a new affective organization that is cultivated through an empathy for the products of human labor ('empathy' understood not as sentimentality, of course, but in the strict sense of *Einfühlung*, namely, the projection of perception onto matter)."²⁴

This raises questions about the specificity of Soviet representations of mechanized (factory) production. Of course, Marxist theory was straightforward in its validation of labor, and the resonance of this in Soviet culture is well known. For Marx, labor marked the fundamental connection between the human and the material worlds that was at the basis of materialist philosophy: "Labor is, in the first place, a process in which both man and Nature participate."²⁵ It was also the site of man's *mastery* of nature, "in which man of his own accord starts, regulates, and controls the material re-actions between himself and Nature."²⁶ The specificity of types of labor was important, however. There is a well-recognized contradiction in Marxist theory between the political validation of labor and a critique of its capitalist conditions. In particular, Marx argued that the replacement of the hand tool by the machine had ruptured the instinctual relationship of skill between the human and the material that was present in traditional craft.²⁷ This created the alienated body of the worker in the conditions of capitalism. The task of communist labor was to remake that relationship: to construct a model of mechanized labor that would be distinct from that of capitalism, and in which the senses would be emancipated.

Homo faber: the Maker

How was this new model of emancipated labor articulated on-screen? Here we turn to one of the most intriguing heroes in Soviet cinema of the 1920s: the eponymous deaf shoemaker in Fridrikh Ermler's 1927 film, *The Parisian Cobbler* (*Parizhskii sapozhnik*). This was much heralded as one of a group of films that came to the screen in 1927 and 1928, in response to demands that cinema focus on the everyday life of real Soviet citizens and offer lessons for its improvement. Ermler had already shown his interest in the embodied experiences of the "simple" Soviet worker in *Kat´ka's Reinette Apples*. In *The Parisian Cobbler* he turned his attention from the "big city" of Leningrad to a transitional space: a provincial town, and its small-scale paper factory. With the explicit aim of provoking discussion at organized screenings, *The Parisian Cobbler* was a short film about the morality of Soviet youth. A young man gets his girlfriend Katia pregnant and refuses to acknowledge her child. A group of young "baddies" try to blame shoemaker Kirik Rudenko for her pregnancy. In a climactic scene, one of the young men is set to rape Katia, but she is rescued by Kirik, who kills the violent youth. "Who is guilty?" the final intertitle asks.

While making this film, director Ermler was running a club for the "study of contemporary urban life." His production team went on an extended expedition to Pskov and used local inhabitants in mass scenes. As such, the film was firmly situated within the realist agenda that was taking shape in the film press in 1927.[28] *The Parisian Cobbler* visualizes the transition between traditional and modern economies, picturing a provincial factory town, where the factory sits amid traditional churches, bells, roaming animals, men washing in the river. This transition is particularly visible in the figure of Kirik—a man engaged in traditional craft amid the emerging industrial economy. Through him, the film asks questions about the act of making, its place in emerging Soviet ideological frameworks and, in broader terms, about the relationship between man and the material world that making encodes. This problematizes the evolution toward industrial economy.

In its plot, the film opposes two different models of Soviet youth: the worthy laboring *komsomol members*, and the indolent hooligans. It is typical of Ermler's subtlety, however, that this binary is not straightforward. The komsomol members are not unambiguously positive characters: they are weak and even passive, unable to stand up against the forceful personalities of the local hooligans. In one scene, young Andrei criticizes his father's petty-bourgeois tendencies—signaled visually in a sequence of shots of an icon, house plants, and a canary in a cage, as well as in the decorative density (swagged curtains, tablecloth) of his home. Yet Andrei himself is revealed as morally corrupt, unwilling to acknowledge the baby that his pregnant girlfriend is carrying. Between these groups—and crucially outside both of them—is the shoemaker.

Kirik is an intriguing hero. The first shot of him shows only a hand, holding a cobbler's knife, cutting through leather. Only subsequently do we see his face and learn his name. He is amid his tools, making and fitting a shoe (figure 4.2). This emphasis is maintained throughout the film. Superficially, Kirik seems to be apart from the socialist everyday in two key ways. First, as both deaf and mute, he is not part of the logos of socialism. He literally cannot speak Soviet. Second, as a lone shoemaker, handcrafting his wares in the "latest Parisian style," he is outside the industrial collectivity of the

Fig. 4.2 The Deaf Shoemaker. Still from *The Parisian Cobbler* (*Parizhskii sapozhnik*, dir. Fridrikh Ermler, production design by Evgenii Mikhailov).

komsomol factory workers. Yet it is Kirik who is the moral center of the film. Why might this be?

In this respect, the ideological value of Kirik's shoemaking is important. Parisian or not, Kirik's craft is one of making, by hand. It is an authentic act, marked by proximity between man and the material. As such, it forms part of an important micronarrative of Soviet socialist construction that is often overlooked. What was the place of making, or handmaking, in the Soviet ideological value system? By placing an artisanal shoemaker in the midst of an industrial context, *The Parisian Cobbler* raises questions about the transformations between those two modes of production.

Here, some broader context on shoemakers in particular is useful. The image of the shoemaker was a potent one in Russian and Soviet culture of the early twentieth century.

> Watch me stoop
> And reach for a shoemaker's knife in my boot

wrote Vladimir Maiakovskii in his "Cloud in Trousers" (1915). Osip Brik listed the shoemaker (with the tailor and the carpenter) as one of the heroic "makers" alongside whom the artist should seek to stand, validated by their production of real objects and their contribution to the collective project.²⁹ The heroes of Barnet's *Outskirts* (*Okraina*, 1933; see chapter 7) are shoemakers; and Pavel Petrov-Bytov's *Cain and Artem* (*Kain i Artem*, 1930) had a Jewish cobbler/revolutionary as its moral center. Nikolai Ekk's *Path to Life* (*Putevka v zhizn'*, 1931), traced the transformation of a group of young, homeless hooligans into future model members of the Soviet collective. Their redemption was, as so often in Soviet Russia, brought about by participation in the act of production. One pivotal scene shows young Mustafa and his friends being taught to use a cobbler's knife to cut leather for boots; the camera focuses closely on the texture and density of the animal skin as the knife moves carefully through it. This cut initiates a striking montage of redemptive labor, intercutting boot-making with carpentry and metalwork. It is a montage of *handwork*: sweating skin, fingers holding planes to create piles of wood shavings, leather being sewn by hand. And the film's plot emphasizes the redemption of its young ruffians' bodies (and minds) through their relationship with their tools and their products.

This sequence in *Path to Life* emphasizes a *reciprocity* between human, tool, material (leather), and end product (boot). This is explicitly framed in the film when Mustafa and his friends handle their finished products (the boot, a chair). This relationship, encoded in handcraft, prompts us to consider the place of making in the Soviet ideological system. Hannah Arendt's development of the Marxist concept of homo faber is useful here. In *The Human Condition*, Arendt makes a distinction between labor and work. For Arendt, labor is constant (demeaning) toil with no product; it is the thankless daily effort needed in order to maintain human life day to day (preparing food, cleaning, etc.). It is what the human has in common with the animal, and it leaves no permanent product—no lasting trace. Work, by contrast, is what distinguishes human from animal. It is an act of making—a contribution to, or intervention in, the construction of society. In Arendt's words:

> The animal *laborans* could be redeemed from its predicament of imprisonment in the ever-recurring cycle of the life process . . . only through the mobilization of another human capacity, the capacity for making, fabricating, and producing of *homo faber*, who as toolmaker not only eases the pain and trouble of laboring but also erects a world of durability. The redemption of life, which is sustained by labor, is worldliness, which is sustained by fabrication.³⁰

This notion of fabrication speaks to Arendt's understanding of human society as "made from objects."³¹ Work signals the participation of the human in the world of things: it produces not just a product, but a relationship with the world. And it does so through the embodied act of making. This was, I suggest, the ideological underpinning of Soviet theories of making—and it helps us to think about Kirik and other Soviet makers on-screen.

For Arendt, homo faber begins as the toolmaker; the originary relationship between man and the world is that between craftsman and tool. This relationship was a point of focus in Soviet culture. There are two main models through which the relationship between (wo)man and tool has historically been understood: either the tool as "projection of a human organ" (an anthropomorphic perspective), or the tool as inscribing itself upon (transforming) the human (the technomorphic).[32] The anthropomorphic model is exemplified in poet Osip Mandel'shtam's 1922 image of the relationship between man and tool as the core of (classical) human civilization: "[Hellenism means] consciously surrounding man with utensils (*utvar'*) instead of indifferent objects; the metamorphosis of these objects into the utensil; the humanization of the surrounding world."[33]

In similar terms, media theorist Viléem Flusser suggests that tools "tear objects from the natural world in order to bring them to the place (produce them) where the human being is."[34] Through the tool, the natural world is *humanized*. Flusser describes any product produced by tools as "informed" by human intention: the object bears the trace of its relationship with its maker, and so exists in a relationship of reciprocity with the human.

In contrast to these anthropomorphic models of the tool, linked to craft, the technomorphic model sees the tool as inscribing itself upon the body: the body is transformed by, and ultimately *becomes*, the tool. Such views are commonly linked to mechanization: where the human controls the tool, the machine implicitly controls the human.[35] And in parallel, machine-produced objects lack the intuitive reciprocity with the human (Flusser's "human intention") that characterizes handwork. In this respect, it is notable that Flusser identifies shoes as a particularly "strongly informed" item, marked by the connection between human and material: the leather (animal skin) is processed and transformed; the finished product bears the mark of the shoemaker's needle and his knife. So it exists in a reciprocal relationship with the human (in this respect, it is surely also important that a shoe is worn).

The example of the shoe points to the third important element of the human-object relationship that is intrinsic to the act of making. That is, the relationship between the maker and the material (here, the leather) from which the product is made. Anthropologist Tim Ingold is one of several recent scholars (in different fields) who have argued for craft, and craftsmanship, as a model for a positive relationship between the human and organic material.[36] The act of making is a skilled act of working *with* the properties of materials. Weaving is prototypical of this model of making, an act of shaping matter into new forms: "In a certain sense, then, we can say that the smith at his forge, or the carpenter at his bench, is actually weaving. Even the bricklayer may be said to weave as he knots bricks with mortar into the fabric of a wall."[37]

Ingold is indebted to Gilles Deleuze and Félix Guattari, who identify the "artisan" as someone who works with material—someone who "is determined in such a way as to follow a flow of matter."[38] The hand of the artisan, and his tool, mark the point of connection between human and material.

In the production-orientated Soviet Union, handcraft occupied an ambiguous and complex place. We have noted (chapter 1) how the VKhUTEMAS core curriculum sought to enable a direct encounter between the producer (artist) and the material (working with clay, etc.). And VKhUTEMAS contained departments of ceramics, textiles, wood- and metalworking, alongside architecture, painting, sculpture and graphics. Yet the evolution of VKhUTEMAS speaks to its uneasy relationship with traditional craft. Where the German Bauhaus was explicit in its continued interest in the act of making that was embedded in craft (exemplified in the weaving workshop[39]), the curriculum in the VKhUTEMAS woodworking workshop, for example, developed rapidly away from that inherited from the Stroganov Institute (which focused on the acquisition of hand skills), toward the design of wooden furniture for mass production. The tool was replaced by the machine, which encodes a different relationship with the material. As Nikolai Tarabukin noted in 1923: the more advanced the processes of modern production, the more divorced is the maker from the object of production.[40] Yet despite all the Soviet emphasis on machine production, the intuitive, sensate, three-way relationship between human, tool, and material that was intrinsic to handcraft did have potent appeal in the Soviet context. It inflected, I suggest, the search for a specific Soviet model of industrial, mechanical production—one in which a new model of human experience itself was at stake.

Tacit Knowledge

This excursion into theories of tools and craft helps us to think about how *The Parisian Cobbler* uses different models of making to represent different modes of being in the world—and, ultimately, different forms of knowledge.

Kirik is at once innocent and highly skilled. Following Ingold, we might say that as craftsman he operates not through language (which is implicitly linked to reason, and detached from the life of the body), but through touch and intuition. His is tacit (and tactile) knowledge. It is interesting in this respect that Grashchenkova claims that Ermler shot a scene—not included in the film's final cut—that showed Kirik dancing alone—his body moving without needing to hear music, finding its own instinctive rhythm.[41] He operates, I suggest, through *sensation*. He is also shown to be in direct contact with the physical material of the world. His domestic space is a space of making: the workshop in which he crafts his shoes, filled with his tools, draped with drying leathers, and distinguished from the other spaces in the film by its sheer textural density.

In its plot, *The Parisian Cobbler* makes a link between the tacit-tactile knowledge that Kirik possesses, which is linked to his traditional handcraft, and the intuitive moral knowledge that enables him to act heroically: to apply that tacit knowledge to the wider world, protect Katia and kill the malign Tundel′. In this film, those with the gift of the (Soviet) gab are revealed as morally corrupt, and the deaf-mute artisan provides an ethical center. His tacit-tactile knowledge is in direct contrast to that represented by the komsomol leader Grisha Kolobov, in spectacles, surrounded by books—whose lack of engagement with "real" bodies is evident in his response to Andrei's request for advice about Katia's pregnancy; Grisha gives Andrei a book entitled "The Problems of Gender (in Russian Literature)." The film ends with the intellectual Grisha removing his spectacles and slowly cleaning them. In his memoirs, Ermler recalled this as a simple metaphor—the intellectual is no longer sure what to think, his certainties are overturned. Indeed, Ermler modestly claimed that it bore no comparison with the kinds of metaphors being "written" in film by directors such as Eisenstein.[42] But it could surely be seen also as a more complex reflection on the knowledge available to different sensory modes of being in the world. The intellectual's heightened vision, symbolized by his spectacles, provides a less powerful form of certainty than the deaf-mute Kirik's world of instinct, sensation, and feeling.

The Parisian Cobbler, then, makes a case for a form of knowledge that is both silent and handheld. In this, of course, silent film could have a particular role to play—and particular potential. When Kirik works, the camera offers first an encounter with the faktura, the texture, of the leather out of which the shoes are sewn. Similarly, in the montage of making in Ekk's *Path to Life*, shots emphasize the cut of the animal hide, the sewing of the leather, the movement of the plane on wood, and even the shavings of wood. Such sequences bring the spectator into proximity with the material - one that, crucially, replicates that of the embodied act of making. Here, of course, the very silence of silent film was important. Like Kirik and other makers, silent film could operate beyond text. In this respect, that tantalizing lost sequence of the deaf Kirik dancing to unheard music is vivid. It raises questions about the particular sensory power of silent cinema. Perhaps the camera lens seemed to have the potential to offer that tacit knowledge—knowledge through the body—that was intrinsic to handcraft.

MACHINES AND MEN

What, then, was the status of mechanized making—of the factory setting—in *The Parisian Cobbler*? It is notable that its scenes of industrial production are far from a typical representation of mechanized labor. They, too, seem to reflect an interest in rukodelie: intercut with frames of spinning cogs and levers, we see hands holding messy poles, swirling the wet pulp that will become paper; and women handling the reams of paper product. As such, industrial production becomes a form of handcraft. These scenes sit alongside scenes of the young protagonists' embodied experience of a life that consists of both labor and leisure. Lunch break at the factory, for example, shows near-naked men lying amid the stones of a river, and young people doing gymnastics on the factory roof. Later, we see our protagonists literally at play in the factory club. Together, such images add up to a vision of socialist labor at odds with the celebration of efficient rationality common to associate with film of this period. Rather, the film emphasizes the messy exuberance of these young workers, their embodied participation in the project of "building socialism."

This points to a more nuanced understanding of Soviet production aesthetics in this transitional period. In 1928, leftist critic Toporkov sought to explicate productionist theory in terms suited to the increasingly complex ideological climate of the late 1920s, and the growing interest in the physical and emotional formation of the new Soviet self. Two elements of Toporkov's argument are important. First, Toporkov argued that the mechanization of labor did mark a shift from an anthropomorphic relationship between man and the instruments of his labor, to a technomorphic one.[43] Rather than reducing the freedom of the human body, however, technology created a new kind of human, who had a new relationship with her/his tools.[44] Countering the charge that the machine operator was nothing more than a knob presser, Toporkov insisted that the operation of machinery demanded skill (*masterstvo*), and that machines were sensitive (*chuvstvitel'nye*) instruments. The operation of machinery was bringing about the rebirth of craft (*remeslo*). This was a new kind of craft, however, and it demanded a new kind of craftsman: the *tekhnik*, whose craft was premised on an affinity between his body and the machine: "As he works with a machine, man unites with it in rhythm, in his breathing, the beating of his heart, his blood."[45] So, Toporkov argued, "technical" art must be characterized by sensory and emotional "intensity."

Toporkov's view of the machine as sensitive and able to evoke feeling runs counter to Arendt's view of mechanical labor as demeaning, and indeed to Marx's vision of the alienation of the body in factory production. It encourages us to think about the Soviet project as seeking a new model of the relationship between the human and the machine-tool in the act of factory production— one that was organic and sensate, and spoke not to a mechanization of the human, but rather to a humanizing of the mechanical. The second level of Toporkov's argument, however, reveals the complexity of this project. Speaking of the relationship between this worker-machine duo and the material with which it/they work, Toporkov seems at first glance to be making a contrary point. Unlike the craftsman, he maintained, "a tekhnik does not rely on his senses for an understanding of his material."[46] The "subjective" sensory (in Ingold's terms, "intuitive") relationship with the material characteristic of the craftsman is replaced by the "objective" relationship characteristic of the machine. And this in turn brings a reeducation of the human senses: the technical apparatus (the microscope, the camera) enables a proximate, close-up knowledge of the material—one determined by science.[47]

This vision of a scientific (nonsensory) relationship with the material seems directly opposed to the emphasis on an embodied knowledge of the material that we have identified as central to the act of making in the Soviet context. In the following case studies, however, we will explore how Soviet production films sought to reconcile these two positions—to articulate a new relationship with the material that was both proximate and handheld. Film in particular seemed uniquely able to do just this. On the one hand, the contradiction identified by Tarabukin—that increased mechanization drew the maker further and further from the object of his making—might seem particularly acute with the apparatus of film and photography. Film is based on distance from the material; the camera eye is disembodied and mechanical. But Soviet film practice was concerned to emphasize just the opposite. Film was certainly technomorphic: its technological lens could permit a scientific encounter with the material that was not normally available to the naked eye. But it could also be anthropomorphic. That is, it could operate proprioceptively, as a substitute for the human senses (the eye, the hand). As such, it was ideally placed to embody (and communicate) the new perspective—to articulate a new relationship with the material. This relationship would be characterized by the sensory and emotional intensity that Toporkov described.

This provides a revealing perspective on production movies of this transitional period—films in which objects were center stage. Here, two films by young Georgian director and LEF activist Leo Esakiia are indicative. Esakiia's first feature film, *Driving a Holtze* (*Verkhom na Khol´te*), was produced in 1929. It tells the story of how a merchant and kulak sets himself up as head of the agricultural organization in a village community, and how, in his hands, the community's first tractor (the Holtze brand that provides the film's title) is an agent of exploitation. Once in the hands of the village peasants, however, the tractor becomes a force for liberation.

Driving a Holtze offers an anthropomorphic vision of the tractor: it is a comrade for the peasants as they grow in political consciousness and take agricultural production literally into their own hands. Like Aleksandr Dovzhenko's *Earth* (*Zemlia*, 1930), the film dwells with almost fetishistic detail on the moving (and unmoving) parts of the tractor. But this camera focuses in particular on the relationship between the bodies (the hands) of the peasant workers, and the machine. In a notable sequence, rapid montage intercuts the work of the tractor with close-ups of the texture of grain, the rough hemp of sacks, and frequent shots of handfuls of grain as grasped by peasants, in a multisensory vision of the transformation of farming by machinery. Such emphasis on the pathos of machines, in harmonious interaction with the human body, was common in Soviet production films of this period. It finds memorable realization in Vertov's many sequences of machine operators (the hands of workers operating textile looms in *Man with a Movie Camera*, for example), and reached an apogee in the extraordinary milk separator sequence in Eisenstein's *The General Line*. Rachel Moore reads that scene in terms suggested by Walter Benjamin as visualizing a transformation from auratic perception (a separation between the viewing subject and the object) to the "tactility" of the optical unconscious: the peasants' viewing of the milk separator closes the distance between them and the object, so that the encounter becomes embodied and ecstatic.[48]

The milk separator is by no means the only machine in *The General Line*, however. And in fact it is that film's later scenes with tractors that speak most directly to the reciprocity between (wo)man and machine that is our subject here. Eisenstein's heroine Marfa Lapkina has a joyous, tactile, and embodied encounter with tractors, when she watches a local farmworker trying to fix his tractor, and, when he needs a rag, offers part of her multilayered underskirt. The tearing away of the strips of cloth initiates a sequence of playful revelry that closes the distance between work and pleasure. Marfa's petticoat symbolizes the embodied relationship of care (zabota) and empathy that Lenin described. Machines are mended by people, and it is through such handling that both are transformed.[49] The thing (the tractor) becomes a social (socialist) thing, and the human, in turn, becomes homo faber: the maker. In *Driving a Holtze*, the sequences of the tractor and its parts reveal it as a coparticipant in embodied labor. Thus, in Shklovskii's terms, the film pictures not just the material (the thing), but "a relationship with the material."

Esakiia's second film, *Amerikanka* (1930), made this emphasis more explicit, focusing not just on a machine, but on a history of making. Set in 1905, *Amerikanka* narrates the building of an underground printing press in Moscow, hidden beneath a large apartment building. The film fulfilled Tret´iakov's call for a "biography of a thing." It revealed the conditions of production behind the work of the printing press, and—crucially—it met his demand for the representation of new kinds of emotion, conveyed through bodily engagement with the object. Although ostensibly about printing and mass communication, *Amerikanka* turns out to be a profoundly human story, with an emphasis on bodies and things.

With its thematic focus on print, *Amerikanka* is explicitly concerned with visual iconography. Its opening sequences show the mechanics of mass communication in the hands of imperial power: a montage of machines spews out photographs of the tsar. The forces of revolution need their own techniques of reproduction. In the next scene the words of Lenin (in exile in Germany) materialize on-screen. He writes a letter, calling for a Moscow-based press to be established as soon as possible. The letter is photographed, transferred as film to Russia itself, and Lenin's words (visually superimposed over a series of filmed sequences) frame the ensuing action. The command initiates action, and the underground printing press is to be built.

Amerikanka is a film about words, and words provide the main source of its cinematographic impact. An early sequence offers a montage of different kinds of print font and political message. Throughout, the shapes and patterns of letters create much of the screen's patterning. But for all its exploitation of the formal potential of letters, *Amerikanka* is notable for its consistent grounding of communication in hands-on making. The first shot of underground printing in exile emphasizes its difference from the mass communication of the imperial propaganda system: the camera focuses on hands working typewriter keys, and the slow production of letters, literally putting together a revolutionary message. This is revolutionary communication as craft. It is laborious, but embodied—and that bodily engagement speaks to commitment and endeavor.

In common with the typage principle of early production movies, this film does not feature three-dimensional characters. There are few close-ups of faces, and no named protagonists. It emphasizes instead the many anonymous individuals that work together to make the free press happen: the suited man who smuggles paper; the woman who carries printed journals in her pram. Human hands, however—and human labor—feature prominently. The underground nature of the press is literalized as we watch men digging deep into the earth, hacking at stone and shoveling mud, as sweat beads on their foreheads. For all its emphasis on the eponymous American printing machine, in this film writing and printing both appear as manual labor—*rukodelie*. Piles of paper are manually packaged; hands are shown setting letters and turning the printing press. Even after the rebels have acquired the mechanical press, sequences emphasize the harmony between the operating body and the machine. The machine is both an extension of the human hand and an agent for the transformation of the body into a maker (and hence into revolutionary subject). As the film progresses, so the pace of labor increases, echoing (and creating) growing revolutionary energy.

This implied remaking of the body is brought about by movement—by embodied participation in the act of making. The rhythm of the press infects activities everywhere. It may be underground, but those above ground are shown to sense its rhythms. In one sequence, the hands of a mother rub soapsuds into linen in firm sweeps that mirror the movement the printing press beneath the building. Another woman irons in a rhythm that matches that of the cogs underground. A man finds himself unable to sleep because of an intangible sensation of mechanical action. These characters' affiliation with the machine takes place through the body: they sense the presence of the machine (whether by vibration or by sound), but are unable to track it down. And so its imperceptible rhythm and pace (the rhythm of revolution) become a part of the energy of everyday life. Printing becomes part of the shared enterprise of embodied making that is the core of the revolutionary project.

This LEF-inspired film, then, presents a vision of technology as both humanized (through its contact with people) and material. It is purposefully distinct from any vision of mass communication (the press, the telegraph) as dematerialized and disembodied. Even writing itself is tangibly material. Woodblock letters are manually set: their volume and texture form part of the film's faktura. Letters are disassociated, combined, and recombined. They add up to a whole, but they are also objects in their singularity. Ultimately, the film tells a story of the word of revolution *made flesh*. Printed text is smuggled in prams, or hidden under piles of grains and dried fruits in a grocery store. Police agents find the metal and wooden letters of the press, rolling them intently between their fingers. As an inspector rifles through the textiles of underwear and ladies' clothes in a luggage check onscreen, the spectator fears that he will find the smuggled paper; the materiality of text is potently felt. The ending of the film carries us forward to 1917, in which the Bolshevik word is triumphant. Now huge majestic printing presses replace the manually operated Amerikanka; now human agency is invisible, the human hand has disappeared. But the film's intertitles make clear that these machines are the descendants of the humble Amerikanka; and as such, they, too, are part of the wider project of Bolshevik making. The new Izvestiia building has its origins in the underground room of 1905. So the Soviet "modern" has its roots in hands-on making.

Esakiia's two films were part of a wider current of production films in Soviet cinema of this period. They are included here because of their emphasis on the tactile communication between the human body and the object world, as an index of a specifically Soviet model of production. And they use the specific potential of cinema to do so. They capture the faktura of their machines and their parts; they break down the monolithic machine, with its potential to alienate the body, into its component elements, and emphasize the human handling upon which it depends. In so doing, they draw the spectator into an encounter with the machine as socialist thing. They lead him/her into *feeling* socialist production.

Industrial Materials

The Parisian Cobbler was much heralded as a komsomol film focused on the real life of industrial workers. As discussed, it used the petty-industrial model of a provincial paper factory to present a subtle meditation on the nature of the transition from handcraft to mechanization. Two other films produced in 1927 also located their action in factories: Room's *Potholes* and Iutkevich's *Lace*. Both featured what Room called "production sequences" (shot sequences focusing on factory machinery).[50] For all their industrial focus, however, like *The Parisian Cobbler*, both films complicated assumptions about factory labor. Most obviously, they featured industrial locations that were surprising in their quest for contemporary Soviet material: crystal and lace-making respectively. The crew for *Potholes* spent three days and nights in the Gus'-Khrustal'nyi and Velikodvor'e glass factories near Vladimir.[51] Iutkevich's group filmed on location in the Livers (Leavers) lace factory on Savvinskaia Embankment in Moscow. The specificity of these factories is important. Both were prerevolutionary: indeed, the Gus'-Khrustal'nyi, founded in 1756, is one of the oldest crystal factories in Europe. Both were also producers of luxury goods. Neither lace nor crystal was ideologically central to the Bolshevik industrialization project. In contrast to the mass production of textiles, lace epitomized bourgeois ideals of beauty and ornament. Similarly, the decorative crystal featuring in *Potholes* was ideologically out of step with the design imperatives of the *novyi byt* (new everyday life). Why, then, did Room and Iutkevich choose these particular industrial contexts?

Certainly, like Ermler's paper factory, these small-scale consumer-product industries enabled their directors to visualize the transition from prerevolutionary to revolutionary models of production. Furthermore, both glass- and lace-making allowed for an exploration of the relationship between handcraftsmanship and mechanical production. But in their focus on glass and lace respectively, these films also marked a shift from the focus on the relationship between the human and the machine that we have discussed thus far, to a focus on the relationship with the product. In this respect, both materials offered considerable cinematographic potential. This was what Shklovskii meant when he wrote of the "ustanovka na material": the cinematic capturing of the faktura of glass and lace was not just a formal imperative, but an ideological one.[52] It could articulate a new relationship with the material world. In both *Potholes* and *Lace*, I suggest, the faktura of material objects was an index of revolutionary transformation itself.

Any detailed analysis of *Potholes* is limited by the fact that the film has not been preserved.[53] As with Room's two previous films, *The Traitor* and *Bed and Sofa*, the screenplay was written by Shklovskii himself, adapted from a short story by worker A. Dmitriev.[54] The narrative is one of moral education. Young Pavel and Tania marry, but Pavel finds himself drawn to another worker, Nastia, and leaves his wife. The ensuing plot charts Pavel's public shaming, repentance, and eventual reconciliation with Tania. In the critical press, much discussion focused on Pavel's narrative in relation to the moral codes of marriage, and the role of the collective in upholding them. Other reviewers (such as worker Vasil'ev) praised the film's realistic portrayal of rabochii byt.[55]

In plot and theme, *Potholes* was a morally educational film about factory life. The material (glass) was tied to plot and ideological message (the formation, or manufacture, of the new Soviet person) by key intertitles at the beginning ("Do you know how glass is made?") and end ("That is how glass is made"). Like glass, Pavel has been "made"; he has been reeducated by the collective. It is clear from extant stills, and from the screenplay, however, that glass was not merely a metaphor, but a material preoccupation. The faktura of glass, and glassmaking, provided a focus for the film's visual style.[56] Large glass bottles appear "filled with light and air, like wine," faces are shot through glass of differing thicknesses, and highly polished surfaces reflect human figures.[57] "The moon streams through the window and illuminates the machinery," and "the glass of bottles gleams."[58] These formal elements were criticized in a number of contemporary reviews: Shneider, for example, described the film's treatment of glass and crystal production as aesthetic and not functional.[59]

This apparent tension between form and theme is symptomatic of filmmaking in this transitional period. It is here, indeed, that my interest lies. I suggest that the formal experiment was central to Room's ideological purpose: *Potholes* attempted to present the evolution of the Soviet individual through a changing relationship with the material, and with the machines that shape it. In Shklovskii's terms, these were experiments in conveying an attitude toward the material, and a "relationship with the object" at the level of form. Abram Room was consistent in his interest in the cinematic treatment of things, and their role in making spectatorship sensory: "We convey a sensation (oshchushchenie) much more effectively when we do so with the help of a thing, an object."[60] Prerelease statements about Room's previous film, *Bed and Sofa* (1927), had gone further, suggesting that things not only reflect but may even create the inner life of those that live with them. The heroine of *Bed and Sofa* is trapped by the bourgeois world of material possessions; her relationship with the world must be remade. In that film, however, Liudmila's "remaking" is off-screen, in an imagined socialist future. *Potholes*, by contrast, attempted to picture its protagonist's path to consciousness on-screen with the help of its factory setting. Industrial production frames a new relationship with the object world—one that is based not on consumption (like that of Liudmila), but on production. Pavel's redemption is brought about through participation in the process of manufacture. His physical commitment to factory work, his embodied participation in glass manufacture, brings his rebirth. For the spectator, whose attention would be consistently drawn to the faktura of glass on-screen, the film sought to enact a parallel process, engaging the eye in a more fully sensory appreciation of the material properties of its filmed objects.

LACE, HANDWORK, AND MATERIAL

Like *Potholes*, Iutkevich's *Lace* sought to link theme and form—to carry out the sensory "re-education" of its protagonists and its spectators in parallel.[61] It, too, tells an ethical tale, tackling the problem of hooliganism, by showing the gradual reeducation of undisciplined youth in a lace factory, their transformation into model Soviet workers.[62] The film had a mixed reception: although the Sovkino administration was initially negative, a series of public screenings and discussions offered much more positive appraisals, praising the relevance of the theme and its head-on confrontation with the problem of hooliganism.[63] Neznamov described it as a "struggle against the disorganization of youth," and "heroic" in its determination to face up to the challenge of representing workers' life on-screen.[64] In general, the film was considered a major step forward in terms of the representation of Soviet reality: "This is life shown in real, familiar detail and muddle. People are shown in flux, changing in relation to other people."[65]

Lace's engagement with the broader task of emotional and sensory reeducation extended beyond its theme, however. In his memoirs, Iutkevich described it as a polemic with cinematic precedent—even with the great master Sergei Eisenstein. He wanted, he says, to replace the latter's faceless masses with "concrete heroes," and at the same time break away from prototypical (Western) plotlines.[66] Thus Iutkevich positioned this project as part of a wider search for a model of cinematic individuality without bourgeois elements: a freeing of the cinematic hero (from romantic complications) into a fully realized place within the collective. Soviet cinema was entering a new stage. Its task was to find a way of representing a remodeled psychology.

Iutkevich's response to this changing agenda lay not only in theme and characterization, but also in his treatment of material. Just as glass in *Potholes* played a role at both thematic and formal levels, so here lace occupies a central position. The film centers on machine-produced lace and, in so doing, engages with the broader history of handmade and machine-produced lace, and its relation to the Russian craft industry. Russian handmade lace had a prestigious reputation and long lineage. Beginning as a traditional peasant craft, it had developed, after Peter the Great, into a growing industry providing Western-style lace for aristocratic costume.[67] Vasili Tropinin's stunning 1823 painting *The Lacemaker* offers an idealized image of a solitary lacemaker, content in her craft (figure 4.3); in reality, this woman was likely a serf employee in a brutal workshop. Machine-made lace was first produced in Saint Petersburg in 1837, and thereafter the mechanized lace industry grew in Russia, in parallel with hand-lace workshops. In the latter part of the nineteenth century, handmade lace was validated as part of the broader turn toward the traditional craft industries (see chapter 3). Sof´ia Aleksandrovna Davydova established the Mariinskii Lace Making School in Saint Petersburg in 1883.[68] Davydova, however, was concerned not just to celebrate traditional craft. She sought also to reveal the historical oppression of female lacemakers in the production of lace for the Russian aristocracy. Her book, *Russian Lace* (1909), sought to uncover that history—just as Marx had criticized the British lace industry as exemplifying the physical oppression of the worker.[69]

In Soviet Russia of the 1920s, then, lace had a multiplicity of different meanings. On the one hand, handmade lace was a traditional craft, and as such could be validated as part of the broader interest in craft, and integrated into the new economy. The second edition of the *Great Soviet Encyclopedia* proclaimed that the Soviet revolution had liberated lacemakers from sweatshop conditions, allowing them to create collective workshops (*arteli*).[70] Evgenii Katsman's remarkable painting of 1928, *Lacemakers of Kaliazin* (figure 4.4), presents an image of just such a new artel, with different generations of female lace-makers, working together by hand in a hybrid picture of the old and the new.[71] On the other hand, the decorative style of lace seemed contrary to the new Soviet aesthetic, a problematic trace of the old world: I. Sokolov's engraving *Lacemaker* (1926) pictures a lone young woman making lace against a dense background of a lace curtain, explicitly coded as bourgeois and retrograde.

In its treatment of lace as both product and object, *Lace* engages with all these potential meanings. Its focus, however, is on machine production. The Livers lace factory that provided its setting was named for the Leavers lace-making machines, first produced in Britain, but rapidly becoming

Fig. 4.3 Vasili Tropinin, *The Lacemaker*, 1823, oil on canvas, 74.7cm × 59.3cm, Courtesy of State Tretyakov Gallery, Moscow.

Fig. 4.4 Postcard of Evgenii Katsman, *Lacemakers of Kaliazin*, (oil on canvas, 1929). Postcard produced circa 1929. Private collection.

the most widespread form of mechanical lace production, and celebrated for their ability to reproduce mechanically the intricate designs that were possible in handmade lace.[72] They were extremely complex devices, operating multiple threads simultaneously: as an American promotion pamphlet of 1949 enthused, "a triumph of mechanical ingenuity."[73] It was perhaps this intricacy—and technical achievement—that first attracted Shklovskii and Iutkevich to the Livers factory in Moscow.

In practice, however, the film's images of lace-making do something more complex than simply to celebrate the achievements of the Leavers machine. *Lace* begins with an extended sequence of shots of mechanized lace-making, plunging the spectator into the material of its title. But from the beginning it uses the materiality of lace to picture an unexpected relationship between handcraft and technology.[74] The delicate filigree of the lace contrasts with the block shapes and horizontal and vertical movements of the machine (figure 4.5).[75] Later, cogs and levers appear themselves like a metal fretwork or lace, an assemblage of rapidly moving shapes and patterns. Thus the iconic production sequences of Soviet montage cinema become something different. Turovskaia suggests that Iutkevich's achievement in this film is to "humanize" machines.[76] I propose further that he deindustrializes machines, bringing mechanical production closer to handwork and craft. The contrast between the mechanized efficiency of this, and subsequent, production sequences, and the soft, fragile unwinding of the finished product as it spools into a bucket at the end of the production line, is striking. It is emphasized in the opening sequence by a cut to an anvil, hammering steel. The symbolic message seems clear: lace production is another form of smelting, a part of the industrial endeavor. Again, however, this message is ambiguous: the blacksmith, after all, is a symbolic figure not of mechanized production, but of a productive encounter between man and metal, between tradition and modernity.[77] And Iutkevich foregrounds the relationship between lacemaker and product: the final finished lace is handled, stretched out, the soft textile threads brushing against the worker's face.

In their emphasis on a three-way relationship between human worker, machine, and product, these sequences problematize assumptions about machine production. They transform machine-workers into something closer to artisans. And as such they reconfigure the vast Leavers machines as delicate extensions of the human hand. In this way, the film closes the gap between anthropomorphic and technomorphic theories of the tool. With or without their machines, characters are shown to have a sensory, embodied

Fig. 4.5 Making. Stills from *Lace* (*Kruzheva*, dir. and production design by S. Iutkevich, 1927).

Fig. 4.5 (Continued).

Fig. 4.5 (*Continued*).

relationship with their product (lace) that goes beyond the scientific/objective relationship described by Toporkov. This lace is touched. Characters make it, handle it, and live with it. Indeed, the film as a whole might be read as an extended commentary on handwork. For all its focus on machines, hands feature prominently throughout, in a symbolic narrative of making. One of the most curious elements of the production design—a revolving art-deco shell that emerges and descends from within a youth club's stage—reveals to us an old woman (custodian of the club), endlessly crocheting and apparently oblivious to her unusual setting. The art of crochet, like lace and lace-making (immortalized in Vermeer's famous painting, *The Lacemaker* [1669]), is emblematic of manual labor. Such validation of the manual—the power of the ordinary worker and his or her capable hands—was central to the ideological discourse of the new age.

Touching the Material

Touching, then, is central to *Lace*. The hand enables (mediates) of the encounter between the human and the material world, and as such is the point of origin for a specifically Soviet way of being in the world. Iutkevich's project was to reveal new Soviet reality, and subjectivity, as enmeshed in the faktura of making. In the plot, manufacture (*manufaktura*) has the potential to reconstruct psychology, drawing the hooligans into a renewed relationship with the material that is a key to their social and personal redemption. The film also exhibits, however, wider sensory fascination with the material properties of things, as its preoccupation with faktura and touch takes form on-screen. Objects appear unmotivated. The young protagonists fool around with gym equipment. White dinosaur bones, props to an unappealingly serious lecture (laid on as entertainment in the youth club), acquire material potency against an otherwise dark background: the jaws of the skull open and close. Just as a hand was shown operating a wooden toy in Vertov's *Film Week* (see chapter 1), so here bored youths, uninspired by the educational talk, play with wooden toys; the camera dwells with fascination on the mechanical movement of wooden chickens' heads bobbing up and down.

In part, this interest in things is evidence of Iutkevich's formalist leanings. This, indeed, was an accusation that contemporary critics made of the film: Neznamov, for one, described the film as cinematographically "extravagant," overfilled with attractions.[78] Certainly, as in Iutkevich's set designs for Room's *The Traitor* (see chapter 2), props and set design here point to a formal interest in the surface of the film, and in how different material properties construct visual impact. Yet this is a distinctly embodied and material cinematic formalism. It is the tactile quality of the objects on-screen that we feel most profoundly: these are things in direct interaction with the human subject. They are touched on-screen and, perhaps most significantly, the camera's close relationship with them offers the spectator what Iutkevich called a "revelation of the faktura of real materials."[79] It provides a fuller apprehension of the concrete reality of the object, through the body as well as through the eye.

In this way, *Lace* seeks to mirror in the spectator its characters' embodied experience of making. This is particularly evident in shots of lace itself. Just as the lace brushes against protagonists' faces, so in the next shot its delicate patterns form the surface of the film screen, first as a filter, and then as a dissolve, leading the spectator's eye through to a shot of workers on the factory floor. Such shots create a sensory relationship with the film screen. The spectator encounters the surface materiality of the textile, its intricate construction, its woven threads. The material is defamiliarized (we do not simply recognize it), and then reencountered, or felt. As such, spectatorial experience is transformed from the purely optical into something embodied and tactile.

Taking its cue from lace, a formal preoccupation with pattern and transparency can be traced through the film. In one sequence, the stretched threads of the lace provide intricate patterns across the screen; skeins of thread are echoed in shots of electrical wires silhouetted against the sky above the factory roof. In later shots, the geometric struts of electrical pylons form a kind of metallic lace. Such designs are key to the film's visual style: interiors are framed by lace curtains; shadows create a trellis on the walls; windows are backlit, patterning the screen.[80] These patterns explore the relationship between surface and depth on the cinematic screen. They articulate the surface, but also incite the spectator to look through that surface, both impeding and enabling vision, giving it a multisensory dimension.

Of course, Iutkevich's use of lace as visual filter is not unique in cinema of this period, in Russia or beyond (see chapter 2); but it is distinct.[81] The association between lace and sensuality had important ideological resonance in the Soviet context. Lace was no ordinary object: as ornamental textile, it was the preserve of bourgeois luxury and individual erotic fantasy. And Soviet filmmakers were of course aware of its sensual allure. In much cinema of the 1920s, lace acted as ideological shorthand for bourgeois aspiration and ideological impurity. In Room's *Bed and Sofa*, Liudmila's face is symbolically obscured when latticework casts a lacelike shadow. In posters for that film, also, her face is obscured by lace.⁸² In Vertov's *Man with a Movie Camera*, the camera observes the awakening of a young woman with an evident, but ironic, pleasure in the textures of lace and textile—a mockery of film's "traditional" voyeurism. In the face of such ideological associations, I suggest that in *Lace*, Iutkevich seeks to redeem lace as material, to reconfigure its sensual allure in materialist terms. In one scene, a young man has stolen lace from the factory and carries it, hidden, wound around his torso. When he is caught red-handed, a fight ensues, and the lace is unwound, bunched up, and torn. Images such as this, together with the film's consistent focus on manufacture, draw attention to the distinct, complex, and textured materiality of lace. As such, they reconfigure it as a thing (material), rather than a symbol. The material pleasures of lace provide an important element of the film's address to the spectator. But, like that of the lace in *New Babylon* (chapter 2), their sensory address is of a different order. We might suggest that Iutkevich's images of lace transform the erotic into the haptic. They substitute conventional erotic pleasure with an alternative model of sensory fulfillment.

Thus, just as the characters in *Lace* are offered a new sensory pleasure (an ideologically appropriate touch) through their embodied experience of making, so the spectator of the film is drawn into a fresh sensory encounter with lace as material. This lace is not recognized, but felt. And it is felt as a woven network of threads and knots, which interpenetrate, but do not fuse. In this sense, for all its retrograde ornamental associations, lace was perhaps ideally suited to modernist (constructivist) reevaluations of things: Tarabukin proposed a new understanding of the material object as a complex, or arrangement (ustanovka) of volumes, surfaces, and energies.⁸³ Iutkevich's haptic images of lace enable an encounter with lace as just such an arrangement. They reveal the weave of the material as a made product; and they offer the spectator a close-up encounter with its madness.

Touching Film

It is clear, then, that the haptic images in *Lace* have direct ideological reference. This prompts us to think about the relationship between haptic looking and the broader ideological project in which Soviet cinema was engaged. Recalling the sights and sounds of factory life on the set for *Potholes*, Shklovskii told a true story of small children whose parents transport them around the factory in industrial trolleys instead of pushchairs: "This is an industrial detail in everyday life," he proclaimed. "Life is built from such details."[84] This statement bears analysis. Life is made out of details, Shklovskii tells us. Cinema's task is to reveal those details, to bring us to an awareness of the real material conditions that shape everyday life. The film camera can offer knowledge both of the object world itself (the "how-it-is-made"), and the relationship between the human and the object world (the "how-it-is-lived"). And this knowledge, crucially, is both embodied and dynamic: it is *felt*.

This first ambition of the Soviet haptic, then, was materialist-Marxist and epistemological: presenting embodied knowledge of the material conditions that frame human life. Film's second purpose, however, went further: it must seek not only to reveal, but also to *shape* a new relationship with those material conditions. Film must provoke in the spectator a new sensory proximity with the world, teaching him/her to see (or feel) the world anew. The cinematic revelation of the material would seek to restore to human experience an embodied, multisensory proximity with the world that had been lost under capitalism.

Finally, the Soviet haptic was inflected by a distinct ambition: to shape the new Soviet spectator and his or her sensory relationship with the world. At its most extreme, the project of film was nothing less than to instill a new bodily way of being in the world. Here we may return to Toporkov, who, in 1929, called for filmmakers to represent the physical gestures of the new "industrial people."[85] Toporkov's challenge to filmmakers came in the context of increasing calls to picture Soviet psychology on-screen.[86] He argued that the conditions of Soviet (industrial) everyday life had created a new kind of gesture, which he called "an object-led (*predmetnyi*) gesture."[87] This gesture was not expressive in the romantic and lyrical sense of the word; it was not superfluous, but was dictated by function. The productive sensate reciprocity between human and machine creates a new kind of human body, an alternative model of sensory pleasure, and eventually, new feelings. Socialist feeling would be dictated by labor: "Man and his activity come together indissolubly."[88] Filmmakers must model the object-led gesture as a mode of (real) Soviet being in the world.[89]

For all its patent contradictions and attempts to stretch productionism to meet changing ideological frameworks, Toporkov's theories exemplify the vision of emotional and sensory affinity between man and material that has been my subject in this chapter. The object-led gesture is based on a dual relationship—with the apparatus, and with the material—that was central to a particularly utopian vision of Soviet making. It draws our attention to the importance of touch and sensation. Here we might return to Dziga Vertov's unrealized plans for the film *Hands*, with which we began this chapter. It is notable that in Vertov's list of shots, his hands are always holding something—grasping objects, operating machines. In January 1928, *Kino* published an article by the American art historian Alfred Barr Jr. entitled "Hands."[90] The essay was an account of a film about hands that *had* been made: Stella Simon and Miklos Blandy's short experimental film, *Hands: The Life and Loves of the Gentler Sex* (*Hände: Das Leben und die Liebe eines Zärtlichen Geschlechts*, 1928), which Barr had seen in Berlin that month. The difference between this film and Vertov's envisaged short is instructive. In Simon and Blandy's work, the movement of hands is abstract and decorative, forming shapes that seek to convey a narrative of love. These hands hardly touch—either objects, or one another. Rather, they form shapes, grasp at empty space, come together, and move apart. Barr suggested that this might represent a possible synthesis of the Russian preoccupation with "real" material, and the experiments of artists such as Fernand Léger with the potential of cinema to picture abstract patterns. But he surely missed the point. Unlike those in Simon and Blandy's film, the Soviet hands in Vertov's film *touch*— and they touch things. They operate within and through the world—and as such, like Toporkov's "object-led gesture," they are a symbol of the proximate relationship between self and world. Here we might also consider the compilation film of Viktor Blium Albrecht, *Hände: Im Schatten der maschine* (1928), in which hands operating machines are a key focus. Here, although Albrecht apparently used shots from Vertov's film The Eleven, the montage works to suggest that the human hand is overcome by machines.

Film as Making

The production films made between 1927 and 1930 that have been our focus in this chapter sought to articulate a new relationship between the human and the material through a reenvisaging of industrial production. They attempted to adapt their avant-garde interest in faktura and material to a changing ideological climate. For contemporary reviewers, however, their attempt was doomed: the social theme and formal experiment were incompatible. The influential critic Khrisanf Khersonskii was uncompromising in his assessment of *Lace*: "Iutkevich perceives the industrial world of machines and people not directly, but impressionistically, and through the prism of that cultural-aesthetic world view that he brings to cinema, as an aesthete above all."[91]

The film was, as one review described it, "contentious," and reviews did not pick up on what Shklovskii had identified as its principle agenda: the articulation of a relationship with the material.[92]

This is not surprising. The reconciliation of Shklovskii's call for a focus on material and the new imperative to represent real people on-screen was not straightforward. Critic E. Arnol'di suggested that filmmakers who were "hypnotized by the material" were unable to elucidate the *significance* of that material.[93] Ieremiia Ioffe went so far as to suggest that silent cinema, with its focus on material, was not equipped to convey psychology.[94] In 1929, Mikhail Bleiman called for a new cinema that would "subdue" material, and he later identified a "rupture" between the plot of films such as *Lace* and *Potholes*, and their material.[95] It is this very rupture that provides my point of interest, however. In a number of key films from this transitional period, what Bleiman called a "thirst for the material" was inflected by a particular ambition: the creation of new Soviet senses.[96] This provides an ideological framing to the broader cinematographic interest in faktura, and distinguishes the Soviet cinematic project from those of its European and American counterparts. Faktura was a means of representing—even of creating—the intensified tactile and dynamic connection with the world that was a condition for a new model of subjecthood.

Four years after the *Film Eye* sequences with which I began this chapter, Vertov's film manifesto *Man with a Movie Camera* presented human life as lived in connection with "the cycles of work and leisure of a city from dawn to dusk within the spectrum of industrial production."[97] The relationship between the human and the material is a core thematic and structural element of the film. It culminates with the hands of *the editor* Svilova, cutting up film and splicing it together. Film, then, is another kind of manufacture, another kind of *handling* of the material. Michelson sees *Man with a Movie Camera* as a Marxist manifesto—and specifically a manifesto for the overcoming of the division between the human and the material world, and the achievement of a: "general and organic unity, a common implication within the movement of industry, the euphoric and intensified sense of a shared end."[98] It is no accident that Vertov devotes time in the film to the labor of a textile factory. All industrial production (weaving, filmmaking) is a form of processing, transforming raw material into a human, social object.

This underlay Vertov's conception of film as a "film-thing," "built with our bare hands." The film is material product, its form dictated by the combination, or processing (montage) of the material (shots).[99] In the materialist labor-led climate of Soviet Russia, Vertov's proud embrace of the title of "the first shoemaker of Russian cinema" is testament to his vision of film as thing.[100] And to its participation in the broader project of making. Could film, then, be a modern form of craft? In the Soviet context, cinema had a double mission—to reveal the textural surfaces, the faktura, of the material world. But also to *handle* and *process* those surfaces, to weave them together into new combinations. The camera's lens is the tool that intervenes between body and world. Could film's own three-way dynamic of material, tool, and spectator create the same reciprocity between the human and the material world that was to be found in craft? Film's task was to articulate a new relationship with the material—which, like that of the shoemaker/craftsman, was proximate, reciprocal and, crucially, handheld—and to provoke the spectator into a multisensory, active form of spectatorship that was a model for a new mode of sensory experience.

NOTES

1. Susanne Strätling, "Das buchstäbliche Erscheinen."
2. Powell, "Hands-on Surrealism," 531.
3. Dziga Vertov, "'Ruki', etude." Tsivian notes that the exact date of the manuscript is unknown, but dates it as 1927 (Tsivian, *Lines of Resistance*, 287 [n. 30]).
4. Tsivian, *Lines of Resistance*, 403.
5. Deleuze describes Vertov as seeking to "carry perception into things," revealing the material interactions between "communist man" and the material world. Deleuze, *Cinema 1*, 81–82.
6. Shukhin, *Animal Capital*, 102–4.
7. Anne Nesbet discusses how an opposition between "man as meat and man as machine" runs through *Stachka*. Nesbet, *Savage Junctures*, 45.
8. Eisenstein, "K voprosu o materialisticheskom podkhode k forme," 114.
9. Fore, "Dziga Vertov," 371.
10. Toporkov, *Tekhnicheskii byt*, 245.
11. Shklovskii, *Ikh nastoiashchee*, 371.
12. Shklovskii was at this point head of the scriptwriting department in Sovkino, and was directly involved in the production of *Potholes* and *Lace*.
13. Shklovskii, "Sherst', steklo i kruzheva."
14. Shklovskii, "Pogranichnaia liniia," 111–12.
15. Davydov, "Order na zhizn,'" 5.
16. N. K., "Byt 'ideologicheskii,'" 5.
17. Fel'dman, "Byt v sovetskom kino," 4.

18. N. K., "Byt 'ideologicheskii,'" 5.

19. Shklovskii, *Zoo*, 114. We should note, incidentally, that for Shklovskii this emphatically did not refer to women!

20. Ibid., 115.

21. The outcome of Bernstein's research into the movement of blacksmiths is most clearly expressed in his later book *O lovkosti i ee razvitii*, which was written in the 1940s but remained unpublished. For discussion of Bernstein's work on motor control see Latash, ed., *Progress in Motor Control*.

22. This kind of interest in the movement of the craftsman was echoed in, for example, Boas's *Primitive Art*. Boas noted how the perfectly controlled rhythmic movement of the craftsman guarantees the form of his finished product, and the instinctual "technical intelligence" of the body of the craftsman. Boas's *Mind of Primitive Man* was published in Russian in 1926. See chapter 5 for further consideration of models of craft in "ethnic" films.

23. Lenin, "A Great Beginning," 427. *Zabota* here is translated as "concern."

24. Fore, "Dziga Vertov," 376.

25. Marx, *Capital*, 197.

26. Ibid., 197.

27. Ibid., 461–55.

28. Ermler, "Avtobiograficheskie zametki," 95. Some two to three hundred local *komsomol'tsy* participated in the mass scenes; real footage was shot; and there is evidence in the local press of considerable interaction with the local community: Ermler, "O 'Parizhskom sapozhnike,'"109.

29. Brik, "Khudozhnik i kommuna," 26 .

30. Arendt, *The Human Condition*, 236.

31. Note that it is the evolution from "labor" to "work" that makes possible Arendt's third stage of human development: "action." It is in "acting" (participating in the community) that humankind reveals itself as free.

32. For a collection of research into the "tool," see Strätling and Holland, eds., *Aesthetics of the Tool*, especially Georg Witte, "Between the Forge and the Assembly Line."

33. Mandel'shtam, "O prirode slova," 182.

34. Flusser, *Towards a Philosophy of Photography*, 23.

35. Ibid., 24.

36. See, for example, Sennett, *The Craftsman*, and Ingold, *Making*.

37. Ingold, *Making*, 29

38. Deleuze and Guattari, *A Thousand Plateaus*, 40.

39. Smith, *Bauhaus Weaving Theory*.

40. Tarabukin, *Ot mol'berta k mashine*. Gough explores this in considerable detail in *The Artist as Producer*, 145–7.

41. Grashchenkova, *Kinoantropologiia*, 549. Sandomirskaia, *Blokada v slove*, discusses deaf-mute culture as a form of resistance to Soviet culture.

42. Ermler, "O 'Parizhskom sapozhnike,'"110.

43. Toporkov, *Tekhnicheskii byt*, 27.

44. Ibid., 30.

45. Ibid., 212.

46. Ibid., 248.

47. Ibid., 254.

48. Moore, *Savage Theory*, 45.

49. It was in fact *The General Line* that prompted Shklovskii's programmatic definition of the new stage of Soviet cinema as "a factory for the relationship with things." Shklovskii, "Pogranichnaia liniia" (see chapter 1).

50. Grashchenkova, "Vospitanie chuvstv," 87.

51. Room, "Kak delalis' 'Ukhaby,'" 5. The crew included cameraman D. Fel'dman and V. Kuznetsov in charge of lighting and Viktor Aden as *khudozhnik* [set designer]). Extensive material relating to *Potholes* has recently been published: Sopin and Tremasov, "'Ukhaby.'"

52. Shklovskii, "Sherst', steklo i kruzheva," 2.

53. The script was published by Irina Grashchenkova as: Room, Shklovskii, "Ukhaby."

54. Both *Potholes* and *Lace* drew their screenplays from short stories by *rabkors* (*rabochie korrespondenty*): Brooks, "Public and Private Values,"; Gorham, "Tongue-tied Writers."

55. Vasil'ev, "Eshche ob 'Ukhabakh,'" 3. The film was not universally considered successful in this respect, however: Shneider accused Room of treating the moral and domestic issues of the film in a retrogressive fashion, with its resolution based on traditional bourgeois familial structures. Shneider, "Ukhaby," 19.

56. For discussion of the glass as metaphor in the Soviet cultural imagination, see Chadaga, "Light in Captivity"; and Chadaga, *Optical Play*.

57. Grashchenkova, "Vospitanie chuvstv," 90.

58. Room, Shklovskii, "Ukhaby," 97.

59. Shneider, "Ukhaby," 21.

60. Room, "Moi kinoubezhdeniia," 5.

61. It is no accident that *Lace* and *Potholes* shared thematic and formal preoccupations. By 1927, Iutkevich had worked twice with Room. Shklovskii's influence on both filmmakers was also significant: it was he who suggested the adaptation of the short story "Stengazeta" into the screenplay for *Lace*, attracted by the setting of the film in a lace *Sobranie sochinenii*, to factory, which "set film on 'materialist' tracks." Iutkevich, *Sobranie sochinenii*, Tom 1, 327.

62. The *stengazeta* (wall newspaper, a "newspaper" posted on a wall in the factory) of the original story plays a vital role in creating a sense of collective responsibility.

63. Vaks, "ODSK na prosmotre 'Kruzhev,'" 5; "O 'Kruzhevakh,'" 3.

64. Neznamov, "Kruzheva." Vladimir Nedobrovo praised the film's "recognizable" characters and its picture of *workers' byt*. Nedobrovo, "O 'Kruzhevakh,'" 3.

65. Vaks, "ODSK na prosmotre 'Kruzhev,'" 5.

66. Iutkevich, *Sobranie sochinenii*, Tom 1, 330.

67. See the entry for lace in the Brokgauz and Efron prerevolutionary encyclopedia. Anon, "Kruzhevo."

68. For further detail on the revival of craft industries see Salmond, *Arts and Crafts in Late Imperial Russia*.

69. See Davydova, *Russkoe kruzhevo*, and Marx, *Capital*, 510–14.

70. "Kruzheva," *BSE*, 2-oe izdanie, 510.

71. But the image stages the tensions inherent in that idea: both of the younger lacemakers look away from their work; another young woman sits side-on to the image and reads aloud. Perhaps the frontal arrangement of the bodies of the lacemakers speaks to their entrapment by their traditional craft, which sits, implicitly, in tension with what is being read to them. The women's faces may figure their engagement with the thoughts that the reading stimulates within them.

72. Indeed, as an American pamphlet of 1949 proclaimed, they could even improve on them. These machines were extremely complex devices, operating multiple threads simultaneously. Rosatto, *Leavers Lace*, 12.

73. Ibid., 12.

74. Shklovskii, "Sherst', steklo i kruzheva," 2.

75. In Eisenstein's *October* (*Oktiabr'*, 1928), we see a similar juxtaposition of the filigree of lace against block shapes of machinery, when the Women's Battalion hangs a lace bra over the solid blocks of a billiard cue stand.

76. Turovskaia and Khaniutin, *Sergei Iutkevich*, 46.

77. This status is exemplified in Preobrazhenskaia's *Women of Riazan Province*, where the blacksmith protagonists represent not the realized industrial future, but a transitional stage. See chapter 3.

78. Neznamov, "Kruzheva," 77. See also Nedobrovo, "O 'Kruzhevakh'"; Strakhov, "Kruzheva."

79. Iutkevich, "Plat'e kartiny," 7.

80. Iutkevich was explicit about his use of shadow as a decorative element in film: Sergei Iutkevich, "Dekoriruem svetom," 43.

81. Iutkevich recalled how he had seen parts of Epstein's *Un Coeur fidèle* (1923) and Kirsanoff's *Ménilmontant* (1926), brought back from Paris by Il'ia Erenburg. Iutkevich, *Sobranie sochinenii*, Tom 1, 329–30. For consideration of the use of lace in film, see Andrew Webber, "Cut and Laced."

82. Cavendish, *Soviet Mainstream Cinematography*, 53.

83. See Witte, "The Tool," 349.

84. Shklovskii, "Sherst', steklo i kruzheva," 2.

85. The lecture was subsequently published: Toporkov, "O predmetnom zheste." The lecture was drawn from Toporkov's book *Predmetnyi zhest*.

86. Toporkov was very much aware of the work of Sergei Volkonskii. Following François Delsarte (and Émile Jacques-Dalcroze) and their interest in bodily expressivity on stage. Volkonskii, who had served as director of the Imperial Theaters until 1902, and had significant influence on the development of Russian dance in particular, had sought to classify all human gestures and their relationship to the expression of emotion. His aim was to provide a theory of gesture, to enable the total choreography of the human body as part of the overall rhythm of a performance. For our purposes, however, it is Volkonskii's attempt to combine emotion and the mechanics of the body that is of particular interest: "Man is a machine; yes, this machine is set in motion by feeling, oiled by feeling." Volkonskii, *Vyrazitel'nyi chelovek*, 132.

87. I opt to translate "predmetnyi zhest" as object-*led* gesture, rather than other possibilities: object/material/objective gesture. These latter options are not, I suggest, what Toporkov means. Toporkov is describing human gestures as they are changed *by* the object (or more broadly by a relationship with objects/technology), and not the gesture *as an object*.

88. Toporkov, "Predmetnyi zhest," 42. The question of "emotion" within leftist mechanistic visions of the transformation of the human body was complex. Ippolit Sokolov, for one, was a clear opponent of Volkonskii's emphasis on rhythm and emotion—and its continued resonance in the 1920s. In his "System for Labor Gymnastics," for example, he had argued for an emotionless, machinelike model of human movement. Sokolov, *Sistema trudovoi gimnastiki*.

89. Toporkov, "Predmetnyi zhest," 41.
90. Barr, "Russian Diary"; Barr ml., "Ruki," 1. Barr was in Russia 1927–1928.
91. Khersonskii, "Chto na ekrane," 23.
92. Strakhov, "Kruzheva," 3. Nedobrovo, "O 'Kruzhevakh,'" 3.
93. Arnol′di, "Fakty—veshch′ upriamaia," 6.
94. Ioffe, "Iz knigi 'Kul′tura i stil,'" 87.
95. Bleiman, "Doloi material," 5; Bleiman, "Chelovek v sovetskoi fil′me, II," 57.
96. Bleiman, "Chelovek v sovetskoi fil′me, III," 27.
97. Michelson, "Introduction," xxxvii.
98. Ibid., xl.
99. Ibid., xxxiii.
100. Fore, "Dziga Vertov," 377.

Chapter Five

PRIMITIVE SENSATIONS

> A tumultuous materialism is ushered into modernity's epistemological fold.
> Michael Taussig, *Mimesis and Alterity*

IN ONE SENSE, this book is an inquiry into the "primitivist" inclinations of early Soviet culture, into the idea that revolution could return to human experience an intuitive sensory encounter with the material world that had a parallel in so-called primitive experience. Handcraft, for example, has emerged as a model relationship between the human and material worlds that had considerable resonance in the formulation of socialist "making." In this chapter we will explore what happened when that primitivist impulse turned its eye upon "primitive" societies themselves, in films made in and about Soviet Central Asia, the Caucasus, and the Far East.

James Clifford has made an important distinction between nineteenth-century exoticism, which "departed from a more or less confident cultural order in search of a temporary *frisson*," and the interest in the primitive "other" that he claims to have distinguished modernist practice.[1] The latter took its point of departure from what Clifford called "a reality deeply in question." This observation may have particular resonance in the Soviet context. The 1917 revolution, after all, threw all existing realities not only into question but even, in the words of the Futurist manifesto of December 1912, "overboard." We might consider, then, the relevance of Clifford's statement that "the 'primitive' societies of the planet were increasingly available as aesthetic, cosmological, and scientific *resources* [my italics]."[2] An interest in the "primitive" mind, and the primitive body, was evident in early Soviet culture, and it was often focused on the "East" (broadly understood, and incorporating the Caucasus, Soviet Central Asia, and the Far East—that is, Siberia, and beyond its borders into China and Asia).[3] How did Soviet Russia's own others function as a conceptual resource during the 1920s and 1930s? Was Soviet Russia's "East" only a backward space to be transformed, brought into the forward-moving temporality of the communist present? Or did it also offer the possibility of rediscovering something that had been lost in human experience with the passage from "primitive" to "civilized" society?

Many films produced in this period operate on a fault line between three competing imperatives. First, the drive toward enlightenment and the overcoming of "backwardness"; second, the need to distinguish Soviet attitudes to the East from those associated with the imperial gaze; and finally, a modernist fascination with primitivism, aligned with a specifically communist/revolutionary interest in "primitive" ways of life as a possible prototype for a new kind of (revolutionary) subject. This chapter will explore these often-intertwined attitudes toward the national republics through the 1920s. In particular, I will suggest that certain key films examine the spaces and peoples of the national republics in search of alternative models of sensory experience. I will trace attempts to appropriate elements of what might be termed a "primitive sensibility" to a specifically Soviet reworking of Orientalist tropes.

Soviet Empires?

The idea of Russian Orientalism—as cultural principle, scholarly enterprise, and imperial strategy—has been much debated. Orientalism, as theorized most famously in its Western context by Edward Said, describes how cultural representations of the exotic "Orient" were part of an imperial structure of power and control, simultaneously reveling in the transgressive pleasures of the East, and containing and controlling them.[4] Considerable recent scholarship has explored the extent to which colonial (and postcolonial) frameworks are helpful in analyzing the Russian Empire.[5] In relation to the Soviet Union, the picture becomes still more complex. Vera Tolz suggests that Said's attempt to deconstruct the underlying imperialist power structures in Western representations of the Orient actually shares an important genealogy with early Soviet anti-Orientalist thinking.[6] As several scholars have noted, early Soviet nationalities policies sought a new model of geopolitical organization to reflect the newness of their social economic structures, avoiding the center-periphery power structures of colonial empires, and celebrating national diversity.⁷ Nevertheless, Douglas Northrop maintains that the Soviet Union can be compared to colonial empires like the Ottoman or Hapsburg Empire, and thus that Orientalist frameworks are useful: "Central Asia remained above all the Other, a land both attractive and repellent, seductive but at root primitive and despotic."⁸ Although the relevance of political models is not my subject here, some awareness of the broad frameworks of pre- and immediately postrevolutionary orientalism and primitivism is relevant. Clearly, Russia's particular geographical positioning between Europe and Asia is part of this story. Diaghilev, after all, had marketed Russia itself as an Orientalist vision for Western audiences in his Ballets Russes productions. In the Ballets Russes, Russia as "barbarian" East performed its exotic otherness for Parisian audiences. Costumes and set designs (those by Leon Bakst and Nikolai Rerikh in particular) drew on a mixed bag of oriental stereotypes in a rich play of luxurious fabrics, colors, and textures; those of Mikhail Larionov and Natalia Goncharova incorporated Russian folk designs into the melting pot.

Members of the prerevolutionary avant-garde were drawn to Russia as a site of convergence between East and West, seeing the Russian Empire's Eastern and Southern peoples as representing an alternative national identity, unspoiled by Westernization.⁹ For the Silver Age Symbolists, this was often conceived as a force of immanent disruption: Andrei Belyi's novel *Petersburg* (1913 and 1922) evoked Russia's Asiatic East as a threat to the false "civilization" of that European-style city; Aleksandr Blok's long poem "On Kulikovo Field" (1908) addressed Russia's Mongol past as a latent force in the present. For Cubo-Futurist visual artists such as Larionov, Goncharova, and David Burliuk, Russia's own Eastern "primitive" offered an uncorrupted starting point for a reinvigoration of visual art. In all these texts, the "primitive" represented both threat and opportunity. In the postrevolutionary context, however, the "primitive" ideal had an ambiguous status. Certainly, the Bolshevik revolution could be cast as a spontaneous uprising of that untamed Eastern energy (stikhiinost'). Blok's emblematic postrevolutionary poem "The Scythians" (1918) begins with the defiant assertion: "Yes, we are Asians." Similarly, Evgenii Zamiatin's essay "Are we Scythians?" (1918), celebrated the Scythian as the prototype of a heretical artist—a force that would overturn existing hierarchies in the creation of a new world.¹⁰

More broadly, although apparently opposed to the Marxist ideal of technological progress, primitivism could have a role to play in the reconceptualization of the self, and of everyday life, that was at the heart of the Bolshevik project. On the one hand, the enlightening arm of Soviet civilization was to reach out and rid the national republics of their obscurantist ways, lifting the veil of the Eastern woman, overcoming the dominance of superstition, and setting the people on the path to modernization. On the other, the non-Russian peoples of Central Asia and the Far East might be, using Clifford's term, a "resource"—representing a model of precapitalist life that was a source of considerable fascination and allure for those seeking a specifically communist reformulation of mind-body experience, and a renewed relationship with the material world. Daniel Miller suggests that "primitivism stands for that aspect of the Romantic movement which is based in the assumption that there exists a form of humanity which is integral, cohesive, and works as a totality."[11]

This latter idea—of a (newly) cohesive form of humanity, a new subjectivity—had clear potency in the postrevolutionary context. And it points to the place of primitivism in the Soviet sensory revolution.

The Turn to the East

In political terms, the First Congress of the Peoples of the East, held in Baku in 1920, marked an explicit turn "to the East" in Bolshevik ambition.[12] The delay in the realization of the anticipated world revolution in Western Europe brought renewed focus on the East. After all, the history of native uprisings in the East against colonial imperialism (whether Russian or British) was a legacy of revolutionary energy that could be appropriated to the Bolshevik propaganda narrative. The peoples of the East, oppressed by imperial powers, their culture unspoiled by Western civilization, could be reinvented as protorevolutionaries. Further, the social and economic organization of those "primitive" societies that were part of the wider Soviet state (such as the Islamic Chechens) could be directly interpreted in terms of Marx and Engels' theories of primitive communism: their horizontal social structures could be viewed as protocommunist, and their transition to socialism might bypass the stage of capitalist industrialization.[13]

In this context, Nergis Ertürk describes the multinational and multilingual First Congress as a utopian space, with diverse peoples united by the dream of "an immanent, heterogeneous common in alterity."[14] This complex statement captures the broad utopian ambition that underlay the Bolshevik vision of the East in the early 1920s, echoes of which can be felt in diverse fields in early Soviet culture. Ertürk's emphasis on "immanence" and "alterity" as two aspects of this dream of a united East alerts us to two aspects of this shared cultural imaginary. "Alterity" indicates how the Soviet revolutionary self-conception was based on the idea of distinction (from the capitalist West, from the "civilized" world). And "immanence" points to the potent sense of a new world about to be born, and hints at the emphasis on a heightened sense of physical presence in the world that would be a core element of it.[15] This latter might have its roots in the "primitive" sensibility of the archaic "East".

The vision of a reconfigured East as a foundation for the new Soviet world was potent. The East was a key space in the imaginary of the Soviet avant-garde.[16] The image of the wild man of nature as protocommunist had considerable resonance through the 1920s—and even into the 1930s. Boris Pil'niak is often seen as a key proponent of primitive communism with his 1922 novel, *The Naked Year*. Vladimir Arsen'ev's *Dersu Uzala* (1921, 1923) told of the author's travels through the Ussuri Basin, with a local guide whose name provides the title of the work. Arsen'ev presented Dersu Uzala, a hunter, as simultaneously culturally backward and morally advanced—a romantic child of nature uncorrupted by civilization. Slezkine sees *Dersu Uzala* as a manifestation of the myth of primitive communism and its potency in shaping Bolshevik attitudes toward the national republics.[17] In related terms, Michael Kunichika interprets Dziga Vertov's *Sixth Part of the World* (1926) in terms of theories of primitive communism, noting that the film appears to accommodate the ongoing presence of the backward, rather than advocating its abolition: "Indeed, it even deems backward socio-economic forms capable of productively participating in the construction of socialism."[18] It is clear, then, that there has been much scholarship devoted to the relationship between primitivism and modernism, both within and beyond Russia and the Soviet Union. My purpose here is not to duplicate that scholarship, but to complement it with a study of cinema. In tracing films produced both in and about the Soviet East, I will uncover a body of film that is rarely studied, and reveal it to be part of a broader interest in "primitive" sensibility, with particular emphasis on a dream of intensified sensory experience of the material world.

Filming in and for the Soviet East

In the eyes of Bolshevik ideologues, cinema could contribute to the creation of a new communist East in three key ways. First, and most obviously, film could spread the Soviet message in the national republics through visual images. Second, it could participate in the project of discovering the Soviet territory—producing and disseminating images of the East for the consumption of the wider population in a cinematic "mapping" of the territory.[19] Finally, it was vital to produce cinema in the republics themselves. There was a growing sense, in the 1920s, that only homegrown cinema could serve the needs of the populations of the Caucasus, Central Asia, and the Far East. Accordingly, the development of "national" film production companies was a priority. In some cases this was a question of starting from scratch; in others, existing film companies were developed and expanded.[20] Building on an existing studio, a Georgian film production company, Goskinprom Gruzii, was set up in 1923, with established Armenian film actor Amo Bek-Nazarov at its head. In 1925, officials converted a mosque in Tashkent into a film studio, suggestively named Stars of the East.[21] In 1924, Bukhkino was established by agreement between the newly established Bukharan Republic and the Leningrad studio Sevzapkino. A Turkmen film studio was established in 1926. Baku was another growing center for film production, with a studio that eventually became Azerkino (and later Azerfilm). In all these cases, local film production was managed by people who had prior experience in Russian cinema.

Bukhkino produced its first feature film, *Minaret of Death* (*Minaret smerti*, dir. Viacheslav Viskovskii) in 1925.[22] In 1924, the Baku studio produced *Legend of the Maiden's Tower* (*Legenda o devich'ei bashne*, 1924), directed by Vladimir Balliuzek. Both Balliuzek and Viskovskii had worked in prerevolutionary cinema; both had also spent periods abroad (Viskovskii was in Hollywood from 1922 to 1924; Balliuzek worked in Paris and other European capitals during the years of the *Ballets Russes*. They were familiar with Western Orientalist visions of the East, and their first feature films were scarcely different from other Eastern-themed films produced by Western film companies (such as *The Thief of Baghdad* [1924], starring Douglas Fairbanks), peddling images of an exotic East for commercial success. *Legend of the Maiden's Tower* adapted an ancient Azeri tale and featured classic tropes of the oriental film: harems, luxuriant exotic decoration, and violent death. Michael Smith describes the style of it, and of other early films produced in Central Asian studios, as "pseudo-national"—catering to a Russian urban audience that "craved" exotica, rather than to local audiences.[23]

If these and similar films were successful in presenting Eastern stereotypes for a Russian urban audience, however, their themes and styles were difficult to square with the developing Soviet ideology. Alongside such entertaining visions of the East, therefore, both Sovkino and local film studios began to produce films focused on the "backward" East (and the need for Soviet enlightenment). An important example of this genre is *In the Name of God* (*Vo imia boga*, directed by Abbas Mirza Sharif-Zade), produced in 1925 by Azerkino. A critique of Islam, this was one of the first in a category of "national-realist" films, which pictured life in the national republics with dark realism, revealing backwardness without romanticism. Such films were linked to propaganda campaigns encouraging the socialist transformation of these spaces. Focusing on the oppression of a woman, moreover, *In the Name of God* was part of a broader project for emancipation and unveiling.[24]

Neither of these tendencies in films about Central Asia was, however, satisfactory—either for audiences, or for ideologues. Writing in 1925, Bolshevik official A. Skachko bemoaned the orientalism that continued to characterize films set in the East, and identified two undesirable trends: "The first is perpetuating old traditions of portraying the Orient in the cinema with the creation of a stereotyped East through piquant fairytales in the style of *A Thousand and One Nights*. Such a vision of the East is just fine for Western city dwellers. But not for either Russian worker-peasants or Eastern audiences. This tendency is found in *Minaret of Death*. The other tendency is exaggerated, narrow propaganda. For example, Dmitri Bassalygo's film *The Muslim Woman*."[25]

There was, nevertheless, a local thirst for films that would present images of the "real everyday life of the East" (attested, according to one critic, by the scale of the audiences that had flocked to see *Minaret of Death* in Bukhara).[26] What was needed, Skachko announced, was a new cadre of *native* film professionals with knowledge of the East, and in particular of the "psychology of its masses."[27] Native professionals would surely make films that expressed a more nuanced relationship with the new Soviet East.

It was partly in response to such views that an overarching Eastern film studio (Vostokkino) was established in 1926. Led by members of the Scientific Oriental Association in Moscow, under the auspices of Sovkino, Vostokkino aimed to provide a structure to unify the diverse production of national film studios, and promote non-Russian artists in cinema.[28] Its explicit aim was to avoid those two pitfalls of Central Asian cinema: exoticism, and overly strong propaganda. Vostokkino operated only from 1928 to 1935, and although much of its work was in documentary cinema, Chomentowski claims that it produced fifty feature films between 1928 and 1935, and describes these films as a "first step toward national cinema."[29] Vostokkino's filmmakers were not necessarily natives of Central Asia. But it was through Vostokkino that many Central Asian natives received their training in film and went on to become filmmakers in their own right.[30]

Much recent writing on cinema from the Caucasus and Central Asia has tended to focus on whether it was a "national" cinema.[31] By contrast, Chomentowski's work on Vostokkino gives a sense of the unified (and unifying) ambitions of "Eastern" cinema in the period. I will attempt to find a middle line between these two approaches. Although it is important to distinguish between the productions emerging from different national film studios, and between films made by Russian filmmakers about the East, and those made by locals, it is also useful to identify features that were common to the representation of the peoples and places of the Caucasus, Central Asia, and the Soviet Far East on screen. There was much contact and two-way travel between Moscow and Leningrad, the Caucasus and Central Asian Republics, and the Far East. As part of the collaborative work on Kuleshov's *Parovoz B 1000*, for example, many members of the avant-garde spent time in Georgia in 1927: Kuleshov's team included Petr Novitskii and Mikhail Kalatozov, Alexander Rodchenko as production designer, and Roman Karmen as cinematographer.[32] Also in 1927, Shklovskii and Tret´iakov spent several months in Tbilisi, working within Goskinprom Gruzii.[33] According to Chomentowski, a wave of Russian directors arrived in Central Asia in 1928—including Iurii Zheliabuzhskii, Mark Donskoi, Vladimir Legoshin, Evgenii Ivanov-Barkov, and Aleksandr Razumnyi.[34] They were often responsible for on-the-ground training of local nationals (who began their careers as actors or production assistants, but went on to direct films themselves).[35] Such territorial mobility was not limited to filmmaking, of course, or constrained to the East. LEF members traveled extensively across the broader territory of the Soviet Union.[36] It points, however, to the internationalist ambitions that characterized cultural production in this rich period, and prompts us to consider the impact of this cultural mobility on the representation of the Eastern "other."

Ethnographic Eyes

The first stage in developing a new cinema for the Soviet East lay in the evolution of what the contemporary press described as an "ethnographic" eye. In this a key role was played by three directors in particular: Bek-Nazarov (Georgia, Armenia), Lev Push (Azerkino), and Nikoloz Shengelaia (Georgia). Bek-Nazarov was an Armenian actor and director, trained in the Moscow Art Theater, who worked with Bauer in the Khanzhonkov studio, and became head of the new Georgian film studio in 1923. In 1925, he moved to the new Armenkino, where he produced his most important films: *Honor* (*Namus*, 1926), *Natela* (1926), *Khaz-Push* (1927), and *Sevil'* (1929). Lev Push, who had begun working in film before the revolution, in a Tbilisi film studio, was based at Azerkino, directing *Giuli* (1927), *Gypsy Blood* (*Tsyganskaia krov'*, 1928), and *Mzago and Gela* (*Mzago i Gela*, produced in 1930, and codirected with Shalva Khuskivadze; released in 1934). Younger still was Georgian Nikoloz Shengelaia, who codirected *Giuli* with Push, and went on to produce many films independently for Goskinprom Gruzii—including *Eliso* (1928, jointly authored by Sergei Tret'iakov), and later the well-known *26 Commissars* (*26 Komissarov*, 1932).

I will begin by considering two films, *Honor* and *Giuli*, which share a number of features and mark a shift, in the mid-1920s, toward new models for Soviet Eastern films. In broad terms, both films sought what was described as an ethnographic (rather than exotic) mode in their representation of everyday life. Both, however, still belong to a category of Eastern melodrama, revealing the mores of traditional life as part of a gripping, and tragic, narrative. Specifically, their narratives focus on the lack of freedom experienced by women in the national republics as a feature of an abusive patriarchal society. Both are set in unspecified local landscapes (Armenia and Georgia), in an unspecified prerevolutionary period. Adapted from a play by Alexander Shirvanzade ("the Armenian Ostrovskii"), *Honor*, Armenkino's first film production, tells a melodramatic tale of a heroine who lacks any control over her own life.[37] Susanna is betrothed as a child to a young man, Seiran; when she grows up, she actually falls in love with her betrothed, and meets with him alone—against Armenian custom. Learning of these trysts, Susanna's father marries her instead to another, older man, Rustam. When Rustam learns of Susanna's shame, however, he kills her. Seiran, learning of Susanna's death, commits suicide himself. *Giuli* tells an equally tragic tale of Giuli, who falls in love with Mitro. Their union is impossible because he is Christian, and she is Muslim. When Giuli's father dies, she is sold by her heartless stepmother into marriage to a wealthy local man, Ali. At its finale, Ali shoots his young wife when she attempts to escape with Mitro.

For all their engagement with the tropes of melodrama (even tragedy), *Honor* and *Giuli* were much praised for their realistic portrayal of Armenian and Georgian life.[38] According to Khersonskii, *Honor* was distinguished by its immersion in the flesh of everyday life in Armenia. Neznamov also praised that film's ethnographic truth to life. Both reviewers, however, emphasized that the film's narrative and cinematic impact was not limited by its ethnographic impulse. Rather, ethnography provided the material, and the director turned that material into an artistic presentation of his own attitude to (and disapproval of) the "barbaric" customs of old Armenia. Using familiar terms, Neznamov praised the film's "good relationship with the material." In this he echoed Khersonskii, whose two reviews made the idea of the film's relationship with its material (Armenian everyday life) central to its value.

This phrase "relationship with the material" had considerable currency in the critical press in this period. We have discussed the importance of material in film theory and practice of the 1920s (see chapter 4). And we have seen how, for Shklovskii and others, film was increasingly envisaged as a means of creating a socialist relationship with the material. In discussions of films set in the national republics, this idea recurred with marked frequency. As Khersonskii said, "Our first Eastern films invited the spectator to take pleasure in the East. Its beauty, its steeds and its beautiful women, its views and its costumes. Not to love the living East, but to *take pleasure in it* [my emphasis]."[39]

In contrast, he claimed that *Honor* revealed its director's real love for "the new Armenia." This distinction—between an implicitly voyeuristic taking of pleasure, and an immersive, reciprocal love—attempts to distinguish the Soviet eye on the East from the Orientalist gaze of imperial Russia. But it also reveals the complexity of that project. Crucially, it did not mean that the visual and sensory pleasure of Armenian everyday life was denied. Neznamov noted that the film's ethnographic material was cinematographic, and that it "demands to be put on celluloid."[40] These reviews suggest, then, that the film seeks to reframe the visual pleasures of the Orientalist gaze.

A close reading of how the style of *Honor* makes a multisensory address to the spectator can help us to understand Khersonskii's attempted distinction. The film's domestic interiors (designed by the young Georgian artist Valerian Sidamon-Eristavi) feature symbols that recur in films set in any period, in any of the Soviet Union's republics. Susanna's father Barkhudar's home is hung with cloth, patterned and unpatterned; Rustam's home too is overwhelmed with decorative textile. In *Giuli* (also designed by Sidamon-Eristavi), the heroine is trapped in a world filled with women and children, and marked by patterned textile: mattresses are piled up, each in contrasting patterns; the competing designs of costume and décor are complemented by the textural complexity of a rough stone wall at the rear (figure 5.1).

Fig. 5.1 Ethnographic Detail. Still from *Giuli* (dir. L. Push, production design by V. Sidamon-Eristov, 1927).

Amid these cluttered, textured, and patterned settings, both films show their characters engaged in manual labor—sewing and potting, specifically. In *Honor*, Barkhudar is a tailor; Seiran's father, Airan, is a potter; and the opening sequences of the film dwell on the objects of their labor. White sheets of unpatterned textile hang about the tailor's home, amid the rich decorative materials of the domestic space. Airan's pots are large, pale, and smooth, piled up against a wooden staircase. The opposition between dense patterned textile and the smooth blank surfaces of pots and sheets gives a densely material quality to the screen; the spectator's multisensory experience implicitly mirrors the tactile relationship with the world that is the characters' way of life. In addition to these male crafts, the film makes an explicit link between femininity and tactile experience ("women's" work). Women bake bread, and the camera dwells on their hands rolling dough, patting and stretching it.

Ultimately, however, as in Preobrazhenskaia's picture of rural peasant life (see chapter 3), the embodied experience of traditional life offers sensory pleasure only to the spectator. Although these characters are engaged in acts

Fig. 5.2 The Weight of Textile. Still from *Honor* (*Namus*, dir. A. Bek-Nazarov, production design by V. Sidamon-Eristov, 1925).

of making, their making is not marked by the redemptive impulse discussed in chapter 4. Rather, in both *Honor* and *Giuli*, the space of female domesticity is one of suffocating textile, signifying entrapment and coercion. Susanna is usually shown draped in fabric, her face framed by a headdress decorated with metal coins that brush against her skin (figure 5.2). For the spectator, women are mere objects for contemplation, decoratively submerged within the film's surface faktura, and not subjects. They are, moreover, complicit in their own captivity: Giuli is forcibly led to Ali's marital bed by other women. After Susanna's brutal paternal beating, women gather to soothe her, but also to instill endurance with the chilling intertitle: "Our fathers beat us, too." In another scene, women sit and gossip about Susanna while they weave, and, as in *Women of Riazan Province*, the skein of thread unspooling is a visual metaphor for the thread of rumor that holds her captive.

Thus, *Honor* and *Giuli* set up a conscious tension between the pleasures and displeasures of the Orientalist gaze. They picture everyday life as enmeshed in and even suffocated by material; and this material provides cinematographic faktura. With their careful representation of lived reality, and their focus on handcraft, the films offer the (urban, Russian) spectator a sensory encounter with Eastern otherness. That faktura, however, is revealed as a source of deceptive allure. The films set out to trouble their sensory relationship with the "material" of the East, using the camera's ethnographic eye to reveal the brutal reality of patriarchal tradition. Here, violence is important: after being beaten by her father, Susanna is, literally, drained of vitality by leeches that are applied to her skin. As the camera dwells on the black leeches sucking on uncovered, unblemished white flesh, there is an uncomfortable sensuality (sexuality) in the spectatorial experience. The desire for the tactile pleasures of the Eastern life is revealed as potentially complicit in its violent tradition.

Revolutionary Sensations

Giuli and *Honor* were consistently singled out for praise and heralded as a new direction for films of the Soviet East, distinguished by their ethnographic eye. Similar terms were used to praise the first film by Shengelaia (who worked with Push on *Giuli*): *Eliso*, produced in Georgia in 1928. Beyond its ethnographic credentials, however, *Eliso* represents another key genre in early Soviet Eastern cinema (and cinema about the Soviet East), which retold the history of the region as a narrative of nascent revolutionary energy.[41] This film, with a screenplay adapted by Sergei Tret′iakov (from a story by Georgian writer Alexander Kazbegi), sought to combine crowd-pleasing love story and political narrative. According to Shengelaia, Tret′iakov's adaptation of the original work "transformed the subjective experiences of the heroes into social moments."[42] *Eliso* was well received, praised for its avoidance of "marmalade Eastern exoticism," and celebrated as a "new direction" for Goskinprom Gruzii.[43]

Set in 1864, *Eliso* tells the story of the forced resettlement of Muslim Chechens from the mountains of the North Caucasus. Chechens and Georgian Christian Khevsurs live peaceably side by side in mountaintop villages. But tsarist officers have a quota to fulfill and wish to appropriate arable lands, so the Chechen community is "banished," rendered homeless and nomadic. Alongside this ethnic-political narrative, the film tells of an impossible love between Chechen girl Eliso and Khevsur Georgian Vazhia. Although their romance is doomed by the gulf between their religions, it also serves to signal a political alliance that can be formed between Georgians and Chechens against their imperialist masters. Vazhia works to overturn the deportation order that is carrying Eliso away. He succeeds too late, but in his overcoming of ethnic allegiance the film envisages a future in which oppressed peoples unite against their common oppressors. Shklovskii interpreted the presentation of Vazhia the mountain man as "a type of Don Quixote, an individual of honor, standing up against the imperial politics of Tsarist Russia."[44] He is both protorevolutionary and primitive epic hero. This combination is important. Describing the "ethnographic mode of representing Georgian identity on screen," Dušan Radunović identifies characters who are "primal and sublime": "He (the Georgian hero) is libidinal, rather than cerebral; visceral, rather than class conscious; natural rather than ideological; familial and private rather than public."[45] *Eliso*'s characters cannot be understood within this simplified framework, however. Vazhia is at once primal and sublime (in Radunović's terms), and political and present. The libidinal and visceral are shown not as opposed to the revolutionary narrative, but as inextricably entwined with it.

In *Eliso*, Tret´iakov and Shengelaia were keen to avoid the false pleasures of exoticism and find a fresh perspective on the Caucasus.[46] The key focus of the film's camera is hardship. The banished Chechens become nomadic: they set up their tents in the middle of the mountain plains, and feed their babies amid the mud and debris of a life uprooted. The camera dwells on the physical realities of survival, and its gaze hovers uncomfortably between disgust and empathy, offering a close-up sensory experience sharply distinct from the visual pleasures of the exotic spectacle. Narrative and montage work together to transform this embodied empathy into protorevolutionary energy. In the plot, the Chechens' forced resettlement begins a process of radicalization that, it is implied, will lead to revolution. When a young mother falls ill and dies, a climactic montage intercuts grief, pain, and anger with shots emphasizing raw physicality and energy in the face of death. The village elder begins to dance (the traditional *lezginka*); as others join in, grief is transformed into a powerful release of latent power. Adrian Piotrovskii identified these final sequences as an example of what he called emotional cinema: "The collective, elemental grief explodes into (*vzryvaetsia*) the passionate, elemental dance of all the people together, amidst the clatter of tambourines, and the blaring of horns."[47]

This emotion is conveyed to the spectator as sensation. The silence of the film notwithstanding, this scene of dance, with its stamping feet and whirling bodies, provokes an affective response that, in turn, seeks to prompt action. Grief becomes rebellion; feeling becomes embodied action.

Shengelaia attributed the politicization of Kazbegi's novel to Sergei Tret´iakov's adaptation.[48] I suggest that Tret´iakov's influence on the film went beyond this, however, and into a particular treatment of filmic material. Tret′iakov had a longstanding interest in the East, and in the liberation of oppressed peoples. He had spent a long period in China (1924–1925) teaching at Peking University, and his articles on China had been widely published and discussed.[49] Tret′iakov was in Georgia from March to October 1927, together with Shklovskii, as a guest of the Georgian film studio.[50] There, in a public lecture about cinema, he praised Shengelaia and Push for their work on *Giuli*, but he noted that Georgian cinema still had some way to go in the search for a "new" film style.[51] Shklovskii was similarly provocative: "The work of Georgian directors will be successful if they are supported by real connections with local history, engineering, economics and botany."[52]

Tret′iakov's attitude to the "primitivism" of the Soviet Caucasus can be traced in articles written while he was in Tbilisi. He went on an expedition with Leo Esakiia to the isolated mountain region of Svanetiia, and published sketches recording his travels in the local newspaper *Dawn of the East*, as well as in *Pravda* and *Novyi LEF*.[53] In these essays, he consciously rejected the false orientalizing of prerevolutionary travel narratives and images of the Caucasus, seeking to construct a new traveling gaze. In an article of 1927, for example, he compared the romanticism of Lermontov's poem "The Novice" (set in the Dzhvary monastery), with the transformation of that space by the ZAGES hydroelectric power station: "ZAGES has taken Kura from the clutches of ethereal romantic poetry and brought it into the fold of down-to-earth Soviet prose."[54] In particular, Tret′iakov was uncompromising in his condemnation of the "god-forsaken middle ages" within which Svanetiia was trapped (see chapter 8), and wrote a screenplay for a film, *The Blind Girl* (*Slepaia*), which was produced (directed by the young Mikhail Kalatozov), but not completed or released.[55] In theme, *The Blind Girl* tells of its eponymous heroine, more or less imprisoned within her smoky, windowless home deep in Svanetiia, whose mistreatment at the hands of an abusive patriarchy serves as an uncompromising indictment of primitive society. Tret′iakov's other unrealized screenplays from this period echo *The Blind Girl* in this direct criticism of patriarchal tradition.[56] *Eliso*, however—the first film that he actually brought to completion in this early period—indicates a more complex relationship with the sensory pleasures of the exotic East.

Edward Tyerman offers an excellent reading of Tret′iakov's engagement with China as part of a quest for an internationalist (or anti-imperial) aesthetics: a way of representing knowledge of the oriental "other," while avoiding the pitfalls of orientalism and exotic pleasure. This mode would reflect the "superior knowledge produced by Marxist tools of analysis," while still maintaining an "aesthetic appeal to the senses."⁵⁷ Here, Tyerman identifies an ambivalence that was inherent to the theory and practice of Tret′iakov's "factography." For all its emphasis on real material, it sought to present a so-called reality (of socialist transformation) that was more vivid than fantasy. Tyerman identifies a simultaneous "discourse of sobriety" (the refusal of exotic pleasure in favor of fact-based, ethnographic study), and a "discourse of rapture" in cultural representations of China in this period, suggesting that the "discourse of sobriety is never entirely free from the inspirational, intoxicating urges that mark the discourse of rapture."⁵⁸ This distinction helps us to consider the intense sensory encounter between the spectator and the material of the Caucasus that we can trace in *Eliso*—and, I argue, in the broader context of representations of the Soviet East. It captures the complex intertwining of condemnation and pleasure, disgust and delight, in Tret′iakov's ethnographic gaze: the attempt to transform the orientalizing gaze of rapture into a new model of sensory pleasure, appropriate to the Soviet modernizing project. Tret′iakov's stated purpose in working with the Georgian film studio was to ensure that its narratives be enmeshed in real life: in work, sleep, production, play. The plot should not dictate the material, but rather real material should create the plot.⁵⁹ This is the ABC of factography, of course. But it can also be considered in relation to the shifting meaning of material in this period. Writing about his experience in China, Tret′iakov envisaged his factographic writing as a means of knowing the real China. This knowledge was made possible by the particular, embodied form of seeing afforded by travel. It was knowledge gathered by feeling by hand (*naoshchup′*).⁶⁰

This term, "naoshchup′," is important in describing a multisensory, embodied form of knowledge (explicitly distinguished from what Tret′iakov called schematic knowledge). It echoes the tacit-tactile knowledge that we have identified as available to the deaf-mute shoemaker Kirik in Ermler's *The Parisian Cobbler* (see chapter 4), but gives it additional cinematic inflection. To discover something naoshchup′ is an embodied, active and participatory form of perception. It suggests an unmediated encounter with material: the viewing self enters the material, and *feels* his/her way around it. In terms that directly anticipate later theories of haptic cinema, Tret′iakov suggested that this tactile encounter is achieved by an "intent gaze" (or close-up; the Russian term *pristal′nyi* carries both meanings). The eye operates as an organ of touch, allowing a new kind of (affectionate) knowledge. At first glance, this tactile close-up appears counter to Tret′iakov's better-known statements on perception. In "Through Unwiped Glasses" (1928), for example, analyzing the power of the aerial gaze, he presented an apparently opposite view: that the view from above enabled a knowledge that could see beyond surface detail and stereotypes in order to reveal the processes that underlie reality.[61] Here, in contrast to the extreme proximity of (haptic) knowledge naoshchup', it is distance that permits a new understanding.

For all their apparent difference, both of these perspectives shared the same goal—and one that we recognize as central to the Soviet avant-garde project: to see the world in new ways. Attention to knowledge naoshchup', however, reveals the embodied, sensory dimension of this project that is too often overlooked. It was premised on a close, reciprocal relationship between the human subject and the material world. In *Eliso*, the close-up ethnographic eye turns the exotic into fact, and reveals the material basis of the lived reality of the ethnic other. For the spectator, an intensely physical encounter with the characters' visceral degradation and suffering acts as a surrogate for sensory pleasure; the camera provokes an embodied "knowledge naoshchup'"—a knowledge that, in Tret'iakov's terms, penetrates to the deeper level of reality. It mobilizes the potential of disgust in order to access sensory empathy.

Primitive Senses

In its anti-imperialist narrative, *Eliso* had elements in common with Bek-Nazarov's *Khaz-Push*, produced for Armenkino and premiering just a few months before *Eliso* in 1927. This film was set in Persia in 1871 and told the true story of the Khaz-push rebel group of peasants and craftsmen, who unite against a monopoly given by the Iranian shah to English merchants for the trade in tobacco. Thus the narrative dynamic is provided, as Zhemchuzhnyi noted, not by a love story, but by the politicization of a starving working class, "and the key figures in this battle are not individual heroes but whole social groups."[62] The East is revealed as "an arena of intense struggle between different imperial forces." Zhemchuzhnyi criticized previous Eastern films as "showing us only the cheap, sugary exotic of the East, and forgetting that beneath this external decorative 'picturesque' flows another life—the degraded life of the Eastern peasant and worker."[63]

Khaz-Push was advertised as the "first artistic-ethnographic film about Persian life"—and this curious combination of terms (artistic-ethnographic) speaks to the complex ambitions shared by many films of this period.[64] In this film, one version of decorative oriental faktura is explicitly revealed as a false surface, masking repressive imperialist politics. Extravagant pavilion sets reproduce the towering vertical spaces of imperial

Fig. 5.3 Surface Pleasure. Still from *Khaz-Push* (dir. A. Bek-Nazarov, production design by M. Arutchian, 1928).

Tehran. The palace of the shah is marked by carefully constructed depth of field (ornate, shaped panels, doors, and windows), and embellished by carpets and patterns (figure 5.3). These spaces are marked, however, by stasis—flattened into mere surface by excess of decoration. As the film progresses, the shah's world is revealed to be in league with the British Empire, enmeshed in Western bourgeois values: its oriental decorativeness is thus revealed as pure simulacrum.

The real faktura of the film is located elsewhere—in the market square (the caravanserai) that is the world of the Khaz-push. Here the visual and textural pleasures of the Orient are still evident, but in contrast to the artifice of the palace, there is an emphasis on authentic life, and a focus on sensory intensity. Camels cross the screen, heavily loaded. Carpets are draped behind stalls selling different wares (figure 5.4). Bundles of tightly packed tobacco leaves create the surface texture of the screen and acquire sensory immediacy when a single leaf is removed, pressed to a nose, and inhaled. A man's head is shaved in the public square. The announcement of the new

Fig. 5.4 Authentic Life. Stills from *Khaz-Push* (dir. A. Bek-Nazarov, production design by M. Arutchian, 1928).

Fig. 5.4 (*Continued*).

trade monopoly brings an abrupt end to this vitality, however. Thereafter, the spectator's "pleasure-taking" gaze is transformed into one of empathy, discovering growing hunger and hardship—uncovering the reality of peasant life. Here, as in *Eliso*, the discourse of rapture shades into one of degradation. Scenes of growing hunger directly reprise earlier images of sensory excess, but as deprivation. A shot of a pile of watermelons contrasts the shiny surface of the fruit with the tattered rags of peasants' clothes, children bite desperately into watermelon skin, and shovel up handfuls of dropped flour. They eat seeds crawling with insects. For the spectator, disgust becomes a surrogate for sensual pleasure. Here cinematic faktura plays a different role: the world of the Khaz-push is marked by a textural density that is in striking contrast to the smooth surfaces of imperial power. The irregular, crumbling stone of the mosque walls and deserted market place frames the growing desperation of the rebels.

As in *Honor* and *Giuli*, an emphasis on handcrafts is evident in this film, but here it has more political significance. The rebellion is fomented by craftsmen. The camera watches closely as the hands of a potter mold clay on a potting wheel (figure 5.5). As metal workers bang steel, a shoemaker nails

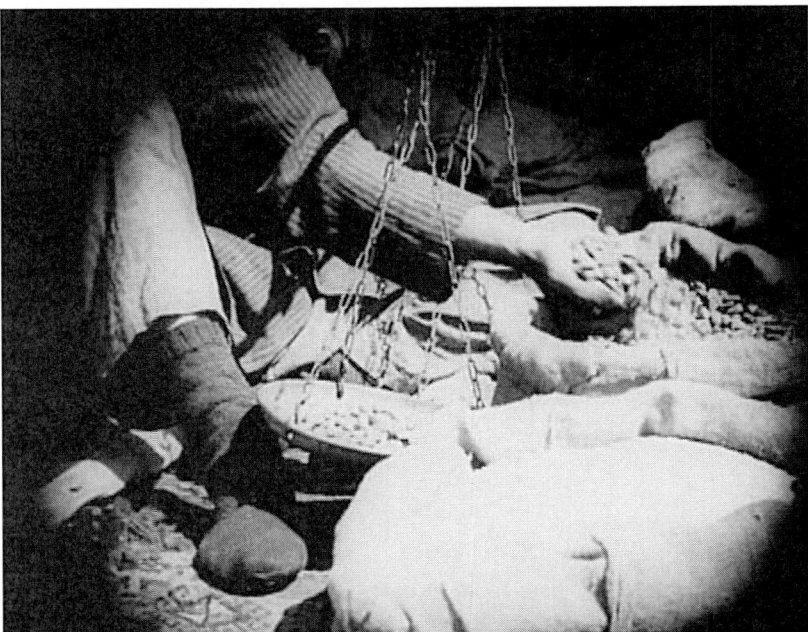

Fig. 5.5 Primitive Senses. Stills from *Khaz-Push* (dir. A. Bek-Nazarov, production design by M. Arutchian, 1928).

Fig. 5.5 (*Continued*).

a metal circle onto the heel of shoes, and tobacco traders touch, sniff and roll tobacco in a series of vivid images. Like the shoemakers and carpenters of chapter 4, these people are "makers." And their proximate relationship with their tools and materials is presented as a precondition for their politicization. As the rebels join forces with political prisoners of the colonial regime, their energized bodies are affiliated with the degraded bodies of the prisoners in a metaphoric exchange that transforms suffering into potential power. Like *Eliso*, then, *Khaz-Push* appropriated negative images that might otherwise signify only the poverty and backwardness of Central Asia (to be overcome) to convey the energy and vitality of the East (to be harnessed). This energy is, the films suggest, intrinsically revolutionary. It is conveyed to the spectator as sensory knowledge—in Tret´iakov's terms, knowledge naoshchup´—through intensified participation in the experience of hardship. The visceral disgust created by these images of abjection acts as a physical form of address: a stimulus to new, Soviet *feeling*. Picturing extreme physical endurance and suffering, the films write their message of rebellion onto the body of the spectator, in an intensified awareness of material life.

Primitive Mimesis

In *Khaz-Push*, texture is the privilege of the underclass: imperial power is presented as a world of hard surfaces, and the revolutionary potential of "primitive" experience lies in embodied intensity. A similar emphasis can be found in one of Soviet cinema's best-known narratives of Eastern revolutionary spirit: Vsevolod Pudovkin's *Storm over Asia* (*Potomok Chingis-Khana*, 1927). This film has been subject to much scholarly analysis.[65] For my purposes, however, it is relevant for its explicit inquiry into the relationship between the film eye and an imagined primitive sensibility. The film tells a story of Bair, a young nomad fur trader who stands up to an English merchant in the trading of a valuable fur pelt, and so puts himself in danger. He finds refuge amid the Soviet partisans, with whom he travels a path to political consciousness, before being captured and sentenced to death by an occupying English army.

According to his memoirs, Pudovkin set out in this film to avoid a decorative orientalism in his presentation of Mongolia: "Mongolia itself . . . will be shown not according to a decorative, ethnographic focus on objects (*predmetnost´*), but through the sensory prism of a (single) man, his emotional experiences, and this perception of existing forms of life and customs."[66]

Pudovkin's emphasis on sensations as opposed to objects here is revealing, for *Storm over Asia* is in many ways a film about things, and relationships with things. The different civilizations that confront one another in the film are symbolized by their different sensory relationships with the material world—and with fur in particular. Fur is implicitly misused and mishandled by capitalism. The film suggests that capitalist commodity relationship involves a lack of connection with the concrete materiality of the object. Although both capitalists and nomad traders are shown appreciating the luxurious weight of a wolf pelt, the cinematography suggests that for the capitalist body, the fur is ornament; for the native body, by contrast, fur is felt through the senses. This is a relationship of reciprocity between human and material. Notably, such appreciation is articulated through touch: they caress and stroke it. The spectator too is encouraged into this tactile relationship: in one particularly striking sequence, the camera dwells in extended close-up on the faktura of Bair's magnificent silver fox pelt, and the minute vibrations of its individually glistening strands (figure 5.6).[67] For the primitive sensibility, then, the fur is almost a living, animate thing, and exists in a heightened sensory relationship with the human body. When Bair is tricked out of his pelt by the capitalist, the betrayal goes beyond the merely financial; it signals the dominance of the wrong system of values.

We can think about the powerful physicality of these scenes of Bair and the fur in terms of the discourse of rapture discussed above. The knowledge that Bair and his fellows have of the object world comes from touch (naoshchup'). This is a knowledge that the film presents as particular to the primitive body. Anthropologist Michael Taussig's concept of "primitive mimesis" is useful here. For Taussig, primitive mimesis is a form of bodily knowledge of the object that was particular to ancient societies.[68] Mimetic behavior is premised on a reciprocal relationship with the world, rather than one of domination and human control over nature. In a mimetic relationship, the human body is immersed into the concreteness of the object in what Taussig calls an "active yielding." Taussig makes an explicit link between primitive mimesis and Marx's vision of how a socialist "emancipation" of the senses might create not only new bodies, but also new "human" objects. He understands Marx's thesis as a modern form of animism, envisaging a coproductive relationship between the human and object worlds.[69]

In *Storm over Asia*, the animate relationship between the primitive body and the object world is contrasted to the sterile world of surfaces that defines

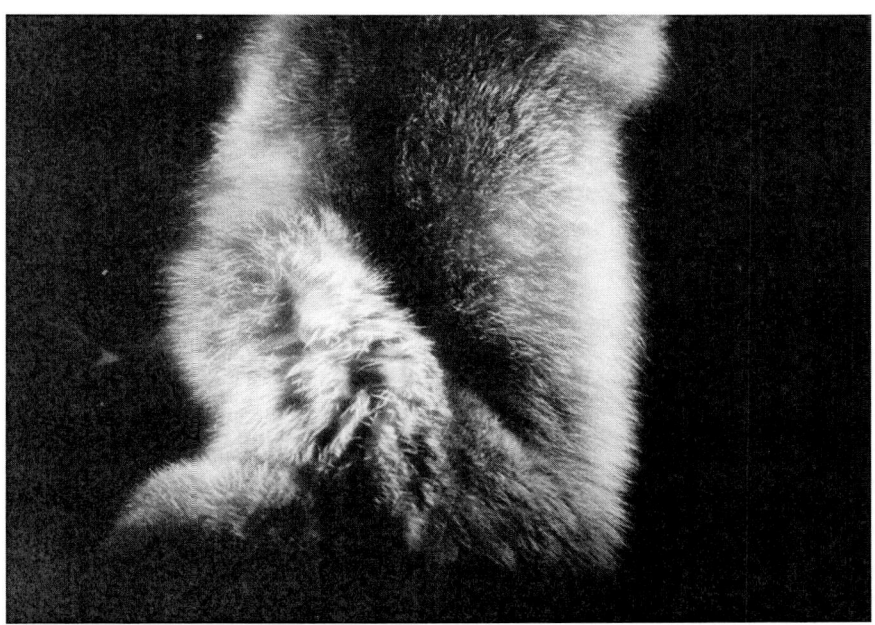

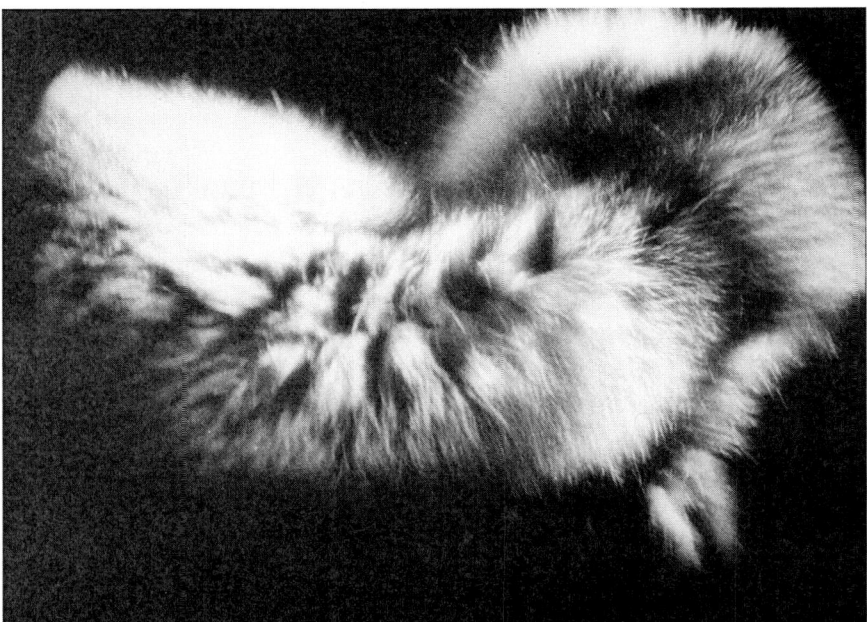

Fig. 5.6 The Faktura of Fur. Stills from *Storm over Asia* (*Potomok Chingiz-Khana*, dir. V. Pudovkin, production design by M. Aronson, S. Kozlovskii, 1928).

Fig. 5.6 (*Continued*).

the capitalist world of the commodity. A striking montage of objects signals the excess of capitalism: rows of shoes, crystal bottles and necklaces, polished shoes, and gloves are woven into a sequence alongside a man shaving, and a woman dressing her hair, tying her corset, and powdering her skin. Pudovkin's montage of objects bears evidence of the influence of concepts of photogénie, but given ideological framing. Falseness is presented as a preoccupation with surface (the capitalist object); this is a fetishistic attitude to the world, which Taussig describes (following Marx) as a "banking" mode: the appropriation of the object as possession.[70] By contrast, Bair represents an embodied, mimetic, fully sensuous, encounter with the object. His is a relationship of reciprocity and not ownership. In these terms, the film presents him as a revolutionary model. Perhaps, in Taussig's terms, Pudovkin asks what a postcapitalist animism might look like?[71]

Storm over Asia is not simplistic in its equation of Easternness with imagined authenticity, however. Its ethnographic eye on the traditional culture of Mongolia does not lack ironic commentary.[72] In one scene, parallel montage makes explicit connections between the preparation of lamas for a religious ceremony and the elaborate coiffure of a British officer and his wife. During the ensuing Buddhist feast and ceremony, the camera dwells at length on the masks and rituals. Like Eisenstein's famous sequence in *October* (1928), which aligns the symbols of Western and Eastern religion alongside the trappings of imperial power in a deconstructive montage, *Storm over Asia* reveals the Buddhist ceremony as *false* ritual, with little of value to distinguish it from the surface decorations of capitalism. The film even mounts a direct critique on the artificial, manufactured exoticism of the Eastern other when, after Bair's near death, the army discovers an amulet that suggests he is a direct descendant of Genghis Khan, and they attempt to stitch him back together, to create a simulacrum, a *fake* Mongolian, as head of a puppet regime. Thus Bair is essentially turned into a facsimile of himself.[73] This "false" primitive cannot be held together, however. The end of the film sees the rebellion of the authentic primitive body, an assertion of a primal (and protorevolutionary) force that cannot be contained: Bair escapes, and the concluding montage sees him and his people galloping headlong across the steppe, swords raised, as the wind swirls around them. Thus a refashioned Mongol primitivism emerges in the film as a true symbol of revolution.

Graphical Thinking

This ending in *Storm over Asia* simplifies—but cannot resolve—a tension central to the complex life of the "Soviet primitive": between the idea of revolutionary order and elemental (primitive) chaos, control, and energy. As an attempt to explore the particular physical and psychological make-up of "primitive" man, however, and its place in the Soviet utopia, *Storm over Asia* was part of a wider context that had its roots in imperial Russia.

Ethnopathology (the classification of race according to particular physical pathologies) was a core element of late tsarist imperial discourse, and such studies continued after the revolution.[74] In the Soviet context, however, scientific interest in "primitive" peoples was complicated by ideological factors. The challenge for ethnographers was to adapt their research to this new discourse; primitive societies were to be viewed as part of an evolutionary model of cultural development.[75] The question of race was broadly replaced with that of class, and that of ethnic essentialism (pathology) by the Marxist doctrine of historical development. Within this overarching framework, however, there were subtle permutations on the theme of backwardness. According to Marxist historical theories, the ethnic "other" could be reimagined as a survival of "primitive communism"—as the as-yet-undeveloped child who would mature into developed communist man. Vera Tolz and Yuri Slezkine discuss the interest, shared by some Soviet Orientalist scholars, in such survivals of primitive forms.[76] The controversial linguist Nikolai Marr is a particularly pertinent example: Marr stressed the "civilizational greatness" of the Islamic minorities in the Caucasus, and was particularly interested in illiterate cultures. Claiming to have uncovered the roots of a shared protolanguage for the peoples of the East, he conceived a new Japhetic world language, which would overcome national and class differences.[77]

Marr's theories are some of the most extreme of a wider range of scholarly endeavors: during the early Soviet period, ethnography, pathology, and pedology came together in their ambition to examine, to catalog (and even to weigh and measure) "primitive" man.[78] During the second half of the 1920s in particular, there was a developing interest in how psychological research might be carried out in order to understand the "primitive" mind. A number of expeditions by teams of psychologists to the Soviet Far East and the Caucasus took place at the beginning of the first Five-Year Plan.[79] Perhaps the best known of them are the two expeditions led by Aleksandr Luriia in Uzbekistan, with the long-distance collaboration of Lev Vygotskii.

The complex and contradictory aims of these Uzbekistan expeditions reflect the tension at the heart of the Bolshevik project—between a materialist interest in how (wo)man is shaped by environment, and desire to reshape her. In 1930, Vygotskii and Luriia published a scientific volume, *Ape, Primitive Man, and Child*, in which they concluded that "a psychology of primitive man has not yet been created."[80] The primary aim of the Uzbek expeditions in 1931 and 1932 was to write that psychology.[81] They sought to explore the mental frameworks of illiterate people, in an attempt to access prelinguistic patterns of thinking. They also aimed, however, to prove a core Marxist hypothesis: that human consciousness was "a product of sociohistorical development," and that the human mind evolves in relation to the social and material environment.[82] The rapid modernization of Central Asia under Bolshevik rule had created particularly favorable conditions in which to study the impact of sociohistorical change on "psychological outlook": in Uzbekistan in 1930 it would be possible to "observe both underdeveloped illiterate groups (living in villages) and groups already involved in modern life, experiencing the first influences of the social realignment."[83] Vygotskii and Luriia were not free of Soviet ideological purpose, however. The Uzbek expeditions had a final additional aim: to *prove* the positive development of consciousness that accompanied the socialist transformation of Uzbekistan.[84]

For all these contradictory ambitions, the Uzbek expeditions were premised on scientific interest in the "primitive" mind. Luriia and Vygotskii operated with the hypothesis that Central Asian native people would have a "primarily graphical reflection of reality."[85] That is, they would think in images. Such a view was commonly expressed by Bolshevik ideologues when discussing the power of visual material in spreading propaganda to the East.[86] In part, the Uzbek project was an attempt to test this hypothesis. And in broad terms, its findings did claim to prove that illiterate "primitive" peoples did have a "graphical-functional" (or "graphical-concrete") reflection of reality, which revealed "a different system of mental process from people with a predominantly abstract, verbal and logical approach to reality."[87] That is, they understood and categorized objects in terms of use in everyday life—as they were *handled* and lived.[88]

The conception of graphical thinking that was central to the Uzbek expedition was closely linked to the theory of eidetic memory that, in *Ape, Primitive Man and Child*, Luriia and Vygotskii found to be characteristic of "primitive" man: "The primitive memory is at once very accurate and very emotional. It retains representations with a great abundance of detail, and always in exactly the same order in which they are really connected to each other."[89] The perception of the object is directly linked with *embodied* memory of its use. Reporting how subjects categorized objects and shapes during experiments with respondents in Uzbekistan, Luriia noted that their graphic recall made direct links with objects as *used* in day-to-day activities. Real-life relations between the subject and the object world provide the structuring basis for perception.

In framing the purposes of his expedition, Luriia cited French anthropologist Lucien Lévy-Bruhl, who had described "primitive thought" as "pre-logical."[90] In Luriia's words, Lévy-Bruhl "believed that primitive thought was magical, reflecting the belief systems and primitive magic rather than the practical relations between human beings and reality."[91] Although accepting the general premise of primitive thought, Luriia challenged Lévy-Bruhl's understanding of such thought as magical. The Uzbek expeditions set out to provide a more ideologically appropriate version of "primitive" thinking—one that emerged directly out of "practical relations between human beings and reality." That is, it is the product of the kind of close relationship (reciprocity) between man and material that we have identified as central to the concept of craft, and making (homo faber). Bodies and things were central here to the ideological framing of a new, Soviet primitive.

Here, a return to Taussig's conception of primitive mimesis is instructive. Mimesis opens up a seam of communication between the self and the other, and the self and the world. At the core of mimesis, according to Taussig, is "a palpable, sensuous connection between the very body of the perceiver and the perceived."[92] Taussig's thesis finds a powerful echo in the theories of Sergei Eisenstein. Eisenstein's interest in premodern thought is well known: we have already quoted his 1944 statement that the role of film is to return human perception to a primordial stage of sensory thinking. Although it was in the later work *Method* that Eisenstein's most sophisticated statement of the relationship between cinema and primitive or sensual/sensory thinking was elaborated, he was preoccupied throughout his life by the relationship between what Kleiman has called the "rationally-logical" and the "sensuous" in a work of art—in its structure, and in the process of perception.[93]

Eisenstein had close personal and professional connections with both Vygotskii and Luriia, and was very much aware of their work from the mid-1920s on.[94] Indeed, Bulgakowa claims that Eisenstein was invited to participate in the Uzbek expeditions. He was also professionally linked to Nikolai Marr. While in France in 1930, Eisenstein read Lévy-Bruhl's *Primitive Mentality* and relished that text's theory of pre- (or proto-) logical *sensuous* thinking.[95] In Mexico, he became directly interested in the relationship between cinema and ethnography; and the direct experience of life in Mexico played a key role in the evolution of his conception of sensuous thought. Returning to Russia in 1932, Eisenstein claims to have set up a working group, together with Luriia, Vygotskii, and Marr, which planned to study systematically "the problems of the developing film language."[96] Little is known about the research actually undertaken by this group (which was cut short by the deaths of Vygotskii and Marr in 1934 and 1935, respectively), but it is clear that a shared interest in primitive thought would have been part of the agenda.

It is not my purpose to make a new contribution to studies of Eisenstein's theoretical work, but it is notable that the model of sensuous thinking had much in common with the conception of primitive mimesis as embodied knowledge. It points to a shared sense of the power of cinema in Soviet culture's particular version of primitive mimesis: the search for a new relationship between human and world. In the essay "Imitation as Mastery" (which may have formed the basis for a talk given at La Sarraz as early as 1929), Eisenstein affirmed that the purpose of film must be to reveal not the external appearance of an object, but its inner essence: "The age of form is drawing to a close. We are penetrating matter. We are penetrating behind appearance to the principle of appearance."[97] The task of film, then—and its unique potential—was to represent not the thing but *knowledge of the thing*. This "knowledge," however, was rooted in the senses. Iampolski finds evidence of how Eisenstein understood this knowledge in an unpublished note in Eisenstein's archives: "To 'think' in a completely deintellectualized fashion: by tracing the contours of objects with our eyes."[98] In Iampolski's words, for Eisenstein: "The initial stage of the creation of meaning depends on the *intuitively magic* [my italics] physiognomic disclosure of the line which lies concealed within the body of the object."[99] It is this knowledge that is intuitively available in primitive mimesis. In a direct echo of Luriia's description of the graphical-functional thinking that was observed in the Uzbek expedition, Eisenstein described it as the ability to "represent [things] to ourselves graphically."[100] For Eisenstein, this was a foundational principle in the theory of cinematic representation that took shape in *Method*: the sensory experience of the body is a prior condition for the creation of meaning.

Tactile Knowledge?

In this chapter, we have undertaken a several-stop journey through Soviet cultural primitivism: from the ethnographic eye of cinema of the 1920s, and its attempt to reframe the pleasures of the East as a multisensory encounter with material of "primitive" life, through Sergei Tret´iakov's search for an embodied form of knowledge of the world, to Pudovkin and Eisenstein's very different conceptions of primitive mimesis. We have revealed that Eisenstein's thinking on sensuous perception—although undoubtedly emerging out of his own unique intellectual and creative preoccupations—was also firmly part of a wider sociopolitical context.

Much of this chapter has been as concerned with the category of manual labor as chapter 4. But here we have been focusing on the manual labor of "primitive" societies—on its relationship with hardship and endurance, but also on the intuitive relationship between man and material that it was seen to enable. Here, too, I have identified the importance of tactile experience as the core of a possible model for revolutionary subjectivity. Hands mattered. And primitive hands were of particular interest. In 1892, anthropologist Frank Cushing (who certainly influenced Lévy-Bruhl who, in turn, influenced Eisenstein and other of our protagonists[101]) wrote an essay with the suggestive title "Manual Concepts." Cushing's purpose was "to suggest that the hand of man has been so intimately associated with the mind of man that it has moulded intangible thoughts no less than the tangible products of his brain."[102]

For many, this notion of tacit-tactile knowledge represented a possible way out of the social, intellectual (and sensory) dead end that capitalism had brought to pass. It was not inimical to modern technology, however. It could even be enabled by it: film could be a modern form of touching. In Benjamin's famous formulation, film made it possible "to get hold of an object at very close range by way of its likeness."[103] Similarly, Tret´iakov's knowledge *naoshchup´* was available not only to the traveler, but also to the lens of the camera. These visions of a close relationship between human and material worlds echo the reciprocal model described as primitive mimesis. It was for that reason that the embodied lives of "primitive" peoples held such interest in Soviet Russia of the 1920s. In Taussig's words: "Might not the mimetic faculty and the sensuous knowledge it embodies be precisely this hard-to-imagine state wherein 'the senses therefore become directly in their practice theoreticians' [Marx]."[104]

NOTES

1. Clifford, "On Ethnographic Surrealism," 542.
2. Ibid. Clifford is referring to the confluence between surrealism and the development of ethnography.
3. This chapter will consider the Caucasus and Central Asia as a linked category in the Soviet East, as the differences were often elided in the contemporary press.
4. Said, *Orientalism*.
5. Notable publications here include Knight, "Grigor´ev in Orenburg"; Layton, *Russian Literature and Empire*; Schimmelpenninck van der Oye, *Russian Orientalism*; Etkind, *Internal Colonization*; Khalid, "Russian History and the Debate over Orientalism"; Knight, "On Russian Orientalism:"; Todorova, "Does Russian Orientalism Have a Russian Soul?" These and other articles from *Kritika* relating to orientalism were republished in David-Fox, Holquist, and Martin, eds., *Orientalism and Empire in Russia*.
6. Tolz, *Russia's Own Orient*.
7. See, for example, Hirsch, *Empire of Nations*. Khalid has claimed that it is inappropriate to think about the Soviet Union as an imperial organization, and that it is better understood as a mobilizing state, like Kemalist Turkey. Khalid, "Backwardness and the Quest for Civilization."
8. Northrop, *Veiled Empire*, 39.
9. Sharp, *Russian Modernism between East and West*, provides an excellent account of the importance of this idea.

10. Michael Kunichika is one of several scholars who have addressed the potent image of the Scythian. He presents a nuanced account of the relationship between the primitive and the modern in Russian modernism: Kunichika, *Our Native Antiquity* (especially chapter 6).

11. Miller, "Primitive Art," 38.

12. Riddell, *To See the Dawn*. See also *Congress of the Peoples of the East*.

13. For discussion of Marx and Engels' theories of primitive communism (and their relation to Leninism), see Gandy, *Marx and History*.

14. See Ertürk, "Baku, Literary Common."

15. This concept is explored in detail in Kunichika, *How Soon is Now*.

16. See Tyerman, "The Search for Internationalist Aesthetics"; Ertürk, "Toward a Literary Communism"; Khomitsky, "World Literature, Soviet Style." For an overview of current research into the international dimensions of Soviet Communism, see Ertürk, "Baku, Literary Common." Of course, the "Eurasian" movement (exemplified in the works of Nikolai Trubetskoi and Lev Gumilev) provides a clear example. See Bassin, "Classical Eurasianism"; Laruelle, *L'idéologie eurasiste russe*. It is notable that the particular nations of Soviet Central Asia were not differentiated in the Eurasian vision of space, which, as Katherine Holt notes, occluded geographical boundaries. See Holt, "The Rise of Insider Iconography," 39.

17. Slezkine, *Arctic Mirrors*, 127. Slezkine argues, however, that the appeal of primitive communism was decisively rejected in favor of the enlightening vision of conquering "backwardness" in Soviet nationalities policy by 1929–1930. Slezkine, 188–93.

18. Kunichika, "'The Ecstasy of Breadth,'" 66.

19. See Widdis, *Visions of a New Land*. See also Sarkisova, *Screening Soviet Nationalities*.

20. For the first account of the cinema of the republics, see Lebedev, *Ocherki istorii sovetskogo kino*. See also the range of essays in Rouland, Abikeyeva, and Beumers, eds., *Cinema in Central Asia*, and Michael G. Smith, "Cinema for the 'Soviet East.'"

21. Rouland, "An Historical Introduction," 4.

22. According to Shoshanna Keller, the film was shot entirely in Leningrad. See her *To Moscow, Not Mecca*, 100–101.

23. Michael G. Smith, "Cinema for the 'Soviet East,'" 652; Holt suggests that the film's high popularity in Uzbekistan "may be linked to the fact that it was one of the first films to depict the Soviet East at all." Holt, "The Rise of Insider Iconography," 46.

24. Bassalygo's *The Muslim Woman* (*Musul'manka*, 1925), Doronin's *The Second Wife* (*Vtoraia zhena*, 1927), and Averbakh's *The Veil* (*Chadra*, 1927) are further examples of this genre. Averbakh began his career in cinema in Kuleshov's studio, and produced *In the Big City*, co-directed with Mark Donskoi, in the same year as *The Veil* (See chapter 6).

25. Skachko, "Kino dlia vostoka," 4. For a retrospective view, see Amo Bek-Nazarov, "Natsional'noe kino v SSSR."

26. Bartenev, "Kino v srednei Azii," 5.

27. Skachko, "Kino dlia vostoka," 3.

28. Chomentowski, "Vostokkino," 34.

29. Ibid., 41–43.

30. Ibid., 35.

31. See, for example, Michael G. Smith, "Cinema for the 'Soviet East.'"

32. For further information see, for example, Kuleshov and Khokhlova, *50 let v kino*, 118. In Georgia, the team had considerable interaction with the established Georgian

avant-garde. Mikhail Kalatozov (Kalatozishvili) was himself Georgian. More broadly, interactions between the Georgian avant-garde and the Soviet avant-garde were particularly fertile through this period. Vladimir Maiakovskii, himself born in Georgia, traveled often to Tbilisi. Leo Esakiia (see chapter 4) contributed to LEF discussions, and published his own essays in *Novyi LEF* in the role of Tbilisi correspondent. Leo Esakiia, "Levoe dvizhenie v iskusstve Gruzii." See also Ram, "Futurist Geographies."

33. Ratiani, *U istokov gruzinskogo kino*, 103.

34. Chomentowski, "Vostokkino,"39.

35. For a revealing account of this kind of mobility, see Makovskii, "Put' na Vostok," especially 111–21. Makovskii recalls professional interaction in Baku with Leo Mur, Sergei Eisenstein, Iakov Protazanov, Ivan Perestiani, Vsevolod Pudovkin, and Igor' Savchenko, among others.

36. Nikolai Aseev, for example, recounts an expedition to Siberia and Altai, telling of time spent with Tret'iakov, Burliuk and Chuzhak, and the establishment of a newspaper in Vladivostok. See Nikolai Aseev, "Oktiabr' v Dal'nem."

37. Tan, "Pervaia armianskaia kartina," 5.

38. See Anon., "Novosti prokata," 3; Khersonskii's two articles on *Namus*; Neznamov, "Khoroshoe otnoshenie k Armenii"; Tret'iakov, "Sem' smertnykh grekhov," 147.

39. Khersonskii, "Namus," 29.

40. Neznamov, "Khoroshoe otnoshenie k Armenii," 3.

41. Several films about the rebellions of Caucasian/Eastern peoples were released in 1926: *Natella* (Bek-Nazarov), about Georgians; *Zare* (Bek-Nazarov), about Kurds; *Dina Dza-Dzu* (Zheliabuzhskii), about Caucasian mountain peoples

42. Shengelaia, "Nado rabotat' druzhno," 5.

43. Vaks, "V obshchestve druzei," 5; Shneider, "Eliso," 5.

44. Shklovskii, "Veter iz Tiflisa," 2.

45. Radunović, "Incommensurable distance," 56.

46. Vaks, "V obshchestve druzei," 5.

47. Piotrovskii, "Khudozhestvennye techeniia v sovetskom kino," 248.

48. Shengelaia, "Nado rabotat' druzhno," 5.

49. Tyerman, "The Search for Internationalist Aesthetics," especially 17–26. Tret'iakov's play, *Roar, China!* (*Rychi, Kitai*) was produced in 1926.

50. Ratiani, ed., *Sergei Mikhailovich Tret'iakov*, 19. Tret'iakov's articles about China continued to be published in *Novyi LEF* through 1927, while he was in Georgia. Shklovskii also published from Georgia in this period: Shklovskii, "60 dnei bez sluzhby," *Novyi LEF* 1927, 6: 17–32; Shklovskii, "Veter iz Tiflisa."

51. Tret'iakov, "Sem' smertnykh grekhov," 145–47.

52. Shklovskii, "Veter iz Tiflisa," 2.

53. Tret'iakov, "Shest' millionov let," 2; "Tri zapora (poezdka v Svanetiiu)," 3.

54. Tret'iakov, "Mtsyri," 150. ZAGES is an acronym for the Zemo-Avchal'skaia Hydroelectric Power station.

55. Ratiani, ed., *Sergei Mikhailovich Tret'iakov*, 336. The screenplay for *The Blind Girl* is published in Ibid., 220–43.

56. For discussion of screenplays that were actually written, and those that were planned, see ibid., 22–23, and Ratiani, *U istokov gruzinskogo kino*, 102–4.

57. Tyerman, "The Search for Internationalist Aesthetics," 17.

58. Ibid, 37. Tyerman derives his categories from Bill Nichols's *Introduction to Documentary*, 36–38.
59. Tret´iakov, "Tekushchie dela," 87–88.
60. Tret´iakov, "Liubit´ Kitai," 10, cited in Tyerman, 19.
61. Tret´iakov, "Skvoz´ neprotertye ochki."
62. Zhemchuzhnyi, "Khaz-Push," 3.
63. Ibid.
64. Anon., advertisement for *Khaz-Push*, *Kino*.
65. See, for example, Karaganov, "Potomok Chingis-khana"; Sargeant, *Storm over Asia and Vsevolod Pudovkin*. See also Sergei Kapterev's excellent commentary on the Hyperkino DVD: *Vsevolod Pudovkin: The Heir to Genghis Khan / Storm Over Asia. 1928*. RUSCICO 2011. For interesting contemporary criticism on Pudovkin, see in particular Iezuitov, *Pudovkin*.
66. Pudovkin, "Potomok Chingis-khana," 60.
67. In 1935, the journal *USSR in Construction* dedicated an issue to fur production, guest edited by Mikhail Prishvin. The cover and inside cover of the issue offered close-up images of the faktura of fur itself. See *SSSR na stroike* 1935, 10. For discussion, see Reischl, "An Exercise with Photographic Literacy."
68. Taussig draws largely on Walter Benjamin's theories of mimesis: "On the Mimetic Faculty." See also Buck-Morss, *Dialectics of Seeing*, 260–5.
69. Taussig, *Mimesis and Alterity*, 36, 98.
70. Ibid., 99.
71. Ibid.
72. The film production itself consisted of a curious blend of authentic and staged material. For the part of Bair, Pudovkin employed the Buriat actor Valerii Inkizhinov (trained in biomechanics in Meierkhol´d's experimental Theater Studio, and part of Kuleshov's workshop). In a published essay about the experience of playing Bair, Inkizhinov described how he had to shed his acquired Russian ways for a "Mongolian 'rebirth.'" Valerii Inkizhinov, "Bair i ia."
73. Cavendish provides a detailed account of the importance of costume in this film in his *The Men with the Movie Camera*, 175–8.
74. See Mogilner's *Homo imperii*, and her "Beyond, against, and with Ethnography." Other notable studies include Bassin, *Imperial Visions*. Many of the scholars and scientists working in prerevolutionary Russia simply continued their work under the new regime. See Hirsch, *Empire of Nations*, 59.
75. Alymov, "Ethnography, Marxism and Soviet Ideology," 135.
76. See Tolz, *Russia's Own Orient*, 139; Slezkine, *Arctic Mirrors*, 127. Trotskii's theories of uneven development should also be considered here, as they emerge out of a similarly complex understanding of the relationship between the primitive/archaic and modernization. His suggestion that countries would inevitably develop along the path of historical development in distinct ways acknowledged the possibility of a coexistence of the primitive and the modern in the formation of a particular Soviet socialism. Trotskii, *The History of the Russian Revolution*, 27.
77. Tolz, *Russia's Own Orient*, 93–95. See also Shlapentokh, "The Fate of Nikolai Marr's Linguistic Theories."
78. For example, Kuczynski, "Steppe und mensch," (1925), published in *Russko-nemetskii meditsinskii zhurnal* in 1925. See Solomon, "Foreign Expertise on Russian Terrain."

79. Anton Iasnitskii has produced an extensive bibliography of published materials relating to scientific expeditions exploring the psychology of national minorities in Soviet Russia between 1928 and 1932. Iasnitskii, "Bibliografiia osnovnykh sovetskikh rabot." See also Proctor, "Kurt Koffka and the Expedition to Central Asia."

80. Luria and Vygotsky, *Ape, Primitive Man, and Child*, 58–59.

81. See Bulgakowa, "From Expressive Movement to the 'Basic Problem,'" 440–45, for further details of this expedition.

82. More broadly, however, they wished to prove the dependence of the evolution of consciousness on social and material conditions. In Luriia's words, "Soviet psychology maintains that consciousness is the highest form of reflection of reality." Thus they would effectively *invert* the traditional consciousness-world binary. Luriia, *Cognitive Development: Its Cultural and Social Foundations*, 8, 19.

83. Luriia, *Cognitive Development*, 14.

84. It is revealing that, also in 1930, Vygotskii published a short essay entitled *The Socialist Alteration of Man*. The results of Luriia's expeditions were suppressed and not published in Soviet Russia, where they were denounced as "pseudo-scientific, anti-Marxist and class-hostile." See Razmyslov, "O kul′turno-istoricheskoi teorii Vygotskogo i Luriia," cited in Proctor, 45. See also Bulgakowa, "From Expressive Movement to the 'Basic Problem,'" 445.

85. Luriia, *Cognitive Development*, 18.

86. See, for example, "For the illiterate audience, the electric beam of the magic motion-picture lamp will define new concepts and images, will make the wealth of knowledge more easily accessible to the backward mind." *Bakinskii rabochii*, 1923 (September 18), cited in Michael G. Smith, "Cinema for the 'Soviet East,'" 645.

87. Luria, *Cognitive Development*, 15. Luriia's findings from the Uzbekistan expedition have a certain infamy in the history of psychology because of a (probably apocryphal) message that he is supposed to have sent to Vygotsky from the field: "The Uzbeks don't have illusions!"

88. Note that studies into affect were being carried out in this period by A. N. Leon′ev, with specific focus on touch. See Leontiev, "The Life and Creative Path of A. N. Leontiev," and Sirotkina, *Shestoe chuvstvo avangarda*, 64.

89. Vygotsky and Luria, *Ape, Primitive Man and Child*, 50.

90. Lévy-Bruhl, *Primitive Mentality*.

91. Luria, *Cognitive Development*, 7.

92. Taussig, *Mimesis and Alterity*, 21.

93. Kleiman, "Introduction." The work on *Method* was begun by Eisenstein in 1931, and continued in Moscow in the 1940s.

94. See Bulgakova, "Sergei Eizenshtein i ego 'psikhologicheskii Berlin,'" and also Bulgakova, "From Expressive Movement to the 'Basic Problem.'" See also Vasil′eva, "Eizenshtein v arkhive A. R. Luriia."

95. He also read Frazer's *The Golden Bough* and Sigmund Freud's *Totem and Taboo*, among other works. See Salazkina, *In Excess*, 34–36 and 41.

96. Eisenstein, *Metod*, Tom 1, 136. See Ivanov "Analiz glubinnykh struktur semioticheskikh system iskusstva," 298; Bulgakowa, *Sergei Eisenstein*, 87–88, and Bulgakova, "Sergei Eizenshtein i ego 'psikhologicheskii Berlin,'" 187. Olenina points out that there is no archival evidence that the group engaged in direct research. Olenina, "Psychomotor Aesthetics," 220.

97. Eisenstein, "Imitation as Mastery," 68. The term used was "stroi veshchei" (the construction of things).

98. Eisenstein developed a conviction that the "line," a "generalizing agent of meaning" was a way of extracting the generalized essence of meaning from things. Eisenstein, archival material from RGALI, f. 1923, op. 2, ed. khr. 239, cited in Iampolski, *The Memory of Tiresias*, 226.

99. Iampol'skii, "The Essential Bone Structure," 187–88.

100. Eisenstein, "Chet-nechet: Razdvoenie edinogo," 235, cited in Iampolski, *The Memory of Tiresias*, 226.

101. Lévy-Bruhl, *How Natives Think*, 140. See Iampolski, *The Memory of Tiresias*, 226. Note that Luria and Vygotskii cite this section of Lévy-Bruhl's work in *Ape, Primitive Man, and Child*, 114–5.

102. Cushing, "Manual Concepts," 308.

103. Benjamin, "The Work of Art in the Age of Mechanical Reproduction," 220.

104. Taussig, *Mimesis and Alterity*, 98.

Chapter Six

MODERN SENSATIONS

> The bricoleur may not ever complete his purpose but
> he always puts something of himself into it.
> — Claude Lévi-Strauss, 1962

IN THIS BOOK, I claim to explore how film was used to picture, and to create, new, revolutionary relationships between human subjects and the material world. Yet my focus so far has been on substances and modes of production that run counter to standard narratives of modernity, on old-fashioned "making." I have discussed patterned textile, weaving, lace, shoemaking, and even "primitive" craft. What, then, of the glass, steel, and white walls that we associate with high modernist style—and with Soviet functionalism? How did they appear on-screen, and what kind of physical experiences could they be seen to encode?

Abram Room's *Potholes* (see chapter 4) was set in a glass factory, and Room exploited the surface faktura of glass on-screen. The camera relished the decorative and ornamental impacts of prerevolutionary crystal vases and chandeliers. Yet it is common to associate glass with the clean lines of utopian rationalism, exemplified in Soviet Russia in constructivist architecture.[1] In Evgenii Zamiatin's dystopian novel *We* (1920), for example, glass symbolizes the One State's culture of surveillance, and its cult of rationality at the expense of human feeling. Outside Russia, in Fritz Lang's *Metropolis* (1927), vast reflective skyscrapers embody the oppressive structures of capitalism. In part, Sergei Eisenstein's unrealized project for *The*

Glass House, which he worked on between 1926 and 1930, can be considered within this discursive framework. Indeed, Eisenstein had visited the sets of *Metropolis* and framed *The Glass House* in polemical response.[2] Eisenstein's eponymous glass house was a glass skyscraper, and the sets were to be made of pure glass. The towering glass apartment block would make it possible to show—simultaneously, in a single frame—the social contradictions (between classes, levels of wealth, etc.) intrinsic to modern capitalism. Transparent walls would enable visual juxtapositions in ways previously possible only through montage.

This ideological emphasis should not obscure the formal complexity of Eisenstein's project, however. It is clear from notes and the various screenplays for *The Glass House* that the plastic potential of glass on-screen was of equal interest to Eisenstein. The prologue in particular emphasizes its protean, mutable qualities: "Prologue—symphony of glass (objectless). Glass-blowing gives shape to all the forms. Glass strands and filaments are stretching out."[3] Glass had formal power on-screen as an agent of distortion, creating changing viewing perspectives, capable of uncovering the plasticity of human bodies and things. He sought also to explore the material itself—its capacity for endless metamorphosis.

This formal experiment is specific to Eisenstein's distinctive aesthetic, of course—but it also points to a wider interest, shared by many Soviet artists in this period, in the interface between material, the human body, and technology (the camera). The project for *The Glass House* was in germination from 1927 to 1930, while Eisenstein worked on and completed two other feature films: *October* (1928) and *The General Line* (1929). In *October*, the glass ornaments in the tsarina's chamber speak to the director's fascination with the cinematographic potential of glass on-screen. In *The General Line*, a future of glass and steel, embodied in the futuristic dairy factory (which constructivist architect Andrei Burov was employed to design) is situated against the mud and hand plows of peasant life.[4]

This factory is a striking instance of the kind of images of modern industrial production and technology that developed in Soviet cinema in the late 1920s. Yet there was a well-recognized need for filmmakers to model not just ways of working, but ways of living—to reframe modernist materials on-screen, creating modern living spaces that would *enable*, rather than repress, the human body. In this chapter, we will examine how these new interiors were articulated, and reveal an abiding focus on two things: the continued importance of the "ordinary" man or woman in constructing (making) his/

her space (see chapter 3), and an emphasis on embodied experience as a marker of the new Soviet life. We will trace the dream of a Soviet "modern," in which a remodeled relationship between human and material world would be created, and cinema's role in picturing this new world.

Homemade Modernism

As we saw in chapter 3, most cinematic interiors in the 1920s—rural and urban—were negatively coded, part of a retrograde world, and far from the socialist ideal. The project of homemaking took place within existing (but, as in Il'ia's room in *Girl with Hatbox*, often bare) domestic spaces. One intriguing exception to this rule, however, was Mark Donskoi and Mikhail Averbakh's *In the Big City* (*V bol'shom gorode*, 1927). Made in the same year as Room's *Bed and Sofa*, this film tells the familiar story of characters from the provinces arriving in the capital. It follows the fate of two young men, Gerasim and Sasha, a poet and an inventor and engineer respectively, as they head to "Red Moscow" to realize their dreams. On arrival in Moscow, Gerasim find success as a poet and is drawn into a decadent demimondain world of writers and performers; Sasha finds work on a construction site, where he is affiliated with a community of "good" Soviet citizens collectively building socialism. The film shows Sasha craft himself a home—both literal and figurative—in the city. Indeed, his real home, a single room in a workers' hostel, is a unique cinematic prototype of a utopian living space. As he proudly shows his new friends Natasha and Galina, Sasha inventively designs his room so that his single bed folds away and can be replaced by a fold-down table and chairs (figure 6.1a). His crockery is stored in a cupboard ingeniously built into the wall; his tea kettle has an innovative whistle; and he moves his simple hanging light via a hook system to suit the changing configurations of the room (figure 6.1b).[5]

This is an exemplary act of homemaking, according to new ideological criteria. It takes seriously the imperatives of collective living, and seeks functional solutions to reduced living space. Crucially, it does so at no sacrifice of either comfort or coziness (*uiut*): Sasha and his friends are shown at home in his space, drinking tea and relaxing. Workers live well in *In the Big City*. Sasha's female coworker Natasha lives in a specially designed commune on the outskirts of Moscow, clearly inspired by contemporary architectural projects for "garden cities."[6] Her home, although lacking the utopian modernism of Sasha's self-built unit, is marked by simple aesthetics. Its walls are plain; Natasha sleeps on a small divan behind a modern

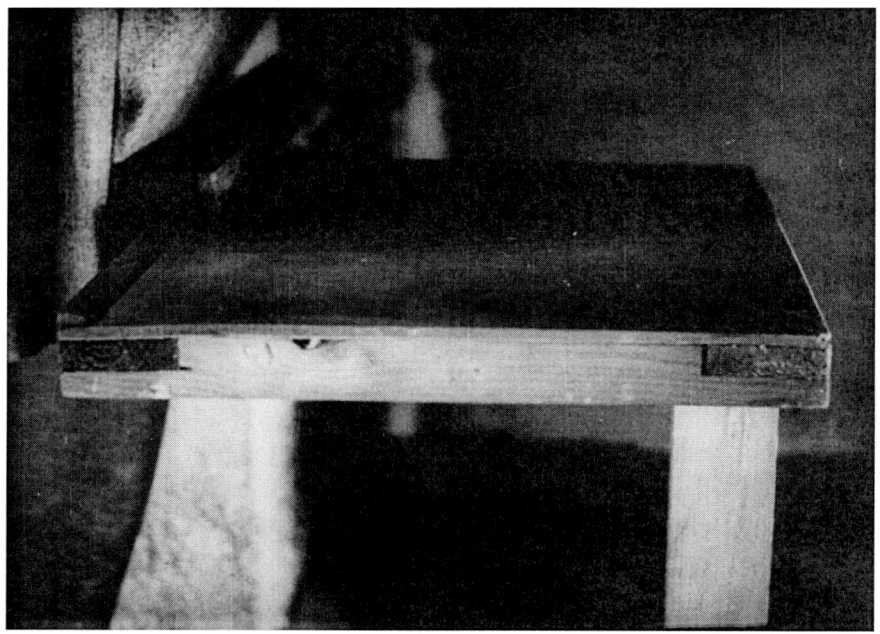

Fig. 6.1 Homemade Modernism. Stills from *In the Big City* (*V bol'shom gorode*, dir. M. Donskoi and M. Averbakh, production design by S. Kozlovskii, 1928).

Fig. 6.1 (*Continued*).

screen, with a bold abstract carpet on the wall behind. This space is at once urban and rural—embedded in the city, and in the city's construction projects (Natasha and her father both work in central city construction; their apartment is filled with plans and materials from Natasha's study at the Technical Construction Institute), but also blessed with light and space, with a rural picket fence marking its entrance. Such ideal workers' spaces are set in visual contrast to the other Moscow of decadent self-indulgence, into which the poet Gerasim falls. Here, in contrast to the plain surfaces that distinguish Sasha's "new" domestic space, we find the patterned textiles and complex textures of bourgeois decoration: ornate candlesticks, drapes, a lushly quilted bed, and a polar bear rug. It is no accident that when Gerasim finally realizes the error of his ways, he throws out not only his dissolute lady friend, but also her cushions, launching them after her in a symbolic rejection of the lure of luxury.

Despite its weak narrative, *In the Big City* stands out in Soviet cinema of this period for its rare portrayal of modernist homemaking. Through Sasha we see a hands-on version of novyi byt—as built from the bottom up, by the ordinary dreamers of Soviet Russia. Technology (electricity, mechanics) is placed in the practical grasp of ordinary men and women: "You are as good as Edison," Natasha tells Sasha admiringly. Sasha's relationship with his living space mirrors the embodied relationship of the maker to his machine and product (see chapter 4); it embeds him firmly within a particularly Soviet value system. But his skills and ambitions are not limited to his own micronarrative: Sasha has also designed a model prototype for an ideal Soviet building, which is proudly displayed to his visiting friends (figure 6.1c). Thus, *In the Big City* offered a tantalizing glimpse of a possible form for the future socialist interior. It pictured, as one reviewer pointed out, "the Moscow of workers building a new world, with great simplicity and sobriety."[7]

Exemplary Life?

In the latter part of the 1920s, there was a growing sense that film could and should do more than simply picture Soviet life *in transition*. It should offer models of an ideal future, making that future visible in the material world. This idea was taken up directly in an article published by Lukhmanov in 1929, inspired in particular by a documentary film, *How You Live*, (*Kak ty zhivesh,*' dir. Shirokov, 1927), which pictured a clean-lined, rationalized modernist domestic environment. Lukhmanov called for fiction films now to take up the challenge of picturing everyday life "as it should be." Cinema must, he said, picture "exemplary" (*obraztsovyi*) life.[8]

How You Live was a celebrated collaboration between architects and film practitioners. Its sets were designed by Gleb Grushchenko, a student in Nikolai Ladovskii's studio. In an article in the avant-garde architecture journal The Construction of Moscow Vitalii Lavrov (another member of Ladovskii's group) described *How You Live* as nothing less than a manifesto for a new vision of living, a prototypical domestic space that sought to remake the relationship between people and things. He began by criticizing previous interior design: "It is characteristic that many things in our rooms misuse their position and, ignoring people, occupy the last few square metres of their already inadequate 'living space.' They are companions of people, yet do not help life, but rather hinder it."[9]

The challenge for architecture, then, was to create new types of things—shaped by and *for* human use. Praising Grushchenko's designs, he noted that "the basic shapes of the furniture are simplified as far as possible. All extraneous details, protrusions, and cavities are removed." This was furniture designed for easy use, and the selection of materials was vital: "The

Fig. 6.2 The Modern Factory (designed by Aleksei Burov). Still from *The General Line* (*General'naia liniia*, dir. S. Eisenstein, production design by A. Burov, V. Kovrinin, V. Rakhal's).

surface of tables is made from glass, wooden parts are polished, the seats of chairs are made from lattice-work, etc." In conclusion, he judged the designs suited to "the eye of the person of this sober, materialist epoch." He might well have added that they were suited "to the body."

Lukhmanov's exhortation for film to picture an exemplary life was echoed by film critic Kolomarov in 1929, who in an essay provocatively entitled "The Thing in Cinema" called for a dialectical presentation of a Soviet new life emerging out of the old.[10] Like Lukhmanov, however, Kolomarov could find only a limited number of feature films to praise for attempting to picture that new world. Naturally, both authors celebrated Burov's futuristic factory in *The General Line* (figure 6.2), but few films had responded to the challenge of picturing—or creating—a new Soviet interior. Nor did the situation change notably in the following few years. *Life in the Palm of Your Hands* (*Zhizn' v rukakh*, dir. David Mar'ian, 1930) pictured life in a new, modernist *dom-kommuna* (communal apartment block), and staged a moral opposition between the light and space of the new way of living and the somber dirtiness of a life of alcoholism and poverty.[11] More interestingly, Bystritskii's *Happy Builders* (*Veselye stroiteli*, 1928) told of a group of young factory workers who, unable to persuade rich dacha (country home) owners to rent them a dacha for a reasonable price, decide to build their own—and eventually their own colony of dachas—outside Moscow.[12] Like Sasha in *In the Big City*, these protagonists were builder-makers, engaged in the project of crafting their own future.

Together, Bystritskii's home-builders and Donskoi and Averbakh's Sasha take their place in Soviet cinema alongside other heroic inventor-makers, and encourage a more nuanced understanding of how modern materials, and their meanings, were transformed and appropriated in the Soviet context. This was a category directly invoked in the first intertitle of Aleksei Popov's gentle comedy *Two Friends, a Model, and a Girlfriend* (*Dva druga, model′ i podruga*, 1927): "The idea of the rationalization of production and of worker-inventors had reached the very furthest outskirts of the Soviet land." This film can be revealingly viewed alongside one of the first Soviet sound films, *Mechanical Traitor* (*Mekhanicheskii predatel′*, dir. Aleksei Dmitriev, 1931). Both films feature inventors, but they are radically different types. In *The Mechanical Traitor*, Professor Rastiapin, the inventor of a new sound-amplifying machine (the "phonovox"), is an archetypal mad scientist, his home a chaos of test tubes, wires, and pulleys, with wallpaper is covered by scribbled formulas (a visual parody of dense floral designs), the inventions sit amid all the paraphernalia of bourgeois life, and his wife summons him regularly to drink tea. He is a prerevolutionary scientist out of place in the new world. He is so distracted by his inventions that he daydreams his way through life, scribbling formulas on parked cars and losing track of his things (as his wife exasperatedly exclaims, "You were inventing again!"). For all the ingeniousness of his inventions (especially the pulley system, which enables him to take his dog for a walk while remaining in place!), Rastiapin is pictured as outside the present moment. And the film's other key protagonist, Prut (played by Igor′ Il′iinskii), commandant of a collective housing block, who eventually becomes the accidental custodian of Rastiapin's miraculous phonovox, is equally out of step with technology—and the Soviet present.

Technology, then—inventions and inventors—is not integrated into real life in *The Mechanical Traitor*. Instead, the film presents characters with a disjunctive relationship with things. The phonovox—the "mechanical traitor" of the film's title—is an unruly object. It leads those who encounter it into muddle and mischief. In Popov's *Two Friends*, by contrast, a quite different image of the inventor (and the invention) appears. The comically named Akhov and Makhov are youthful workers in a provincial soap factory. They too are so busy inventing that they lose track of things—allowing their documents to catch fire, for example, and getting cautioned by their factory manager for insufficient work and too much inventing. But their grand ambition is to create a machine that will make boxes for transporting the factory's soap and reduce dependence on local capitalist cartels: "Our invention must destroy local capitalism!"

Akhov and Makhov are bricoleurs.[13] Their invention appears, at times, to be held together with string. It is conceived from their rough drawings and built out of found materials—a hammer, nails, pieces of wood, cogs, and levers. It is carried on their backs on a handmade river raft, and thrown out of windows. Its first demonstration is an abject and embarrassing failure. It is precisely this series of trials, however—and above all, this hands-on *making*—that dictate its final victory as a triumph of a particularly Soviet kind of invention. This film celebrates invention (and inventiveness) as both handmade and homemade—and, as such, as a kind of game. Indeed, its playfulness is infectious. In the machine's final, triumphant demonstration, Akhov and Makhov feed in pieces of wood; the hammers, wheels, and pulleys surge into action, and suddenly, the first box flies out, then another, and another ... They pile up apparently endlessly—and the watching group of skeptical bureaucrats, gathered to appraise the invention, find themselves climbing gleefully all over them as on an improvised pop-up climbing frame.

Modern Bodies in Modern Spaces

Akhov and Makhov's success is determined by their relationship with their product. Like that of the worker-makers in chapter 4, this relationship is embodied and affectionate: it is one of zabota (care, see Chapter 4). And indeed, the figure of the inventor-maker speaks to the importance of *embodied* experience that we have traced elsewhere. What happened to this relationship in the domestic environment? How did films configure the relationship between human bodies and the furniture and fittings of modern domestic spaces? Such new interiors as did appear in cinema were usually located alongside (and against) those of the past. The power of the socialist interior depended on contrast with that which had preceded it: it was clear what it was not and must not be. But it was much less clear what a modern socialist interior should actually look like—and feel like—itself. Kolomarov, for example, praised the modernist hostel and communal dining room of Fridrikh Ermler's *A Fragment of Empire* (*Oblomok imperii*, 1929).[14] This film tells the story of the peasant Filimonov, injured and losing his memory during the First World War, and awakening to find imperial Russia transformed into the Soviet Union. The narrative traces his doomed attempts to rediscover his lost past, and his gradual affiliation, as worker, to the new world. Brief domestic scenes present a nascent model of collective space, which Filimonov shares with his new worker friends. It has striking large glass doors, geometric shapes, and a lack of decoration. And it is explicitly contrasted with the old-fashioned space where a propaganda worker—now married to Filimonov's former wife—lives, bedecked with crystal chandeliers and white tablecloths, the complete works of Lenin set out alongside porcelain figurines. This ideologue is revealed as a "new man" only in words, and not in deeds—in reality a patriarch with poor manners and poor taste. By contrast, Filimonov and his fellow hostel-inhabitants represent the real socialist future.

In Sergei Komarov's *A Doll with Millions* (*Kukla s millionami*, 1928), for which LEF-member and avant-garde artist Aleksandr Rodchenko designed the sets, another possible shape for a socialist interior emerged.[15] Swimmer Marusia Ivanova lives in a hostel with her fellow athletes, with shared spaces for bathing and exercise. Interior walls are marked by a lack of pattern, appearing as flat midgray on the film stock. A striking geometric grid divides the communal washing area into gendered sections, while allowing for openness and communication. The grid organizes daily life, but rather than rationalizing and repressing the human body, its geometric form enables bodily freedom. On either side of it, young Soviet men and women are pictured engaged in healthy ablutions, free of vanity—and in stark contrast to the satirized, trussed-up bourgeois foreigners, Pierre and Paul, who come to Moscow to seek out Marusia. In another scene, the collective space of the stadium where Marusia competes in a swimming competition is also marked by modernist design.

In this film, modern design is a marker of efficiency and emancipated bodies. It was not always so, however. The geometric patterns of Rodchenko's designs in this film (and in *Al´bidum* [dir. Leonid Obolenskii, 1928], images of which featured in the cinema press) were echoed in several films of the period, and sometimes with very different intent. In Bassalygo's *The Journey of Mr. Lloyd* (*Reis mistera Lloyda*, 1927), designed by Aleksei Utkin, a striking blend of high modernist styles was an indicator of Western corruption.

Similarly, in Kote Mikaberidze's *My Grandmother* (*Moia babushka*, 1929) (which was banned before release), modernist design appeared as a signifier of bureaucratic incompetence and laziness. The film's set focuses on a circular table, around which each large chair, seen from the back, appears like an office door. Inept bureaucrats sit, idly playing with toy cars and allowing endless piles of paper to accumulate. *My Grandmother* makes a direct link between high modernist design and corruption—and it locates this corruption in the body. Like the political worker in *A Fragment of Empire*, these Soviet bureaucrats preach the new world, but their domestic space remains enmeshed in bourgeois clutter. One of the film's most striking scenes is set in the apartment of the chief bureaucrat. It is strewn with mess: a dressing table has open drawers overspilling with stockings, makeup, and jewelry, broken toys and ornaments cover the floor. Heavy silk curtains and oriental carpets show the bureaucrat and his family symbolically entrapped by material. Disgraced and out of a job, he hangs himself amid this stylized excess. And in a grotesque escapade, his wife and son dance madly to celebrate their most recent shopping expedition, ignoring his inert body hanging above them.

The dangling corpse in this scene alerts us to a key index that was used to distinguish the ideal spaces of the new world from the retrograde spaces of the past: the relationship between the body and things. In *A Doll with Millions*, for example, the new space is distinguished by a particular vision of the human body. Marusia and her friends are athletes; they are seen *in motion*, at ease with their healthy bodies. They are clothed in the simple uniform of the komsomol—either in the striped tops and shorts/skirts of sport, or in a simple black skirt and white shirt with red necktie. By contrast, the foreigners Paul and Pierre are distinguished by a lack of physical ease, restricted by their old-fashioned clothing (sometimes literally: Paul is caught by his braces on an iron bedstead, and his tailcoat gets caught in a door). Indeed, instances of such direct encounter between man and object are frequently used in cinema of this period, for satirical effect. In *The Girl with a Hatbox*, for example, Madame Irene finds herself wrapped in a curtain during a fight. In *My Grandmother*, the bureaucrat is trapped in a curtain, and transformed into a billowing column of cavorting fabric. The message appears clear: like the peasants in *Women from Riazan Province*, bourgeois characters are trapped by their material(ism). Like the Western capitalists in Pudovkin's *Storm over Asia*, they lack a mimetic, sensory relationship with the object world that surrounds them.

A similar vision of material entrapment is evident in Protazanov's 1924 film *Aelita*—although here with an unusual twist. *Aelita* is often cited as a rare example of direct overlap between avant-garde art and design and cinema.[16] Made just a year before Protazanov's *The Tailor from Torzhok* (chapter 3), this film's famous constructivist costumes designed by Aleksandra Ekster, and its futuristic sets, appear at first to be a celebration of the avant-garde interest in the possibilities of new design. On-screen, however, those costumes restrict physical movement; the set consists of surfaces, volumes, and forms, rather than texture. In contrast to the real-world shots of 1920s Moscow, with their emphasis on human crowds, and contact between bodies, the abstract shapes and hard surfaces of the Martian set speak to a different code of human interaction. Just as in *Metropolis* glass towers and high-tech communications signal the repression of the workers' bodies, so in Protazanov's Mars, the bodies of workers and leaders alike are oppressed and repressed. In cinematic terms, the Martian sequences offer the spectator what Riegl defined as visual (optical) rather than tactile (haptic) experience. The stunning designs impress, but they do not invite a sensory response. These modern surfaces cannot be appropriated by the body.

Building Modernism?

In one sense, then, *Aelita* and *My Grandmother* were films about "false" modernism. So what distinguished positive visions of modernist design from their negative alter egos? And how could both be used in Soviet film practice, to such different ends? As I have suggested, one key distinguishing element lay in the representation of the body. More specifically, it lay in the relationships between body and material world that were encoded in the physical environment. Here, the film set had a key part to play. This is particularly evident in an experimental film of 1927, directed by Lev Kuleshov. *Your Acquaintance* (*Vasha znakomaia*, originally called *Zhurnalistka*) was the sixth feature film produced by Kuleshov and his collective, with his wife Aleksandra Khokhlova playing the main role, and Aleksandr Rodchenko as production designer.[17] In their memoirs, Kuleshov and Khokhlova describe *Your Acquaintance* as an "antifilm"—that is, as a challenge to conventional narrative cinema: "In essence, it's as if nothing happens in the film. The actors (principally Khokhlova) just live."[18] Claiming simply to picture ordinary people in Soviet reality, *Your Acquaintance* was responding to calls for film to engage with byt. Rodchenko formulated his own role as one of responsibility for the material environment of the film—and hence for the modeling of *living space*: "The 'artist' must make a plan for sets where the people in the film will live."[19] In practice, however, the byt that Rodchenko and Kuleshov sought to reveal was far from ordinary. The film was a celebration of the revolutionary ideals of Soviet modernism, providing prototypical models of the "exemplary" (obraztsovyi) life that had not yet taken real form in Soviet Russia. Produced a year before Donskoi's *In the Big City*, and in the same year as *How You Live*, *Your Acquaintance* featured furniture that echoed the self-made prototypes of functional furniture displayed in Sasha's cozy apartment.

To produce such sets within Sovkino during 1926 and 1927 was no mean feat. Rodchenko bemoaned the lack of "ordinary" furniture in the studio's stores, and lamented the absence of even decent raw material, suggesting that stock was limited to standard props.[20] Faced with this absence, Rodchenko seems to have started from scratch, designing purpose-built furniture for two interior sets: the newspaper office and the home of the heroine, journalist Khokhlova (who takes the name of the actress), which showcased functionalist furniture adapted to the life of a modern woman in a modern city. As Lavrentiev describes it:

> The bed folded up into a cupboard, the upper section of which housed looseleaf binders full of information. In the evening, the doors of the cupboard opened to reveal what amounted to a small bedroom with a lamp in the corner. As for the journalist's work desk, on one side there was a built-in radio with a circuit antenna on top. On the other was a photo-card index and even a light table for viewing slides and negatives. Finally, there was a work surface with a great many little drawers in front for storing supplies, equipment, and so on.[21]

With Rodchenko's involvement, the film's design attracted considerable excitement in the critical press. In an article of November 1926, before *Your Acquaintance* was even released, Rodchenko's designs were upheld as examples of the new functionalism of Soviet everyday life: "Rodchenko ... skillfully captures the logical simplicity and utility of our everyday life ... The struggle for grand forms, a new presentation of the material on the one hand, and the minute facts of life on the other."[22]

This idea of reconciling the ambition for grand forms with minute life facts is an excellent summation of the film's aesthetic ambitions. It describes the highly functional, streamlined spaces that Rodchenko created for his protagonists, bringing revolutionary ideals into ordinary daily life. It also captures the complex relationship with material objects that is our focus here, putting side by side the twin imperatives with which many filmmakers and theorists of the period struggled: how might the formal/ideological imperative of achieving a new presentation of material sit alongside the representation of the real details of the everyday? How might real people live in new spaces? Rather than a simply a homage to modern design, I suggest, *Your Acquaintance* was an experiment in provoking intensified experience through an encounter between the human body (and the spectator's eye) and the material surfaces of a reconfigured world.

THE EMBODIED SPECTATOR

It is common to see Rodchenko's work on *Your Acquaintance* as a precursor to his much better-known work on Anatolii Glebov's play *Inga*, directed by Maksim Tereshkovich at the Theater of the Revolution in 1929.[23] But in designing for a cinematic context, and in interaction with camera-operator and director, Rodchenko's work had the potential to have a different sensory impact on the spectator, using the formal possibilities of the screen to create in its spectators a heightened apprehension of material faktura: to produce a particular kind of spectatorial sensorium.

In this respect, *Your Acquaintance* is of particular interest because of its play with the specificity of cinematic space—the relationship between surface and depth. Production design had a key role to play here. Mikhail Iampolski describes the 1920s as a wholesale rejection of prerevolutionary cinema's preoccupation with the creation of depth. If the principle aim of prerevolutionary set designers had been to create the illusion of three-dimensional space through depth, he suggests, the best Soviet filmmaking of the 1920s was an exercise in pure surface.[24] It is common, indeed, to describe Soviet montage cinema as prioritizing editing over mise-en-scène. This book has sought, however, to complicate that picture—to reveal the abiding importance of texture and material in cinema of that period. How does *Your Acquaintance*—a film produced by the father of the Soviet montage school—fit into my story? How is its presentation of texture and objects linked to its experiments with spectatorial response?

Certainly, in his writings Kuleshov describes how his interest in montage and editing came to predominate over the décor and design that had been his earliest focus (when employed as a set designer for Bauer). This, he claimed, entailed a reenvisaging of the nature of filmic representation itself: "We have to dream of the individual frames of a film as approaching the primitive, flat illustrations on antique vases."[25] Instead of striving to overcome the specificity of the medium—the cinematographic—by creating the illusion of depth, filmmakers must exploit that surface. The power of cinema lies in the contrast between black and white, and in the "formal resolutions in each still."[26] This meant, however, considerable attention to mise-en-scène. Kuleshov describes how the visual style of *Your Acquaintance* was shaped by his growing understanding of the power of contrast. The majority of the set was dark (constructed out of dark brown or black materials), and cinematographer Kuznetsov arranged the lighting so that "the human face, or the object, stands out clearly, in relief (*rel'efno*), against the background."[27]

Kuleshov's term, "rel'efno," is important here, however, for it draws our attention to the three-dimensional materiality of the objects on-screen, which remained of great significance to Kuleshov, for all the dominance of montage in this period. Lighting is used to endow objects and people with a sculptural quality—to reveal their volume and texture. This signals an important contradiction, central to the emergent aesthetics of set design in the period. Despite a growing recognition of the power of camera and lighting to transform physical objects, and of editing to process materials, still the real material of set, props, and costume remained a preoccupation: in Kuleshov's words, "The better the faktura of the set's surfaces, the better the result; it comes out more authentic, more real."[28]

For all Kuleshov's proclaimed focus on the screen as surface, moreover, *Your Acquaintance* is distinguished by its use of light and dark to create depth of field. Exploiting the lessons learned with Bauer, Kuleshov continues to use strong outline shapes (a balustrade, a staircase, etc.) in the foreground, and at middle distance, to articulate the space beyond the frame. Depth is marked by layers of pattern, often created by light. In a shot of the newspaper office by night, for example, light streams through a backlit window placed on the right at middle distance, creating a path of shadow stripes that leads the spectator's eye into the depth of the frame (figure 6.3). This is characteristic: surface pattern in the film is created by the relationship between volumes. Where much film of the period featured patterned textile, either in costume or in décor, *Your Acquaintance* has very little. The heroine's strongly contemporary aesthetic consists of a simple gray dress with a white collar; only her block-striped scarf offers on-screen pattern, and its geometric shapes are in sharp contrast to the patterns of traditional textile. Her long pale neck, short hair, and dark eyes, often hidden by a simple cloche, transform her into an angular composition of contrasting shades of gray. Clothing, indeed, is a distinct part of this film's mise-en-scène: throughout

Fig. 6.3 Depth and Surface. Still from *Your Acquaintance* (*Vasha znakomaia*, dir. L. Kuleshov, production design by A. Rodchenko, 1927).

the film, the scarf acts as a signifier of Khokhlova. Its strong contrasting stripes echo the striking shadow stripes of the newspaper office set, and are a microcosm of the film's overarching aesthetic, in which volume and mass, light and dark, create visual contrast.

Kuleshov's rejection of patterned textile was part of his understanding of cinematic faktura. He later recalled how a growing awareness of the role of the surface in reflecting light had led him to recommend the use of gray velvet for covering volumes and structures in the set, claiming that it offered an ideal reflectivity and evenness of surface.[29] In similar terms, he suggested that the floors of film sets could be covered with the reverse side of carpets to provide a nonreflective midgray surface, rather than the patterns of most carpets.[30] However, this rejection of decorative pattern did not mean a rejection of the patterning of the surface of the cinematic screen per se. As we have shown, shadows and reflections create a grid pattern across the dark surface of the newspaper office floor. Objects play a key role in creating faktura. The office is messy, strewn with scattered cigarette butts and discarded papers. White, this rubbish stands out against the flat gray of the floor, its random distribution making a pattern. They draw attention to the surface of the screen. Unlike mere decoration, however, these objects are not just pattern; they also have volume and faktura. When Khokhlova bends to pick up a broken match, they intervene in the filmic narrative, acquiring a concrete materiality, breaking through the surface of the film, demanding a different kind of sensory spectatorial engagement.

Here, the formal and ideological ambitions of *Your Acquaintance* come together. Things (objects) are central to *Your Acquaintance* in both theme and style, and part of the film's exploration of new models of living. Kuleshov was against the habitual "chaos" that characterized film sets of domestic interiors. His pared-down interiors are usually seen as rejection of "salon beauty and theatricalized prerevolutionary films."[31] He called instead for a small number of carefully selected details. Each element of the décor must have narrative or symbolic significance. Thus a single glass ornament and a coat hanger in an actress's room in *Your Acquaintance* should convey its owner's weakness for the pleasures of consumerism.[32] As Khokhlova sits at the desk of her admirer, Petrovskii, she picks up a toy and fingers it with curiosity, before coquettishly instructing him to give it to her. Just as the young woman in *The Traitor* used a toy as a device for flirtation, here too the touching of the object is an act of seduction. Like the scarf, the toy comes to function as a symbol of Khokhlova herself.

For all Kuleshov's claims, however, these objects are not just symbols. They alert us to the relationship between bodies and material on-screen. Later, after Khokhlova has been chastised for failing to submit her article to deadline, she stands alone in the office. As she walks around the deserted room, she touches its objects one after another, running her finger across their surfaces, dusting them. The material shapes of the space acquire sensory immediacy for the spectator. When she picks up scissors, she first runs their closed blades across her chest, and their dark outline puckers the light gray of her dress, rendering its material (and its materiality) at once tangible and fragile. As she stumbles upon a note announcing that she is to lose her job, the pointed end of the scissors moves to her neck, pressing gently into its flesh, exploiting the spectator's already-heightened senses (figure 6.4). The pointedly tactile impact of these shots is part of the film's broader poetics. Throughout the film, ordinary things acquire a physical intensity: cigarette ends turn into a pattern, scissors become larger than life. According to Rodchenko, the task of the production designer was to enact

Fig. 6.4 Touching Objects. Still from *Your Acquaintance* (*Vasha znakomaia*, dir. L. Kuleshov, production design by A. Rodchenko, 1927).

this transformation: film could reveal the facts of life, and "show ordinary things ... as they have never been seen before."[33] Characters on-screen live their lives alongside—and in connection with—objects. Through the film, the spectator is provoked to do the same.

I am proposing, then, an ideological reading of the formal strategies of this apparently apolitical film. Certainly, *Your Acquaintance* is a formal inquiry into the relationship between surface and depth. Its artfully distributed rubbish is used to *pattern* the surface of the screen. But this is no abstract experiment in visual patterns. Rather, it seeks to provoke intensified, multisensory perception. The film does not allow the spectator to rest on that patterned surface; it draws us immediately into depth of field, only to expel us once again. In one shot, the screen is flattened; in another, it is given material depth and tactile immediacy. Like a child's pop-up picture, it moves explicitly between two- and three-dimensionality. The effect of this is to make the spectator—like the protagonists—intensely aware of the faktura of the material world portrayed. In Soviet Russia, such formal inquiries were linked to ideological frameworks. This was a key moment in the evolution of cinematic language, engaged in a working through of its central questions. And one of the most important of these questions was that of spectatorial engagement. In *Your Acquaintance*, expressive volumes and perspective, and exaggerated "things," prompt the spectator into a constant shift between haptical and optical response. As such, the film aims to bring about an encounter with materiality, to reveal and exploit the faktura of the objects, both animate and inanimate, that it photographs. In its experimental play with surface and depth, we can trace the search for revolutionary modes of experience, a quest for a heightened physical awareness of the world.

Socialist Interiors

In the course of the 1920s, then, Soviet filmmakers responded to the challenge of articulating new modern interiors in two distinct ways. One response lay in the hands-on modernism of the inventor-maker figure who has been a key protagonist of this book, and who builds his/her modern space from the bottom up. The second response lay in the youthful, sentient bodies who populate the few new interior spaces that actually appeared on the film screen during this period. These are characters who live in heightened sensory proximity with the world. In *Your Acquaintance* in particular, that proximity is both pictured on-screen and, through the film's formal strategies, mirrored in the spectator. In both cases, the surfaces and textures of the modern are effectively transformed (appropriated) through the tactile, embodied interface between the human and material that was, I suggest, particular to the Soviet "modern."

Such early experiments notwithstanding, the search for a shape for the socialist worker's domestic space remained a work in progress in cinema through the late 1920s and into the early 1930s. The project of homemaking (see chapter 3) remained imperative—on-screen, as in Soviet reality. It was complicated, however, by shifting ideological imperatives. Two of our familiar protagonists, directors Fridrikh Ermler and Sergei Iutkevich came together in 1932 to make *Counterplan* (*Vstrechnyi*, 1932), one of the first Soviet sound films (with Boris Dubrovskii-Eshke as production designer). As we will see in the following chapter, *Counterplan* was frequently celebrated as a successful move toward a new model for Soviet cinema. What, then, of its domestic space? In the film, two familiar interior spaces—bourgeois and old-Russian provincial—reappear. The flat of the engineer Skvortsov (later exposed as a wrecker) is a high bourgeois space, with drapery, heavy curtains, and a filigree music stand on top of the piano. By contrast, the home of old worker Babchenko, who begins the film as a recalcitrant remnant of the old regime, is styled according to a more traditional provincial Russia, with its samovar and houseplants, marking his resistance to the public spaces—and imperatives—of collectivity.

Alongside these familiar interiors, however, the film features the emergent shape of a new socialist domesticity. This is the living space of the young couple Pavel and Katia Il′in, who appear at first to represent the Soviet future. The film opens with shots of their marital life, in a single room, with a single bed, and makes explicit their need for a home of their own. They move, eventually, into an apartment, in which the openness of space, and lack of ornate decoration, signifies the residence of a new person. Yet this neutral style is also distinctly lacking in markers of the Soviet modern. In cinematographic terms, this space is sterile. Its large volumes seem to dwarf the young couple; they are not shown engaged in the act of (home) making that we have identified as central to the socialist project. Ultimately, the apartment becomes a mark of the separation of Pavel, an engineer, from the collective, and his failure to understand the human implications of his technical decisions; and as such, he must be reeducated. The film's conclusion is marked by withdrawal from the domestic, and a celebration of collective space—represented by the factory floor.

In *Counterplan*, then, the project of finding an appropriate home for the socialist couple implicitly failed. And indeed, in most films produced in the first few years of the 1930s, it was the factory floor, or the collective farm, that remained the workers' implicit home; domestic space continued to figure as a largely negative foil to collective life. This familiar trope is evident, for example, in the little-known *Real (Authentic) Life* (*Nastoiashchaia zhizn′*), directed by Aleksandr Gavronskii and Ol′ga Ulitskaia for Belgoskino in 1930. The film's alternative title, *Lichnaia zhizn′* (*Private Life*), makes clear its thematic stakes: an investigation of the relationship between work and private life in the search for an authentic (real) way of living. It is set in a match factory, and early sequences echo the production films of the 1920s (see chapter 4) in emphasizing the factory floor as a site of playful labor. Vera, a young komsomol member and exemplary machine operator, falls in love with a young journalist (supposedly a communist "new man"), and they set up home. But here too the new domestic space fails to take shape. Vera finds herself—like so many other heroines in films of this period—trapped in bourgeois domesticity. The journalist claims to offer Vera "culture," but the culture that he provides is one that is in direct opposition to his supposed politics. In their ostensibly new home, Vera is caught in that familiar ritual of tea drinking, staring longingly out of a lace-draped window at the simple white buildings of the factory that she has left.

Rejecting the false lure of domesticity, *Real Life* locates its authentic life on the factory floor. It emphasizes the personal satisfaction that comes from the relationship between (wo)man and machine. Indeed, this film shares the thematic focus on hands that we have discussed in chapter 4. Vera has a conversation at a party meeting about her desire to have a private life. "You can't stop work," she is told. "We need every pair of hands." Later, she takes a walk on the riverbank and meets a lone fisherman (a civil-war veteran) who has only one arm. He tells her that he is ashamed to be a cripple, for "we need every pair of hands." This prompts a revelation, and Vera's return to work is marked by an emotional reunion with her machine—and a rejection of domestic space.

The project of homemaking continued to have potency, however. Another film of 1932, *A Refined Life* (*Iziashchnaia zhizn'*, dir. Boris Iurtsev), tells the story of English sailor Fred, who rejects the high-glamour (art deco) world of his ship (and capitalism with it) and eventually finds his home in Soviet Russia, as a brigade worker on the Dneprostroi construction project. Fred is drawn to Russia not just by its socialist values, however, but also by a woman, Marusia, in whose apartment we see another protosocialist domestic space. Like the spaces of Il'ia in *Girl with a Hatbox*, and Kat'ka in *Kat'ka's Reinette Apples*, this home is distinguished by the poignancy of its dressing. It is a bare single room, decorated by a screen shielding the bed, a white-fringed towel hanging on the wall, and a cloth covering the table. Marusia carefully arranges flowers in a vase and biscuits in a bowl as she invites Fred for tea. In this film, such simplicity is in pointed contrast to the decadence of the bourgeois "good life" that repels Fred in the film's early sequences on board ship. Marusia's poignant and careful acts of homemaking present domesticity in Soviet terms.

The studied neutrality of these domestic spaces, produced in the beginning of the 1930s, reveals the failure of the ambitious search for the new Soviet socialist interior, and the new Soviet modern that has been the subject of this chapter. In the early 1930s, the design of contemporary Soviet interior sets provoked considerable debate in the cinematic press. A growing emphasis on the need for a cinema of real heroes, for a more intimate narrative of socialist achievement, made the quest for an appropriate interior for the new socialist hero ever more urgent. In practice, however, a distinctive interior did not emerge in Soviet film design of the 1930s—or after.[34] Indeed, Dashkova goes so far as to identify only one intimate (marital) domestic environment in cinema of the 1930s.[35] Those domestic environments that did appear in film of this period, were primarily *collective*: the hostel rooms of Aleksandr Macheret's *The Private Life of Petr Vinogradov* (*Chastnaia zhizn' Petra Vinogradova*, 1934), designed by Aleksei Utkin; and Eduard Ioganson's *The Crown Prince of the Republic* (*Naslednyi prints respubliki*, 1934), for example. These and other films will be treated in the coming chapters. They show how the question of the ideal Soviet domestic space became tied to a bigger dilemma: that of the shape of the Soviet individual him/herself.

NOTES

1. There is a vast possible frame of reference here. In the Russian context, a core nineteenth-century example of the link between glass and "rationality" lies in Nikolai Chernyshevskii's *What is to Be Done?* (*Chto delat'*, 1863), and its counter, Fedor Dostoevskii's *Notes from Underground* (*Zapiski iz podpol'ia*, 1864). For further explication of the symbolism of glass in Russian culture, see Chadaga, *Optical Play*.

2. Bulgakowa, *Sergej Eisenstein. Drei Utopien*, 109–125.

3. Cited in Kleiman, "'Stekliannyi dom,'" 96.

4. Burov worked alongside Vasilii Rakhal's, who as head of the studio and Eisenstein's accustomed collaborator, had oversight of the production; and the younger Vasilii Kovrigin, who had worked with Eisenstein on *October*, and who produced detailed sketches for the rural interiors. Kovrigin's sketches are preserved in the Muzei kino izobrazitel'nyi fond, Kp. 5353/1–9; 28.

5. See Urussowa, *Das Neue Moskau*, especially 123–9.

6. Frederick Starr, "Visionary Town Planning," 208–11. See also Kopp, *Town and Revolution*, and Widdis, *Visions of a New Land*, 53–58.

7. Fel'dman, "V bol'shom gorode," 8.

8. Lukhmanov, "Zhizn' kakoi ona dolzhna byt'," 37.

9. Lavrov, "Kak ty zhivesh'?" 25–27.

10. Kolomarov, "Veshch' v kino," 29.

11. Grashchenkova, *Kinoantropologiia*, 57–59. The film is described in *Sovetskie khudozhestvennye fil'my*, Tom 1, 371.

12. *Sovetskie khudozhestvennye fil'my*, Tom 1, 250–51; Grashchenkova, *Kinoantropologiia*, 57.

13. I draw here on the concept of the "bricoleur" as articulated by Claude Lévi-Strauss (Lévi-Strauss, *The Savage Mind*), and since taken up by diverse thinkers. For discussion of how this term has been broadened and adapted, see Johnson, "Bricoleur and Bricolage."

14. Kolomarov, "Veshch' v kino," 37

15. Rodchenko worked as a production designer in Sovkino between 1927 and 1928, where his work was confined to four films: *A Doll with Millions* (*Kukla s millionami*), *Your*

Acquaintance (*Vasha znakomaia*, 1927), *Moscow in October* (*Moskva v Oktiabre*) (Barnet, 1927), and *Al'bidum* (Obolenskii, 1928).

16. For recognition of the negative inflections of modernist design in this film, see Christie, "Down to Earth: *Aelita* Relocated."

17. Note that Sergei Komarov, the director of *A Doll with Millions*, which Rodchenko designed after *Your Acquaintance*, was another former member of the Kuleshov collective.

18. Kuleshov and Khokhlova, *50 let v kino*, 106. A pointed refusal to abide by calls for Kuleshov to make films without Khokhlova as actress, *Your Acquaintance* was not well received by contemporary critics.

19. Rodchenko, "Khudozhnik i 'material'naia sreda,'" 14–15.

20. Anon., "Smotr kino-fabrik: otkliki," 26.

21. Alexander Lavrentiev, "Experimental Furniture Design in the 1920s," 157.

22. Anon., "V," 4.

23. The significance of design to the production of *Your Acquaintance* is suggested by the wealth of archival material in Gosfil'mofond (f.1 op. 2, ed. khr. 1: 86). Lengthy inventories detail the film's "décor," which includes itemized bills (47).

24. Iampol'skii, "Rossiia," 13.

25. Kuleshov, "Iskusstvo svetotvorchestva," 62.

26. Ibid., 62.

27. Kuleshov, "Iskusstvo kino (moi opyt)," 188.

28. Ibid., 186

29. Ibid., 187.

30. Ibid., 190.

31. Miasnikov, *Ocherki istorii*, 22.

32. Kuleshov, "Iskusstvo kino (moi opyt)," 189.

33. Rodchenko, "Khudozhnik i 'material'naia sreda,'" 14.

34. Production designers of the 1930s continued to relish the possibilities of costume drama in the growing number of historical-biographical films produced in the latter part of the decade and into the 1940s. The columns, drapery, and textures of high bourgeois interiors returned in the domestic environments of highly placed Soviet officials, as in Pyr'ev's *The Party Card* (*Partiinyi bilet*, 1936) for example. And the patterns and decorative woodwork of the Russian provincial style returned in force in the collective-farm films of Pyr'ev and Grigorii Aleksandrov, among others. The battle for appropriate recognition for the *kino-khudozhnik*, and for appropriate resources, also continued. See Dubrovskii-Eshke, "Voprosy dekoratsionnoi tekhniki," 60–64.

35. Dashkova, *Telesnost'—Ideologiia—Kinematograf*.

Chapter Seven

SOCIALIST FEELINGS

> We have to learn to feel Soviet reality ... as we feel our own organism.
> Pavel Petrov-Bytov

IN THIS BOOK so far, I have identified the late 1920s as a moment when a new model of subjectivity was actively tested on-screen. Cinema seemed uniquely equipped to show human life as enmeshed in, and formed by, material context; and the relationship between self and world was a central focus for filmmakers during the first Five-Year Plan. In this chapter, and those that follow, I will explore how this preoccupation evolved to meet the ideological demands of the emerging Socialist Realist aesthetic between 1932 and 1937. This was a moment of transition in the story of Soviet sensations on-screen.

Writing in 1933, critic Nikolai Iezuitov looked back to 1927 as the beginning of a move toward a cinema "of socialist *feelings* (*sotsialisticheskikh chuvstv*)," to replace the cinema "of concepts/abstractions (*poniatii*)" that he claimed to have dominated Soviet cinema since 1917.[1] The creation of rounded characters—characters with feelings—to replace the one-dimensional types that, according to Iezuitov, had populated revolutionary cinema in the early to mid-1920s was a key task for late silent and early sound cinema. In Iezuitov's words, the "intellectual" style had shown the relationship of the revolution to the person; the "cinema of feelings" would show the relationship of the person to the revolution.[2] What, then, did Iezuitov mean when he called for a cinema of feelings? In previous chapters, I have shown how filmmakers sought to adapt their preoccupation with faktura and sensation to meet the new ideological frameworks—to articulate Sovietness as a new way of being in the world, which operated principally through the body. In the early 1930s, however—and in particular with the emergence of Socialist Realism—this process of adaptation took another turn: discussion of emotions (emotsii) appeared with increasing consistency in the film press, and filmmakers had to shape their work in response.

Here, filmmaking mirrored broader developments in Soviet psychological science, where there was increasing focus on emotional life in relation to studies of the mind. From the early 1930s on, the emphasis on bodily sensation as a determinant of consciousness gave way to increased interest in the psyche, and in the nature of human emotion. Gaivorovskii, for example, used a study of emotion to demonstrate the failure of a "purely physiological" model of consciousness, arguing that human emotion evolved through a matrix of influences: body, psyche, and society.[3] And such science of emotion was intimately linked, for Gaivorovskii and for others, with the project of educating the emotions that became a central aim of Stalinist culture.

Between the Central Committee's Resolution in 1932 on the Restructuring of Literary Artistic Organizations (usually seen as the beginning of Socialist Realism) and the end of the second Five-Year Plan in 1937, there was much debate about the appropriate style for Soviet cinema, to meet increasingly urgent political imperatives. What would Socialist Realism look like on-screen? Ideological shifts were complicated by technological innovations—specifically with the coming of sound technology.[4] The All-Union Conference on Cinema in 1935, marking Soviet cinema's fifteen-year anniversary, provided an occasion for particularly focused self-reflection. This was the first phase of Soviet Socialist Realism, when the shape of the new cinema was in flux. Films produced in this period were, I suggest, testing grounds in the search for an appropriate model for Socialist Realist cinema. Certain elements were fundamental from the beginning. Critic Vaisfel´d defined two key related tasks for the new cinema. First, film was a tool for knowing reality.[5] And, since reality was composed of real people, the second challenge for filmmakers was to picture the communist individual on-screen, "to show a living person, with blood and nerves, feelings and intellect, at work and in their private life."[6] Other critics echoed this exhortation. "The individual is emerging!" Piataev asserted. "The individual builder of Socialism, the many millions of individuals who make up the collective of builders of socialism."[7] These "new people" needed to be pictured not in their professional life, but in their family-everyday life. According to Krinkin, "one of the greatest crimes of film of the rational school is its determined refusal to grant Soviet man those human feelings (chuvstv) that we call intimate. So it appears that our Soviet man does not love, does not suffer, feels no jealousy, and has no friends."[8]

A Soviet feeling, however, could not be just like any other. Konstantin Iukov agreed that art should make its case through "human passions," but specified that those passions must be of a specifically Soviet type: neither abstract nor self-focused, they would instead be goal oriented and collective.[9] What, then, would they look (and feel) like on-screen? In the first half of the 1930s, the answer to this question was by no means clear—and it was caught up in debates about Socialist Realist style.

The complex question of Soviet feelings also had a formal aesthetic element. Central to the search for a model of Socialist Realist cinema was the conviction that film must engage the spectator through feelings.[10] In Iezuitov's words, "The intellectual style did not succeed in putting an end to the opposition between the 'language of logic' and the 'language of feelings' (chuvstv) as Eisenstein hoped. This is what the style of socialist feelings (sotsialisticheskikh chuvstv) will achieve, seeking to create a unity between reason and feelings (chuvstv), understanding and aesthetic pleasure."

These are familiar elements of the Socialist Realist aesthetic, of course: the project of making cinema for the masses, which would be at once educational and entertaining, picturing an ideal Soviet reality, peopled with model heroes. Close attention to the precise terms through which these issues were debated, however, allows us to trace aspects of the imagined poetics—and in particular the sensory and emotional address—of Socialist Realist cinema that are habitually overlooked. Throughout his article, Iezuitov exploited the double meaning of chuvstvo to describe both bodily sensation and emotion. What was the relationship between feeling-as-sensation and feeling-as-emotion? What was the place of pleasure in Socialist Realist film style? And how did the search for a "cinema of socialist feelings" in the first half of the 1930s change the treatment of cinematic material, and of sensation?

This chapter will explore the search for appropriate forms of feeling for the new Soviet subject. It will show how one model of feeling gave way to another (how sensation was replaced by emotion), and how this inflected Soviet cinema's materialist project. This is emphatically not a study of Soviet emotions, however. Indeed, scholarly study of the Stalinist project as one of regulating and controlling the emotions has developed over recent years.[11] I am concerned rather to uncover the hidden history of sensation in early Socialist Realism. In what follows, I will focus on selected films that were directly concerned with the question of what socialist chuvstva might feel like. These films played a part in showing "good" Stalinist feelings, but they were also self-reflexively concerned with the broader question of the relationship between film and feeling, and navigated the complex interface between emotion and sensation. The shape of Socialist Realism—and indeed of Soviet Stalinism—was not yet clear: I suggest that in films produced between 1932 and 1937 there was a search for a peculiarly Stalinist affect—one that would enable film spectators not just to understand, but also to *feel*, the promise of socialism. In 1933, Petrov-Bytov called for sincerity in Soviet film: "We must learn to feel (chuvstvovat´) Soviet reality."[12] Film, he asserted, must communicate with the spectator at the level of the heart, through class intuition. In this early period of Socialist Realism, that project was both sensory and emotional: faktura and material had a key role to play.

Emotional Cinema: The Background

In 1930, Adrian Piotrovskii, then artistic director of the Leningrad film studio, gave a landmark speech to the Communist Academy. In this speech, he distinguished two directions in Soviet cinema during its first decade: "intellectualism," exemplified by the work of Eisenstein, and "emotionalism" (*emotsional'nost'*), represented by Dovzhenko, Pudovkin, Shengelaia, and Evgenii Cherviakov.[13] In part, this speech was Piotrovskii's attempt to distance himself from formalism, through criticism of the intellectual avant-garde. But the opposition was suggestive, and formed the basis for much future discussion—framing, for example, Iezuitov's call for a "cinema of feelings," and a substantial three-part essay by Mikhail Bleiman published in 1933.[14] Both critics followed Piotrovskii in suggesting that emotionalism represented the most productive path for the future of Soviet cinema.

In the speech, Piotrovskii looked back at the 1920s and singled out one film for particular praise. *My Son* (*Moi syn*, 1928) was the second film of Evgenii Cherviakov. His first, *Girl from a Distant River* (*Devushka s dalekoi reki*, 1927) is lost. But *My Son* (recently discovered in an Argentinian film archive) gives us a sense of why Cherviakov was considered such an important director during the 1920s.[15] It also reveals the key challenges that shaped the evolution of so-called psychological cinema in Soviet Russia—and alerts us to the discursive context in which discussion of Soviet feelings emerged.

My Son is directly concerned with psychology, with picturing human suffering. Andrei and Ol'ga are a young married couple, introduced by two close-ups, intercut with inter titles: "The wife" and "The husband." They are at a hospital; Ol'ga gives birth to a baby (off-screen), and then they leave the hospital, carrying a child wrapped in a blanket. They stop at the foot of a staircase. Ol'ga's face is seen in close-up, and she speaks the fatal words (shown on a title card): "Forgive me" (cut to a close-up of her face), "The boy is not your son." The rest of the film tracks Andrei's emotional response to this cataclysmic news, and his attempt to find a way of being a "father" to the baby. It traces his subtle shifts of emotion, examining the nature of fatherhood and parental love. Its end—when Andrei rescues the baby from a fire—provides a possibly redemptive conclusion. He is more of a father to the boy than the real father (who has abandoned him in an attempt to save himself), and achieves a kind of heroism. But the clarity of this moment is ultimately undercut by a questioning title: "Will they get back together? Who knows? . . ."

With its refusal of a simple message, Bagrov has called *My Son* "existential cinema," revealing nothing more (or less) than human emotion itself.[16] It is the antithesis of Abram Room's *Bed and Sofa*—a film produced in the same year, and which treats ostensibly similar material. In *Bed and Sofa*, characters are shown enmeshed in the world; in *My Son*, context is almost absent. As contemporary critic Boris Alpers observed, "Characters fall out of their material surroundings."[17] They are revealed bare. Cherviakov described his project as "showing anger, love, despair, jealously—in a word, all that complicated complex of emotional phenomena," and doing so "without any historical, everyday-life (*bytovye*), industrial, or other accessories."[18] In this sense, the film is an antithesis not only of *Bed and Sofa*, but of the very project that is the subject of this book: the Marxist-inflected attempt to show human life as formed by material context. Certainly, *My Son* was purposefully and pointedly outside the established trajectories of Soviet cinema. In Cherviakov's words, it featured "no things, no masses, no beautiful views, or carefully considered tricks of editing; just people."[19] It is largely composed of extended close-ups that, as contemporary critics and memoirists noted, last for an unusually long time.[20] The camera is largely static; there are few point-of-view shots; lighting is minimal and not atmospheric; set design is minimal (production designer Meinkin pictured the family apartment as empty but for a child's cradle and a stool); and the film as a whole features few physical objects. Robbed of distraction, Bagrov notes, "The spectator can do nothing other than look at these 'pointless' frames."[21]

Fig. 7.1 The Faktura of the Face. Still from *My Son* (*Moi syn*, dir. Ivan Cherviakov, production design by S. Meinkin, 1928).

For all these differences, however, *My Son* does share with other Soviet films of its time the conviction that cinema could be a revelatory tool. It seeks to provide an epistemology of human emotion—to turn the objective eye of the camera onto the human face. Human expression and feeling provide its material (figure 7.1): skin appears as a surface, its pores almost visible; subtle lighting reveals the dips and hollows of the face in nuanced shades of gray; lips and eyes function almost as material things on-screen. Thus the spectator is brought into an affective relationship with the face and its emotions, which moves beyond intellectual understanding into embodied empathy.

Cherviakov's use of the close-up in this film—and his focus on the human face—were unique in the Soviet context, but they had strong links with a wider European context: in particular the work of Delluc and Epstein, and the writings of Béla Balázs. In *The Visible Man*, Balázs analyzed the capacity of film to reveal "the face"—not just of people, but also of things. A close-up of the human face was, for Balázs, one of the most powerful images of cinema: "A face can display the most varied emotions simultaneously.... These are the chords of feeling whose essence is in fact their simultaneity. Such simultaneity cannot be expressed in words."[22]

In similar terms, Epstein identified the human face as one of the most "photogenic" objects. Close-ups of the face, he suggested, could reveal the subtle movements that betray emotion: "Muscular preambles ripple beneath the skin. Shadows shift, tremble, hesitate. Something is being decided. A breeze of emotion underlines the mouth with clouds."[23] Epstein's own 1923 film, *A Faithful Heart*, provided a powerful realization of this idea: like *My Son*, it is a melodrama stripped back to a raw revelation of human emotion. The camera dwells for long shots on the scarcely moving faces of its protagonists, and depends on the capacity of the actors to express minute nuances of feeling.

Both Balázs and Epstein saw cinema as having epistemological ambition—and, crucially, as providing "knowledge" through an embodied (phenomenological) encounter with material. Both, however, lacked the overt ideological dimension that had characterized the Soviet phenomenological impulse in cinema through the 1920s, and which became still more important with the advent of Socialist Realism. This alerts us to the complexity of the lessons for Soviet cinema that Piotrovskii sought in Cherviakov's emotional style. Piotrovskii was explicit in calling his emotional cinema a "cinema of *socialist* passions," and framing it in ideological terms. How, though, could the emotions of *My Son* be seen as specifically Soviet? Piotrovksii's own answer to that question was that the protagonist grapples with the emotional complexities of embracing a new model of socialist fatherhood (determined not by biological paternity but by social responsibility). This is tenuous, however: although a sequence of shots in the film does picture a new model of collective child-rearing, they seem out of place in the narrative, and certainly do not provide its emotional weight.[24] Was there a way of reconciling Cherviakov's bare focus on human emotion with the specificity of the Soviet context? Could there be such a thing as a specifically Soviet psychological cinema? What was particular about Soviet feelings? These complex questions formed a set of preoccupations for filmmakers and critics that stretched through this formative period. They shaped the changing treatment of material and faktura in Soviet cinema between 1932 and 1937.

From Sensation to Feeling

Piotrovskii's overarching argument had operated at two levels. First, Soviet cinema should not be afraid to treat emotional questions: to show fully realized individuals, grappling with emotional challenges. Second, such individually focused cinema would engage the spectator at an emotional, rather than rational, level. These emotions, however, would be of a particularly Soviet type: the problems faced by characters could not be limited to individual narratives and crises; and it followed that spectatorial affect would also be of a new type. Piotrovskii distinguished the curious and light-hearted feeling solicited by an individual plot, from the deeper sensations (oshchushcheniia) and serious emotions (ser'eznye emotsii) that could be elicited by a social theme. Indeed, the task of cinema was to turn oshchushchenie (here understood as precognitive affect) into serious emotion.[25]

The issue was by no means simple, however, and the complexity of debates around "emotional cinema" in the early 1930s is particularly evident in two areas: the screenplay, and the art of acting. In the case of the former, Aleksandr Rzheshevskii's theories of the "emotional scenario" provided a focus for discussion. Rzheshevskii produced screenplays for Zheliabuzhskii's *It is Not Permitted to Enter the City* (*V gorode vkhodit' nel'zia*, 1928), Pudovkin's *Simple Case/Life is Good* (*Prostoi sluchai /Ochen' khorosho zhivetsia*, 1930–1933) and, fatefully, for Eisenstein's *Bezhin Meadow* (*Bezhin lug*, 1937).[26] His brief period of influence was an important moment in the search for a Soviet cinema of feelings. First, it was an experiment in cinematic process: Rzheshevskii sought to use the screenplay not as an iron-clad structure dictating precise shots, and the like, but rather as a stimulus for the director and cameraman's imagination—and most specifically for the notation of mood, emotion, and feeling.[27] Second, it was part of the wider search for what Pudovkin described as "a new kind of psychological cinema."[28]

Life is Good was to be Pudovkin's first sound film; technical (and ideological) difficulties meant, however, that it was finally released in a shortened version, as a silent film, and with a new name, *A Simple Case* (*Prostoi sluchai*) in 1932. Responding to accusations of epic monumentalism in *Storm over Asia*, with this film Pudovkin sought to trace the lived experience of an ordinary Bolshevik, a heroic former soldier in the Civil War, and the emotional challenges he encounters after the war (faced with the temptations of real urban life), in continuing to be "good." Langovoi is married to Masha; and the couple, who met and fell in love as revolutionaries during the Civil War, live in close proximity with their comrades Zheltikov and "Uncle" Sasha. Masha's love for Langovoi is the single constant in the film, and its thematic focus. But the young soldier is weak and betrays her with another woman: the city, implicitly, lures him into moral decline. Although they do not directly voice their disapproval, Langovoi's friends take Masha into their home. Eventually, the errant husband returns to his wife and is forgiven, and the friends are shown united at the end of the film as active members of a Soviet kolkhoz.

Like *My Son*, *Life is Good* stripped its plot back to human feeling. This is echoed in formal strategies. The film is marked by close-ups of faces—in particular the face of Masha. Pudovkin explicitly sought a form of montage that would convey emotional states. Here, however, instead of the fervor of revolutionary endeavor (as in his previous films), the emotions were those of intimacy and marital love. This is a love story in Soviet terms: shared duty and endeavor eventually vanquish temporary infatuation, and the love of a couple is seen as part of a larger social family. *Life is Good* was a troubled film, however; and its troubles give an indication of the intricacies of making psychological cinema in this early period. Shklovskii was highly critical of Rzheshevskii's "emotional scenario"—accusing it of impressionistic vagueness, and an overreliance on emotion.[29] When Pudovkin screened the film's first version, critics lamented its lack of focus, and failure to engage with the real, pressing issues of socialist construction, and accused it of formalism.[30] After all, the question of psychological cinema retained considerable ideological complexity: it was not long since the revolutionary avant-garde had explicitly distanced itself from the Western trap of "psychologism" (satirized in Rodchenko's photomontage).[31] And Pudovkin's experiments with sound, along with his emotional montage, prompted accusations of incomprehensibility.

In addition to the innovation of its screenplay, *Life is Good* was also an experiment in work with actors. Continuing the work he had begun in *Storm over Asia*, Pudovkin used untrained actors and sought to induce "psychological-physical" states in them.[32] Such work was part of his evolving inquiry into the craft of acting, and in particular into the expression of feeling.[33] Cherviakov, too, had explicitly set out to find actors who could work on the expression of emotional states. In their different ways, both directors were responding to changing frameworks shaping the discussion of acting on the Soviet screen. In broad terms, between the late 1920s and mid-1930s there was a shift away from the focus on the body and its reflexes (which had dominated actors' training through the 1920s), and toward "psychology."[34] Yet as Pudovkin's psychological-physical ambition makes clear, the two categories remained closely imbricated during this transitional period. This complexity is vividly expressed in a multipart essay by Abram Room, published in *Kino* in 1932.[35] Room acknowledged the profound influence of his experience in Bekhterev's Neurological Institute on his understanding of actors' craft, but argued that the curriculum in GTK (GIK) had become overly dependent upon mechanized views of the human body, suggesting that biomechanics and reflexology needed to cede to a new "emotionally integrated" vision of film acting.[36]

More research into the evolving norms of Soviet acting, and the relationship between screenplay and film production, would be of great benefit to our knowledge of Soviet cinema in this period. They are not my focus here, however. Rather, I am interested in shifting notions of cinematic material (and sensation), and their link to the agenda of Soviet feelings. Here consideration of the prologue of *Life is Good* is revealing. Spectators were reportedly particularly bemused by this part of the film, which has no diegetic relationship with the main narrative. Initially, in a long take, a lone soldier returns to the embrace of his wife. The couple watch their sleeping child, before the child's awakening and preparation for the day becomes the focus of an extended slow montage sequence that emphatically emphasizes sensory experience. Breeze moves the curtains on their open window and can be imaginatively felt on his bare skin. Water splashes on him; and when he vigorously towels his torso, the camera captures the young boy's embodied, youthful vitality. These characters do not feature again in the film, and are not psychologically developed individuals. They operate on-screen only as bodies that feel, and as such, they provide the sensory-emotional baseline from which the film departs: an ideal model of father, mother, and son, which Pudovkin sets as a standard for the "true" Soviet hero.

The prologue images in *Life is Good* seek to embed ethics in the body—to operate, in Pudovkin's terms, "psycho-physically," providing the spectator with a sensory encounter with the embodied experience of the Soviet hero. Here the phrase "emotional saturation" (*emotsional'naia nasyshchennost'*), which appeared with increasing frequency in discussions focusing on the development of the Soviet style on-screen from the late 1920s on, is relevant. The call for "emotionally saturated" images was above all a challenge to the so-called intellectualism of those avant-garde films designated "Formalist."[37] But the term had wider resonance, and speaks to the complex relationship between emotion and sensation that is our subject here. Abram Room had suggested as early as 1926 that "real cinema is one that is emotionally saturated."[38] Toporkov described the emotional saturation of the *predmetnyi zhest* (see chapter 4). In an important article of 1928, art critic Iakov Tugendkhol'd described the "new realism" of the Association of Easel Painters (OST) as "emotionally saturated," praising its shift from a (Constructivist) focus on pure material to material as "filtered through emotion."[39] This did not mean a rejection of the value of faktura and sensation (oshchushchenie) in visual art, however. It was, rather, an attempt to inflect the avant-garde interest in material with a new ideology of feeling: to capture a new "sensation of the world (*mirooshchushchenie*)."[40]

The complexity of these arguments—and in particular of the concept of emotionally saturated images—directs our attention to the particularities of the early Socialist Realist treatment of filmic material as part of the search for a model of socialist feeling. How do people touch the world, and how does it touch them? And what is the relationship between this touching and their emotional formation? Finally, how do "emotionally saturated" images engage the spectator? What happened to the Soviet haptic in the early 1930s, as the new "cinema of feelings" took shape?

The First Films of Socialist Feeling

The shift described by Tugendkhol'd, from "external *tekhnitsizm*" to "emotionally saturated realism," was echoed in Grigorii Kozintsev's categorization of his 1931 film *Alone* (*Odna*) as a new stage in FEKS's work: "I grew up infatuated with faktura—beloved word of young artists," Kozintsev recalled, "but now I felt ever more clearly that a person, limited on screen to mere external appearance, and to signs of the simplest emotions, will appear artificial, illusory. It's as untrue as doors, drawn on a set wall: you sense that they have no volume (ob"em)."[41]

This was a statement of new purpose for FEKS. For Kozintsev, the opposition between faktura (surface) and ob"em (volume) mirrored the distinction between filmic *material* (and sensation) and *feelings*—between the body and the "inner" self—that is our subject here. In *Alone*, the FEKS collective attempted to bring these two things together.

Alone was one of the first Soviet sound films and, as such, it signals a core transition in Soviet filmmaking. It was, in fact, a transitional film in many respects, and particularly in the story of socialist sensations. It has an explicit and thematic focus on the individual (alone), and was hailed in the cinema press as one of the first films attempting to deal with human psychology, to show the inner struggle of a Soviet person.[42] The plot is straightforward. City resident Kuz'mina has graduated as a teacher, and anticipates a life with her fiancé in the big city. Under some pressure, she agrees to a posting in Altai. There, her idealized visions of teaching stumble against the sordid reality of rural life in this distant corner of the Soviet state. A series of trials allow for Kuz'mina's eventual emergence as a truly committed member of the Soviet collective. As such, the film is a prototype of the familiar Socialist Realist master plot.[43] Beyond its primary ideological message, however, *Alone* asserted the need for the Soviet citizen to renounce his/her dreams of a material "good life." It explored how the new social order changes the relationship between man/woman and the material world.

In a sense, *Alone* reveals the failure of one ideal of the new Soviet modern, located in urban space. The film begins with a sequence of shots of its heroine, waking alone in her single-person room in Moscow: her sleeping head, sunk into a pillow; the lace cuff of her nightdress; a vase of flowers in a window; a transparent curtain. In an attempt to escape the call of her alarm, the heroine buries her head beneath her pillow. Within the otherwise denuded space of her room, the silken bedspread and lace cuff acquire a poignant materiality. They are signs of bourgeois comfort used by our heroine as protection from the onslaught of real (collective) life. In the course of the film, Kuz'mina's relationship with these and other objects in the film serves as an index of her moral and ideological evolution. With her fiancé, she browses in a kitchenware shop. The store-window display here can be viewed as an allusion to the department store that had played a central role in the directors' *New Babylon* (1929) (the fact that it is the same actress underscores this). There, the store display was an orgy of patterned textile, compelling the spectator into an awareness of suffocating texture and materiality. By contrast, these objects do not interact sensuously with the characters on-screen, and surfaces seem to refuse tactile engagement. When our protagonists first admire the crockery, they do so through the glass of a shop window. Later, after Kuz'mina's dreams of the good life are shattered, she returns to the same shop window, and her hand lingers longingly on its glass, the transparent barrier between her and the object (figure 7.2 a, b, c). The camera focuses on a single cup and saucer, simultaneously encouraging and denying an appreciation of their material texture. The reflective white surfaces of the crockery, behind glass, are flat and smooth, rather than textural. In their intransigent and indifferent materiality, these objects seem to look

Fig. 7.2 Look, Don't Touch. Stills from *Alone* (*Odna*, dir. G. Kozintsev and L. Trauberg, production design by E. Enei, 1930).

Fig. 7.2 (*Continued*).

back at Kuz′mina: untouchable. The spectator, too, is refused the sensory pleasure of a haptic encounter with the material.[44]

Thus the first part of *Alone* pictures a world that cannot be touched. It presents the dream of a new, modern, domestic space (of refashioned intimacy), and charts its failure. It suggests that modern urban life is marked by a rupture between bodies and things—by a dulling of physical sensation—and that this is a core problem preventing self-realization in the new Soviet space. This marks an important moment in the story of socialist sensation. In opposition to the dematerialized world of the city, *Alone* makes an intriguing return to the tropes of the Soviet "primitive" that were the subject of chapter 5. In Altai, the smooth surfaces of the objects that surrounded Kuz′mina in the city are replaced by textures, by a more tactile interaction between the human body and the elements. Local men and women shear sheep (figure 7.3 a, b), their hands grasping the wool, cutting, rubbing; a dried horse skin is stretched on poles; close-ups reveal the heavily lined faces of the laboring villagers. The faktura of these images signal the ethnic space, emphasizing the otherness of the native byt. In simple terms, it

Fig. 7.3 Redemptive Touching. Stills from *Alone* (*Odna*, dir. G. Kozintsev and L. Trauberg, production design by E. Enei, 1930).

signifies backwardness. It also, however, establishes an alternative model of experience. A different sensory code structures the screen and directly echoes the model of felt knowledge (naoshchup´) envisaged by Tret´iakov (chapter 5). This is a world lived in close-up. Again, hands act as a symbol of a proximate relationship between man and material: in Altai, Kuz´mina escapes the false, dematerialized surfaces of her previous life, metaphorically touches the world, and is redeemed.

The contemporary critic Sutyrin interpreted this aspect of *Alone* as a self-reflexive statement of purpose, a rejection of the stylization of the director's previous work, and a commitment to a new aesthetic: "And thus FEKS, like the heroine of their new film, became more and more densely [Sutyrin uses the term 'fleshily'] enmeshed in the reality of life."[45] As such, the film was a manifesto for a cinema that engaged in fully sensory ways with the material world, but moved on from the avant-garde preoccupation with material for its own sake. It was an attempt to adapt old preoccupations to new ideological demands. As Kozintsev acknowledged, *Alone* sought to represent human "volume," to make inner life visible. The empty sets in Altai offered a tabula rasa upon which a new (handheld) feeling for the world could be modeled.

Alone was one of a core group of films that were consistently cited as turning points in the development of Soviet cinema. Another fundamental film in this respect was Iutkevich and Ermler's 1932 *Counterplan* (see chapter 6), described by both Iezuitov and Bleiman as heralding a new stage in Soviet cinema. Specifically, it was celebrated for transforming the Soviet production film genre, as a film about "a man building a turbine, and not the other way around."[46] It followed the socialist "path to consciousness" of veteran worker Babchenko, and of young Pavel, both of whom are led to greater virtue by the exemplary young communist Vasia. In distinction from the production films discussed in chapter 4, *Counterplan* was remarkable in trying to give each of its characters a real emotional life. As such, it engaged directly with the new discourse on feelings. Lebedev described it as the first film that had "correctly, on a high ideological level, reflected Soviet reality" in "full-blooded images of concrete living people."[47] For Balázs, *Counterplan* was unique in showing not "the individual amid the masses, but the masses inside the individual."[48] For Iezuitov, it was an exemplary move toward the "cinema of socialist feelings."[49]

The path for the new Soviet film style was by no means clear, however, and *Counterplan* prompted fierce debate about the two key questions facing

Socialist Realist cinema: the shape of the new "realism," and the place of individual psychology in film. How could a film protagonist be at once individual and typical? How could his feelings be both personal and social? Much attention was focused on the directors' inclusion of a love story for the film's positive hero: Vasia is in love with Katia, the wife of Pavel. When her marriage goes through difficulties, Katia and Vasia go for a walk through Leningrad during a long white night, and the lyrical potential of the landscape is exploited as a backdrop for the melancholy of Vasia's unrequited, and even unexpressed, love. For Balázs, this scene was evidence of *Counterplan*'s success in combining individual psychology and a strong socially relevant storyline. Mikhail Bleiman argued, however, that *Counterplan* featured not real human psychology but only the appearance of it.[50] The film featured only superficial psychological moments, but the real psychology of the characters is not revealed.[51]

In his criticism, Bleiman returned to the relationship between the material of cinema, and its capacity for psychological truth-to-life. He accused the film of being based on merely ornamental objects: its naturalistic details were only a decoration on the surface of a film constructed according to a predetermined theme and ideological message.[52] Thus it was not truly realistic in Soviet terms: it failed to show characters' lives *through* (and intertwined with) the details of the material world that they inhabit. It did not allow for the contingent, shifting relationship between man and world. *Counterplan*'s coscreenwriter and codirector, Arnshtam, published a robust response to Bleiman's criticism. He asserted that *Counterplan* was one of the least ornamental films in the history of Soviet cinema, and that its directors had set themselves the challenge of going "into the depths of the material," revealing individual life—and emotion—as formed *in context*, in concrete interaction with the social and material world.[53]

Material and Feeling

How should we understand the use of the term "material" in these discussions, and how is it different from the use of the term in critical and theoretical writings from the 1920s? According to Bleiman, the shift toward individual psychology in film was a rejection of the "thirst for material" that had dominated Soviet cinema of the 1920s.[54] In similar terms, Konstantin Iukov described the new cinema as a liberation from an obsession with the material that had distinguished earlier Soviet cinema.[55] Echoing common criticisms of "Formalist" cinema, Iukov proposed that earlier films based on a particular industrial context (he named Room's *Potholes* here [see chapter 4]), were guilty of turning reality into mere cinematic material focused on the faktura and formal organization of their industrial context.[56] By contrast, the new cinema must be focused not on "*material* in its external expressivity, but on reality (*deistvitel'nost'*) in its deeper processes of meaning."[57] Iukov's use of "material" and "reality" here echoes Kozintsev's distinction between "surface" and "volume" in shaping protagonists on-screen. It also mirrors classic Marxist distinctions between realism and naturalism: a specifically Socialist Realism reveals not the surface appearance of reality (like naturalism), but rather its underlying processes.[58]

What happened, then, to cinematic material in the cinema of the 1930s? Socialist Realist theoreticians were at pains to distinguish Socialist Realism from the naturalist preoccupation with real material for its own sake. In this early period, however, this endeavor was complicated by two things. First, there was an abiding (ideologically sanctioned) interest in the capacity of film to picture the material conditions of Soviet subjectivity: the self is formed in, and by, the home, the workplace, and the world. It is clear from his criticism of *Counterplan* that Bleiman sought to reconcile the materialist impulse of earlier films with the new calls for "socialist feeling": Soviet emotions must emerge out of, and be shaped by, a relationship with the material.

The second key aspect of the emerging Socialist Realist film aesthetic lay in an understanding of the affective power of the image as emerging from a sensory encounter between the spectator and "real" material on-screen. It was a fundamental requirement of Socialist Realist cinema to make such an affective appeal to its spectator, to convey the unique feeling of Soviet reality. Iukov, for example, called for the presentation of "reality" on-screen through what he called "sensorially (*chuvstvenno*) concrete images."[59] As the style of Socialist Realism was tested and shaped during the early 1930s, these two factors shaped discussion. They gave rise to complex and contradictory statements. Although Socialist Realist cinema should take care to avoid the celebration of material for its own sake, it should nevertheless seek to present "emotionally saturated" images.[60] And these "emotionally saturated" images would be "sensorially concrete," operating on the spectator through the senses.

It is clear, then, that the double meaning of chuvstvo as both sensory and emotional was exploited by filmmakers and theorists in their attempt to articulate a new model of Soviet feeling on-screen. Here we can return to Iezuitov's concept of the "*style* of socialist feelings."[61] The new cinema would not just show Soviet feelings through its protagonists and their stories, it would convey them in its style. In his discussion, Iezuitov explicitly distinguished "style" from "form," and referenced art theorist Ieremaia Ioffe in support.[62] Ioffe's evolving views of cinema between 1927 and 1933 mirror shifting ideological frameworks.[63] In 1927, he characterized cinema as enabling an intensified multisensory appreciation of the material world, describing "the unquestionable reality of the viewed objects [which] leads to an unmediated association between vision and touch (*osiazanie*) (the palpating of the screen by peasants)."[64] He praised constructivist cinema for giving life to inanimate objects, but lamented that cinema was not capable of representing the inner world of characters: "Cinema understands embodied man, his actions and his behavior, but not his psychology or his ideas."[65] In 1933, however, articulating his new "synthetic theory" of (Socialist Realist) art, Ioffe returned to the question with a new approach.[66] He argued that the shift in world systems brought about by industrialization, science, and particularly socialist revolution, had radically changed the relationship between the human subject and the object world.[67] The world, he claimed, had "ceased to be external, objective, for man."[68] Thus, in Soviet Russia "the opposition between ... sensibility (*chuvstvennost'*) and consciousness (*soznanie*), between subject and object ... , is obliterated."[69]

Clearly, this was an ideologically astute sleight of hand, but it was a useful one: if the oppositions between sensibility (chuvstvennost') and consciousness, body and mind, and between man and the object world, had been *overcome* by socialism, then Socialist Realist cinema could invoke the full sensory affect of the material in service of its project, in order to present the particular psychology of Sovietness. Sensory faktura and its screened pleasures could be an expression of the perfect union between (wo)man and world enabled by Soviet socialism. Ioffe's terms were echoed in many statements of the period. Balázs, for example, described the new *zhizneoshchushchenie* (life-sensation) of socialist Russia (expressed in *Counterplan*) as the product of "the *organic union* of labour and life in Socialist society."[70] Soviet man or woman would *feel* the world differently; this different bodily feeling would in turn create new, distinctly Soviet, emotions; and in turn it would demand a new kind of art.

Wordless Feeling

Alongside *Counterplan*, Balázs praised Boris Barnet's *Outskirts* (*Okraina*, 1933) for presenting this new, specifically Soviet, life-sensation. *Outskirts*, indeed, was frequently mentioned in these contexts. Although set in prerevolutionary provincial Russia during the First World War, this film is directly concerned with questions of subjectivity, and as such can be seen as part of the search for models of socialist feeling. Produced in 1933, as the tenets of Socialist Realist cinema began to be fixed, it sought to adapt Barnet's already established interest in ordinariness and lived experience to changing ideologies.

The eponymous "outskirt" is a provincial town where Petr Ivanovich and his two sons, Nikolai and Semen, are employed in a shoemaking workshop. The film's opening sequences include a long scene of them, and their community of fellow shoemakers, at work. In contrast to the solitary labor of Kirik in *The Parisian Cobbler* (see chapter 4), this is collective endeavor. The men are surrounded by the tools of their trade, and the camera dwells on their handling of the leather and soles, hammering nails to create shoes. Though the film is set in a factory town, its emphasis is on this act of preindustrial manufacture—and, implicitly, on the kinds of human subjects that such hands-on making produces.

The film's setting amid shoemaking is indicative of its broader poetics, its naturalistic focus on that which is habitually overlooked. Feet figure early in the film: while the shoes and boots are made, a woman sits in the corner and has her feet measured, her legs drawing the attention of the mischievous male workers. Later, the war demands a different kind of footwear: the workshop shifts to the mass production of army boots. At the trenches, Nikolai mends the boot of a fellow soldier, whose foot protrudes below his trousers, heavily wrapped against the cold. There is an explosion; the boy is killed; his lone (now unneeded) boot is thrown symbolically from the trenches. The message is clear: the reality of war is one of sore feet, boots with holes, and acute physical suffering—often as banal as it is tragic. This emphasis on the physicality of lived experience is striking throughout the film. It is, of course, characteristic of Barnet's early work (see chapter 3). As in *Girl with a Hatbox*, when Il'ia sleeps, and his need for comfort is emphasized by a shot of his large body scarcely covered by a small quilt, so in *Outskirts* when the workers sleep, young Semen's bare feet poke out from his small quilt. As Nikolai sets out for war, carefully folding his quilt and blanket, setting aside his kettle, the film offers a vivid understanding of lived experience. These soldiers are ordinary men, their fragility evidenced in the meager comforts that they collect around them. At the front, it is Semen's poignantly felt toothache that leads, with shocking bathos, to his violent death. "What have I done to you?" he screams at the senior officer, who ignores the throbbing pain of his teeth and drags him out of the trench to face the enemy,

In *Outskirts*, the war is shown in terms of its impacts, not its meanings. Indeed, the film emphasizes war's absolute lack of meaning for the ordinary men on both sides who are forced to fight for imperial powers, and those they leave behind. Their suffering is not allowed the grandeur of a higher purpose; but that does not make it less powerful. When Nikolai and Semen have left for the front, their father's pain is poignantly shown as he sits surrounded by the physical traces of their lives. Later, receiving news of Semen's death, Petr Ivanovich's grief is expressed in a single cry of anguish. Ultimately, *Outskirts* celebrates resilience: the capacity of human beings to find comfort, and even small pleasures, amid tragedy. Its redemptive moments of comfort are located in ordinariness, markedly outside established structures of meaning. Crucially, although this was a sound film, they are also located outside language. Barnet's careful use of sound emphasizes silence as much as it does voice, and it is often in moments of silence that the film's most poignant communication takes place. The camera focuses consistently on the experience of hands, and touch: from the nervous hands of a young man courting his lover, to the working hands of the shoemakers. When a young German solder is taken prisoner and sent to the village, it turns out that he is a shoemaker. Petr Ivanovich invites him to work with him, and the craft is the German prisoner's salvation: no words are needed in order for him to feel commonality with his Russian "captors." When a tentative love story develops between the prisoner and local girl Man'ka, their wordless communication bypasses the complexities of national languages and ideologies. They are reduced instead to feeling: they share sunflower seeds; they carefully set out the crockery for a ritual of tea.

In this way *Outskirts* makes a case for international brotherhood. When some members of the community want to punish the German prisoner for Semen's death, it is Petr Ivanovich who protects him: "What does it matter that he's a German? He's a shoemaker like you." This, ultimately, is the film's message. Barnet's attention to the lived experience of ordinariness is a rejection of the grand narratives of history, and the creation of an alternative story of the First World War—one in which the tragedy of workers forced to fight for imperial powers coexists with the creation of class-based bonds and the birth of proletarian consciousness. In this respect it echoes other films of the period such as Dovzhenko's *Arsenal*, and Ermler's *A Fragment of Empire*. Indeed, the only moment of traditional heroism occurs when Nikolai walks alone up out of the trenches and across the front line, waving a white handkerchief, in an assertion of common humanity between ordinary soldiers. It leads to a utopian vision of international brotherhood: "None of us wants to fight."

Outskirts prompted extensive discussion in the film press.[71] In early reviews, Bleiman and other representatives of RosARRK (The Russian Association of Workers in Revolutionary Cinematography) criticized Barnet's image of the provincial setting as principally "lyrical" and "impressionist."[72] They suggested that the film revealed traces of "Formalist Primitivism," and that its style undermined its thematic and ideological message. In a more extended essay, however, Bleiman was more circumspect, suggesting that the film *did* achieve a union of form and meaning. It offered, he suggested, a "formalism of the living human being, rather than the external formalism of previous art."[73] In contrast to *Counterplan*'s "false" psychologism, *Outskirts* succeeded in presenting "empirical man."[74] Where *Counterplan* had used material detail for the surface decoration of an already established idea, the message of *Outskirts* was located *in* the details. Historical events are shown through the prism of real people and real life; emotion is shown as *lived*. In Bleiman's terms, material and emotion came together in a particular Soviet model of feeling.

As prototypes for the new socialist self were tested on-screen in this period, then, *Outskirts* offered one possible vision of Soviet subjectivity. It operated *within* contemporary discourses, and sought to answer contemporary demands. Ivan Popov was clear in identifying the film as a first step on a path to a new model of "synthetic" Socialist Realist cinema—one that represented that union of thought and feeling, man and the object world, that Ioffe had identified as unique to Soviet socialism.[75] Yet the film features characters that seem very different from the classic Socialist Realist hero. Perhaps Barnet's distinctive model of the individual subject offers us a glimpse of an alternative—and ultimately unrealized—future for Socialist Realism? Nikolai is one of many ordinary men, living not according to grand narratives, but enmeshed in the ordinariness of the everyday. According to Evgenii Margolit, "After the revolution as an overcoming of history comes an idyll that is non-heroic in principle. It is hero-less."[76] The film focuses on life as lived, as a goal in itself.

This ambition shaped the film's treatment of material and sensation. Although a sound film, *Outskirts* retained the same focus on embodied, nonlinguistic level of experience as locus of truth that we have identified in

Soviet silent cinema. Its life-sensation is located outside language and communicated through the senses. Here Margolit is again helpful: "In Barnet," he observes, "man returns to his primal, natural unity with the world."[77] This unity is determined by two things: handcraft and domestic ritual. Like the films treated in chapter 4, *Outskirts* presents the act of making as a founding principle for its vision of the socialist subject. It offers a model of (proto-) Soviet selfhood premised on intuition and sentience, and provokes a form of spectatorship that mirrors that proximate relationship between human and material. Ultimately, we might think of *Outskirts* as a direct response to calls, such as that of Petrov-Bytov, for sincerity in Soviet film—and for the film to communicate via class intuition.[78] In *Outskirts*, this class intuition is material and sensory. It works through the body. It is operative and visible (sensible) between the characters on-screen—and it seeks to interpolate the spectator into the same emotional-sensory bond.

Sentience and Sentiment

As Socialist Realism was consolidated, however, the shifting ideological climate seemed to call for a different model of feeling—one based not on intuition and sensation, but on conscious emotion. This, Iezuitov suggested, would be a new Soviet "sentimentalism," distinguished by a unity between feeling and reason.[79] The remaining sections of this chapter will examine two films that span the years 1934–1936: Aleksandr Macheret's *The Private Life of Petr Vinogradov* (1934), and Abram Room's ill-fated collaboration with Iurii Olesha, *A Severe Youth* (1936). Both were self-conscious reflections on the changing shape of socialist feelings: they raise questions about the emerging model of the Soviet subject, about the relationship between sensation and emotion, body and mind, and about film's place in this changing world.

Macheret described *The Private Life of Petr Vinogradov* as a response to increasingly urgent calls for film to offer complex, three-dimensional heroes, and the film was, as the title makes clear, directly engaged with the relation between public and private life. Critics echoed Macheret's emphasis: Evgenii Gabrilovich, for one, saw the film as part of a quest for "full-blooded" (*polnokrovnyi*) art, describing the eponymous Petr Vinogradov as one of the first "complex, temperamental, sharp, multidimensional" characters in Soviet cinema.[80]

The particular complexity of Petr Vinogradov, however, bears further consideration. He is an inventor, a self-made man in progress, an autodidact: he speaks loudly and often, proclaiming the value of science and endeavor in the revolutionary project. Petr moves from the provinces to the city to develop his technical education, and takes up residence in a collective hostel. The white walls of his spartan room are decked with photographs of scientists and learned men, whom he celebrates for their thinking (*myshlenie*). He has a rigorous daily timetable for self-improvement pinned on the wall above his bed, within which there is explicitly no time for pleasure. In this sense, Petr Vinogradov is engaged in a process of self-regulation, eliminating the unruly potentiality of the body (and heart), and transforming himself into what he believes to be an ideal Soviet hero (an ironic double of Chernyshevskii's ambivalent "revolutionary" Rakhmetov, from his 1863 novel *What is to be Done?*). The plot of the film, however, complicates this picture, for Petr's self-regulation leads, in some sense, to his downfall. He may be a successful inventor, but within the film's romantic plotline, he doesn't get the girl. He is so preoccupied with his inventions that he (literally) forgets about love—neglecting his girlfriend from home and failing to read signs of romantic interest from women he meets in the city. This romantic failure represents a much larger lack. Petr is revealed as "uncultured" (with culture understood here broadly, as beauty, pleasure, and sentiment). He is uninterested in art; he behaves badly at a concert performance. And he does not know how to have fun: when he is due to meet a girl at the funfair, Petr arrives late; instead it is his friend Senia who ends up enjoying himself—not just with the pleaures of the fair, but also with the girl.

According to Macheret, Petr Vinogradov suffered from a fatal combination of the enthusiasm of youth and *tekhnitsizm* (an excessive focus on the technical).[81] Like Tugendkhol´d in his descriptions of visual art, Macheret sets tekhnitsizm implicitly against emotional depth. It is important to note, however, that what Petr lacks is the ability to *feel*—through the body. Here the double meaning of chuvstvo, which incorporates both emotion and sensation, is helpful. The failure of tekhnitsizm is that it is insufficiently sensate. Rejecting Toporkov's utopian vision of a tekhnik who would be emotionally—and sensually—energized by his participation in the project of socialist construction (see chapter 4), Macheret pictures Petr Vinogradov as divorced from feelings—both physical and emotional. He does not know how to love or play. So in the context of 1934, the tekhnik Petr is an outmoded Soviet hero, needing remaking, with feelings, for the new age: the film makes a case for a model of Soviet subjectivity where there is a place for both sentiment and sensory pleasure, albeit reconfigured in Soviet socialist terms.

This thematic commentary is intertwined with a self-reflexive inquiry into the changing norms of Soviet cinema itself. Petr Vinogradov's "failure" is marked as an inability to appreciate beauty—either cultural (a symphony) or natural (landscape). This is underscored by the film's formal strategies. Certainly, *The Private Life of Petr Vinogradov* is narrative cinema in the emerging Socialist Realist mode: in simple terms, it uses continuity editing, its camerawork emphasizes stability rather than disruption, and its use of sound is broadly conventional. It lacks the potential of much of 1920s cinema to make a sensory challenge to the spectator at the level of form. This does not mean, however, that the film does not exploit cinematic material and texture to make its point. Production design has a key role to play here: the white walls of Petr's domestic interior are brightly lit. The light and color flatten their faktura. Against these surfaces, the unruly shapes and textures of a single bouquet of flowers stand out as an assertion of nature and beauty. They draw the spectator into an apprehension of the material presence (and necessity) of the flowers and what they symbolize: the need for aesthetic and sensory pleasure.

Such strategies work alongside the consolidating frameworks of Stalinist narrative cinema. They reveal the film's commentary on the changing paradigms of sensation as operating not just thematically, but also formally. Perhaps most strikingly, this early sound film makes the voice of its principal protagonist too loud. Petr speaks in a booming bass; he performs, but he does not listen, and the film mocks his bombastic poetry readings in the (implicitly outmoded) style of Vladimir Maiakovskii. However genuine Petr's commitment to the revolutionary project, it seems that these impassioned, declamatory statements are no longer the required genre for Soviet culture. His loudness is a symbol of his neglect of sensation, and this is a self-reflexive comment on film art itself. Amid the noise of dialogue, it suggests, there remains a place for the sensate encounters of silent cinema. Like Petr, the spectator needs to look and to feel. In this respect, the film provides a lens onto the new discourse on aesthetics (and beauty [*krasota*]) that was evolving in the early to mid-1930s.[82] In a landmark speech opening the 1935 Creative Conference of Soviet Cinema Workers, S. S. Dinamov made a call for the return of "beauty" as a core category in Soviet art.[83] Soviet beauty would be a new kind of beauty, however. It would be, Dinamov asserted, "the beauty of our reality": a "masculine beauty," not the coquettish, superficial beauty of bourgeois art.[84]

In this important speech, Dinamov's emphasis on beauty sat by side with a (by now familiar) call for films that would feature full-blooded characters who would feel on-screen. This juxtaposition prompts us to consider how the new discourse on feelings was linked to evolving ideas about film aesthetics, and specifically about filmic *material*. In this respect, in fact, Dinamov was particularly intriguing. He asserted emphatically, "Marx spoke of the sensory radiance (*chuvstvennyi blesk*) of the material." This sensory radiance needs to surround all our heroes; this sensory radiance needs to be in their actions, their gestures, in everything that they do."[85]

The phrase "chuvstvennyi blesk" here is intriguing. As we have noted, the term "chuvstvo" carries the dual meaning of emotional and sensory impact, and in the early to mid-1930s, in discussions of socialist feelings, it was consistently used to describe emotion, as well as sensation. Dinamov, however, explicitly referenced feeling-as-sensation. He cited Marx's description of chuvstvennyi blesk (taken from Marx's *The Holy Family*, and describing Francis Bacon's materialism[86]), and as such evoked a materialist philosophy of being: the same Marxist-inflected vision of a proximity between man and material that has been the subject of this book so far. Socialism, Dinamov suggested, would enable an encounter with the "sensory radiance" of the material; the task of film was to convey it. Chuvstvennyi blesk is emphatically sensory-sensual in meaning, rather than emotional. It captures the emphasis on affective materiality that underlay discussions of Socialist Realist film in this period. Blurring the distinction between feeling-as-emotion and feeling-as-sensation, Dinamov reveals the complexity of the Soviet aesthetic in these formative years. The dominance of sensation and material in the formulation of socialist models of subjectivity during the 1920s meant that these categories could not simply disappear with the advent of Socialist Realism. Rather, the years up to 1937 were a period of negotiation, a testing ground for Socialist Realism, as revolutionary paradigms of socialist sensation came together with those of the new Soviet "emotions" demanded by the changing ideological climate.

Art Made Flesh

The relationship between these two categories was directly explored in Abram Room's *A Severe Youth*. Like *The Private Life of Petr Vinogradov*, *A Severe Youth* raised questions about the shape of the new Soviet subject—and about the place of feelings (emotional *and* sensory) in particular. Toward the end, the hero Grisha enumerates the "complex of spiritual qualities" that any komsomol member must have. Alongside humanity, humility, sincerity, and generosity, Grisha adds an intriguing "sentimentality" (*sentimental´nost´*). Sentimentality, he elaborates, "that they might love not just marches, but waltzes too." Like Petr Vinogradov, the new Soviet youth must learn to feel. Yet the film's narrative—which tracks Grisha's possible love story with a young woman, Masha, who is married to an older man, an eminent surgeon—suggests that there is no place for sentiment. Masha opts to stay with her husband, the love story has no happy ending, and the plot seems to proclaim the victory of the scientist-surgeon as a scion of rationality and learning.[87]

Room's inquiry into the place of feeling in Soviet subjectivity takes place not only in the film's plot, however, but also in its visual and formal style. Here the apparent certainties of its thematic conclusion become more complex. This is a film in which the camera dwells with evident pleasure on the formal impact of *stuff*: wrought-iron railings, light and water, the marble of statues and bodies. Its opening sequence offers a lingering gaze onto the surface of a venetian blind, through a diaphanous screen to a table set with flowers and crystals, and rests on the black-and-white markings of the large head of a dog. The film abounds in semistill images of patterned, material surfaces. In abstracted close-up, material objects turn into textures and surfaces. The hair of the dog and the crystal of glass are transformed into pure cinematic material: they construct the surface of the screen and their defamiliarization prompts renewed appreciation of their faktura.

This consistent focus on material surfaces alerts us to the film's interrogation of the relationship between looking and feeling, which is carried out at thematic and formal levels. Thematically, through the characters of Stepanov, Masha, and Grisha, *A Severe Youth* stages an encounter between generations, between old and new worlds, coded in part through an opposition between looking and being looked at, between observing and acting. Tsitronov, a permanent guest in the home of Masha and Stepanov, is a corpulent representative of bourgeois greed and passivity. And he is a constant observer—even a voyeur—who watches, but does not act. Returning from her swim, Masha is uncomfortable to find his eyes upon her; later, he watches her alone in her chamber. In another scene, Tsitronov even turns Stepanov into a voyeur, handing him a telescope so that he can see the meeting between Grisha and Masha properly, and his commentary about the two young people provides a voice for the other man's fear of cuckoldry.

As observers, Stepanov and Tsitronov are differentiated from the younger generation, who are the constant objects of their gaze. They can look, but they cannot feel: their bodies are not sentient. By contrast, the young are characterized by action and movement. When Grisha arrives at the home of Masha and Stepanov, the two young people greet one another without dialogue (but with the accompaniment of a musical track). Here, Room turns his sound film into a silent film, as if in a conscious gesture to the narrative associations of the romantic silent rendezvous. But the significance of this silence goes further. Grisha and Masha do not speak because they do not need to. Theirs is a world of action and feeling rather than language, and as such it is differentiated from that of Stepanov and Tsitronov.

The youthful characters in this film are bodies to be admired, part of the film's material. The camera dwells on their bodies as both texture and volume. In one scene, after a stunning display of athletic prowess, Grisha and friends are in a changing room, still in their sports clothing, surrounded by classical statuary (figure 7.4). The equation of these fine living bodies with those of statuary is overt here, and throughout: both are objects to be contemplated. Grisha's discus-player friend Diskobol, whose name consciously evokes the famous Greek statue Discobolus (Diskobólos) of Myron,[88] the most magnificent of all the bodies in the room, lies on a couch, waiting to be massaged. In another scene, his toned body, throwing his discus, assumes the harmonious balance of the statue that provides his name. Masha, too, is explicitly linked to statuary: in her absence, Stepanov gazes at a statue of Venus, positioned alongside a photograph of her. As she moves amid the waves in the film's opening sequence, she is like Venus Anadyomene, an iconic image of the birth of Aphrodite, eternally renewed by the waves.[89] Later, Diskobol moves backstage in a ballet theater, through an underground room populated by classical statues of naked youths: in ballet, as in sculpture, the human body is transformed into a plastic work of art.

Unlike statues, however, the film's young protagonists are not just objects to be observed. They are art made flesh: bodies that act and, crucially, that also feel (the world), living in enhanced sensory relationship with material. It is important in this respect that Diskobol's walk amid the statuary takes place in total silence. Béla Balázs memorably described the capacity of silent film to reveal "the hidden common language of mute things, conversing with each other, recognizing each other's shapes and entering into relations with each other."[90] Such a mute communion is established between Diskobol and the statues here, and powerfully emphasized by the silence of Room's soundtrack. It is, the film suggests, a mode of experience that is unavailable to representatives of the old world. In this sense, the film echoes a core idea of Olesha's 1927 novel *Envy*, whose protagonist, Kavalerov,

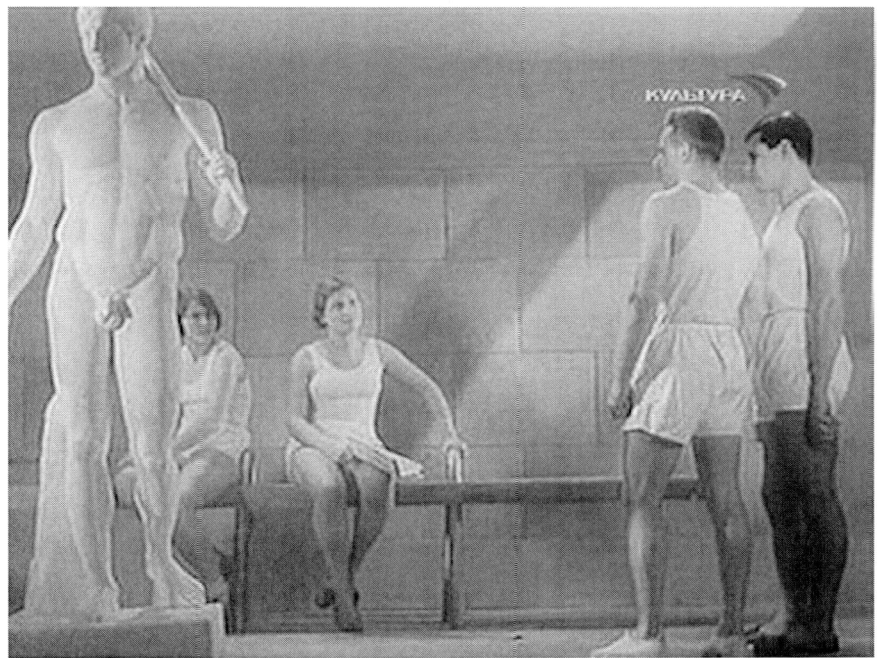

Fig. 7.4 Art Made Flesh. Still from *A Severe Youth* (*Strogii iunosha*, dir. A. Room, production design by M. Umanskii and V. Kaplunovskii, 1934).

exists in a disjunctive relationship with the material world ("Things don't like me"), which distinguishes him from those characters who have easily embraced the new Soviet ideal).[91] A renewed, sentient relationship with objects is a precondition for the new Soviet subject, and exemplified in the young bodies in *A Severe Youth*.

This category of sentience provides a link between its formal preoccupation with surface(s), and the investigation of the moral and emotional frameworks of the new Soviet youth. It also reflects the film's exploration of the power of cinema itself. In this respect, silence is important. Michel Chion suggests that mute figures (such as Diskobol and the statues) hold a particular power in sound cinema, where voice is usually central: they reference cinema's primordial secret, recalling its original silence.[92] Many of those close-up images of pure material in the film (such as the long opening sequence) are accompanied by an entirely empty soundtrack.[93] So in 1936, when sound cinema was firmly established in Soviet Russia, this film consciously summoned a mode of spectatorship that was perhaps at risk in sound film, recalling the faktura of silent cinema and its ability to reveal material texture. It challenged the spectator not to listen but to see and to feel.

This provides a new perspective on *A Severe Youth*. It has been common to consider the film's formal elements as a subversive counter to the emerging narratives and styles of Soviet Socialist Realism. In the censors' report, Room was accused of "chasing after external beauty," while the film was accused of having a "mystical insubstantiality of form."[94] The film's interest in external beauty need not, however, be linked to such claims of pure formalism, or unreality. Rather, *A Severe Youth* revels in the plastic, textural beauty of material objects (and human bodies), and their tangible *presence*. It offers an encounter with the materiality of the world of things—what Dinamov would call its "sensory radiance." And as such it asserts the ideal of socialist sensation that has been the subject of this book, and which was at the center of the revolutionary project.

This is not to suggest, of course, that Room and Olesha present an unproblematic celebration of the ideals of the Soviet 1930s. Rather, *A Severe Youth* might be viewed as a working through of core questions. First, it reflects on the shift in film production from avant-garde to Socialist Realism, and from silence to sound. On the one hand, the film's editing and mise-en-scène operate predominantly within the cinematic codes of narrative cinema. On the other, its close-up focus on material and its haptic emphasis of texture assert an alternative aesthetic that demands a sensory response. Through the textural intensity of the film's call to *look*, and the voiceless space in which this call so often takes place, the film seeks to transform the act of spectatorship into something embodied and multisensory.

Second, *A Severe Youth* questions the place of sensation in the new model of Soviet feeling. In one sense, the young people in this film enact a shift of the category of beauty from the ideal to the real, and embody Dinamov's vision of a new kind of (masculine) beauty. As such, they represent the new, sensate body of the ideal Soviet subject. On the other hand, the film questions the relationship between their feeling bodies and the discourse of Soviet sentimentality that Grisha articulates, and investigates what new Soviet feelings might be. Indeed, scriptwriter Iurii Olesha himself had a longstanding interest in the relationship between bodies and feeling. In *Envy*, the dysfunctional representatives of the "old" world stage an abortive "conspiracy of feelings" (*zagovor chuvstv*) against the regulation and collectivity of the new world. When that novel was adapted for the stage in 1929, Olesha renamed it *Conspiracy of Feelings*, giving added centrality to the place of "feeling" in the new world. In that text, however, the conspiracy of feelings will (and must) fail. Olesha is not calling for a return to bourgeois emotions. But, as *A Severe Youth* shows, nor are the new Soviet sentiments discussed by Grisha and his friends an adequate surrogate.

Finally, then, the film's thematic focus on the moral and psychological qualities that must define the Soviet hero is perhaps a parodic reflection on the distinction between authentic *feeling* (which takes place through the body) and conscious *emotion*. There is a mismatch between Grisha's abstracted discussion of sentiment and the overwhelming presence of the naked, assertively material bodies that surround him: a divorce between words (sound) and filmic material. This can be explicitly linked to the film's own sensory challenge to the spectator. The dialogue works *against* the felt intensity that the film offers at the level of form—and which is contained as active potential within those young bodies. In provoking the spectator to *feel*, the film reveals the hollowness of the discourse of Soviet sentiment. In this respect perhaps *A Severe Youth* was an anticipatory lament for the dream of Soviet sensations amid the consolidating norms of Socialist Realism.

Reason and Feeling

In this chapter so far, we have explored films that engage directly with two questions: first, with the shape of new Soviet feelings, and second, with the role of cinema itself. In part, these inquiries can be seen in relation to the shift from silent to sound cinema. How might the new, nonsilent, art form retain the core purpose of its silent predecessor: to provoke a reanimated engagement with the material world, to give its spectator a heightened ability to see and to feel? But they were also directly linked with the broader changing ideological context. How might that purpose continue to be part of the Soviet revolutionary agenda?

To a greater or lesser extent, these have all been films that challenge language as a principal signifying system. Yet it is common to write about the dominance of the "logos" in Stalinist culture. Mikhail Iampolski has described Soviet cinema as profoundly "logocentric" (and noted that this emphasis on the logos had brought a neglect of the "sensual contact with the world on-screen").[95] Evgenii Dobrenko has written of the growing importance of the word in later Stalinist cinema.[96] In similar terms, Iurii Murashov has suggested that the key task for the spectator of Stalinist cinema was to learn not to look, but to *hear*.[97] In these early Socialist Realist films, however, we can trace an explicit investigation of the limits of language in cinema and its relationship to film's "sensory radiance." This investigation was directly tied to the exploration of emerging models of the new Soviet subject. Made in the years during which the technology of sound cinema was consolidated in Soviet Russia, the films treated in this chapter explicitly linked silence to sentience. They argued *against* language and *for* an appreciation of sensory plenitude. They connected this sensory plenitude explicitly to revolutionary selfhood and asked, ultimately, if sensation had a place in the new Stalinist world.

In the years up to 1937, this question was of increasing concern to filmmakers and critics. It was not limited to filmmaking, of course: Christina Kiaer distinguishes a "lyrical (affective) strand" of in Socialist Realist painting from the "thematic or didactic" trend, which was its principal mode in the later 1930s.[98] Like me, she identifies 1933 as a moment of (unrealized) potential in the formation of the Socialist Realist aesthetic, "an attempt to rework modernist aesthetic strategies to help viewers to *feel*, as well as to comprehend analytically, the meanings and promises of socialism."[99] As we have shown, this project had particularly powerful realization in cinema.

In the course of the 1930s, however, this experimental affective Socialist Realism came under increasing pressure. In schematic terms, we might suggest that the concept of "emotions"—implicitly controlled by the conscious mind—began to dominate that of feelings/sensations as the basis of the new Soviet subjectivity, and filmmaking had to be shaped accordingly. Yet the picture was still not clear. In November 1936, Eisenstein, Room, and Balázs met in VGIK, along with psychologist Artemov, to discuss the pedagogical program for directors, and in particular the foundation course in psychology required for the profession in the future.[100] Despite his assertion in 1932 that filmmaking should turn away from its enslavement to reflexology, Abram Room insisted on focus on the science of sensation.[101] Eisenstein and Balázs agreed, and the meeting resolved to increase classes dedicated to sensation—in order that directors deepen their understanding of spectatorial affect.[102]

This meeting reveals the complexity of debates in this formative period. Balázs's presence here is important. Balázs (who was at that time teaching in VGIK and very much a member of the Soviet film establishment[103]) had published *The Spirit of Film* in Russian earlier in 1936, and it prompted intense discussion about two things: the role of material in cinema, and the capacity of film to provoke spectatorial response. It was frequently accused of formalism for its focus on the power of cinematic material, to which Balázs made a robust reply: "A feeling for the material (chuvstvo materiala) is one of the greatest gifts of any artist, and one of the most necessary qualities of any theorist."[104] In concession to the new political climate, however, Balázs emphasized that the material was not an end in itself.[105] He acknowledged the Socialist Realist emphasis on meaning, while at the same time seeking a place for cinema's powerfully materialist form. As such, we might suggest that he attempted to find a place for oshchushchenie within the new world of Soviet feeling: to harness the productive power of filmic affect *without* its potentially disruptive force.

A similar attempt to reconcile competing—and even contradictory—imperatives is evident in the writings of Soviet critics. Vaisfel´d, for example, criticized Balázs for his emphasis on the the *encounter* with the material, rather than its transformation, but praised his interest in the emotive, intuitive power of film.[106] Vaisfel´d's hedged praise reveals Socialist Realism's vexed relationship with the affective power of cinematic material during this period. In an article of 1936, Iukov criticized Formalist theorists and practitioners for making oshchushchenie the primary goal of their art: "Dialectical materialism, for all its assertions of the material quality of our reason, did not posit oshchushchenie as the only source of our consciousness of objective reality and material life. *Sensation* is only one element, the first decisive step in the material process of human reasoning."[107] The Socialist Realist image must be perceived through the body *and* the mind. It must represent not just the object but, as Shklovskii had written back in the late 1920s, a "relationship to the object." In Iukov's words, "The closer the Soviet artist's representation of reality is to the sincere meaning of this reality, the clearer and more fully the artist reveals his understanding of reality."

These terms, "meaning" and "understanding," were central to Iukov's attempt to reconcile sensation and reason in his new theory of the film image. They echo Iezuitov's definition of Soviet sentimentalism, and point to the particularity of socialist feelings as they took shape in the mid-1930s. As we have seen, these shifts echoed the broader transformation in conceptions of the relationship between body and mind, and the growing emphasis on reason and consciousness in the conceptualization of Soviet subjectivity. According to the second edition of the *Great Soviet Encyclopedia*, reason was the "highest stage of perception"—deeper than feeling.[108] Sensations, meanwhile, were relegated to the merely physiological.[109] Such emphasis was increasingly central to the discussion of screened emotions in this period. Writing in 1934, Popov suggested that "the Communist individual" would be distinguished "by his/her entirely new conscious relationship with the world."[110] The task of cinema was to frame and shape that relationship. This was a complex and uncertain project, however. In this transitional period, the shape of that new Soviet feeling remained unclear. The two remaining chapters of this book will trace the fate of socialist sensation in this changed ideological context, and the search for a new model of feeling. We will see how surface textures and material were used on-screen to test models of Sovietness, and to complicate ideological structures. The story of Soviet sensation was not yet at an end.

NOTES

1. Iezuitov, "O stiliakh sovetskogo kino," 44. This was a continuation of a two-part article published in the previous edition of the journal: "O stiliakh sovetskogo kino (Kontseptsiia razvitiia sovetskogo kinoiskusstva)." The publication was a transcript of a speech presented to the Communist Academy (Komakademiia) on April 22, 1933.

2. Ibid., 41.

3. Gaivorovskii, "Chuvstva i emotsii." Gaivorovskii's distinction between the terms "chuvstva" and "emotsii" in the title of the essay signals the extent to which the term "chuvstva," in this period, was seen to incorporate an implicit emphasis on sensation.

4. For discussion of the transition to sound cinema in relation to ideology, see Kaganovsky, *Voice of Technology*.

5. Vaisfel'd, "Na putiakh k iskusstvu sotsializma," 23.

6. Ibid., 17.

7. Piataev, "Chto takoe individual'nost'?," 3.

8. Krinkin, "Realizm i naturalizm," 19.

9. Iukov, "Zametki k templanu," 7.

10. For discussion of the Stalinist project for "educating the emotions" through film, with particular focus on a psychoanalytic reading of "affect," see the work of Anna Toropova, including Toropova, "'Educating the Emotions.'"

11. See in particular Halfin, *Terror in my Soul*.

12. Petrov-Bytov, "Mirovozzrenie, talant, iskrennost'," 45.

13. Piotrovskii, *Khudozhestvennye techeniia v sovetskom kino*.

14. Bleiman, "Chelovek v sovetskoi fil'me."

15. Cited in Michurin, "Akter v nemom kino," 62.

16. Bagrov, "O Evgenii Cherviakove," 105.

17. Alpers, "Goroda i gody," 8.

18. Cherviakov, "Moi syn," 13.

19. Ibid., 13.

20. Bagrov, "O Evgenii Cherviakove," 109.

21. Ibid.

22. Béla Balázs, "Visible Man, or the Culture of Film," 34.

23. Epstein, "Magnification," 235.
24. See Grashchenkova, *Kinoantropologiia*, 655–665.
25. Piotrovskii, *Khudozhestvennye techeniia v sovetskom kino*, 249.
26. Bagrov notes the possibility that *My Son* had an influence on Pudovkin's collaboration with Rzheshevskii on *Life is Good*. Bagrov, "O Evgenii Cherviakove," 112.
27. For detailed discussion of the "emotional scenario" see Viktor Demin, "'Emotsional′nyi stsenarii.'"
28. Lingart, "Emotsional′nyi stsenarii A. G. Rzheshevskogo," 274.
29. See ibid., 275–80, for discussion of Shklovskii's changing attitude to Rzheshevskii.
30. See, for example, the critical voices questioning Pudovkin in Pudovkin, "25 dekabria 1930g. Vystuplenie na obsuzhdenii fil′ma 'Ochen′ khorosho zhivetsia.'"
31. Kuleshov, "Montazh," 12. See Olenina, "Psychomotor Aesthetics," 143–45.
32. This was memorably recalled by Inkizhinov, who played the young Mongol Bair: Inkizhinov, "Bair i ia," 8–9. In *Life is Good*, Pudovkin was assisted by Mikhail Doller. See Kapterev, "A Simple Case," 128–29.
33. Pudovkin published a book on acting in 1934. Pudovkin, *Akter v fil′me*.
34. See Olenina, "Psychomotor Aesthetics," 214–15.
35. Room, "Akter—polpred idei."
36. Room referenced the theories of Delsarte, Volkonskii, Gastev, and so forth, here.
37. Iezuitov used "emotional saturation," for example, to describe Dovzhenko's *Earth* as a prototype for a new kind of emotional address to the spectator through the image, in distinction from the "abstract" films of Sergei Eisenstein. Iezuitov, "O stiliakh sovetskogo kino 3," 46.
38. Room, "Moi kinoubezhdeniia," 5.
39. Tugendkhol′d, "Iskusstvo i sovremennost′," 219.
40. Ibid., 219–20.
41. Kozintsev, "Glubokii ekran," 191.
42. See, for example, Iukov, "Odna," 3; Aladin, "'Odna,'" 2; Cherennyi, "Vyzov meshchanstvu," 3.
43. Clark, *The Soviet Novel*. Note, however, that *Alone* can also be read as counter to the Socialist Realist master plot, not least in its troubled presentation of technology. See, for example, Kaganovsky, "The Voice of Technology." Also, Neia Zorkaia, "Odna na perekrestkakh." .
44. The film's cinematographer, Andrei Moskvin, used "white on white" cinematography for this film, exploiting a range of pure white tones (usually avoided in black-and-white cinematography) in order to create what critics describe as a "desaturated screen." See Kaganovsky, "The Voice of Technology," 274.
45. Sutyrin, "Ot intelligentskikh illiuzii k real′noi deistvitel′nosti," 17. Note that Kozintsev and Trauberg's *The Overcoat* also offers an oversized teapot; the crockery displays in *Alone* can be seen as a dialogue with that film, as well as with the department store in *New Babylon*. These intertexts provide further support for the reading of this film as a self-reflexive comment on the ideological implications of FEKS's own visual style.
46. Iezuitov, "O stiliakh sovetskogo kino," 44.
47. Lebedev, "Rozhdenie iskusstva," 3.
48. Balázs, "Novye fil′my, novye zhizneoshchushcheniia," 19.
49. Iezuitov, "O stiliakh sovetskogo kino," 41.
50. Bleiman, "Ob ornamentakh," 4.

51. Bleiman, "Chelovek v sovetskoi fil'me I," 35.
52. Bleiman, "Ob ornamentakh," 4.
53. Arnshtam, "Vglub'materiala," 4.
54. Bleiman, "Chelovek v sovetskoi fil'me III," 27. In Evgenii Margolit's words, "human material" replaces "pure" material: Margolit, *Zhivye i mertvoe*, 162.
55. Iukov, "Zametki k templanu," 5.
56. Ibid., 5.
57. Ibid.
58. This debate is familiar in Marxist aesthetics, of course: in Lukács's terms, "realism" is distinguished by its aspiration to reveal social and political dynamics through the representation of reality. As such, it operates with a hierarchy of significance, selecting the "telling detail"; naturalism, by contrast, has a mission of uncovering that which is habitually overlooked, of revealing the minutiae of material context. See, for example, Lukács, "Tolstoy and the Development of Realism."
59. Iukov, "Zametki," 5.
60. Iukov, "Ob odnoi," 7.
61. Iezuitov, "O stiliakh sovetskogo kino (kontseptsiia razvitiia sovetskogo kinoiskusstva)": 39.
62. Semper, *Style*; Wölfflin, *Principles of Art History*; Riegl, *Problems of Style*; Worringer, *Abstraction and Empathy*.
63. Ioffe's key works in the period 1927–1938 were: *Kul'tura i stil'* (1927); *Sinteticheskaia istoriia iskusstv* (1933), *Sinteticheskoe izuchenie iskusstva* (1938).
64. Ioffe, "Iz knigi 'Kul'tura i stil'," 85.
65. Ibid., 87.
66. For extensive discussion of the resonance of this term, "synthetic," in the evolution of the theory of Socialist Realism, see Gutkin, *The Cultural Origins*.
67. Ioffe, "Iz knigi 'Sinteticheskaia istoriia iskusstv,'" 200.
68. Ibid., 201.
69. Ibid., 257.
70. Balázs, "Novye fil'my—novoe zhizneoshchushchenie," 19–20.
71. See the collection of articles "Obsuzhdaem novuiu kartinu Mezhrabpomfil'm—'Okraina,'" 3; Pudovkin, "Na vershiny sovetskoi kul'tury," 2; Brigada Lenbiuro RosARRK, "Bez chutkogo ideinogo zamysla," 3; Popov, "Neobosnovannye obvineniia," May 16, 2; Brigada LenRosARRK, "Ne o kartine," 3; Popov, "Neobosnovannoe obvinenie," June 22, 3; Anon, "Okraina," 2–3. Popov, "Iz dnevnika na proizvodstve," 19–30. A particularly impassioned debate took place between representatives of LenRosARRK (including Bleiman and Kalatozov) and Ivan Popov. LenRosARRK praised the film for its focus on internationalism and class consciousness. They criticized, however, the decision to locate it within the "semiproletarian" world of shoemaking (handcraft), rather than amid the industrial proletariat. In the context of 1933, the ideological validation of the artisan was increasingly under threat. Popov defended Barnet's choice, however, noting the film's emphasis on innate revolutionary fraternalism: shoemakers in *Outskirts* are a protoindustrial force. In the film's opening sequence, as they sit hammering their shoes, they are interrupted by the sound of a strike whistle from the local factory, which acts as an immediate call to arms. Brigada Lenbiuro RosARRK, "Bez chutkogo ideinogo zamysla": 3.
72. Brigada Lenbiuro RosARRK, "Bez chutkogo ideinogo zamysla," 3.
73. Bleiman, "Chelovek v sovetskoi fil'me III," 40.

74. Ibid.
75. I. Popov, "Iz dnevnika na proizvodstve," 30.
76. Margolit, *Zhivye i mertvoe*, 224.
77. Ibid.
78. Petrov-Bytov, "Mirovozrenie, talant, iskrennost'," 44.
79. Ibid., 46.
80. Gabrilovich, "Problema geroia," 3. See also Alpers, "Nadumannost' i narochitost'," 3.
81. Macheret, "Realizovannyi optimizm," 60.
82. For discussion of the "Return of the Aesthetic," see Clark, *Moscow, the Fourth Rome*, 105–35.
83. Dinamov, "Vstupitel'noe slovo," 7.
84. Ibid., 8.
85. Ibid.
86. Marx and Engels, *The Holy Family*, 3.
87. There is some ambiguity in the ending, but the most common interpretation of both film and screenplay is that Masha's final decision involves renouncing Grisha's love and returning to her husband.
88. It is notable that Diskobol is the only one of the characters to have this kind of pseudonymous name—an indication of his importance as athlete (and body) in the film's hierarchies of value
89. As Milena Michalski discusses, and as Bliumbaum explores in considerable detail, Grisha's dream sequence envisages Masha as "music made flesh." Michalski, "Promises Broken, Promise Fulfilled"; Bliumbaum, "Ozhivaiushchaia statuia i voploshchennaia muzyka," 138. See also Belodubrovskaia, "Abram Room, *A Strict Young Man*," and also Belodubrovskaia, "Ekstsentrika stilia v fil'me."
90. Balázs, "The Sound Film," 191.
91. Olesha, "Zavist'," 13.
92. Chion, *The Voice in Cinema*, 100.
93. Siegfried Kracauer, discussing Charlie Chaplin's *Modern Times* (1936), described how Chaplin's "undermining" of naturalistic sound could turn the audience "from naïve listeners to engaged spectators." Kracauer, "Dialogue and the Sound Film," 108.
94. Popov, "Postanovlenie tresta Ukrainfil'm," 2.
95. Iampol'skii, "Kino bez kino," 89, 90. See also Iampolski, "Reality at Second Hand," 166–68, for discussion of the "polemic" around the category of material in Soviet cinema of the late 1920s.
96. Dobrenko, *Stalinist Cinema*, 5.
97. Murashov, "Slepye geroi—slepye zriteli," 417.
98. Ibid., 76.
99. Ibid., 60.
100. Gereb, ed., "Riadom s Eizenshteinom," 235. See "V. A. Artemov," in Karpenko, ed., *Psikhologicheskii leksikon*, np.
101. Ibid., 233.
102. Ibid., 234.
103. Balázs was in the Soviet Union from 1932 until 1945.
104. Balázs, "Otvet moim kritikam," 40.
105. Ibid.

106. Vaisfel´d, "Itogi diskussii," 51.
107. Iukov, "Ob odnoi osobennosti, 21.
108. Anon., "Chuvstvo," *BSE*, 2-oe izdanie, 459.
109. Anon., "Oshchushchenie," *BSE*, 2-oe izdanie, 504.
110. Ibid., 14.

Chapter Eight

SOCIALIST TRANSFORMATIONS

> This sensory radiance needs to surround all our heroes
> S. S. Dinamov, 1935

CHAPTER 7 HAS identified a broad evolution from "sensation" to "emotion" over the course of the 1930s. In broad terms, the utopian dream of a sensory revolution was coming to an end. Yet filmmakers continued to test the parameters of Socialist Realism in their search for a new model of the Soviet subject—and of Soviet film. The remaining two chapters of this book will explore two different "afterlives" of the dream of socialist sensation in this changed context. They will trace how Soviet filmmakers' interest in the material, textural power of cinema, and its capacity to provoke a sensory revolution, endured during the 1930s, and how it was negotiated in relation to new ideological frameworks.

For the first of these afterlives, this chapter returns to the question of the Soviet "East" that formed the subject of chapter 5. Here, however, my focus is not on the East as a possible resource for a refashioned selfhood, but on the East as a space to be transformed. Recent scholarly accounts have concurred in identifying distinct stages in the evolution of Soviet attitudes toward the national republics. Broadly speaking, the 1920s, and in particular the first Five-Year Plan, were characterized by what Slezkine has called an "extravagant celebration of ethnic diversity."[1] In chapter 5, I suggested that they were also marked by an interest in how this diversity might offer possible alternative models of subjecthood. With the consolidation of

Stalinism in the course of the 1930s, this promotion of diversity gave way to a model of homogenization: the "backwardness" of the national republics was to be overcome; a uniform Soviet state was to be created. The process of transformation was one of enlightenment and rationalization.

What happened to the myth of the "East", and the lure of primitive mimesis, in this context? How was the emphasis on rationalization in tension with the drive for "emancipation" and sensory renewal that had been so central to the Soviet narrative? To answer this question, I will step back in time again to 1930, to the middle of the first Five-Year Plan, before moving forward into the 1930s. I will begin by treating two films that were directly engaged with the question of enlightenment and modernization: Viktor Turin's *Turksib* (1929) and Mikhail Kalatozov's *Salt for Svanetiia* (*Sol´ Svanetii*, 1930). Both films, while invested in the project of modernizing a "backward" East, retain a paradoxical investment in the sensory immediacy of "primitive" life. Both seek to reconcile these opposing drives. The second part of the chapter will explore how these and other films navigated the relationship between the (material) ruins of the past, and the construction of the future: I will situate Dziga Vertov's *Three Songs of Lenin* (*Tri pesni o Lenine*, 1934)[2] and Mikhail Romm's *The Thirteen* (*Trinadsat*, 1936) side by side in order to compare their very different responses to the problematic lure of the sensual material of the East. Finally, the chapter will trace the evolution of the distinctive Soviet-Eastern production movie, examining films that picture the integration of a technological future into a primitive present. These films reveal a search for a distinctively Eastern "modern."

Underlying these analyses is a consideration of the categories of visual pleasure and cinematic affect. What was the fate of the embodied pleasures (and sufferings) of the East that we have discussed in chapter 5, in the context of Socialist Realism? What was the relationship between the authentic material of the "backward" East, and the surface pleasures of its faktura, and how did they change in the context of the drive for socialist transformation? What was the link between the idea that cinema could provide an embodied knowledge *naoshchup´* and Dinamov's call for "sensory radiance" on-screen?

Natural Transformations?

Turksib and *Salt for Svanetiia* are usually—and no doubt rightly—seen as unambiguous in their celebration of the capacity of Soviet modernization to overcome "backwardness."[3] They share a basic plot, tracing the construction of transport networks (railway and road, respectively) that transform an isolated space (the Karakum desert, the mountains of Svanetiia) into one connected to the Soviet Union, and hence to modernity. They are focused on the modernization of "primitive" space, on the elimination of ancient culture by the enlightening arm of Soviet civilization. The films' representation of the isolated spaces of Turkmenistan and Svanetiia respectively is more complex than this plot summary would suggest, however. They tread an intriguing line between condemnation of, and fascination with, the "primitive" world. And they configure that world in sensory terms.

Turksib was proclaimed a success because of its achievement in presenting Turkmen and Kazakh life with the potent combination of ethnographic accuracy and aesthetic sensibility that had been commonly cited through the 1920s as an aspiration for films dealing with the national republics (see chapter 5). It focuses on the cotton industries of Turkestan, with a prologue dedicated to cotton as commodity—and, crucially, as material. The film opens with a shot of hands handling unprocessed cotton—pulling apart its puffy whiteness, rubbing its threads, twisting and touching it. Sinewy white ropes of unprocessed cotton are fed into a machine, where they are transformed into thread, and thence into fabric. Sheets of white textile spool out of a machine, pile up in sinuous folds on the floor, and eventually fill the entire screen—their materiality transformed into pure textural surface. The next shot features striped textile; then piles of textile rolls; then items of clothing—both Western and richly patterned Central Asian tunics. This visual lesson in commodity production precedes the film's first "Act." In its emphasis on the relationship between the hands of the workers, the machines that process the cotton, and the concrete materiality of the finished product, the sequence sets up a relationship between the human and the material that is characteristic of the production film in this period.

Turksib conveys a somewhat different message, however. The relationship between the prologue and first act ("Water") sets up a tension between energy (the dynamism of production; the embodied experience of making) and stasis. The peasants of Turkestan are rendered immobile by the lack of water; they cannot continue production. The message is both literal and metaphorical: immobilized, Central Asia stands outside the linear movement of historical time. And hence its laborers are removed from the constructive experience of making.[4] With the building of the railway, however, Turkestan enters time, and moves forward into a productive future. Time and space are blurred: as the stranglehold of the desert's isolation is broken, it is described as the lifting of the "weight of a thousand years." Intertitles refer explicitly to the "breaking" of nature "by the labor of man." And this will enable a new relationship between man (the local inhabitants) and the material world—one configured by production.

Turksib posits three modes of being in the world. The first is the sensually rich experience of manual labor represented by traditional culture. This is conveyed by the film's pronounced formal interest in textures: the fluffiness of the cotton crop, the weave of textile, the cracked surfaces of parched earth. In a commentary on the inefficency of Turkmen fuel, the camera relishes the cinematographic impact of piles of twisted dead wood. As well as representing abstract textures, the film also focuses on hands: the hands of native people, picking and handling cotton; hands manipulating worry beads while "waiting for water"; hands shearing sheep, grasping mounds of wool, tying rope. This is the same world of manual labor that so fascinated Luriia et al. in their inquiries into "primitive" mentality, the "speaking with hands" described by anthropologist Frank Cushing (see chapter 5). And the camera's close-up implicates the spectator in that mode of being. This pleasure in natural, elemental, and "primitive" faktura is tempered, however, by the emphasis on stasis that is the second mode of being that the film presents. This is what has become of traditional life as a result of isolation: a lack of progress, human suffering, and a real and metaphorical drying out not only of the earth, but of the very lifeblood of the people themselves. The geographical (and ideological) isolation of Kazakh and Turkmen people has brought about a rupture between them and the land.

Both the model of natural life, and its negative mirror image of stasis, stand in contrast with the film's central narrative of modernization: technology and mapping. An extended sequence focuses on diagrammatic planning, with a montage of rulers, paper, numbers, and maps, as land surveyors and engineers take conceptual hold over the desert. This is the abstracted ideal of (disembodied) technical mastery. The film's development does not present the simple victory of this kind of modernization, however. Rather, the third (and triumphant) mode of being represented in *Turksib* is that of the embodied energy particular to Soviet modernization, which synthesizes the vitality of natural life with the new dynamic of technology. Throughout the film, technology has its own material textures and sensory pleasures: the wood of railway tracks, the metal of an engine's wheels. In the final scene, mounted nomads race the first train engine to run along the new tracks. The elemental power of nature and the technical force of modernization come together in a celebration of plenty. Becoming incorporated into the wider world, Turkmenia is modernized, and its people are metaphorically reborn into the proximate, embodied relationship with technology that, in turn, enables a reanimated, sensually rich relationship with the natural world. It recaptures *in new form* that which was originally present in "primitive" culture, but which has been lost.

Thus in *Turksib* a new model of sensory embodiment emerges out of a synthesis between the "primitive" and the modern. And this dialectical relationship between different models of being in the world helps us to understand what is at stake in *Salt for Svanetiia*. This was another of Sergei Tret'iakov's film collaborations, produced during his time in Georgia (see chapter 5).[5] In his published writing, Tret'iakov was uncompromising in his presentation of Svanetiia as a repressive, "backward" culture: "Old Svanetiia lives by the tower, by flint threshing equipment, by home-spun dresses, by devouring supplies of stored corn at gluttonous funeral feasts, and by the difficult dream of the murder of a blood relative."[6]

The relationship between Tret'iakov's screenplay and Kalatozov's final film is not entirely straightforward, however, with regard to the presentation of this "primitive" world. Certainly, Old Svanetiia stands entirely outside the modern production economy. The film shows women weaving, and the camera dwells on the movement of fingers. Hair is being cut; simple felt hats are sewn. An extended sequence focuses on the sheep's wool, which is a key feature of the local people's ability to survive: photographed first on the body of the sheep, then on a comb, being stripped and sorted (as in *Alone*) and then woven. Hands touch, manipulate, and work this wool (figure 8.1). There is no romanticism attached to this picture of ethnic craft, however: it is pictured as backbreaking labor and endurance. In his essay "People in Caves," Tret'iakov devoted a long paragraph to a description of female traditional craft: "Women crumple cow-hide and sew soft slippers from the outer skin. They spin hemp . . . and weave nets—round nets, weighted to catch trout; they press goat's hair into wet felt."[7] But he noted damningly, "I have watched them work many times . . . and at length, but never heard them sing."[8]

In the film, traditional labor is framed by inter titles that describe it as primitive and backward. Yet the camera's obvious pleasure in the faktura of the materials shown, its focus on the contact between hand and material, and the emphasis on the tactile immediacy of the life as lived, present a more complex message, particularly in the early parts of the film. These

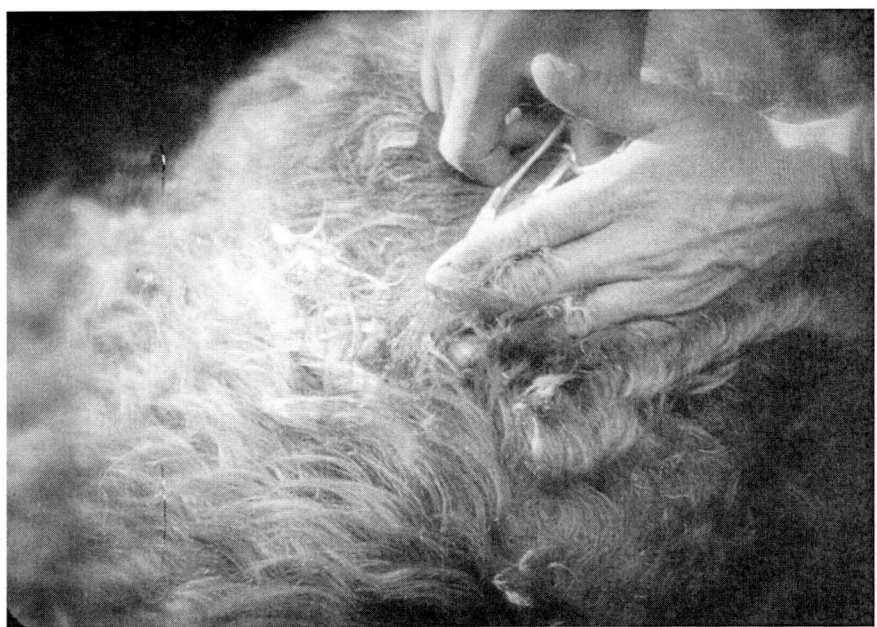

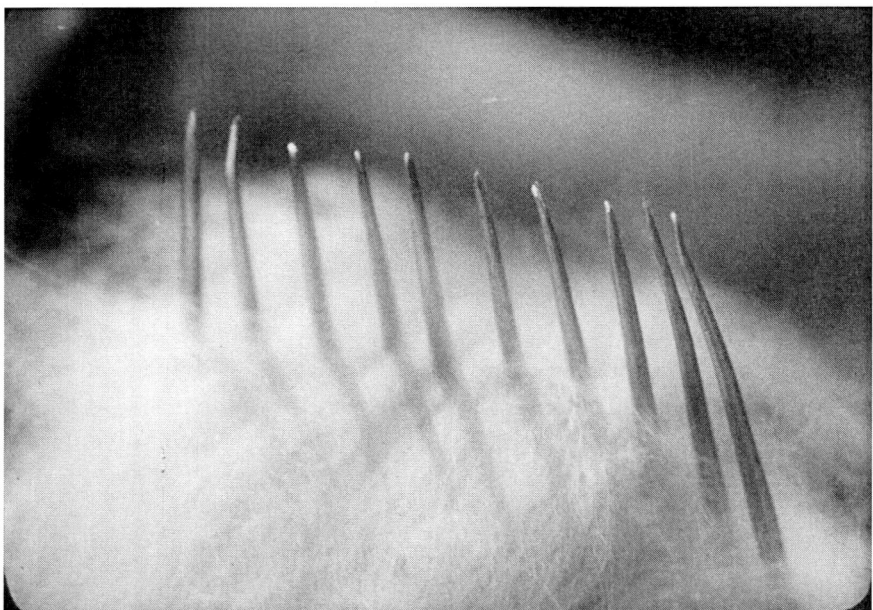

Fig. 8.1 Hands-on Making. Stills from *Salt for Svanetiia* (*Sol' Svanetii*, dir. M. Kalatozov, 1930).

SOCIALIST SENSES

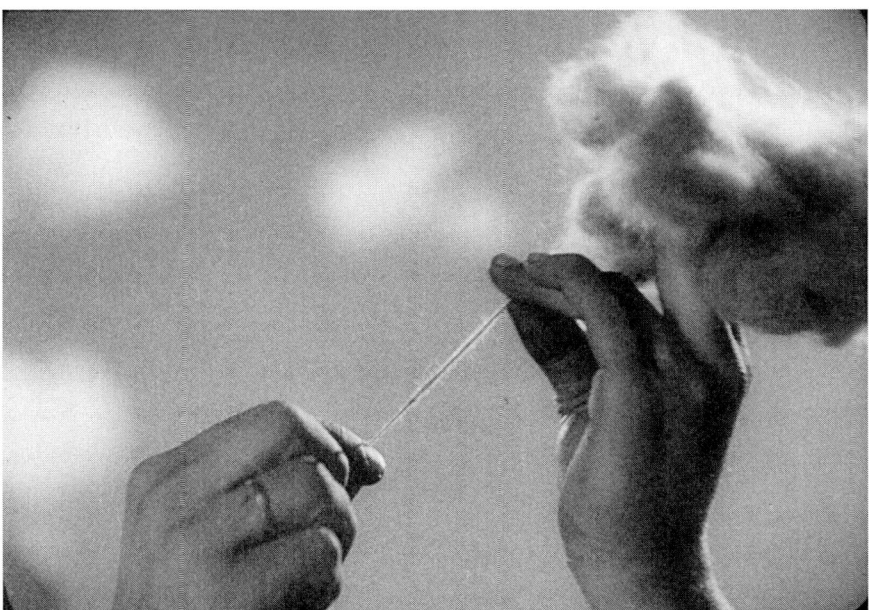

Fig. 8.1 (*Continued*).

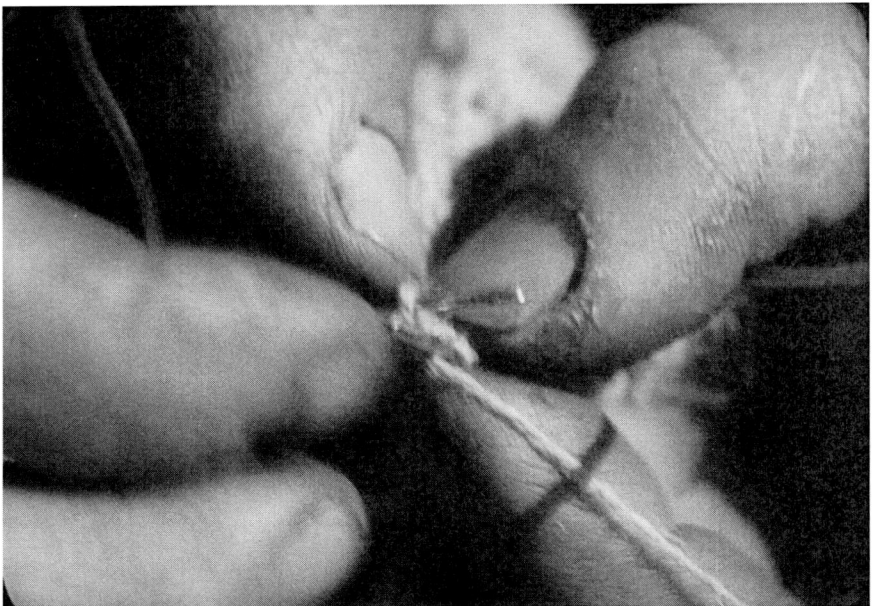

Fig. 8.1 (*Continued*).

close-up shots of working hands, and of the textures of wool, thread, and skin (figure 8.1) move beyond factual information and into sensory affect. Indeed, perhaps their sensory immediacy seeks to provide the tactile "knowledge" (naoshchup´) that Tret´iakov described in his manifesto for a new kind of ethnographic travel writing: to implicate the spectator in a relationship of intense sensory empathy. The Svanetians are locked in a battle for survival against the landscape and the elements. Extreme close-ups provide a sensory encounter with the tactile immediacy of skin and suffering. Animal tongues scour the ground, searching for salt; a dog licks the blood of a baby. Malnourished women desperately squeeze their breasts to make milk for their children. The spectatorial experience is an *embodied* encounter (naoshchup´), not just with suffering, but with the physical intensity of "primitive" life.

In *Salt for Svanetiia*, then, the emphasis on handcraft and sensory intensity has much in common with the "knowledge naoschup" that we discussed in chapter 5. The crucial distinction lies, however, in the film's overarching argument for modernization. The power of the endings of *Salt for Svanetiia* and *Turksib* rests on the overcoming of isolation, bringing the Turkmen peasants, nomadic horsemen, and the Svan into the network of Soviet power; but the affective power of these finales depends upon the success of the films' earlier sensory projects. The spectator has not just *seen* primitive experience; he/she has also felt it. In these terms we might think about the triumphant final scene in *Turksib* when the mounted Turkmen come to to see the new railway and to realize its truth.[9] It is notable that this act of seeing involves the mounted race between nomads and train. It is a race that they are doomed to lose, of course, but that failure is itself part of the embodied encounter with technology that the film stages. So the horsemen do not just see; they also *feel* the forward movement of historical time, into the future. In both *Turksib* and *Salt for Svanetiia*, the dialectical tension between the sensory intensity of the old and the technological mastery of the new prompts a new kind of knowledge, premised on an embodied relationship between the viewing subject and the object. Seeing revolution is not enough; it is necessary to *feel* it. And film has a key role to play in making that happen.

The Past as Lived Material

These two films, then, operate according to a dialectical principle, creating a synthesis between the past and the present in the creation of the future—a synthesis that is partly worked through in terms of the body. But they also reveal the deeply problematic status of the past. In both films, the past appears not only in native peoples' traditional lifestyle, but also as ruined buildings. In *Turksib*, when members of the "advance guard of the new civilization" arrive in Turkestan, they encounter a single ruined tomb (kurgan), diminished and fragile against the powerful landscape that surrounds it. Then follows an extended sequence of ruined kurgans and the inhabited yurts of nomads, and shots of sleeping families, as an inter title announces that "the tombs of the East stand sentry." Thus the film equates the isolation of the desert—its enforced stasis—with its location deep in ancient time. Similarly, in *Salt for Svanetiia*, the old buildings in Ushkul (tombs, towers, and ruins) dramatize the historical continuity that keeps the Svans trapped in the past. In his writings, Tret'iakov made a direct link between the architecture of Svanetiia and backwardness, describing it as trapped by its age-old, windowless towers, its "family fortresses" are prisons. As such, "Socialism in Svanetiia is first and foremost a home with large windows."[10]

As with Kalatozov's close-up images of handwork, however, the ruined towers have a complex status as cinematic material, which complicates such ideological certainties. Early landscape sequences give them historical grandeur amid the looming mountains, and inter titles make clear that they are evidence of the Svans' historical legacy as rebels against feudal power (and as such, of their potential status as survivals of primitive communism). The buildings also mark the Svans' close centuries-long connection with their land: the film shows the backbreaking labor of stone being cut to make the very towers that hold them trapped in eternal cyclical time. The Svans may be metaphorically blind, but as the film makes clear, they can feel. And the film's dialectical achievement is to bring together this innate feeling with a new, modern (technological) vision.

Thus both *Salt for Svanetiia* and *Turksib* prompt us to consider the relationship of the past to the utopian socialist future. Specifically, through their ruins, they explore the affective power of material traces of the past in the present. The pre- and postrevolutionary avant-garde had an ambivalent relationship with the past—and with ruins as its physical manifestation. On the one hand, it was clearly focused on a rejection of the past and all that it represented. Kazimir Malevich criticized those artists who "have not taken the path of Futurism" as doomed "to crawl eternally among old tombstones and feed off the leftovers of olden times."[11] By contrast, the revolutionary avant-garde had a mission of destruction, smashing the oppressive structures of the past. From this perspective, the ruin was, as Schönle notes, "a stubborn resistance to the rhetoric of a clean break from the past, the residue of a humanist notion of self, which resists the avant-garde imagery of progress."[12] In another sense, however, as Kalinin has pointed out, the ruin could be embraced as part of the avant-garde principle of fragmentation.[13] This approach to the ruin, however, depended upon its removal from historical context. Without concre transformed into a "fragment," outside history and without meaning, the ruin could be reconfigured as part of a modernist montage or collage. In Malevich's words, "[the ruin's] meaning for our modernity can obtain only when in its old order an element remained, belonging to my modernity, which I'll take as a contemporary element and put together with my things."[14]

For all this, however, Schönle sees the very presence of the ruin within the avant-garde collage as an acknowledgment of the implication of the past in the present: "To inhabit the ruin is to reconcile oneself with the present's heterogeneity, to recognize its rich texture."[15] In related terms, Michael Kunichika has explored the significance of archeology in Russian modernism, arguing that modernist artists were fascinated by the ruin's capacity to make visible the layers of time that could be seen as "simultaneously present within the revolutionary moment."[16]

In *Salt for Svanetiia* and *Turksib*, the camera reveals a fascination with the shapes and textures of ruins, and their capacity to provoke a sensory relationship with the screen. But it also questions their part in the project of modernity. The material and faktura of the film are in tension with the drive for modernization. In *Salt for Svanetiia*, the film's final explosions link modernization not with ruination, but with annihilation. This marks a key shift in Soviet attitudes to the transformation of the periphery: from a mode of sensory rapprochement between human and nature toward one of control. Georg Simmel memorably described architectural ruins as evidence of a collaboration between the human and natural worlds, evidence of the moment where the balance between human will and nature shifts in favor of nature.[17] He distinguishes "natural" ruination, however, from that "caused by man." In *Salt for Svanetiia* we have two kinds of ruination: the film begins with ruined towers that reveal that fragile balance between the human and the natural; at its end, the "unnatural" explosion that shatters the towers creates unnatural ruins, in which that balance is lost. The explosion marks the domination of man over nature.

Stalinist Ruins

These films' complex treatment of the dialectical relationship between ancient and new, primitive and modern, can be broadly understood within the conceptions of historical time that characterized early revolutionary culture. What happened, then, to ruins in the cinema of Socialist Realism? Vladimir Papernyi suggests that Stalinist culture could not contemplate ruins or decay, arguing that Socialist Realism depended upon the eradication of historical difference in its proclamation of an eternal present utopia. Ruins, as the materialization of historical distance, were inimical to that project.[18] Yet ruins are by no means absent from cinema of the 1930s. How, then, should they be understood? What can the treatment of ruins tell us about changing conceptions of cinematic material and its impact on the spectator? How do they sit alongside narratives of modernization and enlightenment in the Soviet East?

Here we will consider two films that can be productively viewed side by side, despite their radical differences: Dziga Vertov's *Three Songs about Lenin* and Mikhail Romm's *The Thirteen*. These films allow us to think about the changing representation of the ruined places of Central Asia in two related ways: first as cinematic faktura, and second, as comments on historical time and the relationship between the human and the material world. They also allow us to take our story forward into Socialist Realism, showing how films about (or set in) Central Asia during the 1930s continued to be preoccupied by the representation of bodies and their relationship with the material world—but in new ways.

Three Songs About Lenin presents an unambiguous message about the "enlightenment" of Central Asia, and it does so through the familiar metaphor of vision. The first "song" begins with the first-person narrative of a veiled woman in Turkmenistan. "Blind was my life," an inter title proclaims; and the film presents the woman's unveiling as a symbolic unblinding via the "light of Lenin." This first song makes extensive use of the vertical architecture of a ruined mosque, which towers over the veiled woman (figure 8.2). The camera, which moves vertically in circular jumps, seems to mirror either the obscured gaze of the veiled woman as she moves through the city, or (and) the up-and-down movement of the men praying beneath the walls.[19] In its combination of verticality and incompleteness, however, this camera movement also works to comment on the crumbling mosque itself, simultaneously reinforcing its power as a symbol of religious oppression—and suggesting its ruination within the modern city. This degraded religious architecture is later directly contrasted with the clean modern verticals of the factory building, where a woman is shown loading an industrial weaving machine.

Three Songs About Lenin is a film about mourning: the collective sorrow at the death of Lenin.[20] What role do the ruined buildings play in the film's treatment of mourning? What is the relationship between past and present time that is presented in the film? Michael Kunichika has pointed out Vertov's focus, in his earlier film *The Eleventh Year* (*Odinnadtsatyi*, 1928), on the finding of skeletons (by archeologists) amid the construction site of Dneprostroi. He suggests that the buried traces of the past in that film raise a question fundamental to the Soviet rhetoric of progress and the forward march of history: "One must prepare the way to the future, but those efforts create fissures and fractures through which fragments of the deep past emerge from the ground and are recorded for all to see (again and again) preserved in the flickering light of the cinema screen."[21]

To some extent, the flickering presence of ruins in the opening sequence of *Three Songs* poses a similar question. Within the Stalinist present moment—where geographical differences of space are overcome in a temporal simultaneity of mourning at the death of the leader—the past remains materially present. Lenin himself is now part of that past, in a process

Fig. 8.2 The Lure of the Material. Stills from *Three Songs of Lenin* (*Tri pesni o Lenine*, dir. D. Vertov, 1934).

that we might conceive as one of "museification." The camera dwells on the bench where Lenin sat, and the room where he worked; these spaces are the lived past, and film's purpose is to capture them and make them part of the present. But this capturing also marks their transformation from lived (and living) things into signifying objects; just as a museum collection inscribes its objects into a narrative of the past, so the film reveals how these material traces of Lenin will assume symbolic meaning. And through the camera, it raises questions about how film itself negotiates the relationship between material "things" and signifying "objects," and what kind of spectatorial relationships it can encode.

Vertov's interest in the textures and shapes of the ruin in *Three Songs* can be linked to the film's treatment of cinematic sensation, in particular in relation to oriental faktura. In one sense, this film is an overt repudiation of the lure of "false" East and its decorative faktura. In this respect, we might consider the veiled woman with whom the film begins. Completely covered in white cloth, faceless, this woman is an absent presence that dominates the film's first frames (figure 8.2a). Franz Fanon famously equates female unveiling with a colonial act of "taking" in French Algeria: as the veil is removed, it reveals "the flesh of Algeria laid bare."[22] The colonial project depends on this (metaphorical and actual) uncovering. In the Soviet case, however—as is particularly evident in *Three Songs of Lenin*—unveiling was equated not so much with *becoming visible*, as with *becoming able to see*.[23] The veil is removed and the "dark world" is replaced by one in which the woman can proclaim "I see." It is notable, however, that this act of becoming able to see is supplemented with that of becoming able to touch (and feel). Unveiling is also an act of disrobing—unwrapping the voluminous textile within which the female body is enclosed. Just as the modern urban and rural woman liberates herself from the enclosing traps of textile (see chapter 3) so, unveiled, the ethnic woman is permitted a hands-on encounter with socialism. She enters the world of embodied production: inter titles narrow progressively from "My Country" to "My Collective Farm" and finally to "My Hands." It is, the narrative voice proclaims, the woman's own hands that make the Soviet world.

Vertov's treatment of the material of this woman's clothing is not as simple as this would suggest, however. In the words of psychoanalytic critic Joan Copjec, a "rending of clothing" was a fundamental part of the (European) modernist project and its functionalist impulse, proclaiming a victory of human will (consciousness) over sensation.[24] This idea can be traced in the Soviet unveiling projects—and in particular in the symbolic unveilings in films such as *Sevil'* (Sevil', 1929, dir. Bek-Nazarov, see below) and *The Veil* (*Chadra*, dir. Mikhail Averbakh, 1927).[25] Indeed, this conceptual framework—the imposition of consciousness (will) over corporeal sensation and desire—could be seen as central to the Soviet ideological mission. *Three Songs of Lenin*, however, reveals a more complex dynamic. Indeed, Copjec herself alerts us to the ambivalence at the heart of the modern project of "unveiling." She notes that the utilitarian principle can be seen as a curbing of man's will to pleasure; but it is a curbing that is always (and willingly) on the brink of failure. And the veiled female "other" represents the ultimate challenge: "For, on the margins of the utilitarian renunciation of useless enjoyment and all but functional clothes, on the borders of the whole cloth of the greatest happiness, there emerged a fantasmatic figure—veiled, draped in cloth—whose existence, posed as threat, impinged on our consciousnesses."[26]

Copjec's argument is psychoanalytically inflected and based on the idea of desire. In the Soviet context, we find a different kind of tension at work, but one that operates on the same fault line between consciousness (will) and sensation (pleasure). In Vertov's film it operates through an interrogation of the role and impact of cinematic material, and its role in the Soviet sensory revolution. In *Three Songs*, a cinematographic pleasure in faktura is evident: the texture of ruination, the patterns of ethnic costume. These are not repudiated as part of the film's rhetoric of modernization. What is crucial, however, is that that pleasure is focused on the *surface*, in the material. Rather than imagining a fantasy space of desire *beyond* the cloth, the film relocates its pleasure in the textures of the cloth itself. Instead of allowing the architecture of the mosque to dominate the frame with symbolic weight, the camera dwells on the concrete materiality of its crumbling stone. And when, shortly after the opening sequence, we move to watch a young woman sitting in a sunlit room, and it becomes clear that she is, in fact, the same woman who was formerly veiled, we see the textures of her skin, and her youthfulness illuminated. But this is, crucially, not a relationship of voyeurism. She is not uncovered for the pleasure of the spectator; rather she, too, acquires the power to see, and the same tactile knowledge naoshchup' that is offered to the spectator. Such reciprocity is central to Vertov's careful negotiation of the categories of visual pleasure. In Copjec's terms, it is an attempt to celebrate will (consciousness) without relinquishing sensation: to create appropriate socialist sensations in the new context of the 1930s.

I suggest, then, that *Three Songs of Lenin* can be seen as sitting on a borderline between two visions of filmic material. On the one hand, it is clear in its repudiation of the sensory pleasures of "Eastern" faktura. On the other hand, it seeks to reappropriate it in terms that would be appropriate to Socialist Realism. This was the central challenge in cinema of the 1930s. It is at work, in very different ways, in Mikhail Romm's *The Thirteen*—another film with a focus on ruins. This is a film set in Central Asia but emphatically not *about* Central Asia. An example of the emerging Socialist Realist adventure genre, *The Thirteen* transformed the vast and inhospitable territory of the Soviet Union into an epic adventure space. It takes place in the Karakum desert, when a group of Red Army soldiers are returning home after fighting Turkmen insurgents who support the White cause. They are accompanied by a group composed of a border guard, his wife, and an elderly geologist (a roll call of heroic Stalinist professions[27]). On their way, they run into battle with a further group of Basmach insurgents. Most of the group are killed in the process, but they manage to secure the capture of the leader of the Basmachi. As such, they are heroes.

The Thirteen was a film made to order: Romm recounts how he was summoned by Boris Shumiatskii, who had seen John Ford's border guard drama, *The Lost Patrol*, and who instructed him to make a Russian-Soviet equivalent. He recalls Shumiatskii's conditions: "It's important that there is a desert (we have splendid deserts), that there are border guards and Basmachi, and that they all die."[28] Although firmly part of the new adventure genre, *The Thirteen* is in many senses a transitional film. It is stylistically poised between the avant-garde and Socialist Realism, between silent and sound film. Dialogue is kept to a minimum, and it often exploits the potential of the soundtrack for silence. It also exhibits formal qualities that complicate our picture of Socialist Realist cinema.

The Thirteen was praised for its rejection of decorative effects. As a leading cinematographer of the period, Vladimir Nil´sen pointed out, the set was unusually empty: "The decorative element in the normal sense of the word is completely absent. There are not even palm trees to bring to life the landscape of the desert. From the point of view of faktura the whole frame, the entire backdrop, appears as a flat, light-colored surface."[29]

Against this, the film has a single, striking, piece of set, however: a ruined building (possibly a kurgan, possibly a shelter) in the middle of the desert. It is here that the returning Red Army soldiers take shelter, and it eventually becomes their fortress and barricade against the Basmach insurgents. This artificial ruin was designed and built by Vladimir Egorov, and constructed both on location and in the studio.³⁰ In the essentially featureless space of the desert, the lone ruin functions structurally to create cinematic depth and space. For the spectator, and the protagonists, it is the only point of orientation, and throws into relief the need for shelter; it visualizes in stark form a battle between the human drive for safety and the threat of nature. The status of the ruin, however, is more complex than this. It is stylized and even artificial in its lone survival amid the flat, elemental planes of the desert, with its howling winds and shifting sands.

For all its artifice, the ruin plays an important part in the film. We have discussed how ruined buildings raise important questions about time and history. In Georg Simmel's view, ruins hold a sense of a lived past: "Such places, sinking from life, still strike us as settings of a life."³¹ This ruin might represent historical continuity, the constant presence of the past in the present, the lived experience of others in the inhospitable space of the desert. For the Bolsheviks who shelter in it, this is not just a ruin: it is *someone else's* ruin, evidence of *somebody else's* history. And as such it raises questions about the ownership of the desert. Who has the right to shelter? Who has the right to the water of the oasis? If the ruin is testament to lived experience of the past, then the act of inhabiting it can be seen in two ways. Either it is an uprooting of that past in favor of the present, an assertion of Bolshevik ownership, or it is a reconciliation with the heterogeneity of the present, a finding of comfort within the traces of a lived past that will inevitably be carried forward into any future.

Although there is some traction in both of these readings, the most curious fact about this stylized ruin is that it appears *blank*. The ruin hints at being a kurgan, and hence carries the privileged status of the kurgan in the Russian cultural imagination.³² But it is not quite a kurgan. It could be a shelter (and the stone wall that surrounds it hints at that), but it is lone evidence of settlement in an otherwise empty space, so its authentic status is unclear. Ultimately, it is a fantastical construct, which looms as if from nowhere, with no apparent historical roots in the landscape. As such, its capacity to represent a real, lived past is flattened. Instead, the tomb's rootless "ancientness" creates what Gromov calls an "eternal framework" for the film's historical process, just as the the epic style of *The Thirteen*, and its extreme visual economy, serve to take the film out of historical time.³³

The decontextualized status of the ruin in *The Thirteen* indicates an important shift that marks the treatment of Central Asia in cinema of the late

1930s. The ethnographic eye (see chapter 5) is entirely absent in this film. The territory—its ruins, its landscape—are an empty space, void of signification or history. And as such they can be easily appropriated to the Stalinist narrative. In the context of this appropriative relationship with the territory of Turkmenistan, and its ruins, how does *The Thirteen* deal with its native peoples? The plot stages a confrontation between the Bolshevik Red Army and local Basmach insurgents. It reverses the dynamic discussed in chapter 5, which celebrated the protorevolutionary energy of the oppressed native peoples: here the rebellious native "other" celebrated in *Khaz-Push* appears as an enemy of the Bolshevik project. The large hats and exaggerated costume of the Basmach dress are a symbol of their retrograde enslavement to an old order. Ultimately, just as the ruin ceases to signify an authentic lived past, so the film reduces the authentic difference of the Basmach to mere decoration. Indeed, for all their differences, Red and White, Soviet and Basmach, share a common humanity. They are authentically locked in a battle for survival: just as in *Three Songs of Lenin*, the textures of moving sand serve to emphasize the vast distances across which the shared mourning for Lenin extends, so here the faktura of sand works to convey the protagonists' desperate need for water, and their embodied encounter with the intransigence of nature. This is a story of the eternal battle between man and nature—one that does not observe ethnic particularity. In parallel, the film's visual style transforms the ruin into an empty sign.

Technology and Transformation

Three Songs of Lenin and *The Thirteen* are very different films, presenting distinct responses to what we might think of as the "problem" of sensory pleasure in the representation of the Soviet East. Vertov enacts a complex relocation of the allure of the sensory East onto the surface material of ruins and textiles, and presents modernization as a project of learning how to touch (feel) the world. Romm evacuates his (studio-constructed) East of specificity, and presents instead a model of homogeneity, in which the authentic faktura of the ethnic space, and the ethnic "other" is flattened.

This drive toward sameness, evident in *The Thirteen*, was characteristic of films from the mid-1930s on. What role did modernization and mechanization play in this evolution? We have discussed how *Salt for Svanetiia* and *Turksib* construct a dialectical relationship between nature and technology, past and future. And in *Three Songs of Lenin*, technology plays a key role in the project of integration: the radio brings Moscow directly within the walls of a native yurt, as heavily costumed peasants are able to hear (and participate in) Lenin's funeral. The trope of technological transformation is powerful in many films set in the Soviet East, just as it is, of course, in much Soviet film of the 1920s and 1930s. What, if anything, is distinct in the representation of technology in films set in the republics? What happened to the local ethnographic eye in relation to narratives of modernization?

One particularly intriguing attempt to combine an ethnographic eye with a production narrative is evident in *The Last Crusaders* (*Poslednie krestonostsy*, 1934), set in the Caucasus, and directed by the young Siko Dolidze.[34] At one level, *The Last Crusaders* is a film about ethnic rivalry between Christian Khevsurs and Muslim Chechens. Like *Eliso*, the narrative tells of class solidarity overcoming national difference. It takes place amid the transformation of Georgia by Bolshevism. The epic landscape of the Caucasian mountains is dotted with villages on the brink of ruin, held captive by patriarchal tradition. Early sequences focus on the beauty of the landscape, and the romance of a woman singing beside a waterfall, where her young beloved finds her. But such peace cannot last amid this interethnic rivalry, and Bolshevik power makes its way across the mountains.

At the beginning of the film, the Khevsurs have killed two Chechens; according to tradition, the Chechens must seek blood revenge. Instead, young Chechens bring a milk separator as a peace offering. On both sides, it is only the elders who ferment age-old conflict in an effort to maintain the status quo; the young represent a possible future in which ethnic divides are replaced by class solidarity. The narrative revolves around two young Khevsur brothers, Mgeliia and Torgvai. Mgeliia embraces the modern world and communism. He has traveled away from his tribe, and when he returns he attempts to broker a new accord with the Chechens, for the future. When Mgeliia is killed by an unknown hand, however, the Khevsur elders manipulate his brother Torgvai, suggesting that the Chechens were responsible. Torgvai goes to exact revenge, but meets the same young Chechens with whom his brother had found solidarity, and follows Mgeliia in resolving that the tribes should fight together against their common (class) enemy.[35]

The Last Crusaders treads a careful line between sublime landscape, ethnographic material, and its rhetoric of modernization. In places (in costume, and in the representation of customs such as a wedding feast), it is densely ethnographic. But it is concerned also to picture a socialist future for the peoples of the mountains. Torgvai suffers humiliation at first for his refusal of the patriarchal duty of revenge. But he finds redemption through an embrace of technology: he takes the Chechen milk separator, and begins to use it. A striking scene at the local trade cooperative pictures a remarkable medley of national costumes, different ethnic faces, handmade products, old traditions, and new ideals. As a result of his perceived cowardice, young Torgvai is isolated and mocked. His butter, however, is discovered to be far superior to any other, a reconciliation is forged, and the Khevsurs vow to create a dairy collective. In one final trial, the Chechen and Khevsur elders together stage a fake raid designed to perpetuate age-old conflict and prevent modernization. Torgvai heads bravely—now as epic hero seeking revenge—to the Chechen camp. But before he is able to carry out his (primitive) duty, he stumbles upon the elders celebrating their successful plot. Realizing the truth, he embraces his fellow Chechen komsomoltsy: the feud is over and the construction of a new world can begin. Torgvai's "cowardice" is reconfigured as a new form of bravery, appropriate for the modern age. An apparently timeless tale of ethnic rivalry is turned into a narrative of the birth of collective farming in the Georgian mountains.

The success of *The Last Crusaders* lies in its ability to combine its message of modernization with an ethnographic eye, which pictures—and does not smooth over—the radical otherness of the Khevsurs. In the figure of Torgvai, it presents an equivalence between the primal sensibility (of characters such as Vazhia in *Eliso*, see chapter 5) and the modernizing energy of the new world. This fragile balance was not easy to achieve, however, and films about the Soviet East trod a careful line through the 1930s. One of the most intriguing attempts to combine the pleasures of oriental faktura with a celebration of modern technology on-screen is *Mzago and Gela* (*Mzago i Gela*), directed by Lev Push and Shalva Khuskivadze in 1930 (but not released until 1934). *Mzago and Gela* was Push's final production for Goskinprom Gruzii. In one sense, the story is a familiar one of modernization. A silent film, narrated through first-person intertitles, it tells of how an isolated Khevsur village, high in the Georgian mountains, is visited by "proletarian tourists." With them comes technology—specifically radio technology—which prompts a transformation and education of the local youth, and begins the village's move into the modern age.[36]

The film has an explanatory subtitle: "A Khevsur's Tale, produced by photo-recording" (and it begins, strikingly, with a fragmentary recording of an English voice, as part of the film's soundtrack). This pairing of the traditional and the modern (oral narrative and phototechnology) sets an ironic

Fig. 8.3 The Primitive Hero. Still from *Mzago and Gela* (*Mzago i Gela*, dir. L. Push, 1930, production design V. Sidamon-Erastavi (released 1935)).

tone, which frames the film's presentation of "exotic" material as an explicit engagement with the myth of the authentic East. The political narrative of modernization is told through a love story between two young people, Mzago and Gela. Gela is an archetypal Georgian epic hero (figure 8.3), "brave, agile and proud." He sings folk songs, races horses, and loves a beautiful woman, Mzago. She loves him too, but she is no traditional Eastern bride. Mzago has a thirst for knowledge, and a desire to embrace the changing world. When a wounded young communist has to take shelter in the village, Mzago is drawn to him, but her desire is not for the young man himself but above all for his radio and the knowledge that it brings: her eyes (or literally, her ears) are opened to the world beyond. As the young Bolshevik tells her about other wonders of technology, her imagination conjures up images of self-propelled hay carts navigating the snowy mountains (Push uses naïve animation here). She abandons the village—and Gela—and travels to the city to discover the Soviet truth.

Sergei Kapterev describes Push as having a "decorative mind," and notes this film's "pictorialist patterns."[37] It exhibits a clear pleasure in capturing the dense faktura of native village life, and does so within familiar frameworks. The opening sequences convey an isolation that has much in common with the epic shots of *The Last Crusaders* (also focused on Khevsur life), and even with *Salt for Svanetiia*. Semiruined villages huddle on a steep mountainside. A familiar concatenation of patterned textiles and carpets fills the screen. Ethnographic material abounds throughout, but it is framed with ironic discourse. Indeed, the film directs attention explicitly to the exotic and its associated myths and legends. The narrator in the opening sequence observes, "They consider us [the Khevsurs] heirs to the Crusaders, because you will find the design of a cross more often than any other decoration on our national costume." But, it goes on, "we do not always live as the scholars would have it."

This ethnographic eye is purposely playful, appropriating the decorative difference of Khevsur tradition as part of a vision of a joyful Soviet present. The Khevsur village is traditional and tumbledown, but it is not ruined or dark: indeed many of the scenes of local life are set outdoors. Mzago and Gela's modern young faces are framed by their traditional costume; here, the heavy textiles and ornamental accessories are not a weight. More generally, tradition is transformed into a form of play. Mzago and Gela frolic and flirt; the men of the village race horses while the women look on and assess their masculinity. In another scene, Mzago herself gallops joyously across the mountains, in a powerful assertion of her independent spirit. Folk songs are sung, spirit is poured into ceremonial drinking horns, and the community toasts and drinks from them. Children are everywhere.

This playfulness is particularly evident when Gela follows Mzago to Tbilisi, and the familiar trope of the arrival of a "provincial" in the city is given a specifically national/primitive twist. Dressed in his full ceremonial costume, complete with sword and shield, Gela prowls around the city "as if in a forest." He is overwhelmed by urban modernity. He walks past a cinema, where he sees an advertisement for Shengelaia's *Eliso*, with a larger-than-life cutout of the Khevsur hero Vazhia in his national dress (figure 8.4). By this time, *Eliso* was a well-known and successful film, and one in which Vazhia emerged as a heroic prototype for a Georgian national hero. In Gela's present, however, the film makes clear that that prototype is outdated and irrelevant. In traditional dress, Gela is taken for either a bandit or a beggar in the modern city. He is a spectacle for the modern urbanites. Like Filimonov in Ermler's *A Fragment of Empire*, he is disorientated by a tram, unable to find his way in the new world. None of this is grounds for criticism, however.

Fig. 8.4 *Eliso*: An Outdated Primitive. Still from *Mzago and Gela* (*Mzago i Gela*, dir. L. Push, 1930, production design V. Sidamon-Erastavi [released 1935]).

Rather, *Mzago and Gela* smooths over the opposition between the primitive and the modern, rendering it comic and hence implicitly surmountable. It is mere surface, rather than authentic difference.

A similar flattening of conflict between old and new is evident in the integration of the technology of radio into the ethnographic material of traditional village life. The iconic "first encounter" of primitive man with technology is staged in this film in recognizable terms. Adults and children stare at the machine with rapt and suspicious attention. The camera focuses on the wires and dials that enable the radio to spring to life: "It knows a lot, this machine, and talks about everything." Even the village animals are shocked by the explosion of modern technology into their midst. Gradually, however, fear is transformed into excitement, and the new technology is appropriated as a part of village life. Children dance with headphones over their ears (figure 8.5). One evening, during the village festival, as the village indulges ("as always") in "wine, dancing, and more wine," and children are playing with bows and arrows, the radio brings the sound of "urban music"

Fig. 8.5 Technology and Play. Still from *Mzago and Gela* (*Mzago i Gela*, dir. L. Push, 1930, production design by V. Sidamon-Erastavi [released 1935]).

Fig. 8.6 Technology and Play. Still from *Mzago and Gela* (*Mzago i Gela*, dir. L. Push, 1930, production design ny V. Sidamon-Erastavi [released 1935]).

to their ears. Then ensues an intriguing montage in which the traditional and the modern, urban and rural, technical and natural, merge harmoniously to create an atmosphere of hybrid pleasure and free play. Mzago stands with headphones on her head, in traditional dress, dancing to the sound of a distant jazz orchestra (figure 8.6).

For all its naturalization, however, radio technology remains the voice of modernity and modernization. In one scene, the newspaper speaks aloud (the film shows the voices of radio presenters materialized inside the radio speaker as Mzago listens) and Mzago is struck by their pronouncements about backward villages: "They are talking about us." This prompts her illicit nighttime escape to Tbilisi, alone. Initially out of place in her traditional costume, she finds a local office, where she is welcomed by smiling young communist workers and eventually sent to learn dairy production. Her costume covered by an overall, she learns to milk cows. When Gela is eventually reunited with Mzago, who is now transformed by her immersion in urban modernity, he himself vows to change. The film ends with her returning to the village (complete with a milk separator). He stays in the city, and we are told that soon he "will be a radio-engineer."

Mzago and Gela is a remarkable film, distinguished by the wit and levity with which it treats its twin subjects: socialist transformation and the traditions and customs of an ancient tribe. The ethnographic eye of earlier films is replaced here by one that views local costume and custom in terms of pictorial richness. The message of the film is that *within* these outer shells, Mzago and Gela are no different from other Soviet young people. Their "difference" becomes little more than a pleasurable indulgence on the surface of the screen. This signals the beginning of the central transformation that distinguished Stalinist representations of the ethnic space: the reduction of genuine otherness to decorative difference.

Mzago and Gela belongs to a popular genre in late 1920s and 1930s cinema, which narrated the modernization of the national republics. Azerfilm produced two important films within this genre: *Sevil´* (1929) and *Almas,* directed by Aga-Rza Kuliev and Grigorii Braginskii (who also contributed to the script of *Sevil´*) for Azerfilm in 1936 (with Vladimir Aden as production designer). Although separated by several years, these films can be seen as a pair. Both were adaptations of popular plays by young revolutionary playwright Jaafar Jabbarli. *Sevil´* is a story of the liberation of the eponymous heroine, who begins the film as the oppressed, traditionally clothed wife of a westernized Azeri banker, who abandons her for a glamorous bourgeoise. Sevil´ is forced into self-consciousness, casts off her veil and chador, and becomes a modern woman. Its "sequel," *Almas*, is a story of women's liberation in rural Azerbaijan. Set in 1930, it tells a story of the arrival of young teacher, Almas (the same actress who played Sevil´), in a remote village, where she plans not only to teach, but also to transform the place of women in society according to new communist ideology and morality.

Almas effectively takes up where earlier narratives (such as *Sevil´*, and even Room's *Bed and Sofa*) left off. It seeks to picture the future of those heroines whose destinies, in films of the 1920s, were anticipated, but not shown. Indeed, the opening of this film has much in common with the scene in Kozintsev and Trauberg's *Alone*, where Kuz´mina arrives as a teacher in Altai. Here, too, we have a lone woman in a horse and cart; here, too, there is a sense of potential threat (she is told that the previous teacher left because she found the community too difficult); but here there is one crucial difference: *Almas* is returning to her native land. She has been transformed and "modernized" by her education elsewhere, and now she seeks to act as a catalyst for socialist transformation at home.

Much of this book has focused on the ideological and cultural signification of handcrafts. How does that change in cinema of the 1930s? As in *Alone*, the first sequences of *Almas* presenting the native village focus on national craft. Women sit before large boards, weaving carpets. Here, though, the strange otherness that characterized the first sequences of native life in *Alone*, is absent; local life is domesticated and familiar, a curious blend of traditional and modern. Almas seeks to organize the local female carpet weavers into a labor cartel, liberating them from their merchant employer. Thus begins one of Almas's many battles for social transformation. Large weaving equipment begins to arrive, but there is no dedicated space for the workshop. When the corrupt local communist leader resolves that the women may take over the village's old mosque, it causes inevitable resentment among the village's older community—men and women alike. Almas is undeterred, however, and she and her collective successfully transform the mosque into a combined school and weaving workshop.

This is a film focused principally on female liberation and the obstacles that prevent it. The patriarchal system is riddled with corruption: Almas's battle is above all a battle with the power of men. The old men of the village conspire to see her fail; men of the village try to remove their wives and children from her pernicious influence. For all this, however, the film's overarching narrative is one of progress. The village tribunal that is set up to condemn

Almas fails when the children show the villagers what she has taught them: not a devilish dance, but a performance in which komsomol-style marching merges harmoniously with traditional dance. And as the workshop is established, the film features scenes of women weaving together that restage familiar images of women's work (as in *Women of Riazan Province* and *Honor*, see chapters 3 and 5), but in modern, revolutionary terms. Here handcraft is clearly redemptive; the local women's path to political consciousness takes place through shared participation in the act of making.

Almas takes a more serious approach to the challenge of transformation than *Mzago and Gela*, but it shares common features with that film. The appropriation of the mosque acts as a metaphor for a broader process of appropriation that takes place in films of this period: like the mosque, the ethnic space is evacuated of meaning, becoming a vacuum that can be filled with new purpose and new messages. The rich faktura of local costume, interior decoration, and traditional custom becomes visual pleasure on the surface of a homogenous picture of unified Soviet space. The embodied experience of handcraft is transformed into protoindustrial force or harmless traditional diversion. The sensory intensity of the "primitive" is replaced by performative pleasure. In this way, Soviet cinema created its own simulacrum of the East.

In sum, these films of technology mark a transition from an interest in an embodied knowledge naoshchup' (provided by an ethnographic eye) toward a new focus on the "sensory radiance" (see chapter 7) of Easternness. In parallel, they reveal a shift from an interest in the genuine possibilities of alternative modes of subjecthood, toward the celebration of the essential homogeneity of the Soviet man and woman. These arguments may be familiar to us from studies of Socialist Realism and of Stalinist culture. It is notable, however, that all of our case studies reveal a self-reflexive awareness of the dangerous lure of the "wrong" kind of sensory radiance, and the need for films to walk a careful line in representing the material pleasures of the East in the context of Socialist Realism. This is exemplified in the final film that we will examine here.

False Faktura

The Living God (*Zhivoi Bog*) was an early feature for then-young Tadzhik film studio, codirected by Mikhail Verner and Dmitrii Vasil'ev in 1934. This curious film focuses on the Muslim Ismailite faith (a faith that follows the Aga Khan) among the peoples of the Pamir Mountains. This is a film with a clear propaganda purpose. *The Living God* was produced two years before the Soviet state sealed the border with Afghanistan, in an attempt to sever connections between Ismailites.[38] Set in Pamir in the years 1916–1926, it reveals the Aga Khan to be a puppet of imperial power, and the Ismailite faith as a corrupt "secret sect with subtly worked out propaganda."[39]

The film's critique of the trappings and false surfaces of religious culture is clear. It sets up an opposition between "fake" Eastern decoration and authentic primitive life. The Aga Khan is embedded within the luxury of the British imperial power structures: his palace in Bombay is an epitome of Eastern style as simulacrum. It blends the classical structures of Western architecture with the flourishes and patterns of exotic ornament. The Aga Khan himself is a top-hatted lover of horse racing and a puppet of imperial power, whose wealth and prestige are powered by rich tribute from Ismaili states. Visiting leaders from India, Persia, China, Africa, and Pamir itself are treated to a religious show, in which the Aga Khan appears first as a God-child who appears to float before them, surrounded by a cloud of smoke; as an old man ("He is immortal, and so he can be young and old at the same time!"); and finally as himself, his Western suit briefly covered by Ismailite robes. Later, in an extraordinary scene that anticipates the moment of revelation in *The Wizard of Oz*, the camera uncovers the technology that powers this miracle: a man behind a curtain, operating levers and dials, viewing the outcome of his labors on a miniature film screen. Thus the apparatus of the Ismaili faith is revealed as an amalgam of high camp and geopolitical influence. Its "radiance" is pure show.

In opposition to the false glamour and artifice of the high priests of Ismaili power, the film presents the brutal reality of life in Pamir. The poor heroine Nazar-Begim is taken by the local ruling elder into his harem. His palace reproduces the visual tropes of fake oriental style that we have seen with the Aga Khan, but now in degraded and grotesque form. His harem of women is trapped in a sumptuous space bedecked by carpets. The women are grotesque and deformed by captivity, enslaved by their master, and by opium. Their teeth are rotten; they cover their faces with cream, apply clumsy makeup to their heavily lined skin, and fight over scraps of decorated textile. When Nazar-Begim arrives as the latest addition to the harem, it is these women who wash, clothe, and dress her, wrapping her in stiff, shiny fabric, and present her for their master's pleasure. Like the women in *Giuli* and *Honor*, they are profoundly complicit in their own oppression.

The narrative momentum of *The Living God* is provided by an encounter with modernity—in the form of the Bolsheviks. The implied narrator is Abduraim, a young man clothed in the uniform of the Soviet army, telling his comrades the story of his neighbor Nazar-Begim, who was the friend and love of his youth. As Soviet power in Pamir begins a broader process of politicization, so the young boy, now a communist, successfully rescues Nazar-Begim from the clutches of the Ishan, and the film ends with a vision of the future happiness of the young couple, free from oppression.

The tension in *The Living God* is one that runs through cinema of this period: between the ideological call for the "flattening" of difference, the creation of a homogeneous Soviet subject, and an aesthetic fascination with the cinematographic potential of the textures and surfaces of Eastern alterity. Like other films of the 1920s and 1930s, *The Living God* seeks to locate authentic embodied experience in degradation and suffering, in scenes that are dense with sensory empathy. The narrative is clear in its condemnation of the false radiance of the Ismailite faith and the Aga Khan's greedy attempt to dupe his foolish followers. Yet it is the simulacrum of the God-child (for all his technological underpinnings) that provides cinematic dazzle. And as the piles of gold coins collected "for the Aga Khan" glisten before the camera, the camera revels in the exposure of artifice and the shiny textures and surfaces of this world of fakery. In *The Living God*, that fantastical, glistening surface is clearly coded as bad. It is surface without sensation—chuvstvennyi blesk (sensory radiance) without its parallel in embodiment. But in representing this tension, this film—unwittingly or otherwise—poses a core question for Socialist Realist cinema. What was the place of material pleasure in the new world? As we will see in the next chapter, one answer to that difficult question was to relocate it in the apparently harmless space of play.

NOTES

1. Slezkine, "The USSR as Communal Apartment," 414.
2. It should be noted that the date of this film is contentious, and the version referred to here is the one reworked for 1938.
3. See, for example, Honarpisheh, "The Oriental 'Other' in Soviet Cinema, 1929–34," 185–201. Michael Kunichika, however, offers an excellent, more detailed reading of the film in terms that have much in common with my argument here. Kunichika, *How Soon is Now*, chapter 5.

4. Honarpisheh, "The Oriental 'Other' in Soviet Cinema," 186–87.

5. Tret′iakov wrote one other screenplay, together with director Mikhail Chiaureli, for a film produced by Goskinprom Gruzii, and set in Georgia in 1932. Tret′iakov and Chiareli, "Khabarda." The film was produced in 1931.

6. Sergei Tret′iakov, "Liudi v ushchel′iakh," 157.

7. Ibid.

8. Ibid.

9. For further discussion of this film, see, for example, Payne, "The Movie Turksib and Soviet Orientalism."

10. Sergei Tret′iakov, "Strana Svan."

11. Malevich, "Ot kubizma i futurizma k suprematizmu," 42, cited in Schönle, *Architecture of Oblivion*, 126.

12. Schönle, *Architecture of Oblivion*, 151.

13. Kalinin, "Istoriia kak iskusstvo chlenorazdel′nosti," 103–132.

14. Malevich, "1/46 (Eklektika)," 148.

15. Schönle, *Architecture of Oblivion*, 230.

16. Kunichika, *Our Native Antiquity*, 207. Certainly, a complex relationship with the material evidence of the past is also evident in the broader context of Soviet Russia. Orientologists such as Vasilii Bartol′d believed that the preservation of Islamic monuments and tombs in Turkestan, for example, was important: these buildings revealed the ancient strength of Eastern culture, which could be harnessed to the new narrative of the Soviet East. See Tolz, *Russia's Own Orient*, 162–63.

17. Simmel, "The Ruin," 379.

18. Paperny, *Architecture in the Age of Stalin*, 252–54.

19. Mackay, "Allegory and Accommodation," 381.

20. See Michelson, "The Kinetic Icon in the Work of Mourning." Note, however, that Mackay reads the film persuasively as being as much about Stalin as it is about Lenin. Mackay, "Allegory and Accommodation."

21. Kunichika, *Our Native Antiquity*, 278.

22. Fanon, "Algeria Unveiled," 42.

23. Mackay, "Allegory and Accommodation," 381.

24. Copjec, "The Sartorial Superego," 67.

25. For further discussion of films about unveiling, see Rouland, "An Historical Introduction," 6. For contextual information about the Soviet unveiling projects, see Northrop, *Veiled Empire: Gender*; also Massell, *The Surrogate Proletariat*.

26. Copjec, "The Sartorial Superego," 86.

27. See Widdis, *Visions of a New Land*, 143, 147.

28. Romm, quoting Shumiatskii in Romm, "O sebe, o liudiakh, o fil′makh," 146.

29. Nilsen, "O fil′me 'Trinadtsat′,'" 13.

30. Gromov, *Vladimir Egorov*, 77. It seems clear from his diaries that Petr Galadzhev also had a major input into the design for this film. See Galadzhev, "Tvorchestvo konchilos′ do, do . . . ?!," 66–85.

31. Simmel, "The Ruin," 381.

32. For excellent in-depth analysis of the symbolic meaning of the kurgan in the pre- and postrevolutionary period, see Kunichika, *Our Native Antiquity*, 62–107.

33. Gromov, *Vladimir Egorov*, 77.

34. *The Last Crusaders* was produced as a silent film. Sound was added in Georgian, and the Russian inter titles remained, producing, as Evgenii Margolit notes, a powerful "heteroglossia" to the film. See Margolit, "The Problem of Heteroglossia," 124–25.

35. Ibid., 125.

36. For consideration of the role and symbolic significance of radio in early Soviet Russia, see Lovell, *Russia in the Microphone Age*. Lovell mentions *Mzago i Gela* (46).

37. Kapterev, "Mzago and Gela," 82.

38. They also actively restricted the power of the *khalifa* (spiritual leaders of any Ismailite community). See Saikal, *Modern Afghanistan*, especially chapter 3.

39. See Steinberg, *Isma'ili Modern*, 40–51.

Chapter Nine

SOCIALIST PLEASURES

> It seems to me the highest completion of our human activities is that our play becomes labor, and labor becomes celebration and our celebration becomes play.
>
> Johannes Itten

THIS CHAPTER UNCOVERS a second "afterlife" of socialist sensation. In direct dialogue with chapter 4 (Socialist Sensations), it shows how the dream of a refashioned homo faber evolved, in the mid-1930s, into a sanitized vision of *homo ludens*: how the ideal of "making" was transformed into "playing."

In part, this chapter will trace an abiding focus on the cinematic potential of material and texture in Stalinist cinema through the 1930s. Yet it is common in critical literature to discuss cinema of the 1930s—and indeed Stalinist cinema more broadly—in terms of its lack of interest in material objects. This is seen to distinguish the narrative-led cinema of the 1930s from the Formalist experiments of the 1920s. Iampolski accuses Soviet film of having neglected the "sensory" (his term is chuvstvitel'nyi—notable because it adds "sentiment" to the sensory [chuvstvennyi] impact of cinema).[1] Other critics have concurred, suggesting that Socialist Realist cinema is distinguished by its lack of real cinematic faktura (texture). Mamatova, for example, describes how: "The faktura of interiors becomes harder and more glossy. The mise-en-scènes become more static . . . white becomes more noticeably present in clothing . . . white starts to dominate in interiors."[2]

In similar terms, Sal'nikova describes the "bright light" of Socialist Realist visual culture as flattening the faktura of the material world on-screen.[3] Tat'iana Dashkova ascribes the "lack of meaning" of material objects in Soviet cinema before the Second World War to cinema's sacrifice of the real lived experience of individuals to the idealized narratives of Socialist Realism.[4] Such arguments are often linked to comments about Socialist Realist prudery: Dashkova argues that Stalinist cinema is explicitly desexualised, with no "real" bodies.

Throughout this book, I have sought to complicate such pictures—to identify not just ruptures but also continuities in what might be called Soviet cinema's materialist project. In this chapter, I will trace how the cinematic pleasure in texture, touch, and embodied experience endured in 1930s cinema, and how it was part of the negotiation of the consolidating norms of Socialist Realism. What was the ideologically appropriate model for the relationship between human subjects and the material world that surrounded them in the new context of the 1930s?

To help answer this question, I will focus on the category of *play*—with specific reference to childhood, as metaphor and reality. We are accustomed to thinking about socialist leisure and socialist plenty: the carnival scenes of Aleksandr Medvedkin's *New Moscow* (*Novaia Moskva*, 1939); the bathing lidos, circuses, and folk performances of Aleksandrov's musical comedies and other light comedies of the period. Such scenes give us a glimpse of Soviet man and woman at play. But critical writing has tended to think about such representations of socialist leisure as artifice: evidence of the potent myth of the Stalinist "good life." While not challenging the relevance of such readings, I propose that we also consider what might be called "ludic" moments in Socialist Realist cinema: instances of playfulness as a material encounter between body and world. As such they need not be seen as counter to the revolutionary impetus, but as intrinsically part of it, and seeking to negotiate a changing ideological field.

This chapter will elaborate a contextual framework that traces the potent appeal of play, and toys, in the Soviet context. I will then examine the specific development of children's cinema in Russia. To what extent did children's films—and the broader context of child's play—complicate the evolving model of the new Soviet subject, and his/her powerful combination of reason and feeling? Finally, I will offer a broader analysis of the status of play and toys in cinema aimed at adults. How was the model of "making" in dialogue with that of play, and what did that dialogue have to say about changing models of Sovietness?

Play

The term "ludic" is drawn from Johannes Huizinga's distinction between homo faber and homo ludens.[5] In a lecture given in Leiden in 1933, Huizinga concurred with Arendt (see chapter 4) in identifying homo faber as the industrious maker, and posited homo ludens as his vital (and valuable) counterpart. Play, Huizinga asserted, was "a free activity standing quite consciously outside 'ordinary' life as being 'not serious,' but at the same time absorbing the player intensely and utterly."[6] The success of any society depends upon both productivity and play.[7]

What was the status of ludic activity in early Soviet Russia? We are accustomed to thinking about Soviet childhood as a politicized space— a realm of experience appropriated to socialization and to the creation of model citizens.[8] Yet we might also think about the potential of childhood as a metaphor for the (socialist) rebirth of humanity made possible by revolution. Play and playfulness, were at the center of the modernist project—in pre- and postrevolutionary Russia, and in a wider international context. They had particular—but complex, and inevitably ambivalent—resonance for Marxist theorists. In this respect, Huizinga's distinction between homo faber and homo ludens is revealing. In chapter 4, I used Arendt's conception of homo faber to articulate a vision of production that I argued was specific to the Soviet project. What, then, was the place of homo ludens within a Marxist society?

Walter Benjamin provided a particularly developed answer to this question. He was, as is well known, very interested in childhood and child's play—and specifically fascinated by Soviet experimental approaches to children's education and entertainment.[9] Based on his observations in Moscow, Benjamin suggested that Soviet children's clubs had enabled a new level of observation of the child and led to a new understanding: that the "child inhabits his world as dictator."[10] In play, children's gestures are commands and signals: they reimagine the material world for their own purposes. This transformative capacity of play creates new relationships between the child and material objects: in play, objects are reconfigured, take on new forms, entering what Benjamin called "intuitive" (mimetic) relationships with the human subject.[11] This was a reciprocal relationship that had much in common with the ideal relationship between the human and the material world that was so central to the Soviet ideal.

It was thus that play had, for Benjamin, potential as a counter to the dematerialized, "anaesthetized" sensory experience characteristic of modernity.[12] It could be an appropriative mechanism, mobilized in relation to the challenges posed by the (new) technologies of modernity: "By the interest it takes in technological phenomena, its curiosity for all sorts of inventions and machinery, every childhood binds the accomplishments of technology to the old worlds of symbols."[13] The task of the teacher (or theater director) of children was not to instruct, but to release the creative capacities present in play from fantasy and imagination into the world of creative action.[14] As such, play was a model of what Benjamin envisaged as "revolutionary consciousness"[15]: the principle of "innervation" as a "non-destructive, mimetic incorporation of the world."[16]

Benjamin was by no means alone in this vision of play as a form of revolutionary action. The metaphor of play had its own lineage in the Soviet revolutionary context. For members of the prerevolutionary artistic and literary avant-garde, children's art—and children's language—had provided a powerful stimulus for experiment. Futurist Aleksei Kruchenykh, for example, published an anthology of works (written and drawn) by children in 1916, and a second (without drawings) in 1923.[17] Andrei Belyi's *Kotik Letaev* (1920) was explicitly concerned with the creativity of children's language and imagination.[18] After the revolution, an interest in child creativity continued through the 1920s and into the 1930s. VKhUTEMAS had its own studio of children's drawings, art historian Anatolii Bakushinskii published studies of children's art, and early pedagogues and psychologists elaborated theories of children's creativity.[19] As a metaphor, childhood could be seen to represent the iconoclastic force of freedom that underlay the Soviet revolution itself, its shedding of the ("mature") shackles of bourgeois society. It was, to some extent, this possibility of revolutionary rebirth that drew Benjamin to postrevolutionary Russia. As he wrote in his "Moscow" essay of 1927, "The instant one arrives, the childhood stage begins."[20] Benjamin explicitly linked the far-reaching social transformations of Soviet Russia of the 1920s to the category of play: "This astonishing experimentation—it is here called *remonte*—affects not only Moscow; it is Russian. In this ruling passion there is as much naïve desire for improvement as there is boundless curiosity and playfulness."[21]

Benjamin pointed to Soviet experimental culture as playful, but the metaphors of spontaneity and rebirth had broader conceptual underpinning:

Mikhail Bakhtin's early theories of the carnivalesque are perhaps the most obvious examples of what might be called a ludic impulse in early Soviet culture—envisaging revolution as an explosion of transformative playfulness.[22] But the impulse was widespread. For many, the ludic impulse—the imaginative, hands-on quality of play, and its capacity to reshape reality—was the key to the power of art in the revolutionary context. For Alexander Voronskii, play was a central element of the power of art: "In art, everything is constructed conditionally, as in a game. And, as in a game, in art one must believe all that is conditional in order to experience full satisfaction."[23] This celebration of play as iconoclastic liberation ran in parallel with a focus on its capacity for purposeful action and social(ist) transformation.

In the context of the international revolutionary avant-garde, of course, playfulness need not (indeed, must not) be divorced from purpose and productivity. Indeed, it was linked to the intuitive, hands-on relationship with the world that was central to the concept of "making." Johannes Itten, for example, who was responsible for the development of the compulsory foundational course in the Bauhaus between 1919 and 1923, placed play at the center of his pedagogy. Trained as a kindergarten teacher himself, and influenced by the German educational theorist Friedrich Froebel, Itten sought to stimulate the creativity of his Bauhaus pupils by encouraging free play with materials. The principle was twofold. First, the child/artist would become acquainted with the world via the object—and, in particular, via a thoroughly tactile multisensory discovery of the object. Second, they would begin to operate within and upon the world, as a child works with toys and found objects: transforming the object through creative action/improvisation (Ger. *Basteln*). Thus play was brought into the center of human production.[24] For Itten, it was the key to unlocking a new kind of productivity: "It seems to me the highest completion of our human activities is that our play becomes labor, and labor becomes celebration and our celebration becomes play."[25]

This imbrication of work and play was echoed in Benjamin, who envisaged as an ideal "the unfolding of work in play."[26] Modern media had a role here. In contrast to bourgeois art, which lacked the vital play element, new media (in particular cinema) opened up the possibility of a new kind of *Spiel-raum* (room for play), for what Miriam Hansen calls "a technologically-mediated aesthetics of play capable of diverting the destructive, apocalyptic course of history."[27] Here, then, lay the potential of cinema as a counter to the anaesthetizing effect of the sensory assault of modern life. In the eyes of Benjamin, cinema was itself a particularly potent form of play: "The 'prismatic' work of film at once unveils and refracts the everyday, thus making it available for play—for a mimetic appropriation and reconfiguring of its ruined fragments."[28]

TOYS

Benjamin's vision of film as play was metaphorical—tied to the formal capacities of film to provoke embodied spectatorship. But what of more direct engagement, formal and thematic, with the world of childhood and toys? From its beginnings, silent cinema had a privileged relationship with children's play. Thomas Edison's talking dolls—the first attempt at a doll containing a phonograph, which would play a series of nursery rhymes—were marketed briefly in 1877.[29] Although they were not a commercial success, they are evidence of the relationship between dolls/puppets/toys and early recording technologies—a connection that developed powerfully with the advent of cinema. Film technology made possible a visualization of the imagined world of children's play and its material basis: the magic of toys. In Arthur Melbourne-Cooper's short film *A Dream of Toyland* (1908), for example, a boy's dream of bringing his toys to life finds stunning realization on-screen.[30] Similarly, Ernst Lubitsch's *The Doll: Four Amusing Acts from a Toy Box* (1919) sets up a clear relationship between the fantasies of cinema and those of children's play: the director himself appears on-screen, opening up a toy box and assembling an artificial stage set. Throughout the film, as the scenes from the toy box come alive, the juxtaposition of the real (actors' bodies) and the artificial (the drawn set, a stylized sky) is played up: a man rolls down a drawn hill, into an apparently drawn pond, and tumbles into real water. In another example, the famous Laurel and Hardy musical *Babes in Toyland* (1934) presents a grotesque vision of toys running amok. Films such as these relished cinema's capacity to animate the inanimate, but they also often revealed toys as commodities and objects of consumer desire: *A Dream of Toyland* dwells on the experience of the boy in the toy shop, his eyes glued to the shop assistant as he demonstrates a series of different toys. Similar scenes recur in different forms in many films and, as we shall see, have intriguing prominence in the Soviet context.

In Russia, few prerevolutionary films focused explicitly on the potentialities of toys.[31] Władysław Starewicz, usually credited as producing the first animated stop-motion cinema, made extraordinary films using animated (model) insects—most famously *The Cameraman's Revenge* (*Mest' kinematograficheskogo operatora*, 1911).[32] Aleksandr Shiriaev (the discovery of whose films has challenged Starewicz's status as Russia's first animator) made a series of stop-motion films of ballets, using papier-mâché figures.[33] Such films drew on toy-like models, but did not make a direct link to the world of children's play. After 1917, however, toys themselves began to appear more frequently in cinema. As discussed in chapter 4, the first *Film Week* episode (1918) featured a brief sequence of "Handmade Toys," focused on the moving shapes of the wooden toys, their white silhouettes standing out against the disparate textures of the crowds in a market.[34] They are handled and enjoyed by salesman and consumer—as if explicitly for the pleasure of the camera. Children's toys were exploited in feature films of the 1920s for a variety of ends. First, for a focus on *handling*, where the contact between hand and object is the focus of the camera's gaze (Iutkevich's *Lace*, Kuleshov's *Your Acquaintance*); second, for narrative purpose (e.g., Komarov's *A Doll with Millions*, where money is hidden inside the eponymous doll); and for purely formal impact, their forms and textures providing visual surface (e.g., Mikaberidze's *My Grandmother*). In all of these cases, however, the use of toys was linked to an interest in the material properties of objects and their relation to the human body.

The recurrence of toys in Soviet film of this period was caught up in ideological questions, however. In 1930, Aleksandra Khoklova directed an educational film with the title *Toys (Igrushki)*, for which Nikolai Bartram (creator of the Moscow State Museum of Toys in 1918) was consultant. The film studied preschool children playing with historical toys—beginning with natural resources and developing into purpose-made toys.[35] Although the film has been lost, it is evidence of the confluence between scientific interest in play (and in a history of toys) and avant-garde cinema practitioners. It is notable, surely, that Vertov, Benjamin, and our other directors focused on traditional, handmade, wooden toys. These are not mechanized objects, providing access to a fantastical realm of the imagination; they are simple products of craft. They speak not to the relationship between cinema and technology, but rather to a relationship with material and *making*. In this respect, it is useful briefly to consider the particular status of toys in Soviet Russia—both as material objects, and as objects of socialist production. And the linked status of play.

Vertov's market stall was a glimpse of real-life Russia: walking in Moscow in 1927, Walter Benjamin famously noted the presence of handmade toys on market stalls.[36] Toy production in Russia in the 1920s was an underdeveloped industry; and after the revolution, it was caught up in complex ideological questions. In Western Europe, the rapid growth of the toy industry during the nineteenth century had marked the emergence of an understanding of child's play as a realm largely *outside* the direct control of adults.[37] American educator John Dewey made an influential distinction between play and work, which distinguished the purposelessness of play activity from the outcome-driven activities of work.[38] In the Soviet context, this distinction acquired obvious significance: Dewey's works were published in Russia throughout the 1920s, and Dewey visited Russia in 1928.[39] The status of "free play," and of pleasure, was complex, however. According to Catriona Kelly, "The governing image of 'Soviet childhood' over the first decade and a half of the country's existence was rationalistic, anti-bourgeois, and often pro-child and anti-adult."[40] Play could be validated as a site of innate revolutionary transformation. Accordingly, the philosophies of free play, advocated by Dewey, as well as in the Montessori and Froebel theories of kindergarten education, had considerable influence in much discussion of preschool education through the 1920s.

Alongside this interest in child's play as a model of a new kind of experience, however, there was a growing unease in the 1920s about disorganized, unsupervised (purposeless) play. Play was a space for creating citizens of the future, and Soviet educational psychologists elaborated varied and complex theories of play in relation to socialization. The drive toward play should be productively harnessed in service of the "world of work."[41] The well-known work of Anton Makarenko during the 1920s and early 1930s is one of the clearest examples of the attempt to model the ideal adult Soviet citizen through a thoroughly integrated and managed model of childhood, incorporating education and play, and overcoming any distinction between them.[42] Makarenko was an outspoken opponent of the principle of free play, emphasizing the importance of discipline and organization within the collective as a core principle of child pedagogy.

As such, the years from the late 1920s to approximately 1937 were a time of great transition in attitudes toward children's play (and in Soviet educational policy more broadly). Kelly marks 1935 as a turning point, a new phase in Soviet childhoods, when the model of "free education" came under sustained attack.[43] The writing was on the wall even earlier, however. From 1931–1932 on, models of progressive education (along with the science of pedology) were increasingly criticized; school teaching programs swung decisively toward more traditional teaching paradigms. And in 1936, the Central Committee issued a decree that directly criticized the science of pedology.

The twin principles of discipline and purpose became particularly important: "'Happiness' still had to be earned; pleasure was the reward for subordination of the self."[44]

In the context of these many and often contradictory theories and messages regarding child's play, what was the productive purpose of toys? In 1918, a State Museum of Toys was founded in Zagorsk; in 1921, a special commission was set up under the auspices of Narkompros, with the task of assessing existing children's toys; in 1932, it developed into a state-run Scientific Research Institute (linked to the Zagorsk museum) for the study and production of toys, and toy-making fell formally under the oversight of the Ministry of Propaganda.[45] The provision of new socially appropriate toys began in earnest. Narkompros issued regular "Letters on teaching methods," which emphasized the value of wooden bricks (to encourage an interest in buildings), but not dolls (which fostered vanity).[46] In 1935–1936, the debate stepped up. In the first half of 1936, a series of articles appeared in *Pravda* criticizing Soviet toy production.[47] An official journal dedicated to toys—*The Soviet Toy*—was published between 1935 and 1939, with "political-ideological oversight and control of toys."[48] When the first dedicated toy store, Children's World, opened in Leningrad in 1936, it was celebrated in the press as a national event. In reality, however, toys were in short supply—few children had access to any of the kinds of toys displayed in the store or discussed in the press.[49]

It is clear then that in Soviet Russia of the 1920s and 1930s, the toy was a site of ideological complexity and considerable symbolic weight, tied to broader debates in the construction of Soviet subjectivity. Yet its exact function was undetermined. Sal'nikova and Khamitova's analysis of *The Soviet Toy* reveals a more multidimensional picture of the development of the Soviet toy industry, and of the search for appropriate models for Soviet toys, than is sometimes presented in visions of the "happy Soviet childhood" as ideological project. They note in particular that the journal evinced an interest in the child as consumer, focusing on children's emotional responses to particular toys; *The Soviet Toy* even included texts written by children themselves. Thus this journal's short life might testify to a moment, in the late 1930s, when the production of the new model of childhood was envisaged as a two-way process, and when children had something to teach, as well as to learn.

Evolving attitudes to toys during the 1930s testify to this. Sal'nikova suggests that, by the mid-1930s, toys were envisaged as serving a number of key purposes: the development of the child's sensory and motor skills, their self-identification (according to gender and social roles), their socialization within the new Soviet reality, and their education vis-à-vis technology.[50] Nadezhda Krupskaia was one of several ideologues who viewed toys explicitly as tools for the transformation of children into Soviet citizens.[51] The toy was an agent of socialization, and as such part of the state's broader propaganda enterprise. Despite this, however, she continued to articulate the principles of free play throughout the 1930s.[52] As part of his own child-socialization theories, Makarenko distinguished three types of children's toy, to serve different purposes in the child's developmental process. The "ready-made" toy (a car, a castle, a doll) serves to acquaint the child with the real conditions of everyday life; "part-made" toys (such as construction sets) engage the child in the process of construction; while play "materials" (sand, dough, etc.) allow the child a free space for fantasy.[53] And it was in the crucial interplay between these three categories that the potential for the ideological modeling of the future citizen was located.

Within this ideological context, Lev Vygotskii's 1933 lecture "Play and its Role in the Mental Development of a Child" is striking in its resistance to simplistic visions of child's play as a space of simple socialization. Vygotskii rejected theories of play as a symbolic sphere, which could be mapped directly onto the real world: "Play," he wrote, "is never symbolic action in the proper sense of the term."[54] Echoing Huizinga, he emphasized that play (unlike work) is carried out without consciousness of motives or intentions. For Vygotskii, however, another element was important: play is always principally "affective" (Vygotskii uses the term *affektivnyi*).[55] That is, it engages the child both physically and emotionally. The physical response is the primary one. This emphasis on affect shapes Vygotskii's view of the role of toys: play begins as an affective relationship between the child and a material object. It is a crucial transitional zone between the real and the symbolic world. The child is often engaged in an act of symbolic metamorphosis and self-reimagining, but the terms of play are also dictated, to some extent, by the materiality (and hence, agency) of the toy/object itself.[56]

For Vygotskii, then, the toy was both medium and object. It was, I suggest, this *material* aspect of play with toys that was of particular interest to avant-garde theorists and practitioners in Soviet Russia during the 1920s. Toys could be validated as part of the hands-on vision of socialism. This, indeed, was an important element of the Soviet approach to childhood, especially during the first Five-Year Plan. "Give them toys that 'do it themselves,'" an article in *Pravda* exhorted (praising the construction toy Meccano in particular).[57] Even reading could be appropriated to this model. "Do-it-yourself" books (*knizhki-samodelki*) were common in children's publishing during the late 1920s and early 1930s.[58] They included instructions for self-made projects; some included cutout shapes and models for direct construction. One book even encouraged children to create their own films and show them to their friends.[59] In the avant-garde journal *Novyi LEF* in 1927, Rodchenko and Varvara Stepanova collaborated on illustrations to Tret'iakov's children's poems, *Autoanimals*, envisaging pop-out cardboard models that could be shaped and manipulated by child readers, with the exhortation "Do it yourself—act!"[60] Susanne Strätling discusses this project in terms of the neglected ludic qualities of Constructivism, suggesting that its encouragement of hands-on play was an attempt to transform the space of play into a constructive activity.[61]

Yet alongside this ideological agenda, such ludic experiments released Constructivist artists from utilitarian agendas, and opened up "spaces of potentiality."[62] These hands-on books and do-it-yourself models alert us to play as an *embodied* encounter between the child's hand and the material world, and emphasize the potentiality contained within the material fact of the toy as thing. It was this that underlay filmmakers' interest in toys during the 1920s—part of the broader exploration of cinema's capacity to reveal the faktura of the material world.[63] In this respect, Vygotskii's emphasis on play as both affective (emotional-physical) and symbolic provides an intriguing framework through which to think about the cinematic pleasures of toys. Play with toys creates a relationship of reciprocity between the child and the material world that had much in common with the utopian vision of socialist subjectivity.

Developing Children's Cinema in Soviet Russia

It is clear, then, that the 1930s saw a significant transition in attitudes to childhood, and, in parallel, to the relationship between work and play, pleasure and discipline. How, then, were these shifts visible in the cinema—both in the development of children's cinema itself and, more broadly, in the representation of the category of play? The remaining sections of this chapter will explore first the development of specific cinema for children, and how it pictured the complex relationship between free play and the imperative for socialist socialization. Second, I will trace how categories of play—and specifically play with objects—were treated in films about and for adults.

In a 1929 visit to Berlin, Eisenstein (on the recommendation of Luriia and Vygotskii) met with Kurt Lewin, a gestalt psychologist who was working with film to observe and understand children's behavior.[64] Lewin was interested in how a child's total view of the world (social, emotional, material) was visibly manifest in her physical reactions.[65] It was this relational quality—the "unsevered connection between perception and action," and the reciprocity between the child and the world—that Walter Benjamin identified (and valued) in children's play.[66] Like "primitive man" in the Uzbek expeditions and research of Vygotskii and Luriia (see chapter 5), the child was a model for an understanding of human life as rooted in a social and material context.

In Soviet Russia, "child science" flourished in the 1920s and up to the 1936 decree against pedology. The intersections between psychological science, pedology, and artistic experiment are well documented (see chapter 1). How, though, did this extend into consideration of children's cinema—and work with child actors in particular? Here the work of Margarita Barskaia is important. In 1933, Barskaia produced a feature film, *Torn Boots* (*Rvanye bashmaki*), which emerged out of experimental work carried out with children, investigating their movements, gestures, and facial expressions in response to different provocations, and using this as a basis for a new method of filming.[67] As a result of the success of *Torn Boots*, Barskaia was able to set up an experimental studio for in-depth work with children (the All-Union Experimental Children's Film Unit[68]). Terming her research "plastic folklore," Barskaia sought "prompts," which would encourage the children to produce the same movements in front of the camera.[69]

Torn Boots is a story of a workers' strike in Germany, seen through the eyes of the children of the workers. It is a film in which play is important—both thematically and formally. As Lev Kassil´ noted in his review, children actually play in this film: "They run and play, fight and climb, and work ... with an obvious pleasure, infectious energy and simplicity."[70] The use of terms relating to ludic activity is revealing here. Barskaia's method was, Kassil´ described, to involve the children in a long and intricate game, so that they were unaware of acting. As Huizinga notes, ludic activity is totally absorbing and potentially transformative. Kassil´'s observation referred not only to acting technique, however. Play has thematic purpose in this film about childhood—and specifically about the politicization of children in Germany during the rise of Nazism. At the beginning, these young German children play as children should: they dress up as doctors and merchants, they make funny faces, they hide under tables and naughtily make holes in bags of flour. Their play maps symbolically onto the world they live in (they act out an adult's desperate need for food to feed her family, for example), but it is also pure play. Play, indeed, is a source of comedy in the film: in one episode, a child pokes his fingers into a hole in his friend's trouser seat, pulls out his cotton pants, and blows his nose on them. Over the course of the film, however, such raw exuberance is gradually transformed; play is increasingly politicized, as the children are affiliated to their parents' strike. When three-year-old Bubbi is tragically martyred, all the children become political heroes; their youthful joy and their innocent morals come to represent the pioneer spirit of communism.

In the context of this narrative of politicized childhood, incidents of pure play carry particular potency. In one of the most striking scenes, Bubbi gazes in amazement into the window of a toyshop. The camera moves from toy to toy, as Bubbi's expression moves through a gamut of expressions of joy and excitement. As the mechanical mouth of a pig opens and closes, and an electric train whizzes along tiny rails, the boy's body mirrors their actions: his own mouth opens and closes; he emits the noises of the train engine. He exists in a reciprocal, affective relationship with the potentiality of the toy. Deprived of such toys, the boy and his friends work by searching through a rubbish heap for objects that can be salvaged. They collect cigarette ends and old junk for a man who promises to "pay them tomorrow." But this salvage holds the possibility of hope, too: little Emma finds an old motor horn, and it is immediately transformed by her imagination into a doll and becomes a treasured object. In sum, the poor children in *Torn Boots* show the transformative power of play; the pleasures—and above all the potentialities—of childhood are a core element of the film. And yet, at the film's end, childhood is replaced by political activism. Jamie Miller reads the film in part as a warning against the politicization of childhood in Soviet culture.[71] But it might equally be about the centrality of play to the (utopian) Bolshevik vision—one that was increasingly under threat. It presents a model of child's play as, in Benjamin's terms, innervation—a form of revolutionary consciousness.

Barskaia's success with *Torn Boots* gave her considerable leverage within the Soviet film industry, and in particular gained her the powerful support of Boris Shumiatskii. In 1936, in the same year as Natal′ia Sats Children's Theater moved to its own large building, a dedicated studio (Soiuzdetfil′m) was established under Barskaia's leadership.[72] As the strictures of Socialist

Realism were refined and consolidated, children's film, theater, and literature became something of a refuge for several avant-garde artists and writers. Aleksandr Vvedenskii and Daniil Kharms, for example (both members of the OBERIU group), were employed in the late 1920s and 1930s writing children's literature; they worked for periods in the Zagorsk Institute, and were involved in the production of board games, as well as working in children's cinema. Nikolai Oleinikov and Evgenii Shvarts (both avant-garde writers, also associated with OBERIU) jointly wrote a number of screenplays in the 1930s for Barskaia's Soiuzdetfil′m, with a specific child audience in mind.

Oleinikov and Shvarts' two Lenochka films (*Wake Lenochka Up* (*Razbudite Lenochku*, 1934); and *Lenochka and the Grapes* (*Lenochka i vinograd*, 1936)), both directed by Antonina Kudriavtseva, are not only for children, but also *about* childhood—and the pleasures and potentialities of play. *Wake Lenochka Up* introduces its eponymous heroine as a dreamer, whose tendency to stay up late reading ripping adventure yarns leads to endless late arrivals at school. She is, her friends inform her, letting down the collective, and the film celebrates her newfound determination to arrive on time. *Lenochka and the Grapes*—a sound film—is more developed, but here, too, "industry" is carefully balanced with play. In one scene, Lenochka is so determined that her study will not be interrupted that she manages to silence a passing brass marching band—in the end the uniformed musicians are not only not playing their instruments, but are walking on tiptoes! Rewarded for their study, Lenochka and her friends travel to the South, to a collective-farm vineyard. The children's first project on arrival is to build a troop of scarecrows to protect the grape crop. This is a labor project, but marked by the pleasures of childhood and of *samodelka* (do-it-yourself)—a craft project par excellence, with the painted faces and costumes of the scarecrows providing an abundance of cinematic faktura. It turns out that the crows are by no means the only enemy; the children are eventually needed to catch and unmask a saboteur. Above all, however, the children's time in the south is one of play and pleasure. Even the act of spying and catching the saboteur is presented as a kind of game: it is when the children lose their ball and climb into the haystack to retrieve it that they find the stolen grapes.[73]

This balance between pleasure and socialization was central to the emerging genre of children's cinema during the 1930s. In *The Wondrous Garden* (*Divnyi sad*, dir. Lazar′ Frenkel′, 1935), the narrative stages a confrontation between "seriousness" and "play." Len′ka is a talented violinist and is taken to study in a conservatory with a leading professor of music. Yet he is drawn to perform in a circus—to the initial dismay of the professor. Throughout the film, Len'ka and his young friends operate as something akin to a flash mob: they play with gusto and joy, and are ready to erupt into music at any point. The film opens with an extraordinary scene of their extempore orchestra, a fantasy space where the children dream of an expedition to the Arctic. Here there are model animals and seminaked children on a fantastical carousel (figure 9.1). The children play with puppets (and the film's pleasure in the textures of the puppet and the papier-mâché models is clear). Play, then, is intrinsically free, and potentially disruptive. This emphasis is consistent throughout the film: when Len'ka plays his violin in the circus, his friends burst into the ring, overturning the conventions even of that already-transgressive space. At the musical academy itself, play consists not only of regulated outdoor exercise, but also of self-crafted (and more mischievous) entertainment on the beach. Thus the film questions whether these unruly forms of play can work alongside the serious endeavor of musical education. And when Len'ka performs to stunning acclaim in a concert of young musicians, broadcast across the Soviet Union, its answer is a resounding yes. The unruly pleasures of play are not opposed to the development of adult consciousness, but its essential condition.

A similar message emerges in *The Band of Imps* (*Buinaia vataga*, dir. Aleksandr Popov, 1937), set in a school in Baku. Enthused by their geography lesson, the children develop a game called "India." The game begins as a homemade fantasy: the children transform their courtyard into the Indian jungle; they paint their dog to turn him into a tiger. A "do-it-yourself" element develops exponentially: one scene shows a vast shared craft project involving planes, saws, paints, and papier-mâché. And in the film's final scenes, when these children have traveled to the Caspian Sea in reward for hard work at school, the game of India takes on new proportions. The line between fantasy and reality is blurred: adult actors appear as tribesmen; children are riding real donkeys. Finally, the game dissolves into a joyous bathing scene as participants disrobe and leap into the sea.

In one sense, the children in all these films are prototypes for one of the best known—and most important—Soviet children's films: Aleksandr Razumnyi's 1940 adaptation of Arkadii Gaidar's novel *Timur and His Team* (*Timur i ego komanda*, 1940). There are notable differences between our children and Timur and his companions, however. *The Band of Imps*, indicatively, is a film focused almost exclusively on play: its very title signals

Fig. 9.1 The Pleasures of Play. Stills from *The Wondrous Garden* (*Divnyi sad*, dir. L. Frenkel´, production design by A. Bobrovnikov, 1935)

its investment in *mischief* as a core category of childhood. By contrast, Dobrenko reads *Timur and His Team* as a pinnacle of the emergent model of Soviet childhood, blending an ideal of children's "self-organization" with the principles of Soviet socialization. The children combine stikhiinost' (the spontaneity of childhood) and soznatel'nost' (the management of play to accomplish goals for the collective good).[74] The instinctive rules of play coincide with the principles of revolutionary discipline; and pleasure is a reward, not a first principle.

This vision of productive play mirrored the synthesis of reason and (conscious) emotion that we have identified as central to the consolidation of models of an ideal Soviet citizen in the latter part of the 1930s. For children in the mid-1930s, however, productive play coexisted with (and often even dissolved into) fantastical play, as child's play on-screen was a testing ground both for the parameters of Socialist Realism and for the contours of the Soviet subject him/herself.

Adults at Play

Such playfulness was not limited to children's cinema. In 1934, Eduard Ioganson made a film with the title *The Crown Prince of the Republic*. Nikolai—an architect engaged in designing a new residential district—rejects his pregnant wife, Natasha, suggesting that she abort her baby. The baby will, he says, disrupt his work and dreams; the messy, bodily contingency of parenthood is powerfully symbolized by ink that Nikolai spills in his distress, which runs like blood across his careful architectural designs. Natasha, however, goes ahead and has the baby and, by a remarkable (not entirely plausible) narrative coincidence, she loses that baby in the crowded streets of Moscow, and it ends up looked after by Andrei, a young colleague of Nikolai. The film focuses on the effects of this baby on the lives and visions of these idealistic young men, whose work focuses on the design of a Soviet future, staging an encounter between the reality of family life and its abstraction.[75]

Two sequences in the film are of particular relevance to my inquiry here. The first comes when the baby initially takes up residence in the young men's room. This work-live space is dominated by a scale model of the residential complex (*zhil-kombinat*) that the architects are designing—a form of collective living that will be "without individual family sections." It is ironic, then, that these young utopianists, envisaging and planning a residential space that will provide rationalized accommodation for a family, wear headphones to block out the sound of a real, screaming baby right by their side. And, as the plot develops, the intrusion of the noisy, demanding infant, Seriozha, requires a different kind of design project: one that is emphatically hands-on and homemade. Andrei assembles a makeshift cradle for the baby to sleep in; the young men assemble ingenious toys, stringing bells and cylinders across the room. As Andrei struggles to entertain the baby, he steps on and breaks the careful model of the *zhil-kombinat*. Initially horrified, he proceeds to embrace the implicit freedom of its fractured form, transforming it into an object of play.

A second important sequence in the film is set in a "children's palace," to which the young men take Seriozha. While there, initially out of place (and even in disguise), they look into a room where children are gathered around a spiral ramp—which bears more than a passing resemblance to Vladimir Tatlin's Monument to the Third International—playing with building blocks, and putting a baby doll to bed. Drawn into this world, the young architects join in (figure 9.2). They begin to play. For the playing child, as we have seen, the material world exists as much for its material facticity, as for its symbolic status. In the film, the experience of play marks a radical transformation for these idealistic young men. It is an encounter with real material. As they leave the children's home with Seriozha in tow, they are changed. Far from wishing to exclude children—real or imagined—from their idealized visions of collective living, they now embrace a very real baby in their midst. Finally, the baby is reunited with his mother—who rejects her Nikolai and embraces instead a new relationship with Andrei, who is to become a surrogate father to her child.

What, then, have the young architects learned from their encounter with children and play? *The Crown Prince of the Republic* stages an inquiry into the relationship between work and play, between abstract visions of the socialist family and the real, embodied messiness of babies, and of domestic life. The child in the film is a source of *productive chaos*; he introduces the energy of contingency, of lived experience, into the utopian vision. The "design" of the socialist ideal is transformed into a makeshift cradle; the perfect scale model is broken down; Tatlin's tower becomes, symbolically, an object for hands-on play. And the film's "happy ending" shows its young heroes with, implicitly, a renewed understanding of the vision toward which they are working. Here, play and production are directly linked. The model of the tower is transformed into a site of potentiality, and the protagonists' disassembling and reassembling links them to the wider context of hands-on

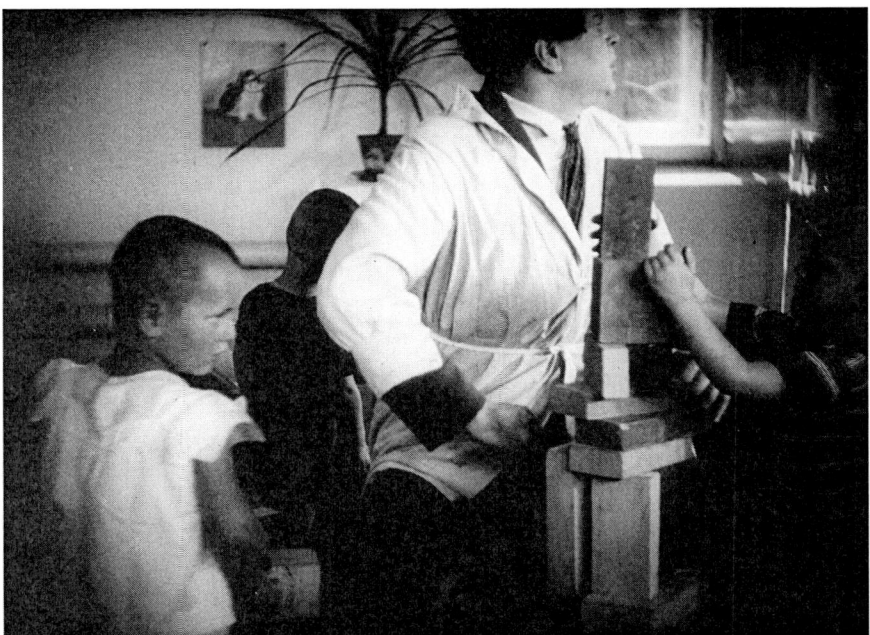

Fig. 9.2 Homo Ludens. Stills from *The Crown Prince of the Republic* (*Naslednyi prints respubliki*, dir. E. Ioganson, production design by P. Betaki and E. Ioganson, 1934).

Fig. 9.2 (*Continued*).

socialism. It is, in a sense, an act of continuous montage, a perpetual process of remaking. Following Benjamin's model of child's play as innervation, the young heroes enter an embodied state of revolutionary consciousness.

In *The Crown Prince of the Republic*, adults learn from play; homo faber meets homo ludens. And both are revealed as vital participants in the Soviet project. This kind of play, then, implicates the film in the story of socialist sensations, tying it to the revolutionary project of sensory revolution. It was a model of play that was increasingly under threat in the Stalinist 1930s, however. Adult play took on various guises in the cinema of the 1930s. Igor´ Savchenko's first sound film, *The Accordion* (*Garmon*), was produced in 1934; and Grigorii Aleksandrov's *The Jolly Fellows* (*Veselye rebiata*) premiered in the same year. Both films, in different ways, interrogate the categories of pleasure and play in a Soviet context. *The Accordion* explored the tension between the regulated body of the laborer, and the potentially disruptive force of music.[76] *The Jolly Fellows* was, as the title suggests, a film that validated play, performance, and dressing up: its heroine, played by Liubov´ Orlova, is eventually rewarded for her tendency to "play act" by a performance in the Bol´shoi Theater. Such playfulness was famously celebrated as the new *bodrost´* (energy/vivacity) needed in Soviet cinema. For all their differences, *The Accordion* and *The Jolly Fellows* raised questions about the relationship between the unruly emancipatory potential of play, and the ideologically sanctioned (and sanitized) category of "merriness" that was taking shape in Soviet culture. This was an issue taken up directly by Savchenko in his next film, *A Chance Encounter* (1936).

A Chance Encounter is set in a provincial toy factory that produces, we are told, "40% of the toys in the Soviet Union." Its opening sequences offer a sideways glance at the iconic symbols of Soviet industrialization: scenes of modern factory buildings are accompanied by a dramatic, even ominous, musical track. Yet, we discover, all of this technology goes into producing objects of *play*. Of course, *A Chance Encounter* is not the only film of this period to present what we might call a softer side to Soviet industrialization. Its focus on the production of consumer objects links it to the textile factory in Aleksandrov's *Radiant Path* of 1940, for example. That this factory produces toys can be seen as a sign of the achievements of Soviet civilization—its capacity to move beyond the brute imperatives of heavy industry.[77] I suggest, however, that there is more to the specificity of toys in this film. Savchenko's film was first screened in 1936—and it was conceived and in production by 1934.[78] As such, *A Chance Encounter* coincides with what we have identified as a key moment in debates about children's play and toy production. I propose that Savchenko's use of toys in the film should be considered as part of the film's broader inquiry into models of Soviet subjectivity. Toys are present throughout *A Chance Encounter* as both visual sign and thematic context; their presence is part of a broader focus on childhood. Toys are not just symbols in this film: they are cinematic *things*. And as such, they are the locus for the film's investigation of the relationship between the human subject and the material world.

A Chance Encounter tells the story of a collision between different ideals of Soviet virtue. The plot follows the arrival of young athletic enthusiast Grisha into the community of factory workers, where he begins work as trainer for their sports teams—most particularly as trainer for the talented young runner, Irina, who is due to compete in an all-union sports contest. Much to the distress of Petr (the other key male protagonist), who has long cherished a secret love for her, Irina and Grisha fall in love and set up home together. Irina falls pregnant and announces to Grisha that she will not run the race, but will raise their child instead. Grisha is outraged by her choice of motherhood over glory, tries but fails to convince her to abort the baby, and the couple part. Irina raises her child, and three years later wins the four-hundred-meter race at the Spartakiada. Grisha is there and attempts a reconciliation with Irina, but she is now in a relationship with Petr, who is helping her to raise her child. Grisha is rejected by Irina and implicitly banished from the wider socialist collective.

It is clear, then, that this film is an inquiry into models of socialist moral probity. But this inquiry is tied to an investigation of the status of *play* in the Soviet 1930s. Once of the film's most visually striking scenes comes when a *kollektiv* of young workers visits the factory director in order to persuade him that Irina should be allowed three months away from work in order to train. The director has previously refused Grisha's impassioned plea, asserting that her role is, above all, that of worker, not athlete. Her colleagues arrive en masse in his office, clutching their various inventions and products. The factory director repeats his refusal to let her go, and then asks them to speak in turn and make their case. At the head of the delegation is Petr, who says simply, "Just watch." And so the factory director (and the spectator) watch as Petr carefully sets down his newest invention: a remote-controlled zeppelin rises from the ground and takes flight. At the same time, the other young workers unwrap their various toys and models, performing their labor productivity for their boss (figure 9.3). The scene transforms into a phantasmagoric display of toys: from the lyricism of Petr's zeppelin to the comedy of a model alligator, a clockwork pig, a toy car, a puppet, and an animated giraffe. Hands wind toys and manipulate glove puppets. The scene reaches its absurd climax in the comic explosion of a model cannon after which it returns to the calm lyricism of the elegant (in Petr's words, *akkuratno*) flight of the model zeppelin.

These young people make their case not with words, but with toys: the scene is one of play—and, in cinematic terms, of visual and material *excess*. The frame is filled with a kaleidoscopic array of textures, surfaces, and shapes. And this argument by objects is, apparently, successful; the factory director relents: Irina has permission to train for the competition. How, then, do they persuade him? Certainly, it could be simply that they convince the factory director of their own increased productivity, so that he can do without Irina's productive prowess. But we can think beyond this. Children are central to *A Chance Encounter*. Irina is "loved by all children in the Soviet Union"; the factory director is unable to understand how anyone in his factory could—like Grisha—be "against" children. Even Irina's eventual athletic victory is explicitly linked to her status as mother. Children are the future; thus the production of toys is part of the creation of this future. Even this interpretation may fail to do full justice to the complexity of *A Chance*

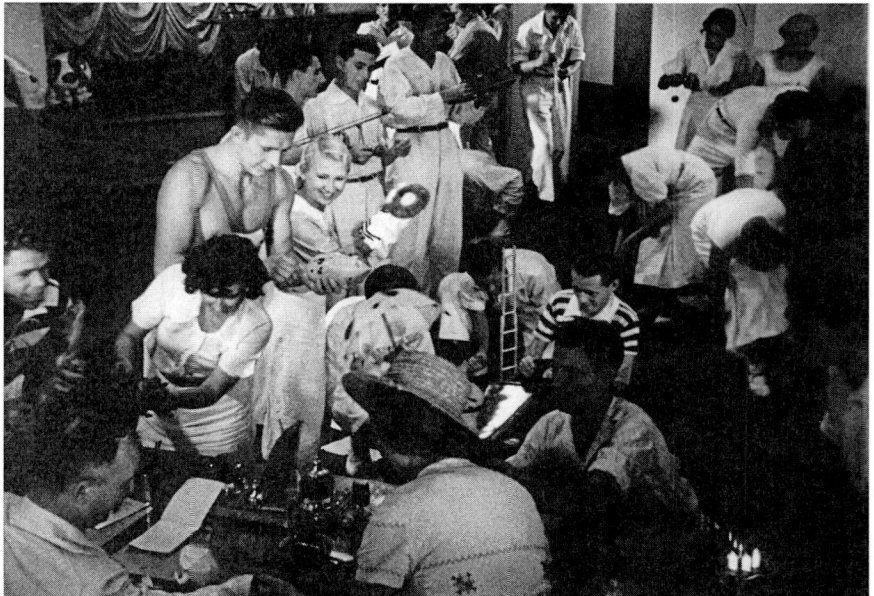

Fig. 9.3 A Phantasmagoria of Toys. Still from *A Chance Encounter* (*Sluchainaia vstrecha*, dir. I. Savchenko, production design by L. Blatova, 1936).

Encounter, however. The film's pervasive infantilization applies to adult characters also.[79] In this scene, we see adults, crucially, at play; they make their case without words—as, we might suggest, children would. The director hears them because he is more attuned to the communicative modes of children than to those of adults.

This is part of Savchenko's inquiry into the nature of the new Soviet hero, where the categories of play and childishness acquire particular potency. Here it is instructive to recall the scene preceding the visual phantasmagoria of objects, when Grisha tries to make *his* case for Irina. As he begins his impassioned speech, Grisha is asked to "speak more quietly." As such, the factory director refuses to allow him to behave like a bombastic hero, to proclaim the slogans and certainties that characterize his speech elsewhere. Perhaps Grisha embodies a type of socialist hero that was becoming increasingly problematic and outmoded in mid-1930s culture? Like Petr Vinogradov in *The Private Life of Petr Vinogradov*, he is *too loud*. The factory director cannot, implicitly, hear the bombastic words of the old-style Soviet message; only when the factory workers speak with *objects*—with toys— is he able to engage. In symbolic terms, the declamatory tone, the "loudspeaker" of the 1920s, must be replaced by a softer tone. This, as we have seen, was a marker of socialist feelings (see chapter 7).

This leads us to look more closely at the film's broader investigation of categories of heroism. We have three male protagonists: the young Grisha and Petr, and the paternal figure of the factory director. Grisha seems a familiar model: driven by ambition for glory (*slava*) and by an innate energy (*azart*), he is a larger-than-life Socialist Realist hero. Petr is distinguished from Grisha in two key—and related—ways. First, in his comparative lack of physical stature and sexual energy. Second, and perhaps more importantly, he lacks the other's confident, and noisy, powers of speech. In the early parts of the film, indeed, it is as if he cannot speak. His initial attempt to declare his love to Irina is interrupted, notably, by children. This deferral— or postponement—of satisfaction appears to be characteristic of Petr's life. By contrast, Grisha captivates Irina, apparently, by his very present vitality. And yet, by the end of the film, it is Petr who is victorious, and Grisha who is the pariah, excluded from society. In part, this reflects an emerging formula in Socialist Realist cinema, exemplified in films such as Iulii Raizman's *Fliers* (*Letchiki*, 1935): the hero who wins in the end does so not because of masculine elan, but because of solidity and sober reflection. Youthful spontaneity is transformed into mature consciousness.[80] Yet Petr is distinct from such heroes, for his heroism is not explicitly linked to maturity. Instead, he is infantilized; unlike Grisha, he is not allowed sexual maturity.

How, then, should we understand this overt opposition between two models of masculinity? I have already suggested that Grisha is too loud. And this loudness acts as a metonym for his one-dimensionality, his failure to leave space for feeling and pleasure (emotional and sensory). As he tries to persuade Irina not to proceed with her pregnancy, his use of the terms *azart* and *slava* acts as a pointer to the film's moral questions. Grisha's case against Irina is that she rejects *azart* (a fervor or enthusiasm that is specifically linked to *achievement*) in favor of an alternative model of pleasure, a different passion—one driven not by rational goals but by emotional, physical, and instinctual imperatives. Indeed, the film's visual style makes clear that in rejecting the opportunity to become a running champion, Irina embraces the corporeal chaos and private pleasures of pregnancy: she is seen swinging in a hammock, surrounded by flowers, singing. Her body has replaced discipline with languor. Grisha's *azart* set in opposition to a model of sensory being in which the natural and the lyrical intertwine. The film pictures an alternative and, crucially, nonsexual, model of physical pleasure.

This helps us to understand how Petr emerges, by the end of the film, as a fully fledged, mature member of the Soviet collective—a new model, perhaps, for Soviet masculinity. The factory director encourages Petr to grow up, "to become a big, strong man." Implicitly, he does so, for the narrative shows him victorious. But what kind of ideal is offered here? How can this factory director be a model of Soviet masculinity? His own office is decorated with flowers; on his desk is a model of a stork carrying a spotted parasol. He appears early in the film as a kind of magician—summoning children to the window of his office as "consumer-consultants," to be captivated by a magic show of the latest toys. The factory director is a father, but he is a father of orphans, and one who is feminized, who rocks his children and tucks them into bed. The masculinity of fatherhood is transformed into a nonsexual model of parenthood and care. In parallel, Petr becomes a surrogate father to Irina's daughter not by virtue of intercourse or insemination. Rather, we might suggest, his victory comes by virtue of making toys. Although as an inventor he is part of the Soviet technological establishment, Petr is infantilized; unlike Grisha, he is not allowed sexual maturity. We could suggest, even, that his sexual desire is sublimated into his invention of toys: his wondrous flying zeppelin is invented while he is explicitly pining for Irina. In *A Chance Encounter*, as in *The Crown Prince*, the sexual act of fathering a child is less important than the fatherhood that is granted to those male characters who know how to *play*.

It is in this respect that the presence of toys in the film acquires particular significance. My suggestion here is that we might view the treatment of toys in *A Chance Encounter* as an explicit delibidinization of tactile pleasure and its relocation in toys and in childhood, for the phantasmagorical carnival of toys that the young people unleash has not only thematic but, crucially, visual and haptic impact. The spectator is brought into a sensory encounter with toys as *things*—handled, animated, textured. The material pleasures of toys—their faktura, their physical presence—become a substitute for other forms of material pleasure. Erotic fulfillment is replaced by an alternative model of sensory plenitude—one located in the tactile and magical pleasures of toys, nature, and childhood. This is what Dinamov described as "sensory radiance." And of course, in the Soviet context, such pleasures were ideologically neutral, in a way that adult "touching" was not. Nadezhda Krupskaia herself pointed to the material, sensory experience of children's encounters with toys: "The child is developing their sense of touch, he/she has to touch everything. They should be given objects that are hard, soft, smooth, rough; they should be taught to distinguish objects by touch, to understand form by touch."[81]

In different ways, both *The Crown Prince of the Republic* and *A Chance Encounter* proclaim the return of a heady combination of sentiment (feeling) and sensation (engagement with the possibilities of material pleasure) as key elements of the moral framework of the new Soviet hero. These young people do not spend all their time in the productive project of building socialism; they also take pleasure in the world. And they indulge in dreams of love and domesticity. Irina and Grisha, indeed, are shown setting up home; another character, Nikonov, gives a party to celebrate his own domestic sphere. And that sphere is figured as also that of the collective—and of the party. "The Party teaches us to care for our family," announces the factory director, the clearest figure of authority in the film. Grisha is excluded—or excludes himself—from this protodomestic sphere, and therefore has no place in the new world.

This is central to the film's thematic interrogation of the relationship between discipline and pleasure, its elaboration of an alternative, nonsexual model of material and sensory pleasure. *A Chance Encounter* could be seen as a self-conscious engagement with Iezuitov's call for "cinema of socialist feelings," his Soviet sentimentalism (see Chapter 7). We can offer many different interpretations of this project, however. First, we can read the messages of the film in terms of the ideological strictures of Socialist Realism: the call for films to tell simple stories about ideal Soviet men and women, to strengthen core party messages—in this case, to reinforce the ideal of the family. In this respect, we can see Savchenko's project as a genuine attempt to elaborate a new model of Soviet sentiment: *A Chance Encounter* makes a crucial link between sentiment and sentience, and locates the space for sentiment (for "socialist feelings") in a delibidinized space of material pleasure. We might also, however, suggest that this vision of Soviet "pleasure" is markedly—and purposefully—sterile, that the film is an ironic comment on the reduction of the utopian dreams of the "new Soviet hero." And in parallel, that the ludic potentiality of the avant-garde toy is reduced here to the rather ominous blank form of Petr's mechanical zeppelin. It is impossible—and reductive—to privilege either of these readings. They exist in productive tension with one another in the very fabric of the film, both in theme and in poetics. In *A Chance Encounter*, the category of play, and the visual and material pleasures of toys, become a site for an investigation not only of Stalinist ideological codes, but of the place and purpose of cinema itself. As such, the toys in the film are not simply a context, but rather the center of its message.

Leisure and Pleasure

A Chance Encounter had a very mixed reception. The film was accused of *both* formalism and naturalism. It was "hyperbolic" and reliant on "external effects."[82] What it did not achieve, according to critics, was (socialist) realism: its characters were not "living."[83] Director of *The Crown Prince of the Republic* Eduard Ioganson also ran into difficulties. In the same year as Savchenko produced *A Chance Encounter*, Ioganson produced his next feature film: *On Vacation* (*Na otdykhe*, 1936), scripted by Shvarts and Oleinikov (writers of the *Lenochka* series). Like *A Chance Encounter*, *On Vacation* suffered severe criticism—in this case so severe that the film was shelved a year after production. *On Vacation* is a thoroughly intriguing film. It is a very light—even sometimes farcical—musical comedy, which directly tackles the vexed question of Soviet pleasure. As such it is poignantly self-reflexive.

The film is set in a holiday resort—a colony (*kurort*)—by the sea. A bearded man arrives by boat, visits a barber to have his beard removed, and enters the colony. The community is excited by the arrival of a new vacationer. He has natural charisma, and strikes up friendships, and even a liaison with the film's young heroine. He is also perplexing, however: in particular, because he will not reveal his "speciality" (his profession). He is apparently determined to hide his identity. The viewer learns that Lebedev is a renowned polar explorer (indeed, in an early scene, Lebedev's eventual love interest, Tania, is coincidentally reading a book containing a photograph of him in his famous bearded incarnation). But Lebedev (and his friend Misha, a decorated aviator, whom he meets also relaxing incognito by the sea) do not allow others to define them by their (heroic) civic role, presenting themselves simply as people in search of harmless pleasure and relaxation.

This is a community entirely dedicated to the pursuit of pleasure, with repeated invocations to "relax." Protagonists young and old climb mountains, play chess and tennis, and frolic on the beach. With ironic humor, the film shows Stalinist society turned on its head: the task of leisure is approached with Stakhanovite fervor (including collective parades), yet it is resolutely purposeless. Homo ludens replaces homo faber. Frequent repetitions of phrases such as "I am relaxing" likewise estrange the pursuit of leisure, turning it into a purposeful renouncing of responsibility.

Indeed, unmotivated leisure provides the film's visual pleasure. One scene offers a feast of perfected socialist bodies in the water, engaged in a panoply of different leisure activities: synchronous swimming, rowing, bathing. Yet the scene is distinguished by two elements that are not characteristic of images of Stalinist *fizkul´tura*: excess and unruliness. This rowing is a heady, chaotic sport carried out with canoe oars and inflatable tires. Men and women frolic on a makeshift floating platform (figure 9.4). And what should we make of the large floating ball that dances on the waves, climbed upon and tossed? Why does the scene begin with a shot of a fully naked child carrying a frilly parasol? These images (not to mention the disconcertingly small bathing trunks that clothe some of the male protagonists in particular) remind us of the sheer *bodilyness* of the bodies on-screen—and of their material pleasures.[84] I have suggested that in *A Chance Encounter* "play" operates as a delibidinized form of sensual pleasure. In *On Vacation* play is still more explicitly linked with (safe) sex. This film, indeed, is rare in Soviet cinema in actually picturing a male-female kiss scene other than as a finale (and *before* the characters—and the spectator—have been reassured of one another's social worth). When Lebedev is brought a parcel on the beach and the courier asked for his documents, his reply—"What documents can a naked man have?"—is a moment of cheeky comedy; but it also draws attention to his unclothed body on-screen, and to the experience of nakedness. It transforms him from object of contemplation into subject; and it aligns the spectator with the haptic sensory experience of his sun-kissed skin.

This link between playfulness and (sublimated) sensual pleasure is also evident in an almost unknown film of 1934, produced for the Azer film studio: *Playing at Love* (*Igra v liubov´*). This film, with "play" (*igra*) in its very title, was directed by established local theater and film director Abbas Mirza Sharifzadeh (Sharifov) from a script by Russian Aleksandr Popov (director of *The Band of Imps*). It is a film about the local working youth—Leila, an attractive young motor mechanic, and her two young suitors, Kerim and Sattar, also mechanics. The film is a remarkable product of the Soviet 1930s—even allowing for the relative freedom possible in the Azeri studio. It is marked by what critics would later condemn in other films as "buffoonery" in a series of set pieces. In one scene, groups of young people are at the beach, sliding down a slide into the water, playing with sand. Sarrat is unable to swim, and is embarrassingly attired in a bizarre contraption of floats; later, he is at a fairground, throwing hoops over bizarre

Fig. 9.4 Adults at Play. Stills from *On Vacation* (*Na otdykhe*, dir. E. Ioganson, production design by P. Zaltsman, 1937).

papier-mâché puppets (the camera dwells with pleasure on their grotesque faces). He wins, and his prize is a tin boat, which he then has to carry around with him. Such scenes accumulate to infantilize the protagonists and turn the entire film into a form of play, so that the final scene where Leila has to decide which one of the two young men to marry appears as much a game as any other part of the film. This emphasis on playfulness is consistent. But there is also an extent to which play is explicitly a form of sublimated desire here, providing a space for the working-through of the film's latent erotic tensions. In one remarkable scene, Kerim claims to be unwell, and Leila and Sattar seem to play at doctors and nurses. The scene is at once entirely childish and sexually charged, as Sattar applies heated glass jars to Kerim's skin, which pools with gleaming droplets of sweat. Kerim's face wears an expression of almost rapturous pleasure at the ministrations of both of his friends.

In a sense, then, Ioganson's *On Vacation* thematized and interrogated the playfulness evident in *Playing at Love* and other films of this period. In *On Vacation*, play provides both character motivation and plot drive. The drama of Lebedev's unmasking is the film's narrative pinnacle. His jealous love rival has found a newspaper article that reveals Lebedev's true identity. When accused, he denies nothing: "What you have read is the truth," he acknowledges. "You have seen right through me." The film suggests, however, that the real truth of Lebedev cannot be reduced to the facts contained in the article. "Give me three days," he asks, "and I will explain myself." He proclaims—and an inter title later repeats—"I must repent in style (*s bleskom*)." This term, "blesk," echoes Sergei Dinamov's call for cinema to convey the sensory radiance of Soviet life (see chapter 7). It draws our attention to questions of performance, magic, and pleasure in Soviet cinema, and in the Soviet everyday.

In *On Vacation*, Lebedev's final self-revelation "s bleskom" takes the form of a performance. He and the other vacationers travel by sailing boat to an island that serves as a phantasmagoric play space. They are clothed in a carnivalesque mixture of wildly disparate ethnic and historic costumes (figure 9.5), and carry cardboard cutout instruments (which they even "play" on the boat). This is a joyous costume ball in which everyone participates, and it culminates in a musical show about an epic, folkloric hero—in which Lebedev plays the central protagonist. Lebedev's "repentance," then, is carried out via *play*. The jealous cultural worker Zhenia leaps up to unmask the imposter with an impassioned, tautological cry: "He is

Fig. 9.5 Performance and Pleasure. Stills from *On Vacation* (*Na otdykhe*, dir. E. Ioganson, production design by P. Zaltsman, 1937).

not he (*on ne on*); that is, he is he, but not the he that you think he is!" This prompts only laughter from the audience, however. So Zhenia calls for Lebedev to undress himself (*razdevaites´*)—and indeed, for all the participants to undress themselves (to "tear off their masks"[85]) and reveal their authentic (social) selves. Zhenia himself, however, is unable—try as he might—to shed the fairy wings that constitute his costume. And others make no move to remove their disguises. This playfulness cannot be cast off.

What, then, is the message about masquerade and playfulness here? At this point in the film, the implication is that Lebedev is *exactly* who he is in the film, despite (or because of) his costume. He may *also* be a polar explorer, but that self is no more significant—no more true—than the other self that he has inhabited at the holiday resort. "I hid my profession," he announces, "because I just wanted to relax." By the end of the film, however, the vacation is over: although the preserved part of the reel ends with Lebedev's self-unmasking, the screenplay indicates that the rest of the film was to show Lebedev departing to lead an expedition to the Arctic; Misha, Tania, and Marusia go with him. As such, we might say, the natural order is restored. Yet *On Vacation*'s overt enjoyment of images of play demands further consideration.

There are several ways in which we can view this film. It participates in the guiding narratives and ideological frameworks of the late 1930s, but it also complicates them. On the one hand, *On Vacation* tells a story of the "complete" Soviet hero. Lebedev is as good at relaxing as he is at being an explorer. As an ideal Soviet type, he is fully comfortable with himself. He has no need to perform a role, and no need of his "position" for self-definition. It is entirely appropriate that Tania falls for him without needing to know of his public persona. Yet the pleasures of play exceed such a straightforward reading. Rather, we might see Ioganson (with Shvarts and Oleinikov) engaged in a direct consideration of the category of socialist pleasure. Where in *The Private Life of Petr Vinogradov*, Petr's work ethic was too strong, and in *A Chance Encounter*, Grisha's competitive *azart* was too dominant, here, Lebedev's extreme, committed "playfulness" draws poignant attention to the very concept of socialist pleasure. Perhaps Ioganson satirizes Soviet society's claims to a culture of leisure by revealing that leisure as artifice and performance. Certainly, he alerts us to the complexity of material pleasure and play in this period. In any case, like *A Severe Youth* and *A Chance Encounter*, *On Vacation* was radically mistimed. In 1936, Iakov Urinov's *The Intriguer* (*Intrigan*) was suppressed for its "buffoonery."[86] In 1937, Nikolai Oleinikov was arrested and shot. Cinema's playful period was coming to a tragic end. *On Vacation* was a casualty of this change: it was removed from the screen in 1937.[87]

Sensory Radiance

In this context, let us turn our attention back directly to toys. In 1937, Aleksandr Vvedenskii wrote the screenplay for a short film, directed by Taisiia Arusinskaia, entitled *An Aerial Adventure* (*Vozdushnoe prikliuchenie*). Possibly produced as advertising for Soiuzkul'torg Toy production (announced in the titles), this entire film is a phantasmagoria of childlike pleasure. Set in a large toy store, it is the story of a dog who is smuggled into the store dressed as a child, escapes, and has a series of adventures, including chasing a toy squirrel, being mistaken for a toy dog, being purchased by a boy, and taking flight in a toy hot air balloon. Like Melbourne-Cooper's *A Dream of Toyland*, this film seems to delight in the games of scale made possible by children's toys. Its opening and closing scenes show children riding model cars down "real" streets,[88] directed by a child-policeman. Several long sequences of animated toys present a medley of model buildings. A vast bear lolls upon a model of the Moscow riverboat station; a giraffe towers over it. A whale spouts water; an oversized doll in Arab dress rests against the wall (figure 9.6).

This phantasmagoria of toys sets the tone for this short film celebrating the pleasures of play. Perhaps because of its status as advertising, *An Aerial Adventure* is remarkable in lacking any political framework. There is no education here, and no socializing endeavor. The film's hermetically sealed world of the toy store allows free rein to the categories of the child's imagination with its ability to manipulate scale and transform reality. This is a world in which children are free: they are masters of their own scale model of the world. In one scene, a little girl walks into a (toy) living room where two dolls and a bear are sitting at a table. She sits with them and talks to them— and they seem to talk back. Later, soft music plays; the little girl drops off to sleep, and gradually the toys do the same. A junior cowboy throws his lasso, opens a window, and allows the balloon to float outside. There is momentary chaos; but the situation can be saved by the children themselves, and the film's scene shows a restoration of order: the boy and the girl drive together in his toy car, her dog alongside them, heading through the streets of toy town. This child-size world of make-believe echoes the happy endings of "grown-up" films.

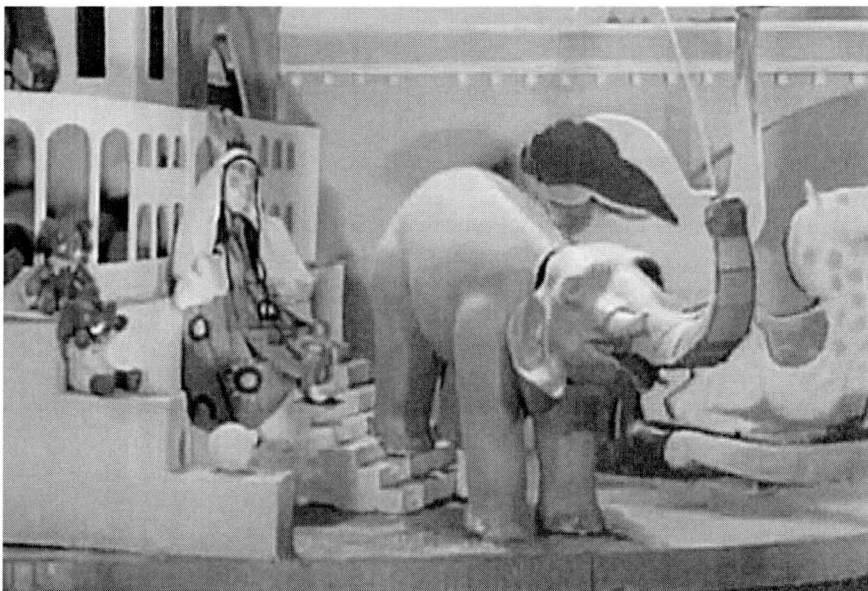

Fig. 9.6 Fantasy Spaces. Stills from *An Aerial Adventure* (*Vozdushnoe prikliuchenie*, dir. T. Anisinskaia, production design by N. Levin, P. Pavlinov, 1937).

Through the screen, the pleasures of toys are here made available to adult and child alike. As we have seen, the shopkeeper scene, in which children stare rapt with wonder at displays of toys, is a familiar trope, and is repeated in *An Aerial Adventure* (figure 9.7). Here, however, it is expanded to incorporate the relationship between the spectator and the film itself. In cinematic terms, the toys in this film provide both animated magic and sensory blesk. Balloons float up like giant gleaming bubbles. Magnificent displays of toys dazzle with their multifarious textures and surfaces. The film is largely contained within a fantasy world: the one scene set outside the store takes place in Gor'kii Park. Outside, a spinning carousel throws sparkling shadows into the darkness. Instead of the familiar monuments of Stalinist culture (like Vera Mukhina's *Worker and Collective Farm Woman*, notably also made in 1937), the statue of a spinning ballerina on a horse at the top of the carousel takes center stage. The world of homo faber is explicitly absent.

An Aerial Adventure configures the world of children's play as a space of potentiality, but ultimately, the separation of this world of toys from that of "real" life speaks to its sterility. It is an explicit celebration of artifice, constrained within the limits of the fantasy world of the store. The toy store contains the transformative, ludic potential of play, and, I suggest, neutralizes it. Like the "safe" sensations of Savchenko's *A Chance Encounter*, this is not play *in life*, but rather life *as play*. It lacks the embodied intensity—and the mimetic reciprocity—that linked child's play to the broader project of sensory revolution that is the subject of this book. Rather than being marked by their materiality, and provoking sensation, the toys in *An Aerial Adventure* appear dematerialized and fantastical. There is no Soviet haptic here. These toys are untouched on-screen; and the spectator is fixed as observer, outside their space of fantasy. In its focus on toys, then, *An Aerial Adventure* is certainly a product of the time. But it also marks a shift. In 1937, the pleasure in material that this film offers is one of pure blesk: it is material that is looked at, but untouched—and untouchable. In that sense it represents a fitting end point for this story of Soviet pleasure.

In this chapter, then, we have traced an evolution in the treatment of toys and play in Soviet cinema to 1937. In the 1920s, and even through the years of the first Five-Year Plan, the ludic potentiality of play could be viewed as a necessary counterpart to the productive endeavors of socialist "making." Play (with toys) could play a part in the emancipation of the senses, enabling a hands-on encounter with materiality. The relationship between child and

Fig. 9.7 Rapt Consumers. Still from *An Aerial Adventure* (*Vozdushnoe prikliuchenie*, dir. T. Anisinskaia, production design by N. Levin, P. Pavlinov, 1937).

toy could mirror that of the craftsman and his tool in its reciprocity and creative potential. Homo faber *needs* homo ludens.

In the course of the 1930s, however, the space of play became increasingly fraught. On-screen, it was a testing ground for new models of Soviet subjectivity, and in particular, for the place of pleasure in an ideal Soviet life. In one sense, we could suggest that the materialist impulse of Soviet cinema went underground, into the safe spaces of children's play. Play and toys function as an "afterlife" for the Soviet haptic, a relocation of faktura and material pleasure. In another sense, however, the very safety of play was part of an ideological shift. The material pleasures of touching that toys offered became a delibidinized surrogate for unsafe touching. The new Soviet subject became a child. Alongside the new discourse on "good" Soviet feelings, consciousness, and reason, lurked a paradoxical emphasis on merriness, which transformed the revolutionary potential of homo faber into a neutered (and neutralized) homo ludens.

NOTES

1. Iampol'skii, "Kino bez kino," 90.
2. Mamatova, "Model' kinomifov 30-kh godov," 111.
3. Sal'nikova, "Evoliutsiia vizual'nogo riada," 339.
4. Dashkova, "Nevidimye miru riushi."
5. Huizinga, *Homo Ludens*. It is not clear that Huizinga ever travelled to Russia; the book was not translated into Russian until 1997.
6. Ibid., 30.
7. Roger Caillois also asserted play's nonpurposive quality: play must be free, separate (from ordinary life), unproductive, and governed by (its own) rules. Caillois, *Les jeux et les hommes*, 42–43. Caillois, however, did acknowledge the power of competition ("agon") in his taxonomy of different kinds of play (50–55).
8. See Kelly, *Children's World*.
9. Benjamin, "Program for a Proletarian Children's Theatre," 201–07. Youth/children's theaters were set up in significant numbers in the years following the revolution. See Kelly, *Children's World*, 465–67.
10. Benjamin, "Program for a Proletarian Children's Theatre," 204.
11. Benjamin, "One Way Street," 449–50.
12. Hansen, "Room for Play," 7.
13. Benjamin, *The Arcades Project*, 475.
14. Hansen, "Room for Play," 7.
15. Buck-Morss, *Dialectics of Seeing*, 263.
16. Hansen, 9.
17. Kruchenykh, *Sobstvennye rasskazy i risunki detei*; *Sobstvennye rasskazy, stikhi i pesni detei*. For discussion of the importance of children's drawing in the evolution of Russian futurism, see Molok, "Children's Drawings in Russian Futurism."

18. Kelly, *Children's World*, 82–84.
19. Anatolii Bakushinskii, *Khudozhestvennoe tvorchestvo i vospitanie*; Bakushinskii, ed., *Iskusstvo detei*, 11–27. Kornei Chukovsky was one of several writers who produced studies of children's language. See Chukovskii, *Malen′kie deti*.
20. See Benjamin, "Moscow," 23.
21. Ibid., 29.
22. Bakhtin's formulation of carnival was in his work on Rabelais: Bakhtin, *Rabelais and His World*.
23. Voronskii, "The Art of Seeing the World," 374.
24. Froebel, *The Education of Man*, 55.
25. Cited in Smith, *Bauhaus Weaving Theory*, 27. Itten's tenure at the head of Bauhaus was distinguished by a particular focus on craft. For discussion of Bauhaus and play, see Kinchin and O'Connor, eds., *Century of the Child*, 74–75.
26. Benjamin, *The Arcades Project*, 361.
27. Hansen, "Room for Play," 30.
28. Ibid., 38
29. See Wood, *Living Dolls*.
30. See also Melbourne-Cooper's *Noah's Ark* (1909), and Martin Justice's *The Toy Shop* (1928).
31. In fact, there are few prerevolutionary films in Russia that feature children at all. One exception is Evgenii Bauer's short *First Love* (*Pervaia liubov′*, 1915), in which a young girl, on her way to a meeting, sees a frog-shaped purse lying on the pavement and becomes convinced that it is real. I thank Rachel Morley for alerting me to this film.
32. See Beumers, "Comforting Creatures," 155–56.
33. See Beumers, Bocharov, and Robinson, eds., *Alexander Shiryaev*.
34. Dziga Vertov's animated documentary, *Soviet Toys* (*Sovetskie igrushki*, 1924), shows a pleasure in the possibilities of animated mechanical toys, but it does so via drawn animation, rather than through material toys, and so does not relate to my argument here.
35. Grashchenkova, *Kinoantropologiia XX/20*, 654–55.
36. Benjamin, "Moscow," 24.
37. For broad discussion of the development of the toy industry in the nineteenth century see the essays collected in Denisoff, ed., *The Nineteenth-Century Child*.
38. Dewey, *Democracy and Education*, 202–4. For discussion of Dewey's reception in Russia, see Mchitarjan, "John Dewey and the Development of Education in Russia."
39. Dewey, *Vvedenie v filosofiiu vospitaniia*; *Shkoly budushchego*; *Shkola i obshchestvo*. Dewey's account of his visit to Russia was originally published in installments in *New Republic* in November and December 1928, and published as a volume in 1929: Dewey, *Impressions of Soviet Russia*.
40. Kelly, *Children's World*, 76. For an excellent discussion of Russian childhood, see Sal′nikova, *Rossiiskoe detstvo*. For discussion of "child science" in Soviet Russia, see especially the work of Andrew Byford.
41. Kelly, *Children's World*, 81.
42. See the collected essays in Kumarin, ed., *Anton Makarenko*.
43. Kelly, *Children's World*, 129, 92.
44. Ibid., 94.
45. Sal′nikova and Khamitova, "Zhurnal 'Sovetskaia igrushka,'" 201. See also Sal′nikova, "Bezglazaia kukla i papin revol′ver"; Sal′nikova, *Rossiiskoe detstvo v XX veke*;

Kostiukhina, *Detskii orakul*, 59, and Sal'nikova and Burmistrov, "Sovetskoe detskoe igrovoe kino 20-kh gg."

46. Kelly, *Children's World*, 71.

47. Kholodnyi, "Starushki i igrushki," 4.

48. *Sovetskaia igrushka*, 1935, 1: 7–8, cited in Sal'nikova and Khamitova, "Zhurnal 'Sovetskaia igrushka,'" 205.

49. Kelly, *Children's World*, 445.

50. Sal'nikova and Khamitova, "Zhurnal 'Sovetskaia igrushka,'" 204–5.

51. Krupskaia. "Ob igrushkakh dlia doshkoliat," 596.

52. Kelly, *Children's World*, 113.

53. Makarenko, *Lektsii o vospitanii detei*, 14.

54. Vygotskii gave this lecture in 1933, but it was not published until the 1960s. Vygotskii, "Play and its Role in the Mental Development of the Child," 540.

55. Ibid., 541; Vygotskii describes the "union of affect and perception" as "characteristic of early childhood" (545).

56. Ibid., 547.

57. Kholodnyi, "Starushki i igrushki," 4.

58. See Borislavov, "Do-It-Yourself!"

59. See Kobrinets, *Knizhka-kino-seans o tom*.

60. Rodchenko and Stepanova, "Fotomul'tiplikatsionnye illiustratsii k detskoi knizhke."

61. Strätling, "Play with Words," 8, 4.

62. Ibid., 9.

63. In the late 1930s, V. Griuntal' took a number of still-life shots of children's toys. See Morozov, *Sovetskaia khudozhestvennaia fotografiia*, 234, 241. Griuntal' also participated in the creation of a children's book *Chto eto takoe* (1932), in which photographs sought to defamiliarize common objects for children, engaging them in a game of working out the identity of the object via an appreciation of its physical and textural characteristics. In a review, Morozov noted how these photographs "renewed the sensation (oshchushchenie) of the objects." S. Morozov, "'Chto eto takoe?'" 18. For further discussion, see Reischl, "An Exercise with Photographic Literacy."

64. See Iasnitskii, "K istorii kul'turno-istoricheskoi geshtal't-psikhologii." Lewin's films, *The Child and Field Forces* (1929), and *The Child and the World* (1931), featured observation of children in different situations—including sustained focus on play activity. See Van Elteren, "Kurt Lewin."

65. Locatelli sees Lewin's picture of the child's mind as a model of film itself as "participative and relational." Locatelli, "Kurt Lewin's Children," 8.

66. Buck-Morss, *The Dialectics of Seeing*, 263.

67. Miloserdova, "Margarita Barskaia," 240.

68. Barskaia and Shumiatskii, "Proizvodstvo detskikh kartin," 3.

69. Miloserdova, "Margarita Barskaia," 240.

70. Kassil', "Rvanye bashmaki," 256.

71. Miller, "Torn Boots," 250.

72. On Natalia Sats, see Victorov, *The Natalia Sats Children's Musical Theatre*.

73. Dobrenko notes the importance of the linking of children's play and political consciousness in the genre. Dobrenko, "The School Tale," 48–49.

74. Ibid.

75. Urussowa discusses this film in the context of urban planning. Urussowa, *Das Neue Moskau*, 257–73.

76. See Kaganovsky, "The Homogeneous Thinking Subject."

77. For discussion of the Stalinist production of luxury, consumer goods, and their ideological framing, see, in particular, Gronow, *Caviar with Champagne*.

78. Savchenko, "*Pravo zapet'*," 59.

79. Graffy, "'An Unpretentious Picture'?"

80. Clark, *The Soviet Novel*, 62–66.

81. Krupskaia, "Ob igrushkakh dlia doshkoliat," 596.

82. Anon., "Pervye itogi obsuzhdeniia statei 'Pravdy,'" 17.

83. Ibid.

84. Such images are not uncommon in Soviet cinema of this period, but *On Vacation* is notable for its self-conscious reflection on the theme of pleasure. Grigorii Aleksandrov's *The Jolly Fellows* (*Veselye rebiata*, 1934) is also notable for its emphasis on unruly pleasure. Particularly notable is the bathing scene near the beginning of the film, when the camera pans left to right along the beach, lens toward the water, allowing the limbs (and even the rears) of sunbathers to construct the foreground, their skin and flesh reflecting the rays of the sun.

85. See Fitzpatrick, *Tear off the Masks!* Also Clark, *Moscow, The Fourth Rome*, 57–60.

86. Margolit and Shmyrov, *Iz''iatoe kino. 1924–1953*, 40.

87. Bagrov, "Eduard Ioganson," 72.

88. Scale-model towns seem to have been built in parks across the Soviet Union in 1936–1937. See Seffer and Buzin, "Schastlivoe detstvo," 212. For research into the place of scale models in Soviet culture, see Bird, *Soul Machine*.

CONCLUSION

The Death of Sensation

THE STORY OF socialist sensations is one of failed ambition. It is the rise, and the decline, of a utopian dream of a remade world, and a remade human subject: a revolutionary animism for the modern age. Such a dream was perhaps inevitably doomed. As early as 1925, Lev Vygotskii anticipated not just its failure, but its implausibility—and even undesirability. In *Psychology of Art*, he reproached the Russian Formalists for "sensualistic one-sidedness"—for a focus on oshchuschenie for its own sake.[1] Art, Vygotskii suggested, certainly had a key role to play in generating emotions and sensory responses; but that was only the first stage. Ultimately, the task of art was to enable the transcendence of those emotions and senses, and "the cultivation of consciousness and will." It could—and must—"socialize" emotion.[2] I have argued that, in its theorization of the new socialist self, Soviet culture followed the trajectory that Vygotskii spelled out here: from an emphasis on sensation, to feeling, and finally to "socialized" emotion. From body to mind, feeling to consciousness. Against that background, I have told the ill-fated story of socialist sensations.

This book has offered a new theoretical and historical framework through which to view Soviet cinema—directing attention to the importance of surfaces, textures, and objects in both formal and thematic terms, and showing how the treatment of "material" was embedded in a wider context, shaped by ideology and utopian aspiration. Filmmakers were closely engaged with their sociopolitical, scientific, and philosophical contexts, so cinema enables us to trace the project for the sensory "remaking" of the newly Soviet self. Film was not just a means of reflecting the relationship between the human body and the material world in the new Soviet reality, however. It sought to create that relationship through its direct address to the spectator, and its capacity to act on bodies and senses.

While this book uses film to narrate Soviet cultural history, it is also a new history of Soviet cinema itself. Beyond, or alongside, my overarching story of socialist sensation, there are other narratives that cut across this book. I have sought to go beyond the established canon: to show how avant-garde theory and practice evolved in dialogue with so-called national cinemas, and mainstream cinema. Certain key protagonists have recurred; some are well known, others much less so. This is in part a story of the avant-garde: the FEKS group, Sergei Iutkevich, Viktor Shklovskii, Abram Room, Vsevolod Pudovkin, Dziga Vertov, and others. I have also returned frequently to the work of Fridrikh Ermler and Boris Barnet—both important members of the filmmaking establishment in this period, and both distinguished by their interest in capturing the everyday reality of Soviet society in transition. I have also, however, shown how the preoccupations that shaped the evolution of these directors' work were shared by others who rarely figure in histories of Soviet cinema. Some of these were members of the avant-garde—either lesser-known (such as Ol′ga Preobrazhenskaia), or non-Russian (Lev Push, Leo Esakiia, Nikolai Shengelaia). Others, such as Aleksei Popov, Eduard Ioganson, and Aleksandr Macheret, occupied a more ambiguous political and artistic position. But all of them sought, I suggest, to shape their filmmaking in relation to the project of presenting new models of human experience. The different case studies and analyses in this book, therefore, seek both to reveal the diversity of filmmaking in this period, and to emphasize its entanglement within a shared, and carefully negotiated, field of meaning. Avant-garde and mainstream, central (Russian) and national filmmakers dealt with the same ideological agendas—and were motivated by shared preoccupations.

Figures other than film directors have also populated this story. In particular, I have traced the unwritten histories of set designers such as Sergei Kozlovskii, Vladimir Egorov, Dmitrii Kolupaev, and others. As such, this book is in part a history of how the evolution of film style was shaped by technical developments and practical possibilities. Montage has dominated our histories of Soviet cinema in this period. This book suggests an alternative narrative: one that emphasizes faktura, material, and surfaces, and that brings mise-en-scène to the fore. I have taken a step in this direction, but there is much work still to be done.[3] Attention to film style reminds us to view cinema in terms of institutional organization, and not just creative individuality; it should prompt consideration of the distinctive visual styles that evolved out of particular film studios (Sovkino, Mezhrabpom, Goskinprom Gruzii, etc.) during the 1920s, and how they were determined not just by individual directors, but by a larger production collective.

There is also a broader intellectual history revealed here. My arguments have drawn heavily on the contemporary film press. Here, too, key individuals play an important role: Mikhail Bleiman, Nikolai Iezuitov, Konstantin Iukov, and others. Such figures played a key part in the creative matrix of filmmaking in this period, shaping aesthetic and ideological frameworks during the complex years that took Soviet cinema from its "revolutionary" birth into established Socialist Realism. Much work can done in uncovering the multiple networks of connections (personal, intellectual, and institutional) that were operative in this period. Further knowledge of the pedagogical evolution of VGIK, for example, and the involvement of individuals such as psychologists Leont'ev and Artemov (chapter 7), would be of great benefit. Research into the studies of audience perception that took place in GAKhN and other institutes during this period would be of help in reinforcing (or challenging) the claims of this book.

What, then, is the broader cultural history that this book uncovers? I began by promising to reveal the place of the sensory in Soviet aesthetics, and show how film participated in the dream of shaping a particular proletarian sensibility: Balázs's new "life-sensation." In early Soviet culture, the hand was a symbol of the newly proximate relationship between the human and the world that was essential to Socialism. Hands, skin (and touch) were the limbs and membrane through which that relationship is mediated. The hand was also significant as a symbol of *making*, another core trope in this book. It is in the act of making that the relationship between human and material is at its most intense and productive. Rather than being uniquely focused on mechanical making and on industry, we have shown how Soviet filmmakers and thinkers were interested in handcrafts (weaving, sewing, potting) as a productive model of connection with the world. Metaphors of making and production focused not just on the how-it-is-made (construction) of objects, but also on the what-is-it-made-from (material). And film seemed to have the unique ability to reveal both of these things.

This is a book about Soviet cinema, but it has used film as a window onto a bigger picture of Soviet cultural history. I have revealed a widespread interest, in early Soviet Russia, in the capacity of revolutionary culture to provoke a new sensory proximity between the human subject and the material world, and traced the range and reach of this interest.[4] The chapters of this book have broadly followed a historical evolution. They have traced how the dream of a sensory revolution, to be brought about by a renewed appreciation of the texture and material of the world, took shape, and then dissolved, in Soviet culture. Although I have not emphasized it unduly, the book divides naturally into three parts, each consisting of three chapters. Together, the first three chapters explore the roots of cinema's implication in the project of sensory "remaking," tracing its theoretical and practical framings. They also narrate the first (chronological) stage of Soviet film's engagement with the project of transforming the relationship between human subject and material world. Chapters 4, 5, and 6 show how that project evolved in the mid to late 1920s by focusing on three distinct areas: production and making; the ethnic "primitive"; and the Soviet "modern." Together, they reveal how filmmakers tried to reconcile conflicting imperatives: the "thirst for material" and the call for a new cinema of "socialist feeling." Chapter 7 reveals how the dream of sensory revolution—of creating socialist sensations—was challenged by changing ideological contexts in the early to mid-1930s, with a growing emphasis on the need for cinema to model Soviet "feelings." This chapter, however, and the two that follow it, show that cinematic material and sensation remained a central preoccupation for filmmakers. This period was a testing ground for appropriate models—of Socialist Realist film style, and of the Soviet subject him/herself. The question of the relationship between sensation and emotion, body and mind, was unresolved. By the end of the 1930s, however, the dream of socialist sensation had come to an end.

I have claimed to be uncovering a hidden history of socialist sensation. There is always a risk in academic writing about bodies that bodies are turned into abstractions: the fleshy lived experience of the body is elided in the theorization of bodily life. Writing about the senses—particularly the tactile senses—runs a still greater risk. Without doubt, many of the characters that I have discussed in the chapters of this book were themselves guilty of just such abstractions. The Soviet "body" was an idea more than it was a reality. It is important not to allow this obvious fact to obscure the nature of their ambition, however. In their discussions of sensation and feeling, my protagonists did attempt to access and understand experience that was outside language and see whether a new world could be based on such experience. I, too, have attempted to tread a line between theories of the senses and their lived reality. Inevitably, this book is principally a story of how bodies and senses were thought about and discussed, and not of how they actually felt. I hope that the study of film nevertheless provides an additional dimension: by looking closely not just at what films show, but at how their images seek to act on a spectator, I try to make at least some socialist sensations *sensible* for the modern viewer.

There are many different conclusions that can be drawn from this material. Am I arguing, for instance, that the dream of sensory revolution is an *unrealized* story of Soviet culture—the what-should-have-been of Socialist Realism? A possible utopian future that did not come to pass? Or do I suggest that in fact it *was* realized—that we have got our theories of Soviet culture wrong? Is this a revisionist history of Soviet culture that overturns theories of control, rationalization, technology in favor of iconoclasm, spontaneity, and feeling? Alternatively, at the other end of the interpretative spectrum, am I telling the story of sensation as a force of resistance against the consolidating norms of Soviet ideology? Was the emphasis on the sensory experience of the body always already oppositional and subversive? In fact, I hope that this book cannot be limited to any of these oversimplified conclusions. I have sought to challenge the assumption that sensation, touch, and affect always contest hegemonic norms, and I have not allowed bodies and senses to be seen as innately challenging to the Soviet dream. Instead, I have shown how early Marxist-phenomenological materialism, as it took shape in Soviet Russia, anticipated many of the concerns of contemporary theories that emphasize the body as the locus of a new kind of knowledge of the world. A vision of reciprocity between the human body and the material was a core element of its utopian vision.

Of course, this vision existed in unresolved tension with a parallel emphasis on human control—the regulation of body and world through the power of reason and consciousness. Cinema in particular was caught between its capacity to enable an (unmediated, fresh) encounter with the material, and its technological processing of that material. It was caught, too, between the twin tasks of provoking sensation and managing emotion. According to Casetti, this was the key to cinema's privileged potential in modernist culture: "The cinema is exactly this: an experience that vacillates between the possibility of an excitement beyond measure, and an adherence to measures that avoid all risk. It is the space between, in which the comings and goings serve to recover a balanced turmoil in order to arrive at what modern man needs: good emotion."[5]

In the Soviet case, I suggest, this vacillation was particularly acute. The tactility and texture of Soviet cinema in this period is distinct from that of other cinemas in its particular ideological inflection. This was no mere formal experiment. Soviet cinema sought to use the potentiality of cinema's address to the spectator as nothing less than a means of modeling new forms of human experience. In its experimental exploration of sensory affect, it envisaged a revolutionary model of selfhood. As such it was at the center of the dream of Socialist Senses.

* * *

The failure of this dream provides the thematic and formal focus of the film with which I will close this book: *Death of (the) Sensation: the Robot of Jim Ripl'* (*Gibel' sensatsii: robot Dzhima Ripl'*, dir. Aleksandr Andrievskii). This film was in production at Mezhrabpom from the mid-1920s on, and was finally screened in April 1935. It spans, therefore, a key period in my history of Soviet sensation. Although the term *sensatsiia* in Russian is not a straight linguistic equivalent of "sensation" in English, with the dual meaning of sense-based sensation (oshchushchenie) and miracle/popular sensation, but rather translates only the latter meaning, it is clear that the film's title plays with the double meaning of the original English. Jim Ripple's robots are a sensation in the sense that they attract great attention and cause great excitement. But the principal meaning of the title seems to lie in the primary meaning of "loss of sensation" in English—that is, the extent to which the automated life of the robot does, or does not, bring about a loss of sensation—of the embodied, proximate relationship between the world and the human subject that has been the subject of this book.

Death of Sensation was the directorial debut of Andrievskii, who worked first as a scriptwriter, composing, among other things, the script for Dmitriev's *Mechanical Traitor* (see chapter 6).[6] The first script for *Death of Sensation* was produced in 1929.[7] Its production design was by Egorov and Kaplunovskii, with work on mannequins and robots supervised by Dubrovskii-Eshke, and carried out by a team in Leningrad supervised by N. Fishman. The film was a loose adaptation of Karel Čapek's 1920 play "RUR" (an acronym standing for Rossum's Universal Robots; Čapek's play coined the term "robot").[8] Other influences no doubt contributed: in 1928, one Eric the Robot made his first appearance in London, opening a Model Engineering Exhibition, standing on a podium, and even speaking to welcome guests. Like the robots in *Death of Sensation*, Eric had the letters RUR stamped on his metal chest, in direct acknowledgment of the relationship with the robots in Čapek's play (but here standing for the name of its maker, I. A. Richards). It was shortly after this London "sensation" that Mezhrabpom commissioned the film.

In public statements, Andrievskii made sure to emphasize that *Death of Sensation* was a fantastic (fantasy) film.[9] Yet it was focused on something that was by no means fantastical: industrial production. According to Andrievskii, the film was based on something that a German academic had once said to Anatolii Lunacharskii: that engineers could be responsible for destroying capitalism.[10] This was a founding principle of Soviet ideology, and has provided a structuring axis for this book. Invention, bricolage, and making were potent symbols of the new world, and part of a reconceptualization of machines and technology. Soviet industry would be different from capitalist industry. And at the heart of this distinction would be a new relationship between the human body and the machine. From the perspective of 1935, *Death of Sensation* can be seen as an interrogation of that idea—of the utopian dream that saw man and machine in a harmonious relationship of mutual care (*zabota*). Although this is a story of robots, it has music, movement, the senses and bodies at its center, and it uses them to ask fundamental questions about spontaneity and regulation, freedom and control.

Death of Sensation sets the capitalist worlds of heavy industry and leisure side by side, and reveals them both as dehumanized, and dehumanizing. It begins in a modern factory in Germany, where a cruel experiment takes place: two young engineers (one of whom is the film's principal protagonist, young Jim Ripple) are forced to increase the pace of the machines on their production line to test the capacity of their human operators to work more quickly: as the mechanical wheel spins, one worker is knocked out, and another reduced to raving. Human bodies are incapable of matching the efficiency possible in machines; and in the eyes of the technocratic factory directors, they are ultimately expendable. Later that day, in a cabaret bar, the moneyed bourgeoisie is shown at play. Here, too, however, the film's thematic focus on production—and specifically on the relationship between bodies and machines—is maintained. As Ripple sits alone, he overhears gossip: workers are threatening to strike, the system is in crisis, another banker has committed suicide. "We must throw out machines and return to handwork," a cigar-smoking capitalist announces.

The picture, then, is of capitalism under threat. And the strange sterility of the world of urban leisure underlines its failure. Jazz musicians play; yet the bourgeois figures sitting at tables do not react to the music. These are bodies without sensation; bourgeois pleasure is presented as a deadened, *disembodied* experience, a marker of an essential separation between capitalism and sensation. It is at this important point in the film that Aleksandra Khokhlova makes a cameo appearance, selling what she describes as "automatic dolls" (figure 10.1). In fact, these dolls appear to be simple puppets—grotesque papier-mâché parodies of the bloated faces of the capitalists that populate the nightclub scene. As she moves through the crowd, Khokhlova's own striking physique mirrors their angular shapes, and the camera dwells disconcertingly on a montage of hands, her long, elegant fingers mirroring the clay fingers of her model as she operates it. Extended shots focus on the distorted faces of the puppets, with their long noses and swollen chins. For Ripple, the combination of the automatic dolls, jazz music, and the capitalist's throwaway assertion that "we need to return to handwork" prompts a revelation. Jim rushes out of the bar, vowing to carry out "a scientific revolution which will change the world." Technology, he claims, will make it possible for robots to replace workers on the factory floor. They will lack the embodied fragility of the human. They will not feel pain. Thus begins Ripple's own utopian dream.

Intriguingly, however, it is not just the automatic dolls that provide the focus of Ripple's interest in this extraordinary scene.[11] Rather he seems equally focused on Khokhlova herself—and through her, I suggest, on the legacy of the Soviet avant-garde and its culture of the body. This reading of the film is not entirely fanciful. According to their memoirs, Andrievskii was a close friend of Kuleshov and Khokhlova, one of their protectors at this difficult time, when both were increasingly ostracized from mainstream filmmaking.[12] No doubt the casting of Khokhlova in this film was part of this protection, but it may go beyond this.[13] In *Death of Sensation*, I suggest, Khokhlova is used to stand in for the revolutionary avant-garde, and specifically to evoke the history of its fascination with puppets, toys, and mechanized movement. We have discussed how, in Kuleshov's *Your Acquaintance*, Khokhlova was shown handling a wooden toy on her desk. Her own feature-documentary, *Toys*, had been produced in 1931.[14] The FEKS collective produced a screenplay for an unrealized film, *Edison's Woman* (*Zhenshchina Edisona*) focused on Thomas Edison's mechanical dolls.[15] And Khokhlova herself had been part of some of Lev Kuleshov's most developed experiments with film's capacity to capture physical reflexes, and to understand human movement as in some sense akin to a machine.[16]

Fig. 10.1 The Return of the Avant-garde. Stills from *Death of Sensation* (*Gibel´ sensatsii*, dir. A. Andrievskii, production design by B. Dubrovskii-Eshke, 1935).

These intertexts prompt us to think about *Death of Sensation* as a reflection on avant-garde conceptions of the relationship between bodies and machines. This is borne out by the complexity of Ripple's robots themselves. Ripple's dream is emphatically not one of the mechanical elimination of human feeling. When he presents his robot prototype to his comrade, its first action is an embrace—its metal arms spread wide. Later, demonstrating a vast full-size robot to his assembled employers, Jim underlines its precision and the speed of its reactions.[17] But again, he does so through showing its capacity to embrace—and even to do so gently. Jim seeks to invent a machine that will not oppress the human, but will work as its comrade. In this first demonstration, his robot operates a small-scale sewing machine. Its hands are sensitive enough to engage in handcraft; they reach out in friendship to a fellow worker. Jim's is a utopian vision of the feeling machine. He is a convinced materialist who believes that there is no distinction between the human and the machine worlds. His robots will be as capable of thinking (myshlenie) as humans themselves because "thinking is also a material process." This emphasis on thinking as "material" is surely an ironic (perhaps even nostalgic) reference to the earlier period of Soviet history that has been a focus of this book: the materialist vision of the self as formed through an encounter with the material world. As the *Pravda* film critic acknowledged, damningly, Jim Ripple is a "utopianist."[18] And his utopian thinking directly echoes that which had had such particular potency in the previous decade.

Death of Sensation does not shy away from the ambiguity and danger of these dreams, however. "Who is this for?" Jim's comrades ask. This forms the principal question in the film, which revolves around questions of discipline, regulation, and control. Jim is signed up by the government and sent to work in the local arms-production industry, where he is given resources and equipment in order to pursue his research. A roll call of negative characters—a banker, a field marshal, and a government minister—appear as the sinister operators behind the scenes of his utopian dream. Unbeknownst to him, these capitalist forces of oppression seek to use the robots as their agents of power—in war, and in the "battle" against the worker. Ultimately, Jim's aspiration for a friendly relationship between machine and worker comes to a tragic end, when he seeks to explain himself to his assembled comrades. Speaking through the mouth of his robot, Jim appeals to them: "I reach out my hand to you so that we might together find a new path . . . build a new world." Intrigued and even seduced, a young man approaches the robot, and they shake hands. However, this putative moment of connection ends in tragedy, as the control system misfires, and—with its characteristic embrace—the robot crushes the curious comrade. This prompts the film's dramatic denouement. The capitalists attempt to put down the workers' strike by means of their robots. Jim tries in vain to avert their course of destruction via his trusted saxophone, but is himself violently crushed by the robots' marauding metal feet, killed by his own creation.

The emphasis of the film overall, however, lies not on the threat of machines, but on their potential. All is not lost. Jim's former comrades— renegade worker-engineers who have refused to follow him into serving the forces of imperial power—manage to bring the robots back under control. Their improvised system (its unruly coils, wires, and pulleys in direct contrast to the high-tech machinery of the armaments factory) is a form of bricolage. And as such it returns to a particularly Soviet vision of invention. As the film concludes, this is its message. In the wrong hands, the robot is a tool for oppression; in the right hands, it is a force for liberation: "Only in the hands of the laboring classes can the machine cease to be a tool of violence."[19]

The film's message goes beyond this, however, to suggest provocatively that robots can have feelings, too. Or rather that they can have sensations. This point is made through music and dance. In a striking scene, Jim, drunk and despairing about his sister Claire's fear of his machines, takes out his saxophone, and his robots dance to his tune. Their movements begin tentatively, but as the music continues they become freer and more expressive— appearing eventually organic and nonmechanical. The machines are responsive to the unpredictable rhythms of jazz. It is here that the engagement of *Death of Sensation* with the history of Soviet bodies becomes evident. Jim's resort to his saxophone is a search for redemption—a refutation of the accusations of treachery. Jazz symbolizes spontaneity, even chaos. It is in one sense directly opposed to the regular rhythms of machines. Yet in this film—and indeed in Soviet Russia more broadly—the picture is more complex.

Jazz was a powerful symbol in Soviet Russia of the early 1930s, and one that had many potential meanings. We have noted the sterility of the jazz performed at the German nightclub at the beginning of the film, and the failure of bourgeois bodies to respond to its imperatives. Here, Nicoletta Misler's assertion that an earlier version of *Death of Sensation* was to feature Valentin Parnakh, dancing his famous *idole-girafe* dance, is important. According to Misler, in a handwritten note in his archives, Parnakh claimed to have danced for Andrievskii in 1924, for the purposes of this film.[20] Indeed, she suggests that the entire second cabaret scene in *Death of Sensation* was shot as early as 1924, and that Parnakh's dance was cut during Andrievskii's editing of accumulated footage before the final film was screened in 1935.[21]

It is difficult to verify this claim or align it with the purported production schedule of *Death of Sensation*, and indeed it is disputed by Grebner's narrative (see note 7 above), but it does prompt us to think further about the film's pointed use of jazz and avant-garde culture. Parnakh was an emblematic figure in the history of avant-garde dance and music, credited with bringing jazz to the Soviet Union. While living in Paris between 1914 and 1922, he had been enthused by performances of African-American jazz bands, and on his return to Moscow, bringing instruments (a banjo, a xylophone, a trombone, silencers), he made himself the spokesman for "new dance" in Soviet Russia in 1922.[22] After the first, legendary impromptu performance of Parnakh's "jazz band" on October 1, 1922 (when Meierkhol'd, Eisenstein, Maiakovskii, and Lunacharskii seem to have been in the audience), Parnakh was invited to perform in Meierkh'old's *DE* (*Daesh' Evropu*). Later that year, Parnakh seems to have performed his *idole-girafe* dance, which he may have composed specifically for Meierkhol'd.[23] He rapidly became an important voice in the developing theory and practice of choreography and movement: he taught, for example, in Ippolit Sokolov's laboratory of rhythmic gymnastics; he was also invited by Sergei Eisenstein to speak in the Proletkul't Central Studio (it is an often-cited anecdote that Eisenstein was so impressed by Parnakh's first performance that he asked him to teach him the foxtrot).[24]

Parnakh's relationships with the Soviet avant-garde reflect a broader interest in the plasticity of the body and freedom of improvisation that seemed to be intrinsic to jazz music and dance. This is important for understanding its role in *Death of Sensation*. Although first screened in 1935, *Death of Sensation* is shot through with references to avant-garde culture. We have already noted the symbolic importance of Aleksandra Khokhlova and her automatic dolls. The second of the film's two nightclub scenes stars Sergei Martinson as a singer, surrounded by dancing girls. Although by 1935 he was working in a "music hall," Martinson's avant-garde credentials were beyond doubt: he had been a prominent member of Vsevolod Meierkhol'd's theater since 1924, and an early member of the FEKS film collective.[25] Meierkhol'd, indeed, can be seen as silent interlocutor in *Death of Sensation*—emblematic of the film's dialogue with the early Soviet avant-garde. His relationship with Parnakh prompts us to revisit the concept of biomechanics, and the relationship between freedom and control, spontaneity and consciousness that has provided a central focus in this book.

What is the relationship between jazz, bodies, and machines in *Death of Sensation*? Misler goes as far as to attribute the film's central focus on jazz, and its capacity to make the machines move, to Parnakh's influence. In jazz, Parnakh saw the possibility of a combination of freedom and control: it reflected the syncopated rhythms of contemporary, mechanized life, but as a force for emancipation and improvisation—a fully embodied sensory response to the potentiality contained within the machine.[26] This sensory response was, according to Parnakh, mimetic: the jazz musician is an "elastic mannequin," embodying the music through her body, and enabling a new relationship between musician and instrument—and, in turn, between musician and audience. This mimetic relationship between the human and the world creates new sensations and new emotions: "a new pathos, gaiety, irony, a new tenderness."[27]

Andrievskii was more than aware of the multiple meanings attached to jazz music and dance, and *Death of Sensation* uses jazz to reflect on core questions. The bourgeois customers in the hall near its beginning have bodies that do not respond to the rhythms of music. They dance without feeling. By contrast, when the robots dance to Ripple's lone saxophone, they do so with the abandon and freedom that Parnakh first saw in those performances in Paris. Rather than representing a mechanized body, these robots are flexible, musical, and responsive—even affectionate (figure 10.2). They represent a dream of a different kind of machine. And of a world where, as Nusinova notes, the saxophone is the weapon of the proletariat. In this utopian vision, reason and science are in accord with human feeling—sensation and emotion. This is the dream of socialist emancipation, of a new relationship between man and machine. It is capitalists, not robots, who are unable to feel.

Yet in *Death of Sensation*, Ripple's flexible, responsive robots (and their creator) are acquired by capitalist industrialists and turned to destructive use. These robots are not allowed to feel. Similarly, Sergei Martinson's show here is not "free": rather than mirroring the spontaneous movements of Parnakh, he is surrounded by lines of dancers in ranked order, like the Tiller girl chorus lines that Siegfried Kracauer would later describe as a "mass ornament."[28] Thus through bodies, music and machines, Andrievskii provides a reflection on the shifting priorities of Soviet culture. By 1935, Valentin Parnakh had fallen out of favor. The place of jazz in the Soviet Union—and

Fig. 10.2 The Dance of the Robots. Still from *Death of Sensation* (*Gibel' sensatsii*, dir. A. Andrievskii, production design by B. Dubrovskii-Eshke, 1935).

its symbolic meaning—was rapidly changing. Grigorii Aleksandrov's well-known (and well-received) *Jolly Fellows* of 1934 provides a direct reflection on this process. It marked, in one sense, the Soviet regime's reconciliation with jazz. Indeed, its very plot narrates the acceptance of jazz onto the main stage of Soviet culture—both literally and metaphorically. Leonid Utesov, one of the first homegrown Soviet jazz musicians, played the main character. Even Parnakh himself played a minor role in *Jolly Fellows*. Here, though, Parnakh explicitly represented a different (and outmoded) form of jazz from the one celebrated in the film (and his name is, notably, not mentioned in the film's titles). This is revealing: *Jolly Fellows* marked jazz's acceptance in Soviet culture; but it also signaled its containment and its sanitization. The chaos and unruly potentiality of jazz, emphasized in the film's plot (most notably in a scene in which music making and play fighting are totally intertwined), is, by its end, contained and sanitized—rendered harmless—by the film's narrative. Valentin Parnakh died in 1951, but his vision was already redundant in 1935: jazz was appropriated to the consolidating Soviet ideology. The emancipatory energy contained in its revolutionary address to the body was transformed into mere entertainment.

It is this sanitized, regulated jazz that provides bourgeois distraction in *The Death of Sensation*. And ultimately, neither people nor machines can realize their emancipatory potential. Andrievskii's film can be read as a self-conscious swan song for avant-garde theories of the body, movement, and emancipation. It interrogates the dreams of the avant-garde—in particular with regard to the body and technology. And it reveals their impossibility. In this respect, the mechanical "devil's wheel" of *Death of Sensation* is perhaps a conscious intertext with FEKS's 1924 *Devil's Wheel* (*Chertovo koleso*), in which the same Sergei Martinson had also played the conductor of an orchestra. The amusement park ride, in that film a symbol of the modernist destabilization of space and time, is reprised here as a sinister industrial device. It tests the strength of the human body. Indeed, it breaks the human body. In 1935, as Socialist Realism took shape, *Death of Sensation* spoke eloquently of the need for a particularly Soviet vision of embodied, fully feeling experience. It was perhaps a lament for the end of that utopian dream.

NOTES

1. Vygotskii, *The Psychology of Art*, 57.
2. Ibid., 214, 243.
3. For instance, Philip Cavendish is exploring experiments in color filming and stereoscopy that took place during this period.
4. An indicative range of primary sources relating to the Soviet "sensory project," drawn from diverse fields, will be published in Emma Widdis, ed., *Revolutionary Bodies, Soviet Minds*.
5. Casetti, *Eye of the Century*, 140.
6. According to the film's scriptwriter Georgii Grebner, Dmitriev was set to be the assistant director of *Death of Sensation*, but had to pull out because of illness. Grebner, "'RUR' ('Gibel' sensatsii')," 244.
7. According to Grebner, the first version of the screenplay was produced in 1929, but was not passed by the censors, although Lunacharskii was a major supporter. See comments in discussion after a screening of the film. Andrievskii, "Prosmotr kartiny 'Gibel' sensatsii,'" 235.
8. Čapek's play was staged in Leningrad by the Peredvizhnoi Theater in 1924. As Nusinova notes, however, the screenplay relied heavily on a development of Čapek's original by Ukrainian writer Vladimir Vadko, whose 1929 story "The Robots are Coming" enjoyed

considerable success in Ukrainian (and in Russian translation). Nusinova, "Gibel' sensatsii (robot Dzhima Ripl')," 73.

9. Andrievskii, "Prosmotr kartiny 'Gibel' sensatsii,'" 234.

10. Ibid.

11. A number of other instances reference the avant-garde interest in marionettes. Meierkhol'd's theories of theater are one clear example. The marionettes of Aleksandra Ekster, developed for an unrealized film project by Danish filmmaker Urban Gad, are another. Bowlt, "The Marionettes of Alexandra Exter."

12. Kuleshov and Khokhlova, *50 let v kino*, 119.

13. In the discussion held after a film screening, Andrievskii recalls that Khokhlova was to have played a much larger part, but that she was excised from the final film as a result of the censors' intervention. Andrievskii, "Prosmotr kartiny 'Gibel' sensatsii,'" 239–40.

14. Kuleshov and Khokhlova, *50 let v kino*, 126–29.

15. See FEKS Collective, "'Zhenshchina Edisona.'"

16. See Olenina, "Psychomotor Aesthetics," 151.

17. Andrievskii gave considerable detail about the construction of the robots. Andrievskii, "Prosmotr kartiny 'Gibel' sensatsii,'" 236–37.

18. Subotskii, "'Gibel' sensatsii,'" 4.

19. Ibid.

20. Misler, "L'idole-girafe," 100.

21. Ibid. Misler also suggests that a "lanky" figure in the cabaret scenes could be Parnakh, but I cannot identify this character.

22. Sirotkina, *Svobodnoe dvizhenie*, 104–8. In English, see Starr, *Red and Hot*, 43–52. In 1922 Parnakh published an article in the avant-garde journal *Veshch'*, describing the music and dances that he had encountered. Parnakh, "Novye tantsy," 25, and "Dzhazband," 25.

23. Evgenii Gabrilovich, a film screenwriter who played the piano in Parnakh's band (because no classical pianist would agree to participate) recalls how he and Parnakh both went to work with Meierkhol'd in this period. Gabrilovich, "Rasskazy o tom, chto proizoshlo," 61–62.

24. Gordon, "Valentin Parnakh," 427.

25. Martinson played Valerian in Meierkho'ld's production of Nikolai Erdman's *The Mandate* (*Mandat*) in 1924, and Khlestakov in his version of Gogol'"s *The Government Inspector* (*Revizor*) in 1925.

26. Misler sees Parnakh's mechanical jazz dances as contesting Soviet Taylorism. Certainly, his most adventurous experiments in dance appeared at the time when the foxtrot and the tango were being eliminated from the permissible dance repertoire in Soviet Russia. For more detail on the Soviet campaign against jazz, see Starr, *Red and Hot*, 37–79 and 157–234. It is important to note, however, that Parnakh's particular vision was not necessarily inimical to machine culture; notably, Parnakh's band played at the first All-Union Exhibition of Agriculture and Cottage Industries in May 1923.

27. Parnakh, "Mimeticheskii tanets," 13.

28. Kracauer, "The Mass Ornament."

GLOSSARY OF RUSSIAN TERMS

byt. Everyday life.
chuvstvennyi blesk. Sensory radiance.
chuvstvo (pl. *chuvstva*). Feeling. The word covers the dual meaning of sense (the five senses) and feeling/emotion.
emotsiia (pl. *emotsii*). Emotion.
emotsional'nost'. Emotionality. The quality of being receptive to, and productive of, emotion.
emotsional'naia nasyshchennost'. Emotional saturation. Used by art and film critics to describe the ability of visual images to communicate emotional-sensory meaning.
faktura. The texture of a work of art, or the material texture of an object.
komsomolets (pl. *komsomoltsy*). Young urban communist(s).
khudozhnik. artist, but used also to describe film production designer.
myshlenie. Reasoning.
naoshchup'. By touch.
novyi byt. The "new everyday life" that Soviet revolution would create.
novyi chelovek. The "new person" that Soviet revolution would create.
obrabotka. Processing. Used by Constructivist theorists to refer to the processing of the "material" of a work of art.
oshchushchenie (pl. *oshchushcheniia*). Feeling or sensation.
predmetnyi (adj), *predmetnost'* (noun). object-led; object-ledness. The quality of being grounded in the material(ist) world of things.

rabochii byt. workers' everyday life.

rukodelie. Handwork, craft.

soznatel′nost′ (soznanie). Consciousness.

tekhnichestvo. The particular qualities of the *tekhnik*.

tekhnik. The new person who would be created by the technological revolution brought about by socialism.

ustanovka na. Describes a particular attitude toward, or tuning of body and mind toward, something.

zabota. The quality of care that marks the socialist relationship with the machine (and the material world).

zhiznestroenie. The constructivist project of "life-building" as the purpose of postrevolutionary art.

BIBLIOGRAPHY*

Abel, Richard, ed. *French Film Theory and Criticism: A History/Anthology*, Vol. 1, 1907–1929. Princeton: Princeton University Press, 1988.

Abramov, A. "Mashinnye tantsy (Ekstsentricheskie tantsy Parnakha)." *Teatr i muzyka* 13 (1922): 363–64.

Adams, Mark B. "Eugenics in Russia, 1900–1940." In *The Wellborn Science: Eugenics in Germany, France, Brazil and Russia*, edited by Mark B. Adams, 153–217. New York and Oxford: Oxford University Press, 1990.

Adamson, Glen, ed. *The Craft Reader*. London: Bloomsbury, 2010.

Adaskina, Natalia. "Constructivist Fabrics and Dress Design." *The Journal of Decorative and Propaganda Arts: Russian/Soviet Themed Issue*, 5 (Summer 1987): 144–159.

Affron, Charles, and Mirella Jona Affron. *Sets in Motion: Art Direction and Film Narrative*. New Brunswick, NJ: Rutgers University Press, 1995.

Agden, V. "Kino-khudozhnik na zapade i v SSSR." *Kino-zhurnal ARK* 3 (1926): 16–18.

Aladin. "'Odna'—krivaia vverkh." *Kino* 64 (November 26, 1931): 2.

Albéra, François. *Albatros: Des russes à Paris, 1919–1929*. Milan: Mazzotta, 1995.

---

*Material emerging from research undertaken for this book appeared in the following publications: "Cinema and the Art of Being: Towards a History of Early Soviet Set Design," in *A Companion to Russian and Soviet Cinema*, edited by Birgit Beumers, 314–336. London: Palgrave Macmillan, 2016; "Making Sense without Speech: the Use of Silence in Early Soviet Sound Film," in *Sound, Speech, Music in Russian and Soviet Cinema*, edited by Lilya Kaganovsky and Maria Salazkina, 100–116. Bloomington: Indiana University Press, 2014; "Child's Play: Pleasure and the Soviet Hero in Savchenko's A Chance Meeting (1936)," *Studies in Russian and Soviet Cinema* 6: 3 (2013), 319–333; "Socialist Feelings: Film and the Creation of Soviet Subjectivity," *Slavic Review* 71, no. 3 (Fall 2012), 590–618. It has been significantly changed in preparation of *Socialist Senses*.

Albrecht, Donald. *Designing Dreams: Modern Architecture in the Movies*. London: Thames and Hudson, 1987.
Alpers, Boris. "Goroda i gody." *Kino i zhizn´* 34–35 (1930): 7–8.
———. "Nadumannost' i narochitost,'" *Kino* 24 (May 22, 1935): 3.
Al´tman, Natan. "Khudozhnik v kino." *Iskusstvo kino* 3 (March 1936): 22.
Alymov, Sergei. "Ethnography, Marxism and Soviet Ideology." In *An Empire of Others: Creating Ethnographic Knowledge in Imperial Russia and the USSR*, edited by Roland Cvetkovski and Alexis Hofmeister, 121–143. Budapest and New York: Central European University Press, 2014.
Amar, Jules (Zhiul´ Amar). *Chelovecheskaia mashina: nauchnye osnovy professional´nogo truda*. Moscow: Gosizdat, 1922.
Andrievskii, A. N. "Prosmotr kartiny 'Gibel´ sensatsii' (25 aprelia 1935 goda)." RGALI. F. 631, op. 2, ed. Khr. 82, l. 1–18, 31–35. Reprinted in "Zabytyi shedevr 30-kh? Iz istorii fil´ma 'Gibel´ sensatsii,'" edited by A. Troshin, 230–44. *Kinovedcheskie zapiski* 45 (2000).
Anley, Maxwell. "The Wisdom of Brainless Knights: Paradox, Dialectics and Literature's Conditions of Possibility." PhD diss., Durham University, 2015.
Anon. "Kruzhevo." *Entsiklopedicheskii slovar´ Brokgauza i Efrona*. Tom 16, 842–47. Saint Petersburg: Semenovskaia tipolitografiia (I. A. Efrona), 1895.
Anon. "Rukodelie." *Zhenskii zhurnal* 3 (March 1926): 24.
Anon. "V." *Gudok* (September 2, 1926): 4.
Anon. "Pokryvalo na divan ili postel´?" *Zhenskii zhurnal* 4 (April 1926): 37.
Anon. "Kak sozdaetsia domashnii uiut?" *Zhenskii zhurnal* 6 (June 1926): 13.
Anon. "Ugolok khoziaiki." *Zhenskii zhurnal* 9 (September 1926): 13.
Anon. "Novosti prokata." *Kino* 39 (September 28, 1926): 3.
Anon. "My v sezone 1926–27 pokazhem...," *Broshiura Mezhrabpom-Rus´*, RGALI f.1921. op. 2. ed. khr. 29: 1. 17.
Anon. "Smotr kino-fabrik: otkliki." *Kinofront* 9 (1927): 25–27
Anon. Advertisement for Khaz-Push. *Kino* 35 (August 20, 1927): 2.
Anon. "Smotrim na etoi nedele: Baby riazanskie." *Kino* 50 (Leningrad) (December 20, 1927): 4.
Anon. "Rezoliutsiia sektsii khudozhnikov arkhitektorov." *Kinofront* 2 (1928): 12–13.
Anon. "Vyshivka aplikatsiei." *Iskusstvo odevat´sia* 5 (May 1928): 14.
Anon. "Port´era iz kholsta." *Iskusstvo odevat´sia* 9 (September 1928): 16.
Anon. "Chto khotiat videt´ rabochie? Svoiu, sovetskuiu zhizn!" *Kino* 5 (January 31, 1928): 20.
Anon. "Trudnyi etap." *Sovetskii ekran* 27 (1928): 3.
Anon. "O 'Kruzhevakh.'" *Kino* 17 (April 24, 1928): 3.
Anon. "Remeslo i prikladnoe iskusstvo." *Zhenskii zhurnal* 4 (April 1930): 4.
Anon. "Obsuzhdaem novuiu kartinu Mezhrabpomfil´m—"Okraina" rezhissera B. Barnet." *Kino* 11 (February 28, 1933): 3.
Anon. "Okraina." *Kino-repertuar* 5 (1933): 2–3.

Anon. "Pervye itogi obsuzhdeniia statei 'Pravdy.'" *Iskusstvo kino* 4 (April 1936): 16–20.
Anon. "Oshchushchenie." *Bol'shaia sovetskaia entsiklopediia*, 1-oe izdanie. Tom 43, 727–732. 1939.
Anon. "Affekt." *Bol'shaia sovetskaia entsiklopediia*, 2-oe izdanie. Tom 3, 557–58. 1950.
Anon. "Kruzheva." *Bol'shaia sovetskaia entsiklopediia*, 2-oe izdanie. Tom 23, 509–11. 1953.
Anon. "Oshchushchenie." *Bol'shaia sovetskaia entsiklopediia*, 2-oe izdanie. Tom 31, 504–6. 1955.
Anon. "Chuvstvo." *Bol'shaia sovetskaia entsiklopediia*, 2-oe izdanie. Tom 47, 458–59. 1957.
Anon. "Emotsii." *Bol'shaia sovetskaia entsiklopediia*, 2-oe izdanie. Tom 49, 31–32. 1957.
Anon. "Frantsuzskie nemye fil'my v sovetskom prokate." *Kino i vremia* 4 (1965): 348–79, 477–81.
Anon. "Postanovlenie tresta Ukrainfil'm o zapreshchenii fil'ma 'Strogii iunosha.'" *Kino* 37 (July 26, 1936): 2.
Antonello, Pierpaolo. "'Out of Touch': F. T. Marinetti's Il tattilismo and the Futurist Critique of Separation." In *Back to the Futurists: The Avant-garde and its Legacy*, edited by Elza Adamowicz and Simona Storchi, 38–55. Manchester: Manchester University Press, 2013.
Arendt, Hannah. *The Human Condition*, 2nd ed. Chicago: University of Chicago Press, 1998.
Arnol'di, E. "Fakty—veshch' upriamaia." *Zhizn' iskusstva* 36 (September 8, 1929): 6–7.
Arnshtam, L. "Vglub' materiala." *Kino* 59 (December 24, 1932): 4.
Artaud, Antonin. "Cinema and Reality." In *French Film Theory and Criticism: A History/Anthology*, Vol. 1, 1907–1929, edited by Richard Abel, 410–412. Princeton: Princeton University Press, (1927) 1988.
Arvatov, Boris. "Everyday Life and the Culture of the Thing (Towards a Formulation of the Question)." Edited and translated by Christina Kiaer. *October* 81 (Summer 1997): 119–128.
Aseev, Nikolai. "Oktiabr' v Dal'nem." *Novyi LEF* 8–9 (1927): 38–49.
B-Shtein, P. "Dvorets i krepost'." *Kino-nedelia* 1 (February 12, 1924): 2.
Babenchikov, M. "Kino—geroi—byt." *Sovetskii ekran* 39 (1927): 13.
Bagrov, Petr. "Eduard Ioganson." *Kinovedcheskie zapiski* 65 (2003): 45–77.
———. "Sovetskii dendi. Siuzhet dlia nebol'shogo romana." *Seans* 21/22 (February 2005): 73–82.
———. "O Evgenii Cherviakove. Rezhisser ekzistentsial'nogo kino." *Iskusstvo kino* 7 (July 2010): 105–116.
Bagrov, Petr, and Natalia Nussinova. "Preobrazhenskaya e Pravov." *Program notes for Il cinema ritrovato 2013*, Cinemateca di Bologna. Accessed September 14, 2015. http://www.cinetecadibologna.it/Preobrazhenskaya_Pravov/ev/programmazione.
Baker, David B., ed. *The Oxford Handbook of the History of Psychology: Global Perspectives*. New York and Oxford: Oxford University Press, 2012.

Bakhtin, Mikhail. "Forms of Time and the Chronotope in the Novel." In *The Dialogic Imagination: Four Essays by M.M. Bakhtin*, edited by Michael Holquist, translated by Caryl Emerson and Michael Holquist, 84–259. Austin: University of Texas Press, 1981.
———. *Rabelais and His World*. Translated by Hélène Izwolsky. Bloomington: Indiana University Press, 1984.
Bakushinskii, Anatolii. *Khudozhestvennoe tvorchestvo i vospitanie*. Moscow: Novaia Moskva, 1925.
Bakushinskii, Anatolii, ed. *Iskusstvo detei. K mezhdunarodnoi vystavke detskogo risunka*. Leningrad: Izdatel′stvo Leningradskogo otdeleniia Soiuza sovetskikh khudozhnikov, 1935.
Balázs, Bela (Bela Balash). *Vidimyi chelovek: Ocherki dramaturgii fil′my*. Translated by K. I. Shutko. Moscow: Proletkul′t, 1925.
———. "Russkaia fil′ma i ee kritika (po povody fil′my 'SVD')." *Kino* 33 (Leningrad) (August 12, 1928): 3.
———. "Sachlichkeit und sozialismus." *Die Weltbühne* 24 (December 18, 1928): 915–18. Russian translation in *Kinovedcheskie zapiski* 100–101 (2011/2012): 384–86.
———. "Novye fil′my, novye zhizhneoshchushcheniia." *Sovetskoe kino* 3–4 (1933): 19–24.
———. "Otvet moim kritikam." *Iskusstvo kino* 6 (1936): 39–45.
———. "Monumentalizm ili kamernost′?" *Iskusstvo kino* 22 (May 11, 1937): 2.
———. "The Close-Up." In *Film Theory and Criticism: Introductory Readings*, edited by Gerald Mast, Marshall Cohen, and Scott Braudy, 260–67. New York and Oxford: Oxford University Press, 1992.
———. "Visible Man or the Culture of Film." In *Béla Balázs: Early Film Theory*, edited by Erica Carter, 1–91. New York and London: Berghahn, 2010.
———. "The Sound Film." In *Béla Balázs: Early Film Theory*, edited by Erica Carter, 183–211. New York and London: Berghahn, 2010.
Balina, Marina, and Larissa Rudova, eds. *Russian Children's Literature and Culture*. New York and London: Routledge, 2008.
Baranova, T. "Kakimi dolzhny byt′ oblozhka, vnutrennie ukrasheniia i format detskoi knigi." *Psikhologiia* 4 (1932): 64–76.
Barker, Jennifer M. *The Tactile Eye: Touch and the Cinematic Experience*. Berkeley and Los Angeles: University of California Press, 2009.
Barr, Alfred H. Jr. (Al′fred Barr, ml.). "Ruki." *Sovetskoe kino* 1 (1928): 26.
Barr, Alfred H. Jr. "Russian Diary 1927–28." *October* 7 (Winter 1978): 10–51.
Barsacq, Leon. *Caligari's Cabinet and Other Grand Illusions: A History of Film Design*. Revised and edited by Elliot Stein. Boston, MA: New York Graphic Society, 1976.
Barskaia, Margarita, and B. Shumiatskii. "Proizvodstvo detskikh kartin." *Pravda* 91, April 2, 1935: 3. Reprinted in "Margarita Barskaia and the Emergence of Children's Cinema," edited by Birgit Beumers, Nikolai Izvolov, Natalia Miloserdova and Natalia Riabchikova, 248–49. *Studies in Russian and Soviet Cinema* 3, no. 2 (2009).

Bartenev. "Kino v srednei Azii." *Kinozhurnal ARK* 10 (1925): 5–6.

Bassin, Mark. *Imperial Visions: Nationalist Imagination and Geographical Expansion in the Russian Far East, 1840–1865*. New York and Cambridge: Cambridge University Press, 1999.

———. "Classical Eurasianism and the Geopolitics of Russian Identity." *Ab Imperio* 2 (2003): 257–67.

Becker, Charles S., Joshua Mendelsohn, and Ksenya Benderskaya. *Russian Urbanization in Soviet and Post-Soviet Eras: Urbanization and Emerging Population Issues*. Working Paper 9. London: International Institute for Environment and Development, November 2012.

Beer, Daniel. *Renovating Russia: The Human Sciences and the Fate of Liberal Modernity, 1880–1930*. Ithaca: Cornell University Press, 2008.

Bek-Nazarov, Amo. "Natsional'noe kino v SSSR." In *20 let sovetskoi kinematografii: sbornik statei*, 74–83. Moscow: Goskinoizdat, 1940.

Bekhterev, Vladimir. "Kinematograf i nauka." *Vestnik kinematografii* 110, no.8 (1915): 39–40.

———. *Kollektivnaia refleksologiia*. Petersburg: Kolos, 1921.

Belodubrovskaia, M. "Ekstsentrika stilia v fil'me A. Rooma 'Strogii iunosha,'" in *Tynianovskii sbornik. Dvenadtsatye—Trinadtsatye—Chetyrnadtsatye tynianovskie chteniia. Issledovaniia. Materialy*, edited by M.O. Chudakova, 318–38. Vypusk 1 (2006).

Benjamin, Walter. "The Work of Art in the Age of Mechanical Reproduction." In Benjamin, Walter, *Illuminations: Essays and Reflections*, edited by Hannah Arendt, translated by Harry Zohn, 211–245. New York: Schocken, 1968.

———. "One Way Street." In *Selected Writings*. Vol. 1, 1913–1926, edited by Marcus Bullock and Michael W. Jennings, translated by Edmund Jephcott, 444–89. Cambridge, MA: Harvard University Press, 1996.

———. "Surrealism." In *Selected Writings*. Vol. 1, 1913–1926, edited by Marcus Bullock and Michael W. Jennings, translated by Edmund Jephcott, 207–18. Cambridge, MA: Harvard University Press, 1996.

———. *Charles Baudelaire: A Lyric Poet in the Era of High Capitalism*. New York and London: Verso, 1997.

———. "Moscow." In *Selected Writings*. Vol. 2, 1927–1934, edited by Marcus Bullock and Michael W. Jennings, 22–47. Cambridge, MA: Harvard University Press, 1999.

———. "Program for a Proletarian Children's Theatre." In *Selected Writings*. Vol. 2, 1927–1934, edited by Marcus Bullock and Michael W. Jennings. 201–7. Cambridge, MA: Harvard University Press, 1999.

———. *The Arcades Project*. Translated by Howard Eiland and Kevin McLaughlin. Cambridge, MA: Harvard University Press, 1999.

———. "The Work of Art in the Age of its Reproducibility: Second Version." In *Selected Writings*. Vol. 3, 1935–38, edited by Marcus Bullock and Michael W. Jennings. 101–133. Cambridge, MA: Harvard University Press, 2002.

———. "On the Mimetic Faculty." In *Selected Writings*. Vol. 2, part 2, 1931–1934, edited by Marcus Bullock and Michael W. Jennings, 720–22. Cambridge, MA: Harvard University Press, 2005.
Bergfelder, Tim, Sue Harris, and Sarah Street. *Film Architecture and the Transnational Imagination: Set Design in 1930s European Cinema*. Amsterdam: Amsterdam University Press, 2007.
Bernshtein, Nikolai. *Obshchaia biomekhanika*. Moscow: 1926.
———. *O lovkosti i ee razvitii*. Edited by M. Feigenberg. Moscow: Izdatel'stvo 'Fizkul'tura i sport,' 1991.
Berthomé, Pierre. *Le décor au cinema*. Paris: Cahiers du cinéma, 2003.
Beumers, Birgit. "Comforting Creatures in Children's Cartoons." In *Russian Children's Literature and Culture*, edited by Marina Balina and Larissa Rudova, 153–73. London: Routledge, 2008.
Beumers, Birgit, Nikolai Izvolov, Natalia Miloserdova, and Natalia Riabchikova, eds. "Margarita Barskaia and the Emergence of Children's Cinema." *Studies in Russian and Soviet Cinema* 3, no. 2 (2009).
Beumers, Birgit, Victor Bocharov, and David Robinson, eds. *Alexander Shiryaev: Master of Movement*. Pordenone: Le Giornate del Cinema Muto, 2009.
Bird, Robert, ed. *Adventures in the Soviet Imaginary: Children's Books and Graphic Art*. Chicago: The University of Chicago Library, 2011.
———. *Soul Machine: Socialist Realism as Model, 1932–1941*. Unpublished manuscript, forthcoming.
Bliakhin, P. A. "K itogam kino-sezona 1927–28 goda." *Kino i kul'tura* 2 (1929): 3–16.
Bleiman, Mikhail. "Shinel'." *Leningradskaia Pravda*, June 12, 1926. Reprinted in Bleiman, Mikhail. *O kino—svidetel'skie pokazaniia*. 62. Moscow: Iskusstvo, 1973.
———. "Kry'lia kholopa." *Leningradskaia Pravda*, August 23, 1926. Reprinted in Bleiman, Mikhail. *O kino—svidetel'skie pokazaniia*. 67–68. Moscow: Iskusstvo, 1973.
———. "Poet i tsar'." *Leningradskaia Pravda*, September 22, 1927. Reprinted in Bleiman, Mikhail. *O kino—svidetel'skie pokazaniia*. 81–82. Moscow: Iskusstvo, 1973.
———. "Dekabristy." *Leningradskaia Pravda*, December 26, 1927. Reprinted in Bleiman, Mikhail. *O kino—svidetel'skie pokazaniia*. 77–78. Moscow: Iskusstvo, 1973.
———. "'Mezhrabpom-Rus''- zhanr." *Kino* (Leningrad) (April 14, 1928): 1.
———. "Doloi material." *Zhizn' iskusstva* 34 (August 25, 1929): 5.
———. "Kuda rastut 'Feksy'?" *Zhizn' iskusstva* 12 (1929): 4–5. Reprinted in Bleiman, Mikhail. *O kino—svidetel'skie pokazaniia*. 112. Moscow: Iskusstvo, 1973.
———. "Ob ornamentakh." *Kino* 59 (December 24, 1932): 4.
———. "Chelovek v sovetskoi fil'me: istoriia odnoi oshibki." *Sovetskoe kino* 5–6 (1933): 48–57.

———. "Chelovek v sovetskoi fil′me II: fil′ma-obozrenie." *Sovetskoe kino* 8 (1933): 51–60.
———. "Chelovek v sovetskoi fil′me III: v poiskakh novogo stilia." *Sovetskoe kino* 9 (1933): 27–42.
Bliumbaum, A. "Ozhivaiushchaia statuia i voploshchennaia muzyka: konteksty 'Strogogo iuncshi." *Novoe literaturnoe obozrenie* 89 (2008): 138–189.
Blok, Aleksandr. "Krushenie gumanizma." In Blok, A. A. *Sobranie sochinenii v 8 tomakh*. Tom 6, 101–114. Moscow: Sovetskii pisatel′, 1962.
Blonskii, Pavel. *Trudovaia shkola*. Moscow: Literaturno-izdatel'skii otdel narodnogo kommissariata po prosveshcheniiu, 1919.
Boas, Franz. *Primitive Art*. Oslo: H. Aschehoug, 1927.
Bogdanov, Igor. *Dym otechestva, ili kratkaia istoriia tabakokureniia*. Moscow: Novoe literaturnoe obozrenie, 2007.
Bois, Yve-Alain. "Malevitch, le carré, le degré zéro." *Macula* 1 (1976): 28–49.
Bokov, Anna. "VKhUTEMAS training." *Pavilion of the Russian Federation at the 14th International Architecture Exhibition*, Venice Biennale, 2014.
Borislavov, Rad. "Do-It-Yourself!" In *Adventures in the Soviet Imaginary: Children's Books and Graphic Art*, edited by Robert Bird, 28–29. Chicago: The University of Chicago Library, 2011.
———. "'O zakonakh kino' V. Shklovskogo: Predislovie k republikatsii." *Novoe literaturnoe obozrenie* 4, no. 128 (2014): 144–148.
Borovskii, Vladimir. "Chto takoe psikhologiia?" *Krasnaia nov′* 4 (1927): 158.
Bowlt, John E. "Constructivism and Russian Stage Design." *Performing Arts Journal* 1, no. 3 (Winter 1977): 62–84.
———. "The Marionettes of Alexandra Exter." *Russian History/ Histoire russe* 8, nos. 1–2 (1981): 219–32.
Boym, Svetlana. *Common Places: Mythologies of Everyday Life in Russia*. Cambridge, MA and London: Harvard University Press, 1994.
Braun, Marta. *Picturing Time: The Work of Etienne Jules-Marey (1830–1904)*. Chicago: University of Chicago Press, 1992.
Brigada Lenbiuro RosARRK M. Bleiman, M. Kalatozov, I. Krinkin, I. Kovarskii, I. Trauberg "Bez chutkogo ideinogo zamysla," *Kino* 23 (May 10, 1933): 3.
Brigada LenRosARRK, M. Bleiman, I. Kovarskii, M. Kalatozov, I. Krinkin, and I. Trauberg. "Ne o kartine." *Kino* 30 (June 22, 1933): 3.
Brik, Osip. "Khudozhnik i kommuna." *Izobrazitel′noe iskusstvo* 1 (1919): 25–26.
———. "Lef i kino: stenograma soveshchaniia." *Novyi LEF* 11–12 (1927): 50–71.
Bristow, Maxine. "Continuity of Touch—Textile as Silent Witness." In *The Textile Reader*, edited by Jessica Hemmings, 44–53. London: Berg, 2012.
Brooks, Jeffrey. "Public and Private Values in the Soviet Press, 1921–1928." *Slavic Review* 48, no. 1 (Spring 1989): 16–35.
Bruno, Giuliana. *Atlas of Emotion: Journeys in Art, Architecture and Film*. New York: Verso, (2002) 2007.
———. *Surface: Matters of Aesthetics, Materiality, and Media*. Chicago: Chicago University Press, 2014.

Buchloh, Benjamin H. C. "From Faktura to Factography." *October* 30 (Autumn 1984): 82–119.
Buck-Morss, Susan. *The Dialectics of Seeing: Walter Benjamin and the Arcades Project.* Cambridge, MA: MIT Press, 1989.
Bukharin, Nikolai. "Enchmeniada (k voprosu ob ideologicheskom vyrozhdenii)." *Krasnaia nov´* 6 (1923): 145–79.
———. *Historical Materialism: A System of Sociology.* New York and Abingdon: Routledge, 2011.
Bulgakowa, Oksana (Oksana Bulgakova). "Sergei Eizenshtein i ego 'psikhologicheskii Berlin': mezhdu psikhoanalizom i strukturnoi psikhologiei." *Kinovedcheskie zapiski* 2 (1988): 174–191.
———. *Sergei Eisenstein. Drei Utopien—Architekturentwürfe zur Filmtheorie.* Berlin: Potemkin, 1996.
———. *Sergei Eisenstein: A Biography.* Berlin: Potemkin, 2001.
———. *Sovetskii slukhoglaz: kino i ego organy chuvstv.* Moscow: Novoe literaturnoe obozrenie, 2010.
———. "From Expressive Movement to the 'Basic Problem': the Vygotsky-Luria-Eisensteinian Theory of Art." In *The Cambridge Handbook of Cultural-Historical Psychology*, edited by Anton Yasnitsky, Renée van der Veer, and Michel Ferrari, 423–48. Cambridge: Cambridge University Press, 2014.
Burch, Noël. *Life to Those Shadows.* Edited and translated by Ben Brewster. Berkeley: University of California Press, 1990.
Caillois, Roger. *Les jeux et les hommes: le masque et le vertige.* Paris: Gallimard, 1958.
Carter, Erica. "Introduction." In *Béla Balázs: Early Film Theory*, edited by Erica Carter, xxiv-xxv. New York and London: Berghahn, 2010.
Casetti, Francesco. *Eye of the Century: Film, Experience, Modernity.* New York: Columbia University Press, 2008.
Cavendish, Philip. "The Hand that Turns the Handle: Camera Operators and the Poetics of the Camera in Pre-Revolutionary Russian Film." *The Slavonic and East European Review* 82, no. 2 (2004): 201–45.
———. *Soviet Mainstream Cinematography: The Silent Era.* London: UCL Arts and Humanities Publications, 2008.
———. *The Men with the Movie Camera: The Poetics of Visual Style in Soviet Avant-Garde Cinema of the 1920s.* New York and Oxford: Berghahn, 2013.
Chadaga, Julia Bekman. "Light in Captivity: Spectacular Glass and Soviet Power in the 1920s and 1930s." *Slavic Review* 66, no. 1 (Spring 2007): 82–105.
———. *Optical Play: Glass, Vision and Spectacle in Russian Culture.* Evanston, IL: Northwestern University Press, 2014.
Chebotarevskii, A. "Kinematograf kak metod." In *Kinematograf: sbornik statei*, 54–62. Moscow: Gosizdat, 1919.
Cherennyi, A. "Vyzov meshchanstvu: o teme 'Odna.'" *Kino* 59 (November 1, 1931): 3.
Cherviakov, E. "Moi syn (k vypusku v prokat)." *Rabochii i teatr* 33 (1928): 13.

Chion, M. *The Voice in Cinema*. Edited and translated by Claudia Gorbman. New York and Chichester: Columbia University Press, 1999.
Chomentowski, Gabrielle. "Vostokkino and the Foundation of Central Asian Cinema." In *Cinema in Central Asia: Rewriting Cultural Histories*, edited by Michael Rouland, Birgit Beumers, and Galina Abikeyeva, 33–45. London: I. B. Tauris, 2013.
Chubarov, Igor'. *Kollektivnaia chuvstvennost': teorii i praktiki levogo avangarda*. Moscow: Izdatel'skii dom Vysshei shkoly ekonomiki, 2014.
Chukovskii, Kornei. *Malen'kie deti*. Moscow: Krasnaia gazeta, 1928.
Chuzhak, Nikolai. "Pod znakom zhiznestroeniia." *LEF* 1 (1923): 12–39.
Christie, Ian. "Down to Earth: Aelita Relocated." In *Inside the Film Factory: New Approaches to Russian and Soviet Cinema*, edited by Ian Christie and Richard Taylor, 80–102. New York and London: Routledge, 1991.
Clark, Katerina. *The Soviet Novel: History as Ritual*, 3rd ed. Bloomington: Indiana University Press, 2000.
———. *Moscow, The Fourth Rome: Stalinism, Cosmopolitanism, and the Evolution of Soviet Culture 1931–41*. Cambridge, MA: Harvard University Press, 2011.
Classen, Constance. *The Deepest Sense: A Cultural History of Touch*. Urbana-Champaign: University of Illinois Press, 2012.
Classen, Constance, and David Howes. *Ways of Sensing: Understanding the Senses in Society*. New York and London: Routledge, 2014.
Clifford, James. "On Ethnographic Surrealism." *Comparative Studies in Society and History* 23, no. 4 (October 1981): 539–64.
Comolli, Jean-Louis. "Machines of the Visible." In *The Cinematic Apparatus*, edited by Teresa De Lauretis and Stephen Heath, 121–50. London: Macmillan, 1980.
Cooke, Catherine. *Russian Avant-garde: Theories of Art, Architecture and the City*. London: Academy Editions, 1995.
Copjec, Joan. "The Sartorial Superego." *October* 50 (Autumn 1989): 56–95.
Crary, Jonathan. *Techniques of the Observer*. Cambridge, MA: MIT Press, 1992.
———. *Suspensions of Perception: Attention, Spectacle, and Modern Culture*. Cambridge, MA: MIT Press, 2001.
Cushing, Frank Hamilton. "Manual Concepts: A Study of the Influence of Hand-Usage on Culture Growth." *American Anthropologist* 5, no. 4 (October 1892): 289–318.
Cvetkovski, Roland, and Alexis Hofmeister, eds. *An Empire of Others: Creating Ethnographic Knowledge in Imperial Russia and the USSR*. Budapest and New York: Central European University Press, 2014.
Danius, Sara. *The Senses of Modernism: Technology, Perception and Aesthetics*. Ithaca: Cornell University Press, 2002.
Dashkova, Tat'iana. "Nevidimye miru riushi: odezhda v sovetskom predvoennom i voennom kino." *Teoriia mody: Odezhda. Telo. Kul'tura* 3 (2007): 149–162.

Republished in Dashkova, Tat′iana. *Telesnost′—Ideologiia—Kinematograf: Vizual′nyi kanon i sovetskaia povsednevnost′*, 104–13. Moscow: Novoe literaturnoe obozrenie, 2013.

———. *Telesnost′—Ideologiia—Kinematograf: Vizual′nyi kanon i sovetskaia povsednevnost′*. Moscow: Novoe literaturnoe obozrenie, 2013.

David-Fox, Michael, Peter Holquist, and Alexander Martin, eds. *Orientalism and Empire in Russia: Kritika Historical Studies 3*. Bloomington, IN: Slavica, 2006.

Davydov, I. "Order na zhizn′." *Sovetskoe kino* 1 (1928): 5–7.

Davydova, S. A. *Russkoe kruzhevo*. Saint Petersburg: Ministerstvo zemledeliia, 1909.

De Lauretis, Teresa, and Stephen Heath, eds. *The Cinematic Apparatus*. London: Macmillan, 1980.

DeBlasio, Alyssa. "Choreographing Space, Time and Dikovinki in the Films of Evgenii Bauer." *The Russian Review* 66, no. 4 (2007): 671–92.

Debord, Guy. *Society of the Spectacle*. Translated by Fredy Perlman. London: Black and Red Books, 1970.

Delaney Grossman, Joan, and Ruth Rischin. *William James in Russian Culture*. Oxford: Lexington, 2003.

Deleuze, Gilles. *Cinema 1: The Movement Image*. London: Athlone, 1986.

———. *Francis Bacon: Logique de la sensation*. Paris: Editions du seuil, 2013.

Deleuze, Gilles, and Félix Guattari. *A Thousand Plateaus*. Translated by Brian Massumi. Minneapolis: University of Minnesota Press, 1987.

Delluc, Louis (L. Delliuk). *Photogénie*. Paris: de Brunhoff, 1920. Reprinted in Delluc, Louis. *Ecrits cinématographiques I: Le cinéma et les cinéastes*. Edited by Pierre Lherminier. 33–77. Paris: Cinémathèque française, 1985.

———. *Fotogeniia kino*. Translated by T. Sorokin. Moscow: Novye vekhi, 1924.

Demin, Viktor. "'Emotsional′nyi stsenarii' (publikatsiia i predislovie D. G. Virena)." *Kinovedcheskie zapiski* 86 (2008): 266–97.

Denisoff, Dennis, ed. *The Nineteenth-Century Child and Consumer Culture*. Aldershot, UK: Ashgate, 2008.

Deriabin, A. S., ed. *Letopis′ rossiiskogo kino 1863–1929*. Moscow: Materik, 2004.

———. *Letopis′ rossiiskogo kino, 1930–1945*. Moscow: Materik, 2007.

Derrida, Jacques. *Le Toucher, Jean-Luc Nancy*. Paris: Galilée, 2000.

Dewey, John (Dzh. D′iui.). *Vvedenie v filosofiiu vospitaniia*. Moscow: Rabotnik prosveshcheniia, 1921.

———. *Shkoly budushchego*. Moscow: Rabotnik prosveshcheniia, 1921.

———. *Shkola i obshchestvo*. Moscow: Rabotnik prosveshcheniia, 1925.

———. *Impressions of Soviet Russia and the Revolutionary World: Mexico-China-Turkey*. New York: New Republic, 1929.

———. *Democracy and Education*. New York: Free Press, 1966 [1915].

Dinamov, S. S. "Vstupitel′noe slovo S. Dinamova." In *Za bol′shoe kinoiskusstvo*. 7–22. Moscow: Finofotoizdat, 1935.

Dobrenko, Evgenii. "The School Tale in Children's Literature of Socialist Realism." In *Russian Children's Literature and Culture*, edited by Marina Balina and Larissa Rudova, 43–66. New York and London: Routledge, 2008.

———. *Stalinist Cinema and the Production of History: Museum of the Revolution*. New Haven, CT: Yale University Press, 2008.

Dobrenko, Evgenii, Marina Balina, and Iurii Murashov, eds. *Sovetskoe bogatstvo: stat′i o kul′ture, literature i kino*. Saint Petersburg: Nevskii prospect, 2002.

Dubrovskii-Eshke, Boris. "Voprosy dekoratsionnoi tekhniki." *Iskusstvo kino* 6 (1937): 60–64.

Douglas, Charlotte (Sharlotta Douglas). "Bespredmetnost′ i dekorativnost′." *Voprosy iskusstvoznaniia* 2–3 (1993): 96–106.

Dunham, Vera. *In Stalin's Time: Middleclass Values in Soviet Fiction*. Cambridge: Cambridge University Press, 1976.

Efimova, Elena. "Traditsionnye biblioteki, biblioteki igrushek i igroteki: istoriia i perspektivy." *Bibliotekovedenie* 1 (2010): 39–45.

Eikhenbaum, Boris. "Kak sdelana 'Shinel′' Gogolia." In *Poetika: sbornik po teorii poeticheskogo iazyka*, edited by Boris Eikhenbaum, 151–166. Petrograd: tip. Leshtukov, 1919. Reprinted in Eikhenbaum, Boris. *O proze. O poezii. Sbornik statei*. 45–63. Leningrad: Khudozhestvennaia literatura, leningradskoe otdelenie, 1985.

———. *Skvoz′ literaturu: sbornik statei*. Leningrad: Academia, 1924.

———. "Problemy kinostilistiki." In *Poetika kino*, edited by Boris Eikhenbaum, 11–52. Moscow: Kinopechat′, 1927. Reprinted in *Poetika kino*, edited by Boris Eikhenbaum, 13–39. Berkeley: Berkeley Slavic Specialties, 1984. Reprinted in English as Eikhenbaum, Boris. "Problems of Film Stylistics." *Screen* 15, no. 3 (Autumn 1974): 7–32.

Eisenstein, Sergei (Sergei Eizenshtein). "K voprosu o materialisticheskom podkhode k forme." *Kinozhurnal ARK* 4–5 (1925): 5–8. Reprinted in Eizenshtein, Sergei. *Izbrannye proizvedeniia v shesti tomakh*. Tom 1, 109–116. Moscow: Iskusstvo, 1964. Excerpt reprinted in English as "The Problem of a Materialist Approach to Form." In *Lines of Resistance: Dziga Vertov and the Twenties*, edited by Yuri Tsivian, 126–128. Sacile: Le Giornate del cinema muto, 2004.

———. "O pozitsii Bela Balasha." *Kino* 29 (July 20, 1926): 3.

———. "Bela zabyvaet nozhnitsy." *Kino* 32 (August 10, 1926): 3.

———. *Metod. Tom 1: Grundproblem*. Edited by N. I. Kleiman. Moscow: Muzei Kino, Eizenshtein-tsentr, 2002.

———. *Metod. Tom 2: Tainy masterov*. Edited by N. I. Kleiman. Moscow: Muzei Kino, Eizenshtein-tsentr, 2002.

———. "Imitation as Mastery." In *Eisenstein Rediscovered*, edited by Ian Christie and Richard Taylor, 65–69. London: Routledge, 2003.

Eizenshtein, Sergei and Sergei Tret′iakov. "Vyrazitel′noe dvizhenie." In *Mnemozina*: 2, edited by Ivanov Viacheslav, 292–305. Moscow: Editorial URSS, 2000.

Published in English as "Expressive Movement." In *Meyerhold, Eisenstein and Biomechanics: Actor Training in Revolutionary Russia*, edited by Alma Law and Mel Gordon, 173–192. Jefferson, NC, and London: McFarland, 1996.

Ekster, A. "V konstruktivnoi odezhde." *Atel´e* 1 (1923): 4.

Elsaesser, Thomas, and Malte Hagener. *Film Theory: An Introduction through the Senses*. New York and London: Routledge, 2010.

Enchmen, E. *Vosemnadsat´ tezisov o teorii 'novoi biologii' (proekt organizatsii Revoliutsionnogo nauchnogo Soveta Respubliki i vvedeniia sistemy fiziologicheskikh pasportov*. Piatigorsk: In. K.O. Severo-Kavkazkogo Revoliutsionnogo Komiteta, 1920.

Epstein, Jean. "Le sens 1 Bis." 27–44. *Bonjour Cinéma*. Paris: Éditions de la sirène, 1921.

———. "Magnification." In *French Film Theory and Criticism: A History/Anthology*. Vol. 1, 1907–1929, edited by Richard Abel, 235–40. Princeton: Princeton University Press, 1988.

Erenburg, Il´ia. "Novoe frantsuzskoe kino." *Sovetskoe kino* 4–5 (1926): 24.

Ermler, Fridrikh. "Avtobiograficheskie zametki." In *Fridrikh Ermler: dokumenty, stat´i, vospominaniia*, 90–97. Leningrad: Iskusstvo, 1974.

———. "O 'Parizhskom sapozhnike.'" In *Fridrikh Ermler: dokumenty, stat´i, vospominaniia*, 109–110. Leningrad: Iskusstvo, 1974.

Ertürk, Nergis. "Toward a Literary Communism: The 1926 Baku Turcological Congress," *Boundary 2*, no. 40, 2 (2013): 183–213.

———. "Baku, Literary Common." The 2014–2015 Report on the State of the Discipline of Comparative Literature. Accessed October 9, 2015. http://stateofthediscipline.acla.org/entry/baku-literary-common.

Esakiia, Leo. "Levoe dvizhenie v iskusstve Gruzii." *Novyi LEF* 19 (1927): 42–46.

Etkind, Alexander. *Eros of the Impossible: The History of Psychoanalysis in Russia*. Translated by Noah and Maria Rubins. Oxford: Westview, 1997.

———. *Internal Colonization: Russia's Imperial Experience*. Cambridge: Polity, 2011.

Fanon, Frantz. "Algeria Unveiled." In Fanon, Frantz, *A Dying Colonialism*, translated by Haakon Chevalier, 35–64. New York: Grove, 1967.

FEKS Collective. "'Zhenshchina Edisona': pervyi stsenarii feksov." Published with an introduction by Natal´ia Nusinova, *Kinovedcheskie zapiski* 7 (1990): 83–97.

Febvre, Lucien. *The Problem of Unbelief in the Sixteenth Century: the Religion of Rabelais*. Translated by Beatrice Gottlieb. Cambridge, MA: Harvard University Press, 1982.

Fel´dman, K. "Byt v sovetskom kino." *Sovetskii ekran* 27 (1928): 4.

———. "V bol´shom gorode." *Sovetskii ekran* 21 (1928): 8.

Fineburg, Jonathan, ed. *Discovering Child Art: Essays on Childhood, Primitivism and Modernism*. Princeton, NJ: Princeton University Press, 2001.

Fischer, Lucy, ed. *Art Direction and Production Design*. New Brunswick, NJ: Rutgers University Press, 2015.

Fitzpatrick, Sheila. *Tear off the Masks! Identity and Imposture in Twentieth-Century Russia*. Princeton, NJ and Oxford: Princeton University Press, 2005.

Flatley, Jonathan. *Affective Mapping: Melancholia and the Politics of Modernism*. Cambridge, MA: Harvard University Press, 2008.
Flusser, Vilém. *Towards a Philosophy of Photography*. London: Reaktion, 2000.
Fore, Devin. "Dziga Vertov, the First Shoemaker of Soviet Cinema." *Configurations* 18, no. 3 (2010): 363–82.
Foucault, Michel. *Discipline and Punish: The Birth of the Prison*. Translated by Alan Sheridan. New York: Pantheon, 1977.
Frankford, Iu. V. "G. I. Chelpanov v roli 'Marksista-psikhologa.'" *Pravda* (October 24, 1926): 2.
Friche, V. M. *Ocherki sotsial'noi istorii iskusstv*. Moscow: Novaia Moskva, 1923.
Fried, Michael. *Absorption and Theatricality: Painting and Beholder in the Age of Diderot*. Chicago: University of Chicago Press, 1988.
Frisby, David and Mike Featherstone, eds. *Simmel on Culture*. London: Sage, 1997.
Froebel, Friedrich. *The Education of Man*. Translated by William Nicholas Hailman. Cambridge MA: D. Appleton, 1887.
Gabrilovich, Evgenii. "Problema geroia." *Kino* 24 (May 22, 1935): 3.
———. "Rasskazy o tom, chto proizoshlo." *Iskusstvo kino* 4 (1964): 60–69.
Gaivorovskii, A. "Chuvstva i emotsii." In *Elementy obshchei psikhologii: osnovnye mekhanizmy chelovecheskogo povedeniia*, edited by K. N. Kornilov, 130–137. Moscow: Izdanie BZO pri pedfake 2 MGU, 1930.
Galadzhev, Petr. "Tvorchestvo konchilos' do, do...?!: Iz dnevnikov Petra Galadzheva." Edited by Natal'ia Galadzheva, 60–114. *Kinovedcheskie zapiski* 99 (2011/12).
Gan, Aleksei. *Konstruktivizm*. Tver': Tverskoe Izdatel'stvo, 1922.
———. "Kinematograf i kinematografiia." *Kinofot* 1 (August 25–31, 1922): 1.
Gandy, David Ross. *Marx and History: From Primitive Society to the Communist Future*. Austin: University of Texas Press, 1979.
Garrington, Abbie. *Haptic Modernism: Touch and the Tactile in Modernist Writing*. Edinburgh: Edinburgh University Press, 2013.
Gastev, Aleksei. *Kak nado rabotat': Osnovnye pravila, razrabotannye Tsentralnym institutom truda*. Odessa: Odesskiy gubprofsovet, 1921. Reprinted as *Kak nado rabotat'*, edited by N. M. Bakhrakh. Moscow: Ekonomika, 1966.
———. *Trudovye ustanovki*. Moscow: Ekonomika, 1924.
Gazdenko, K. "Sovetskii byt na sovetskom ekrane." *Kinofront* 1 (1927): 9–12.
Gereb, Anna, ed. "Riadom s Eizenshteinom...: Bela Balash vo VGIKe." *Kinovedcheskie zapiski* 25 (1995): 229–43.
Gordon, Mel. "Valentin Parnakh: Apostle of Eccentric Dance." *Experiment/Eksperiment* 2 (1996): 423–41.
Gorham, Michael. "Tongue-tied Writers: The Rabsel'kor Movement and the Voice of the 'New Intelligentsia' in Early Soviet Russia." *The Russian Review* 55 (July 1996): 412–29.
Gorshtein. "Igroteka TsPKiO im. M. Gor'kogo." *Sovetskaia igrushka* 1 (1935): 16.
Gough, Maria. "Faktura: The Making of the Russian Avant-garde." *RES: Anthropology and Aesthetics* 36 (Autumn 1999): 33–59.

———. *The Artist as Producer: Russian Constructivism in Revolution*. Berkeley and London: University of California Press, 2005.
Graffy, Julian. *Bed and Sofa*. London: I. B. Tauris, 2000.
———. "'An Unpretentious Picture'?: Igor´ Savchenko's A Chance Encounter." *Studies in Russian and Soviet Cinema* 6, no. 3 (2012): 301–18.
Graham, Loren R. *Science and Philosophy in the Soviet Union*. London: Allen Lane, 1973.
Grashchenkova, Irina. "Vospitanie chuvstv: o stsenarii i fil´me 'Ukhaby.'" *Iz istorii kino* 9 (1974): 86–95.
———. *Abram Room*. Moscow: Iskusstvo, 1977.
———. *Kinoantropologiia XX/20*. Moscow: Izdatel´stvo 'Chelovek', 2014.
Grebner, Grigorii. "'RUR' ('Gibel´ sensatsii')." *Kinovedcheskie zapiski* 45 (2000): 234–44.
Gromov, Iu. *Vladimir Egorov: Khudozhnik v kino*. Moscow: Biuro propagandy sovetskogo kinoiskusstva, 1973.
Gronow, Jukka. *Caviar with Champagne: Common Luxury and the Ideals of the Good Life in Stalin's Russia*. Oxford and New York: Berg, 2003.
Gropius, Walter. "Towards a Living Architecture: Ornament and Modern Architecture." *American Architect and Architecture* (January 1938), cited in Wigley, Mark, *White Walls, Designer Dresses: The Fashioning of Modern Architecture*. 110. Cambridge, MA and London: MIT Press, (1995) 2001.
Groys, Boris and Michael Hagemeister, eds. *Die neue Menschheit: Biopolitische Utopien in Russland des 20 Jahrhunderts*. Frankfurt: Suhrkamp, 2001.
Gurianova, Nina. *Exploring Color: Olga Rozanova and the Early Russian Avant-garde, 1910–1918*. New York and Oxford: Routledge, 2000.
Gutkin, Irina. *The Cultural Origins of the Socialist Realist Aesthetic 1890–1934*. Evanston, IL: Northwestern University Press, 1999.
Halfin, Igal. *Terror in My Soul: Communist Autobiographies on Trial*. Cambridge, MA: Harvard University Press, 2003.
Hansen, Miriam Bratu. "'With Skin and Hair': Kracauer's Theory of Film, Marseille 1940." *Critical Enquiry* 19, no. 3 (Spring 1993): 437–69.
———. "Introduction." In *Theory of Film: The Redemption of Physical Reality*, by Siegfried Kracauer, vii-xlvi. Princeton: Princeton University Press, (1960) 1997.
———. "Room for Play: Benjamin's Gamble with Cinema." *October* 109 (Summer 2004): 1–45.
———. *Cinema and Experience: Siegfried Kracauer, Walter Benjamin, and Theodor W. Adorno*. Berkeley: University of California Press, 2012.
Hansen-Löve, A. (A. Khansen-Leve). *Russkii formalizm: Metologicheskaia rekonstruktsiia razvitiia na osnove printsipa ostraneniia*. Translated by Sergei Romashko. Moscow: Litres, 2013.
Hansen-Löve, Aage, Brigitte Obermayer, and Georg Witte, eds. *Form und Wirkung: Phänomenologische i empirische Kunstwissenschaft in der Sowjetunion der 1920er Jahre*. Paderborn: Wilhelm Fink, 2013.

Hawkings, Stephanie L. "William James, Gustav Fechner and Early Psychophysics." *Frontiers in Physiology* 2 (2011): 1–129.
Heidegger, Martin. *Sein und Zeit*. Tübingen: Max Niemeyer Verlag, (1926) 1993.
Hellbeck, Jochen. *Revolution on My Mind: Writing a Diary under Stalin*. Cambridge MA: Harvard University Press, 2009.
Hellebust, Rolf. *Flesh to Metal: Soviet Literature and the Alchemy of Revolution*. Ithaca: Cornell University Press, 2003.
Heller-Roazan, Daniel. *The Inner Touch: Archaeology of a Sensation*. New York: Zone, 2007.
Hilton, Alison. *Russian Folk Art*. Bloomington: Indiana University Press, 1995.
Hirsch, Francine F. *Empire of Nations: Ethnographic Knowledge and the Making of the Soviet Union*. Ithaca: Cornell University Press, 2005.
Holl, Ute. "Die Bildung des Menschen im Kino-Experiment. Laboratorien, Apparaturen und Dziga Vertovs Kinowahrheit als Medientheorie." In *Laien, Lektüren, Laboratorium: Künste und Wissenschaften in Russland 1860–1960*, edited by Matthias Schwartz, Wladimir Velminski, and Torben Philipp, 347–93. Frankfurt: Peter Lang, 2008.
Holt, Katharine M. "The Rise of Insider Iconography: Visions of Soviet Turkmenia in Russian-Language Literature and Film, 1921–1935." PhD diss., Columbia University, 2013.
Honarpisheh, Farbod. "The Oriental 'Other' in Soviet cinema, 1929–34." *Critique: Critical Middle Eastern Studies* 14, no. 2 (Summer 2005): 185–201.
Huizinga, Johan. *Homo Ludens: A Study of the Play Element in Culture*. London: Roy Publishers, (1938) 1950.
Iampolskii, Anton (Anton Yasnitsky). "K istorii kul'turno-istoricheskoi geshtal't-psikhologii: Vygotskii, Luriia, Koffka, Levin i drugie [A History of Cultural-Historical Gestalt Psychology: Vygotsky, Luria, Koffka, Lewin and Others]." *Dubna Psychological Journal* 5, no. 1 (2015): 60–97.
———. "Bibliografiia osnovnykh sovetskikh rabot po kross-kul'turnoi psikhonerologii i psikhologii natsional'nykh men'shinstv perioda kollektivizatsii, industrializatsii i kul'turnoi revoliutsii (1928–1932)." *Dubna Psychological Journal* 3 (2013): 97–113.
Iampolskii, Anton, Renée van der Veer, and Michel Ferrari, eds. *The Cambridge Handbook of Cultural-Historical Psychology*. Cambridge: Cambridge University Press, 2014.
Iampolskii, Mikhail (Mikhail Yampolsky). "Kino bez kino." *Iskusstvo kino* 6 (1988): 88–94.
———. "Reality at Second Hand." Translated by Derek Spring. *Historical Journal of Film, Radio and Television* 11, no. 2 (1991): 161–71.
———. "Kuleshov's Experiments and the New Anthropology of the Actor." In *Silent Film*, edited by Richard Abel, 45–67. London: Athlone, 1996.
———. *The Memory of Tiresias: Intertextuality and Film*. Berkeley and London: University of California Press, 1998.

———. "The Essential Bone Structure: Mimesis in Eisenstein." In *Eisenstein Rediscovered*, edited by Ian Christie and Richard Taylor, 187–88. London: Routledge, 2003.

———. "Rossiia: kino i kul′tura sovremennosti, ili Regress v roli progressa." *Kinovedcheskie zapiski* 78 (2006): 4–20.

Iasnitskii A. See Yasnitsky, Anton.

Iezuitov, Nikolai. "O stiliakh sovetskogo kino: (Kontseptsiia razvitiia sovetskogo kinoiskusstva)." *Sovetskoe kino* 3–4 (1933): 35–55.

———. "O stiliakh sovetskogo kino 3." *Sovetskoe kino* 5–6, (1933): 31–47.

———. *Pudovkin: puti tvorchestva*. Moscow: 1937.

Ingold, Tim. "The Textility of Making." *Cambridge Journal of Economics* 34 (2010): 91–102.

———. *Making: Anthropology, Archaeology, Art and Architecture*. London: Routledge, 2013.

Inkizhinov, Valerii. "Bair i ia." *Sovetskii ekran* 33 (August 14, 1928): 8–9.

Ioffe, Ieremiia. *Kul′tura i stil′: sistema i printsipy sotsiologii iskusstv*. Leningrad: Priboi, 1927. Reprinted as "Iz knigi 'Kul′tura i stil′.'" In Ioffe, I., *Izbrannoe: 1920-30-e gg.*, edited by M. S. Kagan, I. P. Smirnov, N. Ia. Grigor′eva, 43–101. Saint Petersburg: ID Petropolis, 2006.

———. *Sinteticheskaia istoriia iskusstv: vvedenie v istoriiu khudozhestvennogo myshleniia*. Leningrad: Lenizogiz, 1933. Reprinted as "Iz knigi 'Sinteticheskaia istoriia iskusstv.'" In Ioffe, I., *Izbrannoe: 1920-30-e gg.*, edited by M. S. Kagan, I. P. Smirnov, N. Ia. Grigor′eva, 101–270. Saint Petersburg: ID Petropolis, 2006.

———. *Sinteticheskoe izuchenie iskusstv i zvukovoe kino*. Leningrad: 1938. Reprinted as "Iz knigi 'Sinteticheskoe izuchenie iskusstva i zvukovoe kino.'" In Ioffe, I., *Izbrannoe: 1920–30-e gg.*, edited by M. S. Kagan, I. P. Smirnov, N. Ia. Grigor′eva, 270–485. Saint Petersburg: ID Petropolis, 2006.

———. *Izbrannoe: 1920–30-e gg.*, Edited by M. S. Kagan, I. P. Smirnov, N. Ia. Grigor′eva. Saint Petersburg: ID Petropolis, 2006.

Irinin [pseud.]. "Arkhitektura i dekoratsii." *Sovetskii ekran* 5 (1925): 32.

Ivleva, Viktoria. "Functions of Textile and Sartorial Artifacts in Russian Folktales." *Marvels and Tales* 23, no. 2 (2009): 268–99.

Iukov, K. "Odna." *Kino* 55 (6 October 6, 1931): 3.

———. "Zametki k templanu." *Sovetskoe kino* 11 (1933): 5.

———. "Ob odnoi osobennosti obraza v kinoiskusstve." *Iskusstvo kino* 12, (1936): 21–23.

Iutkevich, Sergei. "Dekoriruem svetom." *Sovetskii ekran* 29 (1925): 43. Reprinted in Iutkevich, Sergei, *Sobranie sochinenii v trekh tomakh*. Tom 1: *Molodost′*. 304–5. Moscow: Iskusstvo, 1990.

———. "Plat′e kartiny." *Sovetskii ekran* 39 (1925): 7.

———. "Dekorativnoe oformlenie fil′ma." In *Predatel′* (brochure to accompany the film's release). Extracts reprinted in Iutekevich, Sergei, *Sobranie sochinenii v trekh tomakh*. Tom 1: *Molodost′*. 315. Moscow: Iskusstvo, 1990.

———. *Chelovek na ekrane: chetyre besedy o kinoiskusstve; dnevnik rezhissera.* Moscow: Goskinoizdat, 1947.
Ivanov, Viacheslav. "Analiz glubinnykh struktur semioticheskikh system iskusstva." In Ivanov, Viacheslav, *Ocherki po istorii semiotiki v SSSR.* Moscow: Nauka, 1976.
Jacobs, Karen. *The Eye's Mind: Literary Modernism and Visual Culture.* Ithaca: Cornell University Press, 2001.
Jameson, Fredric. *Signatures of the Visible.* New York and London: Routledge, 1990.
Jay, Martin. *Downcast Eyes: The Denigration of Vision in Twentieth-Century French Thought.* Berkeley and London: University of California Press, 1993.
Johansson, Kurt. *Aleksej Gastev. Proletarian Bard of the Machine Age.* Stockholm: Almqvist and Wiksell, 1983.
Johnson, Christopher. "Bricoleur and Bricolage: From Metaphor to Universal Concept." *Paragraph* 35, no. 3 (November 2012): 355–72.
Joravsky, David. *Russian Psychology: A Critical History.* Oxford: Blackwell, 1989.
Kaganovsky, Lilya. "The Voice of Technology and the End of Soviet Silent Film: Grigorii Kozintsev and Leonid Trauberg's 'Alone.'" *Studies in Russian and Soviet Cinema* 1, no. 3 (2007): 265–81.
———. *How the Soviet Man was Unmade: Cultural Fantasy and Male Subjectivity Under Stalin.* Pittsburgh: University of Pittsburgh Press, 2008.
———. "The Homogeneous Thinking Subject, or Soviet Cinema Learns to Sing." *Studies in Russian and Soviet Cinema* 6, no. 3 (2012): 281–99.
———. *Voice of Technology: Soviet Cinema's Transition to Sound, 1928–1935.* Bloomington: Indiana University Press, forthcoming 2018.
Kaganovsky, Lilya, and Masha Salazkina, eds. *Sound, Speech, Music in Soviet and Post-Soviet Cinema.* Bloomington: Indiana University Press, 2014.
Kalinin, Il´ia. "Istoriia kak iskusstvo chlenorazdel´nosti (istoricheskii opyt i metaliteraturnaia praktika russkikh formalistov)." *Novoe literaturnoe obozrenie* 71 (2005): 103–32.
Kandinskii, Vasilii. "Plan for the Physico-Psychological Department of the Russian Academy of Artistic Sciences." In *Russian Art of the Avant-Garde: Theory and Criticism, 1902–1934,* rev. ed., edited by John E. Bowlt, 196–98. London: Thames and Hudson, 1988.
Kapterev, Sergei. "Mzago and Gela." *Le giornate del cinema muto, 1–8 ottobre 2011: Catalogo.* 82. Cineteca del Fruili, 2011.
———. "A Simple Case," *Le giornate del cinema muto 2012: Catalogo.* 128–29. Pordenone: La Cineteca del Friuli, 2012.
Karaganov, Aleksandr V. "Potomok Chingis-khana." In Karaganov, Aleksandr, *Vsevolod Pudovkin.* Moscow: Iskusstvo, 1983.
Karpenko, L. A., ed. *Psikhologicheskii leksikon. Entsiklopedicheskii slovar´ v 6-i tomakh.* Tom 1. *Istoriia psikhologii v litsakh.* Personalii. Moscow: Per Se, 2005.
Kassil´, L. "Rvanye bashmaki." *Izvestiia* 315 (December 29, 1933): 4. Reprinted as "Torn Boots" Translated by Jamie Miller. In "Margarita Barskaia and the

Emergence of Children's Cinema," edited by Birgit Beumers, Nikolai Izvolov, Natalia Miloserdova, and Natalia Riabchikova, 256–58. *Studies in Russian and Soviet Cinema* 3, no. 2 (2009).

Kassof, Brian. "A Book of Socialism: Stalinist Culture and the First Edition of the Bol´shaia sovetskaia entsiklopediia." *Kritika: Explorations in Russian and Eurasian History* 6, no. 1 (Winter 2005): 55–95.

Kaufman, N. O. "Veshch´ na ekrane." *Sovetskii ekran* 41 (1927): 5.

Kazanskii, Boris. "O prirode kino." In *Poetika kino*, edited by Boris Eikhenbaum. Moscow: Kinopechat, 1927. Reprinted in *Poetika kino*, edited by Boris Eikhenbaum, 89–135. Berkeley: Berkeley Slavic Specialties, 1984.

Keller, Shoshanna. *To Moscow, Not Mecca: The Soviet Campaign Against Islam in Central Asia*. Westport, CT: Praeger, 2001.

Kelly, Catriona. *Children's World: Growing Up in Russia, 1890–1991*. New Haven, CT: Yale University Press, 2007.

Kelly, Mary B. "The Ritual Fabrics of Russian Village Women." In *Russia—Women—Culture*, edited by Helena Goscilo and Beth Holmgren, 151–76. Bloomington: Indiana University Press, 1996.

Kenez, Peter. "The Cultural Revolution in Cinema." *Slavic Review* 47, no. 3 (Fall 1988): 414–33.

Khalid, Adeeb. "Russian History and the Debate over Orientalism." *Kritika* 1, no. 4 (2000): 691–99.

———. "Backwardness and the Quest for Civilization: Early Soviet Central Asia in Comparative Context." *Slavic Review* 65, no. 2 (Summer 2006): 231–51.

Khanzhonkova, Vera. "Iz vospominanii o dorevoliutsionnom kino." In *Iz istorii kino: materialy i dokumenty* 5, 120–31. Moscow: Akademiia nauk, 1962.

Khersonskii, Kh. "Bor´ba faktov, vzgliadov, idei i sposobov vozdeistviia." *Sovetskoe kino* 9–10 (1926): 21–26.

———. "Kino. Predatel´." *Pravda* 225 (September 30, 1926): 5.

———. "Namus." *Kino* 45 (October 23, 1926): 3.

———. "Chto na ekrane." *Sovetskii ekran* 16 (1928): 23.

Kholodnyi, T. "Starushki i igrushki." *Pravda* 33 (February 3, 1936): 4.

Khomitsky, Maria. "World Literature, Soviet Style: A Forgotten Episode in the History of the Idea." *Ab imperio* 3 (2013): 119–54.

Kiaer, Christina. "Boris Arvatov's Socialist Objects." *October* 81 (Summer 1997): 105–18.

———. *Imagine No Possessions: The Socialist Objects of Russian Constructivism*. Cambridge, MA: MIT Press, 2005.

———. "Lyrical Socialist Realism." *October* 147 (Winter 2014): 56–77.

Kinchin, Juliet, and Aidan O'Connor, eds. *Century of the Child: Growing by Design, 1900–2000*. New York: Museum of Modern Art, 2012.

Kleiman, Naum. "'Stekliannyi dom' S. M. Eizenshteina: K istorii zamysla. Podgotovka teksta i kommentarii." *Iskusstvo kino* 3 (1979): 94–113.

———. "Introduction." In *Eisenstein on Disney*, edited by Naum Kleiman, translated by Alan Upchurch, i–xii. London: Methuen, 1988.

Knight, Nathaniel. "Grigor'ev in Orenburg: Russian Orientalism in the Service of Empire." *Slavic Review* 59, no. 1 (Spring 2000): 74–100.

———. "On Russian Orientalism: A Response to Adeeb Khalid." *Kritika* 1, no. 4 (2000): 701–15.

Kobrinets, F. *Knizhka-kino-seans o tom, kak pioner Gans stachechnyi komitet spas*, illus. by Isaak Eberil'. Leningrad: OGIZ, Molodaia gvardiia, 1931. Last accessed January 10, 2014. https://www.lib.uchicago.edu/e/webexhibits/sovietchildrensbooks/diy.html.

Kolomarov, V. "Veshch' v kino." *Kino i kul'tura* 9–10 (1929): 29–37.

Kolupaev, Dmitrii. "O dekoratsiiakh." *Kino-zhurnal ARK* 2 (1925): 34.

———. "Khudozhnik v kino-proizvodstve." *Kino-zhurnal ARK* 3 (1926): 18.

Kopp, Anatole. *Town and Revolution: Architecture and City Planning, 1917–35*. Translated by Thomas E. Burton. New York: George Brazilier, 1970.

Kornilov, K. N. "Psychology in the Light of Dialectic Materialism." In *Psychologies of 1930*, edited by Carl Murchison, 243–78. Worchester, MA: Clark University Press, 1930.

Korshunov, Ivan. *Detmashstroi, samodel'nye igrushki-mashiny*. Illustrated by L. Kapustin. Leningrad: OGIZ, Molodaia gvardiia, 1931.

Kostiukhina, Marina. *Detskii orakul. Po strannitsam nastol'no-pechatnykh igr*. Moscow: Novoe literaturnoe obozrenie, 2013.

Kozintsev, Grigorii. "Glubokii ekran." In Kozintsev, Grigorii, *Sobranie sochinenii v piati tomakh*. Tom 1, 17–312. Leningrad: Iskusstvo, 1982.

———. "Podgotovitel'nye materialy ko vtoromu izdaniiu 'Glubokogo ekrana.'" In Kozintsev, Grigorii, *Sobranie sochinenii v piati tomakh*. Tom 1, 313–56. Leningrad: Iskusstvo, 1982.

Kozlovskii, S. V. "Tekhnika kinoatel'e." *Kino i kul'tura* 4 (1929): 57–58.

Kozlovskii, S. V., and N. M. Kolin. *Khudozhnik-arkhitektor v kino*. Moscow: Teakinopechat', 1930.

Kozulin, Alex. *Psychology in Utopia: Towards a Social History of Soviet Psychology*. Cambridge, MA and London: MIT Press, 1984.

Kracauer, Siegfried. *The Mass Ornament: Weimar Essays*. Edited and translated by Thomas Y. Levin. Cambridge, MA: Harvard University Press, 1995.

———. *Theory of Film: The Redemption of Physical Reality*. Princeton: Princeton University Press, 1997.

Kravchenko, Al'bert. *Istoriia menedzhmenta*. Moscow: Akademicheskii proekt, 2005

Krementsov, Nikolai. "Eugenics in Russia and the Soviet Union." In *The Oxford Handbook of the History of Eugenics*, edited by Alison Bashford and Philippa Levine, 413–29. New York and Oxford: Oxford University Press, 2010.

Krinitskii, A. "Nuzhen reshiteln'yi sdvig." *Pravda* 72 (March 25, 1928): 4.

Krinkin, I. "Realizm i naturalizm v tvorchestve khudozhnikov kino." *Iskusstvo kino* 1 (1936): 15–20.

Kruchenykh, Aleksei. *Sobstvennye razskazy i risunki detei*. Saint Petersburg: "E U Y," 1914.

———. *Sobstvennye rasskazy, stikhi i pesni detei*. Oakland: Berkeley Slavic Specialties, 1996.

Krupskaia, Nadezhda. "Ob igrushkakh dlia doshkoliat." *Pedagogicheskie sochineniia*. Tom 6, 596. Moscow: Politizdat, 1980.

Krylova, Anna. "Beyond the Spontaneity-Consciousness Paradigm: 'Class Instinct' as a Promising Category of Historical Analysis." *Slavic Review* 62, no. 1 (Spring 2003): 1–23.

Kuleshov, Lev. "O zadachakh khudozhnika v kinematografe." *Vestnik kinematografii* 126 (1917): 15–16. Reprinted in Kuleshov, Lev, *Sobranie sochinenii v trekh tomakh*. Tom 1, *Teoriia. Kritika. Pedagogika*. 57–58. Moscow: Iskusstvo, 1987.

———. "Zadachi khudozhnika v kinematografe." *Vestnik kinematografii* 127 (1917): 37–38. Reprinted in Kuleshov, Lev, *Sobranie sochinenii v trekh tomakh*. Tom 1, *Teoriia. Kritika. Pedagogika*. 59–60. Moscow: Iskusstvo, 1987.

———. "Iskusstvo svetotvorchestva: osnovy myslei." *Kinogazeta* 12 (1918), 1–2. Reprinted in Kuleshov, Lev, *Sobranie sochinenii v trekh tomakh*. Tom 1, *Teoriia. Kritika. Pedagogika*. 61–63. Moscow: Iskusstvo, 1987.

———. "Znamia kinematografii." Published from the autograph copy in Kuleshov, Lev, *Sobranie sochinenii v trekh tomakh*. Tom 1, *Teoriia. Kritika. Pedagogika*. 63–86. Moscow: Iskusstvo, (1920, 1979) 1987.

———. "Montazh," *Kino-fot* 3 (1922): 12.

———. *Iskusstvo kino (moi opyt)*.Teakinopechat', 1929. Reprinted in Kuleshov, Lev, *Sobranie sochinenii v trekh tomakh*. Tom 1, *Teoriia. Kritika. Pedagogika*. 161–227. Moscow: Iskusstvo, 1987.

Kuleshov, Lev, and Aleksandra Khokhlova. *50 let v kino*. Moscow: Iskusstvo, 1975.

Kumarin, V., ed. *Anton Makarenko. His Life and Work in Education*. Moscow: Progress Publishers, 1976.

Kunichika, Michael. "'The Ecstasy of Breadth': The Odic and Whitmanesque in Dziga Vertov's 'One Sixth of the World.'" *Studies in Russian and Soviet Cinema* 6, no. 1 (2012): 53–74.

———. *Our Native Antiquity: Archaeology and Aesthetics in the Culture of Russian Modernism*. Brighton, MA: Academic Studies Press, 2015.

———. *How Soon is Now? Early Soviet Cinema and the Politics of Time*. Unpublished manuscript, forthcoming.

Kurek, Nikolai. "Razrushenie psikhotekhniki." *Novyi mir* 2 (1999): 153–65.

Kut, A. "Iskusstvo muzhestvennoi krasoty: doklad tov. S. S. Dinamova na soveshchanii tvorcheskikh rabotnikov sovetskoi kinematografii." *Sovetskoe iskusstvo* (January 11, 1935): 1.

Kuznetsova, V. A. *Mastera sovetskogo kino: Evgenii Enei*. Leningrad: Iskusstvo-Leningrad, 1966.

Ladovskii, Nikolai. "Psikhotekhnicheskaia laboratoriia arkhitektury (v poriadke postanovki voprosa) 10" *Izvestiia ANOVA* 1 (1926): 7. Reprinted in *Mastera sovetskoi arkhitektury ob arkhitekture: Izbrannye otryvki iz pisem, statei, vystuplenii i traktatov*. Tom 1, edited by M. G. Barkhin and Iu. S. Iaralov, 352. Moscow: Iskusstvo, 1975.

Lamanova, Nadezha. "Russkaia moda." *Krasnaia niva* 30 (1923): 32.

Lant, Antonia. "Haptical Cinema." *October* 74 (Autumn 1995): 45–73.

Lapin, V., *Peterburg: Zapakhi i zvuki*. St. Petersburg: Evropeiskii dom, 2007.

Lapshin, I. "Chuvstvovanie." *Entsiklopedicheskii slovar' Brokgauza i Efrona*. Tom 38, 941–56. Saint Petersburg: Semenovskaia tipolitografiia (I. A. Efrona), 1903.

Laptev, A. *Stroim iz kartona*. Moscow: OGIZ, Molodaia gvardiia, 1932.

Laruelle, Marlène. *L'idéologie eurasiste russe, ou comment penser l'empire*. Paris: L'Harmattan, 1999.

Latash, Mark L., ed. *Progress in Motor Control*. Vol. 1, *Bernstein's Traditions in Movement Studies*. Champaign, IL: Human Kinetics, 1998.

Lavrentiev, Alexander. "Experimental Furniture Design in the 1920s." *The Journal of Decorative and Propaganda Arts* 11, no. 2 (Winter 1989): 142–67.

Lavrov, Vitalii. "Kak ty zhivesh': nauchnoe kino—v pomoshch' arkhitekture." *Stroitel'stvo Moskvy* 11 (1927): 25–27.

Lawder, Standish D. *The Cubist Cinema*. New York: New York University Press, 1975.

Layton, Susan. *Russian Literature and Empire: Conquest of the Caucasus*. New York and Cambridge: Cambridge University Press, 2005.

Lebedev, N. N. "Rozhdenie iskusstva." *Sovetskoe iskusstvo* 2 (1935): 3.

———. *Ocherki istorii sovetskogo kino. Nemoe kino: 1918–1934*. Moscow: Iskusstvo, 1965.

Lebina, N. B. *Povsednevnaia zhizn' sovetskogo goroda: normy i anomalii. 1920-e-1930-e gody*. Saint Petersburg: Zhurnal "Neva" and "Letnii sad," 1999.

Le Corbusier. *L'art décoratif d'aujourd'hui*. Paris: G. Crès, 1925.

Lenin, Vladimir. "A Great Beginning: Heroism of the Workers in the Rear 'Communist Subbotniks.'" In Lenin, V. I., *Collected Works*. Vol. 29, 408–34. Moscow: Progress Publishers, 1965. In Russian: "Velikii pochin," in Lenin, V. I., *Polnoe sobranie sochinenii*. Tom 39, 1–29. Moscow: Politicheskaia literatura, 1956–65.

———. "Materialism and Empirio-criticism: Critical Comments on a Reactionary Philosophy." In V. I. Lenin, *Collected Works*. Vol. 14, 17–362. Moscow: Progress Publishers, 1972.

Leont'ev, A. N. "Nauka dlia kino, kino-nauka." *Kino* 18 (March 21, 1931): 1.

———. "Emotsiia." *Bol'shaia sovetskaia entsiklopediia*, 1-oe izdanie. Tom 64, 190–94. 1934.

Leont'ev, A., and A. Luria. "Issledovanie ob''ektivnykh simptomov affektivnykh reaktskii." In *Problemy sovremennoi psikhologii*. 47–100. Leningrad: 1926.

Leont´ev, A. A. "A. Leont´ev: Biograficheskii ocherk." In *Zhiznennyi i tvorcheskii put´ A. N. Leont´eva*, 8–141. Moscow: Smysl, 2003.
———. "The Life and Creative Path of A. N. Leontiev," *Journal of Russian and East European Psychology* 43, no. 3 (2005): 8–69.
Lévi-Strauss, Claude. *The Savage Mind*. Oxford: Oxford University Press, 1996.
Lévy-Bruhl, Lucien. *Primitive Mentality*. Translated by Lilian A. Clare. New York and London: George Allen and Unwin, 1923.
Leyda, Jay. *Kino: A History of the Russian and Soviet Film*. London: George Allen and Unwin, 1960.
Leys, Ruth. "The Turn to Affect: A Critique." *Critical Enquiry* 37, no. 3 (Spring 2011): 434–72.
Lingart, Liubomir. "Emotsional´nyi stsenarii A. G. Rzheshevskogo." In *Otázky divadla a filmu: theatralia et cinematographica*, 3, edited by A. Závodský, 263–300. Brno: universita J. E. Ourkyne, 1973.
Lisakovskaia, Marina. "Nezamechennyi avangard. Khudozhniki v kino." *Kinovedcheskie zapiski* 99 (2012): 26–34.
Locatelli, M. "Kurt Lewin's Children: Media Images, Perception, Social Acting." Paper presented at the conference "Blending Media: Defining Film in the Modernist Period," Innsbruck University, June 9–10, 2009.
———. "I bimbi di Lewin. Immagini mediali, percezione della realtà, agire sociale." *Immagine: Note di storia del cinema* 6 (2012): 156–72.
Lodder, Christine, and Martin Hammer. *Constructing Modernity, the Art and Career of Naum Gabo*. New Haven, CT, and London: Yale University Press, 2000.
Loos, Adolf. "Ornament and Crime." Translated by William Wang. In *The Architecture of Adolf Loos*, edited by Yehuda Safran and William Wang, 100–3. London: Arts Council of Great Britain, 1985.
Lovell, Stephen. *Russia in the Microphone Age: A History of Soviet Radio, 1919–1970*. New York: Oxford University Press, 2015.
Lukács, Georg. *History and Class Consciousness: Studies in Marxist Dialectics*. Translated by Rodney Livingstone. Cambridge, MA: MIT Press, (1923) 1997.
———. "Tolstoy and the Development of Realism." From *Studies in European Realism: A Sociological Study of the Writings of Stendhal, Zola, Tolstoy, Gorky and Others*. Translated by Edith Bone, 126–205. London: Hillway Publishing Company, 1950. Reprinted in *Marxists on Literature*, edited by David Craig, 282–345. Harmondsworth: Pelican, 1977.
Lukhmanov. "Zhizn´, kakoi ona dolzhna byt´." *Kino i kul´tura* 1 (January 1929): 29–37.
Lunacharskii, Anatolii. "O kino." *Komsomol´skaia Pravda*, (26 August 26, 1925). In *Lunacharskii o kino: stat´i, vyskazyvaniia, stsenarii, dokumenty*, edited by Aleksandr Gak and Nina Glagoleva, 45–55. Moscow: Iskusstvo, 1965.
———. "Mesto kino v oblasti iskusstva." *Krasnaia panorama* 40 (1927). Republished as "Kino" in *Lunacharskii o kino: stat´i, vyskazyvaniia, stsenarii, dokumenty*, edited by Aleksandr Gak and Nina Glagoleva, 98–102. Moscow: Iskusstvo, 1965.

Luria, A. (A. R. Luria). "Affekt." *Bol'shaia sovetskaia entsiklopediia*, 1-oe izdanie, Tom 4, 150–51. 1926.

———. *The Mind of a Mnemonist: A Little Book about a Vast Memory*. New York: Basic, 1968.

———. *Cognitive Development: Its Cultural and Social Foundations*. Harvard: Harvard University Press, 1976.

Luria, A. R., and L. S. Vygostky. *Ape, Primitive Man, and Child: Essays in the History of Behaviou*. Translated by Evelyn Rossiter. Orlando, FL: Paul M. Deutsch, 1992. First published as *Etiudy po istorii povedeniia: Obez''iana. Primitiv. Rebenok*. Moscow, 1930.

Macheret, A. "Realizovannyi optimizm." *Sovetskoe kino* 1–2 (1934): 55–64.

Macheret, A., ed. *Sovetskie khudozhestvennye fil'my: Annotirovannyi katalog*. Tom 1. *Nemye fil'my, 1918–1935*. Moscow: Iskusstvo, 1961.

Mackay, John. "The Kinetic Icon in the Work of: Vertov's Three Songs of Lenin (1934) as a Stalinist Film." *Film History* 18, no. 4 (2006): 376–91.

———. "Film Energy: Process and Metanarrative in Dziga Vertov's The Eleventh Year." *October* 121, (Summer 2007): 41–78.

Maiakovskii, Vladimir. "O driani." In *Sochineniia v dvukh tomakh*. Tom 1, 145. Moscow: Pravda, 1988.

Makarenko, Anton. *Lektsii o vospitanii detei*. Moscow: Gosudarstvennoe uchebno-pedagogicheskoe izdatel'stvo, 1952.

Makovskii, Aleksandr. "Put' na Vostok." In *Zhizn' v kino: veterany o sebe i o svoikh tovarishchakh*. Sbornik 2, edited by O. T. Nesterovich, 107–30. Moscow: Iskusstvo, 1972.

Malevich, Kazimir. "Ot kubizma k suprematizmu: novyi zhivopisnyi realizm" (1915). In Malevich, Kazimir, *Sobranie sochinenii v 5 tomakh*. Tom 1, 35–56. Moscow: Gileia, 1995.

———. "1/46 (Eklektika)." In Malevich, Kazimir, *Sobranie sochinenii v 5 tomakh*. Tom 4, 135–55. Moscow: Gileia, 2003.

Mallet-Stevens, Robert. *Le décor moderne au cinéma*. Paris: Charles Meunier, 1928.

Mamatova, Liliia. "Model' kinomifov 30-kh godov." *Iskusstvo kino* 11 (1990): 103–11.

Mandel'shtam, Osip. "O prirode slova." In Mandel'shtam, *Sochinenii v dvukh tomakh*. Tom 2, 172–186. Moscow: Khudozhestvennaia literatura, 1990.

Marcus, Laura. "Modernism and Visual Culture." In *Handbook of Modernism Studies*, edited by Jean-Michel Rabaté, 239–254. New York: Wiley-Blackwell, 2013.

Margolit, Evgenii. *Zhivye i mertvoe: zametki k istorii sovetskogo kino 1920–1960-kh godov*. Saint Petersburg: Masterskaia Seans, 2012.

———. "The Problem of Heteroglossia in Early Soviet Sound Cinema, 1930–35." In *Sound, Speech, Music in Soviet and Post-Soviet Cinema*, edited by Lilya Kaganovsky and Masha Salazkina, 119–128. Bloomington: Indiana University Press, 2014.

Margolit, Evgenii, and Viacheslav Shmyrov. *Iz"iatoe kino. 1924–1953*. Moscow: Dubl-D, 1995.

Markov, Vladimir. *Printsipy tvorchestva v plasticheskikh iskusstvakh. Faktura.* Saint Petersburg: Soiuz molodezhi, 1914.
Marinetti, Filippo. *Le tactilisme: Un art nouveau inventé par le futurisme.* Paris: Comodia, 1921.
Marks, Laura. *The Skin of the Film: Intercultural Cinema, Embodiment and the Senses.* Durham, NC, and London: Duke University Press, 2000.
———. *Touch: Sensuous Theory and Multisensory Media.* Minneapolis: University of Minnesota Press, 2002.
Martin, Alexander M. "Sewage and the City: Filth, Smell, and Representations of Urban Life in Moscow, 1770–1880." *Russian Review* 67, no. 2 (2008): 243–74.
———. *Enlightened Metropolis: Constructing Imperial Moscow, 1762–1855.* Oxford: Oxford University Press, 2013.
Marx, Karl. "Capital: A Critique of Political Economy, Volume 1." In Karl Marx and Frederick Engels, *Collected Works.* Vol. 35, *Karl Marx, Capital: Volume 1.* London: Lawrence and Wishart, 1996.
Marx, Karl, and Frederick Engels. *The German Ideology: Parts I and III.* Edited and translated by R. Pascal. New York: International Publishers, 1947.
———. *The Holy Family, or Critique of Critical Criticism. Against Bruno Bauer and Co.* Translated by Peter Byrne and Andy Blunden. Moscow: Foreign Languages Publishing House, (1845) 1956.
———. "Economic and Philosophical Manuscripts of 1844." In Karl Marx and Frederick Engels, *Collected Works.* Vol. 3, *Marx and Engels: 1843–44.* 229–349. London: Lawrence and Wishart, 1975.
Massell, Gregory J. *The Surrogate Proletariat: Moslem Women and Revolutionary Strategies in Soviet Central Asia, 1919–1929.* Princeton, NJ: Princeton University Press, 1974.
Mchitarjan, Irina. "John Dewey and the Development of Education in Russia before 1930—Report on a Forgotten Reception." *Studies in Philosophy and Education* 19 (2000): 109–31.
Mead, Margaret, and Rhoda Métraux, eds. *The Study of Culture at a Distance.* New York and Oxford: Berghahn, 2000.
Mencej, Mirjam. "Connecting Threads." *Folklore* 48. Accessed February 5, 2014. http://www.folklore.ee/folklore/vol48/mencej.pdf.
Miasnikov, G. *Ocherki istorii sovetskogo kinodekoratsionnogo iskusstva (1918–1930).* Moscow: VGIK, 1975.
Michalski, Milena. "Promises Broken, Promise Fulfilled: The Critical Failings and Creative Success of Abram Room's Strogii iunosha." *Slavonic and East European Review* 82, no. 4 (October 2004): 820–46.
Michelson, Annette. "Introduction." In *Kinoeye: The Writings of Dziga Vertov*, edited by Annette Michelson, translated by Kevin O'Brien, xvi–lxi. Berkeley and Los Angeles: University of California Press, 1984.

———. "The Kinetic Icon in the Work of Mourning: Prolegomena to the Analysis of a Textual System." *October* 52 (Spring 1990): 16–39.
Michurin, G. "Akter v nemom kino." *Iz istorii Lenfil'ma: stat'i, vospominaniia, dokumenty. 1920-e gody.* Leningrad: Iskusstvo, 1968.
Mikhin, B. "Rozhdenie fundusa." *Iz istorii kino: dokumenty i materialy* 9, 148–55. Moscow: Akademiia nauk, 1979.
Miller, Daniel. "Primitive Art and the Necessity of Primitivism to Art." In *The Myth of Primitivism: Perspectives on Art*, edited by Susan Hiller, 35–53. New York and London: Routledge, 1991.
Miller, Jamie. *Soviet Cinema: Politics and Persuasion under Stalin.* London: I. B. Tauris, 2010.
Miller-Frank, Felicia. "'L'Inhumaine, La Fin du monde': Modernist Utopias and Filmmaking Angels." *Modern Language Notes* 111, no. 5 (1996): 938–53.
Milner, John. *Vladimir Tatlin and the Russian Avant-Garde.* (New Haven, CT, and London: Yale University Press, 1983.
Miloserdova, Natalia. "Margarita Barskaia: Creativity and Destiny." In "Margarita Barskaia and the Emergence of Children's Cinema," edited by Birgit Beumers, Nikolai Izvolov, Natalia Miloserdova, and Natalia Riabchikova, 240–45. *Studies in Russian and Soviet Cinema* 3, no. 2 (2009).
Misler, Nicoletta. "A Citadel of Idealism: RAKhN as Soviet Anomaly." *Experiment/Eksperiment* 3, no. 1 (1997): 14–30.
———. "L'idole-girafe, Moscow, 1920s." *Experiment/Eksperiment* 10, no. 1 (2004): 97–102.
Mogilner, Marina. *Homo imperii: A History of Physical Anthropology in Russia.* Lincoln and London: University of Nebraska Press, 2013.
———. "Beyond, against, and with Ethnography: Physical Anthropology as a Science of Russian Modernity." In *An Empire of Others: Creating Ethnographic Knowledge in Imperial Russia and the USSR*, edited by Roland Cvetkovski and Alexis Hofmeister, 81–121. Budapest and New York: Central European University Press, 2014.
Moldavskii, Dmitrii. *S Maiakovskim v teatre i kino: Kniga o Sergee Iutkeviche.* Moscow: Vserossiiskoe teatral'noe obshchestvo, 1975.
Molok, Yuri. "Children's Drawings in Russian Futurism." In *Discovering Child Art: Essays on Childhood, Primitivism and Modernism*, edited by J. Fineburg, 55–68. Princeton, NJ: Princeton University Press, 2001.
Moore, Rachel O. *Savage Theory: Cinema as Modern Magic.* Durham, NC: Duke University Press, 2000.
Morley, Rachel. "The Incestuous Father in Law." In "A Hundred Years of Russian Film: The forgotten and the under-rated," edited by Julian Graffy. *Studies in Russian and Soviet Cinema* 2, no. 3 (2008): 327–54.
Morozov, S. "'Chto eto takoe?' O detskoi fotoknige V. Griuntalia i G. Iablonskogo." *Proletarskoe kino* 10 (1932): 17–18.

Morozov, S. A. *Sovetskaia khudozhestvennaia fotografiia*. Moscow: Gosudarstvennoe izdatel'stvo "Iskusstvo," 1958.
Moussinac, Léon (Leon Mussinak). "Dekoratsiia i kostium v kino." *Kinofront* 1 (1928): 6–7.
Mukhina, V., and N. Lamanova. Kaftan iz 2-kh vladimirskikh polotents." In *Iskusstvo v bytu: 36 tablits: Igrushka, odezhda, izba-chital'nia, klub, teatr*, edited by Iakov Tugendkhol'd, 19. Moscow: Izvestiia TsIK SSSR i VTsIK, 1925.
Münsterberg, Hugo. *The Photoplay: A Psychological Study*. New York: Appleton, 1916.
Mur, Leo. "Aktivnaia i passivnaia fotogeniia." *Kino-zhurnal ARK* 6 (1925): 4–8.
———. "Fotogeniia." *Kinozhurnal ARK* 6–7 (1925): 3–7.
———. "S"emki na nature i v atel'e," *Kinofront* 2 (1926): 2–7.
Murashov, Iu. "Slepye geroi—slepye zriteli: o statuse zreniia i slova v sovetskom kino." In *Sovetskoe bogatstvo: stat'i o kul'ture, literature i kino*, edited by Evgenii Dobrenko, Marina Balina, and Iurii Murashov, 412–26. Saint Petersburg: Nevskii prospect, 2002. Myzelev, Alla. "Handcrafting Revolution: Ukrainian Avant-garde Embroidery and the Meanings of History." *Craft Research* 3, no. 1 (2012): 11–32.
Naiman, Eric. *Sex in Public: The Incarnation of Early Soviet Ideology*. Princeton, NJ, and Chichester: Princeton University Press, 1997.
———. "On Soviet Subjects and the Scholars Who Make Them." *Russian Review* 60 (July 2001): 305–15.
Nancy, Jean-Luc. *Le Sens du Monde*. Paris: Galilée, 1993.
Nedobrovo, Vladimir. "O 'Kruzhevakh.'" *Kino* 27 (Leningrad) (July 1, 1928): 3.
Nesbet, Anne. *Savage Junctures: Sergei Eisenstein and the Shape of Thinking*. London: I. B. Tauris, 2007.
———. "Emile Zola, Kozintsev and Trauberg, and Film as Department Store." *The Russian Review* 68, no. 1 (2009): 102–21.
Nesterova, Elena. "The Brothers Konstantin and Vladimir Makovskii: One Family, Two Fates." In *From Realism to the Silver Age: New Studies in Russian Artistic Culture*, edited by Rosalind P. Blakesley and Margaret Samu, 27–44. DeKalb: Northern Illinois University Press, 2014.
Neumann, Dietrich, ed. *Film Architecture: Set Designs from Metropolis to Blade Runner*. Munich: Prestel, 1999.
Neznamov, P. "Khoroshoe otnoshenie k Armenii." *Sovetskii ekran* 23 (1926): 3.
———. "Poet i tsar'." *Kino* 39 (September 27, 1927): 3.
———. "Baby riazanskie." *Kino* 52 (December 17, 1927): 3.
———. "Kruzheva." *Sovetskii ekran* 23 (June 5, 1928): 9.
Nil'sen, Vladimir. "O fil'me 'Trinadtsat'.'" *Iskusstvo kino* 4 (April 1937): 10–15.
N. K. "Byt 'ideologicheskii,' byt 'kassovyi', byt zhivoi." *Sovetskii ekran* 27 (1928): 5.
Northrop, Douglas. *Veiled Empire: Gender and Power in Stalinist Central Asia*. Ithaca, NY and London: Cornell University Press, 2003.
Nusinova, N. "Gibel' sensatsii (robot Dzhima Ripl')." In *Uchreditel' kinofestivalia 2015*. 72–73. Moscow: Gosfil'mofond Rossii, 2015.

Oever, Annie van den. "Ostranenie, 'The Montage of Attractions' and Early Cinema's 'Properly Irreducible Alien Quality.'" In *Ostrannenie: On 'Strangeness' and the Moving Image*, edited by Annie van den Oever, 33–61. Amsterdam: Amsterdam University Press, 2010.

Olenina, Ana. "Psychomotor Aesthetics: Conceptions of Gesture and Affect in Russian and American Modernity, 1910s to 1920s." PhD diss., Harvard University, 2011.

Olesha, Iurii. "Zavist'," in *Zavist', Tri tolstiaka. Ni dnia bez strochki*, 12–112. Moscow: Khudozhestvennaia literatura, 1989.

Ol'khovyi, B. S., ed. *Puti kino: Pervoe Vsesoiuznoe partiinoe soveshchanie po kinematografii* Moscow: Teakinopechat', 1929.

Olofsson, Kerstin, ed. *From Orientalism to Postcoloniality*. Stockholm: Södertörns högskola, Research Reports, 2008.

Papazian, Elizabeth. *Manufacturing Truth: The Documentary Moment in Early Soviet Culture*. DeKalb: Northern Illinois University Press, 2009.

Paperny, Vladimir. *Architecture in the Age of Stalin: Culture Two*. Translated by John Hill and Roann Barris. Cambridge: Cambridge University Press, 2002.

Parker, Roszika. *The Subversive Stitch: Embroidery and the Making of the Feminine*. London: I. B. Tauris, (1984) 2010.

Parnakh, Valentin "Novye tantsy." *Veshch'. Gegenstand. Objet* 1–2 (March–April 1922): 25.

———. "Dzhaz-band." *Veshch'. Gegenstand. Objet* 1–2 (March–April 1922): 25.

———. "Mimeticheskii tanets." *Zrelishcha* 7 (Moscow) (October 1922): 13.

———. "The Mimetic Orchestra." Edited by Mel Gordon, translated by Richard Allen, 435–42. *Experiment/Eksperiment* 2, no. 1 (1996).

Paterson, Mark. *The Senses of Touch: Haptics, Affects and Technologies*. New York and Oxford: Berg, 2007.

Payne, Matthew J. "The Movie 'Turksib' and Soviet Orientalism." *The Historical Journal of Film, Radio, and Television* 21, no. 1 (March 2001): 37–62.

———. *Stalin's Railroad: Turksib and the Building of Socialism*. Pittsburgh: University of Pittsburgh Press, 2001.

Pearce, Brian, ed. and trans. *Congress of the Peoples of the East. Baku, September 1920. Stenographic Report*. London: New Park Publications, 1977.

Petrov-Bytov, Pavel. "Mirovozzrenie, talant, iskrennost'." *Sovetskoe kino* 12 (1933): 44–45.

Piataev, A. S. "Chto takoe individual'nost'? V diskussionnom poriadke." *Kino* 40 (1933): 3.

Piotrovskii, Adrian. "Khudozhestvennye techeniia v sovetskom kino." In Piotrovskii, Adrian, *Khudozhestvennye techeniia v sovetskom kino*. Moscow: Teakinopechat', 1930. Reprinted in *Adrian Piotrovskii: Teatr. Kino. Zhizn'*, edited by A. A. Akimova, 232–56. Leningrad: Iskusstvo Leningr. otd-nie, 1969.

———. "E. Cherviakov." *Zhizn' iskusstva* 33 (1928): 8–9.

Plamper, Jan. "Introduction." In "Emotional Turn? Feelings in Russian History and Culture," edited by Jan Plamper, 229–37. Special section of *Slavic Review* 68, no. 2 (Summer 2009).

———. *The History of Emotions: An Introduction*. Translated by Keith Tribe. Oxford: Oxford University Press, 2015.

Plamper, Jan, Shama Shakhadat, and Mark Eli, eds. *Rossiiskaia imperiia chuvstv: Podkhody k kul´turnoi istorii emotsii: Sbornik statei*. Moscow: Novoe literaturnoe obozrenie, 2010.

Platonov, Andrei. "Proletarskaia poeziia." *Kuznitsa* 9 (1922): 3–31.

Popkin, Cathy. *The Pragmatics of Insignificance: Chekhov, Zoshchenko, Gogol*. Stanford: Stanford University Press, 1993.

Popov, I. F. "Neobosnovannye obvineniia ("Okraina")." *Kino* 24 (May 16, 1933): 2.

———. "Neobosnovannoe obvinenie." *Kino* 30 (June 22, 1930): 3.

———. "Iz dnevnika na proizvodstve." *Sovetskoe kino* 5–6 (1933): 19–30.

———. "Obraz kommunista na ekrane." *Sovetskoe kino* 1–2 (1934): 6–14.

———. "Postanovlenie tresta Ukrainfil´m o zapreshchenii fil´ma 'Strogii iunosha.'" *Kino* 37 (July 26, 1936): 2.

Potekhin, Iu. "Predislovie." In Delliuk, L., *Fotogeniia kino*. Translated by T. Sorokin. 3–19. Moscow: Novye vekhi, 1924.

Povelikhina, Anna. "Introducing the Catalogue and Exhibition 'Organica and the Non-objective World of Nature in the Russian Avant-garde.'" *Experiment/Eksperiment* 6, no. 1 (2000): 1–4.

Powell, Kirsten H. "Hands-on Surrealism." *Art History* 20, no. 4 (December 1997): 516–33.

Pozner, Valérie. "Shklovskii/Eizenshtein—dvadtsatye gody. Istoriia plodotvornogo neponimaniia." *Kinovedcheskie zapiski* 46 (2000): 179–189.

———. "Vertov before Vertov: Psychoneurology in Petrograd." In *Dziga Vertov: The Vertov Collection at the Austrian Film Museum*, edited by Thomas Tode and Barbara Wurm, 12–15. Vienna: SYNEMA, 2007.

Pozner, Vladimir. "Frantsuzskii kinematograf v 1924 godu (pis´mo iz Parizha)." *Kinozhurnal ARK* 2 (1925): 27–29.

Pribyl´skaia, E. "Vyshivka v nastoiashchem proizvodstve." *Atel´e* 1 (1923): 7–8.

Prim [pseud.]. "O Predatele." *Vecherniaia Moskva* 217 (September 21, 1927): 3.

Proctor, Hannah. "Kurt Koffka and the Expedition to Central Asia." *Dubna Psychological Journal* 3 (2013): 43–52.

Prokhorov, Alexander. "The Adolescent and the Child in the Cinema of the Thaw." *Studies in Russian and Soviet Cinema* 1, no. 2 (2007): 115–29.

Pudovkin, Vsevolod. "Fotogeniia." *Kino-zhurnal ARK* 4–5 (June-July 1925): 9–12. Reprinted in Pudovkin, Vsevolod, *Sobranie sochinenii v trekh tomakh. Tom 1, O kinostsenarii. Kinorezhissura. Masterstvo kinoaktera*, edited by A. Groshev, A. Golovnia, and V. Zhdan, 90–94. Moscow: Iskusstvo, 1974.

———. "O khudozhnike v kino." *Kino* 10 (March 3, 1925): 2. Reprinted in Pudovkin, Vsevolod, *Sobranie sochinenii v trekh tomakh. Tom 2, O sebe i svoikh fil´makh*.

Kinokritika i publitsistika, edited by A. Groshev, A. Golovnia, V. Zhdan, 117. Moscow: Iskusstvo, 1975.

———. *Kinorezhisser i kinomaterial*. Moscow: Kinopechat, 1926). Reprinted in Pudovkin, Vsevolod, *Sobranie sochinenii v trekh tomakh. Tom 1, O kinostsenarii. Kinorezhissura. Masterstvo kinoaktera*, edited by A. Groshev, A. Golovnia, and V. Zhdan, 95–130. Moscow: Iskusstvo, 1974.

———. "Potomok chingiz-khana" (1928). Reprinted in Pudovkin, Vsevolod, *Sobranie sochinenii v trekh tomakh. Tom 2, O sebe i svoikh fil'makh. Kinokritika i publitsistika*, edited by A. Groshev, A. Golovnia, V. Zhdan, 60–61. Moscow: Iskusstvo, 1975.

———. "25 Dekabria 1930g. Vystuplenie na obsuzhdenii fil'ma 'Ochen' khorosho zhivetsia' ('Prostoi sluchai') na zavode 'Manometr,'" in Pudovkin, Vsevolod, *Sobranie sochinenii v trekh tomakh*. Tom 3, edited by A. Groshev, A. Golovnia, V. Zhdan, 27–32. Moscow: Iskusstvo, 1976.

———. "Na vershiny sovetskoi kul'tury." *Kino* 20 (April 22, 1933): 2.

———. *Akter v fil'me* (Leningrad: Gosudarstvennaia akademiia iskusstvoznaniia, 1934). Reprinted in Pudovkin, Vsevolod, *Sobranie sochinenii v trekh tomakh. Tom 1, O kinostsenarii. Kinorezhissura. Masterstvo kinoaktera*, edited by A. Groshev, A. Golovnia, V. Zhdan, 185–240. Moscow: Iskusstvo, 1974.

Rabaté, Jean-Michel, ed. *Handbook of Modernism Studies*. New York: Wiley-Blackwell, 2013.

Radunović, Dušan. "Incommensurable Distance: versions of national identity in Georgian Soviet cinema." In *Cinema, State Socialism and Society in the Soviet Union and Eastern Europe, 1917–1989: Re Visions*, edited by Sanja Bahun and John Haynes, 49–75. London: Routledge, 2014.

Ram, Harsha. "Futurist Geographies: Uneven Modernities and the Struggle for Aesthetic Autonomy. Paris, Italy, Russia, 1909–1914." In *The Oxford Handbook of Global Modernisms*, edited by Mark Wollaeger and Matt Eatough, 313–41. New York and Oxford: Oxford University Press, 2012.

Ramirez, Juan Antonio. *Architecture for the Screen: A Critical Study of Set Design in Hollywood's Golden Age*. Jefferson, NC: McFarland, 2004.

Ratiani, Irina. *U istokov gruzinskogo kino: vzaimosviaz' literatury, teatra i kino v kul'ture Gruzii*. Moscow: Rossiiskii institut kul'turologii, 2003.

Razmyslov. "O kul'turno-istoricheskoi teorii Vygotskogo i Luriia." *Kniga i proletarskaia revoliutsii* 4 (1934): 78–86.

Reid, Susan E. "Makeshift Modernity: DIY, Craft and the Virtuous Homemaker in New Soviet Housing of the 1960s." *International Journal for History, Culture and Modernity* 2, no. 2 (October 2014): 87–124.

———. "Everyday Aesthetics in the Khrushchev-Era Standard Apartment." In *Everyday Life in Russia: Past and Present*, edited by Choi Chatterjee, David L. Ransel, Mary Cavender, and Karen Petrone, 203–33. Bloomington: Indiana University Press, 2014.

Riddell, John. *To See the Dawn: Baku, 1920—First Congress of the Peoples of the East*. New York and London: Pathfinder, 1993.

Riegl, Alois. *Late Roman Art Industry*. Edited and translated by Rolf Winkes. Rome: Giorgio Bretschneider Editore, 1985.

———. *Problems of Style: Foundations for a History of Ornament*. Translated by Evelyn Kain. Princeton, NJ: Princeton University Press, 1992.

Reischl, Katherine Hill. "An Exercise with Photographic Literacy: Refamiliarizing the Soviet Photo Avant-garde from childrens' books to USSR in Construction." Unpublished manuscript, last modified November 1, 2016. Microsoft Word file.

Rodchenko, Aleksandr. "Khudozhnik i 'material´naia sreda' v igrovoi fil´me: beseda s khudozhnikom A. M. Rodchenko." *Sovetskoe kino* 5–6 (1927): 14–15.

Rodchenko, Aleksandr, and Varvara Stepanova. "Fotomul´tiplikatsionnye illiustratsii k detskoi knizhke 'Samozveri' S. Tret´iakova." *Novyi LEF* 1 (1927): 19–21.

Roginskaia, E. "Problemy kostiuma." *Sovetskoe iskusstvo* 7 (1927): 63–67.

Romaniello, Matthew, and Tricia Starks, eds. *Russian History through the Senses, from 1700 to the Present*. London: Bloomsbury, 2016.

———. *Tobacco in Russian History and Culture from the Seventeenth Century to the Present*. London: Routledge University Press, 2009.

Romm, Mikhail. "O sebe, o liudiakh, o fil´makh." *Izbrannye proizvedeniia v 3-kh tomakh*. Tom 2, 91–339. Moscow: Iskusstvo, 1981.

Room, Abram. "Kino i teatr (diskussionno)." *Sovetskii ekran* 8 (1925): 56–7.

———. "Moi kinoubezhdeniia." *Sovetskii ekran* 8 (1926): 5.

———. "Kak delalis´ 'Ukhaby.'" *Kino* 44 (November 1, 1927): 5.

———. "Akter—polpred idei." *Kino* 7 (1932): 3; *Kino* 11 (1932): 3; *Kino* 15 (1932): 3; *Kino* 17 (1932): 3.

Room, Abram, and Victor Shklovskii, "Ukhaby," *Iz istorii kino*, 9, with an introduction by Irina Grashchenkova, "Vospitanie chuvstv," 96–121. Moscow: Akademiia nauk, 1974.

Rosatto, V. *Leavers Lace: A Handbook of the American Leavers Lace Industry*. Providence, RI: American Lace Makers Association, 1949.

Rouland, Michael. "An Historical Introduction." In *Cinema in Central Asia: Rewriting Cultural Histories*, edited by Michael Rouland, Birgit Beumers, Galina Abikeyeva, 1–33. London: I. B. Tauris, 2013.

Rowell, Margaret. "Vladimir Tatlin: Form/Faktura." *October* 7 (Winter 1978): 83–108.

Said, Edward. *Orientalism*. London: Vintage Books, 1978.

Saikal, Amin. *Modern Afghanistan: A History of Struggle and* Survival. London: I. B. Tauris, 2004.

Salazkina, Maria. *In Excess: Sergei Eisenstein's Mexico*. Chicago, IL: University of Chicago Press, 2009.

Salmond, Wendy. "The Solomenko Embroidery Workshops." *The Journal of Decorative and Propaganda Arts: Russian/Soviet Themed Issue* 5 (Summer 1987): 126–43.

———. *Arts and Crafts in Late Imperial Russia: Reviving the Kustar Art Industries, 1870–1917*. Cambridge: Cambridge University Press, 1996.

Sal′nikova, A. *Rossiiskoe detstvo v XX veke: Istoriia, teoriia i praktika issledovaniia*. Kazan′: Kazan′ State University, 2007.

———. "Bezglazaia kukla i papin revol′ver." *Teoriia mody* 8 (Summer 2008): 119–39.

Sal′nikova, A., and Aю Burmistrov. "Sovetskoe detskoe igrovoe kino 20-kh gg. XX v. i ego iunye zriteli." *Uchenye zapiski Kazanskovo universiteta. Seriia: Gumanitarnye nauki*. 156, no. 3 (2014): 131–41.

Sal′nikova, A, and Zh. Khamitova. "Zhurnal 'Sovetskaia igrushka' kak istochnik ob istorii sovetskogo detstva 1930-kh godov." *Uchenye zapiski Kazanskogo universiteta. Seriia: Gumanitarnye nauki* 155, no. 1 (2013): 200–11.

Sal′nikova, E. "Evoliutsiia vizual′nogo riada v sovetskom kino ot 1930-kh k 1980-m." In *Vizual′naia antropologiia: reizhimy vidimosti pri sotsializme*, edited by Elena Iarskaia-Smirnova and P. V. Romanov, 335–58. Moscow: Variant, 2005.

Sandomirskaia, Irina. "One Sixth of the World: Avant-garde Film, the Revolution of Vision, and the Colonization of the USSR Periphery during the 1920s (Towards a Postcolonial Deconstruction of the Soviet Hegemony)." In *From Orientalism to Postcoloniality*, edited by Kerstin Olofsson, 8–31. Stockholm: Södertörns högskola, Research Reports 2008.

———. *Blokada v slove: ocherki kriticheskoi teorii i biopolitiki iazyka*. Moscow: Novoe literaturnoe obozrenie, 2013.

Sargeant, Amy. *Vsevolod Pudovkin: Classic Films of the Soviet Avant-Garde*. London: I. B. Tauris, 2000.

———. *Storm over Asia*. New York and London: I. B. Tauris, 2008.

Sarkisova, Oksana. *Screening Soviet Nationalities. Kulturfilms from the Far North to Central Asia*. London: I. B. Tauris, 2016.

Savchenko, Igor′. "Pravo zapet′. K postanovke kinooperetty 'Garmon′' i 'Irinkin rekord.'" *Sovetskoe kino* 5 (1934): 59. Reprinted as Igor Savchenko, "The Right to Sing." Edited by Emma Widdis and translated by Susan Larsen, 373–79. *Studies in Russian and Soviet Cinema* 6, no. 3 (2012).

Schimmelpenninck van der Oye, David. *Russian Orientalism: Asia in the Russian Mind from Peter the Great until the Emigration*. New Haven, CT: Yale University Press, 2010.

Schivelbusch, Wolfgang. *The Railway Journey: The Industrialization of Time and Space in the Nineteenth Century*. Berkeley: University of California Press, 2014.

Schönle, Andreas. *Architecture of Oblivion: Ruins and Historical Consciousness in Modern Russia*. DeKalb: Northern Illinois University Press, 2011.

Schwarz, Matthias, Wladimir Velminski, Torben Philipp, eds. *Laien, Lektören, Laboratorium: Künst und Wissenschaften in Russland 1860–1960*. Frankfurt: Peter Lang, 2008.

Seffer, V., and A. Buzin. "Schastlivoe detstvo." *Ogonek* 23 (1937): 212.

Semashko, N. A. "Gigiena kostiuma." *Iskusstvo odevat′sia* 3 (1928): 5.

Semper, Gottfried. *Style in the Technical and Tectonic Arts, or, Practical Aesthetics (Texts and Documents)*. Edited by Harry Francis Mallgrave and Michael

Robinson, translated by Harry Francis Mallgrave. Los Angeles: Getty Research Institute, 2004.

Sennett, Richard. *The Craftsman*. New Haven, CT: Yale University Press, 2009.

Seremetakis, C. Nadia. "The Memory of the Senses, Part 1: Marks of the Transitory." In *The Senses Still: Perception and Memory as Material Culture in Modernity*, edited by C. Nadia Seremetakis, 1–18. Chicago: Chicago University Press, (1994) 1996.

Serres, Michel. *Les Cinq sens*. Paris: Grasset, 1990.

Sharp, Jane Ashton. *Russian Modernism between East and West: Natalia Goncharova and the Moscow Avant-Garde, 1905–1914*. New York and Cambridge: Cambridge University Press, 2006.

Shaw, Claire. *Deaf in the USSR: Marginality, Community and Soviet Identity, 1917–1991*. Ithaca: Cornell University Press, 2017.

———. "'We Have No Need to Lock Ourselves Away': Space, Marginality, and the Negotiation of Deaf Identity in Late Soviet Moscow." *Slavic Review* 74, no. 1 (2015): 57–78.

Shengelaia, N. "Nado rabotat' druzhno." *Literaturnaia gazeta* (January 13, 1933): 5.

Shklovskii, Viktor. "Iskusstvo kak priem." *Sborniki po teorii poeticheskogo iazyka* 2. in *O teorii prozy*. 7–20. Moscow: Krug, 1925. First published in Sborniki po teorii poeticheskogo iazyka 2. Leningrad: 18-aia Gos. Tipografiia, 1917. In English as "Art as Device," in *Theory of Prose*, translated by Benjamin Sher, 1–15. Normal, IL: Dalkey Archive, 1990.

———. "O poezii i zaumnom iazyke." *Poetika. Sborniki po teorii poeticheskogo iazyka*. 13–26. Petrograd: 18-aia Gos. Tipografiia, 1919.

———. "O fakture i kontr-rel'efakh." *Khod konia: sbornik stat'ei*. 101–7. Moscow, Berlin: Helikon, 1923.

———. "O zakonakh kino." *Russkii sovremennik* 1 (1924): 245–52.

———. "Semantika kino." *Kino-zhurnal ARK* 8–9 (1925): 5. Reprinted in Shklovskii, Viktor, *Za 60 let. Raboty o kino*. 30–32. Moscow: Iskusstvo, 1985.

———. "Kuda shagaet Dziga Vertov?" *Sovetskii ekran* 32 (1926): 4.

———. "Pogranichnaia liniia." *Kino* 12 (March 22, 1927): 2. Reprinted in Shklovskii, Viktor, *Za 60 let. Raboty o kino*. 110–13. Moscow: Iskusstvo, 1985.

———. *Ikh nastoiashchee*. Moscow: Kinopechat', 1927. Reprinted in Shklovskii, Viktor, *Za 60 let. Raboty o kino*. 334–81. Moscow: Iskusstvo, 1985.

———. "Sherst', steklo i kruzheva." *Kino* 32 (August 9, 1927): 2.

———. "60 dnei bez sluzhby." *Novyi LEF* 6 (1927): 17–32.

———. "Veter iz Tiflisa." *Kino* 35 (1927): 2.

———. *Kak pisat' stsenarii*. Moscow: Gosudarstvennoe izdatel'stvo khudozhestvennoi literatury, 1931.

———. *Zoo, or Letters not about Love*. Translated by Richard Sheldon. Champaign, IL: Dalkey Archive, 2012.

Shlapentokh, Dmitrii. "The Fate of Nikolai Marr's Linguistic Theories: The case of Linguistics in Political Context." *Journal of Eurasian Studies* 2, no. 1 (January 2011): 60–73.

Shneider, M. "SVD." *Kinofront* 9–10 (1927): 18–20.
———. "Ukhaby." *Kinofront* 1 (1928): 19–22.
———. "Eliso." *Kino* 44 (October 30, 1928): 5.
Shukhin, Nicole. *Animal Capital: Rendering Life in Biopolitical Times*. Minneapolis: Minnesota University Press, 2009.
Simmel, Georg. "Architecture in the Age of Stalin." Translated by David Kettler. In Georg Simmel, "Two Essays," *The Hudson Review* 11, no. 3 (Autumn 1958): 371–85.
———. "The Metropolis and Mental Life." In *Simmel on Culture*, edited by David Frisby and Mike Featherstone, 174–87. London: Sage, 1997.
Sirotkina, Irina. "Nikolai Bernstein: The Years Before the 'Pavlovian Session.'" *Russian Studies in History* 34, no. 2 (1995): 24–36.
———. *Diagnosing Literary Genius: A Cultural History of Psychiatry in Russia, 1880–1930*. Baltimore: Johns Hopkins University Press, 2000.
———. "The Ubicuitous Reflex and its Critics in Post-Revolutionary Russia." *Berichte zur Wissenschaftsgeschichte* 32, no. 1 (2009): 70–81.
———. "The Art and Science of Movement in France and Russia." In *History of the Neurosciences in France and Russia: From Charcot and Sechenov to IBRO*, edited by Irina Sirotkina, Jean-Gaël Barbara, and Jean-Claude Dupont, 183–93. Paris: Hermann, 2011.
———. *Svobodnoe dvizhenie i plasticheskii tanets v Rossii*. Moscow: Novoe literaturnoe obozrenie, 2012.
———. *Shestoe chuvstvo avangarda: tanets, dvizhenie, kinesteziia v zhizni poetov i khudozhnikov*. Saint Petersburg: Evropeiskii universitet v Sankt Peterburge, 2014.
Sirotkina, Irina, and Roger Smith. "The Russian Federation." in *The Oxford Handbook of the History of Psychology: Global Perspectives*, edited by David B. Baker, 412–42. New York and Oxford: Oxford University Press, 2012.
Sirotkina, Irina, Jean-Gaël Barbara, and Jean-Claude Dupont, eds. *History of the Neurosciences in France and Russia: From Charcot and Sechenov to IBRO*. Paris: Hermann, 2011.
Skachko, A. "Kino dlia vostoka." *Kino-zhurnal ARK* 10 (1925): 3.
Slezkine, Yuri. "The USSR as Communal Apartment, or How a Socialist State Promoted Ethnic Particularism." *Slavic Review* 53, no. 2 (1994): 414–52.
———. *Arctic Mirrors: Russia and the Small Peoples of the North*, Ithaca: Cornell University Press, 1994.
Smith, Alison K. *Recipes for Russia: Food and Nationhood under the Tsars*. DeKalb: Northern Illinois University Press, 2008.
Smith, Mark D. *Sensing the Past: Seeing, Hearing, Smelling, Tasting and Touching in History*. Berkeley and Los Angeles: University of California Press, 2008.
Smith, T'ai. *Bauhaus Weaving Theory: From Feminine Craft to Mode of Design*. Minneapolis: Minnesota University Press, 2014.
Smith, Michael G. "Cinema for the 'Soviet East': National Fact and Revolutionary Fiction in Early Azerbaijani Film." *Slavic Review* 56, no. 4 (Winter 1997): 645–78.

Sobchak, Vivian. *Carnal Thoughts: Embodiment and Moving Image Culture.* Berkeley and Los Angeles: University of California Press, 2004.
Sobolev, R. P. *Liudi i fil'my dorevoliutsionnogo kino.* Moscow: Iskusstvo, 1961.
Sokolov, I. *Sistema trudovoi gimnastiki.* Moscow: R. Ts, 1922.
———. "Industrial'naia zhestikuliatsiia." *Ermitazh* 10 (July 1922): 6–7.
———. "Skrizhal' veka." *Kino-fot* 1 (1922): 3.
———. "Shinel'." *Kinofront* 5–6 (1926): 28.
———. "SVD." *Kinofront* 9–10 (1927): 20–23.
Solomon, Susan Gross. "Foreign Expertise on Russian Terrain: Max Kuczynski on the Kirghiz Steppe, 1923–4." In *Soviet Medicine: Culture, Practice and Science,* edited by Frances Bernstein, Christopher Burton, and Dan Healey, 71–92. DeKalb: Northern Illinois University Press, 2010.
Sopin, A., and A. Tremasov. "'Ukhaby': materialy o nesokhranivshemsia 'rabochem boevike.'" *Kinovedcheskie zapiski* 108–9 (2015): 15–35.
Starr, Frederick S. "The Revival and Schism of Urban Planning in Twentieth-Century Russia." In *The City in Russian History,* edited by Michael F. Hamm, 230–40. Lexington: University of Kentucky Press, 1976.
———. "Visionary Town Planning During the Revolution." In *Cultural Revolution in Russia, 1928–31,* edited by Sheila Fitzpatrick, 208–11. Bloomington: Indiana University Press, 1984.
———. *Red and Hot: The Fate of Jazz in the Soviet Union 1917–1991.* New York: Limelight, 1994.
Steinberg, Jonah. *Isma'ili Modern: Globalization and Identity in a Muslim Community.* Chapel Hill: University of North Carolina Press, 2011.
Steinberg, Mark D., and Valerie Sobol, eds., *Interpreting Emotions in Russia and Eastern Europe.* DeKalb: Northern Illinois University Press, 2011.
Strakhov, V. "Kruzheva." *Kino* 38 (Leningrad) (July 8, 1928): 2.
Strätling, Susanne. "Das buchstäbliche Erscheinen und Verschwinden. Zur De-Materialisierung von Schriftflächen zwischen konstruktiv und konkret (El' Lisickij und Carlfriedrich Claus)." *Plurale. Zeitschrift für Denkversionen,* 0 (2001): 107–39.
———. "Play with Words: Hands-on Aesthetics in Constructivist Book Design." Conference paper delivered at "Design without Frontiers: Interdisciplinarity and Collaboration in Soviet Art, Architecture and Design," Cambridge University, September 20–21, 2012.
Strätling, Susanne, and Jocelyn Holland, eds. "Aesthetics of the Tool." Special issue of *Configurations. A Journal of Literature, Science, and Technology* 18, no. 3 (Fall 2010).
Strizhenova, Tat'iana. *Iz istorii sovetskogo kostiuma.* Moscow: Sovetskii khudozhnik, 1972.
Subotskii, Ia. "'Gibel' sensatsii': novaia kartina Mezhrabpomfil'ma." *Pravda* 112 (April 23, 1935): 4.
Sutyrin, V. "Ot intelligentskikh illiuzii k real'noi deistvitel'nosti." *Proletarskoe kino* 5–6 (1931): 14–24.

Tan. "Pervaia armianskaia kartina." *Sovetskii ekran* 14 (1926): 5.
Tarabukin, Nikolai. *Ot mol′berta k mashine*. Moscow: Rabotnik prosveshcheniia, 1923.
Tarkhanov, I. "Oshchushchenie." *Entsiklopedicheskii slovar′ Brokgauza i Efrona*. Tom 22, 537–41. Saint Petersburg: Semenovskaia tipolitografiia (I. A. Efrona), 1897.
Tashiro, Charles S. *Pretty Pictures: Production Design and the History Film*. Austin: University of Texas Press, 1998.
Tatlin, Vladimir, Tevel′ Shapiro, Iosif Meerson, and Pavel Vinogradov. "Nasha predstoiashchaia rabota." *VIII s′′ezd Sovetov. Ezhednevnyi biulleten′ s′ezda* (January 1, 1921): 11.
Taussig, Michael. *Mimesis and Alterity: A Particular History of the Senses*. New York and London: Routledge, 1993.
Taylor, Richard. *The Politics of the Soviet Cinema, 1917–1929*. Cambridge: Cambridge University Press, 1979.
Teplov, V. "Chuvstvo." *Bol′shaia sovetskaia entsiklopediia*, 1-oe izdanie. Tom 61, 727–29. 1934.
Tihanov, Galin. "The Politics of Estrangement: The Case of Early Shklovsky." *Poetics Today* 26, no. 4 (Winter 2005): 665–96.
———. "Gustav Shpet's Literary and Theater Affiliations." In *Gustav Shpet's Contribution to Philosophy and Cultural Theory*, edited by Galin Tihanov, 56–82. West Lafayette, IN: Purdue University Press, 2009.
Tikhonov, N. "Fot." *Kinofot* 8 (September 15, 1922): 4.
Til′berg, Margareta. *Tsvetnaia vselennaia: Mikhail Matiushin ob iskusstve i zrenii*. Moscow: Novoe literaturnoe obozrenie, 2008.
Todes, Daniel P. *Ivan Pavlov. A Russian Life in Science*. Oxford: Oxford University Press, 2014.
Todorova, Maria. "Does Russian Orientalism Have a Russian Soul? A Contribution to the Debate between Nathaniel Knight and Adeeb Khalid." *Kritika* 1, no. 4 (2000): 717–27.
Tolz, Vera. *Russia's Own Orient: The Politics of Identity and Oriental Studies in the Late Imperial and Early Soviet Periods*. Oxford: Oxford University Press, 2011.
Toporkov, A. K. *Tekhnicheskii byt i sovremennoe iskussstvo* (Leningrad: Gosizdat, 1928).
———. "O predmetnom zheste v kino." *Kino i kul′tura* 2 (February 1929): 33–42.
———. *Predmetnyi zhest*. Moscow: Teakinopechat′, 1929.
Toropova, Anna. "'Educating the Emotions': Affect and Stylistic Excess in the Stalinist Melodrama." *English Language Notes* 48, no. 1 (Spring/Summer 2010): 49–63.
———. "Educating the Emotions: Affect, Genre Film, and Ideology under Stalin." PhD diss., University College London, 2012.
Tret′iakov, Sergei. "Otkuda i kuda?—Perspektivy futurizma." *LEF* 1 (1923): 192–203.
———. "Liubit′ Kitai." *Shkval* 25 (1925): 14–15. Reprinted in Tret′iakov, Sergei, *Chzhungo*, 7–10. Moscow-Leningrad: Gosizdat, 1927.
———. "Tekushchie dela." *Novyi LEF* 8–9 (1927): 87–88.

———. "Strana Svan." *Novyi LEF* 11–12 (1927): 12–25.

———. "Sem′ smertnykh grekhov nashei kinematografii (na doklade S. Tret′iakova, 2 aprelia)." *Zaria Vostoka* 1443, (April 5, 1927). Reprinted in Tret′iakov, Sergei, *Kinematograficheskoe nasledie. Stat′i, ocherki, stenogrammy vystuplenii, doklady. Stsenarii*, edited by Irina Ratiani, 145–47. Saint Petersburg: Nestor-Istoriia, 2010.

———. "Mtsyri," *Pravda* 90 (April 21, 1927): 4.

———. "Shest′ millionov let (poezdka v Svanetiiu)." *Zaria Vostoka* 1597, (October 9, 1927): 2. Reprinted in Tret′iakov, Sergei, *Kinematograficheskoe nasledie. Stat′i, ocherki, stenogrammy vystuplenii, doklady. Stsenarii*, edited by Irina Ratiani, 150–53. Saint Petersburg: Nestor-Istoriia, 2010.

———. "Tri zapora (Poezdka v Svanetiiu)." *Zaria Vostoka* 1599 (October 12, 1927): 3. Reprinted in Tret′iakov, Sergei, *Kinematograficheskoe nasledie. Stat′i, ocherki, stenogrammy vystuplenii, doklady. Stsenarii*, edited by Irina Ratiani, 154–56. Saint Petersburg: Nestor-Istoriia, 2010.

———. "Chem zhivo kino?" *Novyi LEF* 5 (1928): 23–28.

———. "Liudi v ushchel′iakh." *Pravda* (April 15, 1928): 4. Reprinted in Tret′iakov, Sergei, *Kinematograficheskoe nasledie: stat′i, ocherki, stenogrammy vystuplenii, doklady. Stsenarii*, edited by Irina Ratiani, 156–160. Saint Petersburg: Nestor-Istoriia, 2010.

———. "Skvoz′ neprotertye ochki." *Novyi LEF* 9 (1928): 20–24.

———. "Biografiia veshchi." In *Literatura fakta: pervyi sbornik materialov rabotnikov LEFa*, edited by N. Chuzhak, 29–34. Moscow: Zakharov, (1929) 2000.

———. *Kinematograficheskoe nasledie: stat′i, ocherki, stenogrammy vystuplenii, doklady. Stsenarii*. Edited by Irina Ratiani. Saint Petersburg: Nestor-Istoriia, 2010.

Tret′iakov, Sergei and M. E. Chiaureli. "Khabarda! (Postoronis′!) Kinopamflet v shesti chastiakh." In Tret′iakov, Sergei, *Kinematograficheskoe nasledie: stat′i, ocherki, stenogrammy vystuplenii, doklady. Stsenarii*, edited by Irina Ratiani, 295–335. Saint Petersburg: Nestor-Istoriia, 2010.

Trotter, David. *Cinema and Modernism*. Malden, MA and Oxford: Blackwell, 2008.

———. *Literature in the First Media Age: Britain between the Wars*. Cambridge, MA: Harvard University Press, 2013.

Trotskii, Lev. *Literatura i revoliutsiia*. Moscow: 1923.

———. *Literature and Revolution*. Ann Arbor: University of Michigan Press, 1975.

Tsivian, Yuri. "Two 'Stylists' of the Teens: Franz Hofer and Evgenii Bauer." In *A Second Life: German Cinema's First Decades*, edited by Thomas Elsaesser and Michael Wedel, 264–76. Amsterdam: Amsterdam University Press, 1996.

Tsivian, Yury (Yuri), ed. *Lines of Resistance: Dziga Vertov and the Twenties*. Sacile: Le Giornate del cinema muto, 2004.

Tugendkhol′d, Iakov. "Iskusstvo i sovremennost′." In Tugendkhol′d, Iakov, *Iskusstvo Oktiabr′skoi epokhi*. Leningrad: Akademiia, 1930. Reprinted in *Bor′ba za realism v iskusstve 20-kh godov: materialy, dokumenty, vospominaniia*, edited by V. N. Perel′man, 216–22. Moscow: Sovetskii khudozhnik, 1961.

Turovskaia, M., and I. Khaniutin. *Sergei Iutkevich*. Moscow: Biuro propagandy sovetskogo kinoiskusstva, 1968.
Turovskaia, M. I., and Y. Chanutin, *Sergei Jutkewitsch*. Berlin: Henschelverlag, 1968.
Turvey, Malcolm. "Balázs: Realist or Modernist?" *October* 115 (Winter 2006): 77–87.
Tyerman, Edward. "The Search for Internationalist Aesthetics: Soviet Images of China, 1920–1935." PhD diss., Columbia University, 2014.
Tynianov, Iurii. "Libretto kino-film'a 'Shinel'.'" In *Iz istorii Lenfil'ma, III (Stat'i, vospominaniia, dokumenty: 1920–1930e gody)*, edited by N. S. Gornitskaia, 78. Leningrad: Iskusstvo, leningradskoe otdelenie, 1973.
———. "O feksakh." *Sovetskii ekran* 14 (1929): 10.
Urussova, Janina. *Das neue Moskau: Die Stadt der Sowjets im Film 1917–41*. Cologne, Weimar, Vienna: Bohlau verlag, 2004.
Vaingurt, Julia. "Poetry of Labour and the Labour of Poetry: The Universal Language of Alexei Gastev's Theory of Biomechanics." *Russian Review* 67, no. 2 (April 2008): 209–29.
Vainshtein, O. *Aromaty i zapakhi v kul'ture*, 2 volumes. Moscow: Novoe literaturnoe obozrenie, 2010.
Vaisfel'd, I. "Na putiakh k iskusstvu sotsializma." *Sovetskoe kino* 1–2 (1934): 15–23.
———. "Itogi diskussii o 'Dukhe fil'my.'" *Iskusstvo kino* 6 (1936): 46–51.
Vaks, L. "ODSK na prosmotre 'Kruzhev.'" *Kino* 21, (May 22, 1928): 5.
———. "V obshchestve druzei sovetskoi kinematografii: 'Eliso.'" *Kino* 39 (September 25, 1928): 5.
Van Elteren, Mel. "Kurt Lewin as Filmmaker and Methodologist." *Canadian Psychology/Psychologie canadienne* 33, no. 3 (July 1992): 599–608.
Vasil'ev, Al. "Eshche ob 'Ukhabakh.'" *Kino* 9 (February 28, 1928): 3.
Vasil'eva, Iu. (Julia Vassilieva). "Eizenshtein v arkhive A. R. Luriia." *Kinovedcheskie zapiski* 8 (1990): 79–96.
———. "Eisenstein/Vygotsky/Luria's Project: Cinematic Thinking and the Integrative Science of Mind and Brain." *Screening the Past* (2013): 12. Accessed September 8, 2015. http://www.screeningthepast.com/2013/12/eisenstein-vygotsky-luria%E2%80%99s-project-cinematic-thinking-and-the-integrative-science-of-mind-and-brain/#_ednref61.
Vertov, Dziga. "Kinoki. Perevorot." *LEF* 3 (1923): 141.
———. "Ruki, etude," 1927?, RGALI 2091-2-22. Reproduced in *Lines of Resistance: Dziga Vertov and the Twenties*, edited by Yury Tsivian, 282–85. Sacile: Le Giornate del cinema muto, 2004.
Victorov, Viktor. *The Natalia Sats Children's Musical Theatre*. Translated by Miriam Morton. Moscow: Raduga, 1986.
Vishnevskii, Vsevolod. "Protiv kamernoi kinematografii." *Kino* 20 (April 29, 1937): 2.
Voevodin, V. "V. Egorov—Khudozhnik fil'ma V. Meierkhol'da 'Portret Doriana Greia.'" *Kinovedcheskie zapiski* 13 (1992): 214–24.

Vöhringer, Margarete. *Avantgarde und Psychotechnik: Wissenschaft, Kunst und Technik der Wahrnehmungsexperimente in der frühen Sowjetunion*. Gottingen: Wallstein Verlag, 2007.

———. "Professionalisiertes Laientum: Nikolaj Ladovskijs Psychotechnisches Labor für Architektur." In *Laien, Lektören, Laboratorium: Künst und Wissenschaften in Russland 1860–1960*, edited by Matthias Schwarz,Wladimir Velminski, and Torben Philipp, 325–47. Frankfurt: Peter Lang, 2008.

Volkonskii, Sergei. *Vyrazitel'nyi chelovek*. Saint Petersburg: Apollon, 1913.

Voronskii, Aleksandr. *Iskusstvo videt' mir: O novom realizme*. Moscow: Krug, 1928.

———. "The Art of Seeing the World (The New Realism)." In *Art as the Cognition of Life: Selected Writings 1911–1936*. Edited and translated by Frederick S. Choate, 361–91. Oak Park, MI: Mehring Books, 1998.

Vygotskii, Lev (Lev Vygotskii). "Igra i ee rol' v psikhicheskom razvitii rebenka." *Voprosy psikhologii* 6 (1966): 62–76.

———. *The Psychology of Art*. Cambridge, MA: MIT Press, (1925) 1971.

———. "Istoricheskii smysl psikhologicheskogo krizisa." *Sobranie sochinenii v 6-ti tomakh*. Tom 1, *Voprosy teorii i istorii psikhologii*, edited A. R. by Luriia and M. G. Iaroshevskii, 291–436. Moscow: Pedagogika, 1982. Published in English as "The Historical Meaning of the Crisis in Psychology: A Methodological Investigation." In *The Collected Works of L. S. Vygotskii*. Vol. 3, *Problems of the Theory and History of Psychology*, edited by Robert W. Rieber and Jeffrey Wollock, 233–343. New York: Plenum Press, 1997.

———. "Soznanie kak problema psikhologii povedeniia." In *Sobranie sochinenii v 6-ti tomakh*. Tom 1, *Voprosy teorii i istorii psikhologii*, edited by A. R. Luriia and M. G. Iaroshevskii, 78–98. Moscow: Pedagogika, 1982.

———. "Play and its Role in the Mental Development of the Child." In *Play: Its Role in Development and Evolution*, edited by Jerome S. Bruner, Alison Jolly, and Kathy Sylva, 537–55. Harmondsworth: Penguin, 1985.

Wall-Romana, Christophe. *Jean Epstein: Corporeal Cinema and Film Philosophy*. Manchester: Manchester University Press, 2013.

Ward, Chris. *Russia's Cotton Workers and the New Economic Policy: Shop Floor Culture and State Policy, 1921–1929*. Cambridge: Cambridge University Press, 1990.

Webber, Andrew. "Cut and Laced: Traumatism in Luis Buñuel's Un Chien Andalou." In *Projected Shadows: Psychoanalytic Reflections on the Representation of Loss in European Cinema*, edited by Andrea Sabbadini, 92–101. London: Routledge, 2007.

Widdis, Emma. *Visions of a New Land: Soviet Film from the Revolution to the Second World War*. New Haven and London: Yale University Press, 2003.

———. "Cinema and the Art of Being: Towards a History of Early Soviet Set Design." In *Companion to Russian Cinema*, edited by Birgit Beumers. Malden, MA: Wiley-Blackwell, 2016.

———. *Revolutionary Bodies, Soviet Minds: A Source Book, 1917–1941*. Bloomington: Indiana University Press, forthcoming 2018.

Wigley, Mark. *White Walls, Designer Dresses: The Fashioning of Modern Architecture*. Cambridge, MA: MIT Press, 2001.
Witte, Georg. "Between the Forge and the Assembly Line. The False Time of the Tool in the Work of Andrej Platonov." In "Aesthetics of the Tool," edited by Susanne Strätling and Jocelyn Holland. Special Issue of *Configurations. A Journal of Literature, Science, and Technology* 18, no. 3 (Fall 2010): 203–9.
———. "Die Emotionen der Kunst." In *Form und Wirkung: Phänomenologische i empirische Kunstwissenschaft in der Sowjetunion der 1920er Jahre*, edited by Aage Hansen-Löve, Brigitte Obermayer, and Georg Witte, 343–85. Paderborn, Germany: Wilhelm Fink, 2013.
Wölfflin, Heinrich. *Principles of Art History: The Problem of Style in Later Art*. Mineola, NY: Dover Publications, 2012.
Wollen, Peter. "Fashion/Orientalism/The Body." *New Formations* 1 (Spring 1987): 5–33.
Wood, Gaby. *Living Dolls: A Magical History of the Quest for Mechanized Life*. London: Faber & Faber, 2003.
Worringer, Wilhelm. *Abstraction and Empathy: Problems in the Psychology of Style*. Chicago, IL: Ivan Dee, 2009.
Wünsche, Isabel. "The Evolution of Human Eyesight: Mikhail Matiushin's Organic Culture in Russian Avant-garde Art." *Australian & New Zealand Journal of Art* 12, no. 1 (2012): 25–41.
———. *Kunst & Leben: Michail Matjuschin und die russische Avantgarde in St. Petersburg*. Cologne: Böhlau, 2012.
Wurm, Barbara. "Gastevs Medien: Das 'Foto-Kino-Labor' des CIT." In *Laien, Lektüren, Laboratorium: Künste und Wissenschaften in Russland 1860–1960*, edited by Matthias Schwartz, Wladimir Velminski, and Torben Philipp, 347–93. Frankfurt: Peter Lang, 2008.
Yampolsky, Mikhail, see Iampolskii Mikhail.
Youngblood, Denise J. *Soviet Cinema in the Silent Era, 1918–1935*. Austin: Texas University Press, 1991.
Zacharias, Kyllikki. "Movement within Nature: Boris Ender and the Geptakhor Studio." *Experiment/Eksperiment* 2, no. 1 (1996): 293–305.
Zalkind, Aron. *Ocherki kul'tury revoliutsionnogo vremeni*. Moscow: 1924.
———. "Refleksologiia i nasha sovremennost'." In *Novoe v refleksologii i fiziologii nervnoi sistemy*, edited by V. M. Bekhterev, v–vii. Moscow: Gos. Izdatel'stvo, 1925.
———. "Psikhologiia cheloveka budushchego (sotsial'no-psikhologicheskii ocherk)." Reprinted as "Die Psychologie des Menschen der Zukunft" translated by Dagmar Kassek. In *Die neue Menschheit: Biopolitische Utopien in Russland des 20 Jahrhunderts*, edited by Boris Groys and Michael Hagemeister, 608–89. Frankfurt: Suhrkamp, 2001.
Zhdan, Antonina. "Art History and Psychology at RAKhN: An Experiment in Collaboration." *Experiment/Eksperiment* 3, no. 1 (1997): 69–75.
Zhemchuzhnyi, Vit. "Khaz-Push." *Kino* 5 (January 31, 1928): 3.
Zorkaia, Neia. "Odna na perekrestakh." *Kinovedcheskie zapiski* 74 (2005): 143–59.

INDEX

Accordion, The. See Savchenko, Igor'
acting, 34, 234, 235–237, 261n33, 308–309
Aelita. See Protazanov, Iakov
Aerial Adventure, An. See Arusinskaia, Tat'iana
affekt/affect, 5; contemporary theory of, 43–44, 341; 17, 75, 127–128, 131–132, 200n88, 229, 233, 234, 245, 258, 259, 260n10, 266, 272, 342; affective power of cinema and production design), 41, 52, 61, 63, 73, 75–76, 128–129, 178; in Socialist Realist cinema, 232, 244–245, 252, 258–259, 273, 274; power of play, 306–307, 309, 335n54
Al'tman, Natan, 58
Albatros, l'. See Meerson, Lazar, 55–56
Aleksandrov, Grigorii, 225n34, 298; *Jolly Fellows*, 316, 317, 336n84, 350; *Radiant Path,* 317
All-Russian Neurological conference, 11
All-Union Conference on Cinema (1935), 228
All-Union Experimental Children's Film Unit, 308
All-Union Party Conference on Film (1928), 85
Almas. See Braginskii, Grigorii
Almas. See Kuliev, Aga-Rza
Alone. See FEKS
Amerikanka. See Esakiia, Leo
Andreev, Andrei: production designer, 58, 62

Andrievskii, Aleksandr: *Death of Sensation,* 342–344, 347–349, 351
appliqué, 106–108, 109–111, 118, 121n42
Arendt, Hannah: concept of *homo faber,* 135–136
Armenkino, 173, 181
Arsen'ev, Vladimir, 169
Artaud, Antonin, 37
artisan. *See also* handcraft, rukodelie, craft, 128, 134, 137, 138, 150, 262n71
Arusinskaia, Tatiana, *An Aerial Adventure,* 329–333
Arvatov, Boris, 32–33
Atel'e, 107
avant-garde, 2, 7, 18; theory, 27–33, 43, 45n12, n20, 46n34, 338, 344, 346, 348, 351; influence on theatre and film set design 55–56, 65, 208, 212, 214; filmmaking, 70, 79, 86, 158; and folk craft, 107–109; and hands, 109–110, 131, 274, 338; and the national republics, 167, 169, 172, 181, 197n32; 235; and adaptation to Socialist Realism, 236, 237, 242, 256, 280; and the past, 274–275; and children's culture, 300–303, 306–307, 310, 322, 344
Averbakh, Mikhail: *In the Big City,* 205–208
Azerkino, 170, 171, 172, 173, 324; Azerfilm (from 1935), 289

backwardness: as description of provincial Russia, 99; of national republics, 166, 171, 187, 191, 197n17, 241, 266, 273, 269
Bakst, Leon, 167
Balázs, Béla, 21–22, 39–41, 232–233, 242–245, 258–259, 339; on historical cinema, 73–75
Ballets Russes, 55, 68, 167, 170
Balliuzek, Vladimir, 55, 56; *Legend of the Maiden's Tower*, 170
Band of Imps, The. See Popov, Aleksandr
Barnet, Boris, 111, 338; *Girl with a Hatbox*, 112–116; *House on Trubnaia Square*, 112; *Outskirts*, 135, 245–249, 262n71
Barskaia, Margarita: and children's cinema, 308, 309–310; *Torn Boots*, 308–309
Battleship Potemkin. See Eisenstein, Sergei
Bauer, Evgenii, 53, 173, 334n31; and set design, 53–55, 54, 80n12, 216–217
Bed and Sofa. See Room, Abram
Bek-Nazarov, Amo, 172–173; *Honour*, 173–177; *Khaz-Push*, 181–187; *Sevil*, 289–290
Bekhterev, Vladimir, 13, 14; and cinema, 35–36, 47n54, 236
Belyi, Andrei, 167, 300
Benjamin, Walter: and experience of modernity, 4, 37; and "innervation," 21, 26n88, 300, 309, 316; and cinema's "optical unconscious," 37–38, 141, 196; and toys and children's play, 299–302, 303, 308, 316
Bernstein, Nikolai, 34, 131; and "technical intelligence," 131
Bezhin Meadow. See Eisenstein, Sergei
biomechanics, 34–35, 131, 199n72, 235, 349
blacksmith, 106, 123, 131, 150, 161n21, 163n77
Bleiman, Mikhail: critic, 61–62, 71–73,159, 230, 242–244, 248, 262n71
Blok, Aleksandr: on revolutionary iconoclasm, 5, 167
Boas, Franz, 161n22
Bodrost'. See merriness, 316
body: regulation and/or emancipation of, 5, 10, 21–22, 34–35, 88, 163n, 212, 254–257, 316, 341, 348–351; research into movement and sensations of, 33–35, 131, 354; in early and contemporary film theory, 36–38, 43–44, 214–216, 298; and mind in Soviet psychological theory, 12–16, 17–18,

25n64, 26n77, 235–36, 245, 337, 340; and relationship with material world, ix, 1–7, 8–11, 17, 18, 19, 27, 28–29, 31–33, 37–38, 130–131, 204, 209, 213–214, 228, 240, 337, 341, 354; and relationship with tools/machines, 103, 106, 132, 136–143, 155, 157, 160, 161n22, 163n86, 343, 346–351; film spectatorship of and through the, 76, 92, 101, 103, 113–116, 127, 155, 187, 216, 235, 237, 246, 249, 250, 273, 309; imagined "primitive," 166, 168, 188–189, 194–195, 278, 346–347; in Socialist Realism, 254–257, 259, 263n88, 278, 298, 303, 320, 324; as abstraction, 7, 340. *See also* sensation, 341, 343
Borovskii, Vladimir: psychologist, 12, 14
bourgeois, 127, 147, 162n55, 182, 212, 223, 283, 289, 300, 304, relationships with things, 31–32, 78, 146, 213, 253; art and cinema, 58, 251, 301; decoration and design, 58, 75–76, 87, 107–108, 111–114, 115, 119, 133, 145, 148, 155, 207, 210, 213, 221–222, 223, 225n34, 238; entertainment, 343–344, 347, 351; bodies, 348–349; emotions, 257
Braginskii, Grigorii, *Almas*, 289–291
bricolage, bricoleur. *See also* do-it-yourself, 203, 211, 224n13, 343, 347
Brik, Osip, 134
Bukharin, Nikolai, 2, 11, 13–14, 25n65
Bukhkino, 170
bulls, 125–127
Burliuk, David, 29, 167, 198n36
byt: imperative to show on screen, 61, 72, 86, 128, 214–215; *novyi*, 145, 207; *rabochii*, 128, 146; native, 240, definition of, 356

Cain i Artem. See Petrov–Bytov, Pavel
capitalism sensory relationship with objects and material world under, 1, 37–38, 44, 125, 157, 188, 190, 191, 196, 203–204, 223, 343; alienated labour of, 132, 211, 243
Caucasus, 19, 165, 166, 170, 172, 177, 178, 179, 180, 192, 283
Central Asia, 196, 197n16, 267, 275, 276, 280, 281
Chance Encounter, A. See Savchenko, Igor'
Chelpanov, Georgii: psychologist, 13, 14, 46n35

Cherviakov, Ivan: as actor, 71; as exemplary of "emotional cinema," 230–231; *My Son*, 230–234
childhood, 20, 298, 299–300, 302; state's attitude to, 303–307; as model for revolutionary selfhood, 299–300, 308, 312, 314, 321; films about, 308–309, 310–313
children, 96, 109, 114, 158, 174, 184, 272, 286, 287, 290, 291; cinema for, 298, 307–313; state's attitude to, 299–300, 303–307, 318; scientific study of, 308; and play, 302, 304–307; and do-it-yourself, 306–307, 310–311
chuvstvennyi blesk. See sensory radiance
chuvstvo, chuvstva. See also feelings, 6, 73; definition of 16–18, 20, 23n18; as both sensory and emotional, 224, 250, 252, 259, 260n3; "a cinema of socialist," 227–230; search for appropriate Soviet, 229–230; *chuvstvitelnost´*, 22; *chuvstvovanie*, 16, 30–31
Chuzhak, Nikolai, 30–31, 46n24, 198n36
cinematography, 20, 62, 73, 261n44
clay, 31, 137, 184, 343
cloth. See also textile, fabric, 85, 91, 94, 96–97, 115, 118, 120n21, 142, 174, 223, 267, 278–279
clothes: clothing, 63, 86, 91, 92, 97, 113, 115, 117, 142, 144, 184, 267, 278–279, 297, 289, 292, 297; design for new Soviet, 107–109, 213, 217, 254; in Socialist Realist cinema, 297, 324, 326
cobbler. See also shoemaker, 124, 133, 135; see *The Parisian Cobbler*
consciousness. See also *soznatel´nost´*, 4, 5, 6, 8, 20–21; relationship between "spontaneity" and, 5, 23n13, 313, 320, 349; as discussed in Soviet psychology, 13, 15–16, 17, 18, 25n64, 192, 200n82, 228, 245, 259; conquest of over sensation, 279, 337, 341; and cinema, 35–36; development of political, 127, 141, 147, 187, 193, 242, 247, 289, 291, 311, 316, 320, 333; 278, 279, 311, 313
Constructivism, and "material," 30–33, 128, 131; and set design, 55, 60; and craft, 107; ludic qualities of, 307
control (*ovladenie*): as central metaphor for Soviet culture, 4, 191, 341, 343, 346,
349; of self, 16–17, 35, 229, 258; of the material world, 28, 36, 42, 132, 188, 275; of the spectator through film, 40. See also mastery, regulation
costume drama. See also historical film, 19, 58, 60–79; prerevolutionary, 60; ideological difficulty of, 60–62
costume: design in film, 19, 51, 55, 58, 59, 62, 71, 72, 73, 81n25; avant-garde 214, 217; traditional peasant/folk, 96, 97, 99, 107, 217, 326; national, 167, 174, 279, 282, 283–284, 286, 289, 291; in Socialist Realist cinema, 326, 328
cotton, 267, 268
Counterplan. See Ermler, Frikrikh
craft, 19, 94, 103, 106, 107–111, 123, 143, 148, 353; as processing, 109, 119; in the domestic interior, 109–111; as model of "making," 130, 133, 134, 136–138, 140, 160, 161n22, 162n71, 205, 247, 303, 334n25; in "primitive" societies, 175, 181, 194, 203, 269, 290; and children, 310–311. See also handcraft, folk craft
Crown Prince of the Republic, The. See Ioganson, Eduard
curtains, 54, 69, 118, 133, 155, 213, 221, 236

Danish film school, 56
Davydova, Natal´ia, 108, 148
Decembrists, The. See Ivanovskii, Aleksandr
decoration, decorative: in production design, 52, 55, 58, 60, 63, 66, 72, 85–86, 96, 187; inappropriateness of in Soviet world, 59, 86–87, 107, 110–111, 112, 118, 145, 148, 203, 212, 218–219, 222; ambivalence of attitudes towards, 111, 116, 218; in films set in national republics, 170, 174–176, 181–182, 187, 278, 280, 282, 285, 286, 291; in bourgeois space, 207; opposition between "decorative" and volume in production design, 55, 59–60, 71, 76; opposition between "decorative" and "authentic" material in production design, 61, 94, 96, 101. See also ornament, production design
defamiliarization. See also *ostranenie*, 42
Delluc, Louis, 39–40, 41–43, 48n82, 81n35, 128, 232

Delsarte, François, 163n86
design: of new Soviet future, 31–33, 86–87, 107–111, 145, 204–210, 212–214, 215–216, 221–222, 313–314
Dewey, John, 304
Diagilev, Sergei, 55, 167
dialectic: dialectical, 5, 17, 30–31, 35, 209, 259, 269, 273–275, 282
dikovinka, 54, 80n12. *See also* set design
Dinghaftigkeit, 37. *See also* Lukacs
disgust, 178, 180–181, 184, 187
Dmitriev, Aleksei: *The Mechanical Traitor*, 210–211
do-it-yourself, 110, 211–212; children's play, 306–307, 310–311. *See also samodelka, rukodelie*, homemade, craft, handcraft, making
Dokuchaev, Nikolai, 31
Dolidze, Siko, *The Last Crusaders*, 283–284
domestic space, 62, 85–87; in films set in provincial Russia, 88–92; in "everyday" films, 111–115, 205–208, 208–210, 213, 221–224; in real Soviet homes, 109–11; in films of national republics, 174–175. *See also* interiors
Donskoi, Mark, 172; *In the Big City*, 205–208, 210, 215
Dovzhenko, Aleksandr, 230, 247; *Earth*, 141, 261n37
drapery, 54, 80n12, 112, 222, 225n34
Driving a Holtze. *See* Esakiia, Leo

Earth. *See* Dovzhenko, Aleksandr
East, Soviet East, 166–196, 265–293. *See also* orient, primitive
Eggert, Konstantin, 60
Egorov, Vladimir: set designer, 54, 55, 56, 60, 66, 80n18, 82n71, 328; and *The Tailor from Torzhok*, 88, 89; and *The Thirteen*, 281
Eikhenbaum, Boris, 41–42, 49n104
Einfühlung, 132. *See also* empathy
Eisenstein, Sergei, 53, 86, 138, 147, 198n35, 348; and psychology, 36, 194, 258–259, 308; and montage as a recarving of "material," 40, 49n97; and "expressive movement," 36; 40; and "sensuous thinking," 194–196, 229; and "primitive" thought, 194–195; and children, 308; *Strike*, 58, 127; *Battleship Potemkin*, 59; *The General Line*, 141–142, 204–205, 224n4; *October*, 163n75, 191; *The Glass House*, 203–205; *Bezhin Meadow*, 234
Ekk, Nikolai, *A Path to Life*, 135–136, 138
Ekster, Aleksandra, 108, 214, 251n11
El Lissitzkii, 3, 4, 12
Eleventh Year, The. *See* Vertov, Dziga
Eliso. *See* Shengelaia, Nikolai
emancipation, (of the body and senses), 1, 5, 8, 104, 171, 188, 331, 349, 351; tension between regulation and, 5, 44, 266
embroidery, 103, 107–109, 113
emotion: in Soviet psychological science, 13–16, 228; definition of 16–18, 26n77; in art and cinema, 33, 36, 163n88, 178; search for specifically Soviet model of, 142, 222, 233, 237 243, 248, 257, 313; regulation/education of, 228, 234, 249, 257, 337
emotional cinema. *See* psychological cinema
emotional saturation. *See emotsional'naia nasyshchennost'*
emotional scenario, 235
Rzheshevskii, Aleksandr, 235. *See* emotional scenario
empathy: between human and thing, 127, 132, 142; in film spectatorship, 178, 181, 184, 272, 293. *See also* reciprocity
Enchmen, Emanuil, 25n64, 25n65
Enei, Evgenii, set designer, 56, 57; and *The Overcoat*, 62–63, 64; and *SVD*, 73–75; *New Babylon*, 75–77; *Alone*, 237–243
Epstein, Jean, 48n78, 74, 81n35, 82n72, 163n81, 232–233
Ermler, Frikrikh, 83n92, 238; *Kat'ka-bumaznyi ranet*, 114–115; *The Parisian Cobbler*, 132–139; *Fragment of an Empire*, 212, 247, 286; *Counterplan*, 221–222, 242
Ermol'ev studio, 55, 88
Esakiia, Leo, 179, 197n32, 338; *Driving a Holtze*, 141–142; *Amerikanka*, 142–144
ethnography, 95–96, 191–193, 283, 287; ethnographic eye of camera, 172–177, 181, 187, 190, 195, 282–284, 286, 289, 291; detail in set design, 59, 95–96, 172–177, 181, 286–287
ethnopathology, 191–192

everyday (life): transformation of, 2, 32, 37, 108–109, 118, 127, 124, 168, 208–209, 215, 306; (call for) films about, 19, 38, 61, 72, 86, 87, 111, 113, 115, 128–130, 132, 133, 157, 215–216, 228, 248, 302; industrial, 157; in the national republics, 171, 173, 174–176, 193, 338. See also *byt*
exotic (exoticism): as criticism of film production design, 61, 66, 171, 173, 177, 178, 181, 191, 285, 286, 292; in attitudes toward the "East," 165–167, 170, 179; complexity of relationships toward, 179–181

fabric, 85; in set design, 63, 68–69, 73, 75, 89–91, 96, 113, 118, 167; in avant-garde theory, 107; in home decoration, 110, 111, 118; the production of, 267; in images of "traditional" and "backward" cultures, 176, 213, 292. See also textile, weaving, sewing, embroidery
factography, 180
faktura, 18, 19, 20, 28, 41, 99; definition of, 29–30; of language, 29; and set design, 59, 60, 65; and historical film, 62–63; 116, 118, 144, 145, 159, 176, 188, 216, 266, 269; oriental, 279, 282, 284, 310, 321
fashion, 107–109, 118, 213
Feeling(s). See *chuvtvo*, emotion, sensation
FEKS (Factory of the Eccentric Actor), 338, 348, 351; and costume drama, 61–65, 71–79; *The Overcoat*, 62–63; *SVD*, 71–75; *New Babylon*, 75–79; *Alone*, 237–242, 261n45; and puppets, 344
Film Eye. See Vertov, Dziga
Film Week. See Vertov, Dziga
First Congress of the Peoples of the East, 168
First Exhibition of Modern Decorative Art, 108
Five Year Plan, 6, 19, 85, 116, 123, 192, 227, 228, 265, 266, 306, 331
Fliers. See Raizman, Iurii
folk: as style in film making, 59, 88, 96, 113, 285, 298, 326; craft (see also craft), 103; craft and avant-garde, 107–109; 111, 118, 167

Formalism, formalist, 29–30, 337; and *Photogénie*, 41–42; and cinema, 41–43; and "material," 49n106, 49n108, 128; as (often negative) description of film/art, 65, 82n63, 154–155, 230, 235, 248, 256, 258–259, 297, 323
Fragment of an Empire. See Ermler, Frikrikh
Frank, Semen, psychologist, 13
Frenkel', Lazar', *The Wondrous Garden*, 310–312
Fundus, 53, 57, 80n8, 80n24. See also production design
fur, 79, 188, 203–204, 199n67
Futurists, Futurism, 29, 45, 68, 167, 181, 274, 290, 316, 333n17

Gaivorovskii, Aleksandr, psychologist, 16, 228, 260n3
GAKHN, 33–34, 46n34, 49–50, 339; laboratory of choreology, 34
Gan, Aleksei, 30, 37
Gardin, Vladimir, *The Poet and the Tsar*, 60, 71, 72
Gastev, Aleksei, 34
Gavronskii, Aleksandr, *Real Life*, 222–224
General Line, The. See Eisenstein, Sergei
Geptakhor Dance Studio, 34–35
GIK. See VGIK
Girl with a Hatbox, see Barnet, Boris
Giuli. See Push, Lev
Glass House, The. See Eisenstein, Sergei
glass, 128, 145–147, 161, 162n56, 163, 190, 203–205, 212, 214, 219, 220, 224n1, 238, 253; as system for lighting in pre-revolutionary cinema, 53–54, 80n24
Golden Series (Prerevolutionary cinema), 60, 88
Goncharova, Natalia, 167
Goskinofabrika, 57. See also Sovkino
Goskinprom Gruzii, 170, 172, 173, 177, 284, 294n5, 339
graphical thinking, 191–195
Gropius, Walter, 107
GTK (Gosudarstvennyi tekhnikum kinoiskusstva), 57, 61, 81n25, 236. See also (V)GIK (Gosudarstvennyi institut kinoiskusstva), 81n25, 258, 339

hand(s), 11, 19, 21, 27, 31, 63, 76, 92, 106, 111, 119, 124, 223, 238, 242, 247, 267–269, 272, 278, 318, 339, 344; in the avant-garde, 123–124, 125–127, 154, 158–159; and "making." *See also* handcraft, handmade, handwork, handling, 133–134, 135, 137, 141, 143–144, 148, 175, 184–187, 195–196, 240, 268–269

handcraft, 11, 18–19, 37, 118, 249, 272, 290–291, 339, 346; and relationship with models of production, 103–107, 123, 130, 133–139, 145, 150, 165; in "primitive" culture, 176, 184–187, 272, 291; in the home, 109–111. *See also* handwork, *rukodelie*

handling, 30, 139, 144, 159, 246, 267–268; film as, 159–160; of objects, 193, 303; and play, 307, 314, 344, 318

handmade: ideological value of, 107, 125, 148–150, 211, 284, 303; practical need for, 110. *See also* handwork, craft, making, do-it-yourself

handwork, 19, 123, 132, 135–136, 147–154, 273, 343, 3. *See also rukodelie*

haptic, film theory, 6, 8–11, 43–45, 70, 82n78; specifically Soviet haptic, 10, 43–45, 124, 156, 157–159, 180–181, 237, 331; in Socialist Realist cinema, 256, 321, 324, 331, 333; 51, 70, 79, 116, 221, 240, 324

historical film. *See also* costume drama, 60–79

homemade: do-it-yourself, 109–110, 119, 205, 206, 211, 311, 314. *See also* self-made

homemaking, 19, 110–111, 113–115, 118, 121n43, 205–208, 221–223

homo faber, 132–137, 142, 194, 297, 299, 316, 323, 331, 333

homo ludens, 297, 299, 315, 316, 323, 333

Honour. *See* Bek-Nazarov, Amo

House on Trubnaia Square. *See* Barnet, Boris

How You Live, 208–209

Iezuitov, Nikolai: critic, on the "cinema of socialist feelings," 227–230, 242, 244, 249, 259, 261n37; on "style," 245

In the Big City. *See* Averbakh

INKhUK (Institut khudozhestvennoi kul´tury), 31, 33, 46n25

innervation, Walter Benjamin's theory of, 21, 26n88, 300, 309, 316

interiors: in prerevolutionary production design, 53–54 creation and representation of new Soviet 86–87, 109–111, 118, 205–210, 219; 221–224; ideological coding of, 61, 68, 71, 88, 111–115, 174, 204, 205–211, 221–224, 212–220; in Stalinist cinema, 297. *See also* domestic

Intriguer, The. *See* Urinov, Iakov

inventors, 210–211

Ioffe, Ieremaia: art theorist, 159, 245, 248, 262n63

Ioganson, Eduard, 338; *The Crown Prince of the Republic*, 224, 313–316; *On Vacation*, 323–329

Iukov, Konstantin: critic, 229, 243–244, 259, 339

Iurtsev, Boris: *A Refined Life*, 223

Iutkevich, Sergei: as set designer of *The Traitor*, 65–70; as director of *Lace*, 128, 144, 145, 147–156, 303; as director of *Counterplan*, 221–222, 242

Ivanov-Barkov, Evgenii: director, 172

Ivanovskii, Aleksandr, 60; *Palace and Fortress*, 61; *The Decembrists*, 71

Jacques-Dalcroze, Emile, 163n86

James, William, 12, 48n93

Jazz, 289, 343–344, 347–351

Kalatozov, Mikhail: *The Blind Girl*, 179; *Salt for Svanetiia*, 269–273

Kandinskii, Vasilii, 33, 46n34

Kaplunovskii, Vladimir: set designer, 57, 342

Kassil´, Lev, 308

Kat´ka–bumaznyi ranet. *See* Ermler, Frikrikh

Katsman, Evgeni, 148, *149*

Kazankii, Boris, 41

Khaz-Push. *See* Bek-Nazarov, Amo

Khersonskii, Khrisanf: critic, 65, 82n61, 158, 173–174

Khokhlova, Aleksandra: in *Your Acquaintance*, 214–219, 225n18; and toys, 303, 344, 348, 352n13

Khuskivadze, Shalva, 173, 284

Kolupaev, Dmitrii: set designer, 55, 57–58, 59, 82n58, 328; and *Women of Riazan Province*, 96–101; and *A Major Nuisance*, 117

Kornilov, Nikolai: psychologist, 14, 26n70, 36
Kozintsev, 62, 70, 71, 74, 75, 76, 78, 79; on surface and volume, 237, 242, 244. *See also* FEKS
Kozlovskii, Sergei: set designer, 56, 57, 59, 80n24, 81n29, 111, 238; and *Girl with a Hatbox*, 113–115; and *Storm over Asia*, 189; and *In the Big City*, 206
Kracauer, Siegfried, 38, 47n70, 263n93, 349
Krinskii, Vladimir, 31
Kruchenykh, Aleksei, 300
Krupskaia, Nadezhda: on toys, 306–307, 321–322
Kudriavtsev, Antonina: *Wake up, Lenochka*, 310; *Lenochka and the Grapes*, 310
Kuleshov, Lev, 172, 197n24, and reflexology, 36, 344; and set design/as set designer, 56, 58, 80n12; *Your Acquaintance*, 214–221
Kuliev, Aga-Rza: *Almas*, 289–292
Kustar. *See also* folk craft, 107–108, 125
Kustodiev, Boris: artist, 89, 90, 119n9

labor, 19, 76, 94, 99, 103–106, 109, 119, 124, 130–132, 135; distinction between proletarian and traditional/capitalist, specificity of new Soviet, 131–132, 139–44, 145, 222, 240, 267–270, 297, 316; Aleksei Gastev's Institute of, 34–35; Hannah Arendt on labor as distinct from work and "making," 135–136; manual, 76, 79, 143, 154, 175, 195, 240, 267–270, 274; as means of overcoming nature, 268
lace-making, 107–108, 145, 148, 150, 154
lace, 75, 78, 107, 112, 115, 116, 128, 147–156, 203; traditional production of, 148, 154, mechanical production of, 149–150; as bourgeois, 145, 148, 155–156; as erotic, 78–79, 155–156, 163n75; *Lace* (dir. Iutkevich), 128, 145, 147–159, 151–152, 303; material structure of, 150, 155–156
Lace. See Iutkevich, Sergei
Lacemakers: representations of, 148, 149, 162n71
Ladovskii, Nikolai: architect, 31, 208
Lamanova, Nadezhda: couturier, 108
Langman, Eleazar: photographer, 123

Larionov, Mikhail: artist, 167
Last Crusaders, The. See Dolidze, Siko
laundry, 76, 85, 92, 94, 96, 113, 117, 119n10, 124
Lavrov, Vitalii: architect, 208
Le Corbusier, architect, 86–87
LEF, 30–31, 32, 41–42, 131, 141, 144, 172, 179, 197n32, 212, 307
Legend of the Maiden's Tower. See Balliuzek
leisure: images of in Soviet cinema, 139, 159, 298, 323–328, 343
Lenin, Vladimir: and psychology, 5–6, 11, 12, 24n48; on Soviet labour and relationship with the machine, 131–132, 142; *Three Songs About*, 276–280
Lenochka and the Grapes. See Kudriavtsev, Antonina
Leont'ev, Aleksei: psychologist, 17, 26n77; and cinema, 36, 339
Lévy-Bruhl, Lucien, 193–194
Lewin, Kurt: psychologist, 308
Life in the Palm of your Hands. See Mar'ian, David
Life is Good. See Pudovkin, Vsevolod
lighting: in production design, 51, 53–54, 62, 63, 73, 79, 80n24, 120n19, 162n51, 217, 231–232
Living God, The. See Verner, Mikhail
Loos, Adolf, 86
Losskii, Nikolai: psychologist, 13
ludic, 298; definition of, 299–301, 308; as model for revolution, 300–301, 331; importance in the avant-garde and Constructivism, 307; 308, 322, 331
Lukács, Georg: and "Dinghaftigkeit," 37; and realism, 262n58
Lunacharskii, Anatolii: as philosopher, 24n48; on cinema, 37; 343, 348, 351n7
Luriia, Aleksandr, 14, 15, 17, 26n77, 35, 36; expedition to Uzbekistan, 192–195, 200n82, 200n83, 200n84, 200n85, 200n87, 200n94, 268, 308; and Eisenstein, 194–195, 308
lyric, lyrical, lyricism, 39, 88, 157, 243, 248, 258, 318, 320

Mach, Ernst: Lenin's response to, 24n48
Macheret, Aleksandr, 338; *The Private Life of Petr Vinogradov*, 224, 249–252

INDEX 401

machine(s), human as, 16, 25n56, 34, 160n7, 163n86, 163n88, 343, 344; centrality of as metaphor in Soviet culture, 22; humanization of, 140–144, 150, 346–347; relationship between human and, 106, 106, 117, 131–132, 136–137, 139–144, 145, 149–150, 157, 208, 223, 267, 287, 300, 343, 344, 347–350; as distinct from/in relation to handcraft, 11, 124, 130, 145, 148–150, *151–152*, 211, 267, 343

Maiakovskii, Vladimir, 87, 134, 197n32, 251, 348

Major Nuisance, A. See Popov, Aleksei

Makarenko, Anton: educator, 304, 306

making, 19, 106, 115, 118–119, 130, 210–211, 208, 210–211; as distinct from "labor," 135; in traditional society, 175–176; as bricolage, 211. *See also* craft

Malevich, Kazimir, 108, 274

Mallet Stevens, Robert, 66, 68

Man with a Movie Camera. See Vertov, Dziga

Mandel'shtam, Osip: on tools, 136

manufacture, 103, 154. *See also* making

Mar'ian, David: *Life in the Palm of your Hands*, 209–210

Marinetti, Filippo, 27

Markov, Vladimir: theorist of art, 29

Marr, Nikolai, 36, 192; and Eisenstein, 194

Marx, Karl: on sensuous human activity, 1, 2, 4, 31–32, 33, 127, 188; and the commodity, 125, 190, 197n13; and alienation of the body in mechanical production, 106, 132, 140, 148; and primitive communism, 168; and "sensory radiance," 252

mastery (*ovladenie*): of self, 14, 17; of the material world (nature), 36, 42, 132, 268, 273

material (world): (Formalist) definitions of, 42, 128–30, 174, as changed by Socialist Realism, 243–245, 248, 252, 257–260, 280–282; human relationship with, 1–2, 11, 30–32, 40–45, 124–125, 127, 128–130, 187–189, 213, 238–243, 249, 257, 275, 298, 346 (in making) 131–134, 135–139, 140–142, 146–154, 157–160, 195–196, 214, 268–70, 303, (in play) 299–300, 306–307; tension between encountering and processing/organization of, 15–16, 30–33, 37–39, 41–43, 107, 141, 229; in historical cinema, 60–63, 72–75, 78–79. *See also* reciprocity

Materialism (materialist): emphasis of psychological science, 10, 12–15, 33, 192; as foundational principle, 21, 30–32, 36–37, 252, 259; in film theory, 37–45, 128–130, 131, 157, 233, 349

Matiushin, Mikhail, 33; organic school of, 34

Mechanical Traitor, The. See Dmitriev, Aleksei

Mechanics of the Brain. See Pudovkin, Vsevolod

Medvedkin, Aleksandr, 298

Meerson, Lazar: set designer, 55

Meierkhol'd, Vsevolod, 55, 348; and biomechanics, 34, 199n72; *Picture of Dorian Grey*, 56; and set design, 55–56

Mel'nikov, Konstantin: architect, 31, 57

Melodrama. *See also* costume drama, historical film, 61, 95

merriness, 317, 333. See also *bodrost'*

Mezhrabpom, 34, 57, 80–81n24, 112, 339, 342–343

Mikaberidze, Kote: *My Grandmother*, 213, 303

mimetic (relationship with things), 213

Minaret of Death. See Viskovskii, Viacheslav

modern, interiors and design, 212–213, 214–216, 313

Moholy-Nagy, Lazlo, 28

monism, 12. *See also* psychology

Moscow Institute of Psychology, 14

Moskvin, Andrei: cinematographer, 62, 73, 74, 76, 261n44

mosque, 184, 276, 279; as film studio, 170; as school, 290–219

Munsterberg, Hugo, 36

Mur, Leo: critic, 48n87, 86, 198n35

My Grandmother. See Mikaberidze, Kote

My Son. See Cherviakov, Ivan

Mzago and Gela. See Push, Lev

naoshchup (knowledge naoshchup'), 180–181, 187, 188, 196, 242, 266, 272, 279, 291, 353

Narkompros, 12, 305

nasyshchennost, emotsional'naia nasyshchennost'. See also emotional saturation, 236–237, 261n37
national republics, 19, 20, 166, 265–267, 283, 289; producing cinema in, 168–174, 197n20; and legacy of rebellion, 275
needlework. *See also* sewing, embroidery, 118
New Babylon. See FEKS
New Economic Policy (NEP), 6, 110, 115
New man (*novyi chelovek*), 3, 4, 13, 22n6, 212, 222, 353
Neznamov, Petr: critic, 72, 147, 154, 173–174

OBERIU (Ob''edinenie real'nogo iskusstva), 310, 329
Object(s), 1, 2, 9–11, 211, 337; in production design, 51, 52, 53, 54, 59, 60–63, 74–76, 80n12, 115–116, 243; lack of in Socialist Realist cinema, 297–298; remaking of the human relationship with, 29–32, 85, 87, 92, 107–110, 113, 115, 118, 123, 124–126, 128, 130–147, 187–194, 213–221, 231, 238–240, 259; in play, 299–301, 302, 303, 306–307, 309, 314, 317–322, 324, 325n63; film and capacity for new discovery of, 37–45, 115–116, 146–158, 195–196, 215, 245, 248, 253, 258, 278, 297–298, 319. *See* material, things, *predmetnost'*
obrabotka: as principle of Constructivism, 30, 107, 253
October. See Eisenstein, Sergei
Oleinikov, Nikolai, 310, 323; *On Vacation*, 328
On Vacation. See Ioganson, Eduard
Organic school. *See* Matiushin
oriental: decoration, 112, 115, 170, 181–182, 213, 278, 284, 292
Orientalism, orientalist, 166–168, 170, 171, 174, 176, 179, 187, 192
Orlova, Liubov', 316
Ornament: ornamental art, 9; in modernism, 55, 60; in production design, 63, 68, 94, 112, 155–156, 188; ideological suspicion of, 85–87, 107, 112, 243; complexity of attitudes toward, 87, 107–109, 111, 188, 213. *See also* decoration
Oshchushchenie: definition and importance of, 5–6, 12, 16–18, 24n18, 20, 353; in visual art/photography, 18, 29, 237, 335n63; Shklovskii and, 27, 29, 41; Vertov and, 27; cinematic sensation, 27, 41, 130, 146; changing conceptions of in Soviet culture, 234, 237, 245, 259. *See also* sensation
Ostranenie. See also defamiliarization, 29, 38, 41
Outskirts. See Barnet, Boris
Overcoat, The. See FEKS
Ovladenie. See mastery

Palace and Fortress. See Ivanovskii, Aleksandr
Parisian Cobbler, The. See Ermler, Fridrikh
Parnakh, Valentin: musician, 347–350
past: representations of in historical film, 61–62, 72–73; complexity of relationship between the present and the, 92, 167, 212, 213, 266, 273–282, 294n16
Path to Life, A. See Ekk, Nikolai
Pattern: on film screen, 52, 54, 55, 63–70, 71, 73–79, 91, 96–101, 112, 116, 143, 150, 155–156, 158, 216–220, 238, 253; as signifier of the past, 87, 92, 99, 112, 114, 118, 174–175, 182, 203, 279, 286, 292; rejection of in set design, 212–218, 285. *See also* textile, cloth
Pavlov, Ivan: psychologist/physiologist, 13, 25n57, 35
peasants: in Soviet Russia 88, images of 88, 99, 141, 267, 272, 283; and craft, 107–109, 181; in *Women of Riazan Province*, 95
pedology. *See also* psychology, children, 25n67, 192, 304–305, 308
Petrov-Bytov, Pavel, *Whirlpool*, 120n14; *Cain i Artem*, 135; 127, 230, 249
photogénie, 39–43; formalist response to, 41–42; 128, 190
physiology: science of, 12, 25n67
Pil'niak, Boris, 169
Piotrovskii, Adrian: on "emotional cinema," 178, 230–231, 233–234
play, 20, 211, 289, 293, 298–334; as revolutionary action, 299–302, 308, 309, 316; children's, 287, 288, 298; and relationship with labour, 139, 141, 211, 222, 297–299, 301, 314; theories of in Soviet Russia, 304–307; cinema as, 70, 74, 79,

91, 300–301; as unruly and disruptive, 311, 313; as 'safe' pleasure in Socialist Realist cinema, 322–329, 329–333; playfulness, 286, 298, 300, 313; in children's cinema, 307–313; for and by adults, 154, 313–323, 326–329, 328; as distinct from *bodrost'*, 316

Playing at Love. See Sharifzadeh (Sharifov), Mirza

pleasure: sensory pleasure, sensual pleasure, 184, 333; of technology, 268; 323; disembodied qualities of bourgeois, 343–344

Poet and the tsar, The. See Gardin, Vladimir

Popov, Aleksandr: *The Band of Imps*, 311

Popov, Aleksei: *A Major Nuisance*, 116–119; *Two Friends, a Model and a Girlfriend*, 210–211

Popova, Liubov', 31, 108

Potholes. See Room, Abram

pottery, potting, 175, 184, *186*, 339

Pozniakov, Nikolai, 34

Pravov, Ivan: *Women from Riazan Province*, 88, 94–107

predmetnyi, predmetnost', 157, 187, 237. See object, things

Preobrazhenskaia, Ol'ga, 338; *Women from Riazan Province*, 88, 94–107, 175

Pribyl'skaia, Evgeniia, 107, 108

primitive communism, 168, 169, 191–192, 197n17, 274

primitive mimesis, 187–190, 194–195, 196, 266

primitive, 19, 165–168, 191; complex relationship between condemnation of and fascination with, 165–167, 169, 178–180, 191, 267–273; and intensified sensory relationship with the world, 187–189, 191–196, 240–242, 269–273; transformation of attitudes towards, 287–293; primitivism, and modernism, 165–169, 179, 191, 195

Private Life of Petr Vinogradov, The. See Macheret, Aleksandr

processing: of the material/material world, (as principle of art), 30–31, 40–42, 44, 159, 341, 353; (as principle of making/labor), 101–106, 107, 109, 119, 159. See also *obrabotka*

production design, 18–19, 51–79; scholarship on, 51–52, 56–57; debates about, 57–59, 65; prerevolutionary, 53–56; and Constructivism, 55; outside Russia, 56; and the organization of space, 65

production movies/films, 130, 140–141, 143, 144, 148, 222, 242, 266–267

Protazanov, Iakov: *The Tailor from Torzhok*, 88–94, 95, 106, 214; *Aelita*, 214

Provincial, style, 59, 87–89, 92, 112, 117, 221–222, 225n34; setting, 19, 117, 132, 144, 211, 246, 248, 317

prudery, of Soviet cinema. See also pleaure, 298

psychological (emotional) cinema: prerevolutionary, 53; in Soviet Russia, 230–236

psychological science. See also reflexology, pedology, 2, 11–16, 16–18, 129 applied psychology: influence on the arts, 33, 129; and cinema, 35–37, 258. See also psychotechnics, 33–35

psychology (of Soviet subject on screen), 129, 147, 154, 157, 159, 231, 238, 243, 245

psychotechnics, 14–15, 24n67, 33; and cinema, 36

Pudovkin, Vsevolod, 35, 39–40; on set design, 53; *Mechanics of the Brain*, 34; *Storm over Asia*, 187–191; *A Simple Case/Life is Good*, 234–237; on "psychological" cinema, 234–237; and actors, 235–236, 261n33

puppets. See also toys, 302, 311, 318, 326, 342, 344

Push, Lev, 172–173, 338; *Giuli*, 173–176, 179; *Mzago and Gela*, 284–290

radio, 282, 284–285, 287, 289

Raizman, Iurii: *Fliers*, 320

Rakhal's, Vasilii: set designer, 56, 57, 59, 224n4

Razumnyi, Aleksandr: *Timur and his Team*, 311, 313

Reactology. See also reflexology, 15

Real Life. See Gavronskii, Aleksandr

reciprocity, between human and world, 124, 131, 188, 190, 193–194, 341; in act of making, 131, 135–136, 142, 157, 193–194; in child's play, 299–300, 307–308, 331–332; in "primitive" experience, 188, 193–194; cinema as creating relationship of, 9, 44, 160

Refined Life, A. See Iurtsev, Boris

reflexology, 13–15, 16, 17, 33, 34; and influence on culture, 33, 36; and cinema, 35–37; and Kuleshov, 36; and Vertov, 35; and Eisenstein, 36; and Room, 235–236, 258

regulation: as core metaphor for modern (and especially Soviet) project, 4, 8, 21; tension between emancipation and, 5, 341, 343; of emotion, 250, 256. *See also* control, mastery, body

Riegl, Alois: art theorist, 9, 24n36, 43, 70, 82n78, 214

Rodchenko, Aleksandr: artist, 31; and children's books, 307; as production designer, 58; 123, 172, 214–216

Roginskaia, Frida: critic, 107

Romm, Mikhail, *The Thirteen*, 266, 275, 280–282

Room, Abram, 52, 257, and reflexology, 35, 236, 258; on acting, 236, 261n36, *The Traitor*, 63–70, 154; *Bed and Sofa*, 65, 155, 205, 231, 290; *Potholes*, 128, 145–147, 162n55, 203, 244; *A Severe Youth*, 249, 252–257

Rozanova, Ol′ga: artist, 108

Ruins, 266, 274–282

rukodelie. See also handcraft, 109–111, 119, 123, 139, 143, 353

rural. *See* provincial, peasant

Sabiński, Czesław, 55, 80n8
Salt for Svanetiia. See Kalatozov, Mikhail
Samodelka. See also do-it-yourself, 310
Sats, Natal′ia, 309–310
Savchenko, Igor′, 316; *The Accordion*, 316; *A Chance Encounter*, 316–323, 331
Sechenov, Ivan: psychologist, 12–13
self-made. *See also* do-it-yourself, handmade, 215, 307
sensation. *See oshchushchenie*, feeling

sensibility: Balazs's theory of proletarian, 22, 339; "primitive," 166, 169, 187–188, 284; specifics of a Soviet, 245

sensory history, 6–7

sensory pleasure, 20, 63, 78, 87, 92, 110, 156–157, 174–175, 179–181, 240, 250–251, 268, 280–282, 322

sensory radiance (*chuvstvennyi blesk*): as description of qualities of Socialist Realist art, 252, 266, 291, 293, 321, 326, 329–332, 293

set design. *See* production design

Severe Youth, A. See Room, Abram

Sevil. See Bek-Nazarov, Amo

Sevzapkino, 170

sewing. *See also* needlework, 63, 116, 174, 269, 339

sexual energy, 25n63, 298, 320, 321, 322, 326

sexuality: Soviet models of, 321, 324, 333

Sharifzadeh (Sharifov), Mirza, *Playing at Love*, 324, 326

sheets. *See also* laundry, 112, 116

Shengelaia, Nikolai, 173, 177, 338; *Eliso*, 177–178, 179, 286; as representative of "emotional cinema," 230

Shiriaev, Aleksandr, 302–303

Shklovskii, Viktor: and *ostranenie*, 27, 29, 38, 41, 116; and *oshchushchenie*, 29, 30, 45n16; and *faktura*, 29, 128; and cinema, 41–43, 131, 142, 145–146, 158–159, 160n12, 235, 259; and material, 29, 45n15, 49n108, 128–131, 142, 146, 174; and *Lace*, 150, 162n61; in Georgia, 172, 177–178, 179, 198n50

shoemaker. *See also* cobbler, 76, 132–136, 180, 184, 186–187, 203, 246–247; Vertov as, 160

shoes, 136

Shpielrein, Isaak: psychologist, 15, 25n67

Shvarts, Evgenii, 310; *On Vacation*, 328

Sidamon-Erestavi, Valerian: set designer, and *Honour*, 174, 175; and *Mzago and Gela*, 288

silence, 138–139, 280

Simmel, Georg, 4; on ruins, 275, 281

Simov, Valentin: set designer, 55, 56

Simple Case, A. See Pudovkin, Vsevolod

skin, 116, 135, 272, 339

Socialist Realism (Socialist Realist), 6, 20, 44, 228–229, 245; search for a film style, 44, 227–228, 248, 265; "feelings," 229–230, 237, 243–245, 252, 258; and heroism, 248, 249–250, 320–322; and reason, 257–260; and pleasure, 229, 293, 265, 291, 297–298; and children's culture, 309–10, 351; and the past, 275–282

Soiuzdetfil'm. *See* cinema for children, 309–310

Sokolov, Ippolit, "labour gymnastics," 47n46, 163n88, 348; as film critic, 62, 73, 75, 163n88

sound, 280, 284, 310, 316, 324

Soviet haptic. *See* haptic

Sovkino, 57, 58, 86, 117, 119n2, 147, 160n12, 170, 171, 215, 224n15, 339

sport, 213, 254, 317–318

Stanislavskii, Konstantin, 55

Starewicz, Władysław, 302–303

State Film Institute/Academy. *See* GTK, VGIK

Stepanova, Varvara: at VKhUTEMAS, 31; 123; and children's books, 307

stikhiinost'. *See* consciousness

Storm over Asia. *See* Pudovkin, Vsevolod

Strike. *See* Eisenstein, Sergei

Stroganov Institute for Technical Drawing, the, 54, 55

Sublimation: of desire in Socialist Realist cinema, 321, 324–325

Svanetiia, 179

SVD. *See* FEKS

Svetozavrov, Boris, 128

Tactility: and the avant-garde, 27–29, 31–32; as model for new relationship with the world, 38, 118, 124, 138, 142, 175, 180–181, 195–196, 238–242, 269, 301; and film spectatorship, 78, 90, 92, 155, 159, 214, 219–221, 269. *See also naoshchup'*

Tailor from Torzhok, The. *See* Protazanov, Igor

tailors, 63, 64, 88, 89, 90, 123, 124, 134, 175

Tarabukin, Nikolai, 29, 46n34, 137, 140, 156

Tarich, Iurii: *Wings of a Serf*, 60–61

Tatlin, Vladimir: artist, and "material," 28–29, 31, 33; and the tactile, 28, 31; Monument to the Third International, 314

Taylor, Frederick, 34

Technology. *See* machine

tekhnik, 139–141, 250, 253, 254

textile, 19, 54, 62–63, 107–109, 116, 159; and set design, 66, 217–218; in *The Tailor from Torzhok*, 89–92; in *Women of Riazan Province*, 96–106; in *A Major Nuisance*, 116–118; in ethnic interiors and costume, 174; 213, 286

Thiemann and Reinhardt Studio, 60

things. *See also* objects, 32–33, 86, 87; on-screen, 52; 125, 219–220; relationships with, 129–130, 193–194, 208–209; Tret'iakov and the biography of a, 142; in *Storm over Asia*, 188–189; in *Your Acquaintance*, 219–221

Thirteen, The. *See* Romm, Mikhail

Three Songs of Lenin. *See* Vertov, Dziga

Timur and his Team. *See* Razumnyi, Aleksandr

tool, 19, 124, 130–132, 133, 135, 136–137, 139–140, 187, 246, 333; theories of, 135–137, 150; film camera as, 160

Toporkov, Aleksei: leftist critic and theorist, 128; on the *tekhnik* and his/her relationship with the machine and the product of work, 139–141, 154, 250; and the "object-led gesture" on screen, 157–158, 163n86, 163n87, 237

Torn Boots. *See* Barskaia, Margarita

toys, 109, 124–125, 219, 301; as represented in film, 302–303; theories of in Soviet Russia, 303–307; production in Russia, 303–304; State Museum of, 305; Scientific Research Institute on (Zagorsk), 305, 310; in *An Aerial Adventure*, 329–333

Traitor, The. *See* Room, Abram

Trauberg, Leonid. *See* FEKS

Tret'iakov, Sergei: on cinema and the role of the artist, 5, 28, 49n97, 142, 180; and the "biography of the thing," 142; poems for children, 307; in Georgia, 172, 173;177–181, 198n50; and *Eliso*, 173, 177–179; complexity

of attitudes to "primitive" life, 179–181, and *Salt for Svanetiia* 269–273. *See also* knowledge *naoshchup'*
Tropinin, Vasilii: painter, 148, *149*
Trotskii, Lev: on the new Soviet person, 4, 33; on uneven development, 199n76
Turin, Viktor: *Turksib*, 266–269
Two Friends, a Model and a Girlfriend. See Popov, Aleksei
Tynianov, Iurii: and *The Overcoat*, 62; and *SVD*, 72–73

Ulitskaia, Liudmila: *Real Life*, 222–224
Urinov, Iakov: *The Intriguer*, 328–329
Ustanovka. See also things, material, human relationship with, 34, 128, 129, 131, 145, 156, 354
Utkin, Aleksei: set designer, 54, 56, 60, 66, 212

Vasil'iev, Dmitri: *The Living God*, 291–293
veil, 78, 168, 171, 276–279, 290
Verbovka (embroidery workshop), 108, 111
Verner, Mikhail: *The Living God*, 291–293
Vertov, Dziga, 5, 338; the senses and "film sensation," 27, 127, 279; and reflexology, 35; film eye's relationship with material world, 42, 127, 160; and hands, 124–127, 158; and machines, 141; and toys, 154, 303, 334n34; *Film Week*, 124–125; *Man with a Movie Camera*, 124, 141, 158–159; *Film Eye*, 125–128, 159; *Three Songs of Lenin*, 266, 275–280, 282; *The Eleventh Year*, 276
VGIK (Gosudarstvennyi institut kinoiskusstva), 8:n25, 258, 268, 273, 339

village. *See* province, peasant, on film, 59, 94–95, 96, 99, 106, 112, 117–118, 286, 387
Viskovskii, Viacheslav: *Minaret of Death*, 170
VKHUTEMAS, 31, 32, 46n26, 57, 137, 300; as VKhUTEIN, 60
Volkonskii, Sergei, 163n86, 163n88, 261n36
vostok (vostochnyi). See East, 20
Vostokkino, 171–172
Vvedenskii, Aleksandr, 310; *An Aerial Adventure*, 329
Vygotskii, 11, 17; and the "crisis" in psychology, 14–15; and "inner speech," 49n104; and the "primitive," 192–193, 200n84, 308; and Eisenstein, 36, 194–195, 308; on play, 306–307, 335n55; and art, 337

Wake up, Lenochka. See Kudriavtsev, Antonina
weaver, 123, 290
weaving, 103–106, 137, 159, 176, 203, 269, 290–291, 339
Whirlpool. See Petrov-Bytov, Pavel
Wiene, Robert: *Cabinet of Dr. Caligari*, 56, 58–59; *Raskolnikow*, 59
Wings of a Serf. See Tarich, Iurii
Women of Riazan Province. See Preobrazhenskaia, Olga
Wondrous Garden, The. See Frenkel', Lazar'

Your Acquaintance. See Kuleshov, Lev

zabota, 131, 142, 211
Zalkind, Aron, 11, 14, 25n63, 33, 34, 35, 36
Zamiatin, Evgenii, 167, 203
Zhiznestroenie, 31, 46n24, 354
Zoshchenko, Mikhail, 117

EMMA WIDDIS is Reader in Russian Studies at the University of Cambridge and a Fellow of Trinity College. She is author of *Visions of a New Land: Soviet Cinema from the Revolution to the Second World War* (Yale University Press, 2003) and *Alexander Medvedkin* (I. B. Tauris, 2014), and editor with Simon Franklin of *National Identity in Russian Culture* (Cambridge University Press, 2014). She is the director of the Cambridge Russian Sensory History Network (CRUSH).